P9-DMT-794

www.wadsworth.com

wadsworth.com is the World Wide Web site for Wadsworth and is your direct source to dozens of online resources.

At *wadsworth.com* you can find out about supplements, demonstration software, and student resources. You can also send email to many of our authors and preview new publications and exciting new technologies.

wadsworth.com
Changing the way the world learns®

4th Edition

CONTEMPORARY BEHAVIOR THERAPY

Michael D. Spiegler
Providence College

David C. Guevremont
Woonsocket Education Department

THOMSON
™
WADSWORTH

Australia • Canada • Mexico • Singapore • Spain • United Kingdom • United States

WADSWORTH

THOMSON LEARNING

Publisher: Vicki Knight
Assistant Editor: Jennifer Wilkinson
Editorial Assistant: Lucy Faridany
Marketing Manager: Kathleen Morgan
Marketing Assistant: Laurel Anderson
Advertising Project Manager:
   Shemika Britt
Project Manager, Editorial Production:
   Paula Berman
Print/Media Buyer: Nancy Panziera
Permissions Editor: Joohee Lee
Production Service and Compositor:
   Graphic World Inc.
Photo Researcher: Kathleen Olson

Copy Editor: Linda Purrington
Cover Designer: Denise Davidson
Cover Image: J. David
   Andrews/Masterfile
Text Printer: RR Donnelley

COPYRIGHT © 2003 Wadsworth, a division of Thomson Learning, Inc. Thomson Learning™ is a trademark used herein under license.

ALL RIGHTS RESERVED. No part of this work covered by the copyright hereon may be reproduced or used in any form or by any means—graphic, electronic, or mechanical, including but not limited to photocopying, recording, taping, Web distribution, information networks, or information storage and retrieval systems—without the written permission of the publisher.

Printed in the United States of America
5 6 7 06

For more information about our products, contact us at:

**Thomson Learning Academic Resource Center
1-800-423-0563**

For permission to use material from this text, contact us by:

Phone: 1-800-730-2214
Fax: 1-800-730-2215
Web: http://www.thomsonrights.com

Wadsworth/Thomson Learning
10 Davis Drive
Belmont, CA 94002-3098
USA

Asia
Thomson Learning
5 Shenton Way #01-01
UIC Building
Singapore 068808

Australia
Nelson Thomson Learning
102 Dodds Street
South Melbourne, Victoria 3205
Australia

Canada
Nelson Thomson Learning
1120 Birchmount Road
Toronto, Ontario M1K 5G4
Canada

Europe/Middle East/Africa
Thomson Learning
High Holborn House
50/51 Bedford Row
London WC1R 4LR
United Kingdom

Latin America
Thomson Learning
Seneca, 53
Colonia Polanco
11560 Mexico D.F.
Mexico

Spain
Paraninfo Thomson Learning
Calle/Magallanes, 25
28015 Madrid, Spain

Library of Congress Control Number:
   2002107284
ISBN 0-534-54651-X

To Arlene
who makes all the difference in my life
MDS

To Jeannine Guevremont
for being the mother of all aunts
DCG

Michael D. Spiegler (Ph.D., clinical psychology, Vanderbilt University) is Professor of Psychology at Providence College and was formerly Director of the Community Training Center at the Palo Alto VA Hospital and Assistant Professor of Psychology at the University of Texas at Austin. He was a pioneer in developing skills training as a treatment for chronic psychiatric disorders and film modeling therapy. His other areas of research include observational learning, anxiety, the treatment of obesity, and active learning. Professor Spiegler is coauthor of *Personality: Strategies and Issues* and *The Community Training Center.* His nonprofessional passions include his wife, flying his plane, rock climbing, skiing, listening to early music, savoring wine, and hosting a nighttime comedy show.

David C. Guevremont (Ph.D, clinical child psychology, West Virginia University) is Clinical Psychologist for the Woonsocket Education Department. He was previously Associate Professor of Psychiatry at the University of Massachusetts Medical Center, taught at Assumption College, and was Director of the Attention Deficit Hyperactivity Disorder (ADHD) Clinic at Blackstone Valley Psychological Institute. His research and clinical interests have focused on the assessment and treatment of children with attention deficit and disruptive behavior disorders. He has published extensively in areas related to ADHD, behavioral assessment and treatment, and children's peer relations. His avocational interests include sports, music, food, and watching reruns of Seinfeld.

Thank you for reading this preface. Few people read prefaces, so we want to reinforce your extraordinary behavior by answering one of the questions you may be curious about: How is this book different from other behavior therapy textbooks?

Contemporary Behavior Therapy is simultaneously an introduction for beginning students and a comprehensive, scholarly review and resource for advanced students and professionals. To make this a "teaching book"—one from which students easily can learn—we have written in a casual, inviting style and have employed many pedagogical features, including the following:

◆ *Unifying principles and themes* that are initially presented in brief, introductory chapters and then illustrated throughout the book
◆ *A consistent behavioral perspective,* including using behavioral principles—such as prompting, shaping, reinforcement, modeling, and behavior rehearsal—to teach behavioral principles and procedures, as well as using behavioral rather than trait descriptions in referring to disorders
◆ *Unique conceptual schemes* that organize the currently diverse field of behavior therapy
◆ *Numerous Cases,* integrated into the textual discussion, that provide rich detail about the application of behavior therapy to a wide array of problems and disorders
◆ *Unique Participation Exercises* that provide students with hands-on experience with behavior therapy principles and procedures and promote active learning
◆ *Many illustrations* (including photographs and cartoons) that are functional rather than decorative
◆ *Integration of clinical, research, professional, and ethical facets* of the practice of behavior therapy

Contemporary Behavior Therapy is written for readers in a variety of disciplines. Applications and examples are drawn from diverse fields. Moreover, no previous background is needed because all the basic concepts are presented in Chapters 3 and 4. Theoretical issues in behavior therapy are set off as In Theory boxes so that they can be omitted in courses that do not cover theory.

What makes this book a scholarly review of behavior therapy is its comprehensiveness and critical evaluation. All of the major behavior therapy procedures are discussed, and the coverage has been guided by a series of surveys of practicing behavior therapists, which we have conducted over the past 13 years. The latest research findings are presented, synthesized, and evaluated; the literature review is documented with more than 2200 references, including 450 that are new since the publication of the last edition.

What's new to the fourth edition of *Contemporary Behavior Therapy?* Looking at the book as a whole:

◆ The text has been shortened judiciously—to make it more suitable for a one-semester course—by tightening up the writing and abbreviating content less prominent in the field today.
◆ The Participation Exercises have been simplified to make them more accessible for students.
◆ A new glossary of psychological disorders and problems treated by behavior therapy has been added, which is useful for students who have little or no background in abnormal psychology.
◆ The text has been thoroughly updated to reflect the field of behavior therapy at the beginning of the 21st century.
◆ Ethical issues have been integrated throughout the text at points where they are most relevant (rather than in a separate chapter at the end).

And here is a sample of the new content we've included.

◆ Expanded coverage of stimulus control interventions, including new guidelines for using prompting and a new section on setting events
◆ New coverage of the latest variations of differential reinforcement procedures, including noncontingent reinforcement and functional communication training
◆ Expanded discussion of behavioral child management training, including planned activity scheduling and updated outcome research
◆ New coverage of the many variations of exposure therapy and strategies for enhancing its efficacy
◆ New discussion of the ethicality of using poorly validated behavioral treatments
◆ New discussion of strategies for promoting transfer and generalization in social skills training
◆ New section on schema-focused cognitive therapy
◆ Expanded coverage of culturally competent behavior therapy
◆ New discussion of dissemination of behavior therapy and manual-based treatments
◆ New section on premature acceptance of new treatments
◆ New coverage on assuring effectiveness of behavior therapy in clinical settings

This book is divided into three parts. Part I presents the fundamental principles of behavior therapy, which are repeatedly illustrated and drawn on in subsequent chapters. Part II covers all the major behavior therapy procedures used today. Part III first illustrates broader applications of behavior therapy principles and procedures to behavioral medicine and psychological disorders with primary physical characteristics;

then, it presents a final evaluation of and commentary on the present status and future of behavior therapy.

We have written *Contemporary Behavior Therapy,* fourth edition, as teachers, researchers, and clinicians. As teachers, we have incorporated many features that enhance learning, such as stressing general principles and providing numerous examples, including everyday illustrations to which students can relate. As researchers, we appreciate the importance of empirically validating treatment procedures. Thus, not only have we presented the evidence for the efficacy of behavior therapy procedures by describing studies, but we also have critically evaluated their limitations. As clinicians, we find the practice of behavior therapy to be challenging, stimulating, and reinforcing, and we have tried to impart this in our writing.

Acknowledgments

We are indebted to many people who have contributed in various ways to this book.

We thank our students who have assisted our work in numerous ways: Mia Geraci, Emily LaPolice, and Christine Tangel. Samantha Samberg played a major role in the extensive literature review required for the book. Karen Sherman competently prepared the name index. Annmarie Mullen performed myriad secretarial tasks with her usual efficiency and cheerfulness.

We are grateful to Arlene Spiegler, who read numerous drafts of the book with a discerning eye, offered valuable suggestions, and provided wise third opinions—all of which enhanced the final product.

We thank our reviewers for their suggestions:

Frank Fulkerson, Western Illinois State University
Robert Hoff, Mercyhurst College
Dennis Larson, Augustana College
Timothy Lionetti, Montclair State University
Raymond Miltenberger, North Dakota State University
James Olson, University of Texas–Permian Basin
Heather Vonderfecht, Walla Walla College

Special thanks are due Suzanne Kastner, who competently shepherded the book through its production with knowledge, creativeness, care, and good humor.

The book has benefited from the consultation of our colleagues Haig Agigian, Mary O'Keeffe, and George Raymond. We appreciate the support we received from Theodore Bosack.

On a personal note, we are grateful for having Jane and Gordon in the background. Although the book certainly could have been written without Sharie Sasson, the experience would not have been the same.

For understanding or at least accepting the priority of "the book," I (M.D.S.) thank my family and friends. My work on this book, and all I do, is partially maintained by the modeling and reinforcement provided by the two people who picked me up from the steps, my loving parents,

Lillian and Julie Spiegler. Although my dad died last year, his influence is unabated. Finally, and most important, for the love and support I receive daily from my wife and soul mate, Arlene, I am grateful, always and forever.

I (D.C.G.) am grateful to my family and colleagues for their support during the process of writing this fourth edition.

Preparation of *Contemporary Behavior Therapy,* fourth edition, has consumed much of our lives during the past couple of years. Fortunately, our professional and personal collaboration continues to be a most satisfying enterprise. Accordingly, we want to acknowledge the debt we owe to each other for making the process of writing *Contemporary Behavior Therapy* so reinforcing.

Michael D. Spiegler
David C. Guevremont

Contents

Chapter 15 APPLICATIONS TO PSYCHOLOGICAL DISORDERS
WITH PRIMARY PHYSICAL CHARACTERISTICS **414**

Chapter 16 CONTEMPORARY BEHAVIOR THERAPY IN PERSPECTIVE:
STRENGTHS, CHALLENGES, AND CONTROVERSIES **446**

Case Studies, Participation Exercises, and In Theory Boxes

Participation Exercises

In Theory Boxes

A Note to Readers

To aid your journey through this book, you should be aware of several topographical features we've included to help you learn about behavior therapy and to make your reading easier. Each chapter begins with an outline of its contents, and we suggest you look it over before starting to read. References are designated by superscript numbers that correspond to reference notes at the end of each chapter. All major behavior therapy terms are printed in **boldface type** at the point where they are first defined in detail. These terms also are defined succinctly in a comprehensive Glossary of Behavior Therapy Terms at the back of the book. A Glossary of Psychological Disorders and Problems provides brief definitions of the major disorders and problems treated by behavior therapy.

Three features are set off from the main text by gray bars. *Cases* are a continuous part of the text discussion, so you should read them as you come to them. *Participation Exercises* give you direct experience with behavior therapy principles and procedures. Instructions for when to read and carry out the Participation Exercises are provided in the text or a footnote. Some of the Participation Exercises require work sheets and some have answers, both of which you will find in the Student Resource Materials, a booklet that comes with new copies of the book. *In Theory* boxes describe theoretical and professional issues related to behavior therapy, and you should read them as soon as you have come to logical pauses in the text.

We have written *Contemporary Behavior Therapy,* fourth edition, specifically for students and have incorporated many suggestions from students who have used the previous editions. We'd appreciate your comments and feedback. You can communicate with us by mail at: Michael D. Spiegler, Department of Psychology, Providence College, Providence, RI 02918-0001; or by email at: spiegler@providence.edu. We'd like to hear from you, and we'll reply.

Happy reading and learning.

BASIC PRINCIPLES

Imagine that you are about to partake of a delicious four-course dinner. You can think of each of the four parts of this book as one of the courses. In Part I, we serve the appetizers: the ideas that will prepare your palate for the rest of the dinner. We begin with an overview of the field of behavior therapy in Chapter 1, followed in Chapter 2 by a look at the historical events that shaped contemporary behavior therapy. Next, Chapter 3 introduces the behavioral model, the principles that underlie behavior therapy. Chapter 4 explains how the behavioral model is applied to behavior therapy, describes the basic processes involved in implementing behavior therapy, and discusses how the success of behavior therapy is evaluated. Finally, Chapter 5 describes behavioral assessment, the procedures for gathering information about clients' problems and measuring clients' progress in therapy.

The first course is about to be served. Please join us.

What Is Behavior Therapy?

Opening a textbook for the first time is like walking into a psychotherapist's office for the first visit. Both students and clients (as recipients in behavior therapy are usually called) arrive with general expectations for what is about to happen. Students assume the author will teach them, just as new clients in psychotherapy expect the therapist will help them with their problems.

Being taught and *being helped* are passive processes. As teachers and behavior therapists, we believe that for education and psychotherapy to be maximally effective, students and clients must actively participate in the process. In behavior therapy, clients actively engage in therapy procedures. In education, students learn best when they actively engage in learning, and we have written this book with that goal in mind.

One way you will actively learn about behavior therapy is through Participation Exercises that will give you hands-on experience with the ideas, concepts, and procedures used in behavior therapy. Some Participation Exercises take a very brief time to complete, and these should be done when you come to them in the chapter. Others require a bit more time; it is optimal to do them before continuing your reading, but you can do them later. Finally, some exercises need to be carried out over a number of days or require the assistance of another person and therefore must be done after you read the chapter. We will make suggestions as to when to do each Participation Exercise, either in the text or in a footnote. The first Participation Exercise is an example of one you should do right now.

◆ ▮▮▮

Participation   ASSESSING YOUR INITIAL IDEAS ABOUT BEHAVIOR THERAPY
Exercise 1-1
You have no doubt heard about behavior therapy. How accurate is your picture of behavior therapy? This exercise can help answer that question. Read each of the following statements, and write down whether you think it is primarily true or primarily false.

1. Behavior therapy is the application of well-established laws of learning.
2. Behavior therapy directly changes symptoms of a disorder.
3. A trusting relationship between client and therapist is not necessary for behavior therapy to be effective.
4. Behavior therapy does not deal with problems of feelings, such as depression and anger.
5. Generally, little verbal interchange takes place between the therapist and client in behavior therapy. ·
6. The client's cooperation is not necessary for behavior therapy to be successful.
7. Most clients in behavior therapy are treated in fewer than five sessions.
8. Behavior therapy is not applicable to changing mental processes such as thoughts and beliefs.
9. Positive reinforcement works better with children than with adults.
10. Many behavior therapy procedures use painful or aversive treatments.
11. Behavior therapy primarily deals with relatively simple problems, such as phobias (for example, fear of snakes) or undesirable habits (for instance, smoking).

12. The behavior therapist determines the goals of therapy.
13. The behavior therapist primarily is responsible for the success of therapy.

You may have recognized that many of the statements are false. In fact, all these statements are predominantly false. They are all myths or misconceptions about behavior therapy.

◆

TERMINOLOGY AND SCOPE

Behavior therapy also is called *behavior modification* and *cognitive-behavioral therapy*. Behavior therapists occasionally distinguish among the terms, but the distinctions are not standard.[1] *Behavior modification* originally referred to procedures that primarily changed the consequences of behaviors (such as reinforcement) and also changed the stimulus conditions that elicited behaviors (such as the environmental setting). However, *behavior modification* sometimes is used as a generic term to refer to *any* procedure that modifies behaviors, including some rather radical procedures ranging from lobotomies to wilderness survival courses,[2] which are totally unrelated to behavior therapy. The term **cognitive-behavioral therapy** specifically refers to treatments that change cognitions (such as thoughts and beliefs) that are influencing psychological problems. *Behavior therapy* is the broadest and "purest" term.

The major goal of behavior therapy is to help clients with psychological problems, a goal it shares with other forms of psychotherapy. Examples of psychological problems include anxiety, depression, interpersonal difficulties, problems with sexual functioning, bizarre behaviors (such as hearing voices), and being unable to function in one's everyday life. Psychological problems often are personally distressing to clients, may be disturbing to other people (for example, parents may be upset by their child's aggressive acts), and may violate social norms. The common terms for *psychological problems* such as *mental illness, emotional disturbance, psychopathology,* and *abnormal behavior* have particular connotations. In this book, we use more neutral terms: *psychological problem, psychological* or *psychiatric disorder, problem behavior,* and *problem.*

In addition to treating psychological disorders, the principles and procedures of behavior therapy have been adapted to improve everyday functioning, such as work productivity and child rearing;[3] to deal with societal problems, such as promoting safety and conserving energy;[4] and to prevent and treat the physical and psychological effects of medical disorders.

WHAT IS BEHAVIOR THERAPY? DEFINING THEMES AND CHARACTERISTICS

If the statements in Participation Exercise 1-1 reveal something of what behavior therapy is *not*, then just what *is* behavior therapy? Unfortunately, no single, agreed-on definition exists.[5] Behavior therapy is both diverse and evolving, so it is difficult to define concisely.

Instead of a general definition, we present four defining themes that are at the core of behavior therapy: scientific, active, present focus, and learning focus.[6] These themes are interrelated and overlap in their influence on the practice of behavior therapy.

Scientific

The essence of behavior therapy is a commitment to a scientific approach that involves *precision* and *empirical evaluation*.[7] All aspects of behavior therapy are defined precisely, including the behaviors targeted for change, treatment goals, and assessment and therapy procedures. Treatment protocols that spell out the details of particular therapy procedures have been developed for a number of behavior therapies.[8] Using such protocols enables therapists to employ the same procedures that have already proven effective. As another example of precision, clients' progress is monitored before, during, and after therapy using quantitative measurements of the behaviors to be changed.

Behavior therapy consists of procedures that have been *empirically validated*.[9] This means that conclusions about the effectiveness of therapies are based on research—involving controlled studies that other researchers can independently replicate (repeat)—rather than on a therapist's own experiences and beliefs, the opinions of authorities, or testimonials (as from satisfied clients).[10]

Active

In behavior therapy, clients engage in specific actions to alleviate their problems. In other words, clients *do* something about their difficulties, rather than just talk about them. Behavior therapy is an *action therapy,* in contrast to a *verbal therapy* (such as psychoanalysis or client-centered therapy). In verbal psychotherapies, the dialogue between the client and therapist is the major mode through which therapy techniques are implemented. In action therapies, the therapy techniques involve tasks the client does, and the conversation between the client and therapist is primarily for exchanging information. For example, clients in behavior therapy may monitor their behaviors during the course of their daily activities, learn and practice coping skills, and role-play problem situations in therapy sessions. Specific therapeutic tasks that clients perform in their everyday environments, called **homework assignments,** are an integral part of behavior therapy.[11]

Behavior therapy often is carried out, at least in part, in the client's natural environment. The logic is simple. The client's problem is treated where it is occurring, which is in the client's everyday life. "Taking therapy home" makes it more likely that the changes that occur during therapy will transfer to the client's life and continue after therapy has ended.[12]

The term **in vivo** (Latin for "in life") is used to designate therapy procedures that are implemented in the client's natural environment. In vivo therapy is implemented in one of three ways. First, the therapist may work directly with the client in the client's natural environment. This approach is costly in terms of therapists' time and is therefore used only occasionally. Second, the therapist can train people in the client's life, such as parents, spouses, and teachers, to provide information related to the client's problem and to assist in the treatment itself, such as by administering reinforcers.[13] Third, clients can serve as their own change agents by carrying out therapy procedures by themselves, with the guidance of the therapist.[14] Thus, those responsible for implementing treatment include not only behavior therapists but also nontherapist agents of change, including relatives, friends, teachers, and clients themselves. We refer to this latter group as *change agents*.

Clients' serving as their own change agents illustrates the **self-control approach** commonly used in behavior therapy.[15] A self-control approach has three important advantages. First, clients who are instrumental in changing their own behaviors are more likely to maintain the change. Second, being responsible for the change is personally empowering.[16] Third, clients who become skilled in dealing with their problems may be able to cope with future problems on their own,[17] which makes a self-control approach cost-effective in the long run.

A final way in which behavior therapy is active involves the essential collaboration between the therapist and client. Behavior therapists share their expertise so that clients become knowledgeable partners in their therapy. Decisions about therapy goals and treatment procedures are made jointly. For example, behavior therapists provide information about treatment options, describing what each of the appropriate therapies entails and the effectiveness of each (based on research findings). Clients then can decide on the type of treatment that is best suited to their needs and preferences. In contrast to this close collaboration between behavior therapists and their clients, in some forms of psychotherapy the therapist creates a "therapeutic mystique," which sets the therapist apart from the client by virtue of the therapist's special knowledge.

Present Focus

The focus of behavior therapy is in the present. Behavior therapists assume that clients' problems, which occur in the present, are influenced by current conditions. Accordingly, behavioral assessment focuses on the client's current, rather than past, circumstances to find the factors responsible for the client's problems. Then, behavior therapy procedures are employed to change the current factors that are affecting the client's behaviors. This emphasis contrasts with other types of psychotherapy, such as psychoanalytic therapy, which assume that the major influences on clients' problems lie in the past.

Learning Focus

An emphasis on learning is a final theme that distinguishes behavior therapy from other types of psychotherapy. Learning is important in three different respects. First, the behavioral model holds that most problem behaviors develop, are maintained, and change primarily through learning. Behavior therapists do not believe that *all* behaviors come about through learning because some are strongly influenced by heredity and biology. Nonetheless, virtually all behaviors are influenced by learning, even if they have biological components.

Second, behavior therapy provides clients with learning experiences in which new (adaptive) behaviors replace old (maladaptive) behaviors. Indeed, there is a strong *educational* component in behavior therapy, and behavior therapists often serve as teachers.

Third, the development of some behavior therapies was originally based on basic learning principles, and theories of learning (such as classical conditioning) often are used to explain why behavior therapy procedures work.

Other Common Characteristics of Behavior Therapy

In addition to the fundamental themes in behavior therapy just described, four common characteristics of behavior therapies help distinguish behavior therapy from other forms of psychotherapy: individualized therapy, stepwise progression, treatment packages, and brevity.

INDIVIDUALIZED THERAPY

Although standard therapy and assessment procedures are used in behavior therapy, they are tailored to each client's unique problem, the specific circumstances in which the problem occurs, and the client's personal characteristics. For instance, reinforcement is used to get clients of all ages to engage in adaptive behaviors. However, the specific reinforcer (such as playing a game or attending a concert) is likely to vary with the client's age. Moreover, activities that serve as a reinforcer for one 6-year-old might differ from activities that work for another 6-year-old.

STEPWISE PROGRESSION

Behavior therapy often proceeds in a stepwise progression, moving from simple to complex, from easier to harder, or from less threatening to more threatening. For example, a girl who was socially withdrawn was taught—through modeling and reinforcement procedures—to interact with peers in steps: initially playing by herself in the presence of peers, then playing with peers, and finally initiating play with peers. Similarly, a man who was afraid of heights gradually was exposed to higher elevations during treatment, beginning a few feet off the ground and ending on top of a 10-story building.

TREATMENT PACKAGES

Two or more behavior therapy procedures often are combined in a **treatment package** to increase the effectiveness of the therapy.[18] This practice is analogous to the treatment of many medical problems, such as the combination of medication, diet, and exercise for cardiovascular disease. Although treatment packages can be more effective than specific treatments, combining therapies may lengthen treatment, which is not surprising.[19]

BREVITY

Behavior therapy is relatively brief, generally involving fewer therapy sessions and often less overall time than many other types of therapy. This results, in part, from the use of homework assignments in particular and the self-control approach in general. Length of therapy varies considerably with the problem being treated. Often, the more complex and severe the problem, the longer the treatment duration. For example, one survey revealed that the average number of hours required to treat specific phobias was 13.4, compared with 46.4 for obsessive-compulsive disorder.[20] Treatment duration also varies with the therapy used.

THERAPIST–CLIENT RELATIONSHIP IN BEHAVIOR THERAPY

The relationship between the therapist and the client is important in all forms of psychotherapy,[21] and with some psychotherapies it is considered the most critical factor. In behavior therapy, the relationship is considered a necessary but not a sufficient condition for successful treatment.[22] In other words, behavior therapists presume that their clients are helped primarily by the specific change techniques used rather than by their relationship with the therapist. Interestingly, clients in behavior therapy may attribute their improvement more to the therapist–client relationship than to the therapy procedures.[23] Nonetheless, from the behavior therapist's perspective, the therapist–client relationship is analogous to the role of anesthesia in surgery.

> Somebody goes . . . for surgery because there are certain procedures that need to be implemented. In order for these procedures to take place, the person must be under anesthesia; the anesthesia facilitates what is really important. However, if anything goes wrong with the anesthesia during the surgery, then that becomes the priority. Similarly . . . a good . . . [therapist–client relationship] is necessary and often crucial. Without it you just can't proceed.[24]

The therapist–client relationship in behavior therapy facilitates the implementation of specific therapy procedures in a variety of ways, including increasing the client's positive expectations and hope for success; encouraging the client to complete homework assignments that may involve risk taking; overcoming obstacles that arise in therapy, including noncompliance; and increasing the potency of the therapist's praise and approval.[25]

MANY VARIETIES OF BEHAVIOR THERAPY

Behavior therapy is not a single technique. There are many different forms of behavior therapy—in other words, many behavior therapies.

These therapies are unified by the defining themes and common characteristics you read about earlier. The following examples illustrate the variety of behavior therapy procedures that exist. (The chapters in which they are introduced are given in parentheses.)

◆ *Positive Reinforcement* (Chapter 6): A sixth-grade boy was doing poorly in school because he was spending an average of only 20 minutes a day doing homework. The therapist suggested that his parents have him earn privileges by doing appropriate amounts of homework. The boy was allowed to play with friends, have an evening snack, and watch television only after doing predetermined amounts of homework.

◆ *Modeling and Behavior Rehearsal* (Chapter 11): A woman was intimidated by her boss and consequently was unable to speak to him about problems at work. She learned to express her desires appropriately to her boss by observing the therapist demonstrate effective ways to tell superiors politely yet forcefully about dissatisfactions and personal preferences (modeling). The woman then practiced these behaviors—initially with the therapist and later with less threatening people than her boss (behavior reversal).

◆ *Response Cost* (Chapter 7): A 7-year-old boy, who was big for his age, frequently bullied smaller children. To decrease the boy's bullying, the boy's teacher instituted a rule specifying that he would miss recess or gym, his favorite school activities, each time he was caught fighting.

◆ *Cognitive Restructuring* (Chapter 12): To increase a woman's self-esteem, her therapist taught her to substitute positive, self-enhancing thoughts (such as "I look nice today" or "I'm doing a great job") for her habitual negative, self-effacing ideas (such as "I look a mess today" or "I can't do anything right").

◆ *Stress Inoculation Training* (Chapter 13): A business executive drank excessively when he arrived home each evening after a frustrating day at the office. To help the man deal with his frustration, the therapist taught him appropriate coping skills, including relaxation and cognitive restructuring. In therapy, the client role-played being in various frustrating situations and practiced applying the coping skills. He then used the skills in his everyday life whenever he felt frustrated and had the urge to drink.

◆ *Systematic Desensitization* (Chapter 9): A college student was doing poorly in school because she panicked during examinations. To overcome her test anxiety, the student first was taught muscle relaxation. While relaxed, she visualized increasingly more anxiety-evoking situations (beginning with hearing the announcement that an exam would be given in 2 weeks and ending with being unable to answer an exam question). The objective was to substitute relaxation for the anxiety associated with test situations.

◆ *Extinction and Differential Reinforcement of Other Behaviors* (Chapter 7): On several occasions, a young mother had beaten her 3-year-old son when he had a temper tantrum. The more the mother tried to get her son to stop crying, the angrier she got; eventually she beat the child. The mother was taught to ignore her son during a temper tantrum (extinction) and to reinforce him with attention when he began engaging in any other behaviors (differential reinforcement of other behaviors). This treatment package was designed not only to reduce the frequency and duration of her son's temper tantrums but also to help the mother cope with her frustration and eliminate abusing her child.

◆ *Token Economy and Shaping* (Chapters 8 and 6, respectively): A 36-year-old man who was hospitalized for the treatment of schizophrenia was extremely socially withdrawn. He was placed in a token economy program in which he earned tokens (poker chips) for engaging in increasing levels of social interaction. At first he earned tokens for engaging in minimal social contacts (for instance, asking a nurse for something he wanted) and later for extended social interactions (for example, having a conversation with another patient while they worked on a project together) (shaping). The man could exchange the tokens he earned for a variety of reinforcers (such as watching TV and playing pool).

◆ *Cognitive-Behavioral Couple Therapy* (Chapter 13): A married couple sought help because they believed that they no longer loved each other and they had difficulty resolving conflicts. For the couple's first complaint, the therapist instructed each spouse to perform several behaviors each day that the other spouse considered an indication of caring. For dealing with conflicts, they were taught problem-solving strategies. These strategies involved generating a variety of potential solutions to disagreements and then evaluating them to select the optimal solution.

Even from the small sample of behavior therapy procedures just presented, it is clear that many diverse behavior therapies are used to treat a wide array of problems, including some very serious and complex psychological disorders.

ETHICAL ISSUES IN BEHAVIOR THERAPY

In considering ethical issues related to behavior therapy, two points should be kept in mind. First, ethical issues potentially arise whenever one person's behavior is changed directly or indirectly by another person. This is true in psychotherapy as well as in many other areas, including education, advertising, and religion. Second, the ethical issues that can arise in behavior therapy are relevant to all psychotherapies.

The two major potential ethical issues in behavior therapy concern depriving clients of their rights and harming clients. Throughout this book, we will, from time to time, raise ethical questions in relevant contexts. As you read, be alert for instances where ethical issues could occur. In addition, consider the ways in which behavior therapy protects clients from ethical violations. For example, you have already read about the active role clients play in deciding on their treatment goals and the specific therapy procedures used to achieve them. This practice not only affords clients freedom of choice but also increases the chances that the treatment will be successful because clients are actively involved in their therapy.[26]

Ethical violations occasionally occur in behavior therapy, and there are a small number of well-documented incidents. Most have been perpetrated against people who have little or no power, especially institutionalized individuals such as prison inmates.[27] To help prevent such incidents, behavior therapists have developed guidelines for the ethical practice of behavior therapy.[28] Table 1-1 presents examples of the questions that should be answered for each therapy case.

PURPOSE OF THIS BOOK

The purpose of this book is to introduce you to contemporary behavior therapy. We first will present its general principles and then illustrate how they are applied to treat clients' problems. Although this book is not intended to teach you to be a behavior therapist, you may be able to apply many of the principles and some of the procedures to deal with

Table 1-1 Examples of ethical questions that should be answered for each therapy case
SOURCE: Adapted from *Ethical issues for human services,* 1977, pp. v–vi.

A. Have the goals of treatment been adequately considered?
  1. To ensure that the goals are explicit, are they written?
  2. Has the client's understanding of the goals been ensured by having the client restate them orally or in writing?
  3. Have the therapist and client agreed on the goals of therapy?
  4. Will serving the client's immediate interests be contrary to the client's long-term interest?
B. Has the choice of treatment methods been adequately considered?
  1. Does the published literature show the procedure to be the best one available for that problem?
  2. Has the client been told of alternative procedures that might be preferred by the client on the basis of significant differences in discomfort, treatment time, cost, or degree of demonstrated effectiveness?
C. Is the client's participation voluntary?
  1. Have possible sources of coercion on the client's participation been considered?
  2. If treatment is legally mandated, has the available range of treatments and therapists been offered?
  3. Can the client withdraw from treatment without a penalty or financial loss that exceeds actual clinical costs?
D. Has the adequacy of treatment been evaluated?
  1. Have quantitative measures of the problem and its progress been obtained?
  2. Have the measures of the problem and its progress been made available to the client during treatment?
E. Has the confidentiality of the treatment relationship been protected?
  1. Has the client been told who has access to the records?
  2. Are records available only to authorized persons?
F. Is the therapist qualified to provide treatment?
  1. Has the therapist had training or experience in treating problems like the client's?
  2. If deficits exist in the therapist's qualifications, has the client been informed?
  3. If the therapist is not adequately qualified, is the client referred to other therapists or has supervision by a qualified therapist been provided? Is the client informed of the supervisory relation?

minor problems in your everyday life. However, if you develop a psychological problem that seriously affects your life and does not resolve itself quickly, you should consult with a professional. You can find guidelines for choosing a behavior therapist in the Appendix.

SUMMARY

1. The basic aim of behavior therapy is to help clients deal with psychological problems. Behavior therapy principles and procedures also are used to modify everyday problems.
2. There is no single, agreed-on definition of behavior therapy. Behavior therapy can be characterized by four defining themes: scientific, active, present focus, and learning focus.
3. The scientific approach entails precisely defining treatment goals, assessment procedures, and therapy procedures; continuously monitoring clients' progress using quantitative measurements; and evaluating the effectiveness of procedures through controlled research.
4. Behavior therapy is active in that clients do more than just talk about their problems. They play an active role in determining the goals for therapy and the specific treatment procedures that are employed. Clients may be taught to carry out therapeutic procedures on their own in their home environments.
5. Behavior therapy focuses on the present. Current conditions are assumed to influence the clients' present problems, and behavior therapy procedures change these current maintaining conditions.
6. In behavior therapy, problem behaviors are assumed to be learned and/or changeable through learning; therapy therefore focuses on learning. Also, theories of learning often are used to explain why behavior therapies work.
7. Four common characteristics further define behavior therapy. Behavior therapy is individualized for each client, proceeds in a stepwise progression, often involves the combination of two or more therapies in a treatment package, and tends to be relatively brief.
8. Behavior therapy consists of a wide variety of different treatment procedures.
9. As with all psychotherapies, ethical issues can arise in behavior therapy. The two major potential issues are depriving clients of their rights and harming clients. Behavior therapy practices provide for some internal protections against ethical violations.

REFERENCE NOTES

1. Martin & Pear, 1996; Wilson, 1978.
2. For example, Krakauer, 1995, p. 75.
3. Hawkins & Forsyth, 1997.
4. For example, Fantuzzo & Thompson, 1991; Glenwick & Jason, 1980; Jason & Glenwick, 1984; Spiegler & Guevremont, 1998, Chapter 16.
5. Kazdin & Wilson, 1978.
6. Compare with Cottraux, 1993.
7. Wilson, 1997a.
8. For example, Dobson & Shaw, 1989; Meichenbaum, 1994; compare with Addis & Carpenter, 1997; Chorpita, 1995; Raw, 1993.

9. Chambless & Hollon, 1998; Kendall, 1998; Spiegler & Guevremont, 1994.

10. Date, 1996; Persons, 1994.

11. For example, Addis & Jacobson, 2000; Bryant, Simons, & Thase, 1999; Burns & Nolen-Hoeksema, 1992; Burns & Sprangler, 2000; Edelman & Chambless, 1995; Mahrer, Nordin, & Miller, 1995; Startup & Edmonds, 1994.

12. For example, Edelman & Chambless, 1993; Risley, 1995.

13. Petronko, Harris, & Kormann, 1994.

14. For example, Israel, Guile, Baker, & Silverman, 1994; Rehm & Rokke, 1988; Rokke, Tomhave, & Jocic, 1999, 2000; Silverman, Ginsburg, & Kurtines, 1995; Watson & Tharp, 1989.

15. Rehm & Rokke, 1988.

16. For example, Israel, Guile, Baker, & Silverman, 1994; Suarez, Peters, Crowe, Easterling, & Adams, 1988.

17. For example, Otto & Gould, 1995; Otto & Pollack, 1994; Otto, Pollack, Meltzer-Brody, & Rosenbaum, 1992; Otto, Pollack, Sachs, Reiter, Meltzer-Brody, & Rosenbaum, 1993.

18. For example, Carr & Carlson, 1993; Gould & Otto, 1995; Otto & Gould, 1995; Otto, Pava, & Sprich-Buckminster, 1995.

19. For example, Turner, Beidel, Spaulding, & Brown, 1995.

20. Turner, Beidel, Spaulding, & Brown, 1995.

21. Gaston, Goldfried, Greenberg, Horvath, Raue, & Watson, 1995.

22. Fleece, 1995; Raue, Castonguay, & Goldfried, 1993; Raue & Goldfried, 1994; Schapp, Bennun, Schindler, & Hoogduin, 1993.

23. Raue & Goldfried, 1994.

24. Gaston, Goldfried, Greenberg, Horvath, Raue, & Watson, 1995, p. 5, italics in original.

25. Gaston, Goldfried, Greenberg, Horvath, Raue, & Watson, 1995; Keijsers, Schaap, & Hoogduin, 2000; Kohlenberg & Tsai, 1991, 1994, 1995; Raue & Goldfried, 1994.

26. Bandura, 1969.

27. For example, Cotter, 1967.

28. For example, Davison, 1976; Davison & Stuart, 1975; Stolz, 1977.

Chapter 2

Antecedents of Contemporary Behavior Therapy

Behavior therapy has "a long past but a short history."[1] In rudimentary forms, behavior therapy is very old. Humans have been using behavioral principles to modify people's behaviors for thousands of years; parents rewarding children for doing chores is an obvious example. These everyday applications are haphazard, but they can be effective. To treat more serious problems, a systematic approach is necessary. The formal, systematic application of behavioral principles to treat psychological problems—that is, behavior therapy—is about 50 years old.

HISTORICAL PRECURSORS

A number of historical treatments for psychological disorders closely resemble contemporary behavior therapies. For example, Pliny the Elder, a 1st-century C.E. Roman scholar, treated drinking problems using the fundamental principle of aversion therapy. He created an aversion to alcohol by putting putrid spiders at the bottom of the problem drinker's glass.[2] An early account of a cognitive therapy strategy in treating depression is portrayed in a 10th-century Icelandic story.[3] In Egil's saga, a daughter helps her grieving father overcome his severe depression by getting him to engage in sequentially more active behaviors, which results in his feeling better about himself.

At the close of the 18th century, Jean-Marc-Gaspard Itard attempted to socialize the "Wild Boy of Aveyron," a child who grew up without human contact.[4] To teach the boy language and other social behaviors, Itard employed procedures similar to contemporary behavior therapies used to treat children with autistic disorder. These procedures included modeling, prompting, shaping, and time out from positive reinforcement.[5]

In the early 19th century, Alexander Maconochie, a captain in the Royal Navy, had the dubious distinction of being in charge of one of the worst British penal colonies, located on Norfolk Island, Australia.[6] To rehabilitate the prisoners, Maconochie established a point system that allowed each prisoner to redeem himself by performing appropriate tasks and social behaviors. In Maconochie's words, "When a man keeps the key of his own prison, he is soon persuaded to fit it into the lock." Despite the apparent success of this early token economy, Maconochie's superiors disapproved of his innovative methods and denigrated their effectiveness.[7]

An 1845 paper presented to the Royal Academy of Medicine in Paris reported that François Leuret, a physician, treated a 30-year-old wine merchant for his obsessional thoughts. Leuret had the man recite song lyrics, behaviors that competed with his disturbing, repetitive thoughts.[8] This procedure is similar to some present-day cognitive-behavioral interventions.

These early harbingers of behavior therapy procedures have only historical significance and interest, having had no real influence on the development of contemporary behavior therapy.[9]

EARLY EXPERIMENTAL WORK

The inspiration for contemporary behavior therapy came from experimental work on learning carried out at the beginning of the 20th century.

Pavlov (center) in his lab

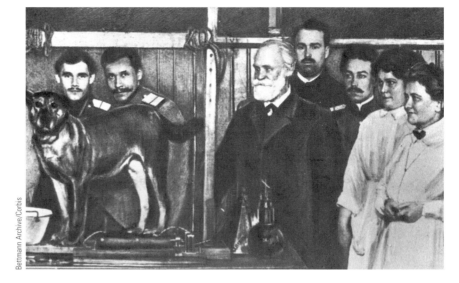

Bettmann Archive/Corbis

Russian physiologist Ivan Pavlov is credited with the first systematic account of what has come to be called *classical* (or *Pavlovian*) *conditioning*.[10] In this form of learning, a neutral stimulus (one that elicits no particular response) is repeatedly paired with a stimulus that naturally elicits a particular response. The result is that eventually the neutral stimulus alone elicits the response. In Pavlov's well-known experiments with dogs, a neutral stimulus, such as a light or a tone, was paired with food, a stimulus that reflexively produces salivation. After repeated pairings of these two stimuli, the light or tone alone began to elicit salivation. This classical conditioning process is shown in Figure 2-1.

Figure 2-1 The classical conditioning process recognized by Pavlov

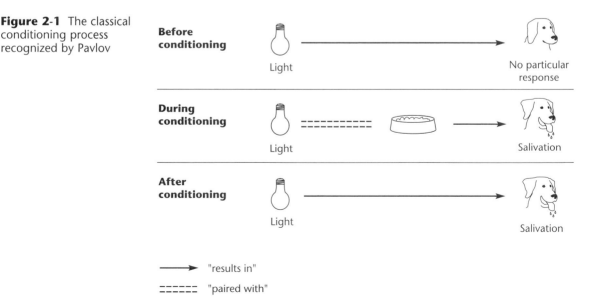

Archives of the History of American Psychology, University of Akron

John B. Watson

Archives of the History of American Psychology, University of Akron

Mary Cover Jones

In addition to his important laboratory experiments with animals, Pavlov wrote about the application of learning procedures to treat psychological disorders.[11] Pavlov's critical contribution to behavior therapy, however, was the influence his work had on John B. Watson, an experimental psychologist at Johns Hopkins University. Watson is the founder of *behaviorism*, the school of psychology on which behavior therapy is largely based. Behaviorism emphasizes the importance of objectively studying behaviors by dealing only with directly observable stimuli and responses. Watson's behaviorism rejected mentalistic concepts such as consciousness, thought, and imagery.[12]

In 1924, Mary Cover Jones, one of Watson's students, successfully treated a 3-year-old boy named Peter, who had an intense fear of rabbits.[13] The therapy consisted of two basic procedures. First, Peter watched other children happily playing with a rabbit, which may have led Peter to realize that rabbits were not necessarily frightening. Then, Jones gradually exposed Peter to the rabbit. She placed a caged rabbit in the room while Peter was eating a favorite food. The cage was at a sufficient distance so that its presence did not interfere with Peter's eating and did not upset him. Gradually, over a period of days, Jones brought the rabbit closer to Peter, always keeping it at a distance with which Peter was comfortable. Jones eventually took the rabbit out of the cage and gradually brought it closer to Peter. After this treatment, Peter was able to comfortably hold and play with the rabbit. Years later, Jones' two therapy procedures—modeling and in vivo exposure—were refined and now are widely used behavior therapies for the treatment of fears.

Hobart and Willie Mowrer also were influenced by Pavlov's classical conditioning principles. In 1935, they began a treatment program for

Courtesy of the University of Illinois at Urbana-Champaign Archives

Willie & Hobart Mowrer

Edward Thorndike

nocturnal enuresis (bedwetting) at the New Haven Children's Center.[14] The treatment taught children to awaken when they felt tension in their bladder so that they could go to the toilet to urinate rather than wet the bed. To accomplish this, a special pad under the bedsheet activated a bell when urine contacted it.[15] Thus, as soon as children began to urinate, they were awakened by the bell. After bladder tension and waking up were paired a number of times, a full bladder alone woke the child. Their bell-and-pad technique proved highly successful and is still used today.

At the same time that Pavlov was studying classical conditioning, psychologist Edward Thorndike at Columbia University was investigating increasing or decreasing behaviors by systematically changing their consequences.[16] This type of learning came to be called *operant* (or *instrumental*) *conditioning*.

In a different arena, Edmund Jacobson, a physiologist at the University of Chicago in the 1930s, was experimenting with muscle relaxation as a treatment for tension associated with a wide array of psychological and physical disorders, including generalized anxiety, phobias, depression, hypertension, colitis, tics, and stuttering.[17] Jacobson's *progressive relaxation* is the basis for the extensive use of muscle relaxation in behavior therapy.

GROWING DISCONTENT WITH PSYCHOANALYSIS

Despite the effectiveness of some early behavior therapies,[18] contemporary behavior therapy did not begin in earnest until the 1950s.[19] The events that occurred at that time must be understood in relation to the nature and status of psychoanalysis, the then prevailing model of psychotherapy.

Psychoanalysis, originally developed by Sigmund Freud, focuses on exploring clients' early childhood experiences and attempting to uncover unconscious conflicts and desires. The objective is for clients to gain insight about the origin of their problems. Insight is believed to be the key to change; for this reason, psychoanalysis and similar therapies are called *insight therapies*.

Psychoanalysis was the only major approach to psychotherapy during the first half of the 20th century. However, after World War II, doubts about the usefulness of psychoanalysis as a general treatment method began to mount. Because psychoanalysis is such a lengthy process—often requiring several years—it could not meet the needs of the large number of veterans who required psychological treatment as a result of the war.

This growing discontent with traditional psychoanalytic psychotherapy received a major impetus from a retrospective study by British psychologist Hans Eysenck (pronounced EYE-zink) published in 1952.[20] Eysenck investigated the effectiveness of insight therapies by examining records from hospitals and insurance companies. He concluded that people treated by traditional insight psychotherapy were no more likely to improve than those who received no treatment at all. Subsequent reanalysis of Eysenck's data showed that his conclusion was exaggerated.[21] Nonetheless, Eysenck's original conclusion did serve as an impetus for psychotherapists to seriously question the benefits of traditional

Hans Eysenck

psychotherapy and to seek more effective alternatives. One of those alternatives was behavior therapy.

FORMAL BEGINNINGS OF CONTEMPORARY BEHAVIOR THERAPY

Contemporary behavior therapy had its formal beginnings in the 1950s, simultaneously in the United States and Canada, South Africa, and Great Britain.

Developments in North America

B. F. Skinner

Beginning in the 1930s, psychologist B. F. Skinner, at Harvard University, began his extensive investigation of operant conditioning, using pigeons and rats as subjects. Like Pavlov, Skinner speculated about the therapeutic uses of learning principles,[22] but he himself did not carry his ideas to fruition. It remained for his students and followers to apply operant principles to therapy.

In the early 1950s, Ogden Lindsley, then a graduate student working with Skinner at Harvard, directed a series of studies to determine the feasibility of applying operant conditioning procedures to adults with psychiatric disorders.[23] His initial research demonstrated that patients in psychiatric hospitals whose behaviors seemed aimless would consistently perform simple tasks when given meaningful reinforcers. Lindsley's investigations could not legitimately be considered therapy. However, they led to the development of sophisticated procedures, derived from operant conditioning principles, to treat complex human problems. Incidentally, Lindsley may have been the first person to formally use the term *behavior therapy* to describe the systematic use of learning procedures to treat psychological disorders.[24]

Ogden Lindsley

In the late 1950s, Teodoro Ayllon (pronounced eye-YONE), at the Saskatchewan Hospital in Canada, performed now-classic demonstrations of the effectiveness of operant principles in modifying severely disturbed behaviors of patients with psychiatric disorders.[25] Ayllon's demonstrations were instrumental in overcoming the widespread resistance to the behavioral model. According to psychoanalysis, the model still prevailing at the time, psychological disorders are the result of deep-seated, unconscious conflicts. This implied that successful treatment had to delve into those conflicts.[26] To indirectly challenge these psychoanalytic notions, Ayllon and his colleague Eric Haughton showed that a behavior that might be considered a symptom of a psychiatric disorder could be created simply by reinforcing it and then could be eliminated simply by withdrawing the reinforcement.[27] They chose holding a broom in an upright position (see Figure 2-2) as the behavior, and their subject was a 54-year-old female patient with schizophrenia who had been hospitalized for 23 years and who spent most of her time lying in bed or sitting on a couch. A psychiatrist who was unaware of the origins of the patient's broom-holding made the following comments after observing the patient's behavior.

Courtesy of Harvard University Archives

Courtesy of University of Kansas, University Archives

Figure 2-2 Sketch of the patient's stance that Haughton and Ayllon reinforced in their demonstration study
SOURCE: Haughton & Ayllon, 1965, p. 96.

Her constant and compulsive pacing holding a broom . . . could be seen as a ritualistic procedure, a magical action. When regression conquers the associative process, primitive and archaic forms of thinking control the behavior. Symbolism is a predominant mode of expression of deep seated unfulfilled desires and instinctual impulses. . . .

Her broom could then be:

1. a child that gives her love and she gives him in return her devotion;
2. a phallic symbol;
3. the sceptre of an omnipotent queen.[28]

This explanation is consistent with the psychoanalytic model that postulates complex and deep-rooted causes of behavior. However, Haughton and Ayllon's study demonstrated that alternative and much simpler and more straightforward explanations for psychiatric symptoms might exist, a revolutionary idea at the time.

In 1961, Ayllon collaborated with Nathan Azrin, another of Skinner's former students, to design the first comprehensive token economy at Anna State Hospital in Illinois.[29] A token economy provides clients with token reinforcers (such as poker chips or points) to motivate them to perform desired behaviors; the patient can exchange tokens for actual reinforcers (for instance, a snack or time watching TV). The Anna State Hospital token economy paved the way for the widespread application of this treatment method.

In setting up their token economy, Ayllon and Azrin, like most other early behavior therapists, encountered considerable resistance from the hospital staff. Most of the staff did not believe that the new behavioral treatment methods could be effective and were reluctant to support Ayllon and Azrin's program. As was typical of behavior therapy efforts at the time, the Anna State Hospital token economy was set up as an experimental program funded by a research grant, which separated it from the mainstream hospital programs. Resisting the new treatment model, the staffs of other hospital programs were reluctant to provide patients for the token economy, especially patients with whom they were having some success. Therefore, the patients who were referred to Ayllon and Azrin's experimental program were those who had not responded to traditional treatments and were considered incurable. Naturally, this "stacked the deck" against the new behavior therapy program. Ironically, these unfavorable conditions turned out to be a blessing in disguise. The token economy resulted in remarkable changes in the so-called incurable patients, which strengthened the case for the effectiveness of behavior therapy procedures. This cycle of facing *skepticism* from traditional professionals, having to work under *adverse conditions,* and nonetheless *demonstrating effectiveness* was a common experience for early behavior therapists through at least the mid-1970s.

Developments in South Africa

Meanwhile, in South Africa, psychiatrist Joseph Wolpe had become disenchanted with psychoanalytic methods of treatment. In the 1950s, he

Courtesy of Arnold Lazarus

Arnold Lazarus

Courtesy of Stanley Rachman

Stanley Rachman

developed several keystone behavior therapies, most notably systematic desensitization, for treating problems such as irrational fears and anxiety. Wolpe's treatment approach involved replacing debilitating anxiety with more adaptive reactions such as deep muscle relaxation (based on Jacobson's progressive relaxation). Wolpe explained his procedures in terms of classical conditioning and neurophysiological concepts.[30] His work has had a major influence on behavior therapy, and he is sometimes referred to as the founder of behavior therapy.[31]

Prominent among the professionals Wolpe trained in South Africa were Arnold Lazarus and Stanley Rachman. Lazarus initially made important contributions by adapting systematic desensitization to groups of clients and to children.[32] Throughout his career, Lazarus has strongly advocated extending the boundaries of behavior therapy. He has developed innovative therapy techniques on the basis of their effectiveness rather than their being derived from existing theories—in contrast to Wolpe, whose work always was tightly bound to learning theory.[33] Since 1966, Lazarus has practiced and taught behavior therapy in the United States. Rachman, who had collaborated with Lazarus in South Africa, emigrated to Great Britain in 1959 to work closely with Eysenck. Rachman introduced desensitization to British behavior therapists, and he became one of behavior therapy's foremost advocates and researchers in Great Britain.[34]

Developments in Great Britain

Great Britain was the third major seat of contemporary behavior therapy's origins in the 1950s. The development of behavior therapy in Great Britain was spearheaded by Eysenck at the Institute of Psychiatry at the University of London. This work was facilitated by M. B. Shapiro,[35] who, as director of the Clinical-Teaching Section, championed the intensive study of individual cases, as did Skinner and his associates.[36] This emphasis is but one commonality among the early behavior therapists in North America, South Africa, and Great Britain. As is often the case in the history of science, similar approaches apparently developed simultaneously and independently. Nonetheless, behavior therapy in North America, South Africa, and Great Britain in the 1950s presented a strong and fairly unified alternative to traditional psychoanalytic therapy.

EARLY ETHICAL CONCERNS ABOUT BEHAVIOR THERAPY

Some early criticisms of behavior therapy in its formative years involved ethical concerns that were in large measure artifacts of the time. For example, one ethical criticism involved the possible danger that behavior therapy techniques would be used to control people. In part, this notion may have arisen from misunderstandings about some of the terminology that behavior therapists used, such as references to "controlling variables," "experimental control," and the "manipulation of contingencies." Coincidentally, behavior therapy emerged in a period of heightened concern about external control (such as by government), about the invasion of personal privacy (as through electronic eavesdropping and computer storage of personal information), and about the abuse of civil liberties (for instance, of institutionalized patients and prisoners). "Reacting to the seemingly unchecked growth of these influences, many citizens . . . [came] to adopt positions that are highly critical of any and all behavior influence efforts."[37]

A number of early ethical criticisms of behavior therapy arose out of confusion as to what behavior therapy was and what it was not. These criticisms occurred most frequently when the term *behavior modification* was used (rather than *behavior therapy*). *Behavior modification* was mistakenly confused with *any* procedure that modifies behavior, including psychosurgery (such as lobotomies), electroconvulsive shock therapy (ECT), drugs, brainwashing, sensory deprivation, and even torture.[38] A survey of articles indexed under *behavior modification* in the *New York Times* over a 5-year period revealed that the term was incorrectly used approximately half the time.[39] In some cases, the treatment procedures had absolutely no relationship to behavior therapy. For example, the use of a drug that causes a brief period of paralysis of the muscles (including those of the respiratory system) as punishment for prisoners was erroneously called *behavior modification*.[40]

The extent to which the name of a therapy procedure can influence people's perceptions of it is illustrated by a study titled "A Rose by Any Other Name . . . : Labeling Bias and Attitudes Toward Behavior Modification."[41] In this experiment, undergraduate and graduate students evaluated a video of a teacher using reinforcement procedures in a special education class. All the students saw the same video, but half were told that it illustrated "behavior modification" and half were told that it illustrated "humanistic education." Interestingly, compared with students who viewed it as "behavior modification," those who viewed it as "humanistic education" gave the teacher significantly more favorable ratings and considered the teaching method significantly more likely to promote academic learning and emotional growth.

ACCEPTANCE AND GROWTH OF BEHAVIOR THERAPY

In the 1960s, there were few behavior therapists in private practice, and those working in psychiatric hospitals and outpatient facilities were still encountering resistance from traditional psychotherapists. Even in academic settings, which are among the most accepting and nurturing atmospheres for new ideas, behavior therapists often were isolated because their colleagues viewed behavior therapy as a radical departure from mainstream psychology.

To overcome these barriers to acceptance and growth, behavior therapists in the late 1950s and early 1960s spent considerable time gathering evidence that behavior therapy was a viable alternative to traditional psychotherapy. This effort included publication of demonstration projects, such as Ayllon's studies. These studies showed that a wide array of clinical problems could be treated successfully in a relatively brief period with behavior therapy techniques.[42]

Albert Bandura

Chuck Painter, Stanford University News Service

In the 1960s, while already established behavior therapy procedures (such as token economies and systematic desensitization) were being refined, another major approach to behavior therapy was born. Psychologist Albert Bandura at Stanford University developed a social learning theory that included not only principles of classical and operant conditioning but also *observational learning*[43]—the process of changing one's own behaviors by observing the behaviors of another person (a model). In addition, Bandura's *social learning theory*[44] emphasized the critical role that cognitions (such as thoughts, images, and expectations) play in psychological functioning, including their role in the development and treatment of psychological disorders. Indeed, Bandura now calls his theoretical approach *social cognitive theory*.[45]

Making cognitions a legitimate focus of behavior therapy was antithetical to Watson's behaviorism because cognitions are not directly observable by others. Watson's behaviorism may have been a useful position for early behavior therapists to adopt. It countered the deeply entrenched psychoanalytic perspective emphasizing unconscious forces that, of course, cannot be observed directly. Today, most behavior therapists believe that dealing only with directly observable behaviors is too restrictive.[46] After all, humans *do* think, expect, plan, and imagine, and these cognitive processes clearly influence how people act.

During the 1960s, several prominent behavior therapists created cognitive-behavioral therapy, which changes clients' maladaptive cognitions that contribute to psychological disorders. Independently, Aaron Beck at the University of Pennsylvania developed *cognitive therapy*,[47] and Albert Ellis, in private practice in New York City, designed *rational emotive therapy*[48] (which he renamed *rational emotive behavior therapy* in 1993[49]). Both therapies seek to modify the negative and illogical thoughts associated with many psychological disorders, such as depression and anxiety. Donald Meichenbaum (pronounced MIKE-en-baum), at the University of Waterloo in Ontario, developed cognitive-behavioral treatment packages, such as *self-instructional training* and *stress inoculation training* that are used to treat a wide range of psychological problems, including impulsive behaviors, anxiety, anger, pain, and schizophrenic behaviors.[50] Meichenbaum was among the first to apply cognitive-behavioral interventions with children. Initially, cognitive-behavioral therapies served as supplements to existing behavior therapy procedures, but they rapidly evolved as a major approach in the field. Indeed, today, a majority of behavior therapists use cognitive-behavioral therapies.

In 1966, the Association for Advancement of Behavior Therapy was established in the United States. Cyril Franks, who previously had worked with Eysenck and Rachman at the Institute of Psychiatry in London, was its first president. It has become the major professional organization that advocates for behavior therapy and facilitates the field's further development. Additionally, by 1970 four major professional journals were devoted exclusively to behavior therapy.

Still, some critics voiced the opinion that behavior therapy would soon fade into oblivion, along with a host of other "faddish" therapies that arose in the 1960s, such as encounter groups. However, developments in the 1970s clearly showed that behavior therapy was much more than a

Cyril Franks

Courtesy of Cyril Franks

passing fancy. Behavior therapy was beginning to be acknowledged as an acceptable form of treatment, and even a *treatment of choice* (that is, an optimal treatment) for certain psychological problems.

EMERGENCE OF BEHAVIOR THERAPY

In the 1970s, behavior therapy emerged as a major force in psychology and made a significant impact on psychiatry, social work, and education. The principles and techniques of behavior therapy also were adapted to enhance the everyday functioning of people in areas as diverse as business and industry,[51] child rearing,[52] ecology,[53] and the arts.[54] Applications include improving athletic performance,[55] increasing people's willingness to take prescribed medications,[56] enhancing the quality of life of nursing home residents and geriatric patients,[57] and more efficiently teaching young children to play musical instruments.[58] Examples of larger-scale behavioral interventions include promoting energy conservation,[59] preventing crimes,[60] providing individual instruction for large college classes,[61] and influencing entire communities to engage in behaviors that lower the risk of cardiovascular disease.[62]

During the 1980s, two important developments in the field of behavior therapy increased its applicability and acceptance. First, cognitive-behavioral therapy emerged as a major force. Second, behavior therapy began to make significant contributions to the field of *behavioral medicine,* which involves the treatment and prevention of medical problems.[63]

By 1990, the Association for Advancement of Behavior Therapy was a quarter of a century old, having grown in membership from 18 (in 1966) to approximately 4,000. Other influential behavior therapy societies had been founded in other countries, including Argentina, France, Germany, Great Britain, Israel, Japan, Mexico, the Netherlands, and Sweden.[64] More than 20 major journals devoted solely to behavior therapy had been established, and empirical research on behavior therapy filled the leading clinical psychology journals as well as many prestigious publications in psychiatry, social work, and education. Although behavior therapy had its origins in South Africa, Great Britain, and North America, today it is practiced around the world in such diverse countries as Russia,[65] Poland,[66] Argentina,[67] Puerto Rico,[68] Italy,[69] Japan,[70] Singapore,[71] New Zealand,[72] and Cuba,[73] to name a few.

One indication of the increasing maturity of the field of behavior therapy is the fact that for more than 20 years, its strongest critics have been its proponents rather than its opponents. In effect, the field of behavior therapy had reached the point where convincing skeptical outsiders was no longer a priority.[74] Instead, behavior therapists began to scrutinize their own therapy methods and the impact they were having on clients and on the broad field of psychotherapy.[75]

SUMMARY

1. Behavioral principles have been used for thousands of years to change people's problematic behaviors. However, only in the past 50 years have they been applied systematically.

2. There are a number of historical accounts of treatment procedures that resemble those of contemporary behavior therapy. However, the immediate impetus for the development of behavior therapy came from experimental research on learning conducted in the early part of the 20th century. This included the work of Pavlov, who conceptualized classical conditioning; Watson, who founded behaviorism, an approach that only dealt with observable behaviors; Jones, who designed an early learning-based treatment of fear; and the Mowrers, who designed the bell-and-pad treatment for bedwetting, based on classical conditioning.

3. Contemporary behavior therapy began in the 1950s, in part because of a growing discontent with psychoanalysis. It started simultaneously in North America, South Africa, and Great Britain. In the United States, Lindsley used the operant conditioning principles developed by Thorndike and Skinner to influence the behaviors of patients with psychiatric disorders, and Ayllon and Azrin developed the first token economy. In South Africa, Wolpe developed systematic desensitization, and Lazarus broadened its application. Rachman brought behavior therapy from South Africa to England and collaborated with Eysenck, an advocate for behavior therapy and critic of psychoanalytic therapy.

4. Early behavior therapy efforts were met with strong criticism and resistance from traditional psychotherapists. Initially, behavior therapists had to focus on demonstrating that behavior therapy could be effective.

5. A number of early ethical criticisms of behavior therapy arose because of a heightened concern about the possible dangers of external control and because of confusion about what constitutes behavior therapy.

6. In the 1960s, Bandura developed a social learning theory that combined observational learning with classical and operant conditioning. The theory emphasized the critical role that cognition (thinking) plays in psychological functioning—a drastic departure from Watson's behaviorism.

7. Cognitive-behavioral therapy changes clients' cognitions that maintain psychological disorders. Originally developed by Ellis, Beck, and Meichenbaum, cognitive-behavioral therapy began as a supplement to existing behavior therapy procedures but rapidly evolved into a major behavior therapy approach.

8. In the 1970s, behavior therapy emerged as a major force among psychotherapy approaches.

9. The Association for Advancement of Behavior Therapy was established in 1966 in the United States to advocate for behavior therapy and has served as its major professional organization.

10. Although behavior therapy had its origins in South Africa, Great Britain, and North America, today it is practiced in many diverse countries.

REFERENCE NOTES

1. Franks & Wilson, 1973.
2. Franks, 1963.
3. Arnarson, 1994; Fell, 1975.
4. Itard, 1962.
5. Lovaas, 1977.
6. Kazdin, 1978.
7. Pitts, 1976.
8. Stewart, 1961.
9. Franks, 1969.
10. Pavlov, 1927.
11. Kazdin, 1978.
12. Watson, 1914.
13. Jones, 1924; compare with Kornfeld, 1989.
14. Kazdin, 1978.
15. Mowrer & Mowrer, 1938.
16. Thorndike, 1911, 1931, 1933.
17. Jacobson, 1929, 1934.
18. Yates, 1970.
19. Sobell, 1994.
20. Eysenck, 1952.
21. For example, Cartwright, 1955; Luborsky, 1954; Smith & Glass, 1977.
22. Skinner, 1953.
23. Lindsley, 1956, 1960, 1963; Skinner, 1954; Skinner, Solomon, & Lindsley, 1953; Skinner, Solomon, Lindsley, & Richards, 1954.
24. Skinner, Solomon, & Lindsley, 1953.
25. For example, Ayllon, 1963, 1965; Ayllon & Michael, 1959.
26. Freud, 1909/1955.
27. Haughton & Ayllon, 1965.
28. Haughton & Ayllon, 1965, pp. 97–98.
29. Ayllon & Azrin, 1968.
30. Wolpe, 1958.
31. Wolpe, 1990.
32. Lazarus, 1959, 1961; Lazarus & Abramovitz, 1962.
33. Lazarus, 1966, 1967, 1971, 1976.
34. Rachman, 1959, 1967, 1972, 1990; Rachman & Eysenck, 1966.
35. For example, Shapiro, 1951, 1952, 1957, 1961a, 1961b, 1966.
36. Skinner, 1953.
37. Davison & Stuart, 1975, p. 756.
38. Franks & Wilson, 1978.
39. Turkat & Feuerstein, 1978.
40. Reimringer, Morgan, & Bramwell, 1970.
41. Woolfolk, Woolfolk, & Wilson, 1977.
42. Ullmann & Krasner, 1965.
43. Bandura, 1969, 1977b, 1986b; Bandura & Walters, 1963.
44. Bandura & Walters, 1963.
45. Bandura, 1986b, 1997.
46. For example, Cloitre, 1995.
47. Beck, 1963, 1972, 1976.

48. Ellis, 1962, 1970.
49. Ellis, 1993.
50. Meichenbaum, 1974, 1975, 1977; Meichenbaum & Cameron, 1972, 1973.
51. Hermann, de Montes, Dominguez, Montes, & Hopkins, 1973; New tool, 1971; Pedalino & Gamboa, 1974.
52. For example, Becker, 1971; Christophersen, 1977; Patterson, 1975; Patterson & Gullion, 1976.
53. Kazdin, 1977b.
54. Madsen, Greer, & Madsen, 1975.
55. For example, Rachman & Hodgson, 1980; Rachman & Teasdale, 1969; Rushall & Siedentop, 1972.
56. For example, Epstein & Masek, 1978; Lowe & Lutzker, 1979.
57. For example, Libb & Clements, 1969; Sachs, 1975.
58. Madsen, Greer, & Madsen, 1975.
59. Kazdin, 1977b.
60. For example, McNees, Egli, Marshall, Schnelle, Schnelle, & Risley, 1976; Schnelle, Kirchner, Macrae, McNees, Eck, Snodgrass, Casey, & Uselton, 1978; Schnelle, Kirchner, McNees, & Lawler, 1975.
61. For example, Keller, 1968.
62. Maccoby, Farquhar, Wood, & Alexander, 1977.
63. Arnkoff & Glass, 1992; Glass & Arnkoff, 1992.
64. Kazdin, 1978.
65. Lauterbach, 1999.
66. Kokoszaka, Popiel, & Sitarz, 2000.
67. Torres-Martinez & Spinetta, 1997.
68. Martinez-Taboas & Navas-Robleto, 2000.
69. Sanavio, 1999.
70. Sakuta, 1999.
71. Banarjee, 1999.
72. Blampied, 1999.
73. Dattilio, 1999.
74. Nezu, 1996.
75. For example, Baer, Hurley, Minichiello, Ott, Penzel, & Ricciardi, 1992; Kazdin & Wilson, 1978; Krasner, 1976; Stolz & Associates, 1978.

The Behavioral Model

To appreciate the nature of behavior therapy, you must understand the model on which it is based. In this chapter we describe the general model of human behavior that forms the basis of behavior therapy. Then, in Chapter 4, we outline the principles of behavior therapy derived from the model. Thus, Chapters 3 and 4 present the core of behavior therapy.

WE ARE WHAT WE DO: PREEMINENCE OF BEHAVIOR

How do we define who a person is? What makes you unique? According to the behavioral model, each of us is defined by our **behaviors**—in other words, by what we *do*. *We are what we do.*

Overt and Covert Behaviors

There are two broad categories of behaviors: overt and covert. **Overt behaviors** are *actions* that other people can directly observe; in a sense, they are public behaviors. Examples include eating, walking, talking, kissing, driving a car, writing a sentence, cooking, laughing, and singing—all behaviors we can "see" others engaging in.

Covert behaviors are things we do that others cannot directly observe. They are private behaviors that we usually are aware of when we ourselves engage in them. Covert behaviors include *thinking* (and other cognitive processes such as remembering), *feeling* (emotions), and *physiological responses* (for example, decreasing blood pressure and relaxing muscles). Cognitions, emotions, and physiological responses, together with overt actions, constitute the four **modes of behavior** that are assessed and treated in behavior therapy. Participation Exercise 3-1 can help you distinguish between overt and covert behaviors. Incidentally, *covert behaviors* do not refer to secretive actions, such as cheating on an exam or hiding an object, which are overt behaviors that others can observe.

◆

Participation Exercise 3-1

DISTINGUISHING BETWEEN OVERT AND COVERT BEHAVIORS*

Distinguishing between overt (public) and covert (private) behaviors is easy. If you can directly observe other people engaging in the behavior, it is overt. If you cannot directly observe the behavior, it is covert.

Number from 1 to 20 on a sheet of paper, and for each of the behaviors listed, put an *O* for overt behaviors and *C* for covert behaviors. Then, check the answers found in your Student Resource Materials.

1. Singing
2. Thinking
3. Smiling

4. Learning
5. Eating
6. Remembering

*You should do this Participation Exercise before you continue reading.

7. Liking	14. Dreaming
8. Staring	15. Drinking
9. Enjoying	16. Smoking
10. Writing	17. Hoping
11. Listening	18. Touching
12. Observing	19. Concentrating
13. Speaking	20. Sighing

Covert Behaviors: Special Considerations

Covert behaviors are no less important than overt behaviors. Indeed, many behaviors that supposedly set us apart from our relatives in the animal kingdom are covert, including complex thinking and reasoning. Although behavior therapists deal with both overt and covert behaviors, this was not always the case. Early behavior therapists followed the tradition of Watson's behaviorism and dealt only with overt behaviors (see Chapter 2).

Assessing overt behaviors is relatively straightforward because they are directly observable. In contrast, covert behaviors are private, which makes assessing them more complicated. Each of us has direct knowledge of our own covert behaviors, but we have only indirect knowledge of other people's covert behaviors.

The covert behaviors of others are inferred from their overt behaviors. (An exception is physiological responses that can be measured by instruments, such as a stethoscope and a polygraph.) Most often we learn of others' covert behaviors when they tell us about their thoughts and feelings. *Talking* about one's private experiences is an overt behavior. The other way we learn about someone's covert behaviors is by observing what the person does and inferring from his or her overt actions what is "going on inside of the person." For instance, if you see someone smiling and laughing, you are likely to conclude that the individual is feeling happy. You could say that you have "anchored" covert behavior with overt behavior.[1] Table 3-1 gives examples of overt behaviors that serve as anchors for common covert behaviors. Participation Exercise 3-2 will give you practice in the anchoring process that behavior therapists employ to assess clients' covert behaviors.

Table 3-1 Examples of overt behaviors that serve as anchors for covert behaviors

Overt Behaviors	Covert Behaviors
Telling others what's "on your mind"	Thinking
Missing an appointment	Forgetting
Staring, wrinkling one's brow, remaining motionless	Concentrating
Trembling, pacing, biting one's nails	Feeling frightened
Hugging, kissing, saying "I love you"	Feeling in love
Applauding, thanking	Appreciating

Participation Exercise 3-2 **FINDING OVERT BEHAVIORAL ANCHORS FOR COVERT BEHAVIORS***

For each of six common covert behaviors listed, think of one or more overt behavioral anchors. In other words, think of *observable* behaviors that most people would agree are likely to indicate that a person is engaging in the covert behavior. As an example, note that you've just been asked to perform a covert behavior, namely to *think* of overt behavioral anchors. If you want other people, such as your course instructor, to know that you've thought of overt behavioral anchors, you'll have to perform an overt behavior that indicates this covert behavior. *Writing* overt behavioral anchors for each of the following covert behaviors is an overt behavior. When you have finished, compare the overt behavioral anchors you have written with those in your Student Resource Materials.

1. Feeling happy
2. Reading silently
3. Worrying
4. Being interested (in a particular topic)
5. Listening (to a speaker)
6. Liking (a particular person)

Behavioral Versus Trait Descriptions

Before reading further, take a few minutes to do a simple demonstration. Think of someone you know well. Write a brief description of that person so that someone who doesn't know the person could get a feel for what he or she is like. When you have finished, continue reading.

When describing someone, as you just did, most people refer to the individual's traits rather than to their behaviors. *Traits* are personality characteristics that we *attribute* to others and ourselves, such as friendly, smart, interesting, and honest. Traits are theoretical constructs that do not actually exist. They are convenient ways of describing people and are inferred from behaviors. For example, when we observe someone holding the door open for people and stopping to let other motorists enter the flow of traffic, we say the individual is *courteous*. It is important to note that traits are abstract concepts, not covert behaviors.

Trait descriptions *appear* to provide a great deal of information about a person, but they provide generalizations rather than specific information. Consider the following example. When friends are upset, Juanita tries to comfort them, whereas Juan respects their privacy and stays away. Both Juanita and Juan can be considered *caring*. However, referring to either of them as *caring* tells us little about how they will behave.

To understand what is meant by a trait for a particular person, one must refer to the person's behaviors that led to inferring the trait. Notice the circular reasoning here. The process begins with observing behaviors, then

*You should do this Participation Exercise before you continue reading.

infers a trait from the behaviors, and finally returns to the behaviors to explain what is meant by the trait. This makes the use of traits superfluous.

In contrast, the behavioral model simply describes people in terms of their behaviors. Behavioral descriptions are specific and much more detailed than trait descriptions. On the downside, they are lengthier. Compare the inference "Lillian is conscientious" with the observation "Lillian studies at least four hours a day, plans her work carefully, and usually finishes her assignments ahead of time." The accuracy and therefore the usefulness of the behavioral description outweighs its disadvantage of being lengthier.

There are several interrelated advantages of describing clients' problems in terms of behaviors rather than traits. Behavioral descriptions are more precise, and they promote individuality. In contrast, trait descriptions classify clients' problems into broad categories (such as depression and schizophrenia). Further, behavioral descriptions provide the detailed information needed to design a treatment plan tailored to the unique characteristics of each client's problems.

Being able to distinguish behaviors from traits is important for understanding the behavioral model. Descriptions that concern what people *do* refer to behaviors, whereas descriptions that concern what people *are* or characteristics that they possess refer to traits. Participation Exercise 3-3 provides a check of your understanding of this distinction.

◆

Participation Exercise 3-3

DISTINGUISHING BETWEEN TRAITS AND BEHAVIORS*

See if you can differentiate between traits and behavioral descriptions in the following paragraph. On a sheet of paper, number from 1 to 20. Then, write the letter *T* for trait or *B* for behavior for each of the numbered statements.

> (1) Ramon is extremely perceptive. (2) He notices even small changes in others' emotions and (3) accurately tells them how they are feeling. (4) He reads a great deal and (5) is very knowledgeable about many topics. (6) He is very intelligent, and (7) he can recall facts he learned years ago. (8) Ramon is a warm, sincere, good-natured person. (9) He is a good friend, (10) goes out of his way to help other people and (11) is generous. (12) He always dresses neatly. (13) Ramon works hard, and (14) he is a dedicated worker. (15) He is a good athlete. (16) He swims during the summer and ice skates during the winter. (17) He is an active person (18) who is very energetic. (19) Although he is gregarious, (20) Ramon frequently spends time alone.

You can check your answers in your Student Resource Materials. Look at the descriptions you mislabeled and apply the following rule: What a person *does* is a behavior; what a person *is* or *possesses* is a trait.

◆

*You should do this Participation Exercise before you continue reading.

Behavior therapists deal with clients' behaviors, not their traits. However, clients often describe themselves and their problems by using traits (for example, "I'm shy and withdrawn"). Thus, behavior therapists must "translate" traits into behaviors. This involves identifying the behaviors that are associated with clients' trait descriptions. The key question the therapist asks is, *"What specific things do you do that lead you to describe yourself as [the trait]?"* As you can see in Table 3-2, a trait description may be associated with a variety of specific behaviors. Participation Exercise 3-4 can give you experience in translating traits into behaviors.

Participation Exercise 3-4

TRANSLATING TRAITS INTO BEHAVIORS*

Translating trait descriptions into behavioral descriptions involves finding behaviors that could be indicative of particular traits. On a sheet of paper, list several behaviors that might help describe individuals with the following traits.

1. Sociable	5. Dependable
2. Hostile	6. Smart
3. Helpful	7. Patient
4. Thrifty	8. Healthy

The behaviors you listed should be activities individuals *do* (in other words, behaviors) that most people would agree indicate the particular trait. You will find sample behaviors for each trait in your Student Resource Materials.

WHY DO WE BEHAVE THE WAY WE DO?

How often have you asked, "Why did I do that?" or "Why did so-and-so act that way?" People are fascinated by "why questions" about human behavior, and psychologists have developed many theories to explain human behavior. According to the behavioral model, *a person's behaviors*

Table 3-2 Examples of overt behaviors that might indicate particular traits

Behaviors	Trait
Smiling; laughing; talking about feelings of joy	Happy
Crying; sitting alone; moving slowly; saying that one is depressed ("down" or unhappy)	Depressed
Greeting people; smiling at others	Friendly
Arriving on time to appointments; carrying out assigned tasks; keeping secrets	Trustworthy
Volunteering to help others; frequently paying for the check when dining with others	Generous

*You should do this Participation Exercise before you continue reading.

are caused by present events that occur before and after the behaviors have been performed. **Antecedents** are events that occur or are present *before* the person performs the behavior. **Consequences** are events that occur *after* and *as a result of* the behavior. For example, feeling tired is an antecedent for sleeping, and feeling rested the next day is a consequence of sleeping.

The ABC Model

The **ABC model** describes the temporal sequence of antecedents, behavior, and consequences (see Figure 3-1). The specific antecedents and consequences that cause an individual to perform a behavior are its **maintaining conditions.**[2] Not all antecedents and consequences of a behavior are its maintaining conditions. Only a relatively small number of antecedents and consequences *maintain* (influence) a behavior, and we refer to these as **maintaining antecedents** and **maintaining consequences.**

MAINTAINING ANTECEDENTS

There are two categories of maintaining antecedents—*prerequisites* and *stimulus control*—each of which can occur naturally or can be introduced intentionally to change a behavior.

To engage in a behavior, you must first have the requisite knowledge, skills, and resources. For example, *going to the movies* requires knowing where the theater is located and what time the movie starts, being able to get to the theater, and having enough money to pay for a ticket. If these prerequisites seem trivial, consider whether you could go to a movie without them.

Stimulus control involves cues or conditions that "set the stage" for behaviors to occur.[3] There are two types of stimulus control: *prompts* and *setting events*. **Prompts** are *cues* to perform a behavior, such as when a parent says, "Go wash your hands," to a child before dinner. **Setting events** are environmental *conditions* that elicit a behavior; they are broader and more complex than prompts. For example, you are more likely to study for a test if you are in a quiet room with others who are studying than if you were in a room where other people are socializing.

Figure 3-1 The ABC model

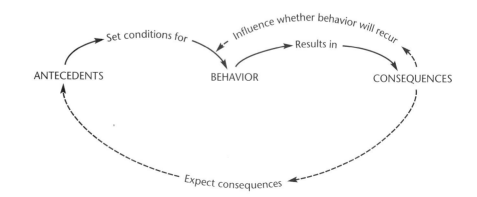

Similarly, think about how your behavior differs when you are in class, at a party, with close friends, and with strangers. Besides the specific circumstances, setting events may include who is present and what they are doing, the time of day, and the physical arrangement of the environment. People frequently alter setting events in their daily lives to influence their own behaviors. For instance, a woman wishing to lose weight and improve her health might remove all high-fat foods from the house and keep healthy foods prominently displayed. Behavior therapists use prompts and setting events in therapy to change problem behaviors.

◆   **In Theory 3-1**

IT'S WHERE YOU ARE (NOT WHO YOU ARE) THAT COUNTS: BEHAVIOR IS SITUATION SPECIFIC

Our predictions about how people in our lives will act often are correct because people generally behave *consistently*. Many theories have been developed to explain the source of this consistency. According to the behavioral model, the consistency is determined by the situation in which the behavior is performed. *Situation* refers to the context, including where we are, whom we are with, and what is happening. Setting events indicate which behaviors are expected in the particular circumstances and therefore are likely to result in positive consequences. The environmental cues also may tell us which behaviors are inappropriate in the setting and likely to result in negative consequences. Our personal views about what is expected or appropriate behavior in the situation, based on our previous experiences with similar situations, also are important.

Because the cues in each situation in which we find ourselves influence our behavior, how we act is likely to be consistent in the same or similar situations. The most reliable information we have to predict another person's behaviors is the context in which those behaviors occur. Thus, we say that behavior is **situation specific.**[4]

A simple example can illustrate what is meant by situation specificity. Wilberto is a college student who typically sits quietly in each of his lecture classes, usually talks at a moderate volume whenever he eats with friends at the cafeteria, and often yells at basketball games until he becomes hoarse. In each instance, the social expectations and restrictions associated with the specific context influence how loudly Wilberto speaks. Wilberto's speech volume is consistent in similar situations, but it varies in different situations. Further, although Wilberto sits quietly in all his lecture classes, he often speaks up in seminars and discussion sections, where the demands are different from the demands in lectures.

By way of contrast, the major alternative to the situation-specificity explanation of the consistency of behavior is to attribute the consistency to a person's traits. We might call Wilberto quiet or loud. However, both these descriptions are inaccurate because *quiet* does not predict Wilberto's behavior at basketball games and *loud* does not predict Wilberto's behavior in lecture classes. A description of Wilberto's behavior in different situations is more accurate.

MAINTAINING CONSEQUENCES

Whereas maintaining antecedents are responsible for a behavior's being performed in the first place, *maintaining consequences determine whether the behavior will occur again.* In general, when the consequences of performing a behavior are favorable, the individual is more likely to repeat the behavior. Unfavorable consequences make it less likely that the person will engage in the behavior in the future. Consequences include what happens directly to the person, to other people, and to the physical environment as a result of the behavior. Consequences can be immediate or delayed.

You may be wondering how events that occur *after* a behavior has been performed can influence that behavior. In fact, the actual consequences of a behavior can influence only the future occurrence of the behavior. However, *expectations* about the probable consequences, which are *antecedents,* influence whether a person will perform a behavior in the present (see Figure 3-1). In other words, a person's prediction about what is likely to happen as a result of performing a particular behavior is one factor that determines whether the person will perform the behavior. Our expectations about the maintaining consequences of our actions are largely a product of the consequences we have experienced for similar behaviors in the past. *Maintaining consequences for today's actions are the maintaining antecedents of tomorrow's actions.* For example, if Julius' dinner guests praised his Caesar salad last week, he will be tempted to make one this week. His guests' praise was a consequence of making a Caesar salad last week, but it becomes an antecedent of the same behavior this week. Clearly, remembering the consequences of a behavior is necessary if the consequences are to affect the future occurrence of the behavior.[5]

IDENTIFYING MAINTAINING ANTECEDENTS AND
MAINTAINING CONSEQUENCES

Contrary to the popular misconception, behavior therapy does not *directly* change symptoms or behaviors. *Behavior therapy treats problem behaviors by directly changing their maintaining conditions.*[6] And before the maintaining

CALVIN AND HOBBES copyright 1990 Watterson. Dist. by UNIVERSAL PRESS SYNDICATE. Reprinted with permission.
All rights reserved.

conditions can be changed, they first must be identified. This process begins by identifying the antecedents and consequences of the behavior, some of which are its maintaining conditions.

◆

Participation Exercise 3-5

IDENTIFYING ANTECEDENTS AND CONSEQUENCES*

This exercise contains a list of six specific behaviors and the details surrounding each. From the details, list the antecedents and consequences of each designated behavior. Include all the antecedents and consequences actually in the scenario, but do not assume any that are not mentioned. When you have finished, check your answers with those in your Student Resource Materials.

Behavior 1: *Calling the police.* One hot summer evening, Mrs. Kriegel was sitting in her second-floor apartment. As she looked out the window, she saw two young men attack an elderly woman and then run off with the woman's purse. She immediately called the police. The police thanked her and then rushed to the scene of the crime. Mrs. Kriegel realized she had done the right thing.

Behavior 2: *Going to a play.* Quanisha read about a new play in town. It had received especially good reviews. She knew she could get a student pass to see it and that she could earn extra credit for her English class if she saw the play. As it turned out, she was disappointed in the play and felt it was a waste of time. The extra credit, however, did boost her grade.

Behavior 3: *Getting up late.* Al did not go to bed until after 3 A.M. He was so drunk he forgot to set his alarm clock. He awoke 2 hours late the next morning and missed the last bus to the office. When he finally arrived at his office, he discovered that he had missed two important appointments with clients.

Behavior 4: *Cooking a fancy meal.* Brendan's parents were coming for a visit, and he wanted to make a good impression. It was the perfect opportunity for him to try out a new recipe, and besides, he enjoyed preparing a fancy meal. Although his efforts turned the kitchen into a complete disaster area, the meal itself was a success and his parents enjoyed the dinner. Brendan also enjoyed the dinner and was satisfied with the evening as a whole.

Behavior 5: *Shopping for new clothes.* Jane needed new clothes, and she had saved enough money during the summer to go shopping. She got directions to the new shopping mall and borrowed the family car. Jane came home with a comfortable and stylish new wardrobe. She felt good about her new clothes, and her mother and friends commented on how good she looked in them.

Behavior 6: *Pulling a fire alarm.* Manny spotted a fire alarm box at the corner. He wanted to impress his friends and thought of all the excitement that

---

*The Participation Exercise can be done before you continue reading or later.

would occur if he pulled the alarm. After reading the instructions on the fire alarm and looking to see that no one was around, he pulled the alarm. Fire trucks raced to the scene within minutes. A crowd quickly gathered. The angry fire chief announced that it was a false alarm. The fire marshal began an investigation, while the crowd slowly dispersed and the fire trucks returned to the station.

As we have said, not all the antecedents and consequences of a behavior are its maintaining conditions. In behavior therapy, the therapist and client identify those antecedents and consequences that appear to be influencing (causing) the problem behavior. It is these **probable maintaining conditions** of a behavior that are changed to modify the behavior.

An example may help clarify the concept of maintaining antecedents and maintaining consequences and their roles in determining behaviors. Consider the behavior you are engaging in right now—reading a chapter in your textbook. What prerequisites, prompts, and setting events have led to your reading the chapter? What are the likely consequences of reading the chapter? Take a moment to write down these antecedents and consequences, and then look at the examples in Figure 3-2 on page 40.

Present Maintaining Conditions Versus Past Originating Conditions: A Critical Distinction

According to the behavioral model, *present* conditions cause our behavior. What role do our past experiences play in determining our current behaviors? The answer is that past events only indirectly influence present behaviors. The factors that directly cause present behaviors are occurring now.

Let's look at a personal example. When was the last time you dressed yourself? Unless you are lounging at home in your sleeping attire, the answer probably is "sometime earlier today." In fact, you dress yourself one or more times a day, every day. What are the maintaining conditions of *dressing yourself?* The maintaining antecedents may include knowing how to dress yourself, having clothes, waking up in the morning, and anticipating going somewhere outside your home. The maintaining consequences may include feeling properly dressed, being complimented on your attire, and not getting arrested for indecent exposure.

Do you recall your first attempts to dress yourself? You may have resisted dressing yourself initially. After all, you had been used to having others dress you, and dressing yourself was difficult and frustrating. Nonetheless, you learned to dress yourself. What conditions resulted in your learning to dress yourself? The major maintaining antecedent probably was your parents' telling you to get dressed. The maintaining consequences probably included praise from your parents and permission to engage in some desirable activity (such as going outside to play) that required being dressed.

This example illustrates that the same behavior—dressing yourself—is maintained today by conditions that are very different from the conditions in which it originated. This is the essence of a crucial distinction between present maintaining conditions and past originating conditions.

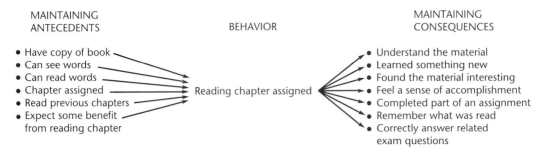

Figure 3-2 Some of the possible maintaining antecedents and maintaining consequences of performing a specific behavior: reading an assigned chapter

Past events can have an *indirect* influence on current behaviors, as when the memory of previous events affects your current behaviors.[7] For instance, *recalling* how pleasant it was to be comforted by your mother when you cried can help maintain your crying years after you received your mother's sympathy. However, note that your mother's actual comfort is not directly influencing your current behavior. Rather, a *memory* of being comforted is serving as a maintaining condition—and memories are *present* events.

To summarize, behavior therapists assume that present conditions directly influence behaviors occurring in the present. In other words, *present behaviors are maintained by present maintaining conditions*. Thus, the way to change a present behavior is to change its present maintaining conditions.

Learning and Environment Versus Heredity and Biology

According to the behavioral model, most of our behaviors develop, are maintained, and change primarily through learning. *Learning* is the process by which environmental factors influence behaviors. The **environment** comprises all external influences on behaviors, including the physical setting and conditions as well as the people who are present. What, then, is the role of hereditary and biological factors in determining behaviors, from the behavioral perspective?

Hereditary and biological factors are thought to set broad upper limits on a person's psychological characteristics. For example, considerable evidence shows that intelligence has a strong genetic component.[8] Within the broad limits established by one's genetic endowment, however, intelligence can be substantially increased (as by an enriched intellectual environment) or decreased (as by minimal intellectual stimulation).[9] Similarly, activity level—how active a person generally is—also has a heritable component.[10] Nevertheless, environmental factors also contribute to activity level, as the following hypothetical example illustrates.

At birth, Hyman exhibited a high activity level, whereas Lois exhibited a low activity level. When Hyman grows up, we would expect to see him doing things quickly, being involved in many activities, and usually being on the go with abundant energy. In contrast, we would anticipate that as an adult Lois would generally move slowly, engage in only a few activities, and spend much time in sedentary behaviors.

◆ **In Theory 3-2**

DON'T LOOK BACK: THE ROLE OF PAST EVENTS ON CURRENT BEHAVIORS

The idea that past events have only a weak and indirect influence on our present behaviors may seem contrary to the widely held view that our past, especially early childhood, has a profound effect on our current lives. The notion that "the child is parent to the adult" is rooted in psychoanalysis, and like other psychoanalytic concepts, it has become part of our common belief system.

The behavioral and psychoanalytic views are not completely contradictory. Both hold that adults are products of their previous experiences. The two perspectives differ, however, in how they view the nature of that influence. Psychoanalysis postulates that early experiences have a direct and permanent effect on later behaviors, implying that current circumstances have little or no influence on adult (or later childhood) behaviors. The behavioral model holds that the behaviors that result from early experiences can, with appropriate learning, be changed so that these early experiences exert little or no influence on later behaviors.

Looking to the past for the determinants of present behaviors can be problematic. Examining past events is difficult and involves gathering information that is *retrospective*, which often is inaccurate. Not only do we forget the specifics of past events, but also we inevitably reconstruct history, as when we fill in missing details or adjust apparent inconsistencies in our recollections. Moreover, even if it were possible to collect reliable accounts of past events, there is no way to ascertain whether particular events that occurred in the past caused a behavior because we cannot go back in time and test such hypotheses.

In contrast, the *current* factors that are influencing the way we behave are considerably easier to assess. First, because they are occurring in the present, obtaining accurate information is more feasible. Second, because the factors are currently active, it is possible to systematically alter them and observe the effects on behaviors. This makes it possible to test the validity of hypotheses about the influence of current factors on behaviors.

Viewing the past from the present has its limitations.
PEANUTS Reprinted by permission of UFS, Inc.

However, suppose in adulthood Hyman's wife models and encourages a slow-paced life, and Lois' husband displays and promotes a fast-paced life. Under these circumstances, it is possible that Lois and Hyman might show comparable levels of activity as adults. Hyman's activity would be below his "biological" level, and Lois' activity would be above hers. However, Lois is not likely to engage in the very high level of activity that Hyman could potentially engage in.

Learning can influence many behaviors, even if they have heritable or biological components.[11] Thus, learning can change some psychological disorders that seem to have substantial heritable or biological origins (for example, autistic disorder, depression, and schizophrenia[12]). Also, behavior therapy procedures that teach clients more adaptive ways of behaving can change biological functioning, such as central nervous system activity.[13] To summarize, heredity and biology set wide boundaries for behaviors. Within these limits, learning and environmental factors play a significant role in influencing behaviors.[14]

In Theory 3-3

FREEDOM IN RECIPROCAL DETERMINISM

According to the behavioral model, environmental factors play a major role in determining how we behave. If you interpret this statement as your "being controlled by the environment," then you will view it as limiting your options. However, just the opposite is true. There are reciprocal or give-and-take relationships among the environment, overt behavior, and covert behavior. Each of these factors influences and is influenced by the two other factors, which is to say that they are *reciprocally determined,* as Figure 3-3 depicts.[15] As an example, consider how the environment, covert behaviors, and overt behaviors might reciprocally influence one another in the case of writing a paper. Table 3-3 illustrates the various combinations of determinism.

The concept of reciprocal determinism has important implications for personal freedom. How we behave is not rigidly determined by external forces. We can alter or create the factors that influence our behaviors. For instance, a woman who rarely exercises can join a health club, which will increase the chances that she will exercise regularly. Likewise, a man who thinks poorly of himself because he is unsuccessful in his work can select a job at which he can succeed, which, in turn, will influence his thoughts about himself. A key to personal freedom lies in understanding the factors that influence our behaviors and accepting responsibility for controlling them.

Figure 3-3 According to the principle of reciprocal determinism, the environment, overt behaviors, and covert behaviors each influence and are influenced by the two other factors

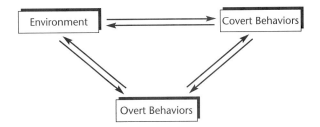

Table 3-3 Examples of how the environment, covert behaviors, and overt behaviors might reciprocally determine one another in the case of writing a paper

ENVIRONMENT influences OVERT BEHAVIOR

When Chung writes in a quiet place, he gets more writing done.

OVERT BEHAVIOR influences ENVIRONMENT

When Megan starts to write in her dorm room, her understanding roommates lower the volume on the stereo.

COVERT BEHAVIOR influences OVERT BEHAVIOR

When Joan thinks that a particular topic is interesting, she spends more time writing about it.

OVERT BEHAVIOR influences COVERT BEHAVIOR

When Carlos successfully completes a difficult paper, he feels competent as a student.

ENVIRONMENT influences COVERT BEHAVIOR

When Manny waits until the night before to write a paper, he gets anxious.

COVERT BEHAVIOR influences ENVIRONMENT

When Indiana is concentrating on writing a paper, her roommate stops talking to her.

SUMMARY

1. The behavioral model defines people in terms of their behaviors.
2. Behavior is anything a person does. Overt behaviors are actions that other people can directly observe. Covert behaviors are private behaviors, consisting of thoughts, feelings, and physiological responses. Covert behaviors are inferred from overt behaviors, with the exception of physiological responses, which can be measured by instruments.
3. The most common way of describing people is in terms of their traits. The problem with trait descriptions is that they are general rather than specific. Behavioral descriptions are more precise than trait descriptions and preserve individuality.
4. The ABC model describes the temporal sequence of antecedents, behavior, and consequences. The specific antecedents and consequences that cause an individual to perform a behavior are its maintaining conditions. Maintaining antecedents establish the conditions for the behavior to occur and consist of prerequisites, prompts (cues to perform the behavior), and setting events (environmental conditions that elicit the behavior). Maintaining consequences determine whether the behavior will occur again.
5. Behavior therapy treats problem behaviors by directly changing their maintaining conditions.
6. The past originating conditions of a behavior—those conditions that account for its initial development—have only an indirect influence on our present behaviors.

7. Our behaviors are situation specific. They are consistent in the same or a similar situation and vary in different situations.
8. Most of our behaviors develop, are maintained, and change primarily through learning. Heredity and biology set broad upper limits for some behaviors, but learning and environmental factors still play a significant role in influencing them.
9. One's environment, covert behaviors, and overt behaviors are reciprocally determined; each factor influences and is influenced by the two other factors.

REFERENCE NOTES

1. Craighead, Kazdin, & Mahoney, 1976.
2. For example, Ellingson, Miltenberger, Stricker, Galensky, & Garlinghouse, 2000; Ellingson, Miltenberger, Stricker, Garlinghouse, Roberts, & Galensky, 2000; Iwata, Wallace, Kahng, Lindberg, Roscoe, Conners, Hanley, Thompson, & Worsdell, 2000; Mace, 1994; Rapp, Miltenberger, Galensky, Ellingson, & Long, 1999.
3. For example, Kennedy & Itkonen, 1993; Smith & Iwata, 1997.
4. Mischel, 1968, 1973.
5. Compare with Greene, 2001.
6. Compare with Cautela, 1993; Ellingson, Miltenberger, & Long, 1999.
7. For example, Sahakian & Charlesworth, 1994.
8. Willerman, 1979.
9. For example, Lee, 1951; Skeels, 1966.
10. For example, Buss, Plomin, & Willerman, 1973; Torgersen, 1985.
11. For example, Baxter, Schwartz, Bergman, Szuba, Guze, Mazziotta, Akazraju, Selin, Ferng, Munford, & Phelps, 1992; Iwata, 1994; Otto & Pollack, 1994; Schwartz, Stoessel, Baxter, Martin, & Phelps, 1996.
12. O'Leary & Wilson, 1975.
13. For example, Baxter, Schwartz, Bergman, Szuba, Guze, Mazziotta, Akazraju, Selin, Ferng, Munford, & Phelps, 1992.
14. Weissberg & Owen, 1999.
15. Compare with Bandura, 1986a, 1986b.

Chapter 4

The Process of Behavior Therapy

The behavioral model described in Chapter 3 is the basis for behavior therapy. In this chapter, we provide an overview of how that model is applied in behavior therapy.

We begin with a classic case published in 1965. The senior therapist was Arnold Lazarus, one of the founders of behavior therapy. The case illustrates many of the principles of the behavioral model. It also provides examples of some of the defining themes and common characteristics of behavior therapy described in Chapter 1. As you read the case, see if you can identify those themes and characteristics that are clearly evident.

Case 4-1

THE BEHAVIORAL ANALYSIS OF A PHOBIA IN A 9-YEAR-OLD BOY[1]*

Background

When he was referred for therapy, Paul, age nine, had been absent from school for three weeks. The summer vacation had ended six weeks previously, and on entering the fourth grade, Paul avoided the classroom situation. He was often found hiding in the cloak-room and subsequently began spending less time at school each day. Thereafter, neither threats, bribes, nor punishments could induce him to reenter school.

Paul's history revealed a series of similar episodes. During his first day of kindergarten, he succeeded in climbing over an extremely high wall and fled home. His first-grade teacher considered him to be "disturbed." Serious difficulties regarding school attendance were first exhibited when Paul entered the second grade. . . . he became progressively more reluctant to enter the school and finally refused entirely. A psychiatrist was consulted and is reported to have advised the parents to use coercion, whereupon Paul was literally dragged screaming to school by a truant officer. . . .

A series of specific traumatic events commenced with [Paul's] near-drowning when five years old . . . he underwent a serious appendectomy with critical complications . . . he witnessed a drowning [that] upset him considerably. Following his entry into the fourth grade, the sudden death of a . . . close friend of his elder sister, profoundly affected the entire family. . . . Paul's father experienced personal stress in his work situation . . . immediately preceding fourth grade. Finally, Paul seemed to have been intimidated by a warning from his eldest sister that fourth-grade schoolwork was particularly difficult. . . .

*The title we have given this case is intended to be a humorous counterpoint to Freud's (1909/1955) classic case, "The Analysis of a Phobia in a Five-Year-Old Boy." The similarity between the two cases, especially with respect to the treatment, ends with the titles.

Treatment Plan

After the initial interview, it was evident that Paul's school phobia was the most disruptive response pattern of a generally bewildered and intimidated child. Although subsequent interviews revealed the plethora of familial tensions, situational crises, and [a history of] . . . specific traumatic events [described earlier] . . . the initial therapeutic objective was to reinstate normal school attendance. . . .

The school was situated two and one-half blocks away from the home. The routine was for Paul to leave for school at 8:30 A.M. in order to arrive by 8:40. The first recess was from 10:00–10:30, lunch break from 12:00–1:00, and classes ended at 3:30 P.M. At the time when therapy was initiated, the boy was extremely surly and dejected in the mornings (as reported by the parents), refused breakfast, rarely dressed himself, and became noticeably more fearful toward 8:30. Parental attempts at reassurance, coaxing, or coercion elicited only sobbing and further withdrawal.

Accordingly, the boy was exposed to the following increasingly [more] difficult steps along the main dimensions of his school phobia:

1. On a Sunday afternoon, accompanied by [two of] the therapists, he walked from his house to the school. The therapists were able to allay Paul's anxiety by means of distraction and humor, so that his initial exposure was relatively pleasant.

2. On the next two days at 8:30 A.M., accompanied by one of the therapists, he walked from his house into the schoolyard. Again, Paul's feelings of anxiety were reduced by means of coaxing, encouragement, relaxation, and the use of "emotive imagery" (i.e., the deliberate picturing of subjectively pleasant images such as Christmas and a visit to Disneyland while relating them to the school situation). . . . Approximately 15 minutes were spent roaming around the school grounds, after which Paul returned home.

3. After school was over for the day, the therapist was able to persuade the boy to enter the classroom and sit down at his desk. Part of the normal school routine was then playfully enacted.

4. On the following three mornings, the therapist accompanied the boy into the classroom with the other children. They chatted with the teacher, and left immediately after the opening exercises.

5. A week after beginning this program, Paul spent the entire morning in class. The therapist sat in the classroom and smiled approvingly at Paul whenever he interacted with his classmates or the teacher.

6. Two days later when Paul and the therapist arrived at school, the boy lined up with the other children and allowed the therapist to wait for him inside the classroom. This was the first time that Paul had not insisted on having the therapist in constant view.

7. Thereafter, the therapist sat in the school library adjoining the classroom.

8. It was then agreed that the therapist would leave at 2:30 P.M. while Paul remained for the last hour of school.

9. On the following day, Paul remained alone at school from 1:45 P.M. until 2:45 P.M.. . . .

10. [On the next day] instead of fetching the boy at his home, the therapist arranged to meet him at the school gate at 8:30 A.M. Paul also agreed to remain alone at school from 10:45 A.M. until noon provided that the therapist return to eat lunch with him. At 1:45 P.M. the therapist left again with the promise that if the boy remained until school ended (3:30 P.M.) he would visit Paul that evening and play the guitar for him.

11. Occasional setbacks made it necessary to instruct the lad's mother not to allow the boy into the house during school hours. In addition, the teacher was asked to provide special jobs for the boy so as to increase his active participation and make school more attractive.. . .

12. After meeting the boy in the mornings, the therapist gradually left him alone at school for progressively longer periods of time. After six days of this procedure, the therapist was able to leave at 10 A.M.

13. The boy was assured that the therapist would be in the faculty room until 10 A.M., if needed. Thus, he came to school knowing the therapist was present, but not actually seeing him.

14. With Paul's consent the therapist arrived at school shortly after the boy entered the classroom at 8:40 A.M.

15. School attendance independent of the therapist's presence was achieved by means of specific rewards (a comic book and variously colored tokens [that] would eventually procure a baseball glove) contingent upon his entering school and remaining there alone. He was at liberty to telephone the therapist in the morning if he wanted him at school, in which event he would forfeit his rewards for that day.

16. Since the therapist's presence seemed to have at least as much reward value as the comic books and tokens, it was necessary to enlist the mother's cooperation to effect the therapist's final withdrawal. The overall diminution of the boy's anxieties, together with the general gains [that] had accrued to his home situation, made it therapeutically feasible for the mother to emphasize the fact that school attendance was compulsory.. . .

17. Approximately three weeks later, Paul had accumulated enough tokens to procure his baseball glove. He then agreed with his parents that rewards of this kind were no longer necessary.

Outcome

Paul's therapy was carried out over 4½ months, during which there were a number of setbacks. However, at the end of treatment, Paul was not only attending school regularly but, according to his mother's reports, his behavior had improved outside of school. For example, Paul had become less moody, more willing to participate in household chores, more congenial in his relationships with his peers, and more self-sufficient. Ten months after the termination of therapy, Paul's mother reported that Paul had not only maintained the positive changes but he also had progressed further.

Defining Themes and Common Characteristics of Behavior Therapy in Case 4-1

Many features of the treatment for Paul's school-phobic behaviors are typical of behavior therapy. The *scientific approach* taken in Paul's case is evident in the precision of the assessment and treatment. For example, highly specific details regarding the circumstances surrounding the problem behaviors, such as precise times, were gathered. Treatment focused on specific, clearly defined overt behaviors: staying away from school and going to school.

The therapist encouraged Paul to engage in *active* procedures that helped reduce his fear and increase his school attendance and his positive feelings about being in school. This approach contrasts with verbal psychotherapy, in which Paul would only have talked about his problems. Further, Paul's therapy took place in vivo. That is, the therapists worked directly with Paul in the school setting, where the problem was occurring. Because a therapist had to be at school with Paul for many hours, multiple therapists were employed. Using multiple therapists is not typical, but with children it is common to enlist the aid of nonprofessional change agents, such as Paul's mother and teacher, to implement specific aspects of the treatment.

The focus of therapy was clearly in the *present*. It is abundantly evident that Paul had a difficult, and at times traumatic, childhood before his presenting problem at the beginning of the fourth grade. Although these events no doubt affected Paul, treatment for his school avoidance (a present problem) focused on current conditions because they were the factors maintaining his problem.

Consistent with the *collaborative nature* of behavior therapy, the therapists consulted Paul about a variety of treatment decisions even though he was only 9 years old. Although standard therapy procedures were employed, they were *individualized* to fit Paul's unique case (for example, the reinforcers for school attendance, such as a baseball glove, were matched to Paul's interests). Paul's treatment involved a *stepwise progression* in which Paul was gradually exposed to increasingly more anxiety-evoking events. Finally, a variety of behavior therapy procedures were combined in a *treatment package* (including emotive imagery, in vivo exposure, shaping, and reinforcement).

The Process of Behavior Therapy: An Overview

The process of behavior therapy involves a series of interrelated steps, shown schematically in Figure 4-1. The steps are:

1. Clarifying the client's problem
2. Formulating initial goals for therapy
3. Designing a target behavior (the specific behavior that will be changed)
4. Identifying the maintaining conditions of the target behavior
5. Designing a treatment plan (specific therapy procedures) to change the maintaining conditions

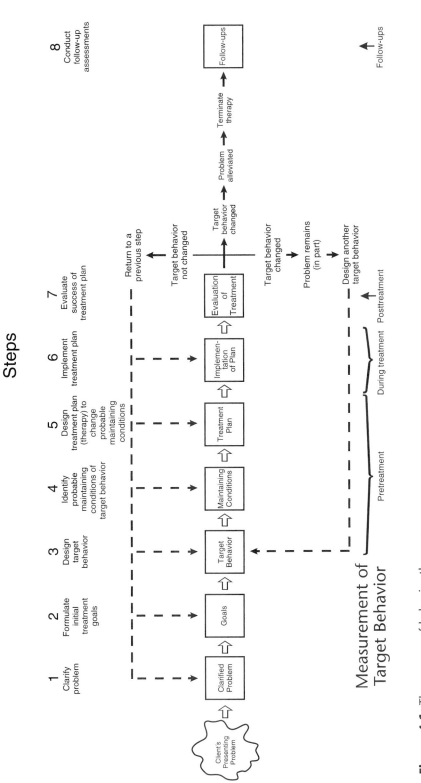

Figure 4-1 The process of behavior therapy
© 2002 Michael D. Spiegler and David C. Guevremont

6. Implementing the treatment plan
7. Evaluating the success of the treatment plan
8. Conducting follow-up assessment

Additionally, measurement of the target behavior begins immediately after the target behavior has been designed (step 3) and continues through the evaluation of therapy (step 7).

If the therapy has successfully changed the target behavior, then the therapy either (1) is terminated or (2) the process is begun again with another target behavior. If the therapy procedures have not succeeded, the therapist and client return to the step where the process broke down. For instance, the target behavior may not have been defined precisely enough or the therapy procedures may not have been implemented correctly.

STEP 1: CLARIFYING THE PROBLEM

Clients usually describe their problems in broad, vague terms (for instance, "I'm unhappy much of the time" or "I can't seem to cope with my job"). The first step in behavior therapy is to clarify the client's presenting problem. For example, for a client whose presenting problem is "I'm stressed out a lot," specifying what the client means by "stressed out" and "a lot" is crucial.

Clients often come to therapy with multiple problems. Behavior therapy begins by narrowing the client's complaints to one or two problems to be worked on initially. Treating one problem at a time has three advantages. First, clients can focus their attention more easily on one task than on multiple tasks. Second, concentrating on a single problem often results in relatively quick change, which may motivate the client to continue working on other problems. Third, problems may be related to one another, so alleviating one problem may reduce or even eliminate other problems (as with Paul in Case 4-1).[2] Thus, treating one problem at a time is efficient in the long run.

STEP 2: FORMULATING INITIAL TREATMENT GOALS

Once the client's problem has been clarified, the next step is to formulate initial goals for therapy, which will direct subsequent steps in the treatment process. Clients always enter therapy with some goals, although they may be implicit and very general (for instance, "getting help with my problem" or "feeling better"). Once the client's problem is clarified, more specific goals can be formulated.

The client is given the major responsibility for deciding on the therapy goals, and the goals always are individualized. The therapist helps the client clarify expectations about the outcome of treatment. The therapist takes a more active role in goal setting in two circumstances: (1) when the client's goals are clearly unrealistic (for example, never getting angry with one's children) or (2) when the goals are likely to have negative consequences for the client or others (for instance, a high school senior's wanting to lose 20 pounds in the 2 weeks before her prom). Once goals have been established, the therapist helps the client state them so that they are specific, unambiguous, and measurable.

Clients' goals may be reevaluated and changed at various points in the course of therapy. For example, clients may raise or lower their expectations about the degree to which the target behavior might change, based on its ongoing assessment.

STEP 3: DESIGNING A TARGET BEHAVIOR

After treatment goals are formulated, the next step in behavior therapy is to design a target behavior. A **target behavior** is a narrow, discrete aspect of the problem that can be defined clearly and measured easily. Table 4-1 lists the sequential target behaviors used to treat Paul's fear of going to school (in Case 4-1). The target behaviors were arranged in order of increasing difficulty, and each was dealt with in sequence, starting with the easiest and least anxiety provoking. The same advantages of focusing on one or two problems hold for treating one or two target behaviors at a time.

Characteristics of Good Target Behaviors

Target behaviors should meet four requirements:

1. *Narrow in scope.* The target behavior usually addresses one part of the problem rather than the entire problem. For example, *going out with close friends* might be a target behavior for a client whose problem is pervasive social anxiety. Further, the definition of the target behavior may include a specific time when and place where it is appro-

Table 4-1 Target behaviors selected for Paul (Case 4-1), in order of increasing difficulty
SOURCE: © Michael D. Spiegler and David C. Guevremont

1. Walking from the house to the school with the therapist on a nonschool day
2. Walking from the house to the schoolyard with the therapist at an appropriate time (that is, 8:30 A.M.) on a school day
3. Spending 15 minutes in the schoolyard with the therapist
4. Entering the classroom and sitting at a desk with the therapist present after school hours
5. "Playing school" in the classroom with the therapist after school hours
6. Entering the classroom and talking with the teacher in the presence of the therapist
7. Spending the morning in the classroom with the therapist present
8. Spending the day at school without the therapist in sight (but available in the school building)
9. Walking to school alone
10. Spending all day in school with the therapist unavailable part of the day
11. Spending all day in school with the therapist unavailable (that is, normal school attendance—the total target behavior)

priate to engage in (for example, *making one's bed before leaving the house*).

2. *Unambiguously defined.* A target behavior that is defined precisely can be assessed reliably. In the case of an overt behavior, knowing the definition of the target behavior should allow anyone observing the client to know whether the client is engaging in the target behavior or not.

3. *Measurable.* Whenever possible, the target behavior should be quantified. Discrete numbers are more precise than qualitative categories (such as "improved" versus "unimproved"). The measurements can be of (1) *frequency* (how often), (2) *duration* (length of time), (3) *intensity* (strength), or (4) *amount of by-product* of the target behavior (for example, the amount of liquid soap remaining in a soap dispenser as an indication of hand washing[3]). Table 4-2 describes these measures and provides examples. The type of measure employed depends on such factors as the nature of the target behavior, the treatment goals, and practical considerations.

4. *Appropriate and adaptive.* The target behavior must fit the unique problem and be adaptive for the client. This requirement includes not causing other problems (for instance, in the treatment of obesity,

Table 4-2 Types of measures used to assess target behaviors

Type	Description	Examples
FREQUENCY	Number of times the behavior occurs	1. Number of days child attends school 2. Number of cigarettes smoked
DURATION	a. Length of time spent engaging in target behavior	1. Hours child spends in school 2. Minutes spent smoking
	b. Latency (length of time to begin a target behavior)	1. Minutes to enter school after being dropped off by parents 2. Minutes to light up after sitting down at desk
	c. Interval between responses (length of time between the occurrence of instances of the target behavior)	1. Number of days preceding an absence 2. Minutes between cigarettes smoked
INTENSITY	Strength of the target behavior	1. How anxious (on scale of 1–10) child feels while in school 2. Strength of inhalation
AMOUNT OF BY-PRODUCT	Number of by-products of engaging in the target behavior	1. Number of punches in lunch meal ticket 2. Number of cigarette butts left in ashtray

smoking as a substitute for snacking between meals results in its own health hazards). The target behavior also must suit the particular client's circumstances and abilities. For example, a therapist would not ask a visually impaired client to read cue cards as reminders to eat healthy snacks.

Two Types of Target Behaviors: Acceleration and Deceleration

There are two types of target behaviors. **Acceleration target behaviors** are increased, and **deceleration target behaviors** are decreased. Acceleration target behaviors are established for **behavioral deficits,** which are adaptive behaviors that clients are not performing often enough, long enough, or strongly enough (for instance, paying attention in class and standing up for one's rights). Deceleration target behaviors are established for **behavioral excesses,** which are maladaptive behaviors that clients are performing too often, for too long a time, or too strongly (for example, fighting and smoking).

Dealing with acceleration target behaviors is simple and straightforward. Behavior therapy procedures are used to increase the acceleration target behavior directly. For example, if social interaction was the acceleration

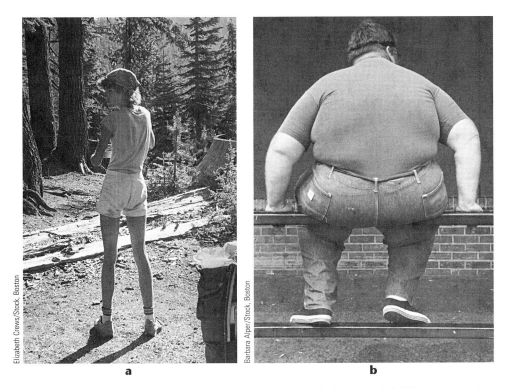

Elizabeth Crews/Stock, Boston

Barbara Alper/Stock, Boston

a   b

Photos 4-1a and 4-1b Examples of the effects of (a) a behavioral deficit in eating and (b) a behavioral excess in eating

target behavior for a hospitalized client who was depressed, the nurses might praise the client each time they saw the client interacting with someone. Dealing with deceleration target behaviors is more complicated.

SPECIAL CONSIDERATIONS FOR DECELERATION TARGET BEHAVIORS

Two basic strategies are used to treat deceleration target behaviors. One is to decrease the deceleration target behavior directly, as parents often try to do by punishing a child's misbehavior. This simple strategy often results in an incomplete solution. When a problem behavior is eliminated or substantially decreased, a void is created in the person's life. No matter how disruptive the problem behavior was, it served some function for the person and filled periods of time in the person's life.

The preferred strategy for treating deceleration target behaviors fills the functional and temporal void with an appropriate adaptive behavior. This is done by substituting an acceleration target behavior for the deceleration target behavior. For instance, if the deceleration target behavior is criticizing friends, then complimenting friends would be a suitable acceleration target behavior. Often, the therapist implements both strategies simultaneously. In other words, the deceleration target behavior is decreased at the same time that an appropriate substitute acceleration target behavior is increased.

An acceleration target behavior used as a substitute for a deceleration target behavior must meet three requirements. First, it must serve the same general function (compliments and criticisms, for example, are both ways of communicating feedback). Second, it should be adaptive; nothing is gained by substituting one maladaptive behavior for another. Third, the acceleration and deceleration target behaviors should be **competing responses;** that is, it should be difficult to perform both at the same time (as is true of complimenting and criticizing). The more the client performs the acceleration target behavior, the fewer opportunities the client has to engage in the deceleration target behavior. It is standard practice in behavior therapy to include an acceleration target behavior in treatment plans that involve a deceleration target behavior. Table 4-3 has examples of deceleration target behaviors and suitable competing acceleration target behaviors.

Table 4-3 Examples of acceleration target behaviors that compete with deceleration target behaviors

Deceleration Target Behavior	Competing Acceleration Target Behavior
Studying in front of the television	Studying in the library
Biting fingernails	Keeping hands in pockets or at sides
Driving home from parties drunk	Taking a taxi home
Staying up until 3 A.M.	Getting into bed and turning out the lights at 1 A.M.
Talking to "voices" (that is, hallucinating)	Talking to other people
Criticizing others	Praising others

◆

| **Participation** | FINDING COMPETING ACCELERATION TARGET BEHAVIORS TO |
| **Exercise 4-1** | SUBSTITUTE FOR UNDESIRABLE BEHAVIORS* |

For each undesirable behavior listed, write one or more acceleration target behaviors that compete with it—in other words, behaviors that, when performed, make it unlikely that the undesirable behavior will occur. Be sure each of your acceleration target behaviors meets the requirements for a good target behavior (described earlier in the chapter).

1. Eating junk food between meals
2. Cramming for exams
3. "Blowing" an entire paycheck
4. Using foul language
5. Leaving lights on that are not in use
6. Wasting time
7. Being late for classes
8. Procrastinating in paying bills
9. Littering

Examples of appropriate competing acceleration target behaviors are given in your Student Resource Materials.

◆

THE DEAD PERSON RULE

Whereas acceleration target behaviors indicate what a client is expected to do, deceleration target behaviors indicate only what the client should *not* do, which poses a problem. Consider a typical scene in an elementary school classroom. Katie is disrupting the class by talking to Heather when the teacher wants the class to read silently. If the teacher tells Katie, "Don't talk to Heather" (a deceleration target behavior), all Katie knows is that she is *not* allowed to talk to Heather. She could obey her teacher by talking to Nigel or by dancing in the aisle. It would be more useful if the teacher told Katie, "Read your book," the acceleration target behavior the teacher wants Katie to perform.

When dealing with behavioral excesses, it often is easier, but less beneficial, to specify what a client should *not* do than what the client should do. To avoid making this mistake, behavior therapists follow the **dead person rule:** *Never ask a client to do something a dead person can do.* Only dead people are capable of *not* behaving! *Don't talk* violates the dead person rule because dead people "can" not talk. Applying the dead person rule means that the client is asked to do something *active.* "Read your book" follows the dead person rule because dead people can't read books.

Ironically, the dead person rule violates itself. "Never ask a client to do something a dead person can do" is something a dead person *could* do.

*Do this Participation Exercise before you continue reading.

The general principle could be rephrased as a *live person rule:* "Always ask a client to do something that only a live person can do." However, the purpose of the dead person rule is to remind therapists to formulate target behaviors that clients can actively perform. This function is better served by the catchy dead person rule. Participation Exercise 4-2 gives you a chance to apply the dead person rule to common violations of the rule.

Participation Exercise 4-2

RESURRECTING THE DEAD: IDENTIFYING AND CORRECTING DEAD PERSON BEHAVIORS*

The dead person rule often is violated in everyday life. This exercise will make you aware of common violations of the rule and give you practice in rephrasing dead person behaviors as live person behaviors.

Part I: Changing Dead Person Behaviors to Live Person Behaviors

A series of frequently heard or seen instructions are listed in Table 4-4. Each instruction requests someone to perform a dead person behavior. For each instruction, write a *live person behavior* that is appropriate for the situation. When you have finished, compare your answers with those in your Student Resource Materials.

*You should do Part I of the Participation Exercise before you continue reading, but you will need to do Part II later.

Table 4-4 Common
instructions that violate
the dead person rule

Situation/Context	Instruction
Parent to child	"Don't be impolite."
Sign in park	DO NOT LITTER
Teacher to student	"No running in the hallway."
Sign on one of two side-by-side doors	DO NOT ENTER
Parent to young boy having trouble tying his shoe	"Don't cry; big boys don't cry."
Parent to child at dinner table	"Don't eat with your fingers."
Sign at petting zoo	DO NOT FEED THE ANIMALS
Parent to child being put to bed	"I don't want to hear another word out of you."
Traffic sign at fork in road	NO LEFT TURN
Teacher to student	"Don't' look at other students' tests."
Instructions on a written form	DO NOT WRITE BELOW THE RED LINE
Lifeguard to swimmer	"No diving off the side."
Parent to child	"Don't hit your sister when she takes your toy."

Part II: Identifying Common Dead Person Behaviors

Over the next few days, look for violations of the dead person rule you hear in people's instructions to others and see in written instructions. Briefly note the situation or context (following the models in Table 4-4), then write the dead person instruction, and finally rephrase the instruction so that it refers to a live person behavior.

◆

MEASURING THE TARGET BEHAVIOR

Measurement of the target behavior begins as soon as it has been designed and before therapy begins. This initial measurement provides a **baseline,** which consists of the repeated measurement of a target behavior as it occurs naturally—that is, before treatment. A baseline provides a standard for evaluating how much a target behavior changes after treatment has begun.[4] Measurement of the target behavior continues throughout the remainder of the therapy process as an ongoing check of the client's progress.

STEP 4: IDENTIFYING MAINTAINING CONDITIONS

Identifying the maintaining conditions of the target behavior is a crucial step because it is these conditions that will be changed in order to change the target behavior.[5] A variety of behavioral assessment procedures (covered in depth in Chapter 5) are employed to pinpoint maintaining antecedents and maintaining consequences.

The assessment typically begins with an interview in which the therapist questions the client in detail about the antecedents and consequences of the target behavior.[6] The questions would include "In what situations do you engage in the target behavior most frequently and least frequently?" "What are you thinking and how are you feeling right before you perform the target behavior?" "What happens right after you perform the target behavior?" and "What are the long-term effects of engaging in the target behavior?"

The retrospective information gathered in interviews may be checked out with other assessment procedures.[7] The therapist may ask the client to keep a record of when the target behavior occurs during the week and to note the antecedents and consequences in each case. Parents may be instructed to observe the circumstances in which their child engages in the target behavior. Sometimes the therapist sets up a simulated situation in which possible maintaining conditions are systematically presented and removed and the effects on the target behavior are noted.[8] For example, a child who has trouble concentrating on schoolwork might be asked to work on an assignment with and without an adult present.

Steps 5 and 6: Designing and Implementing a Treatment Plan

Target behaviors are changed indirectly by directly changing their maintaining conditions. In Case 4-1, for example, Paul's acceleration target behavior—school attendance—occurred infrequently because its consequences (anxiety) were negative. Accordingly, the treatment plan for Paul involved increasing his attending school by making the consequences of school attendance positive, which included the support and friendship of the therapists and specific tangible reinforcers. A **treatment plan** consists of the specific, individualized details of how the therapy procedures will be implemented for a particular client.

Most behaviors are maintained by multiple antecedents and consequences. For example, among the common maintaining consequences of self-injurious behaviors (such as head banging) associated with severe developmental disorders are social attention, direct sensory stimulation, and removal of clients from frustrating tasks.[9] Generally, it is not feasible or necessary to change all the maintaining conditions to change the behavior because the maintaining conditions of a behavior tend to be interrelated. Behavior therapists select for change those maintaining conditions (1) that appear to exert the greatest control over the target behavior and (2) that available behavior therapy procedures are most likely to modify efficiently.

Although behavior therapists are the experts in the methods used to change target behaviors, the client is the one who will undergo the treatment. Accordingly, clients in behavior therapy play a role in selecting the particular therapy procedures to be used. In most cases, several different behavior therapies are likely to be effective for the client's problem. Before any treatment begins, the therapist describes each viable alternative therapy procedure to the client. The descriptions include (1) the underlying rationale, (2) what the therapy entails, (3) what the client is expected to do, (4) an estimate of how long the therapy will take to work, and (5) the general success rate of the therapy for the client's type of problem. Finally, the therapist describes the advantages and disadvantages of each therapy.

Once the client and therapist agree on the therapy procedures and the specifics of how they will be implemented for the client, the treatment begins. The target behavior continues to be measured to assess progress during treatment. When problems or setbacks arise, which is common, the treatment plan is adjusted.

Steps 7 and 8: Evaluating the Success of Therapy and Follow-up Assessment

Evaluating the success of therapy first involves determining whether the target behavior has changed significantly from the baseline—that is, from before the therapy was implemented. If the target behavior has not changed, then it is necessary to return to one of the previous steps and correct any mistakes made (for example, not having correctly identified a maintaining condition of the target behavior). If the target behavior has changed, has this alleviated the client's presenting problem and met the treatment goals? Remember that a target behavior usually is related to an *aspect* of the problem. It may be necessary to change one or more additional target behaviors before the problem is fully alleviated (as in Case 4-1, in which a series of target behaviors were changed—see Table 4-1, page 52).

When the treatment goals have been met, therapy is terminated. However, the therapist and client may set up periodic checks (for example, first in 3 months and then in a year) to ascertain whether the client's treatment gains have continued to be maintained. This is called **follow-up assessment** (or **follow-up,** for short). If a follow-up assessment indicates that the client needs additional treatment, that can be arranged.

Behavior Therapy Research

Research is an integral part of behavior therapy. *Process research* identifies the effective components of a therapy procedure—in other words, what makes it work.[10] *Outcome research* evaluates the effectiveness of therapy procedures and is the major type of research that behavior therapists do. Outcome research has two purposes: (1) to evaluate the effectiveness of a specific treatment for a particular client and (2) to validate the effectiveness of a therapy procedure in general. *Case studies* and *single-subject studies* are used to assess the success of an individual client's treatment and, occasionally, to provide evidence about the general effectiveness of a treatment. Experiments, which involve groups of clients, are employed only to validate the general effectiveness of a therapy procedure.*

Case Studies

A **case study,** such as Case 4-1 at the beginning of this chapter, is a detailed description of what transpires during the treatment of a specific client.[11] Besides documenting the success of therapy for individuals, case studies also are useful for describing new therapy procedures and novel applications of existing therapies.[12] The case studies in this book provide a behind-the-scenes look at the practice of behavior therapy. (Be aware that the sections in this book designated "Case," such as Case 4-1, contain single-subject studies and experiments as well as case studies.)

The major limitation of case studies is that generalizations to other clients cannot be made because a single case cannot be considered representative of all or even of most people. Sometimes, however, a series of case studies that evaluate the effectiveness of a therapy procedure with a number of clients is used to document the effectiveness of the procedure.[13] Another limitation of case studies is that they cannot rule out the possibility that factors other than the treatment may have contributed to the changes obtained. For example, variations in a client's life circumstances—such as beginning a new job—that occur concurrently with therapy may be responsible for changes in the client's problems.

Single-Subject Studies

Single-subject studies systematically compare what happens when a client's target behavior is treated and when it is not treated. If a target behavior changes only after the therapy is introduced, this effect provides evidence that the changes were caused by the therapy.[14] Thus, compared with case studies, single-subject studies allow more definitive conclusions to be drawn about the effects of a treatment.

Single-subject studies are especially useful in clinical practice to evaluate the effectiveness of therapy procedures for a particular client. They also may be a viable alternative to experiments involving groups of clients for demonstrating the efficacy of therapies when a limited number of clients are available for research.[15] The two most common types of single-subject studies are reversal studies and multiple baseline studies.

---

*Contrary to everyday usage, some therapy researchers have made a distinction between the terms *effectiveness* and *efficacy* (for example, Seligman, 1995). *Efficacy* refers to the success of therapy when it is assessed under "ideal" conditions—in research settings using rigorous controls and standardized procedures. *Effectiveness* refers to the success of therapy when it is measured in "real" clinical settings (such as community-based clinics and private practice), where rigorous controls and standardization may be lacking. The distinction is problematic for two reasons. Categorizing therapy outcome studies as measuring efficacy or effectiveness can be difficult and arbitrary, and the distinction is made inconsistently by researchers (for example, Persons, 1997). Accordingly, we have chosen to use the terms interchangeably in this book.

REVERSAL STUDIES

Reversal studies systematically introduce and withdraw the therapy and examine what happens to the client's target behavior. Reversal studies always involve a minimum of three phases: baseline, treatment, and reversal. In the first phase, a *baseline* level of the target behavior is obtained to provide a basis for comparison.

In the second phase, the *treatment* is begun and the target behavior continues to be assessed. If the therapy is effective, the client's target behavior will change from the baseline level. An acceleration target behavior will increase, and a deceleration target behavior will decrease. Figure 4-2 shows the expected change for an acceleration target behavior.

Change in the target behavior from the baseline to the treatment phase is not necessarily caused by the therapy. Some unaccounted-for factors in the client's life may have caused the change. To determine whether the therapy was influencing the change in the target behavior, a third phase of the study is introduced. The therapy is terminated, but the target behavior continues to be assessed. This is called a **reversal phase** because the conditions are reversed to the baseline conditions where the target behavior only was assessed. If the therapy is responsible for the change in the target behavior, then the target behavior will return to near baseline levels when the therapy is withdrawn (as depicted in Figure 4-2).

These three phases—baseline, treatment, and reversal—make up an **ABA study.** *A* stands for no therapy (assessment only)—in the baseline and reversal phases—and *B* stands for treatment. An ABA study provides evidence that the therapy was responsible for changes in the target behavior. However, ending with the reversal phase leaves clients back where they started—that is, at the baseline level. Thus, a fourth phase, *reinstatement of treatment,* is added so that the client can continue to benefit from the therapy. The study thus becomes an **ABAB study,** with the second *B* standing for the reinstatement of therapy. If the therapy is effective, the target behavior will again change in the desired direction (see Figure 4-2). The second B phase provides additional evidence that the therapy is responsible for the change in the target behavior. Compared

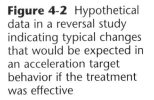

Figure 4-2 Hypothetical data in a reversal study indicating typical changes that would be expected in an acceleration target behavior if the treatment was effective

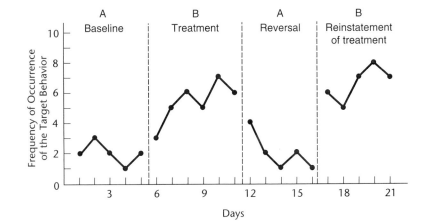

with an ABA study, an ABAB study, by virtue of its additional confirming evidence, provides greater confidence that change is the result of the therapy. Table 4-5 summarizes the phases of an ABAB reversal study.

Reversal studies have three major limitations. First, they cannot be used to evaluate the success of therapy with all target behaviors. Reversal studies are appropriate when target behaviors are maintained by external factors, such as privileges given to a teenage girl for studying and getting good grades. In contrast, reversal studies are inappropriate when the target behaviors that are learned in therapy become relatively permanent behaviors in the client's repertoire, such as study skills, and thus are unlikely to change when the therapy is withdrawn.

Second, it is not legitimate to generalize from the success of a single client's therapy to clients in general. As with case studies, this limitation can be circumvented in part by conducting a series of reversal studies on a particular therapy procedure for the same problem with multiple clients.[16]

Third, withdrawing therapy in reversal studies may be unethical. If a treatment reduces a client's self-destructive behavior, such as driving while intoxicated, then it would be unethical to remove the treatment during a reversal phase, even though it is important to assess the effectiveness of the treatment. Multiple baseline studies circumvent this limitation.

MULTIPLE BASELINE STUDIES

In a **multiple baseline study,** a particular therapy procedure is introduced sequentially for different target behaviors, clients, or settings, depending on the purpose of the study. One purpose is to ascertain whether the therapy is effective for multiple target behaviors, a second purpose is to determine whether the therapy is effective with different clients, and a third purpose is to assess whether the therapy is effective in

Table 4-5 Phases of a reversal study

	PHASES		
	A Baseline	B Treatment	A Reversal	B Reinstatement of Treatment
Procedure	Measure target behavior	Introduce treatment; measure target behavior	Withdraw treatment; measure target behavior	Reinstate treatment; measure target behavior
Purpose	Assess normal level of target behavior	Change target behavior	Check whether treatment is responsible for change in target behavior	Reinstate change in target behavior
Expectation	None	Target behavior will change in desired direction	Target behavior will return to baseline level	Target behavior will change in desired direction

Table 4-6 Variables that change and remain constant in multiple baseline studies

Type of Study	VARIABLES		
	Target Behaviors	Clients	Settings
Across target behaviors	Different	Same	Same
Across clients	Same	Different	Same
Across settings	Same	Same	Different

different settings (such as at home and at work). If the therapy is responsible for the changes in a target behavior, then change should occur *only* when the therapy is introduced and not before. Table 4-6 summarizes the differences between the three types of multiple baseline studies.

We'll illustrate the rationale and basic procedures of multiple baseline studies by examining a hypothetical example of a multiple baseline study across target behaviors. The study examined the effectiveness of Therapy X on three different acceleration target behaviors, for the same client and in the same setting.

As you can see in Figure 4-3, following 5 days of baseline, the therapy was introduced for behavior 1 but not for behaviors 2 and 3, for which baseline assessment just continued. Notice in Figure 4-3 that only the target behavior being treated (behavior 1) increased, presumably because of the therapy. Behaviors 2 and 3 did not change, presumably because they received no treatment.

Next, on day 10, the therapy was introduced for behavior 2, which increased, providing additional evidence of the therapy's effectiveness. In contrast, behavior 3 remained unchanged from its baseline level, which is what would be expected if the therapy was responsible for the changes.

Finally, the therapy was applied to behavior 3 on day 14. As with the other two target behaviors, behavior 3 increased when the therapy was introduced, further substantiating the claim that the therapy was responsible. Because each target behavior changed *only* after the therapy was applied to it and because the client and setting were held constant, it is reasonable to conclude that the changes were attributable to the therapy and not to other factors.

Both reversal studies and multiple baseline studies provide more information about the causal effects of the therapy than case studies. However, because multiple baseline studies, like reversal studies, evaluate the effects of therapy for single subjects, there are limits on the generalizability of their findings to other clients.* Determining the general efficacy of a particular therapy requires groups of clients.

Experiments

Experiments study groups of clients, all of whom are dealt with in the same way except that some clients receive the therapy being tested and

---

*Multiple baseline studies across clients are single-subject studies because each client in the study is considered separately and the results for all the clients are not averaged, as in experiments (which are described later).

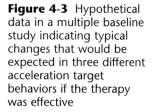

Figure 4-3 Hypothetical data in a multiple baseline study indicating typical changes that would be expected in three different acceleration target behaviors if the therapy was effective

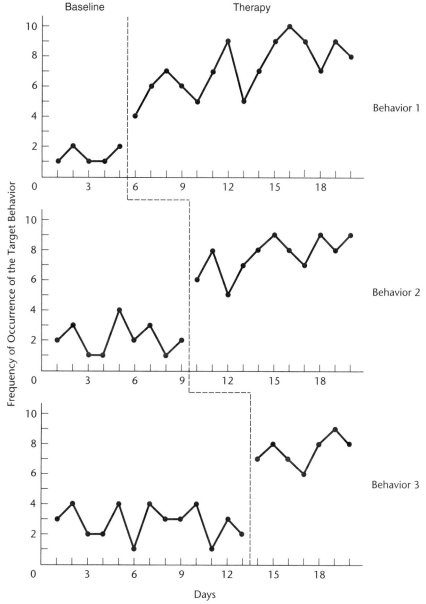

others do not. Experiments are the primary research method used to evaluate the overall efficacy of a treatment, as opposed to its effectiveness in a particular case. Experiments definitively address the question "Is the therapy being evaluated responsible for the changes in clients' behaviors?" This question can be answered because experiments *control*, or account for, the influence of *extraneous factors*—that is, factors other than the therapy that are likely to affect clients' problems (such as motivation to change and life circumstances that might help alleviate problems).

In the simplest experiment, researchers randomly assign clients to two groups. *Random assignment* means that each client has an equal chance of being assigned to each group. The **treatment group** receives the therapy, whereas the other group does not, thus serving as a comparison or **control group** (see Table 4-7). The two groups are made equivalent, *except* that one group receives therapy and the other does not.* Thus, if clients in the treatment group improve significantly more than clients in the control group, then we can confidently conclude that the improvement was caused by the therapy and not by extraneous factors.

Once the efficacy of a therapy has been demonstrated, researchers may carry out additional experiments to assess its relative effectiveness compared with other therapies. In such experiments, the comparison groups consist of clients treated by other therapies and a control group itself may not be necessary.

The findings of experiments are more generalizable than the findings of case studies or single-subject studies because the results of experiments represent averages for a number of clients. However, the accuracy of generalizations to other clients depends on how similar the clients and their problems in the experiment are to the clients to whom the generalizations are made. This issue is particularly relevant to analogue experiments.

ANALOGUE EXPERIMENTS

Ideally, the effectiveness of therapy procedures should be evaluated in clinical settings—that is, with actual clients who seek treatment for psychological disorders. Because of practical and ethical constraints, this goal cannot always be met. Practically, for example, it may be difficult to find clients with similar problems, to ensure that all clients receive identical therapy procedures, and to control extraneous factors. Important ethical issues include treating clients who are in serious need of therapy with new, untested therapies and assigning such clients to control groups.

Analogue experiments can circumvent some practical and ethical problems.[17] In **analogue experiments,** the conditions of the study are similar (analogous), but not identical, to the conditions that exist in actual clinical practice. Analogue experiments primarily differ from clinical experiments in terms of the problems and the people treated. For instance, the problem might be mild social anxiety that makes people feel uneasy around others but that is not debilitating in the sense of preventing social interactions; the subjects in an analogue experiment may be college students who volunteer to participate in a therapy study rather than clients who are actively seeking therapy.

Analogue experiments are easier to carry out and may control for extraneous factors better than actual clinical studies. They also do not pose some of the ethical problems associated with clinical research. The major

---

*The groups are made equivalent with respect to extraneous factors in two ways. First, random assignment usually ensures that, overall, subjects in one group do not differ from subjects in the other group in terms of preexisting characteristics among the clients. Second, the two groups are dealt with in the same way (for instance, they are given the same assessment measures), except for the presence or absence of therapy.

disadvantage of analogue experiments is that the generalizability of findings to actual clinical conditions may be limited. Accordingly, analogue research is most useful as an initial step in evaluating therapy—before it is used with actual clients. If such preliminary testing indicates that the

Table 4-7 Types of control groups commonly used in behavior therapy outcome experiments

Control Group	Description	Purpose	Example
NO TREATMENT	Clients receive no therapy. Target behaviors are assessed at the same time that clients in the therapy group receive pretherapy and posttherapy assessments.	To control for improvements in clients' problems that are due to factors other than the specific therapy procedures.	A young child was referred for therapy because of aggressive behaviors. The child's aggressive behaviors were assessed and then reassessed 10 weeks later.
WAIT-LIST	Clients initially receive no therapy. Target behaviors are assessed at the same time that clients in the therapy group receive pretherapy and posttherapy assessments. After the therapy group's final assessment, clients receive therapy.	To control for the influence of clients' expectations that they will receive therapy.	Couples seeking help for their marital conflict had their marital relationship assessed and then reassessed two months later. They then participated in two months of marital therapy, after which their marital relationship was assessed again.
NO CONTACT	Clients receive no therapy. Target behaviors are assessed without the clients' being aware that they are part of a therapy study and without direct contact with the therapist or researcher.	To control for improvements in clients' problems that are due to being participants in a therapy study rather than to the specific therapy procedures.	All people between the ages of 21 and 35 in a community were mailed a questionnaire to complete about their anxiety three days after an earthquake struck and then again five months later.
ATTENTION	Clients meet with a therapist for the same amount of time as clients in the therapy condition but receive no therapy.	To control for improvements in clients' problems that are due to the therapists' attention rather than to the specific therapy procedures.	College students with severe test anxiety met with a therapist once a week for 12 sessions and discussed theories of the development and course of test anxiety.
PLACEBO	Clients receive a therapy-like procedure that they are led to believe is highly effective but in fact has no proven efficacy.	To control for improvements in clients' problems that are due to clients' expectations that the therapy they are receiving will be effective rather than to the specific therapy procedures.	Clients who were depressed were told that listening to a specially prepared audiotape of rhythmic clicking sounds before they went to sleep for three weeks would result in dramatic improvements in their mood.

therapy is effective, the next step is to perform experiments with actual clients (for example, people who meet the diagnostic criteria for clinical depression rather than people who are sad).[18]

WHAT CONSTITUTES EFFECTIVE BEHAVIOR THERAPY?

Four *outcome measures,* or criteria, are used to evaluate the effectiveness of behavior therapy: meaningfulness of change, transfer and generalization

---

◆   **In Theory 4-1**

BEHAVIOR THERAPY AS AN EXPERIMENT

Behavior therapy is analogous to an experiment. An experiment begins with a hypothesis that a particular *independent variable* (a condition that is directly varied) influences a particular *dependent variable* (the behavior being studied). To test the hypothesis, researchers vary the independent variable and measure the dependent variable to see if it changes. They do this while controlling extraneous factors that might affect the dependent variable. If the dependent variable changes when the independent variable is introduced, the hypothesis is supported. In other words, the experiment has produced evidence that the independent variable has a causative effect on the dependent variable.

You can see the parallels between an experiment and the process of behavior therapy if you substitute the terms *maintaining conditions* for *independent variable* and *target behavior* for *dependent variable.* The behavior therapist hypothesizes that certain conditions are maintaining the target behavior. The therapist tests the hypothesis by changing the maintaining conditions in therapy and by observing whether the target behavior changes. If the target behavior changes (in the desired direction), then the hypothesis is supported and the therapy is successful. If the target

behavior does not change (in the desired direction), the hypothesis is not supported and the treatment is unsuccessful. Table 4-8 details the parallels between behavior therapy and an experiment.

One major difference exists between behavior therapy and an experiment. In an experiment, control procedures prevent factors other than the independent variable from influencing the dependent variable. Accordingly, experiments can establish cause-and-effect relationships with a high degree of certainty. This is less true for behavior therapy. If the hypothesized maintaining conditions are changed and the target behavior changes, then therapy is successful. However, generally it is not possible to know definitively that modifying the hypothesized maintaining conditions caused the change. The reason is that with therapy, it usually is not possible to control for the effects of many extraneous variables. For example, changes in a client's life that occur during therapy may have a beneficial affect on the problem (such as recovering from an illness or starting a new romantic relationship). Not knowing definitively what accounts for the success of therapy usually is acceptable in clinical practice because the goal is to alleviate a client's problem.

Table 4-8 Parallels between behavior therapy and an experiment

Step	Behavior Therapy	Experiment
1. Define what is to be changed	Target behavior	Dependent variable*
2. Assess baseline level	Pretherapy measurement of target behavior	Preexperiment measurement of dependent variable
3. Search for influential factors	Identify maintaining antecedents and maintaining consequences of target behavior	Decide on independent variable*
4. Formulate hypothesis	"If correct maintaining conditions have been identified, then modifying them will change the target behavior."	"If the independent variable does influence the dependent variable, then varying the independent variable will result in the dependent variable changing."
5. Test hypothesis	Implement therapy (that is, modify maintaining conditions)	Carry out experiment (that is, vary independent variable)
6. Examine outcome	Posttherapy measurement of target behavior	Postexperiment measurement of dependent variable
7. Draw conclusions when		
a. Change is in expected direction	Therapy successful	Hypothesis confirmed
b. No change or change is in unexpected direction	Reassess maintaining conditions (that is, return to step 3)	Find other independent variable (that is, return to step 3)

*In an experiment, the condition that is directly varied is called the *independent variable.* The object of an experiment is to observe the influence of the independent variable on subjects' behaviors. The specific behavior under investigation is called the *dependent variable* because it is hypothesized to depend on or be influenced by the condition varied by the experimenter (that is, the independent variable).

of change, maintenance of change over time, and acceptability of the therapy. These outcome measures are applicable both to research (typically experiments) that evaluates the efficacy of a therapy for clients in general and to the determination of the effectiveness of a therapy with a particular client in clinical practice.

Meaningfulness of Change

Effective therapy should result in a change that is clearly meaningful for the client, which is known as **clinical significance.**[19]* Informally, for individual clients, clinical significance amounts to meeting the goals for therapy. More formally, clinical significance depends primarily on one or both of two criteria. First, clinical significance is evaluated with reference to relevant norms.[20] Consider the hypothetical case of Mai Lee, a 5-year-old girl who interacts with her peers only 5% of the time that she is with other children at her preschool. Suppose that after therapy Mai Lee is spending 35% of her time at preschool interacting with other children. Although 35% clearly is a substantial change, if the norm for social interaction for 5-year-old girls were 55%, then the therapy outcome would not be considered clinically significant.

Second, clinical significance can be evaluated in terms of general standards for adaptive or acceptable functioning, which is referred to as **social validity.**[21] Social validity usually is assessed by having knowledgeable people judge whether the client's behaviors following therapy are adaptive or acceptable.[22] Using the example of Mai Lee, in addition to assessing the amount of peer interaction she engaged in, the goals of therapy might specify that her interactions involve making appropriate overtures to peers and engaging in cooperative play with them. Mai Lee's teacher might be asked to observe her peer interactions and rate them in terms of how appropriate they were and whether they involved cooperative play.

Transfer and Generalization of Change

The purpose of therapy is to bring about changes in the client's everyday life. Obviously, then, effective treatment requires that changes that are achieved in therapy *transfer* to the client's life. In other words, **transfer** occurs when what is learned and practiced in therapy carries over to other settings. For example, a man who learns problem-solving skills in therapy sessions to control his anger when confronted with frustrating situations, must also be able to control his anger when he encounters such situations during the course of his daily living. Moreover, the man should be able to use problem solving to deal with anger in diverse settings, such as work and home.

Additionally, in most cases, the therapeutic benefits should impact behaviors and aspects of the client's life other than those that were specif-

---

Clinical significance is not *statistical significance,* which refers only to the reliability of an outcome. A statistically significant outcome means that there is a high probability that the outcome would occur again if the therapy were applied in other cases, but it implies nothing about the meaningfulness of the outcome. For example, suppose a treatment for smoking cessation results in an average reduction of cigarettes smoked from 36 to 33 per day. Given a sufficient number of clients in the treatment group, this could be a reliable finding. In other words, there is a high probability that the treatment would reduce cigarettes smoked in other studies using the same treatment. However, because three fewer cigarettes per day would not improve the clients' health, the results of the study are not *clinically significant.*

ically addressed in treatment, a process called **generalization.**[23] The man in the previous example might use problem solving to deal with his excessive drinking and work-related stress in addition to his anger.[24]

Transfer and generalization of change are not always a natural outcome of successful treatment, so it often is necessary to include in the treatment plan procedures that create transfer and generalization. For instance, with children who are socially withdrawn, social skills training can be carried out with multiple peers (to enhance generalization) and in a variety of settings (to enhance transfer).[25]

Durability of Change

Changes that result from therapy must endure long after the treatment has ended. Endurance of therapeutic effects typically is referred to as **long-term maintenance** (or **maintenance,** for short).

Maintenance of treatment effects is determined by assessing the client's functioning at various time intervals after therapy has been terminated—optimally, extending several years.[26] Such follow-up assessment has become a standard measure in behavior therapy outcome research. Typically, the results of follow-up assessments are reported in the research literature using phrasing such as "the treatment gains were maintained up to 2 years." Such phrasing can be misleading. What is meant is that at a 2-year follow-up, the treatment gains were maintained, and not that the treatment effects only lasted 2 years or less. The major practical obstacle to obtaining follow-up assessments is keeping track of clients' whereabouts and getting clients to undergo additional assessment procedures.[27]

Maintenance of treatment gains, like transfer and generalization, is not guaranteed by an initially successful therapy outcome. Specific procedures may need to be included during and after therapy to ensure durability over time. For example, a residential treatment program for antisocial behaviors reinforces teenage clients for socially appropriate behaviors with spending money. As clients are nearing the end of the program, the reinforcers are switched to verbal praise because outside the program appropriate behaviors are more likely to be reinforced by praise than money. Additionally, significant people in the clients' lives, such as parents and teachers, may need to be trained to continue the social reinforcement of appropriate behaviors the clients have adopted. This can help ensure that clients will continue to perform the behaviors after they have left the program.

As you may have realized, long-term maintenance partially depends on transfer and generalization. To begin with, maintenance is an issue only if the changes transfer to the client's everyday life. Further, the more situations to which therapeutic changes transfer and the more behaviors to which the changes generalize, the greater the likelihood that the behaviors will become habitual.

Acceptability of the Therapy

A final outcome measure concerns the acceptability of the treatment procedures to the client and sometimes to significant others, as in the case of children.[28] In this context, **acceptability** refers to how palatable the therapy procedures are. It does not refer to whether the client believes the therapy is effective.[29]

Some forms of behavior therapy are more likely to be acceptable than others. As with many treatments for medical problems, effective behavioral treatments sometimes involve discomfort and may be intrusive (for example, they interfere with the client's normal activities). How much discomfort and intrusion clients are willing to tolerate to alleviate their problems is a matter of individual preference.[30] However, all other things being equal, therapy procedures that are more acceptable to clients are more useful because clients are more likely to seek therapy and remain in treatment.[31] Conversely, clients tend to drop out of treatments that have low acceptability.[32]

Acceptability of treatments to behavior therapists is a factor that determines whether therapists will apply them. For many reasons independent of the demonstrated efficacy of a treatment, therapists may not want to use it with clients. As just one example, therapists may find a therapy difficult or boring to administer. Similarly, nonprofessional change agents, such as parents and teachers, are more likely to continue to administer therapy procedures that they find acceptable and discontinue or inconsistently employ procedures that they find unacceptable.[33] The bottom line is that even the most effective therapies can be helpful only if they are used, which partly depends on their being acceptable first to the clinician who recommends and administers the treatments and then to the client who must undergo them.

SUMMARY

1. The process of behavior therapy involves eight basic steps: clarifying the client's problem, formulating goals, designing a target behavior, identifying maintaining conditions of the target behavior, designing a treatment plan to change the maintaining conditions, implementing the treatment plan, evaluating its effectiveness, and conducting follow-up assessment. Assessment begins after the target behavior is designed and continues through the course of therapy and after therapy is terminated.

2. Only one or two problems are treated simultaneously. Each problem is defined as a target behavior, an aspect of the problem that is relatively small, discrete, and measurable. A good target behavior is narrow in scope, unambiguously defined, measurable, and appropriate and adaptive for the client and the problem.

3. Acceleration target behaviors are increased and are designed for behavioral deficits, adaptive behaviors clients are not performing enough. An acceleration target behavior is treated by increasing it directly. Deceleration target behaviors are decreased and are designed for behavioral excesses, maladaptive behaviors clients are performing too much. A deceleration target behavior can be decreased directly. However, the preferred strategy is to decrease

it indirectly by increasing an adaptive acceleration target behavior that competes with the deceleration target behavior.

4. The dead person rule states "Never ask a client to do something a dead person can do." Its purpose is to remind therapists to formulate target behaviors that clients can actively perform.

5. Once a target behavior has been selected, its probable maintaining conditions are identified. A treatment plan is then developed to change the maintaining conditions, which will change the target behavior.

6. The effectiveness of the treatment plan is evaluated in terms of the treatment goals. If the plan was successful, therapy is terminated and periodic follow-up assessments are conducted. If the treatment plan has not alleviated the problem, then additional target behaviors are designed and treated.

7. Process research identifies the effective components of a therapy. Outcome research evaluates whether therapy is effective, both for individual clients and for a therapy procedure in general.

8. Case studies are detailed, descriptive accounts of what transpired in the treatment of individual clients. Case studies are limited in terms of the generalizability of their findings to other clients and in terms of determining whether the therapy itself caused the changes in the target behavior.

9. Single-subject studies systematically compare what happens when a client's target behaviors are treated and when they are not treated. Reversal designs systematically introduce and withdraw the therapy to assess its effects on the client's target behavior. In multiple baseline studies, a particular therapy procedure is introduced sequentially for different target behaviors, clients, or settings. Single-subject studies provide more information about the causal effect of the therapy than case studies, but they are limited in terms of the generalizability of their findings.

10. Experiments study groups of clients and control for the effects of extraneous variables. In a simple experiment, clients are randomly assigned to two groups. One group receives therapy and the other does not, serving as a control or comparison group. Experiments provide results that can be generalized and that most definitively indicate whether the therapy itself has resulted in the changes in clients' target behaviors.

11. Analogue experiments set up conditions that are similar, but not identical, to the conditions that exist in actual clinical practice and thereby circumvent some practical and ethical problems of clinical research. However, because they do not replicate clinical practice, analogue experiments are most useful as initial investigations of the effectiveness of therapy.

12. Behavior therapy can be viewed as a scientific experiment in which hypotheses about the causes of the client's target behaviors are tested.

13. Four outcome measures are used to evaluate the effectiveness of behavior therapy: meaningfulness of change, transfer and generalization of change, durability of change, and acceptability of the therapy.

REFERENCE NOTES

1. Lazarus, Davison, & Polefka, 1965, pp. 225–227, 229.
2. Rosales-Ruiz & Baer, 1997; Voeltz & Evans, 1982.
3. Finney, Miller, & Adler, 1993.
4. Barlow & Hersen, 1984.
5. For example, Derby, Wacker, Sasso, Steege, Northup, Cigland, & Asinus, 1992; Iwata, Vollmer, & Zarcone, 1990.
6. O'Neill, Horner, Albin, Storey, & Sprague, 1990.
7. For example, Storey, Lawry, Ashworth, Danko, & Strain, 1994.
8. For example, Chapman, Fisher, Piazza, & Kurtz, 1993.
9. For example, Smith, Iwata, Vollmer, & Zarcone, 1993.
10. Whisman, 1993.
11. For example, Campbell & Lutzker, 1993.
12. For example, Cautela & Kearney, 1993; Davison & Lazarus, 1995.
13. For example, Mathews, Teasdale, Munby, Johnston, & Shaw, 1977; Perlis, Aloia, Millikan, Boehmler, Smith, Greenblatt, & Giles, 2000; Wolpe, 1958.
14. Haynes, Spain, & Oliveira, 1993; Kazdin, 1993; Morgan & Morgan, 2001.
15. Hilliard, 1993; Peterson & Bell-Dolan, 1995.
16. Baer, Osnes, & Stokes, 1983; Baer, Williams, Osnes, & Stokes, 1983; Guevremont, Osnes, & Stokes, 1986a, 1986b.
17. For example, McGlynn, Moore, Rose, & Lazarte, 1995.
18. For example, Paul, 1969a.
19. For example, Jacobson, 1988; Jacobson, Follette, & Revenstorf, 1984; Kazdin, 1977a, 1999; Kendall & Norton-Ford, 1982; Wolf, 1978.
20. Jacobson, 1988.
21. Carr & Carlson, 1993; Foster & Mash, 1999; Kazdin, 1977a; Wolf, 1978.
22. For example, Finney, Rapoff, Hall, & Christopherson, 1983; Frisch & Froberg, 1987; Jones, Kazdin, & Haney, 1981; Minkin, Braukmann, Minkin, Timbers, Timbers, Fixsen, Phillips, & Wolf, 1976; Romano & Bellack, 1980.
23. Risley, 1995.
24. Belchic & Harris, 1994.
25. For example, Beidel & Turner, 1998; Beidel, Turner, & Morris, 2000.
26. For example, Foxx & Faw, 1990.
27. For example, Heimberg, Salzman, Holt, & Blendell, 1993.
28. For example, Jones, Eyberg, Adams, & Boggs, 1998; Miller & Kelley, 1992; Smith & Linscheid, 1994.
29. For example, Cox, Fergus, & Swinson, 1994; Newton, Hartley, & Sturmey, 1993.
30. Renfrey, 1992; Tarnowski, Simonian, Bekeny, & Park, 1992.
31. Meichenbaum, 1991.
32. For example, Callahan & Leitenberg, 1973; Smith, Marcus, & Eldredge, 1994; Wilson & Tracey, 1976.
33. McConnachie & Carr, 1997.

Chapter 5

Behavioral Assessment

Behavioral assessment is to behavior therapy what a banana is to a banana split—indispensable. Behavioral assessment procedures provide the data that guide the development of a unique treatment plan for the client and measure its effectiveness.

Behavioral assessment gathers information to (1) clarify the problem, (2) set initial goals, (3) select and define target behaviors precisely, (4) identify the maintaining conditions of the target behaviors, (5) design a treatment plan, and (6) monitor the client's progress.

Our discussion focuses on the eight most frequently used behavioral assessment methods: interview, direct self-report inventory, self-recording, checklist/rating scale, systematic naturalistic observation, simulated observation, role-playing, and physiological measurement (see Table 5-1).[1] The first three methods—interview, self-report inventory, and self-recording—gather information from clients' reports about themselves. On one hand, self-report measures have a number of advantages, including their efficiency and ability to tap covert behaviors directly. On the other hand, self-reports are subject to various unintentional and intentional errors, such as distorting the data so that they "look good." Accordingly, some behavioral assessment procedures employ other people to assess clients' behaviors—checklist/rating scale, naturalistic and simulated observation, and role-playing. These methods also have their strengths and limitations, as you will see. Finally, physiological measurements primarily rely on instrumentation to provide information. In subsequent chapters, you will learn about a number of specific applications of the basic methods of behavioral assessment presented in this chapter.

Before reading further in the text, take a few minutes to read the examples in Table 5-2. They provide a preview of this chapter's content.

MULTIMETHOD AND MULTIMODAL ASSESSMENT

In practice, more than one method of assessment generally is used to gather information.[2] **Multimethod assessment** leads to a more compre-

Table 5-1 Most frequently used methods of behavioral assessment
SOURCE: Based on data from Guevremont & Spiegler, 1990.

Rank	Method	Percentage of Behavior Therapists Using Frequently*
1	Interview	90
2	Direct self-report inventory	63
3	Self-recording	56
4	Checklist or rating scale	51
5	Systematic naturalistic observation	30
6	Simulated observation	23
7	Role-playing	20
8	Physiological measurement	19

*Percentage of behavior therapists indicating that they used the method with six or more clients in the past year.

hensive assessment than does employing a single method, and it provides corroborative evidence from different assessment procedures, which increases the validity of the assessment. Finally, each method has its particular strengths and limitations, so using multiple methods yields a balanced assessment.

In behavioral assessment, information about more than one *mode* of behavior usually is obtained.[3] **Multimodal assessment** is important because psychological disorders generally involve more than one mode.[4] Depression, for example, may consist of reduced activity (overt behavior),

Table 5-2 Examples of behavioral assessment methods used to assess *anger* and *aggressive behaviors* (examples of commonly used methods are printed in **boldface**)

Method	Modes of Behavior			
	Overt Behaviors	*Cognitions*	*Emotions*	*Physiological Responses*
Interview	"Describe what you do when you get angry at your wife."	"What thoughts go through your mind when you get angry at your wife?"	"How are you feeling when you hit your wife?"	"What specific bodily reactions do you have when you get angry at your wife?"
Direct self-report inventory	True or false: "I often use physical violence to get my way."	True or false: "When I get angry, I think about attacking someone."	True or false: "When I am angry, I feel like I am going to explode."	True or false: "When I get angry, I start to sweat."
Checklist and rating scale	**Parents check the specific aggressive acts a teenager engaged in last week.**	Not used.	Teacher rates the severity of a student's anger using a 5-point scale.	Mother checks off possible physiological responses (such as sweating and shaking) she observes in her son that may indicate anger.
Self-recording	**Client keeps diary of incidents of aggressive acts.**	**Client keeps diary of thoughts before, during, and after incidents of anger and aggressive behaviors.**	**Client records occurrences of angry feelings during the day.**	**Client records pulse when provoked to anger.**
Systematic naturalistic observation	**Therapist observes parent–child interactions at home, coding examples of parental verbally and physically aggressive behaviors.**	Not used.	Therapist observes overt behaviors (such as shaking fist or making threatening remarks) that may indicate client feels angry.	In client's home, therapist observes overt signs of physiological reactions (for example, face flushing and rapid breathing).

(continued)

Table 5-2 *(continued)*

	Modes of Behavior			
Method	*Overt Behaviors*	*Cognitions*	*Emotions*	*Physiological Responses*
Simulated observation	**Therapist deliberately provokes client and notes client's overt responses.**	Not used.	Therapist deliberately provokes client and notes client's overt behaviors (such as shaking fist or making threatening remarks) that may indicate client feels angry.	Therapist deliberately provokes client and notes overt signs of physiological reactions (for example, face flushed and rapid breathing).
Role-playing	**Scenario is presented of client's boss' criticizing client for being late. Therapist role-plays boss, and client responds to boss's criticism. Therapist observes what client says.**	Scenario is presented of client's boss' criticizing client for being late. Therapist role-plays boss and client responds to boss's criticism. Client describes thoughts while responding to criticism.	Scenario is presented of client's boss' criticizing client for being late. Therapist role-plays boss, and client responds to boss's criticism. Therapist observes client's overt responses (such as grimaces) that may indicate anger.	Scenario is presented of client's boss' criticizing client for being late. Therapist role-plays boss, and client responds to boss's criticism. Therapist observes client's overt signs of physiological reactions (such as face flushing).
Physiological measurement	Not used.	Not used.	Heart rate and blood pressure, signs of arousal that may indicate anger, are measured while client thinks about frustrating situations.	**A father's heart rate, blood pressure, and galvanic skin response are measured before, during, and after he watches a video of his children's misbehaving.**

thoughts of hopelessness (cognition), sadness (emotion), and weight loss (physiological response).

The particular modes of behavior assessed and the methods used depend on the nature of the problem and on practical considerations. Table 5-2 gives examples of how anger and aggressive behaviors might be assessed using each of the eight most common behavioral assessment methods for each of the four modes of behavior. As the table indicates, certain methods of assessment are optimal for each mode of behavior, and not all methods are appropriate for each of the modes.[5] In assessing a client's thoughts, for example, interviews, self-report inventories, and self-recordings are the optimal methods, and role-playing could possibly be used; however, the remaining four assessment methods are not applicable. In practice, the most efficient and least costly methods of assessment typically are chosen, which is one reason why behavioral interviews are used most frequently.

CHARACTERISTICS OF BEHAVIORAL ASSESSMENT

In a sense, behavioral assessment is defined independently of the methods used. What constitutes behavioral assessment depends on *how* an assessment procedure is implemented. For instance, the interview is the most common method of psychological assessment, so it is hardly unique to behavioral assessment. However, the emphases in a behavioral interview (such as focusing on current circumstances) distinguish it from interviews in other types of assessment. Some of the general differences between behavioral and nonbehavioral (traditional) approaches to assessment are summarized in Table 5-3.

Behavioral assessment procedures share five characteristics. Behavioral assessment (1) is individualized, (2) focuses on the present, (3) directly samples relevant behaviors, (4) has a narrow focus, and (5) is integrated with therapy. These emphases are consistent with the behavioral model

Table 5-3 Comparison of behavioral and traditional assessment
SOURCE: Adapted from Barios, 1988.

	Behavioral	*Traditional*
Aims	To identify target behaviors	To describe personality functioning
	To identify maintaining conditions	To identify etiology (origin)
	To select appropriate treatment	To diagnose or classify
	To evaluate and revise treatment	
Assumptions		
1. Role of behavior	Sample of client's typical behaviors in specific situations	Sign of client's personality (for example, traits and intrapsychic dynamics)
2. Role of past	Unimportant (present behavior caused by present events)	Crucial (present behavior caused by past events)
3. Consistency of behavior	Consistent in the same situation	Consistent in different situations
Interpretation		
1. Direct or indirect	Direct (sample)	Indirect (sign)
2. Degree of inference	Low (behavior to behavior)	High (behavior to personality)

and overlap with the defining themes and common characteristics of behavior therapy described in Chapter 1.

Individualized

Behavioral assessment is used to gather unique and detailed information about a client's problem and its maintaining conditions.[6] The particular assessment methods are chosen with the particular client and the client's problem in mind. Additionally, standard tests and procedures may be customized to fit the needs of the assessment. These practices are consistent with behavior therapy's individualized approach. Individualized behavioral assessment directly contrasts with the practice of diagnosing psychological problems, as you will see in In Theory 5-1.

◆   **In Theory 5-1**

IS THERE A PLACE FOR DIAGNOSIS IN BEHAVIOR THERAPY?

Diagnosis involves classifying clients' problems into discrete categories of disorders. The American Psychiatric Association developed the standard diagnostic categories used today to classify psychological disorders. These categories appear in the 1994 publication of the *Diagnostic and Statistical Manual of Mental Disorders* (4th edition),[7] which is referred to as *DSM-IV*, and in a minor revision published in 2000.[8]

Philosophically, diagnosis is antithetical to fundamental premises of behavior therapy and behavioral assessment.[9] In contrast to the individualistic approach of behavior therapy and assessment, diagnosis groups clients' problems into categories.[10] For example, rather than dealing with a client's particular anxiety-related behaviors, DSM-IV views the client as having a *posttraumatic stress disorder*. The client's individual problem now is indistinguishable from the problems of all people whose behavior has the same diagnosis. This often results in two false assumptions: (1) that all individuals with the same disorder display the same behaviors and

(2) that an individual whose problem has been given a particular diagnosis displays all, or even most, of the symptoms that are supposedly characteristic of the diagnosis. Thus, based on a diagnosis, one may attribute characteristics to a client that the client does not possess.

Diagnosis is a trait concept, which is another basic way in which diagnosis runs counter to the behavioral approach. Strictly speaking, a diagnosis refers to people's behaviors rather than to people themselves. Unfortunately, this fact often is forgotten. The client becomes the diagnosis, which leads to viewing the client as a *schizophrenic* rather than as an *individual with schizophrenia*, for example. This unfortunate error results in people being stigmatized and discriminated against. Further, in the case of some disorders, it is assumed that, once diagnosed, the person always has the disorder, although the symptoms may not always be present.[11] This unsupported assumption accounts for such well-known expressions as "Once an alcoholic, always an alcoholic." That expression, incidentally, embodies our earlier point regarding the regrettable common practice of equating the person with the diagnosis. You may have noticed already in your reading of this book that behavior therapists view clients as *having* disorders, rather than *being* disordered.

Diagnosis often does not provide information critical to a meaningful behavioral assessment of an individual client's problem and to designing behavior therapy procedures for treating the problem. Diagnosis does not specify (1) the specific behaviors that are problematic for an individual client; (2) under which conditions they are problematic; (3) their frequency, intensity, and duration; or (4) the maintaining conditions of the problem behaviors.

Does this mean behavior therapists do not use diagnostic labels in referring to their clients' problems? No, it does not. In fact, most behavior therapists do assign DSM-IV diagnoses. In clinical practice, the major reason for doing so is that official diagnoses are required by clinics, hospitals, schools, and social service agencies before treatment and services can be offered and by health insurance and health care providers before the treatment will be paid for.

One potential benefit of diagnosis is that in some cases—but certainly not all—a diagnosis provides information that is helpful for comprehensive planning of clients' treatment (for example, considering medication for a client with bipolar disorder). However, even when useful information comes from a diagnosis, it is never sufficient to design a comprehensive treatment plan. The unique aspects of each client's problem must be considered, which requires a thorough behavioral assessment of its particular maintaining conditions.

Another potential benefit of diagnosis is that it provides a common language for clinicians to communicate about disorders and for different researchers to be assured that they are studying the same *basic* clinical phenomena.

The behavioral alternative to diagnosis is a detailed description of a client's unique problem and the antecedents and consequences that are maintaining it. On one hand, the end product of a thorough behavioral assessment is much lengthier and makes comparisons between clients (such as for research) much more difficult. On the other hand, behavioral assessment provides the necessary information for designing individualized treatment that is most likely to be effective.

Present Focus

The focus of behavioral assessment, like behavior therapy, is on relevant information about the client's current functioning and life conditions. Isolating the causes of problem behaviors involves assessing the current maintaining conditions. Details about the client's past, especially early childhood, are considered relatively unimportant.

Directly Samples Relevant Behaviors

Behavioral assessment procedures examine *samples* of a client's behaviors to provide information about how the client typically functions in particular situations. To predict a teenage girl's typical ability to remain focused on schoolwork, the therapist might give the girl several different classroom assignments and observe her on-task behaviors (such as writing answers) and her off-task behaviors (such as looking around the room). This is a direct approach, in which *behaviors* are used to predict other *behaviors*. In contrast, nonbehavioral, traditional assessment is *indirect*. Behaviors are used as *signs* (of traits or psychological states), rather than samples, of something other than behavior. Consider the example of a person's frequently watching football games. In behavioral assessment, this is likely to indicate that the person enjoys football. In traditional assessment, the same observation might be interpreted as an indication of the individual's underlying aggressiveness.

Narrow Focus

Behavioral assessment deals with discrete behaviors and specific circumstances rather than a client's total personality or lifestyle as traditional assessment does. This tactic is consistent with the fact that behavior therapy focuses on target behaviors. It also makes behavioral assessment more efficient.

Integrated with Therapy

Behavioral assessment is an integral and continuous part of therapy. Assessment of the client's problem and its maintaining conditions are initial steps in behavior therapy, and assessment continues throughout therapy to evaluate changes in the client's target behavior. In fact, often it is difficult to distinguish between behavior therapy and assessment.[12] For example, in the treatment of obesity, maintaining records of all the food clients eat is important. Besides providing the therapist with valuable information, keeping food records makes clients aware of the food they consume and of their eating habits. Such awareness is an important component in the treatment of obesity.

Behavioral Interviews

An interview usually is the first assessment method used in behavior therapy.[13] Initial interviews have four major goals: (1) establishing rapport with the client, (2) understanding the client's problem and selecting a target behavior, (3) gathering data about maintaining conditions,[14] and (4) educating the client about the behavioral approach to treatment and issues of confidentiality. Establishing rapport and informing clients about the behavioral approach are not assessment procedures themselves, but they are essential parts of an initial interview.

Building *rapport,* the first goal, involves developing a relationship of mutual trust.[15] Listening attentively and nonjudgmentally and letting clients know that they are understood are among the ways the therapist builds rapport with the client.

The second goal is for the therapist to begin to understand the client's problem thoroughly. Clients often describe their problems in vague, trait terms. They may say that they are "shy" or "hot-headed." The therapist questions the client to elicit the specific details of the client's unique problem. It is not enough to know that the client "has trouble in relationships with men," for example. Does "trouble" mean that she cannot approach men or that she feels uneasy in their company? Is the client referring to casual or intimate "relationships"? Once the specifics of the problem are delineated, the client and therapist can select a target behavior.

The third goal of the initial interview is to begin assessing the maintaining conditions of the target behavior. The therapist asks about the antecedents and consequences of the behavior. Specifically, *when* and *where* (under what circumstances) does the client get anxious with men? What happens to the client and to the interaction with men, both immediately and afterward, when the client experiences anxiety?

The fourth goal is to provide clients with information so that they know what to expect from behavior therapy and can decide whether the behavioral approach is right for them. The therapist describes the behavioral model and how it views psychological problems, as well as the general nature of behavior therapy (which amounts to a very condensed version of the material you read in Chapters 3 and 4). The therapist also explains the ethical and legal rules of confidentiality that are followed in psychotherapy.

The standard questions in a behavioral interview (as well as those implicitly asked by other behavioral assessment methods) ask *what, when, where, how,* and *how often?* They provide information concerning the specific nature of the problem and its maintaining conditions. In contrast, traditional assessment emphasizes "why questions" to gather information about the causes of the client's problem. One problem with "why questions" is that clients often are not aware of what causes their behaviors (which is one reason they have come to therapy). Further, according to the behavioral model, the causes of a behavior are its maintaining conditions, which are assessed by the standard behavioral interview questions (what, when, where, how, and how often?).

The focus in the behavioral interview is on the present rather than the past. You can see these emphases in the examples of questions a therapist

Table 5-4 Examples of information typically gathered in initial behavioral interviews

1. What brings you here today?
2. When did the problem begin?
3. How often does the problem occur?
4. When (in what situations) does the problem occur?
5. What tends to occur before the problem (antecedents)?
6. What tends to occur after the problem, and how does the problem affect your life (consequences)?
7. What do you think about when the problem is occurring?
8. What do you feel when the problem is occurring?
9. What steps have you already taken to alleviate the problem, and with what results?

typically asks in an initial behavioral interview in Table 5-4. Besides the client, the therapist may interview significant people in the client's life (such as a parent or spouse) to provide additional and corroborating information.

◆

| **Participation Exercise 5-1** | BEHAVIORAL QUESTIONING: WHAT, WHEN, WHERE, HOW, AND HOW OFTEN?* |

Clients typically describe their problems in vague, general terms. Behavioral interviewing clarifies the nature of the problem so that goals for therapy can be established, target behaviors can be selected and defined, and probable maintaining conditions can be identified.

In this exercise, you will find brief problem descriptions as might be given by a client or a client's advocate (such as a daughter for an elderly parent) in the first therapy session. For each description, write five questions that you think would be helpful for a behavior therapist to ask the client or the client's advocate. Direct your questions at clarifying the problem, selecting target behaviors, and identifying probable maintaining conditions. Make sure the format of your questions is appropriate for a *behavioral* interview (refer to the title of the Participation Exercise for a reminder). When you have finished, compare your questions with the examples in your Student Resource Materials to get an idea of the *type* of questions that would be appropriate.

1. The father of a 9-year-old girl reports, "My daughter's self-concept is so poor and she has so little confidence that she fails at most things she tries."
2. A 37-year-old business executive says, "There has been so much pressure on me lately. Between work and family responsibilities, I feel like I'm just going to explode."
3. The mother of a 5-year-old boy reports, "My son can be an absolute monster. He has no respect for authority and always has to have things his own way or else he acts up."
4. Two college juniors, boyfriend and girlfriend, report, "We are either best friends or at each others' throats. We seem to have a Jekyll and Hyde relationship."
5. A 22-year-old woman says, "I have this habit of avoiding responsibility, and it makes me feel like a coward. I lost two jobs in the past 6 months because of my stupid attitude."

◆

DIRECT SELF-REPORT INVENTORIES

Direct self-report inventories are questionnaires containing brief statements or questions that require a simple response from the client, such as answering "yes" or "no" or rating how true a statement is on a 5-point

*This Participation Exercise can be done before you continue reading or later.

scale. Behavioral self-report inventories are *direct* because they ask straightforward questions and because the answers are taken at face value. For instance, when a client responds "yes" or "often" to the item "I avoid going to parties," the answer provides a behavior therapist with information about a specific situation the client avoids. In contrast, the same answer might be used in traditional assessment to *indirectly infer* a trait of shyness.[16] This contrast illustrates how behavioral assessment is defined by the way in which assessment procedures are applied rather than by the methods themselves.

Many direct self-report inventories have been developed to assess an array of problem behaviors, including fear and anxiety;[17] depressive behaviors;[18] social skills, including assertive behaviors;[19] health-related disorders, such as premenstrual syndrome, Type A behavior, and eating disorders;[20] sexual dysfunctions;[21] and marital problems.[22] Direct self-report inventories have been developed for adults[23] and children.[24] Table 5-5 gives examples of items that might appear on direct self-report inventories for different problem behaviors. (*Item* is the term typically used for the statements or questions that clients respond to in a self-report inventory.)

Direct self-report inventories are highly efficient, which is the major reason behavior therapists use them frequently. Clients complete them on their own, and the inventories can be scored quickly. Because self-report inventories contain standard questions that pertain to people in general, they do not yield specific and detailed information about an individual client. Accordingly, when self-report inventories are employed to elucidate the problems the client is experiencing, they are most useful for initial screening, after which more individualized assessment, such as an interview, is required. Similarly, self-report inventories that focus on a particular problem, such as the Beck Depression Inventory,[25] often are used as general measures of changes over the course of therapy.

The validity of self-report inventories depends on clients' ability and willingness to provide honest and accurate answers. This may not occur

Table 5-5 Examples of items used in direct self-report inventories

Problem	Sample Item
Unassertive behavior	When the food you are served at a restaurant is not done to your satisfaction, you complain about it to the waiter or waitress. (*Agree* or *Disagree*)
Depression	I cry often. (*True* or *False*)
Anxiety/Fear	Enclosed spaces (Rate on scale from 1–5, with 1 being *no discomfort* and 5 being *extreme discomfort in the situation*.)
Obesity	I have one or more between-meal snacks each day. (*True* or *False*)
Sexual dysfunction	I become aroused by sexual fantasies. (*Agree* or *Disagree*)
Social skills	I often share my toys with other kids. (*Yes* or *No*)
Marital discord	My partner does not understand me. (*Usually, Sometimes,* or *Never*)

for various reasons, including the inclination to present oneself in a favorable light, the tendency to overestimate or underestimate one's own behaviors, and the frequent discrepancy between what people say and what they do.

◆

<table>
<tr><td>**Participation
Exercise 5-2**</td><td>ARE YOU IN THE HABIT OF GOOD STUDY HABITS? FIND OUT
WITH A DIRECT SELF-REPORT INVENTORY*</td></tr>
</table>

Rate how often you engage in each of the 15 study habits, using the following scale.

> 3 = Consistently
> 2 = Usually
> 1 = Occasionally
> 0 = Rarely or never

1. I review my class notes each evening.
2. I study in a setting free of distractions.
3. I read assigned material before class but do not study it until shortly before the exam on the material.
4. I look up the meaning of words I do not know while I am reading.
5. I get a good night's sleep before important exams.
6. I use background music to relax me while studying.
7. I start studying for exams at least 3 days before the exam.
8. Before reading course material, I survey (skim) the reading to get an idea of what it includes.
9. While reading course material, I underline or highlight as many important points as possible rather than make brief notes as I read.
10. I take practice tests (such as in a study guide) when they are available.
11. When I get back an exam, I make sure I know the correct answers to the questions that I got wrong.
12. If I do not understand something a teacher says in class, I write it in my notes and try to figure it out later.
13. I read the chapter summary before and after I read the chapter.
14. After completing a reading assignment, I write down the key ideas.
15. I read all my assignments at the same speed.

The major purpose of this Participation Exercise was to give you the experience of completing a direct self-report inventory. So, before checking "how you did," think about the experience. To what extent do you think the inventory adequately assessed your study skills? Were you completely honest in your responses? For instance, did you note any tendency to respond as you think you *should* study rather than how you *do* study? What advantages of self-report inventories emerged? What limitations did you become aware of?

If you'd like to score the inventory, first reverse the scoring of the items that describe poor study habits. For items 3, 6, 9, 12, and 15, change *3* to *0*,

*This Participation Exercise can be done before you continue reading or later.

change *2* to *1*, change *1* to *2*, and change *0* to *3*. Now add the scores for all 15 items. The higher the sum (the closer to 45), the better are your study habits. You may find it helpful to consider changing the study habits that you assigned a *0* or a *1* (after reversing scores). Also, if you are unsure about why a particular study habit is good or poor, consult with a teacher, your learning assistance center, or a book on study skills.

◆

SELF-RECORDING

Self-recording (or **self-monitoring**) involves clients' observing and recording their own behaviors. Self-recording capitalizes on the fact that clients almost always are available to observe and record their behaviors. Compared with observations made by others, self-recording is time efficient, especially for infrequent behaviors (such as panic attacks) that would necessitate constant observation by an outsider.[26] Self-recordings can be made of both overt and covert behaviors, which can include such subjective states as fear and pain.[27] Clients' privacy is protected with self-recording, which is not the case when others make the observations.

In the simplest form of self-recording, clients record the number of times they perform a target behavior. This can be done, for example, by making tally marks on a small card or by using an inexpensive golf or knitting counter (see Photos 5-1a, b, and c).[28] Clients can record their observations in diaries or on simple forms, such as the one in Figure 5-1.[29] More elaborate recording devices also have been developed,[30] such as a cigarette pack that indicates the number of cigarettes removed.[31]

Three potential problems are associated with self-recording: (1) clients' making inaccurate recordings, (2) self-recording interfering with ongoing behaviors, and (3) behaviors' changing due to their being recorded.

First, the usefulness of self-recording depends on the client's ability and willingness to make careful and candid recordings. The accuracy and honesty of self-recording can be increased by simplifying recording

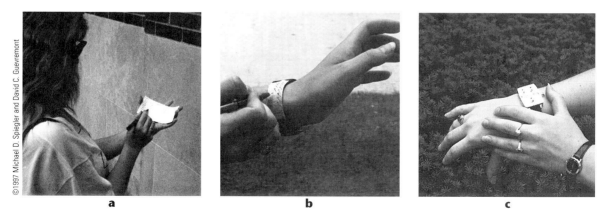

©1997 Michael D. Spiegler and David C. Guevremont

a　　　　　　　　　　b　　　　　　　　　　c

Photo 5-1a, b, and c Examples of simple, inexpensive self-recording devices

Figure 5-1 Sample form used to record binge eating, including relevant environmental circumstances, thoughts, and feelings

Date	Time	Place	Activity	Thoughts	Feelings
9/6	2:45 PM	home	watching TV	I'm wasting time. I'm lazy.	depressed helpless lonely
9/8	10:00 AM	work	on break	I'm going to have to stay late again to finish my work.	upset mad frustrated
9/13	7:30 PM	home	getting ready for a date	Will I look good enough? Will I say stupid things? What's going to happen at the end of the evening?	nervous anxious

procedures, recording as soon after the observation as possible, and having independent observers make occasional spot checks.

A second potential problem is that self-recording tends to interrupt ongoing activities. Clients usually must stop whatever they are doing, at least briefly, to record. If the target behavior occurs frequently, numerous interruptions will occur. Not surprisingly, clients may find self-recording irritating, which can result in their failing to record.

The third potential problem with self-recording is that the behavior may change *because* it is being recorded.

Reactivity

When clients are aware that their behaviors are being assessed, they may behave atypically. This phenomenon, known as **reactivity,** results in an inaccurate picture of the client's typical behaviors.[32] For example, when children self-monitor their remaining at an assigned task in the classroom, their on-task behaviors increase substantially.[33] Likewise, when clients monitor their self-destructive hair-pulling, the habitual behavior decreases dramatically.[34] Reactivity can occur whenever clients are aware that they are being assessed, which means it is a potential problem with any direct observational assessment procedure, but not with retrospective observational procedures, such as checklists and rating scales, which are discussed in the next section.

Reactivity may occur with self-recording for at least two reasons.[35] First, the client may find it annoying and bothersome to record each instance of a deceleration target behavior. The result is that self-recording serves as an aversive consequence for performing the deceleration target behavior, which reduces its occurrence. Second, self-recording an acceleration target behavior may serve as positive feedback, which reinforces the behaviors.

Self-recording does not always result in reactivity, and some measures tend to be more reactive than others. For instance, self-recording caloric intake may result in weight loss for some clients, but self-recording of eating habits is not likely to be associated with weight loss.[36] Thus, the major protection against reactivity during self-recording is to employ measures that tend to be less reactive.

So far, we have been talking about reactivity as a problem. On one hand, reactivity is a problem when accurate information about the current status of a client's target behavior is required, such as to establish a baseline level. On the other hand, if the client's self-recording changes the target behavior in the desired direction, why not harness reactivity in the service of therapy? In fact, self-recording occasionally is used as a therapy procedure.[37] However, the changes produced through self-recording tend to be relatively small and short-lived.[38] Accordingly, self-recording as a therapy procedure generally is employed as one component of a treatment package rather than as the only treatment.[39]

Participation Exercise 5-3 provides an experience analogous to clients' self-recording target behaviors. Because this Participation Exercise must be done over a number of days, you will not be able to do it now. However, read through it now (and carry it out in the coming week) because some of the procedures involved in self-recording are discussed in the instructions.

◆

Participation Exercise 5-3

SELF-RECORDING YOUR BEHAVIOR

Before you begin self-recording, there are three preparatory steps.

1. First, choose a behavior to self-record. Table 5-6 contains examples of behaviors that will work. If you choose a behavior not listed, be sure that it (a) is relatively easy to observe, (b) can be quickly recorded without disrupting the behavior, and (c) occurs at a moderate rate. If you perform the behavior very often (for example, blinking), it will be difficult to record; if you rarely engage in the behavior (for example, buying a new car or getting married), you will have nothing to record.
2. Decide on an appropriate unit of behavior (such as pages read, miles jogged, or minutes on the phone) and a unit of time (for example, an hour or a day) for the behavior.
3. Finally, devise a recording device. The simplest procedure is to divide a 3-by-5-inch index card into intervals and make a check mark each time you perform the behavior, as shown in Figure 5-2. At the end of your

Table 5-6 Examples of units of behavior and time appropriate for various behaviors
SOURCE: Based on Liebert & Spiegler (1994).

Behavior	Unit of Behavior	Unit of Time
Reading	Pages	Day or hour
Writing	Lines	Day or hour
Jogging	Quarter-miles	Day
Swimming	Laps in a pool	Day
Being late	Times late	Day
Daydreaming	Minutes spent	Day or hour
Talking on the telephone	Minutes spent	Day or hour
Swearing	Curse words	Day or hour
Studying	Minutes spent	Day
Drinking		Day or hour
Coffee	Cups	
Beer	Ounces	
Smoking	Cigarettes	Day or hour

designated time period, total the number of check marks (for example, 56 "four-letter words" per day). Also include on your record brief notes about the events in your life while you are recording; they will help you understand variations in your rates of performing the behavior.

You are now ready to observe and record your behavior. Be sure you carry your index card with you whenever you might be engaging in the behavior. Make your observations over the course of a week so that you can observe the behavior under various conditions.

When you have finished your observations, plot them on a graph on which the horizontal axis represents units of time and the vertical axis represents units

Figure 5-2 Example of an index card record of pages read in a week

		Total Per Day
Mon.	︴︴ ︴︴ ︴︴ ︴︴ ︴︴ ︴	26
Tues.	︴︴ ︴︴ ︴︴ ︴︴ ︴︴ ︴︴︴	28
Wed.	︴︴ ︴︴ ︴︴ ︴︴ ︴︴ ︴︴︴	28
Thurs.	︴︴ ︴︴ ︴︴ ︴︴ ︴︴ ︴︴ ︴︴ ︴︴ ︴︴ ︴︴ ︴︴ ︴	56
Fri.	︴︴ ︴︴ ︴︴ ︴︴ ︴︴ ︴︴ ︴︴ ︴︴ ︴︴ ︴︴ ︴︴ ︴︴	57
Sat.	︴︴ ︴︴ ︴︴ ︴︴ ︴︴ ︴︴	30
Sun.		0
Sat. night big date		
Sunday slept till 1:30 PM		

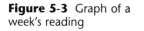

Figure 5-3 Graph of a week's reading

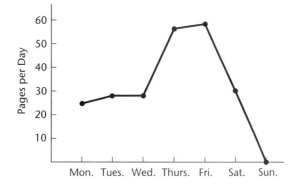

of behavior (see Figure 5-3). The graph, along with your notes of what was happening during the recording, will succinctly tell you something about your behavior. For example, the graph in Figure 5-3 shows that the person read approximately the same number of pages (between 26 and 28) for the first 3 days. On Thursday the number of pages nearly doubled, and it remained the same on Friday. On Saturday the number of pages dropped to approximately the same rate as for Monday through Wednesday, perhaps because of the interference of a Saturday evening social engagement. And on the seventh day no pages were read—perhaps because the person rested. The daily notes can provide clues regarding the factors that might account for the daily variations in reading rate (see Figure 5-3).

Your experiences in doing this Participation Exercise may have been similar to those of clients who are asked to self-record target behaviors. For example, you may have found it inconvenient to record the behavior, especially when you were engaged in other activities. Accordingly, you may have put off recording until later, which may have led to inaccurate recording or forgetting to record altogether. You may have found your behavior changing as a result of self-recording (reactivity). In addition, you may have learned something about your target behavior, such as how often it actually occurs and the circumstances in which you engage in the behavior more frequently and less frequently.

♦

BEHAVIORAL CHECKLISTS AND RATING SCALES

Checklists and rating scales are similar in format to self-report inventories, but they are completed by someone other than the client, such as a parent, teacher, or spouse. Checklists and rating scales list potential problem behaviors. With a **checklist,** the informant checks off those behaviors that are problematic for the client. With a **rating scale,** the informant evaluates each behavior by indicating how frequently it occurs or how severe it is. Thus, rating scales provide more information than checklists.[40] Checklists and rating scales are completed retrospectively; that is, they are based on the informant's recollections of the client's behaviors.

For example, after school hours a teacher might complete a checklist of a student's behaviors that day.

Although checklists and rating scales typically are used to assess target behaviors, they also can be used to identify maintaining conditions. For example, using the Children's Headache Assessment Scale, parents rate environmental antecedents associated with their child's headaches.[41]

Many checklists and rating scales have been developed for both adults and children.[42] Some are broad, measuring problem behaviors in general; others are narrow, assessing specific problem areas. For example, the Child Behavior Checklist includes 113 common problem areas associated with childhood.[43] In contrast, the Children's Attention Profile is a rating scale designed specifically to assess inattention and hyperactivity in children within a classroom setting (see Figure 5-4).[44]

Many of the same advantages and limitations that were described for self-report inventories also apply to checklists and rating scales. They are

Figure 5-4 The Children's Attention Profile
SOURCE: Adapted from © 1986 Craig Edelbrock

CAP Rating Scale

Child's Name:	FOR OFFICE USE ONLY
Today's Date:	
Filled Out By:	

Below is a list of items that describes pupils. For each item that describes the pupil *now* or *within the past week*, check whether the item is Not True, Somewhat or Sometimes True, or Very or Often True. Please check all items as well as you can, even if some do not seem to apply to this pupil.

	Not True	Somewhat or Sometimes True	Very or Often True
1. Fails to finish things he/she starts	☐	☐	☐
2. Can't concentrate, can't pay attention for long	☐	☐	☐
3. Can't sit still, restless, or hyperactive	☐	☐	☐
4. Fidgets	☐	☐	☐
5. Daydreams or gets lost in his/her thoughts	☐	☐	☐
6. Impulsive or acts without thinking	☐	☐	☐
7. Difficulty following directions	☐	☐	☐
8. Talks out of turn	☐	☐	☐
9. Messy work	☐	☐	☐
10. Inattentive, easily distracted	☐	☐	☐
11. Talks too much	☐	☐	☐
12. Fails to carry out assigned tasks	☐	☐	☐

Please feel free to write any comments about the pupil's work or behavior in the last week.

efficient; most can be completed in 15 minutes or less. Generally they are used for initial screening purposes and as global measures of change. Sometimes they are used to select target behaviors.[45]

The utility of checklists and rating scales depends on informants' accurately observing the client's behaviors and making reliable ratings.[46] *Reliability,* in general, refers to the consistency or dependability of observations. The specific type of reliability germane to checklists and rating scales is **interrater reliability,** which is the degree to which two or more raters agree. It is measured by comparing the responses of the raters and calculating the percentage of agreement.

Participation Exercise 5-4 gives you a chance to use a behavioral checklist—and probably have fun in the process.

◆

Participation Exercise 5-4

CHECKING OUT A PROFESSOR*

The checklist in this Participation Exercise, like most behavioral checklists, will take only a few minutes to complete. Table 5-7 contains a list of 40 behaviors in which professors might engage. Choose one of your current or past professors whose class you have been in for at least a month. Using Work Sheet 5-1,† place a check mark next to each of the behaviors that the professor has performed on *at least one occasion.* Complete the checklist anytime you are not in the professor's class, which is analogous to how checklists are used in behavioral assessment.

Table 5-7 Behaviors in which professors might engage

Paces	Coughs	Drinks coffee in class
Fumbles with notes	Makes eye contact	Ridicules students
Arrives late	Speaks softly	Listens attentively to students
Speaks in monotone	Keeps class late	
Talks with hands	Picks nose	Gives hard exams
Smiles	Rubs eyes	Tells personal stories
Taps pen on desk	Strokes beard	Falls asleep
Pauses for long time	Tells jokes	Cracks knuckles
Plays with hair	Stutters	Uses blackboard
Talks rapidly	Loses train of thought	Talks to students before class
Hums	Argues with students	
Dismisses class early	Reads notes	Talks to students after class
Checks watch	Fiddles with clothing	Cancels class
Sits on desk	Repeats self	Takes attendance

*You should complete the checklist before you continue reading, but you will need to check your interrater reliability later.
†You will find this work sheet in your Student Resource Materials.

To ascertain how reliable your responses to the checklist are, you will need the help of another student who has been in the professor's class. Ask this student to fill out the checklist using the duplicate copy of Work Sheet 5-1.* Then compare your two checklists to obtain your interrater reliability. To assess the number of agreements, count the number of times you agree on whether the professor exhibits a behavior (both of you checked a behavior) or the professor does not exhibit a behavior (neither of you have checked a behavior). Divide the number of agreements by 40, and multiply by 100 to get the *percentage of agreement.*

Doing this Participation Exercise should give you some insight into the checklist method. Obviously, it can be done quickly. Did you have any problems completing the checklist? Were you clear about what each behavior referred to so that you could easily say whether you've noticed the professor engaging in each behavior? How reliable were your observations? Any ambiguity in what was meant by the behaviors on the checklist would lower interrater reliability. What other factors might account for your having less than 100% agreement?

◆

Systematic Naturalistic Observation

Systematic naturalistic observation consists of someone observing and recording specific, predetermined overt behaviors as the client naturally engages in them.[47]† Precise definitions of the behaviors, including criteria for differentiating each target behavior from similar behaviors, are essential. Table 5-8 contains sample definitions of three different behaviors along with examples of behaviors that are consistent and inconsistent with the definition.

The type of measure used—such as frequency, time, or strength—depends on the nature of the target behavior and the purpose of the assessment.[48] When observations are made *continuously* over a relatively brief time, such as an hour or two, considerable observer time is required. A more efficient procedure is *time sampling,* in which observations are restricted to specific time intervals, such as the first 5 minutes of each hour.[49] Devices used to make recordings range from simple to complex, including paper and pencil; clocks and counters; electromechanical devices, such as event recorders and keyboards; and audio and video recordings.

Training observers, often nonprofessionals such as parents and teachers, is essential.[50] Observers first study the definitions of the behaviors and familiarize themselves with the recording system. They then practice making observations until their observations are highly accurate, which

---

*You will find this duplicate work sheet in your Student Resource Materials.
†Naturalistic observation need not be systematic, as it is in behavior therapy. Rather than looking for discrete behaviors, as in systematic naturalistic observation, the observer can record all behaviors that a person performs, similar to the qualitative, narrative description typical of many case studies. Obviously, systematic and open-ended naturalistic observations yield very different data.

is determined by **interobserver reliability** (the equivalent of inter-rater reliability). The minimum level of acceptable agreement among observers usually is between 80% and 90%.[51]

Systematic naturalistic observation has three potential problems: (1) reactivity, (2) observer error or bias, and (3) impracticality.

Reactivity when being observed by others is a common phenomenon. Sometimes our performance is enhanced by others watching us, as when

Table 5-8 Examples of definitions used for behavioral observations

---

PHYSICALLY AGGRESSIVE BEHAVIORS

Definition: The client physically strikes another person with any part of his or her body or with an object, with potential for inflicting pain on the other person.

Examples: Hitting, slapping, punching, tripping, tackling, pushing, biting, kicking, throwing an object at another person, hitting another person with a stick.

Nonexamples: Spitting, making faces, calling another person names, making verbal threats or threatening gestures at another person.

VERBALLY EXPRESSING ADMIRATION

Definition: The client verbally praises, compliments, expresses a liking or admiration for another person, or expresses a sense of awe about another person's behavior or accomplishment.

Examples: "You did a nice job," "I really like you," "You look very handsome," "How did you get that done so quickly?" "I enjoy talking with you very much," "Your fast ball is incredible."

Nonexamples: "Would you like to have dinner with me?" "How about a kiss?" "What do you know, he finally got a good grade" (a backhanded compliment), hugging, kissing, embracing, or any other physical show of affection without concomitant verbal affection.

INITIATING SOCIAL CONTACT

Definition: (1) The client initiates social contact by verbally greeting or *starting* an interaction with another person, (2) uses a neutral or pleasant tone of voice when talking to the person, (3) directly looks at the person when initiating contact, and (4) is within 15 feet of the other person at the time the social contact is begun.

Examples: Introducing oneself to another person, asking another person a question (for example, "Can you please tell me where the exit is?"), calling another person by name, or starting a conversation with another person through a comment (for instance, "The team played well today").

Nonexamples: Yelling at or otherwise using an unpleasant tone of voice, talking to another person *only* after that person initiated the contact, talking to someone without looking at the person, or initiating social contact from a distance of greater than 15 feet.

THE FAR SIDE® By GARY LARSON

© 1984 FarWorks, Inc. All Rights Reserved/Dist. by Creators Syndicate

"Anthropologists! Anthropologists!"

children in a race run faster because their parents are watching. In other instances, we may perform less well because we are being watched, such as when we are trying to type fast and someone is looking over our shoulder.

The fundamental principle employed to reduce reactivity during naturalistic observation is to minimize clients' awareness that they are being observed. This involves making *unobtrusive observations,* such as when the observer is out of sight or a hidden camera records the behavior.

When unobtrusive observations are not possible, reactivity may be minimized by an **adaptation period** in which clients get accustomed to the observation procedures before the actual observations begin.[52] In this way, they may ignore or forget about the fact that their behavior is being observed. For example, if a child were being observed in a classroom, the observer might simulate recording observations (for example, by taking notes on a clipboard) in the room for short periods over the course of a few days before starting the actual observations. It is likely that the children would adapt to the observer's presence, much as we tend to stop noticing a new piece of furniture after it has been there for a while.

Photo 5-2 Systematic naturalistic observation of a 4-year-old child interacting with her peers in a preschool playground. Following an adaptation period, the children have become accustomed to the observer's presence.

©1997 Michael D. Spiegler and David C. Guevremont

Most observational errors occur because the behaviors being observed are defined ambiguously. Even when the behaviors are clearly defined, observers' personal biases may make the observations invalid. Observers' expectations about how the target behaviors are likely to change as a result of therapy are a major source of bias.[53] Failure to take into account the cultural context of behaviors is another source of bias. Consider the following interaction observed in an African-American family.[54]

> ADOLESCENT: I thought you were my friend.
> PARENT: I am no pal to you.

European-American observers recorded this interaction as "harsh discipline." However, African-American observers, who were more familiar with the cultural context, recorded it as "constructive discipline." Cultural issues must be considered when using standard observational codes because codes developed for one population may not apply to other populations.[55]

Assessment through systematic naturalistic observations often is impractical.[56] Considerable observer time is required, such as for training, travel to the client's natural environment, and the actual observations. If the client performs the target behavior infrequently, an observer may spend an inordinate amount of time waiting for it to occur. Further, naturalistic observation may not be possible because it invades a client's privacy, as would be the case in a client's home or professional office. When these practical or ethical limitations make systematic naturalistic observation impractical, simulated observation is an alternative.

SIMULATED OBSERVATION

In **simulated observation,** conditions are designed to resemble the natural environment in which the client's problem is occurring.[57] This often is done in a room that allows observers to see and hear the client through a one-way mirror and intercom. Having the observers out of sight generally minimizes reactivity. Simulated observation is more efficient, in terms of the observers' time, than systematic naturalistic observation.[58]

Using simulated observations, behavior therapists can test hypotheses concerning external maintaining conditions by systematically varying them and observing changes in the client's target behavior.[59] For example, suppose the therapist suspects that a couple communicates least effectively when they talk about financial matters. To test this hypothesis, the therapist can observe the couple interacting while they attempt to solve problems concerning money and a variety of other topics.[60]

A **behavioral avoidance test** is a simulated observation procedure used to assess fear. The therapist asks a client to engage in a series of steps that involve progressively more fear-inducing behaviors. The number of steps the client can complete is used as a measure of fear. For example, to assess how fearful a client is of snakes, the therapist might ask the client to (1) approach a snake that was in a glass cage 20 feet away, (2) put on a pair of gloves and touch the snake, (3) then hold the snake for a moment, (4) next take off the gloves and touch the snake, (5) then hold the snake for a moment, and finally (6) pick up the snake, walk to a chair, and sit down with the snake in his or her lap.

Therapists often use simulated observation procedures that have been previously developed and validated for particular problems. An example is the Restricted Academic Situations Test, which assesses children's ability to pay attention while working independently on written assignments in the classroom.[61] The child is seated at a desk in the observation room and told to complete a written assignment while remaining seated at the desk. From

Photo 5-3 Observing a child's aggressive behaviors from behind a one-way mirror

Cary Wolinsky/Stock, Boston

behind a one-way mirror, the therapist records the child's behaviors in 30-second intervals for 20 minutes (see Figure 5-5). The specific behaviors recorded are leaving the seat, playing with objects around the desk, fidgeting in the seat, talking out loud, and looking away from the written work. The observer simply places a check mark in the appropriate behavior category anytime the behavior occurs during the 30-second interval. The proportion of time the child engages in each behavior provides data

Figure 5-5 Sample recording sheet used for the Restricted Academic Situations Test

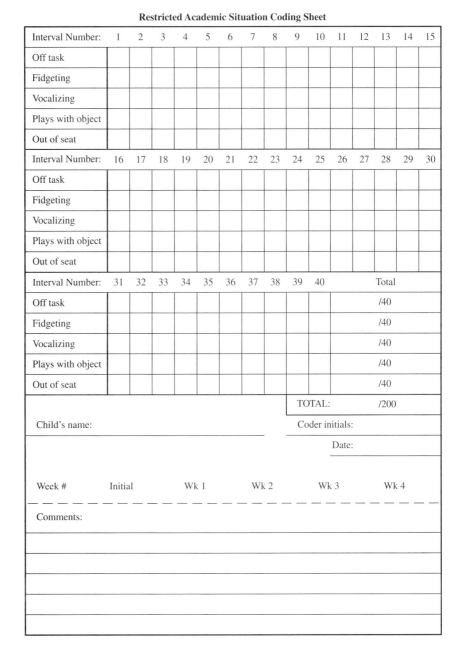

Restricted Academic Situation Coding Sheet

Interval Number:	1	2	3	4	5	6	7	8	9	10	11	12	13	14	15
Off task															
Fidgeting															
Vocalizing															
Plays with object															
Out of seat															

Interval Number:	16	17	18	19	20	21	22	23	24	25	26	27	28	29	30
Off task															
Fidgeting															
Vocalizing															
Plays with object															
Out of seat															

Interval Number:	31	32	33	34	35	36	37	38	39	40		Total
Off task												/40
Fidgeting												/40
Vocalizing												/40
Plays with object												/40
Out of seat												/40

TOTAL: /200

Child's name: _____   Coder initials: _____

Date: _____

Week #   Initial   Wk 1   Wk 2   Wk 3   Wk 4

Comments:

that can be used to pinpoint target behaviors and assess progress during and after therapy.

The primary limitation of simulated observation is the ability to generalize from observations made under a simulated condition to the client's natural environment. The more closely the simulation approximates the natural conditions, the greater will be the generalizability.[62]

ROLE-PLAYING

In **role-playing,** clients enact problem situations to provide the therapist with samples of how they typically behave in those situations. Role-playing is especially useful in assessing social skills, such as assertive behaviors.[63]

Role-playing is an efficient form of simulated observation. No special physical arrangements are needed because the relevant environmental conditions are imagined—clients act as *if* they were in the problem situation. With interpersonal problems, the therapist plays the roles of other people. For example, a client who reported difficulty in giving her secretary work was asked to make work-related requests of the therapist, who played the role of the secretary.

Generalizability is a potential limitation of role-playing. The more clients are able to behave *as if* they were in the actual situations, the more likely the behaviors observed will be valid indications of how they typically act. Many clients initially feel uneasy or awkward engaging in role-playing. With practice, however, most clients can "get into" role-playing. The therapist also must be able to play roles realistically, which requires *specific* knowledge of how other people interact with the client. This includes avoiding stereotypic concepts of role relationships, such as how fathers "typically" deal with sons. Reactivity is a potential problem in role-playing, such as when clients act more appropriately during role-playing than they typically do in actual situations.

PHYSIOLOGICAL MEASUREMENTS

When physiological components of a target behavior are relevant to treatment, physiological responses are measured. The most frequent measures are heart rate, blood pressure, respiration rate, muscle tension, and skin electrical conductivity.[64] These responses are used to assess complex behaviors, such as feeling anxious[65] and being sexually aroused.[66] Physiological responses can be the sole target behavior, as when lowering a client's blood pressure is the aim of relaxation training for hypertension (see Chapter 14).

Physiological measurements most often are carried out in specially equipped research laboratories. The high cost of the instrumentation required to obtain accurate physiological measures precludes general application in most clinics or private offices. Ideally, physiological recordings should be made in clients' natural environments as their problems occur. Portable measurement devices, which increasingly are becoming available, can be used for this purpose. However, portable devices tend to be less reliable than stationary laboratory apparatus. In the future, technological advances may make in vivo physiological recording more feasible.[67]

Physiological measurements are no more or less valid than other assessment methods, although people sometimes give them more credence either because they seem to be "pure" measures or because technology is involved. Physiological measurements are relevant for assessing some behaviors and not for others.

Pulse rate is a simple measure of anxiety that clients can assess easily in their natural environments. If you'd like to see how your heart rate changes in various situations, do Participation Exercise 5-5 over the course of the next few days.

Participation Exercise 5-5

GETTING TO THE HEART OF THE MATTER: MEASURING YOUR PULSE

To experience how clients use their heart rates to assess anxiety in actual life situations, compare your heart rate at rest with your heart rate in anxiety-evoking situations. Because people's normal heart rates can differ widely, *changes* in heart rate from the individual's resting base rate are used, rather than the absolute rate.

Part I: Taking Your Pulse

You can measure your pulse easily from your radial artery or carotid artery. Your radial artery is located on the thumb side of your wrist. To locate it, turn one of your palms upward. Place the index and middle fingers of your other hand (not your thumb, which has a pulse of its own) over the artery, as shown in Photo 5-4. You should not be wearing a watch or bracelet on the wrist from which you are taking your pulse.

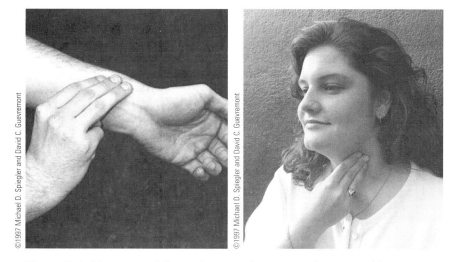

©1997 Michael D. Spiegler and David C. Guevremont

Photo 5-4 Placement of fingers for taking the radial pulse

Photo 5-5 Placement of fingers for taking the carotid pulse

The carotid artery runs up the side of your neck. Gently place the index and middle fingers of your right hand along the left side of your esophagus, as shown in Photo 5-5 (see page 101). Don't exert too much pressure on the carotid artery because that can decrease your heart rate.

Try taking both your radial and carotid pulses and decide which gives you the stronger pulse. Using a watch or clock that displays seconds, count for 15 seconds and multiply by 4 to obtain your *heartbeats per minute.*

Part II: Assessing Your Resting Heart Rate

To measure your resting heart rate, lie down or sit in a very comfortable chair (such as a recliner) for about 5 minutes. Listen to some relaxing music; imagine calm, pleasant scenes; think calming thoughts; or otherwise relax. When you feel very relaxed, count your pulse for 15 seconds; then continue to relax for another minute. Again, count your pulse for 15 seconds. Add these two counts, and multiply by 2 to get your resting heart rate.

On an index card, copy the information in the sample index card in Figure 5-6. In the space shown, record your resting pulse.

Part III: Assessing Your Heart Rate In Vivo

To provide you with an analogue of how clients assess their heart rate as a measure of anxiety, you will take your pulse in various situations in which you typically feel anxious (for example, right before an exam is handed out, as you are about to meet a date for the first time, and waiting to be called on in class). Over the next few days, carry the index card with you. When you find yourself in a situation in which you feel some anxiety, take your pulse for 15 seconds and multiply by 4; write your pulse rate in the second column ("Rate per minute"). Then, assign a number from 1 to 5 that best indicates the level of anxiety you feel according to the following scale.

1	2	3	4	5
calm				anxious

On the index card, write that scale score in the fourth column ("Anxiety rating") and then, in the first column ("Situation"), write a brief description of the situation you are in. Finally, subtract your resting pulse from your "Rate

Figure 5-6 Index card for recording pulse rate

Resting pulse _____			
Situation	Rate per minute	Change	Anxiety rating
1.			
2.			
3.			
4.			
5.			
6.			
7.			
8.			

per minute" (second column), and write the difference in the third column ("Change"). If your pulse rate in the anxiety-evoking situation is higher than your resting rate, you will have an increase, or a positive number; if your pulse rate in the anxiety-evoking situation is lower than your resting rate, you will have a decrease, or a negative number.

Sample at least five different situations in which you typically experience anxiety.

Part IV: Evaluation

When you have completed your assessment, examine the data on your index card. Most likely, you will find that your pulse rates for the in vivo situations are higher (positive changes in the "Change" column) than your resting pulse rate; however, some people's heart rates decrease when they are anxious, which is another reason why change from resting pulse is the critical measure. In either case, by comparing the last two columns you may see a relationship between your heart rate changes and your anxiety ratings.

◆

We have examined each of the eight major methods of behavioral assessment individually. Now we will illustrate the multimethod/multi-modal nature of behavioral assessment in the case of a woman who was treated for excessive anger and violent behaviors.

Case 5-1

BEHAVIORAL ASSESSMENT IN A CASE OF DOMESTIC VIOLENCE

Tina T. was a 36-year-old college graduate who worked as a computer sales representative. She had a 5-year history of violence toward her husband and 10-year-old daughter. Tina contacted a behavior therapist when her husband threatened to move to another city with their daughter if she did not seek help.

In the initial interview, Tina admitted that she had a serious problem, which she described as "uncontrollable fits of anger." The therapist asked Tina a series of questions to elucidate the nature of her problem and its maintaining conditions. The questions included the following:

1. When you have an "uncontrollable fit of anger," what do you do? How do you feel? What are you thinking? What bodily reactions do you experience?

2. What seems to precipitate your "anger fits"? Are they associated with something your husband or daughter says or does? Are there any situations that make you more prone to have a "fit"? Where do your "fits" usually occur? Who is there at the time? At what time of day and on which days of the week? What feelings and thoughts do you have right before an "anger fit"?

3. What happens after your "anger fits"? How do your husband and daughter react to your "fits"? What do they do and say? How long do

their reactions last? What do you do after your "fits"? How do you feel? What thoughts run through your mind?

4. What strategies have you used to deal with your problem and how successful have they been?

In the initial interview, Tina told the therapist that her "anger fits" initially involved yelling and cursing, then throwing objects at her daughter and husband, and finally beating them with her fists and household objects. She became angry whenever she was frustrated about a situation she believed she could not handle (such as unreasonable demands from others). Her "fits" most often occurred shortly after returning home from work. A "fit," which rarely lasted more than 5 minutes, would gradually subside and become less violent as she "vented her anger." At that point, she would start to cry and beg for her family's forgiveness, which usually was forthcoming.

Other assessment procedures were instituted to confirm the accuracy of the information Tina gave in the interview and to provide additional data.

1. Tina filled out the Novaco Anger Inventory, a questionnaire that assesses anger reactions in a wide array of situations.[68] The inventory contains descriptions of 80 situations, and clients rate the degree of anger they would expect to feel if the situation actually occurred.

2. Tina started an *anger diary* in which she (1) described each instance when she became angry, (2) rated the intensity of her anger (using a scale ranging from "no anger" to "rage"), (3) noted how she reacted (including overt and covert behaviors), and (4) described the consequences of her reactions.[69] The anger diary provided the therapist with information about the situations that elicited Tina's anger, the ways in which she typically responded, and the consequences of her anger. It also helped Tina become more aware of her anger and her reactions to it. Tina used the anger diary throughout her treatment as an ongoing measure of her progress.

3. The therapist visited Tina's house on three consecutive Tuesdays, shortly after she arrived home from work, to directly observe her behaviors. Besides assessing Tina's aggressive acts toward her daughter and husband (for example, yelling and hitting), the therapist recorded positive behaviors (such as praising and physical affection). Using a modified Patterson Coding System[70] that listed 18 different aggressive and positive behaviors, the therapist recorded each of these behaviors he observed Tina perform over the course of 30 minutes.

4. In the third therapy session, Tina and her therapist role-played several troublesome situations revealed in her anger diary and Anger Inventory. The therapist played the role of either husband or daughter and observed Tina's reactions to provocations. Tina's heart rate and blood pressure were monitored during the role-playing and compared with baseline recordings taken when Tina was calm and not at all angry.

On the basis of the information gathered from these assessment procedures, the therapist and Tina designed a treatment plan for two related behaviors: positive interactions with family members and adaptive reactions to frustration. Among the findings of the behavioral assessment, the home observations revealed that Tina rarely had positive interactions with her husband and daughter. Thus, one component of Tina's therapy involved teaching Tina specific ways to engage positively with her family. In both the home observations and role-playing, the therapist observed that Tina reacted to provocation impulsively. Accordingly, another component of Tina's treatment was self-instructional training, in which she learned strategies to help her pause and think before reacting. From the interview, anger diary, and home observations, it became clear that a critical maintaining consequence of her anger and aggression was the sympathetic responses from her family to the remorse Tina expressed after one of her "fits." Consequently, part of the therapy involved training family members to withhold their sympathy when Tina indicated that she was sorry about an "anger fit."

Tina's anger diary provided a continuous measure of her progress over the course of the 5½ months of her therapy. The diary revealed steady improvement. Two home observations in the last weeks of therapy indicated that Tina now handled frustration and other potential provocations with restraint and often with prosocial responses. At the end of therapy, Tina again filled out the Anger Inventory; both the number of different situations that evoked anger and the intensity of the anger she experienced had decreased significantly. Additionally, role-playing with concurrent physiological recording during the last therapy session showed that Tina became less aroused in potentially provocative situations and that she responded in more socially appropriate ways than she had at the beginning of therapy. Two long-term follow-up telephone interviews with Tina, 6 and 12 months after treatment indicated that her anger and violence were no longer problematic for her or for her family.

Case 5-1 highlights essentials of behavioral assessment. Assessment procedures supplied information to clarify the problem, set initial goals, design target behaviors, identify maintaining conditions, and then design a treatment plan and monitor the client's progress. The assessment proceeded in a stepwise fashion, by cumulatively gathering and substantiating data. Employing a multimethod/multimodal approach provided a comprehensive assessment. Finally, behavior therapy and assessment were closely linked.

◆ ALL THINGS CONSIDERED: BEHAVIORAL ASSESSMENT

If we liken behavior therapy to a pilot, behavioral assessment is the navigator. Behavioral assessment determines the direction in which therapy will proceed, provides the necessary course corrections along the way, and indicates when the destination has been reached.

Multimethod/multimodal assessment are essential ingredients of behavioral assessment. Assessing more than one mode of a problem behavior can result in more effective treatment. For example, anxiety may involve a client's thoughts, feelings, and actions. To assess only one of these modes might result in incomplete treatment. Different modes of a problem behavior may be optimally assessed by different methods because assessment methods vary in their ability to tap each mode of behavior[71] (as you saw in Table 5-2, pages 77–78). In addition, information gathered by one assessment method may be verified by other methods.

In this chapter, we have sketched a picture of behavioral assessment at the beginning of the new millennium. Behavioral assessment has evolved over the past 40 years, and its basic nature continues to change. For example, historically behavioral assessment (and therapy) focused on overt behaviors. Behavior therapists considered systematic naturalistic observation the optimal method of assessment and viewed self-report measures as less valid.

Today, systematic naturalistic observation is no longer considered the sine qua non of behavioral assessment.[72] However, systematic naturalistic observation remains a highly desirable method for many target behaviors,[73] and it is frequently used in research.[74] Self-report methods, such as direct self-report inventories and self-recording, have become more popular both for their efficiency and their ability to directly tap cognitive and emotional modes of behavior, which is not possible with systematic naturalistic observation.[75]

Although assessment has always been recognized as important in behavior therapy, developments in behavioral assessment have escalated in recent years. Literally hundreds of behavioral assessment procedures and instruments have been developed, with the aim of providing behavior therapists with more reliable, valid, and practical methods. Still, the developments in behavioral assessment are not of the same magnitude as developments in behavioral treatment procedures. Given current trends in the field, we predict that behavioral assessment in the future will continue to be refined, will address the need for specialized techniques for clients from diverse cultures (see Chapter 16),[76] and increasingly will be integrated with traditional methods of assessment (consistent with the trend toward integration of behavior therapy discussed in Chapter 16).[77]

SUMMARY

1. Behavioral assessment is an indispensable part of behavior therapy. Behavioral assessment gathers information to clarify the problem, set initial goals, design target behaviors, identify maintaining conditions, and then design a treatment plan and monitor the client's progress.

2. Behavioral assessment is multimethod (using more than one method of assessment) and multimodal (assessing more than one mode of behavior).

3. Behavioral assessment procedures share five characteristics: is individualized, focuses on the present, directly samples relevant behaviors, has a narrow focus, and is integrated with therapy.

4. For the most part, diagnosis of disorders is antithetical to funda-mental premises of behavioral assessment and behavior therapy. The behavioral alternative involves detailed descriptions of client's unique problems and their specific maintaining conditions.

5. An interview is usually the first assessment method used. The four goals of initial behavioral interviews are to establish rapport with the client, to gather information about the client's problem, to obtain data about its maintaining conditions, and to educate the client about the behavioral approach. The interview focuses on the present and asks questions concerning what, when, where, and how often rather than why.

6. Direct self-report inventories are questionnaires containing brief statements or questions about behaviors and maintaining condi-tions that require a simple response or rating. They are highly effi-cient and are most often used for initial screening. Their validity depends on clients' responding honestly and accurately.

7. Self-recording involves clients' observing and keeping records of their own behaviors. It is time efficient and can be used to assess both covert and overt behaviors. Clients must be motivated to self-record and must make accurate recordings. Reactivity—a change in clients' behaviors because the clients know their behaviors are being observed—is a potential problem with most observational assessment procedures.

8. Behavioral checklists and rating scales contain lists of potential problem behaviors, about which someone who knows the client well responds. With checklists, the informant indicates all the behaviors the client performs. With rating scales, the informant uses a scale of frequency or severity to evaluate the client on each behavior. Checklists and rating scales are efficient.

9. Systematic naturalistic observations are made in the situations in which the target behavior normally occurs. These observations are most accurate when the target behaviors are defined clearly and observers are well trained. The reliability of the observations is assessed by comparing the observations of two or more independ-ent observers. Three potential problems with systematic naturalis-tic observations are reactivity, observer error and bias, and imprac-ticality.

10. Simulated observations are made under conditions set up to resemble the client's natural environment. A one-way observation mirror often is used. A potential limitation is the ability to gener-alize what is observed in the simulation to the client's natural environment.

11. In role-playing, a form of simulated observation, clients enact problem situations to provide the therapist with samples of how they typically behave. Generalization to the natural environment can be limited because clients may behave differently from the way they typically do.

12. Physiological measurements assess physiological responses associ-ated with the target behavior. They usually take place in specially

equipped laboratories, but increasingly portable recording devices are being used.

13. Each behavioral assessment method has its strengths and limitations. Multimethod/multimodal assessment helps overcome the limitations of single methods and provides more complete information about clients' problems.

14. Initially, behavioral assessment focused on overt behaviors and systematic naturalistic observations. Today, direct self-report inventories and self-recording that can tap cognitive and emotional modes of behavior frequently are employed.

REFERENCE NOTES

1. Guevremont & Spiegler, 1990; compare with Swan & MacDonald, 1978.
2. King, Ollendick, Murphy, & Tibge, 1997; Schwartz, Houlihan, Krueger, & Simon, 1997.
3. Eifert & Wilson, 1991; Kazdin, 1992; Peterson & Bell-Dolan, 1995.
4. Compare with Jorgensen & Carey, 1994; Lazarus, 1989a.
5. For example, Wilfley, Schwartz, Spurrell, & Fairburn, 1997.
6. Goldfried & Sprafkin, 1974.
7. American Psychiatric Association, 1994.
8. American Psychiatric Association, 2000.
9. Tryon, 1999.
10. Compare with Kutchins & Kirk, 1995.
11. For example, Rosenhan, 1973.
12. Goldfried & Sprafkin, 1974.
13. Morganstern, 1976.
14. For example, Storey, Lawry, Ashworth, Danko, & Strain, 1994.
15. Marquis, 1972; Peterson, 1968; Rimm & Masters, 1979.
16. Liebert & Spiegler, 1994.
17. Beidel, Turner, & Morris, 1995; Glass & Arnkoff, 1994; Nietzel, Bernstein, & Russell, 1988.
18. Beck & Steer, 1993; Rehm, 1988.
19. Becker & Heimberg, 1988.
20. Williamson, Davis, & Prather, 1988.
21. McConaghy, 1988.
22. Margolin, Michelli, & Jacobson, 1988.
23. For example, Peters, 2000; Sedlar & Hansen, 2001.
24. For example, Burham & Gullone, 1997; Reitman, Hummel, Franz, & Gross, 1998.
25. Beck & Steer, 1993.
26. Aiken, 1996.
27. For example, Gil, Porter, Ready, Workman, Sedway, & Anthony, 2000; Peterson & Tremblay, 1999.
28. Lindsley, 1968.
29. For example, Gil, Porter, Ready, Workman, Sedway, & Anthony, 2000; Tarrier, Sommerfield, Reynolds, & Pilgrim, 1999.
30. Schwitzgebel & Schwitzgebel, 1973.
31. Azrin & Powell, 1968.
32. For example, Johnson & Bolstad, 1973; Kirby, Fowler, & Bear, 1991.
33. Reid, 1996.
34. Rothbaum, 1992.
35. Kazdin, 1974e.
36. Green, 1978.
37. For example, Clees, 1994–1995; Critchfield & Vargas, 1991; Maletzky, 1974; Spiegler, 1983, pp. 294–295.
38. Thoresen & Mahoney, 1974.
39. For example, Azrin & Peterson, 1990; Kazdin, 1994.
40. Aiken, 1996.
41. Budd, Workman, Lemsky, & Quick, 1994.
42. Gross & Wixted, 1988; Morrison, 1988.
43. Achenbach, 1978.
44. For example, Guevremont, DuPaul, & Barkley, 1990.
45. Gross & Wixted, 1988.
46. Glaser, Kronsnoble, & Worner Forkner, 1997; Smith, Pelham, Gnagy, Molina, & Evans, 2000.
47. For example, Cook, Peterson, & DiLillo, 1999; Heiman, 1995; Hummel & Gross, 2001; Messer & Gross, 1995.
48. Foster, Bell-Dolan, & Burge, 1988.

49. For example, Davis & Chittum, 1994.
50. For example, Barton & Ascione, 1984; Hartmann & Wood, 1982.
51. Hartmann, 1982.
52. Haynes, 1978.
53. Kent & Foster, 1977; Rosenthal, 1969.
54. Cauce, 1995.
55. Markman, Leber, Cordova, & St. Peters, 1995.
56. Wade, Baker, & Hartmann, 1979.
57. Jones & Friman, 1999.
58. Foster, Bell-Dolan, & Burge, 1988.
59. For example, Guevremont & Dumas, 1996.
60. For example, Burman, Margolin, & John, 1993.
61. Guevremont, DuPaul, & Barkley, 1990.
62. Bellack, Hersen, & Turner, 1979; Foster & Cone, 1980; Reisinger & Ora, 1977.
63. For example, Blumberg, Hovell, Werner, Kelley, Sipan, Burkham, & Hoffstetter, 1997; Eisler, Hersen, Miller, & Blanchard, 1975; McFall & Marston, 1970; Prince, 1975.
64. Sturgis & Gramling, 1988.
65. Nietzel, Bernstein, & Russell, 1988.
66. Gordon & Carey, 1995; McConaghy, 1988.
67. For example, Holden & Barlow, 1986.
68. Novaco, 1975.
69. Bornstein, Hamilton, & Bornstein, 1986; Nomellini & Katz, 1983; Novaco, 1975.
70. Patterson, Ray, Shaw, & Cobb, 1969.
71. Tryon & Pinto, 1994.
72. Guevremont & Spiegler, 1990; Jacobson, 1985.
73. Cone, 1998; Foster & Cone, 1986.
74. Cone, 1993.
75. Jensen & Hayes, 1986; Kendall, 1987b.
76. Ollendick & Greene, 1998.
77. Barrios, 1988; Bellack & Hersen, 1988; Kendall, 1987a.

PART II

BEHAVIOR THERAPY

Now that we've whetted your appetite, you are ready for the elaborate main course: behavior therapy with all the trimmings. We'll begin by presenting relatively simple therapy procedures and proceed to more complex ones. The presentation is cumulative, so to fully appreciate the therapies described later, you need to digest previously discussed therapies.

Chapter 6 deals with stimulus control and reinforcement procedures that increase clients' adaptive behaviors. Chapter 7 covers deceleration behavior therapies that decrease clients' maladaptive behaviors. The token economy, contingency contract, and behavioral child management training—the topics of Chapter 8—are treatment packages based on the procedures and principles presented in Chapters 6 and 7. Exposure therapies, covered in Chapters 9 and 10, treat anxiety and other exaggerated negative emotions by safely exposing clients to threatening situations. Modeling therapy and skills training are the topics of Chapter 11. Finally, Chapters 12 and 13 discuss cognitive-behavioral therapies, which change clients' cognitions that maintain their psychological disorders.

Now that you've seen the menu, we invite you to really bite into behavior therapy.

Stimulus Control and Reinforcement Therapy

To treat clients' problems, behavior therapies modify maintaining antecedents, maintaining consequences, or both. In this chapter, we first explore therapy procedures that elicit or initiate target behaviors through antecedent control and then turn to therapy procedures that change the reinforcing consequences of target behaviors.

STIMULUS CONTROL: ANTECEDENTS THAT ELICIT BEHAVIORS

Antecedents, the *A* in the ABC model (discussed in Chapter 3), "set the stage" for behaviors to occur. In some cases, a client may not be performing a desirable behavior because no antecedents exist to elicit it. For such acceleration target behaviors, stimulus control procedures introduce antecedents to elicit the desirable behavior. In other cases, existing antecedents elicit an undesirable behavior. For such deceleration target behaviors, stimulus control procedures change the antecedents. These interventions involve either prompts or setting events, the two broad categories of stimulus control.

Prompting

Driving down the road, you see a sign for the street you're looking for and you slow down. Your friend, sitting next to you, tells you to turn left on the street. You slow down and turn left because you have been prompted to do so. In fact, many times each day your behavior is initiated by cues indicating that it is appropriate to perform a particular behavior.

Prompting provides people with cues, or prompts, that remind or instruct them to perform a behavior. Every day we rely on prompts to guide our behaviors, such as when we stop at a red light or check our appointment book. There are four types of prompts: verbal, environmental, physical, and behavioral. Each type of prompt may be used alone or in combination with others.[1]

Verbal prompts involve telling clients what they are expected to do. In an unusual application of prompting, children were taught to prompt

HAGAR reprinted with special permission of King Features Syndicate, Inc.

their teacher to praise their good behaviors.[2] As an example, children would approach the teacher with a completed assignment and say, "I finished all my math problems," to remind the teacher to praise them. Behavior therapists often use verbal prompts together with modeling and reinforcement. Verbal prompts can also be employed on their own in such diverse applications as increasing people's use of seat belts while driving[3] and increasing the taking of free condoms at a treatment clinic for substance abuse.[4]

Environmental prompts are cues in the environment, such as signs, that remind clients to perform behaviors. Some examples are alarms to remind older adults to take their medications,[5] written cue cards to prompt adults with mild handicaps to perform home maintenance tasks,[6] pictorial signs to remind children with autistic disorder to perform daily living skills (such as getting dressed),[7] and written prompts for people with diabetes to remind them to self-monitor their blood glucose levels.[8]

Physical prompts (also called *physical guidance*) involve someone's physically directing a client in performing a behavior. An example is teaching a child to write by holding the child's hand and helping the child make the required movements. Physical prompts are used extensively to teach self-care skills to individuals with developmental disabilities, such as training children who are both deaf and blind in self-feeding skills.[9]

Behavioral prompts involve one behavior cuing another. For example, a husband in marital therapy learned to use his wife's crying as a signal to respond with sympathy rather than annoyance. An individual's own behavior can serve as a prompt to engage in another behavior. For instance, parents may learn to use their feeling angry at their child as a cue to leave the room to "cool off."

© 1997 Michael D. Spiegler and David C. Guevremont

Photo 6-1 How many different types of environmental prompts can you identify in this picture?

Guidelines for administering prompts include the following: (1) administer a prompt just before it is appropriate to perform the target behavior, (2) make the prompt salient so that the client is aware of it, (3) make a prompt specific and unambiguous, (4) have the prompt remind clients about the consequences of engaging in the desired behavior (such as a sign reading, "Taking Your Medication Will Make You Feel Better"), and (5) follow up prompts with positive reinforcement for engaging in the prompted behavior.[10]

Prompting usually is a temporary measure. As the client performs the behavior more frequently (because it is reinforced), prompts become less necessary and are gradually withdrawn—a process called **fading.** Prompting (in conjunction with modeling and shaping) is a standard procedure for eliciting behaviors that a client performs rarely. Teaching language and social interaction skills to children with autistic disorder is a prime example.[11] To teach the names of objects, for instance, the therapist points to the object and says, "What is this? *Pencil.*" (The therapist's saying the word *pencil* is a verbal prompt.) As the child begins to imitate the prompt, the therapist fades the prompt by saying it at successively lower volumes. Eventually the therapist whispers the prompt, then merely mouths it, and finally asks the child, "What is this?" without any prompt.

Setting Events

Setting events are broad and sometimes complex conditions in the immediate environment that influence the likelihood that certain behaviors will be performed. When a setting event is identified as a maintaining antecedent of a problematic target behavior, it is modified to create the desired change in the behavior. Consider the case of a boy with autistic disorder who behaved aggressively toward his baby sibling. A detailed behavioral assessment showed that one of the setting events for the boy's aggressive behaviors was the noise the sibling made when eating off of a metal plate. The sibling's metal plate was replaced with a plastic one that made little noise. This simple, yet potent intervention reduced the client's aggressive behaviors.[12]

Like prompts, setting events usually are part of a treatment package aimed at changing more than one maintaining condition of a target behavior.[13] However, when a target behavior is maintained primarily by a setting event, simply changing the setting event may be sufficient, as in the previous example. In another case, modifying setting events was the sole treatment for two boys with attention deficit hyperactivity disorder (ADHD) who interacted inappropriately during play.[14] The boys' inappropriate social interactions (such as calling each other names and refusing to share toys) occurred in a playroom containing 12 different toys and where there were no rules or adult supervision. A dramatic decline in negative behaviors and an increase in positive social interactions occurred when the therapist rearranged the playroom so that there were only two toys, specific rules for behaving, and an adult supervisor.

Therapists often change setting events to increase on-task behaviors and to reduce or prevent problem behaviors of children in classrooms.[15]

Examples include rearranging seating (for example, placing a disruptive student close to the teacher), removing distractions (such as lowering window shades so children cannot look outside),[16] and modifying work (for instance, reducing the number of problems on a work sheet to make the assignment more manageable).

Although modifying setting events generally is employed with children, this approach also is used to treat adults with various problem behaviors. Examples include facilitating weight loss,[17] reducing pathological gambling,[18] promoting cholesterol-lowering diets,[19] and treating trichotillomania (compulsive pulling out of one's hair).[20] Changing setting events is used extensively in the treatment of insomnia in adults, as you will see in Chapter 15.[21]

Stimulus Control in Perspective

Stimulus control procedures typically are part of a treatment package, although sometimes they serve as the sole intervention. In the former case, the role stimulus control plays often is not assessed (in other words, the treatment package is shown to be effective without looking at the specific contributions of the treatment components). Accordingly, there is less direct empirical support for stimulus control procedures than for many other behavior therapies. When stimulus control is the primary intervention, such as in treating insomnia by modifying setting events, the effectiveness of the techniques has been empirically validated.

Compared with other behavior therapy interventions that accelerate adaptive behaviors, stimulus control procedures can be very efficient because they can be easily implemented with little time and effort required. Instructing a client to do something and posting a sign that reminds the client to perform a particular behavior are examples of efficient prompts. Making simple changes in environmental conditions, such as removing alcohol from the house of a person who has a drinking problem, also can be implemented relatively efficiently.

Another advantage of stimulus control interventions is that they can prevent maladaptive behaviors. When the setting events that promote an undesirable behavior have been identified, these conditions can be systematically modified to prevent the behavior. For example, if a client trying to quit smoking is tempted to smoke when at a sports bar that allows cigarette smoking, the client could patronize only establishments that prohibit smoking.

Similarly, in **planned activity scheduling** behavior change agents arrange for clients to engage in *active* desirable behaviors in situations likely to elicit problem behaviors, which reduces opportunities for misbehavior.[22] For example, on a long-distance driving trip, in anticipation of sulking and sibling conflicts, parents can introduce a variety of activities for their children, such as having them play favorite games. Planned activity scheduling generally is employed with children, but therapists have effectively used it in treating adults with head injuries and adults with schizophrenia.[23]

In the case of serious maladaptive behaviors that are maintained by both antecedents and consequences, it may sometimes be possible to intervene primarily through stimulus control. For instance, if a teenage boy often gets into fights after playing violent video games, his access to videos could be limited to nonviolent games only. The advantage of treating the behavior by modifying antecedents rather than consequences is that effective consequential intervention may involve the use of aversive consequences. In general, behavior therapists avoid using aversive procedures whenever possible because of humanitarian and practical problems that you will read about in Chapter 7.

The purpose of stimulus control procedures is to get clients to perform a target behavior. Ultimately, however, for the behavior to continue, it must be reinforced.

REINFORCEMENT: CONSEQUENCES THAT ACCELERATE BEHAVIORS

Teachers motivate students to learn by awarding high grades for good test performance. Parents get children to do chores by letting them watch TV if they complete their chores. Employers ensure continued work output by paying employees. These are common examples of the use of reinforcement in everyday life. People have always reinforced other people's behaviors (and their own) to get others (and themselves) to act in particular ways. Clearly, behavior therapists did not invent the concept of reinforcement. What behavior therapists have done, however, is uncover the basic principles of reinforcement and systematically apply them to change behaviors effectively and reliably.

What Is Reinforcement?

To reinforce is to strengthen. The term *reinforcement* refers to strengthening a behavior so that the person will continue to perform it. Formally, **reinforcement** occurs when the consequences of a behavior increase the likelihood that the person will repeat the behavior. This is an *empirical definition* because it is based on the *observation* that the behavior recurs.

The reinforcing consequence is a **reinforcer.** The person receives the reinforcer only if he or she engages in the behavior. Another way of saying this is, "The reinforcer is *contingent* on the behavior being performed." Reinforcers usually are pleasant or desirable. However, whether a consequence is a reinforcer depends on its effects on the behavior, not on its subjective properties for the person. In other words, reinforcers are defined by their accelerating effects on the behaviors they follow.

Reinforcers differ from rewards. *Rewards* are pleasant consequences of a behavior that do not necessarily make it more likely that the person will perform the behavior again.[24] Receiving your driver's license is an example. You are rewarded for passing the driving test, but obviously the reward does not increase the taking of driving tests!

Behavior therapists do not assume that a consequence will serve as a reinforcer. A *potential* reinforcer is identified and then made contingent on the client's engaging in the target behavior. If the behavior increases, then the therapist knows the consequence was a reinforcer.

Besides increasing the likelihood that the behavior will recur, reinforcers provide positive feedback.[25] Reinforcers indicate that people are engaging in an appropriate behavior and are performing it properly. When you receive an *A* for a poem in a writing class, the grade tells you that you have written a good poem and may increase the chances of your continuing to write poetry.

Positive and Negative Reinforcement

Reinforcement always *increases* the frequency of a behavior. This accelerating effect can come about in two ways. One way is when an event—usually a pleasant one—is *presented* (added) as a consequence of a person's performing a behavior. This is known as **positive reinforcement,** and the consequence is a **positive reinforcer.** For instance, you hold the door open for your friend who is behind you, and your friend says, "Thank you." If hearing "thank you" makes you more likely to hold the door for your friend (or other people) in the future, then "thank you" is a positive reinforcer and positive reinforcement has occurred.

The other way that a behavior is accelerated occurs when an event—usually an unpleasant one—is *removed* or *avoided* (subtracted) as a consequence of a person's performing a behavior. This is **negative reinforcement,** and the consequence is a **negative reinforcer.** Many everyday behaviors are maintained by negative reinforcement. For example, taking aspirin is reinforced by relief from pain, napping is reinforced by decreasing fatigue, turning in a paper on time is reinforced by avoiding a loss of points, and driving at the speed limit is reinforced by avoiding a ticket. In each instance, we avoid or escape from something undesirable. Such was the case with a 19-year-old man with autistic disorder who had been stealing and ingesting pills whenever and wherever he could find them.[26] In searching for the maintaining conditions of this dangerous behavior, the therapist learned that when the man ingested pills, he immediately was taken away from his job—a job he disliked. Apparently, leaving work was negatively reinforcing his potentially life-threatening behavior.

Although negative reinforcement plays an important role in maintaining people's behaviors, therapists use it only occasionally.[27] Accordingly, this chapter deals almost exclusively with positive reinforcement.

Many people, including professionals, mistakenly use the term *negative reinforcement* to refer to procedures that decelerate a behavior and erroneously equate negative reinforcement with *punishment* (see Chapter 7).[28] Remember: *Reinforcement,* positive or negative, always refers to the *acceleration* or strengthening of a behavior. It may help to think of the terms *positive* and *negative* as mathematical signs that merely indicate whether the consequence is *added* (positive) or *subtracted* (negative) to increase the frequency of the behavior.[29]

Before reading any further, take 2 minutes to list specific things that you believe can serve as reinforcers for your behaviors—in other words, things that would get you to perform various behaviors. Save this list to use later in Participation Exercise 6-2.

Categories of Positive Reinforcers

Positive reinforcers can be grouped into four major categories: tangible reinforcers, social reinforcers, token reinforcers, and reinforcing activities. Some reinforcers fit into more than one category.

TANGIBLE REINFORCERS

Many of your own reinforcers that you just listed were probably **tangible reinforcers,** which are material objects. Food, clothes, electronic gadgets, jewelry, CDs, books, cars, and recreational equipment are examples of tangible items that are reinforcers for many adults.[30] Although it is common to associate reinforcers exclusively with tangible reinforcers, they are only one type of reinforcer.

SOCIAL REINFORCERS

Social reinforcers consist of attention, praise, approval, and acknowledgment from other people.[31] These reinforcers are administered verbally (for example, "Great job!"), in writing (for instance, a thank you note), physically (as with a pat on the back), and through gestures (such as smiling).[32] Attention, a potent social reinforcer, can result in rapid and dramatic changes in clients' behaviors, as illustrated in Figure 6-1; the graph shows the number of items of clothing a 6-year-old girl left lying on her bedroom floor before and after her mother began giving her attention for putting clothes away.[33]

Social reinforcers have four advantages. First, they are easy to administer. All that is needed is another person. Second, social reinforcers don't cost anything; people have a limitless supply of social reinforcers to give to others. Third, social reinforcers generally can be administered immediately after the person has performed the target behavior, which increases the effectiveness of a reinforcer. Fourth, social reinforcers are **natural reinforcers**—that is, consequences that people receive as a regular part of their daily lives. Using social reinforcers during therapy increases the chances that the target behavior will be maintained after therapy has ended because the reinforcers will continue to be available.[34]

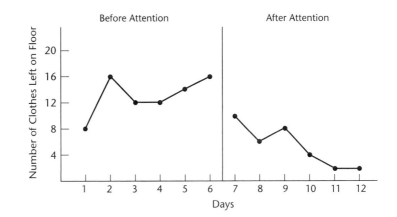

Figure 6-1 Number of items of clothes a 6-year-old girl left on her bedroom floor before and after her mother gave her attention for putting clothes away

SOURCE: Hall & Hall, 1998b.

Social reinforcers are among the most powerful consequences for initiating and maintaining behaviors. People of all ages, including very young children, actively seek attention, affection, and praise from others for engaging in desirable behaviors.[35] Think about how your own daily behaviors (such as the way you dress) are influenced by other people's approval and attention. Social reinforcement was the major component used in Case 6-1 to treat a patient whose legs were paralyzed due to psychological rather than physical causes, a problem called *conversion disorder.*

Case 6-1   TREATMENT OF A CONVERSION DISORDER BY SOCIAL REINFORCEMENT[36]

On admission to a psychiatric hospital, a 42-year-old married man was bent forward at the waist, unable to straighten his body or move his legs. For 15 years, he had complained of lower back pain, despite two orthopedic surgeries. Every 4 to 6 weeks, he had 10- to 14-day episodes of being totally unable to walk, which he referred to as "drawing over." The patient had been hospitalized numerous times and treated with heat and muscle relaxants.

Orthopedic and neurological evaluations revealed no abnormalities. Behavioral assessment, however, indicated that the patient received considerable reinforcement for his physical complaints, such as being served breakfast in bed and not having to do household chores.

Treatment began in the hospital, where it was administered by an attractive young female assistant. The assistant asked the patient to leave his wheelchair and to stand and walk as far as possible, and she praised his efforts (for example, "You're standing very well today" and "I'm very proud of you").

In Phase 1, only standing was reinforced. As Figure 6-2 shows, this resulted in minimal walking. When both standing and walking were reinforced in Phase 2, walking increased. To check whether social reinforcement specifically for walking was responsible for the increase, a 5-day reversal period, in which only standing was reinforced, was instituted in Phase 3. The patient did not increase his walking distance, except on day 11. When reinforcement for both standing and walking was reinstated in Phase 4A, walking further increased. The social reinforcement for both standing and walking led to additional increases when a walker was substituted for the wheelchair (Phase 4B) and then when the walker was taken away (Phase 4C). By day 18, the patient was walking normally and was discharged from the hospital. Four weeks later, the patient had increased his walking to an average of 350 yards a day.

Immediately after the follow-up assessment (see Figure 6-2), the patient had a severe "drawing over" episode and was readmitted to the hospital, unable to walk. The therapist learned that the patient's family had reinforced his "sick-role" behaviors with social attention.

The patient began walking again when social reinforcers were reintroduced for standing (Phase 5 in Figure 6-2). His walking dramatically increased when the social reinforcers were administered for both standing and walking (Phase 6). During this last phase of therapy, the family

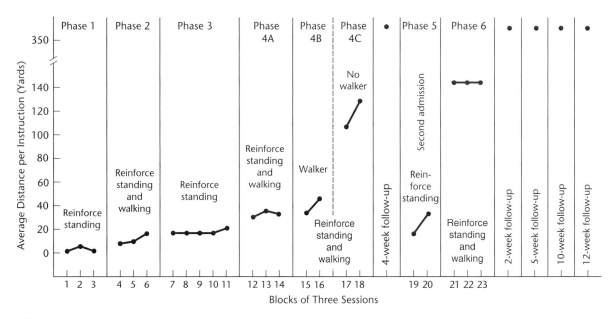

Figure 6-2 Average distance that the patient walked during all phases of treatment and follow-up
SOURCE: Kallman, Hersen, & O'Toole, 1975, p. 412.

members were videotaped while interacting with the patient. Analysis of the tape revealed that they generally ignored his "well-role" behaviors. Accordingly, the family was taught to socially reinforce the patient's attempts to stand and walk and to ignore his physical complaints. The social reinforcement procedures previously used by the assistant in the hospital were modeled for family members. After his second hospital discharge, the patient again increased his daily walking to an average of 350 yards. Follow-up assessments over the next 12 weeks indicated that he continued to walk normally.

Case 6-1 illustrates the potency of social reinforcement. Initially, the client's physical complaints seemed to be exacerbated by the attention he received from family members. Later, the attention and praise of a hospital assistant accelerated the client's walking. The case also points out that changes achieved in therapy do not automatically transfer to the client's natural environment. Usually, specific procedures must be implemented to ensure the transfer of treatment effects. This was accomplished in Case 6-1 by making sure that the reinforcement contingencies used in therapy continued in the client's home environment.

TOKEN REINFORCERS

A third category of positive reinforcers are **token reinforcers,** symbolic items that have value because of what they can be exchanged for or what they stand for. Money is a token reinforcer because people can exchange it for valued goods and services.[37] Other everyday examples of token reinforcers include good grades and merit salary increases.

Reinforcement is most effective when the reinforcer immediately follows the behavior. However, for many reinforcers it is impractical to provide the reinforcer immediately. For instance, Kavitha's parents want to use bike riding after school as a reinforcer for Kavitha's making her bed in the morning. When Kavitha makes her bed in the morning, her parents immediately place a sticker of a bicycle on the calendar for the current day, which indicates that she may ride her bike that afternoon. The sticker is a token reinforcer that serves the important function of bridging the time between the behavior and the substantive reinforcer.

Examples of token reinforcers used to increase adaptive behaviors of clients in behavior therapy include points and vouchers used to purchase retail items[38] and food and gas coupons to promote abstinence in clients with drug abuse problems,[39] stickers to increase school attendance in children with severe anxiety,[40] and fast food coupons (such as for free pizza) to promote cooperation among disruptive adolescents in an inner city school.[41] The most extensive use of token reinforcers is in token economies (see Chapter 8).

REINFORCING ACTIVITIES

Engaging in activities is the fourth category of positive reinforcers. Examples of activities that often serve as reinforcers for many people are shopping, watching TV, playing sports, listening to music, surfing the Internet, playing computer games, getting a massage, socializing with friends, talking on the telephone, sleeping late, going out to eat, dating, going on vacations, and spending time on hobbies.[42]

Reinforcing activities usually are pleasurable. However, activities in which a person frequently engages—but does not necessarily enjoy—can serve as reinforcers. This is the basis of the Premack principle.

Premack Principle

Kaj, like many of us, turns on the radio every time she starts her car. She does not fasten her seat belt, however. What do you think would happen if Kaj could turn on her car radio *only after* she had put on her seat belt? Most likely, Kaj would start wearing her seat belt.

More than 30 years ago, David Premack discovered that higher probability behaviors—whether they are considered enjoyable or not—can serve as reinforcers for lower probability behaviors. This has come to be called the **Premack principle.**[43]

The Premack principle lends itself to creative applications in behavior therapy.[44] Typically, *probability* is measured by *frequency of occurrence.**

*According to Premack's (1965) original formulation, frequency and probability are not equivalent (although they are correlated). Thus, the use of higher frequency behaviors to reinforce lower frequency behaviors is not strictly the Premack principle. However, the term *Premack principle* is generally used in behavior therapy to indicate using higher frequency behaviors as reinforcers, and we are following that convention.

Acceleration target behaviors often are low-probability behaviors—that is, they occur infrequently, which is why they need to be accelerated. Thus, high-probability behaviors can be used as reinforcers for many acceleration target behaviors.[45] Although the high-probability behaviors need not be pleasurable to serve as reinforcers, high-probability behaviors that are especially *aversive* to the individual generally do not function as reinforcers.[46] Additionally, the high-probability behaviors must not be occurring so often that they lose their effectiveness in motivating clients to engage in the low-probability target behavior. As the familiar adage tells us, too much of a good thing can be bad.[47]

Employing high-probability behaviors as reinforcers is especially useful with clients for whom other potential reinforcers are difficult to identify. A prime example is hospitalized patients with chronic psychiatric disorders for whom tangible and social consequences may be ineffective as reinforcers.[48] If we observe such patients' daily activities, we note such typical behaviors as standing, staring out the window, pacing, and sleeping in a chair. These simple, mundane activities (that might erroneously be labeled "doing nothing") are high-probability behaviors. Thus, they can serve as reinforcers according to the Premack principle, as Case 6-2 illustrates.

Case 6-2 ## INCREASING SOCIAL INTERACTION WITH THE PREMACK PRINCIPLE[49]

B. H. was a 44-year-old female patient in a psychiatric hospital who rarely interacted with other patients or staff members. She responded to questions by nodding or giving one-word answers. The staff reported that they had "never observed B. H. enjoying anything." She spent almost all her waking hours sitting in a specific chair in the day room. The ward staff decided to use this high-probability behavior to reinforce social interactions, which were decidedly low-probability behaviors for B. H.

The ward psychologist informed B. H. that she would be permitted to sit in her favorite chair only after she had interacted with another patient or staff member. Initially, 2 minutes of social interaction was required for 30 minutes of sitting. B. H. nodded that she understood, at which point the psychologist immediately reinforced their interchange by permitting her to sit in her chair for 30 minutes. The psychologist made the contingency explicit by telling B. H. that she had just earned sitting time by listening and communicating that she understood.

At the end of the first 30-minute period, a staff member approached B. H. and suggested that they have a cup of coffee together, reminding B. H. that she had to spend 2 minutes interacting with others in order to sit in her chair. B. H. reluctantly accepted the invitation. For the rest of the day, one of the ward staff approached B. H. after each 30-minute period of sitting and suggested some minimal social activity that would allow her to continue sitting.

On each successive day, 1 minute of social interaction was added to the criterion required for 30 minutes of sitting. As B. H. progressed, the staff gave her fewer and fewer suggestions about how she might socialize and made B. H. responsible for deciding how she wanted to spend time with others, drawing on the examples the staff had initially provided. By the 12th day, B. H. was getting up from her chair after 30 minutes without having to be prompted by a staff member.

Within 3 weeks, B. H. was spending more than the criterion time socializing and less than 30 minutes sitting in her chair. For example, she often played dominoes with a particular patient. Initially, she would get up in the middle of the game as soon as she had accumulated enough socializing time to sit in her chair. After a while, she would finish a game first, which took more than 30 minutes. Eventually, B. H. was spending the majority of each day in some social activity.

In using the Premack principle to accelerate B. H.'s social behaviors, the ward staff did not assume that she enjoyed sitting in her chair. All they knew was that sitting in the chair had a higher probability of occurring than social interaction. From the increases observed in B. H.'s social behaviors, it appeared that sitting in the chair was a reinforcer. The Premack principle will work for you as well, as you'll find out by doing Participation Exercise 6-1 over the course of the next couple of weeks.

Participation Exercise 6-1

DOING WHAT COMES UNNATURALLY: APPLYING THE PREMACK PRINCIPLE*

You can easily see how well the Premack principle works by using it to accelerate one of your own low-probability behaviors. Choose a behavior that *you "should" be doing at least once a day but that you rarely do.* For many people, examples would be washing dishes right after meals, flossing their teeth, making their bed, and exercising (although these may not be examples for you). Keep a record for a week of the number of times each day you perform the low-probability behavior you have chosen. This record will provide a baseline.

Next, make a list of your routine high-probability behaviors, those you perform at least once a day without fail. These might include such routine behaviors as taking a shower, shaving, putting on makeup, combing your hair, eating breakfast, and checking the mail (or whatever your routine behaviors are). You do not have to consider the routine behaviors enjoyable.

Select one of these high-probability behaviors as a reinforcer. It must generally occur *after* you engage in the low-probability behavior. For example, if your low-probability behavior were making your bed before leaving the house in the morning, then you could reinforce it with any high-probability behavior that you typically do after leaving the house in the morning, such as listening to the car radio or stopping for a cup of coffee.

After a week of recording a baseline, implement the Premack principle by following the rule: *Engage in the high-probability behavior only after you have*

*You will need to do this Participation Exercise later, but you should read it now.

performed the low-probability behavior. Continue to record the number of times you perform the low-probability behavior each day. You will likely observe an increase in the frequency of your low-probability behavior.

◆

Identifying Reinforcers

Reinforcers are most effective when they are individualized for each client. Behavior therapists do not assume that consequences that serve as reinforcers for one person will be reinforcers for all people. *Potential* reinforcers are first identified and then tested to see if they indeed accelerate the target behavior. Behavior therapists use a variety of methods to identify potential reinforcers, including directly questioning the client, selecting from generalized reinforcers, and observing the clients' routine behaviors.

QUESTIONING CLIENTS

Asking clients about potential reinforcers is the easiest and most frequently used procedure. The therapist might start with a general question, such as, "What things do you find enjoyable or rewarding?" Then, the questions would get more specific, asking about narrow categories of reinforcers (for example, "What do you like to do in the evenings?" "If you had some extra money, what would you buy with it?" or "Where would you like to go if you had a day off?").

Direct questioning has its limitations. For instance, it does not work for clients with severely limited intellectual and verbal abilities. Clients who are suffering from depression often cannot think of reinforcers because nothing seems pleasant or worthwhile to them. In such cases, the therapist can question people who know the client.

EXPOSING CLIENTS TO GENERALIZED REINFORCERS

Consequences that are reinforcing for many people are called **generalized reinforcers.**[50] Common examples include food, money, and social attention. Generalized reinforcers vary with clients' demographic characteristics, such as age, gender, and cultural background.[51] For example, food is a generalized reinforcer for most people. However, the specific food is likely to be different for young children and adults, as well as for Hispanic and Japanese individuals. Similarly, generalized reinforcers may vary with specialized clinical populations. For instance, the privilege of taking methadone at home rather than at a clinic is a generalized reinforcer for clients who are dependent on heroin.[52]

One method of identifying potential reinforcers is to expose clients to an array of generalized reinforcers and asking them to select those that they think will serve as reinforcers for them. For example, children can be taken to a toy store and asked to pick out toys they would like to have. Adults might make selections from a merchandise catalogue or the entertainment section of the Sunday newspaper. Special procedures have been developed for clients with very limited intellectual and verbal capacities.[53] For instance, clients with severe mental impairments spent time in a room containing 16 potential reinforcers, such as a fan, juice, and a swing.[54] Reinforcer preference was determined by the frequency with which clients approached each of the objects. Whether these preferred items were serving as reinforcers was tested empirically by seeing if they accelerated target behaviors.

Behavior therapists have developed standardized lists of generalized reinforcers to aid in finding potential reinforcers for clients. The Reinforcement Survey Schedule is a direct self-report inventory that lists common generalized reinforcers (such as watching television, shopping, and solving problems).[55] Clients rate the degree to which they enjoy each on a 5-point scale ranging from "not at all" to "very much." The Children's Reinforcement Survey Schedule contains generalized reinforcers for children (for example, playing games, eating sweets, going on family outings, and playing with friends).[56] An adult checks off valued generalized reinforcers for the child. With the Pleasant Events Schedule, the client rates an extensive list of behaviors on two dimensions: (1) the frequency of engaging in each behavior and (2) the amount of pleasure derived from engaging in each behavior.[57] Reinforcement menus such as the one shown in Figure 6-3 allow children to point to pictures of generalized reinforcers they prefer.[58]

OBSERVING CLIENTS' ROUTINE BEHAVIORS

A third method of identifying reinforcers is to observe clients in their natural environments and note the behaviors they engage in most frequently and spend the most time doing. These high-probability behaviors can serve as reinforcing activities following the Premack principle.

Figure 6-3 Part of a reinforcement menu
SOURCE: Adapted from Daley, 1969, p. 44.

◆

Participation Exercise 6-2

IDENTIFYING YOUR OWN POTENTIAL REINFORCERS*

Earlier, you made a list of your potential reinforcers. Now, you can compile a more complete list, using two of the methods you have just read about for identifying potential reinforcers.

Part I: Direct Questioning

As you answer the following questions, keep a running list of potential reinforcers that are elicited by the questions, eliminating duplicates. Some of the questions directly identify reinforcers, whereas others are designed to cue areas in your life in which you may find potential reinforcers.

1. What things do you like to use? Buy? Consume (for example, what kind of food)?
2. What would you like as a gift?
3. What items do you see in stores, ads, or catalogues that draw your attention?
4. What activities do you enjoy?
5. What do you like to do in your spare time?
6. What do you like to do most in your work?
7. What do you consider a fun night out? Night at home? Weekend? Vacation?
8. What accomplishments give you satisfaction?
9. What are you doing when you feel happy? Alive? Useful? Important?
10. What types of social interactions do you enjoy? Do you engage in?
11. What types of social events do you like? What types do you go to?
12. What do you like other people to do for you? Say to you?
13. With whom do you like to spend your time?
14. What do you like to happen when you finish doing something well?
15. What allows you to persevere at difficult and long tasks?

Part II: Identifying Pleasant Activities

Table 6-1 contains 50 activities that are potential reinforcers. Rate each item twice. First, answer the question, "How often have I engaged in the activity during the past 30 days?" For each item, use the following scale.

1 = *Not at all* in the past 30 days
2 = *A few times* (1–6) in the past 30 days
3 = *Often* (7 or more) in the past 30 days

Write the number in the Frequency column of Work Sheet 6-1.†

After rating the frequency of the 50 activities, read each item again and using the following scale, answer the question, "How pleasant, enjoyable, or rewarding was the activity during the past month?"

*You will need to do this Participation Exercise later, but you should read it now.
†You will find this work sheet in your Student Resource Materials.

Table 6-1 Common activities that are potential reinforcers
<small>SOURCE: Adapted from MacPhillamy & Lewinsohn, 1971.</small>

Attending a club meeting	Playing video games
Attending a concert	Playing sports
Being alone	Playing a musical instrument
Being with my parents	Playing with a pet
Complimenting or praising someone	Reading fiction
Cooking	Reading the newspaper
Dancing	Riding a bike
Dating	Saying prayers
Daydreaming	Sending and receiving emails
Doing art work	Shopping
Doing volunteer work	Sleeping late
Driving	Staying up late
Eating out	Straightening up (house or car)
Eating snacks	Surfing the Internet
Exercising	Taking a nap
Getting dressed up	Taking a shower
Getting or giving a massage or back rub	Taking a walk
Getting up early in the morning	Talking on the telephone
Going on vacation	Telling stories and jokes
Going to a mall	Watching a TV program
Going to a party	Watching a video
Going to the movies	Watching people
Helping someone	Watching sports events
Listening to music	Writing letters
Listening to or watching the news	
Listening to radio talk shows	

1 = This activity was *not* pleasant. (It was either unpleasant or neutral.)

2 = This activity was *somewhat* pleasant. (It was mildly or moderately pleasant.)

3 = This activity was *very* pleasant. (It was strongly or extremely pleasant.)

Write the number in the Pleasantness column of the work sheet. If you've engaged in an activity more than once in the past month, make an average pleasantness rating. If you have not engaged in an activity during the past month, rate it according to how enjoyable you think it *would have been.*

When you have rated the activities twice, multiply the frequency and pleasantness ratings for each activity and write the product in the Frequency × Pleasantness column. Higher products indicate more frequent and more pleasant activities that may be potential reinforcers. Add the activities with the highest products to your list of potential reinforcers that you compiled in Part I, eliminating duplicates. Remember that an activity is an *actual* reinforcer only if it accelerates a behavior that it follows.

Alternatives to Identifying Reinforcers

Sometimes it is difficult to identify reinforcers, especially ones that are practical as well as potent. In such instances, generalized reinforcers can be tried, drawing from generalized reinforcers that are appropriate for the particular client's demographic characteristics (such as gender and age). The odds are good that one or more will work for the client.

It also is possible to create a reinforcer by making a generalized reinforcer desirable and valuable to a particular client. **Reinforcer sampling** is a procedure in which clients are first given a generalized reinforcer noncontingently—that is, without having to do anything to obtain it.[59] The aim is to "hook" the client on the generalized reinforcer. When the client begins to enjoy the reinforcer and wants more of it, the client is then required to perform the target behavior to obtain the reinforcer. For example, to get him to clean his room, a mother taught her son a new game that they played together each night for a week. The boy came to enjoy the game and to look forward to playing it. At this point, the mother made playing the game contingent on the boy's cleaning his room. Reinforcer sampling had established the game as a reinforcer, as evidenced by the fact that the boy began to clean his room. Businesses use an analogous strategy when they give customers free samples to induce them to buy a product. For instance, bakeries often provide pieces of the special bread or cake of the day for customers to munch on while they wait to be served.

Another way to create reinforcers is to expose the client to other people (models) who are partaking of the reinforcer and who clearly are enjoying it. What we find enjoyable or valuable is determined in part by what we observe others enjoying and valuing. Humor is a good example. The next time you watch a comedy show on TV, check to see if your laughter coincides with the laugh track (an indispensable feature of TV comedy).

Administering Reinforcers

After identifying a client's potential reinforcers, the next step is to design procedures for administering them when the client performs the target behavior.

SOURCES OF REINFORCERS

Reinforcers can be administered (1) by other people and (2) by clients themselves, and reinforcers also can be (3) a natural consequence of the behavior. In behavior therapy, other people most often dispense reinforcers for a client. These **reinforcing agents** include therapists,[60] parents,[61] teachers,[62] spouses,[63] siblings,[64] and peers.[65] Adults usually reinforce children's behaviors, but sometimes children reinforce adults' behaviors, as when a 6-year-old girl's display of joy at seeing her parents when they pick her up on time from school increases the parents' coming on time.[66]

Clients can reinforce their own behaviors, which is called **self-reinforcement.**[67] Self-reinforcement has a number of advantages over reinforcement provided by others. Because the reinforcing agent is always present, reinforcement can occur immediately after the target behavior is performed and when clients are alone.[68] Self-reinforcement is likely to increase transfer, generalization, and long-term maintenance of the target behavior. Self-reinforcement also has the advantage of making clients responsible for their behavior changes. The major limitation of self-reinforcement is that clients may be less reliable in administering reinforcers than are other people who are specifically charged with that task.

Besides coming from reinforcing agents, reinforcers may occur as a natural result of engaging in the target behavior. For instance, increased endurance and energy often are natural reinforcers of regular aerobic exercise.

CONTINUOUS VERSUS INTERMITTENT REINFORCEMENT

Reinforcers are administered on two basic schedules. A *reinforcement schedule* is a rule that specifies which occurrences of a target behavior will be reinforced. With a **continuous reinforcement schedule,** a behavior is reinforced *every time* a person engages in it. With an **intermittent reinforcement schedule,** only *some* of the occurrences of the target behavior are reinforced. When an intermittent schedule of reinforcement is based on a specified interval of *time* (for instance, a reinforcer is given after every 5-minute interval in which the individual performs the behavior one or more times), it is known as an *interval schedule.* When the schedule is based on the *number* of times the behavior must be performed for it to be reinforced (for example, after every five times the person engages in the behavior), it is called a *ratio schedule.*

Continuous reinforcement is most useful when the client is first learning to perform a target behavior. Once the behavior is established, the client is usually switched to an intermittent schedule. Intermittent reinforcement is more economical than continuous reinforcement. Both the cost of reinforcers (such as with tangible reinforcers) and the time required to reinforce behaviors are less. The most important advantage of intermittent reinforcement is that it promotes transfer, generalization, and long-term maintenance of the target behavior.[69] Intermittent reinforcement simulates what occurs in clients' natural environments, where behaviors are reinforced some but not all of the time. To appreciate just how powerful intermittent reinforcement can be in maintaining behaviors over prolonged periods, consider what happens in compulsive gambling. Although gamblers are reinforced (by winning) only occasionally, they will continue to place countless bets after their last payoff.

INDIVIDUAL VERSUS GROUP CONTINGENCIES

Reinforcers most often are administered through **individual contingencies** in which the consequences a person receives (or fails to receive) depend only on his or her behavior. An example in a classroom is when any student who scores at least 80 on a quiz gets 5 extra minutes of recess. In contrast, with a **group contingency** all members of a group receive (or fail to receive) the same consequences, depending on the performance of the group.

In one type of group contingency, each group member must meet a specified performance criterion for all the group members to receive the reinforcer. For instance, if all students get 80 or higher on a quiz, then the whole class receives 5 extra minutes of recess. Another type of group contingency depends on the total or average performance of all the group members to determine whether the entire group receives the reinforcer.[70] For example, if the average of all the students' quizzes is 80, the entire class gets extra recess.

The decision to use individual or group contingencies when a group of clients is being treated varies with the particular application.[71] For instance, using a group contingency requires that all members of the group be able to perform the target behavior.[72] Potential advantages of group contingencies over individual contingencies include (1) efficient use of reinforcement with a group of clients (such as an entire classroom), (2) the fact that group members are more likely to reinforce each other's appropriate behaviors, and (3) the development of implicit or explicit group pressure to perform the target behavior. Potential disadvantages of group contingencies include (1) group members' using excessive pressure or coercion to influence others—the downside of group pressure, (2) one or more members' of the group intentionally sabotaging the program, and (3) the unfairness of withholding reinforcers from individuals whose behavior was appropriate.[73]

GUIDELINES FOR ADMINISTERING REINFORCERS AND FOSTERING MAINTENANCE

Behavior therapists have developed guidelines for administering reinforcers and fostering maintenance. The following are seven important guidelines.

1. *Reinforcers should be contingent on the client's performing the target behavior.* The reinforcer is administered only *after* the client has performed the target behavior. Providing a potentially reinforcing item or activity *before* the client engages in the target behavior will not accelerate it.

2. *The reinforcer should be administered immediately after the client performs the target behavior.* Immediate reinforcement is more effective than delayed reinforcement, especially when the client is initially learning a target behavior.

3. *Reinforcers should be administered consistently.* All reinforcing agents for a client should use the same criteria for administering reinforcers.

4. *The client should be made aware that the reinforcer is a consequence of the target behavior.* The simplest way to do this is to tell the client the reason for the reinforcer as it is administered (for example, "You did a great job finishing the project, so take the rest of the day off"). This helps the client remember the consequence, which is important because reinforcement affects the future performance of a behavior.[74]

5. *Continuous reinforcement should be used initially, followed by intermittent reinforcement.* Continuous reinforcement is optimal for initially accelerating a target behavior, and intermittent reinforcement facilitates transfer, generalization, and long-term maintenance.[75]

6. *Natural reinforcers should be used in therapy.* Employing reinforcers that the client is likely to receive outside therapy also enhances transfer, generalization, and long-term maintenance.[76]

7. *Reinforcers should be kept potent.* Reinforcers can lose their potency with repeated use because clients become satiated on them (as we become satiated with food after Thanksgiving dinner). Conversely, the more a client is deprived of a specific reinforcer, the greater is that reinforcer's potency (as when we don't eat before Thanksgiving dinner). The internal states of satiation and deprivation that can change the potency of reinforcers are called *establishing operations* because they establish how reinforcers will operate on (influence) clients' target behaviors.[77] Procedures for maintaining the potency of reinforcers include (1) using reinforcers to which clients have not had access recently,[78] (2) dispensing reinforcers in small amounts, (3) switching reinforcers periodically, and (4) using reinforcers that are less likely to lead to satiation (for example, praise rather than food).

Shaping

Do you remember playing the game "hot and cold" as a child? One child has to locate a particular object while a playmate directs the child toward the object by saying "hot" when the child gets closer and "cold" when the child starts to move farther away from the object. The game is a variation of a reinforcement procedure known as *shaping.*[79]

In **shaping,** the *components* of a target behavior are reinforced rather than the complete target behavior. Successively closer approximations of the total behavior are reinforced so that finally the complete behavior is being reinforced. Figure 6-4 shows this process schematically.

Therapists use shaping to accelerate target behaviors that a client is performing infrequently or that are difficult or complex for a client, such as in teaching emergency fire-exiting skills to a 9-year-old girl with autistic disorder.[80] The therapist breaks down the total behavior into its logical component parts or steps and then reinforces each component as it occurs. The process is cumulative in that each component plus all preceding

Shaping involves reinforcing successive steps required for a complex behavior.
Reprinted with permission of Mal Hancock.

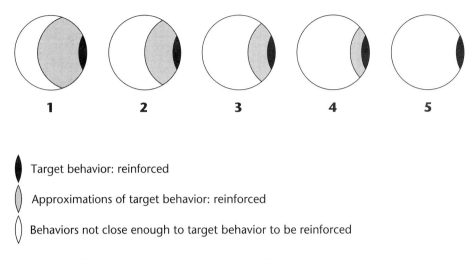

Target behavior: reinforced

Approximations of target behavior: reinforced

Behaviors not close enough to target behavior to be reinforced

Figure 6-4 Schematic diagram representing the principle of shaping
SOURCE: © Michael D. Spiegler and David C. Guevremont

components are reinforced. For instance, suppose a therapist were teaching a child to say the sentence, "I want milk." The therapist would first reinforce "I," then "I want," and finally "I want milk." Shaping generally is part of a treatment package and often is combined with prompting.

Shaping was used in the treatment of a 3-year-old girl who had to be fed through a gastronomy tube because she refused to eat.[81] Jenny's parents were taught to praise her and briefly engage in a game (such as pat-a-cake) for each bite of food she accepted. After an assessment of the foods Jenny would and would not tolerate, the intervention began with baby food that was soft and watery and gradually increased in thickness and texture as Jenny began to eat. Jenny showed significant increases in the amount of food she consumed at home, and these results transferred to her preschool. By the end of the intervention, Jenny frequently fed herself a jar of baby food.

Case 6-3 illustrates the use of shaping to accelerate talking in a man who had not spoken in 19 years.

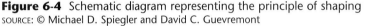

Case 6-3 SHAPING AND PROMPTING USED TO INSTITUTE SPEECH IN A PATIENT WITH LONG-STANDING SELECTIVE MUTISM[82]

A 40-year-old male patient in a psychiatric hospital had been completely mute and virtually unresponsive during 19 years of hospitalization. For example, in group therapy he remained impassive, staring straight ahead even when he was offered a cigarette, which other patients were accepting. During one group therapy session, the therapist accidentally dropped a package of chewing gum, and the patient momentarily moved his eyes toward it. This response was chosen as a starting point to shape the patient's speaking.

Individual therapy sessions were held three times a week. The therapist began by holding a stick of gum in front of the patient's face and waited until he looked at it, at which point the patient was given the gum. When the patient consistently looked at the gum, the therapist waited for any lip movement before reinforcing the response with gum. Then, in order, looking at the gum, lip movements, and any sound were required for the reinforcer. Next, the therapist used the prompt, "Say *gum, gum,*" and made the reinforcer contingent on closer and closer approximations of *gum.*

At the end of the 18th therapy session, the patient spontaneously said, "Gum, please." This breakthrough was accompanied by other verbal responses, such as answering questions about his name and age. Thereafter, the patient responded to other questions the therapist asked, but he did not respond to other staff members. To generalize his responding to other people, a nurse was brought into the therapy sessions. After a month, the patient was responding to the nurse's questions. Finally, the patient's verbal requests were shaped and generalized by having all the staff members with whom the patient had contact do things for the patient only when he specifically asked for them.

Employing shaping to initiate speech in a man who had been mute for essentially all his adult life is an impressive demonstration of the efficacy of shaping. Case 6-3 also illustrates the use of specific procedures to foster generalization of his speaking with different people.

Shaping requires careful observation of the client's actions to make fine discriminations among the components of the target behavior. Participation Exercise 6-3 can help you appreciate the subtle skills required for effective shaping.

Participation Exercise 6-3

SHAPING YOUR SHAPING SKILLS*

To do this exercise, you will need the help of a friend for about 20 minutes.

Choose a behavior that is (1) simple, (2) brief (taking less than 1 minute), and (3) easily broken down into component parts or steps. Examples of suitable behaviors are opening and closing a book, removing the top of a pen and replacing it, standing up and sitting down, opening and closing a window, and talking about a particular topic (such as schoolwork or the weather).

List the major components of the behavior in their appropriate order. Table 6-2 lists the major components of two simple behaviors as examples. Keep your list in mind as you shape your friend's behavior. However, your friend may not perform each component and is likely to perform some steps that fall between the major components you've identified. The key to effective shaping is to be able to notice differences among responses so that you are *always reinforcing closer approximations to the behavior.*

*You will need to do this Participation Exercise later, but you should read it now.

Table 6-2 Major components of two simple behaviors

Opening and closing a book

1. Movement of either hand
2. Movement of either hand in the direction of the book
3. Touching the book with the hand
4. Opening the book partially
5. Opening the book fully
6. Closing the book partially
7. Closing the book fully

Criticizing

1. Any verbal utterance
2. Any statement (as opposed to a question)
3. Any negative statement
4. Any negative statement that is a criticism

When your friend arrives, say something like the following:

> I am going to try to get you to perform a simple behavior—nothing embarrassing. I'll do this by saying "good" every time you get closer to performing the behavior. I can't give you any hints about what I want you to do. I will give you feedback as you get closer to the behavior by saying "good."

Your friend may appear quizzical or skeptical ("You want me to do something but you won't tell me what?"). Just be sure your friend understands the instructions. If at any time your friend asks a question such as, "What do you want me to do?" answer, "Just get me to say 'good.'"

At first, your friend may remain motionless and speechless for several minutes (as he or she tries to figure out what to do or say). To get started, reinforce—by saying "good"—the first movement (or utterance, in the case of a verbal behavior) your friend makes (as the therapist did in Case 6-3). Then, reinforce behaviors that are closer and closer to the target behavior. It is crucial that you say "good" *immediately* after the component response is made. Otherwise, your friend may associate the reinforcer with some other response that he or she made at about the same time.

When your friend finally performs the behavior, congratulate him or her, describe the shaping procedure you were using, and ask your friend to comment on the process. Your friend may raise questions and issues that will enhance your understanding of shaping.

◆

Reinforcement Therapy in Perspective

Reinforcement therapy is consistently effective in accelerating many different target behaviors for clients of all ages and intellectual and physical capabilities.[83] For example, reinforcement procedures are indispensable in promoting socially adaptive behaviors of clients with schizophrenia, brain damage, and mental retardation.[84]

The key to effective application of reinforcement entails *(1) consistently administering potent reinforcers, which have been (2) specifically identified for the client, (3) immediately following the behavior.* After a client is successfully performing the target behavior, specific steps must be taken to ensure that the client will perform the behavior in different situations in his or her natural environment (if this is appropriate), and will continue to do so over the long run. Four procedures are employed to promote transfer, generalization, and long-term maintenance: (1) using natural reinforcers, (2) using self-reinforcement, (3) reinforcing the target behavior in the client's natural environment by natural reinforcing agents, and (4) administering reinforcers intermittently. The first three ensure that the target behavior will continue to be reinforced. The fourth procedure increases the chances that the client will continue to perform the behavior even when it is reinforced only occasionally in the client's natural environment, which is typical. Behaviors will be maintained only if they are reinforced. Although this principle may appear obvious, many people harbor the illusion that once a person is engaging in a behavior, the behavior should magically continue—that is, without further reinforcement. In other words, reinforcement mistakenly is viewed as a quick cure, like taking an aspirin to relieve a headache. Behaviors must be reinforced at least occasionally (intermittently) if they are to continue being performed.

Reinforcement therapy is used to accelerate socially adaptive and desirable behaviors. Some critics have argued that clients should perform socially desirable behaviors without their having to be reinforced because the natural consequences of the behaviors are intrinsically worthwhile. However, if this were so, then why don't the clients engage in these "intrinsically worthwhile" behaviors on their own? Apparently, the behaviors do *not* have intrinsic worth to the clients, which is why extrinsic reinforcers are needed to initiate and maintain socially desirable behaviors that are not being performed.

A related ethical criticism of reinforcement is as follows: By fostering socially desirable behaviors, reinforcement therapy deprives clients of an aspect of their personal freedom, namely, to act however they wish, which includes socially undesirable or nonconformist behaviors. In fact, clients who need to be taught socially desirable behaviors often do not have these behaviors in their repertoire. Thus, the new behaviors increase the options clients have for how they behave, which in effect increases their personal freedom.

Another common criticism of reinforcement is that it is a form of bribery. *Bribery* is offering something valuable, such as money or a favor, to influence someone to act, usually dishonestly or illegally. Bribes are given *before* the behavior is performed, whereas reinforcers are always given *after* the behavior occurs. Receiving reinforcers for engaging in appropriate or adaptive behaviors is no more a form of bribery than being paid a salary for a day's work. Furthermore, reinforcers are not used in behavior therapy to accelerate dishonest or illegal behaviors.

Although reinforcement therapy is not a panacea, it is perhaps the most widely applicable behavior therapy, and its effectiveness has been demonstrated by a large body of empirical research. Accelerating desirable behaviors with reinforcement has no major negative side effects, and clients consistently rate it as an acceptable treatment.[85] Reinforcement therapy provides clients with new, adaptive behaviors that are alternatives to their maladaptive problem behaviors. In doing so, reinforcement therapy increases clients' freedom by giving them more options for how to behave and enhances clients' dignity as human beings.

SUMMARY

1. Stimulus control procedures change antecedents that elicit behaviors. Prompting provides the cues that remind or instruct clients to perform target behaviors. Prompts can be verbal, environmental, physical, or behavioral. After the client is performing the behavior, prompts are faded (gradually withdrawn).
2. Setting events are environmental conditions that elicit behaviors. When a setting event is identified as a maintaining antecedent of a target behavior, it is modified to create the desired change in the behavior.
3. Reinforcement occurs whenever the consequences of a behavior increase the likelihood that the behavior will be repeated. Reinforcers usually are pleasant or desirable consequences, but whether a consequence is a reinforcer depends on its accelerating effects.
4. Reinforcers provide feedback that a behavior is being performed properly.
5. Reinforcement can be positive or negative, depending on whether the consequence is added or removed, respectively.
6. The four major categories of positive reinforcers are tangible reinforcers, social reinforcers, token reinforcers, and reinforcing activities.
7. Social reinforcers are versatile because they are easy to administer, usually can be administered immediately, and are natural reinforcers.
8. The Premack principle uses high-probability behaviors as reinforcers for low-probability behaviors.
9. Reinforcers are identified by questioning clients, exposing them to generalized reinforcers, and observing their frequent activities.
10. Reinforcers can be created by reinforcer sampling and exposure to models' enjoying potential reinforcers.
11. Reinforcers are administered by other people and by clients themselves, and they can occur as a natural consequence of the behavior.
12. Continuous reinforcement is used to teach behaviors initially; intermittent reinforcement fosters long-term maintenance as well as transfer and generalization.
13. With groups of clients, reinforcers can be administered in a group contingency. All members of the group receive or fail to receive the reinforcers, depending on the performance of the group.
14. Shaping involves reinforcing components of a target behavior in sequence until the full target behavior is performed. Shaping is

used to accelerate difficult or complex target behaviors or behaviors that occur infrequently.

15. Reinforcement therapy consistently has been effective in accelerating many different types of target behaviors for clients of all ages and intellectual and physical capabilities.

16. Behavior is maintained only if it is reinforced. Procedures for enhancing long-term maintenance as well as transfer and generalization employ natural reinforcers, self-reinforcement, natural reinforcing agents, and intermittent reinforcement.

Reference Notes

1. For example, Ninness, Ellis, & Ninness, 1999.
2. Hrydowy, Stokes, & Martin, 1984.
3. Austin, Alvero, & Olson, 1998; Cox, Cox, & Cox, 2000; Engerman, Austin, & Bailey, 1997.
4. Kirby, Marlowe, Carrigan, & Platt, 1998.
5. Lemsky, 1996.
6. McAdam & Cuvo, 1994.
7. Pierce & Schreibman, 1994; Van Houten, 1998.
8. Wagner, 1998.
9. Luiselli, 1993.
10. Van Houten, 1998.
11. Lovaas, 1977; Zanolli & Daggett, 1998.
12. Koegel, Stiebel, & Koegel, 1998.
13. For example, Chandler, Fowler, & Lubek, 1992; Davis & Fox, 1999; Sasso, Mundschenk, Melloy, & Casey, 1998.
14. Guevremont & Dumas, 2002.
15. Davis & Fox, 1999.
16. Kern & Dunlap, 1998.
17. Grave, 1999.
18. Hodgins, Wynne, & Makarchuck, 1999.
19. Shah, Coyle, Kavanaugh, Adams-Huet, & Lipskey, 2000.
20. Rothbaum & Ninan, 1999.
21. Backhaus, Hohagen, Voderholzer, & Riemann, 2001; Bootzin & Epstein, 2000; King, Dudley, Melvin, Pallant, & Morawetz, 2001; Lichstein, Wilson, & Johnson, 2000; Reidel & Lichstein, 2000.
22. Bigelow & Lutzker, 1998; Close, 2000; Lutzker, Huynen, & Bigelow, 1998.
23. Lutzker, Huynen, & Bigelow, 1998.
24. Kazdin, 1989.
25. For example, Babcock, Sulzer-Azaroff, Sanderson, & Scibak, 1992; Pollack, Fleming, & Sulzer-Azaroff, 1994.
26. Chapman, Fisher, Piazza, & Kurtz, 1993.
27. Compare with Bloxham, Long, Alderman, & Hollin, 1993; Iwata, 1987; Kitfield & Masalsky, 2000; Marcus & Vollmer, 1995.
28. Guevremont & Spiegler, 1990; McConnell, 1990.
29. Compare with Michael, 1975.
30. For example, Cooper, Wacker, Brown, McComas, Peck, Drew, Asmus, & Kayser, 1999; McCain & Kelley, 1993; Williamson, Williamson, Watkins, & Hughes, 1992.
31. For example, Griffiths, Feldman, & Tough, 1997; Hall & Hall, 1998b.
32. For example, Luiselli, 1993.
33. From the author's (DCG) case files.
34. For example, Stark, Knapp, Bowen, Powers, Jelalian, Evans, Passero, Mulvihill, & Hovell, 1993.
35. For example, Borrego & Urquiza, 1998; Connell, Carta, & Baer, 1993; Grandy & Peck, 1997; McConnachie & Carr, 1997.
36. Kallman, Hersen, & O'Toole, 1975.
37. For example, Ninness, Ellis, & Ninness, 1999.
38. Budney, Higgins, Radonovich, & Novy, 2000; Higgins, Budney, Bickel, Hughes, Foerg, & Badger, 1993; Higgins, Wong, Badger, Ogden, & Dantona, 2000; Iguchi, Belding, Morral, Lamb, & Husband, 1997.
39. Rowan-Szal, Joe, Chatham, & Simpson, 1994.
40. Hagopian & Slifer, 1993.
41. Brigham, Bakken, Scruggs, & Mastropiere, 1992.
42. For example, Axelrod & Hall, 1999; Davis & Chittum, 1994; Hall & Hall, 1998a.
43. Premack, 1965.
44. For example, Carrington, Lehrer, & Wittenstrom, 1997; Danaher, 1974.
45. For example, Homme, C'de Baca, Devine, Steinhorst, & Rickert, 1963; Horan & Johnson, 1971; Roberts, 1969; Wasik, 1970.

46. Watson & Tharp, 1972.
47. Timberlake & Farmer-Dougan, 1991.
48. Spiegler & Agigian, 1977.
49. From the author's (MDS) case files.
50. Bandura, 1969.
51. Axelrod & Hall, 1999.
52. Schmitz, Rhoades, & Grabowski, 1994.
53. For example, Bigelow, Huynen, & Lutzker, 1993; Fox & DeShaw, 1993a, 1993b.
54. Pace, Ivancic, Edwards, Iwata, & Page, 1985.
55. Cautela & Kastenbaum, 1967.
56. Phillips, Fischer, & Singh, 1977.
57. MacPhillamy & Lewinsohn, 1971.
58. Daley, 1969; Homme, 1971.
59. For example, Bigelow, Huynen, & Lutzker, 1993; Steed, Bigelow, Huynen, & Lutzker, 1995.
60. For example, Kallman, Hersen, & O'Toole, 1975.
61. For example, Wahler, 1969.
62. For example, Stark, Collins, Osnes, & Stokes, 1986; Thomas, Becker, & Armstrong, 1968.
63. For example, Stuart, 1969, 1980.
64. For example, James & Egel, 1986.
65. For example, Solomon & Wahler, 1973; Strain, 1981.
66. For example, Graubard, Rosenberg, & Miller, 1974.
67. For example, Ajibola & Clement, 1995; Christian & Poling, 1997.
68. For example, Rokke, Tomhave, & Jocic, 2000; Solomon, Flynn, Worden, Mickey, Skelly, Geller, Peluso, & Webster, 1998.
69. For example, Ducharme & Holborn, 1997; Esveldt-Dawson & Kazdin, 1998.
70. For example, Brigham, Bakken, Scruggs, & Mastropiere, 1992; Davis & Chittum, 1994.
71. For example, Pigott & Heggie, 1986; Shapiro, Albright, & Ager, 1986.
72. Axelrod, 1998.
73. For example, Axelrod, 1998; Kazdin & Geesey, 1977.
74. Compare with Greene, 2001.
75. Esveldt-Dawson & Kazdin, 1998; Zanolli & Daggett, 1998.
76. Baer, 1999; Esveldt-Dawson & Kazdin, 1998.
77. Berg, Peck, Wacker, Harding, McComas, Richman, & Brown, 2000; Brown, Wacker, Derby, Peck, Richman, Sasso, Knutson, & Harding, 2000; Friman, 2000; Kennedy & Meyer, 1998; Worsdell, Iwata, Conners, Kahng, & Thompson, 2000.
78. Michael, 2000.
79. Morgan, 1974.
80. Bigelow, Huynen, & Lutzker, 1993.
81. Gutentag & Hammer, 2000.
82. Isaacs, Thomas, & Goldiamond, 1960.
83. Kazdin & Wilson, 1978.
84. Rachman & Wilson, 1980.
85. For example, Jones, Eyberg, Adams, & Boggs, 1998; Miller & Kelley, 1992.

Chapter 7

Deceleration Behavior Therapy

Reinforcement therapy is used to accelerate desirable and adaptive behaviors. For decelerating undesirable and maladaptive behaviors, behavior therapists employ a number of strategies. In this chapter, we discuss three major deceleration strategies: differential reinforcement, consequential deceleration therapy, and aversion therapy.

The preferred strategy for decelerating an undesirable behavior is to reinforce an acceleration target behavior that is an alternative to the deceleration target behavior, a procedure called **differential reinforcement.** For example, to reduce a client's criticizing people, the client might be reinforced for complimenting others. As this example shows, differential reinforcement changes the deceleration target behavior *indirectly.*

DIFFERENTIAL REINFORCEMENT: INDIRECTLY DECELERATING UNDESIRABLE BEHAVIORS

Differential reinforcement works because *the more the client engages in the alternative behavior, the less opportunity the client has to engage in the deceleration target behavior.* Consider the case of a young girl with severe mental retardation who frequently hit herself.[1] To reduce her self-destructive behavior, she was reinforced for using her hands to play with a puzzle. Differential reinforcement was effective because while her hands were engaged in playing with the puzzle, she could not use them to hit herself.

Four major strategies of differential reinforcement are used to indirectly decelerate undesirable behaviors. In order of most to least desirable, they are differential reinforcement of (1) incompatible behaviors, (2) competing behaviors, (3) any other behaviors, and (4) a lowered frequency of the undesirable behavior.

Differential Reinforcement of Incompatible Behaviors

The optimal strategy for decelerating undesirable behaviors is to reinforce acceleration target behaviors that are *incompatible* with them—that is, **differential reinforcement of incompatible behaviors.** *Incompatible* means that the acceleration and deceleration target behaviors cannot occur simultaneously. Thus, while a person is performing the acceleration target behavior, it is *impossible* for the person to perform the deceleration behavior. For example, differential reinforcement of incompatible behavior was used as part of a treatment package to reduce excessive crying associated with infant colic.[2] The parents played music and attended to the infant (such as by making eye contact with and gently touching the infant) whenever the infant was quiet and alert for 30 seconds or more. This procedure reduced the infant's crying by 75%.

Designing acceleration target behaviors that are incompatible with undesirable behaviors involves ingenuity and is even more challenging than devising *competing* acceleration target behaviors, which you did in Participation Exercise 4-1. You will get a feel for this process by taking a few minutes to do Participation Exercise 7-1 before you read about the next form of differential reinforcement.

◆

FINDING INCOMPATIBLE ACCELERATION TARGET BEHAVIORS
TO SUBSTITUTE FOR UNDESIRABLE BEHAVIORS

For each undesirable behavior that follows, write an *incompatible* acceleration target behavior. Be sure the acceleration target behavior meets the standards for a good target behavior described in Chapter 4 (page 52), including making the target behavior appropriate and realistic. You will know you have designed an incompatible behavior if it is *impossible* to engage *simultaneously* in the behavior you have devised and the undesirable behavior.

1. Biting one's nails
2. Interrupting others during conversations
3. Sleeping in class
4. Making self-deprecating statements (such as "I'm just no good")
5. Leaving clothes on the floor

◆

Differential Reinforcement of Competing Behaviors

Although reinforcement of incompatible behaviors is the optimal strategy for reducing undesirable behaviors, in practice finding appropriate incompatible behaviors often is not possible. In such cases, the next best strategy is **differential reinforcement of competing behaviors.** Engaging in a competing acceleration target behavior reduces, but does not eliminate, the opportunity to engage simultaneously in the undesirable behavior.[3] For a 9-year-old girl, "doing math problems" competes with "wandering around the classroom," but she can still do math problems while wandering!

Differential Reinforcement of Other Behaviors

Reinforcing an incompatible or competing behavior has the advantage that an adaptive behavior is substituted for a maladaptive behavior. However, this approach is not always possible, as when an alternative acceleration target behavior cannot be identified. If a target behavior is seriously maladaptive, it may be necessary to reinforce *any other* behavior to decrease the maladaptive behavior quickly; this is known as **differential reinforcement of other behaviors.**

Differential reinforcement of other behaviors is employed primarily for high-frequency behaviors that are either dangerous to others (such as hitting people)[4] or self-injurious (such as head banging).[5] In such cases, engaging in virtually any other behavior is preferable to engaging in the deceleration target behavior. For example, a child who frequently hurled objects at other people was reinforced for throwing objects at anything but a person. Although throwing things at inanimate objects is undesirable, it is *less* undesirable than injuring people (being the lesser of two evils). Differential reinforcement of other behaviors occasionally is used for reducing less severe maladaptive behaviors, such as noncompliance in preschoolers,[6] sibling conflict, and nervous habits, such as vocal tics,[7] and wandering of geriatric patients with dementia.[8]

Differential Reinforcement of Low Response Rates

Occasionally, it is unreasonable to expect that the client can completely stop engaging in the maladaptive behavior (go "cold turkey," so to speak), as when the rate of performing the behavior is very high. In such cases, the client can be reinforced for performing the deceleration target behavior less often, which is called **differential reinforcement of low response rates.**[9] This strategy was used with an adolescent boy who frequently talked out inappropriately in a special education class.[10] The teacher told the boy that she would spend extra time with him if he talked out inappropriately three times or less during a class period. This contingency lowered the rate of the boy's talking out from an average of more than 30 times a class period to an average of less than 3 times a period.

Differential reinforcement of low response rates can eliminate a behavior completely if the criterion for reinforcement is gradually decreased to zero. For example, first the client might be reinforced for 10 or fewer responses, then for 5 or fewer, next for 2 or fewer, and finally, for no responses.[11]

Variants of Differential Reinforcement

Both differential reinforcement of other behaviors and low response rates often are used to treat severely maladaptive behaviors. Two variants of differential reinforcement—noncontingent reinforcement and functional communication training—have received increasing attention in recent years for such problem behaviors.

NONCONTINGENT REINFORCEMENT

In **noncontingent reinforcement,** the reinforcer identified as maintaining a problem behavior is administered on a frequent fixed-interval schedule (for example, every 15 seconds), regardless of whether the client engages in the deceleration target behavior.[12] In other words, the client still receives the reinforcer but usually not after performing the target behavior. In this way, the reinforcement is not contingent on the behavior.

The reductions in behavior following noncontingent reinforcement therapy are believed to be related to satiation and extinction.[13] Because the reinforcer is administered frequently, the client becomes satiated on it, which decreases its effectiveness. Extinction (which you will read about shortly) involves withholding the reinforcer that typically follows the problem behavior, resulting in a decrease in the behavior.

Noncontingent reinforcement as a treatment for serious maladaptive behaviors still is in its early stages of development. However, initial studies have suggested that noncontingent reinforcement can successfully reduce aggressive, self-injurious, and disruptive behaviors, particularly when social attention maintains them.[14]

FUNCTIONAL COMMUNICATION TRAINING

Sometimes clients engage in aggressive and disruptive behaviors to obtain desired reinforcers. For example, 4-year-old Batya has learned that when she has a temper tantrum, one of her parents or her nursery school teacher comes over to ask what is wrong. Thus, Batya engages in temper tantrums specifically to obtain adult attention. Similarly, when 6-year-old Ari becomes frustrated with a task at school, he bangs loudly on his desk; this behavior results in his being permitted to take a break or do some other task. Ari's disruptive behavior is negatively reinforced because he gets to escape from doing the frustrating task. Such scenarios are especially likely when the client lacks appropriate communication skills and therefore communicates desires inappropriately.

Functional communication training teaches clients to use acceptable ways of communicating the desire for a reinforcer as an alternative to their typical unacceptable means of communicating the same message.[15] In our previous example, Batya would be taught to communicate that she wanted attention in a more acceptable way, as by saying simply, "I want you," or by waving a small flag that is a prearranged signal for wanting attention. And Ari might be taught to say "break" or make the hand gesture for "cut" (side of the hand across the throat) to communicate his need to terminate a frustrating task. Functional communication training has been used to treat aggressive and disruptive behaviors of children and adults who have very limited communication skills, such as people with developmental disabilities and autistic disorder.[16]

The first step in functional communication training is to identify the reinforcer maintaining the problem behavior. Second, the client is taught to use an appropriate communication behavior that will result in the client obtaining the reinforcer. Because the training often is used with clients with severe developmental disabilities, a wide range of acceptable communication responses are employed, including simple verbalizations, manual signs, picture cards, and gestures. Typically, clients are taught to use several different communication responses.[17] Third, the alternative, acceptable ways of communicating are reinforced by the client's obtaining the desired reinforcer, and the reinforcer is withheld (extinction) for the inappropriate communication behaviors. Functional communication training appears to reduce problem behaviors relatively quickly, and studies have found that the effects of the training persist for at least 2 years.[18]

In contrast to standard differential reinforcement procedures, the alternative behavior that is reinforced in functional communication training is specifically taught to the client rather than being a naturally occurring behavior. Moreover, clients in functional communication training control when the alternative behavior will be reinforced by their appropriately communicating their need or desire for the reinforcer.

DECELERATION BEHAVIOR THERAPY: DIRECTLY DECELERATING UNDESIRABLE BEHAVIORS

In some cases, differential reinforcement may not reduce the undesirable behavior sufficiently or fast enough. This is likely to happen in three circumstances.

First, sometimes it is difficult to find a suitable acceleration target behavior. With substance abuse, for example, few alternative behaviors are as immediately satisfying as the physical effects of some drugs.

Second, increasing the acceleration target behavior may only partially decrease the maladaptive target behavior. For instance, accelerating *complimenting* may not result in an acceptable decrease in *criticizing* because a person can compliment and criticize someone virtually in the same breath (for example, "I love your suit, but that tie just doesn't make it").

Third, differential reinforcement typically decreases the deceleration target behavior *gradually,* which may not be fast enough. This would be the case with behaviors (1) that are potentially dangerous to the client (for instance, self-mutilation) or to other people (such as physically aggressive acts) and (2) that infringe on others' rights (for example, destroying someone's property).

Two forms of deceleration behavior therapy are used to reduce undesirable behaviors directly. **Consequential deceleration therapy** *changes the consequences* of the maladaptive target behavior. **Aversion therapy** *associates the maladaptive target behavior with something unpleasant.* Consequential deceleration therapy is more broadly applicable and is used much more frequently than aversion therapy.

Both forms of deceleration therapy can be used in conjunction with procedures, such as differential reinforcement, that accelerate alternative, desirable behavior. Indeed, treating an acceleration target behavior along with a deceleration target behavior is standard practice in behavior therapy.

CONSEQUENTIAL DECELERATION THERAPY

Consequential deceleration therapies either (1) *eliminate reinforcement for the target behavior* (extinction and time out from positive reinforcement) or (2) *make the consequences of the behavior undesirable* (response cost, overcorrection, and physically aversive consequences). We first turn to the two procedures that eliminate reinforcement.

Extinction

All behaviors are maintained by reinforcement. When the reinforcers maintaining a behavior are no longer administered, the person eventually stops performing the behavior. The process of eliminating (withdrawing or withholding) reinforcers is called **extinction.** Case 7-1 is a classic example of extinction.

ELIMINATING BEDTIME TEMPER TANTRUMS BY EXTINCTION[19]

The client was a 21-month-old boy who engaged in prolonged temper tantrums at bedtime. When his parents put the boy to bed and left the room, he screamed and cried. The parents responded by remaining in the room until the child fell asleep (from ½ hour to 2 hours). Thus, it appeared that the child's parents' attention was reinforcing his temper tantrums.

The therapist suggested an extinction procedure. The parents put the child in his bed as usual. However, after remaining in the child's bedroom for a short time, they left the room and did not return even when the child cried. As Figure 7-1 shows, after the boy cried for 45 minutes the first night of extinction, the length of crying quickly declined to zero. By the 10th night the child even smiled when the parents left his bedroom, and he continued to go to sleep without incident for the next week.

At this point, an unfortunate event occurred. The child's aunt put the boy to bed, and when he cried as she began to leave the room, she stayed in his bedroom until he fell asleep. This positively reinforced the tantrum behavior that had been eliminated. In fact, this single reinforcer increased the child's crying to its pretreatment level.

The parents instituted the extinction procedures again. The broken line in Figure 7-1 shows that the child's crying reached zero by the seventh night of the second extinction attempt, indicating that the procedures were successful. At a 2-year follow-up, the parents reported that no additional bedtime temper tantrums had occurred.

Figure 7-1 Results of two attempts to eliminate, through extinction, bedtime temper tantrums of a 21-month-old child
SOURCE: Adapted from Williams, 1959, p. 269.

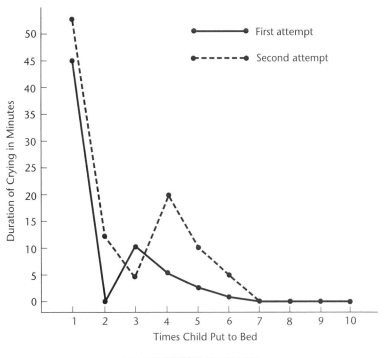

For extinction to work, it is crucial to correctly identify the reinforcer that is maintaining the deceleration target behavior.[20] In Case 7-1, social attention was reinforcing the child's bedtime temper tantrums, so extinction appropriately involved ignoring the behavior. Extinction often is used to reduce behaviors that are reinforced by social attention. (You are likely to have used extinction in social situations, as when you ignore a friend who is bragging obnoxiously.)

Some people mistakenly equate *ignoring* and *extinction*. Ignoring as an extinction procedure is appropriate *only* when social attention is maintaining the deceleration target behavior. Consider the example of a 9-year-old boy who regularly stole money from his mother's purse. The boy's mother decided to pretend not to see her son taking money from her purse and to say nothing to him. She believed she was using extinction. However, not surprisingly, her son's stealing continued because the behavior was reinforced by the money rather than by social attention.

Extinction can be effective as the sole treatment, as in Case 7-1. Generally, however, it is more effective when it is combined with other therapies, such as differential reinforcement.[21]

Extinction has four potential problems. First, in some, but certainly not all, cases, extinction may work relatively slowly. This is a problem with target behaviors that must be decelerated rapidly, such as self-injurious behaviors.[22]

Second, in 1 of every 4 cases, extinction results in an *extinction burst,* an initial intensification of the target behavior before it begins to decrease.[23] And for certain target behaviors, such as self-injurious behaviors where extinction bursts are especially undesirable,[24] extinction bursts occur in as many as half the cases treated with extinction.[25] Extinction bursts are reduced when extinction is combined with other deceleration procedures, such as differential reinforcement.[26]

Third, the effects of extinction may not transfer to circumstances other than the specific one in which the extinction was carried out. This may have occurred in Case 7-1. The boy had not cried for a week and a half with his parents, who had administered the extinction procedure. However, when his aunt put him to bed, the circumstances changed and he cried.

The fourth potential problem with extinction is that the target behavior may recur temporarily after it has been eliminated, which is known as *spontaneous recovery*. Spontaneous recovery is another factor that may have accounted for the return of the boy's crying in Case 7-1. Spontaneous recovery is *not* an indication that extinction has been ineffective. In fact, the intensity of the deceleration target behavior generally is weaker during spontaneous recovery than it was before extinction was implemented, and the target behavior soon begins to decline again. When using extinction, the therapist should tell people involved in the procedure that the deceleration target behavior may recur temporarily.[27]

Extinction also has two practical limitations. First, the reinforcer maintaining the target behavior must be identified, which is not always possible. Second, for extinction to be most effective, the reinforcer must be *completely* withheld.[28] As you saw in Case 7-1, even a single, isolated exception can reinstate the deceleration target behavior and maintain it for a considerable time thereafter. In effect, the behavior was placed on an intermittent reinforcement schedule, which increased the durability of the behavior.

Time Out from Positive Reinforcement

Time out from positive reinforcement (or **time out,** for short) involves *temporarily* withdrawing a client's access to generalized reinforcers immediately after the client performs the deceleration target behavior. When parents have their child stand in a corner for several minutes following a misbehavior, they are using time out. In part, time out is time-limited extinction. However, in contrast to extinction, the actual reinforcers for the deceleration target behavior are not identified. In fact, what is temporarily denied is access to a range of generalized reinforcers.[29] Technically, then, the term *time out from positive reinforcement* is a misnomer, and the procedure should be called *time out from generalized reinforcers.*

Typically, time out requires the client, usually a child, to leave the situation in which the undesirable behavior occurs and spend a specified amount of time in a designated time-out area. This may be an isolated corner or a special **time-out room** that does not allow access to generalized reinforcers (such as windows to look out of or objects to play with).[30]

Practical considerations often make it impossible to completely eliminate reinforcers during the time-out period. For example, in a school setting, a

Photo 7-1 A child spending a few minutes in a corner is a common way that time out from positive reinforcement is implemented.

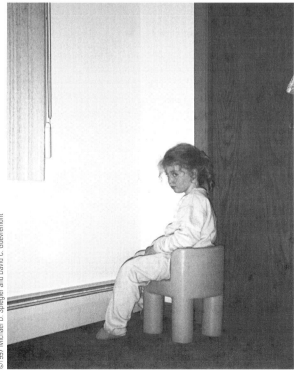

©1997 Michael D. Spiegler and David C. Guevremont

time-out room may not be available, so children are put in a remote corner of the classroom for time out. Although many of the previously available generalized reinforcers have been removed (such as interacting with other children), the child still has access to some generalized reinforcers (such as observing other children, albeit from a distance).[31] Such "partial" time out tends to be less effective than "total" time out in which all generalized reinforcers are removed.[32]

Time out from positive reinforcement is most effective when the following six conditions are met.

1. *The client should be aware of the reason for time out and its duration.* This can be done most easily by telling the client the reason for the time out and how long it will be (for instance, "For speaking disrespectfully, you have a 3-minute time out").

2. *The duration of time out should be brief.* Usually, 5 minutes or less is sufficient. Time-out periods as short as 15 seconds have reduced inappropriate eating behaviors and table manners in institutionalized children with mental retardation.[33] For children up to age 5, a rule of thumb is that the duration of time out should not exceed approximately 1 minute for each year of the child's age.[34] Relatively short periods are effective, and lengthening the time period does not necessarily increase the effectiveness of time out.[35] Incidentally, time out from positive reinforcement is not simply isolation (seclusion).[36] Isolation is not a behavior therapy procedure. The duration of time out is brief and specified ahead of time, whereas isolation often is for a long, indeterminate period.

3. *No reinforcers should be present or introduced during the time-out period.* For example, an adult should not respond to a child's questions (such as, "Is the time up yet?"), thereby giving the child social attention.

4. *Time out should be terminated only when the specified time has elapsed.* If the child is removed from time out beforehand, the time out may be less effective in the future.

5. *Time out should be terminated only when the child is behaving appropriately,* which means not engaging in any undesirable behaviors. This provision ensures that an undesirable behavior, such as screaming, is not inadvertently negatively reinforced by termination of time out or positively reinforced by once again gaining access to generalized reinforcers.

6. *Time out should not allow clients to escape or avoid situations they find unpleasant, including responsibilities.* If a child dislikes schoolwork, for example, then removing the student from the classroom allows the student to avoid schoolwork.

Time out from positive reinforcement has been used to decelerate a variety of maladaptive behaviors of children, adolescents, and occasionally, adults. Target behaviors have included self-injurious behaviors of children with autistic disorder,[37] inappropriate table manners and eating habits of institutionalized children with mental retardation,[38] verbal and physical aggression of children and adolescents,[39] disruptive social behaviors of adults with psychiatric disorders,[40] and alcohol consumption by clients with a history of substance abuse.[41]

Many parents apply time out when their young children do not comply with instructions or rules,[42] and elementary school teachers use time out as a standard discipline procedure.[43] When applied correctly, time out is highly effective and efficient. Children easily learn the time-out routine and generally comply with it. Furthermore, the threat of time out can serve as a deterrent for future misbehaviors (for example, "The next time you eat with your fingers, you'll have a time out").

An interesting positive side effect of time out used in the home or school is that it gives adults a "time out" of sorts—not from positive reinforcement but from aversive elements of the child's misbehavior. The brief respite may lessen the chances that the adults will become overly upset and even abusive.

The widespread use of time out by parents and teachers who have little or no training in its correct implementation often results in misapplication. For example, many parents send their children to their room for misbehavior, which, given the contents of most children's rooms, hardly constitutes a time out from generalized reinforcers.

Although correctly applied time out from positive reinforcement is effective with most children, it does not work well with all clients. Some clients, such as children with attention deficit hyperactivity disorder, may not remain in time out for even a minute or two.[44] In such cases, undesirable consequences for failure to stay in time out may be added to the time-out procedure.

The second category of consequential deceleration therapy makes the consequences of the maladaptive behavior undesirable. Both extinction and time out from positive reinforcement also may involve undesirable consequences, in that clients generally experience removal of reinforcers as unpleasant. But this is a side effect of the primary operation of extinction and time out, which is removing reinforcers. The three major therapies that introduce undesirable consequences are response cost, overcorrection, and physically aversive consequences.

Response Cost

The undesirable consequence in **response cost** is the removal of a valued item or privilege that the client possesses or is entitled to.[45] Many everyday behaviors are influenced by response cost, including fines (such as for illegal parking and failure to return library books), the loss of points for turning in school assignments late, and the loss of TV time or a favorite dessert for misbehavior. In each case, there is a *cost* for performing a particular behavior.

In behavior therapy, one way of implementing response cost is for the client to deposit items of value with the therapist (for example, favorite articles of clothing). If the client performs the deceleration target behavior, the therapist or the client disposes of one of the items.

An alternative procedure has clients write checks to their least favorite cause or charity. When clients perform the deceleration target behavior, the therapist automatically mails one of the checks. In one application of this procedure, an African-American client who was abusing amphetamines gave his therapist $50 checks made out to the Ku Klux Klan; the checks were to be mailed to the Klan if the client used the drug. The client forfeited $50 just once. At a 15-month follow-up, the client reported that

Photo 7-2 Parking fines are an all-too-familiar form of response cost.

©1997 Michael D. Spiegler and David C. Guevremont

he had not taken any amphetamines.[46] As in this case, clients usually forfeit very few valuables because the mere threat of response cost often is sufficient incentive to eliminate the maladaptive behavior.[47]

Ogden Lindsley developed a response cost procedure for reducing the number of personal items that his family left lying around the house.[48] Whoever found an item in an inappropriate place (such as a jacket on the piano bench) put it in a large box, called the Sunday Box. The owner was not permitted to retrieve the item until the following Sunday. Lindsley discovered the power of his response cost procedure the day he left his briefcase on the coffee table. He had to live without the briefcase and its contents until the beginning of the next week. You can discover for yourself how well the Sunday Box works—without necessarily repeating Lindsley's experience—by doing Participation Exercise 7-2 over the course of the next few weeks.

◆

Participation Exercise 7-2

BOXING YOUR WAY TO A NEATER ROOM[49]

If you are a member of the Messy Room Club, this Participation Exercise is for you. It is a variation of the Sunday Box technique, and it is easy to do by following six steps.

1. Make a list of the items that are frequently out of place in one room in your house. Knowing the possible fate of the items you list, you may be

reluctant to include items that you "cannot do without." However, remember that the more valuable the items, the more likely it is that the procedures will help you keep them in their proper places.

2. Next to each item on your list, write the precise location in which it belongs (for example, "books on bookshelf," "hair dryer on hook in bathroom," "socks in top dresser drawer").
3. Find a cardboard box or other suitable container large enough to hold all the items on your list.
4. Specify a particular time each day for inspecting the room. A good time is when you return home in the afternoon or evening.
5. Every day at the inspection time, place all the items on your list that are out of their designated locations in the box, and *leave them there until the predetermined retrieval time* (see step 6). An alternative procedure is to have a friend inspect the room each day and put out-of-place items in the box. (Roommates who would like your common living space to be neater may be delighted to assume this responsibility.)
6. Every fourth day, at the designated inspection time, count the number of items in the box and record this number. Then remove all the items. They are yours to keep—for at least the next 24 hours!

Follow these steps for at least 4 cycles (16 days). A declining number of items in your box in successive 4-day cycles will indicate that the response cost is working. You may even have your Messy Room Club membership revoked.

Response cost has been used extensively with children in school.[50] Its effectiveness can be equal to or greater than that achieved by using reinforcement procedures.[51] For example, in the treatment of attention deficit hyperactivity disorder, loss of token reinforcers (response cost) was more effective than access to token reinforcers in improving accuracy on an arithmetic task.[52] Therapists have taught similar procedures to parents to decrease children's misbehaviors at home.[53]

CALVIN AND HOBBES copyright 1986 Watterson. Dist. by UNIVERSAL PRESS SYNDICATE. Reprinted with permission. All rights reserved.

To treat problems with paying attention in the classroom, a battery-operated device has been developed for administering response cost combined with reinforcement.[54] A small box on the student's desk displays the cumulative points the student has earned. The student can exchange the points later for desired reinforcers. The student earns a point automatically, once per minute, as long as the student continues to pay attention to his or her work. The teacher deducts points using a handheld, remote-control device whenever the child is observed not paying attention to a task. When a point is deducted, a red light on top of the box on the student's desk comes on for 15 seconds. These procedures have significantly improved attention to schoolwork in boys with attention deficit hyperactivity disorder.[55] One reason the procedures have been effective is that they simultaneously accelerate a desirable behavior (on-task behavior) while decelerating an undesirable behavior (off-task behavior).

Response cost can be a highly effective procedure for decelerating a variety of target behaviors with children, adolescents, and adults. It even can be effective for severely aberrant behavior. For example, a 33-year-old woman with mental retardation showed an 87% reduction in self-injurious and aggressive behaviors after being treated with response cost (for example, being deprived of music for 30 seconds).[56] The effects of response cost may endure when the procedure is terminated.[57] Furthermore, most people view response cost as an acceptable deceleration therapy, which facilitates its application.[58]

Overcorrection

Overcorrection decelerates maladaptive behaviors by having clients correct the effects of their actions and then intensively practice an appropriate alternative behavior.[59] Richard Foxx and Nathan Azrin originally developed overcorrection to treat behaviors that harm and annoy others or that are destructive.[60] Overcorrection also is used for behaviors that have negative consequences primarily for the client, including self-injurious behaviors,[61] bedwetting,[62] excessive and stereotypic behaviors (such as walking in circles),[63] and persistent eating of nonnutritive substances (pica), such as dirt, paper, and buttons.[64]

Overcorrection has two phases: (1) *restitution,* in which the client makes amends for the damage done, and (2) *positive practice,* in which the client performs an appropriate adaptive behavior in an exaggerated fashion (usually repeatedly). Case 7-2 illustrates both phases of overcorrection.

REDUCING OBJECT THROWING BY OVERCORRECTION[65]

Case 7-2

A 62-year-old woman, who had been a patient in a psychiatric hospital for 43 years, engaged in a number of inappropriate and dangerous behaviors, including throwing objects from the floor at other people. Overcorrection was instituted to decelerate object throwing.

In the restitution phase, the patient was instructed by a staff member to apologize to individuals who had been hit. If the patient refused, the staff member apologized on the patient's behalf and prompted her to nod in agreement.

Positive practice consisted of 5 minutes of picking up trash on the floor and putting it into a garbage can. Initially, the patient refused to do the positive practice, so the staff member physically guided her through the clean-up activity. The physical prompting was discontinued when, after several sessions, the patient began to perform the positive practice voluntarily.

Before the overcorrection procedure was instituted, the patient threw objects at other people an average of 13 times a day. After 2 weeks of overcorrection, the frequency of the target behavior decreased to an average of less than one incident per day. The frequency remained at or below that level for 4 months, at which point observations were terminated.

Sometimes only one phase of overcorrection is employed. When restitution alone is used, it may involve an exaggerated or augmented form of making amends.[66] This procedure was used for 34 hospitalized adults with mental retardation who frequently stole from one another, especially food at mealtimes or snacktimes.[67] Before the augmented restitution was instituted, staff members had the clients return the food (or what was left of it) to its owner. This intervention was not potent enough, and the stealing continued at a high rate (see Figure 7-2). Accordingly, the staff tried overcorrection consisting of augmented restitution, a procedure called **theft reversal.** The offender not only returns stolen items but also buys similar items for the victim (additional food in this case). As Figure 7-2 shows, theft reversal dramatically reduced the number of thefts.

When the maladaptive behavior results in a consequence that cannot easily be corrected, as with behaviors that do not affect others or the environment, positive practice is used without restitution.[68] For example, children in a classroom had problems with speaking out and leaving their

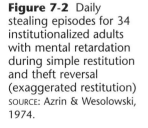

Figure 7-2 Daily stealing episodes for 34 institutionalized adults with mental retardation during simple restitution and theft reversal (exaggerated restitution) SOURCE: Azrin & Wesolowski, 1974.

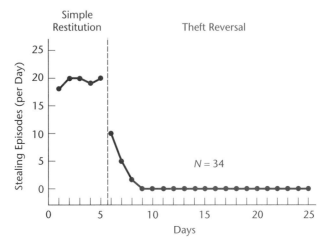

seats at inappropriate times.[69] During recess, the children were asked to practice appropriate classroom behaviors, such as raising their hands and asking permission to leave their seats. They practiced these behaviors repeatedly for 5 minutes. Compared with response cost (losing recess time), this positive practice markedly improved classroom behaviors.

Two general issues concerning the practice of overcorrection are worth noting. First, although overcorrection generally is applied immediately after the target behavior is performed,[70] it also appears to be effective when it is delayed, as in the example just described.[71] Second, increasing the duration of positive practice does not result in greater reductions in maladaptive behaviors, and sometimes very brief periods are effective. For example, positive practice lasting 30 seconds was as effective as positive practice durations of 2 and 8 minutes in reducing self-stimulatory behaviors (such as repetitive rocking) of adults with severe developmental disabilities.[72]

Overcorrection has been compared with time out from positive reinforcement in treating conflicts between siblings.[73] Overcorrection consisted of making an apology as restitution for the undesirable behavior and then positively practicing a prosocial alternative, such as giving toys to or complimenting the sibling. Positive practice was continued for a time comparable to time-out durations, which was set at 1 minute per age of the child. Time out and overcorrection were *equally* effective in reducing sibling conflicts, and the children's parents rated both as acceptable deceleration strategies.

Overcorrection can augment other deceleration strategies.[74] For instance, with a group of clients who had developmental disabilities and were deaf and blind, differential reinforcement of other behaviors alone was ineffective in reducing self-injurious behaviors and hitting others. Adding overcorrection to the differential reinforcement procedure rapidly reduced the maladaptive behaviors.[75] In contrast to other consequential decelerating therapies that only decelerate the maladaptive behaviors, overcorrection that includes positive practice has the distinct advantage of accelerating alternative adaptive behaviors.[76]

Overcorrection is more limited in its range of applications than other consequential deceleration therapies. It is appropriate primarily for behaviors that have correctable adverse effects. For such problems, overcorrection procedures have been demonstrated to be effective in decelerating a variety of maladaptive behaviors, especially when both phases are employed.[77] Moreover, overcorrection is viewed as an acceptable treatment, which minimizes resistance to using it.[78] However, not surprisingly, parents consistently rate overcorrection as less acceptable than positive reinforcement procedures for changing their children's behaviors.[79]

Overcorrection has potential uses outside therapy. When businesses are found negligent, for example, some consumer protection laws mandate that the business automatically pay the consumer several times the amount of loss or damage the consumer incurred. Community service as an alternative to fines or incarceration for convicted criminals is a form of overcorrection. Ecological problems, such as littering or wasting energy, also seem to be suitable targets for overcorrection.

◆

DESIGNING NOVEL OVERCORRECTIONS*

In this Participation Exercise, you will design procedures for novel applications of overcorrection to everyday undesirable behaviors. In the process, you may discover some useful ideas for reducing some of your own unwanted behaviors. At the very least, you will check your understanding of overcorrection.

For each of the behaviors in the list that follows, describe one or more procedures for restitution and for positive practice. Then, compare your procedures with the samples in your Student Resource Materials.

1. Littering in a park
2. Misspelling words in a paper
3. Leaving clothes in inappropriate places
4. Arriving late for classes or appointments
5. Trashing the neighbor's lawn
6. Leaving unnecessary lights on at home
7. Putting dishes in the sink without washing them

◆

Physically Aversive Consequences

Physically aversive consequences are stimuli that result in unpleasant physical sensations, including pain. Most people associate deceleration behavior therapy with physically aversive consequences, as when a parent spanks a child. In fact, behavior therapy uses physically aversive consequences infrequently.[80] A number of potential undesirable side effects as well as ethical and humanitarian objections are associated with their use, and these will be discussed later in the chapter.

Time out from positive reinforcement, response cost, and overcorrection are effective and do not use physically aversive consequences. However, these therapy procedures often take longer to work than do physically aversive consequences. Thus, when rapid deceleration of a maladaptive behavior is required, physically aversive consequences may be the treatment of choice.

Self-injurious behaviors (such as hitting or scratching oneself) are the major target behaviors treated by physically aversive consequences. These behaviors can result in serious physical harm and, in extreme cases, death. They occur most frequently with clients who have severe psychological problems, such as autistic disorder.

Ironically, mild electric shock often is an effective and efficient means of significantly reducing self-injurious behaviors.[81] The shock itself lasts only a second or two. It results in a sharp, stinging sensation that lasts for no more than a few minutes, and no permanent tissue damage occurs. (The shock used in deceleration therapies is *not* the same as that

*This Participation Exercise can be done before you continue reading or later.

used in electroconvulsive therapy [ECT]).* The use of shock may be justified by a cost-benefit analysis, as you will see in Case 7-3.

<table>
<tr><td>**Case 7-3**</td><td># ELIMINATING SELF-DESTRUCTIVE BEHAVIOR USING CONTINGENT SHOCK[82]</td></tr>
</table>

A 6-year-old girl with diffuse brain damage and no verbal communication skills frequently climbed in high places (for instance, on furniture and window sills), which posed a serious threat to her physical well-being. "Her body bore multiple scars from past falls, her front teeth were missing, having been imbedded in molding from which she had fallen while climbing outside the second story of her house."

The initial behavioral assessment revealed that her mother's attention was probably maintaining the child's climbing. Time out from positive reinforcement, extinction, and differential reinforcement of competing behaviors (such as sitting at a table) were tried to no avail. At this point, because of the seriousness of the problem, the therapist, in consultation with the child's parents, decided to use contingent electric shock.

The room in which therapy was conducted had a small table with chairs in the center and a high bookcase next to the door. Each therapy session began with the therapist and child seated at the table. Whenever the girl climbed on the bookcase, the therapist shouted, "No!" and immediately applied a 1-second shock to her calf or lower thigh. The therapist then returned to his chair. The shock was delivered by a handheld, battery-powered device resembling a long flashlight. The pain lasted only for the 1-second duration of the shock, and there were no aftereffects (such as redness, swelling, tingling, or aching).

The contingent shock rapidly reduced the girl's climbing, as can be seen in Figure 7-3. In the first session, the child climbed 9 times; in the second, 3 times; and thereafter, only twice in the next 18 sessions.

Although the girl stopped climbing in the therapy sessions, she continued to climb at home. The treatment effects were specific to the therapy room and especially to the therapist. Accordingly, the girl's mother—who had observed the therapy sessions from behind a one-way mirror—began to implement the therapy at home. When her daughter began to climb, the mother shouted, "No!" and applied the shock as the therapist had done. She then resumed whatever she had been doing without further interaction with the child.

In the 16 days before the therapy was instituted at home, the mother had observed her daughter's climbing an average of 29 times per day. Within 4 days after therapy began at home, the rate of climbing declined to an average of twice a day. After 33 days, the number of climbing inci-

---

*Electroconvulsive therapy is a medical treatment primarily used for severe depression that has not responded to psychotherapy and medication. It involves passing electricity through the brain while the patient is sedated; this leads to a convulsion, temporary unconsciousness, and amnesia for the experience. Electroconvulsive shock therapy is *not* a behavior therapy.

Figure 7-3 Rapid decline of the child's climbing when the therapist administered mild shock contingent on climbing
SOURCE: Data from Risley, 1968.

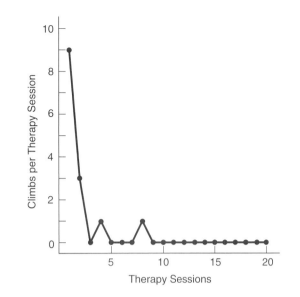

dents decreased to zero and, with one exception, did not recur in the next 15 days, at which point the therapy was terminated.

Sophisticated and precise means of monitoring self-injurious behaviors and administering electric shock have been developed. The Self-Injurious Behavior Inhibiting System (SIBIS; pronounced SEYE-biss), for example, is a lightweight device that a client wears on the part of the body that is subject to injury (see Photo 7-3).[83] The device measures the impact of the blow and automatically delivers a mild electric shock whenever the force of the impact exceeds a preprogrammed level (which is based on the

Photo 7-3 A child with autistic disorder wearing the Self-Injurious Behavior Inhibiting System (SIBIS).

The Johns Hopkins University Applied Physics Laboratory

intensity of the impact that will cause physical damage). The strength of the shock is like that of a rubber band snapped on the arm. The SIBIS can detect self-injurious behaviors and administer contingent electric shock more precisely and consistently than a therapist can. Moreover, the client does not develop negative associations with the person who directly administers the shock.

A small number of studies have evaluated the effectiveness of the SIBIS. Although it can result in rapid and dramatic decreases in self-injurious behaviors,[84] its effectiveness varies considerably with individual clients.[85]

Electric shock is a good aversive stimulus for four reasons. First, it is easily administered. Second, it can be activated instantaneously (at the press of a switch). Third, its intensity can be controlled precisely. Ease and precision of administration are important because physically aversive consequences are most potent when delivered immediately after the client performs the target behavior. Fourth, most clients experience electric shock as aversive.

Many people, including some behavior therapists, consider electric shock an unacceptable treatment (for example, because they think it too harsh).[86] A number of less innocuous physically aversive stimuli have been employed to treat a variety of problem behaviors, and some of these are listed in Table 7-1.

POTENTIAL NEGATIVE SIDE EFFECTS OF PHYSICALLY
AVERSIVE CONSEQUENCES

Negative side effects of physically aversive consequences actually are uncommon. In general, they occur less often when deceleration procedures are combined with procedures that accelerate alternative adaptive behaviors than when deceleration procedures are used alone.[87] Also, the milder the aversive consequences are, the fewer are the undesirable side effects observed.[88] Most negative side effects fall into three categories: avoidance behaviors, emotional responses, and perpetuation effects.

Avoidance Behaviors Deceleration therapy may lead clients to develop negative associations toward the therapy situation—including the thera-

Table 7-1 Examples of "more acceptable" physically aversive consequences

Aversive Consequence	Problem Behavior
Rubber band snapped on wrist	Trichotillomania (pulling out hair)
Noxious odor	Self-stimulating behaviors
Cigarette smoke	Compulsive eating
Lemon juice	Head banging
Bitter substance	Nail biting
Mild mouthwash	Biting other children
Water mist sprayed in face	Face slapping
Loud noise	Bruxism (teeth grinding)
Bright light	Dangerous nocturnal rocking

pist and anyone else administering the treatment (such as parents and teachers)—and subsequently to avoid it.[89] Children may run away from the therapist who administers the treatment; adults may fail to show up for therapy sessions.

Avoidance behaviors can be minimized by having more than one person administer the therapy (for example, both parents) and by varying the setting in which the treatment takes place. The people administering the undesirable consequences also should provide positive consequences for alternative behaviors (so that these individuals are not seen solely as "bearers of bad news"). This is especially important when these people have ongoing relationships with the client (as with parents).

Emotional Responses Clients treated with physically aversive consequences sometimes exhibit disruptive emotional responses, such as crying, tantrums, soiling and wetting their clothes, and fear.[90] Occasionally, clients become physically aggressive toward the therapist or others carrying out the procedures[91] and toward themselves.[92] Besides creating additional psychological problems for clients, these emotional responses interfere with the therapy process by making the procedure more difficult to use. They also may add to clients' negative associations to the therapy situation.

Perpetuation Effects Despite their legitimate application in behavior therapy, using physically aversive consequences is never a preferred strategy and is used infrequently. Thus, it is regrettable that one possible side effect of physically aversive consequences is that clients may learn this strategy as a means of controlling other people's behaviors. One revealing finding is that children whose parents use physically aversive consequences are more likely to behave aggressively.[93]

A related side effect is that the use of physically aversive consequences may be reinforced in the change agent, especially in nonprofessionals such as parents.[94] Physically aversive consequences often lead to a rapid reduction of the deceleration target behavior. Thus, their use is negatively reinforced by the relief the change agent experiences when the client stops performing the target behavior. The result is that nonprofessionals may be more likely to use physically aversive consequences in the future when a professional is no longer supervising their behavior change efforts.

Guidelines for the Effective Use of Consequential Deceleration Therapy

Behavior therapists have developed guidelines for administering consequential deceleration therapy. The following are seven important guidelines.

1. *The consequence (removal of reinforcers or introduction of undesirable consequences) should occur immediately after the target behavior.* The closer in time the consequence is to the target behavior, the greater is its effectiveness because the client is more likely to associate the consequence with the target behavior.

◆ **In Theory 7-1**

PUNISHMENT: WHAT'S IN A NAME?

You may have noticed the conspicuous absence of the word *punishment* when you were reading about physically aversive consequences and perhaps even before. Technically, **punishment** occurs whenever a consequence of a behavior results in that behaviors being performed less frequently in the future. (This empirical definition directly parallels the empirical definition of reinforcement.) Not surprisingly, then, using physically aversive consequences is a form of punishment. However, you may not have realized that *all* consequential deceleration therapies are types of punishment. We deliberately have avoided using the term *punishment* so as not to prejudice you against these therapies.

Most people think that punishment is synonymous with physically aversive consequences. Humanitarian objections to inflicting physical discomfort or pain have merit, and the use of physically aversive consequences, even when justified, has a bad public reputation. Because the term *punishment* is primarily associated with physically aversive consequences, all punishment procedures become guilty by association.

What we call something strongly affects how we view it and our attitude toward it. Shakespeare's Juliet was wrong when she said that "a rose by any other name would smell as sweet." Similarly, punishment by any other name would not smell as sour. *Response cost,* for example, clearly does not have the same negative connotation as *punishment.* Because this book is an introduction to behavior therapy, we did not want to bias you before you had learned about how consequential deceleration therapies operate, their role in behavior therapy, and how effective they can be. We wanted you to draw your own conclusions about their merits. Although we have chosen not to use the term *punishment,* you will encounter it in the behavior therapy literature as the generic name for consequential deceleration therapies.

---

2. *The consequence should be administered each time the target behavior occurs.* Greater suppression results from the continuous (that is, for each occurrence) and consistent (that is, by all change agents involved) administration of the consequence, especially at the beginning of treatment.

3. *The client should be made aware of the target behavior for which the consequence will be administered.* The client should be told and reminded about the contingency between the target behavior and the consequence (for example, reminding a student, "When you turn in an assignment late, you will lose one letter grade").

4. *Reinforcement should not closely follow the delivery of the consequence.* The consequence should not be a signal to the client that a reinforcer is forthcoming (for example, comforting a child who is crying after a reprimand for a misbehavior). This may lead to an *increase* in the deceleration target behavior.

5. *The consequence should be preceded by a warning cue.* After the cue (for example, "No!") becomes associated with the negative consequence, the cue alone may serve to decelerate the target behavior.

6. *An adaptive behavior that competes with the undesirable target behavior should be reinforced in conjunction with decelerating the maladaptive behavior.* Engaging in a competing adaptive behavior decreases the opportunities to engage in the maladaptive target behavior.

7. *If physically aversive consequences are employed, their potential negative side effects should be kept in mind and minimized if they occur.*

AVERSION THERAPY

When physically aversive consequences are used, an unpleasant event is administered immediately *after* the client performs the maladaptive behavior. In contrast, in *aversion therapy* an aversive stimulus is introduced *while* the client is engaging in the maladaptive behavior. The aversive stimulus is terminated as soon as the client stops performing the behavior. The objective is for the client to *associate* performing the maladaptive behavior with the aversive stimulus so that performing the behavior becomes aversive.

The same kind of association between a behavior and an aversive stimulus sometimes inadvertently occurs in everyday circumstances. A person may get airsick when a plane encounters turbulence. Subsequently, the individual may avoid traveling by plane, which is associated with getting sick.

Aversion therapy primarily has been used to treat two classes of maladaptive behaviors: substance abuse and *paraphilias,* which are sexually deviant behaviors (such as exhibitionism and pedophilia).

Basic Procedures

Maladaptive behaviors can be paired with any stimulus that the client finds aversive (unpleasant, distasteful, or painful). Shock and nausea-producing drugs are the most frequently used physically aversive stimuli, and occasionally noxious odors, and hot air and smoke (to decelerate cigarette smoking) are employed. The shock in aversion therapy is the same as that used in consequential deceleration therapy and shares the same advantages described earlier (page 160). Psychologically aversive stimuli include feelings of humiliation and unpleasant thoughts.

The aversive stimulus used may depend on the target behavior. For example, nausea generally is more effective than shock in treating alcohol abuse.[95] The client determines the strength of the stimulus. For the therapy to be effective, the client must honestly tell the therapist the intensity at which the stimulus becomes aversive. Clients for whom aversion therapy is successful must be willing to experience a truly aversive stimulus, which generally means that the clients are highly motivated to change their maladaptive behavior.

The aversive stimulus is associated with the target behavior in one of three ways. Ideally, the association is created as the client is (1) *actually engaging in the target behavior.* Because this is not always possible or efficient, the client can be (2) *symbolically exposed to the target behavior,* as by viewing pictures of the target behavior or listening to a verbal description of it, or by (3) *imagining performing the target behavior.* The first method is illustrated in Case 7-4.

Case 7-4 ELIMINATING CHRONIC RUMINATIVE VOMITING BY AVERSION THERAPY[96]

Nine-month-old Mark was hospitalized for malnutrition and weight loss caused by *ruminative vomiting,* a potentially fatal condition characterized by regurgitating, chewing, and reswallowing food. Mark had begun vomiting after meals when he was 6 months old, and medical and psychological treatments over the next 3½ months were unsuccessful. The critical nature of Mark's condition warranted the use of aversion therapy. Figure 7-4 shows Mark's weight during a 3-week baseline period.

Mild shocks were administered for ½-second intervals as Mark vomited and were terminated as soon as he stopped vomiting. The electrodes were strapped lightly to his calf, and the shock was activated by a remote switch. This arrangement made it possible for Mark to move about freely.

The therapy was initially conducted in Mark's hospital room with Mark in various locations (for example, in his bed, in a highchair, and playing on the floor) and with several observers present. Sometimes Mark was left alone and observed via closed circuit TV. To facilitate transfer, the therapy procedures were introduced while Mark and his mother were alone under circumstances approximating those in their home.

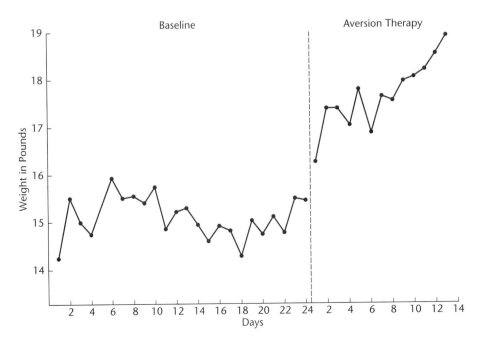

Figure 7-4 Mark's weight during baseline and aversion therapy
SOURCE: Adapted from Cunningham & Lindscheid, 1976.

After 2 weeks of aversion therapy, Mark's ruminative vomiting had ceased completely. He had gained almost 3 pounds (see Figure 7-4), and other behaviors had improved, including his crying less frequently and starting to babble again. At a 6-month follow-up assessment, ruminative vomiting had not recurred, Mark continued to gain weight, and his parents reported no further problems.

One limitation of aversion therapy (as well as many other therapies) is that the treatment effects may remain specific to the therapy situation—in other words, they may not transfer to other situations. One way to foster transfer is to conduct the therapy in various settings, especially those where the client is likely to be after treatment. Such transfer procedures were part of Mark's therapy and may have been one of the factors contributing to its success.

Whereas Mark's behavior was self-injurious, Case 7-5 provides an example of an adult who wanted to change a sexual habit that was harmless to him and others. The case illustrates how clients can be exposed symbolically to the target behavior and the use of drug-induced nausea as the aversive stimulus.

Case 7-5 ## TREATMENT OF TRANSVESTIC (CROSS-DRESSING) BEHAVIORS BY AVERSION THERAPY[97]

A 22-year-old married truck driver reported that he had experienced the desire to dress as a woman since he was 8 years old. From the age of 15 and through his military service and marriage, he had derived erotic pleasure from dressing in female clothes and viewing himself in the mirror. At the same time, he maintained a good sexual relationship with his wife. He was strongly motivated to seek therapy because of his fear of being detected wearing women's clothes and because of the urging of his wife, who had just recently learned of her husband's cross-dressing.

The therapist prepared slides of the client in various stages of female dress and had the client prepare an audio tape that described these activities. The client was then exposed to the slides and tape to confirm that they induced sexual excitement.

The treatment involved pairing the transvestic experience with nausea, produced by injection of the drug apomorphine. As soon as the injection began to take effect, the slides and tape were presented, and they were terminated only after the client began to vomit. The treatment was administered several times a day for 6 days, which was sufficient to completely eliminate the client's desire to dress in female attire. Follow-up over a 6-month period, including interviews with both the client and his wife, indicated that the client no longer cross-dressed.

One limitation of aversion therapy is that its effects may not be durable because the association between the maladaptive behavior and the aversive stimulus may not last. To deal with this problem, clients are asked to return periodically (such as every couple of months) for additional therapy sessions called **booster treatments.**[98] Re-exposing the client to the target behavior and the aversive stimulus keeps that association "active." For example, booster treatments for alcohol abuse significantly increase the chances of continued abstinence.[99] Also, as with consequential deceleration therapy, it is essential for clients to adopt new, adaptive behaviors that substitute for the maladaptive behavior that has been decelerated. For instance, if the client in Case 7-5 continued to abstain from cross-dressing, it is likely that he was obtaining the erotic pleasure he derived from cross-dressing in another way, such as in his sexual relations with his wife.

Covert Sensitization

In **covert sensitization,** the therapist verbally describes both the client's engaging in the deceleration target behavior and the concomitant aversive stimulus, usually nausea. The following description was used with a college professor who wanted to stop smoking.

> You are preparing your lectures. . . . As soon as you start reaching for the cigarette, you get a nauseated feeling in your stomach . . . like you are about to vomit. You touch the pack of cigarettes and bitter spit comes into your mouth; when you take the cigarette out of the pack some pieces of food come into your throat. Now you feel sick and your stomach cramps. As you are about to put the cigarette in your mouth, you puke. . . . The cigarette in your hand is very soggy and full of green vomit. There is a stink coming from the vomit. Snot is coming from your nose. Your hands feel all slimy and full of vomit. . . . Your clothes are all full of puke. You get up from your desk and turn away from the . . . cigarettes. You immediately begin to feel better being away from the . . . cigarettes.[100]

Covert sensitization has four advantages over other aversion therapies: (1) no equipment, such as a shock apparatus, is needed; (2) unlike some drug-induced aversion, covert sensitization can be safely carried out without medical supervision; (3) with an aversive *image,* clients can self-administer covert sensitization in vivo; and (4) clients may consider it more acceptable, which is an important consideration because of the high dropout rate with aversion therapy.[101]

Developed by Joseph Cautela,[102] covert sensitization most frequently has been used to treat paraphilias,[103] overeating,[104] alcohol abuse,[105] and smoking,[106] and it is used almost exclusively with adults.[107] Support for the efficacy of covert sensitization is tenuous; most of the research has been case studies,[108] and some of the few controlled studies have yielded equivocal findings.[109]

ETHICAL ISSUES IN THE USE OF AVERSIVE THERAPIES

Physically aversive consequences and aversion therapy are the behavior therapies that have come under closest scrutiny regarding ethical concerns. Because these treatments involve physical discomfort or pain, they have the *potential* of infringing on clients' fundamental human rights. Some people believe that aversive treatments should not be used at all, especially not with clients who are vulnerable to abuse and unable to make informed decisions about their own treatment, such as clients institutionalized for schizophrenia and mental retardation.[110]

In considering the ethicality of aversive procedures, keep two points in mind. First, the aversive stimulus is relatively brief and has no long-term ill effects. For example, when shock is used, it is administered for only a second or two. The sharp, stinging sensation that the client experiences lasts no more than a few minutes, and no permanent tissue damage results. Second, there is nothing inherently unethical about treatment involving discomfort or pain. After all, we do not think it is unethical to have our teeth drilled or to receive an injection to prevent or cure a disease, not to mention the extreme discomfort of chemotherapy. Because the benefits of these treatments outweigh their unpleasantness, we do not consider them unethical.

The potential for harm by aversive procedures has been exaggerated due to widely held misconceptions about the extent and nature of aversive procedures used in behavior therapy. After briefly examining these misconceptions, we will discuss the ethical issues relevant to the actual use of aversive procedures in behavior therapy.

Misconceptions About Aversive Procedures in Behavior Therapy

There is a widespread misconception that aversive procedures are used extensively in behavior therapy. Indeed, some people even think of aversive procedures as synonymous with behavior therapy. In fact, aversive procedures constitute a small proportion of behavior therapy techniques, and they are employed infrequently.[111] One reason for their limited use is that aversive procedures generally are relatively weak treatments, especially for producing lasting change.

Exaggerated and inaccurate popular depictions of techniques that only remotely resemble behavior therapy procedures have spurred the myth that aversive behavior therapy procedures are powerful and evil forces. A prime example is *A Clockwork Orange,* a popular book[112] that was made into a movie. A young man named Alex has committed a series of sadistic and brutal attacks on innocent people. He is taken to a prison hospital for treatment. Strapped to a chair with his eyelids pinned open, Alex is forced to watch films depicting violence while experiencing drug-induced nausea and panic. The hospital staff ignore Alex's pleas to terminate the treatment. Supposedly, after a few such treatments, even the thought of violence makes him extremely anxious, and Alex is considered cured of his antisocial behaviors.

To begin with, Alex's so-called treatment is *not* an example of behavior therapy because aversion therapy never involves restraining clients and subjecting them to treatment against their will. Furthermore, the story is grossly inaccurate regarding the potential of aversive conditioning.[113] In fact, it is extremely difficult, and often impossible, to change a person's behavior when the individual does not want to change.[114] Thus, the procedures depicted in *A Clockwork Orange* are science fiction, not science.

Principle of Utility

Aversive techniques usually are instituted as a last resort, when other therapy procedures have failed to decelerate serious debilitating behaviors. In each case, a cost-benefit analysis is made. Does the potential outcome of therapy—the reduction of a serious, maladaptive behavior—outweigh the potential negative effects of the aversive procedure, such as temporary discomfort? This question follows from the ethical *principle of utility,* which holds that an action is morally right if, when compared with alternative actions, it produces more benefit than harm.[115]

The excerpt that follows addresses the question, "Do the ends justify the means?" with respect to using physically aversive consequences to reduce self-destructive behaviors.[116] As you read it, consider the ethical issues it raises.

> A colleague . . . showed us a deeply moving film. The heroine was an institutionalized primary-grade girl. She . . . [frequently engaged in head banging], so a padded football helmet was put on her head. Because she could take it off, her hands were tied down in her crib. She kept tossing her neck and tore out her hair at every opportunity. She accordingly had a perpetually bruised face on a hairless head, with a neck almost as thick as that of a horse. She was nonverbal.
>
> My colleague and his staff carefully planned a program for her, using all kinds of reinforcers . . . but [she] persisted in her typical behavior. In desperation, the ultimate weapon was unwrapped. When she tossed her head, my colleague yelled "Don't!" simultaneously delivering a sharp slap to her cheek. She subsided for a brief period, tossed again, and the punishment was delivered. My colleague reports that less than a dozen slaps were ever delivered and the word "Don't!" yelled even from across the room was effective. Its use was shortly down to once a week and was discontinued in a few weeks. In the meantime, the football helmet was removed and the girl began to eat at the table. She slept in a regular bed. Her hair grew out, and she turned out to be a very pretty little blonde girl with delicate features and a delicate neck. In less than a year, she started to move toward joining a group of older girls whose behavior, it was hoped, she would [imitate]. She smiled often.
>
> [When the girl's] . . . parents discovered that she had been slapped . . ., they immediately withdrew her from the custody of my colleague's staff. The last part of the film shows her back at the institution. She is strapped down in her crib. Her hands are tied to a side. She is wearing a football helmet. [Once again] her hair is torn out, her face is a mass of bruises and her neck is almost as thick as that of a horse.[117]

There is no doubt that the therapist violated ethical guidelines by not completely informing the girl's parents about the treatment procedures.

When this case occurred 30 years ago, behavior therapists were not as sensitized as they are today to the importance of fully disclosing treatment procedures and obtaining consent for their use.

The case also raises another critical ethical question. Given the self-destructive nature of the girl's behaviors, was the treatment ethically justified? Looking at the case from a different perspective, was it ethical to stop the treatment? Was the principle of utility violated? How would you answer these questions?

Finally, consider a more recent case of a 31-year-old man with a severe developmental disability who engaged in life-threatening voluntary vomiting.[118] Because alternative nonaversive treatments could not be found, two behavior therapists recommended that short-term contingent shock be used. After a court ruled against this recommendation, the man was subjected to an intrusive medical procedure (permanent nasogastric intubation) and a severely restricted environment for the next year. How would you evaluate the ethicality of the court's conservative decision made in this case? Was the principle of utility violated?

The principle of utility also may be applicable when clients voluntarily seek treatment for psychological problems that seriously interfere with their living normal lives. In the treatment of paraphilias and substance abuse, aversion therapy can be an important component of a treatment package that includes procedures to accelerate alternative, socially desirable and adaptive behaviors. The brief discomfort experienced in aversion therapy is minimal compared with the extensive disruption of work and family life, the social ostracism, and the self-depreciation that result from long-standing socially unacceptable and personally maladaptive behaviors.[119]

Misuse, Abuse, and Safeguards

Aversive procedures occasionally are misused and abused. Misuse is usually perpetrated by nonprofessional change agents who have had minimal training and experience with the procedures. For example, aversive consequences often need be applied only briefly to be effective.[120] Inexperienced change agents, including some behavior therapists, may continue the aversive consequences long after they have had their desired effect. This practice not only is unlikely to produce a further decrease in the target behavior but is also likely to produce negative side effects, such as aggressive behaviors. Moreover, such treatment justifiably would be considered harsh.

Abuses of aversive techniques are more likely to arise when the deceleration target behavior is disturbing to others, as with a patient on a psychiatric ward who disrupts the ongoing activities with inappropriate outbursts. Overburdened hospital staff may apply aversive procedures because they are, in the short run, more efficient. Generally, it is easier to devise an aversive consequence to stop disturbing behaviors immediately than to identify and then to gradually accelerate alternative, competing prosocial behaviors. However, the client's best interests must take precedence over other people's interests.

A variety of guidelines have been proposed to promote the ethical use of aversive procedures, including the following.

1. Aversive procedures should be considered only after it is clear that alternatives are not possible or would be ineffective or inefficient.[121]

2. When possible, deceleration therapies that are not *physically* aversive (such as response cost and time out from positive reinforcement) should be tried before physically aversive procedures are employed.

3. If a physically aversive procedure is used, a physician should be consulted to be sure that it will be medically safe for the client.

4. The client or the client's legal guardian must be aware of the nature of the treatment and agree to it—what is known as *informed consent.*

5. The procedures should be implemented only by a competent professional.

6. Aversive techniques should be used along with procedures that simultaneously accelerate alternative behaviors to take the place of the behaviors being eliminated.

7. Clear-cut measures of the target behavior should be collected before, during, and after therapy to document its effectiveness (or ineffectiveness).

Such guidelines for the *ethical* use of aversive procedures supplement the guidelines for the *effective* use of consequential deceleration therapy in general presented earlier in the chapter (page 161). Another way to safeguard clients from potentially harmful therapies is to have special committees monitor their use.[122] These committees should consist of both professionals and concerned laypersons who are competent to evaluate treatment ethicality.[123] Finally, institutionalized clients would benefit from an independent advocate who was available to hear clients' complaints and ensure that they received proper consideration.[124]

Ethical problems are far less likely to arise when clients freely volunteer to receive aversive procedures, as did the man who wished to stop cross-dressing, in Case 7-5. Few people would consider it unethical for consenting adults to subject themselves to a series of mild shocks to eliminate their abuse of alcohol or cigarettes. In contrast, ethical issues regarding aversive procedures are prominent in the treatment of clients who are *required* to be in therapy, such as adults committed to institutions.

◆ ALL THINGS CONSIDERED: DECELERATION BEHAVIOR THERAPY

Deceleration behavior therapy is an important part of the behavior therapist's armamentarium. It can be effective and efficient in treating maladaptive behaviors. In general, success rates for consequential deceleration therapy have been higher than for aversion therapy. This difference is due, at least in part, to the fact that the primary targets of aversion therapy—substance abuse and paraphilias—are highly resistant to treatment of any kind.[125]

It is obvious that therapies that accelerate adaptive behaviors enhance clients' personal freedom by increasing the number of alternative behaviors they can choose to engage in. Therapies that decelerate undesirable behaviors also serve this function. A woman whose excessive drinking has been alleviated by aversion therapy is freer because now she has many more options in her life. She can engage in activities once impaired by intoxication, including holding a job and interacting with family and friends. With either acceleration or deceleration behavior therapy procedures, *after successful treatment the client has more options for behaving than before treatment.*

With both consequential deceleration therapy and aversion therapy, the reduction of the target behavior may be only temporary, which can be a major limitation of these treatments.[126] However, in some cases, as with self-injurious and highly disruptive behaviors, even temporary suppression of the target behavior is desirable, especially when no other treatments have been effective. Moreover, temporary suppression provides the opportunity to reinforce alternative adaptive behaviors, which is the optimal strategy for creating durable change.

Besides the ethical issues discussed earlier regarding deceleration behavior therapy, two other concerns militate against its application: undesirable side effects and practical problems. The potential undesirable side effects of physically aversive consequences we discussed earlier (pages 160–161) are relevant to aversion therapy as well. However, to put this concern in perspective, the undesirable side effects are not inevitable. In fact, they are the exception rather than the rule; when they do occur, they are usually temporary, declining over the course of therapy.[127] Nonetheless, behavior therapists must be alert to their occurrence.

Practical problems also are associated with deceleration therapy procedures. These approaches are less acceptable to both clients and therapists than other behavior therapies. Clients generally do not want to subject themselves to discomfort or pain, or even to the loss of reinforcers. And, some therapists find it distasteful to administer aversive stimuli.

A related problem concerns the client's motivation to change. High motivation is necessary to enter and remain in treatment that has distinctly negative aspects. Clients who are not highly motivated to change are less likely to cooperate with the therapy procedures and more likely to drop out of therapy altogether.[128]

In sum, deceleration behavior therapy procedures can be effective means of treating maladaptive behaviors, especially when time is crucial. Otherwise, deceleration therapy should be used after more acceptable therapies have been tried and have not been effective. Finally, deceleration therapy techniques always should be part of a treatment package that includes procedures for accelerating alternative adaptive behaviors.

Summary

1. The preferred strategy for decelerating an undesirable behavior is to reinforce an acceleration target behavior that is an alternative to the deceleration target behavior. This differential reinforcement can be of incompatible behaviors, of competing behaviors, of any other behaviors, and of low response rates of the target behavior. Two variants of differential reinforcement are noncontingent reinforcement and functional communication training.

2. The two strategies that decrease maladaptive behaviors directly are consequential deceleration therapy, which changes the consequences of maladaptive behaviors, and aversion therapy, which associates unpleasant events with maladaptive behaviors.

3. Extinction and time out from positive reinforcement remove the reinforcers maintaining the deceleration target behavior. Extinction does this by permanently removing or withholding the reinforcers that maintain the behavior.

4. Time out from positive reinforcement involves immediately and temporarily removing the client's access to generalized reinforcers. Time out always is brief and often is implemented in a special area, such as a time-out room.

5. Response cost, overcorrection, and physically aversive consequences introduce undesirable consequences to decelerate maladaptive behaviors. Response cost involves removing a valued item or privilege when a maladaptive behavior is performed.

6. Overcorrection decelerates maladaptive behaviors by having clients correct the effects of their actions (restitution) and then intensively practice an appropriate alternative behavior (positive practice).

7. Physically aversive consequences can decelerate undesirable behaviors rapidly. Painful but harmless shock frequently serves as the aversive consequence. Physically aversive consequences are used rarely in behavior therapy because they have potential negative side effects—avoidance behaviors, emotional responses, and perpetuation effects—and because of ethical and humanitarian objections.

8. Technically, punishment refers to any procedure that decelerates a behavior by changing its consequences. All consequential deceleration therapies are examples of punishment.

9. In aversion therapy, an unpleasant or painful stimulus is introduced while the client is engaging in the maladaptive behavior. The client comes to associate the target behavior with the unpleasant stimulus (most often shock or nausea). The association is created in one of three ways: as the client is actually engaging in the target behavior, is symbolically exposed to the behavior, or is imagining performing the behavior. Aversion therapy is used primarily to treat substance abuse and paraphilias. Because the effects of aversion therapy may be temporary, booster treatments may be required to increase its durability.

10. In covert sensitization, the client imagines both the target behavior and the aversive stimulus, which is usually nausea created by the therapist's vivid descriptions of disgusting events.

11. Aversive procedures have come under the closest scrutiny regarding ethical violations. In fact, aversive procedures constitute a small proportion of behavior therapy techniques and are used infrequently. When aversive procedures are used, a cost-benefit analysis is performed for each case.

12. Misuses and abuses of aversive procedures most often are perpetrated by change agents who have limited experience with the pro-

cedures and who employ them because they are easier to implement than alternative therapy approaches.

13. Success rates have been higher for consequential deceleration therapy than for aversion therapy. Deceleration therapies, like acceleration therapies, increase clients' freedom by expanding their options for behaving. A major limitation of deceleration therapies is that their effectiveness may be only temporary, which is one reason for simultaneously accelerating alternative adaptive behaviors. Three issues that militate against the use of deceleration behavior therapy are ethical and humanitarian objections, undesirable side effects, and practical problems. Clients' being highly motivated to change is especially important with deceleration behavior therapies.

REFERENCE NOTES

1. For example, Nunes, Murphy, & Ruprecht, 1977.
2. Larson & Ayllon, 1990.
3. For example, Ayllon, Layman, & Kandel, 1975; Deitz, Repp, & Deitz, 1976; Shafto & Sulzbacher, 1977.
4. Hegel & Ferguson, 2000; Luiselli & Greenridge, 1982.
5. For example, Conrin, Pennypacker, Johnston, & Rast, 1982; Lindberg, Iwata, Kahng, & DeLeon, 1999; Thompson, Iwata, Conners, & Roscoe, 1999; Vollmer, Iwata, Zarcone, Smith, & Mazaleski, 1993; Volmer, Roane, Ringdahl, & Marcus, 1999.
6. Goetz, Holmberg, & LeBlanc, 1975.
7. Leitenberg, Burchard, Burchard, Fuller, & Lysaght, 1977; Wagaman, Miltenberger, & Williams, 1995.
8. Heard & Watson, 1999.
9. For example, Deitz, 1977; Lennox, Miltenberger, & Donnelly, 1987; Poling & Ryan, 1982; Singh, Dawson, & Manning, 1981.
10. Deitz & Repp, 1973.
11. Deitz, 1977.
12. Tucker, Sigafoos, & Bushell, 1998.
13. Hagopian, Crockett, van Stone, DeLeon, & Bowman, 2000.
14. Lallo, Casey, & Kates, 1997; Tucker, Sigafoos, & Bushell, 1998.
15. Carr & Durand, 1985; Duran, 1999; Worsdell, Iwata, Hanley, Thompson, & Kahng, 2000.
16. Carr, Levin, McConnachie, Carlson, Kemp, & Smith, 1994; Kahng, Hendrickson, & Vu, 2000.
17. Brown, Wacker, Derby, Peck, Richman, Sasso, Knutson, & Harding, 2000; Kahng, Hendrickson, & Vu, 2000; Shirley, Iwata, Kahng, Mazaleski, & Lerman, 1997.
18. Derby, Wacker, Berg, DeRaad, Ulrich, Asmus, Harding, Prouty, Laffey, & Stoner, 1997.
19. Williams, 1959.
20. For example, Ducharme & Van Houten, 1994; Magee & Ellis, 2000.
21. For example, Coe, Babbitt, Williams, Hajimihalis, Snyder, Ballard, & Efron, 1997; Mazaleski, Iwata, Vollmer, Zarcone, & Smith, 1993.
22. For example, Allen, Turner, & Everett, 1970; Lerman & Iwata, 1996; Neisworth & Moore, 1972.
23. Cooper, Heron, & Heward, 1987; Lerman & Iwata, 1996.
24. For example, LaVigna & Donnellan, 1986; Lerman, Iwata, & Wallace, 1999.
25. Lerman, Iwata, & Wallace, 1999.
26. Ducharme & Van Houten, 1994; Kazdin, 1994; Lerman & Iwata, 1995.
27. Ducharme & Van Houten, 1994.
28. For example, Lawton, France, & Blampied, 1991.
29. Ducharme & Van Houten, 1994.
30. For example, Bloxham, Long, Alderman, & Hollin, 1993.
31. Kazdin, 1994.
32. Costenbader & Reading-Brown, 1995; Twyman, Johnson, Buie, & Nelson, 1994.
33. Barton, Guess, Garcia, & Baer, 1970.
34. Barkley, 1987.
35. For example, White, Nielson, & Johnson, 1972.
36. Compare with Williams & Williams, 1995.
37. For example, Tate & Baroff, 1966.
38. Barton, Guess, Garcia, & Baer, 1970.
39. For example, Kendall, Nay, & Jeffers, 1975.
40. Cayner & Kiland, 1974.

41. For example, Bigelow, Liebson, & Griffiths, 1974; Griffiths, Bigelow, & Liebson, 1974.
42. For example, Forehand & McMahon, 1981; Rortvedt & Miltenberger, 1994.
43. Marlow, Tingstrom, Olmi, & Edwards, 1997.
44. For example, McNeil, Clemens-Mowrer, Gurwitch, & Funderburk, 1994.
45. Kazdin, 1972.
46. Boudin, 1972.
47. For example, Mann, 1972, 1976.
48. Lindsley, 1966.
49. Spiegler, 1989, 2000.
50. For example, McCain & Kelley, 1994; Reynolds & Kelley, 1997.
51. For example, Sullivan & O'Leary, 1990.
52. Carlson, Mann, & Alexander, 2000; Carlson & Tamm, 2000.
53. Barkley, 1987.
54. Polaha & Allen, 2000.
55. DuPaul, Guevremont, & Barkley, 1992; Evans, Ferre, Ford, & Green, 1995.
56. Keeney, Fisher, Adelinis, & Wilder, 2000.
57. Armstrong & Drabman, 1998; Sullivan & O'Leary, 1990.
58. Blampied & Kahan, 1992; Jones, Eyberg, Adams, & Boggs, 1998; Reynolds & Kelley, 1997.
59. MacKenzie-Keating & McDonald, 1990.
60. Foxx & Azrin, 1972.
61. For example, Harris & Romanczyk, 1976.
62. Azrin, Sneed, & Foxx, 1973.
63. Rojahn, Hammer, & Kroeger, 1997; Rollings, Baumeister, & Baumeister, 1977.
64. Ellis, Singh, Crews, Bonaventura, Gehin, & Ricketts, 1997.
65. Foxx & Azrin, 1972.
66. Tremblay & Drabman, 1997.
67. Azrin & Wesolowski, 1974.
68. Azrin & Besalel, 1999.
69. Azrin & Powers, 1975.
70. Axelrod, Brantner, & Meddock, 1978; Ollendick & Matson, 1978.
71. Azrin & Powers, 1975.
72. Cole, Montgomery, Wilson, & Milan, 2000.
73. Adams & Kelley, 1992.
74. For example, Testal, Francisco, Ortiz, Angel, Santos, & Dolores, 1998.
75. Sisson, Van Hasselt, & Hersen, 1993.
76. Carey & Bucher, 1981, 1986.
77. Axelrod, Brantner, & Meddock, 1978; Ollendick & Matson, 1978.
78. Jones, Eyberg, Adams, & Boggs, 1998.
79. Jones, Eyberg, Adams, Boggs, 1998; Miller, Manne, & Palevsky, 1998.
80. Guevremont & Spiegler, 1990; Spiegler & Guevremont, 1994, 2002.
81. For example, Bucher & Lovaas, 1968; Prochaska, Smith, Marzilli, Colby, & Donovan, 1974.
82. Risley, 1968; quotation from p. 22.
83. Linscheid, Iwata, Ricketts, Williams, & Griffin, 1990.
84. Linscheid, Iwata, Ricketts, Williams, & Griffin, 1990.
85. Linscheid, Hartel, & Cooley, 1993; Williams, Kirkpatrick-Sanchez, & Crocker, 1994.
86. Kazdin, 1980.
87. For example, Carey & Bucher, 1986.
88. Kazdin, 1989.
89. For example, Azrin & Holz, 1966.
90. For example, Azrin & Wesolowski, 1975; Carey & Bucher, 1981.
91. For example, Foxx & Azrin, 1972; Knight & McKenzie, 1974; Mayhew & Harris, 1978.
92. For example, Azrin, Gottlieb, Hughart, Wesolowski, & Rahn, 1975; Rollings, Baumeister, & Baumeister, 1977.
93. Kazdin, 1987; Timberlake, 1981.
94. Kazdin, 1989.
95. Nathan, 1976.
96. Cunningham & Linscheid, 1976.
97. Lavin, Thorpe, Barker, Blakemore, & Conway, 1961.
98. Rachman & Teasdale, 1969.
99. Voegtlin, Lemere, Broz, & O'Hollaren, 1941.
100. Cautela, 1972, pp. 88-89.
101. For example, Callahan & Leitenberg, 1973; Wilson & Tracey, 1976.
102. Cautela, 1966, 1967.
103. For example, Barlow, 1993; Dougher, 1993; Krop & Burgess, 1993a; Maletzky, 1993.
104. For example, Cautela, 1966; Janda & Rimm, 1972; Stuart, 1967.
105. For example, Anant, 1968; Ashem & Donner, 1968; Cautela, 1967, 1970, 1971; Cautela & Wisocki, 1969; Hedberg & Campbell, 1974; Smith & Gregory, 1976.
106. For example, Lawson & May, 1970; Sipich, Russell, & Tobias, 1974; Tooley & Pratt, 1967; Wagner & Bragg, 1970.
107. Compare with Cautela, 1982.
108. For example, Cautela & Kearney, 1993.

109. Rachman & Wilson, 1980.
110. Tustin, Pennington, & Byrne, 1994.
111. Guevremont & Spiegler, 1990; Spiegler & Guevremont, 1994, 2002.
112. Burgess, 1962.
113. Franks & Wilson, 1975.
114. Bandura, 1969.
115. Beauchamp & Walters, 1978.
116. For example, Lovaas & Simmons, 1969.
117. Goldiamond, 1974, pp. 62-63.
118. Mudford, 1995.
119. Bandura, 1969.
120. For example, Cole, Montgomery, Wilson, & Milan, 2000; Lovaas & Simmons, 1969; White, Nielson, & Johnson, 1972.
121. Carr & Durand, 1985; Emerson, 1993.
122. For example, Risley & Twardosz, 1974.
123. Kassirer, 1974.
124. Bootzin, 1975, p. 152.
125. Kazdin & Wilson, 1978.
126. Compare with Linscheid, Hartel, & Cooley, 1993.
127. Kazdin, 1989.
128. For example, Callahan & Leitenberg, 1973; Wilson & Tracey, 1976.

Chapter 8

Token Economy, Contingency Contract, and Behavioral Child Management Training

Now that you are familiar with the basic principles and procedures of consequential behavior therapy, let's explore their application in three standard treatment packages: token economy, contingency contract, and behavioral child management training. A wide array of acceleration and deceleration problem behaviors have been modified with these treatment packages, including independent living skills of clients with limited capacities, delinquent behaviors, and young children's compliance with parental instructions.

TOKEN ECONOMY

Even if you are unfamiliar with the term *token economy,* you are familiar with the concept. Every day you participate in an elaborate token economy—our monetary system.

What Is a Token Economy?

Courtesy of Teodoro Ayllon

Teodoro Ayllon

A **token economy** is a system for motivating clients to perform desirable behaviors and to refrain from performing undesirable behaviors.[1] Clients earn **tokens**—token reinforcers such as poker chips or points—for adaptive behaviors and lose tokens for maladaptive behaviors. The clients exchange tokens for actual reinforcers called **backup reinforcers.** The token economy provides detailed, explicit procedures for clients' earning, losing, and spending tokens. Token economies are used more often for groups of clients than for individuals, so most of our discussion deals with group programs.

Modern token economies have some highly innovative historical precursors. In Chapter 2, you read about Maconochie's point system for prisoners in Australia at the beginning of the 19th century.[2] At about the same time in England, Joseph Lancaster set up an elaborate token reinforcement system to motivate students' learning.[3] Because the school had a large number of students and few teachers, superior students tutored other students in small groups. The students, as well as their tutors, received token reinforcers based on the students' performance. By the late 19th century, a number of school systems in the United States were using token reinforcement to promote learning and foster appropriate classroom behaviors (such as arriving on time for school).[4] The token economy as we know it today began with a program for hospitalized patients with chronic psychiatric disorders, developed by Teodoro Ayllon and Nathan Azrin in 1961 at Anna State Hospital in southern Illinois.[5]

Courtesy of Nathan Azrin

Nathan Azrin

Basic Elements

A token economy consists of four basic elements:

1. *A list of acceleration and deceleration target behaviors and the number of tokens that clients can earn or lose for performing each.* Token economies primarily deal with acceleration target behaviors that vary with clients' problems. For individuals with mental retardation, dressing might be a

target behavior, whereas for students a target behavior might be completing an assignment.

2. *A list of backup reinforcers and the token cost of each.* The list of backup reinforcers is general to all the clients in the program and includes some reinforcers that will motivate each of the clients.

3. *The type of token.* Tokens can be tangible or symbolic. Tangible tokens include poker chips (different colors for different values), metal washers, specially designed paper currency, stars on a chart, and money itself. Points are symbolic tokens.

4. *Specific procedures and rules for the operation of the token economy* (for example, when clients can exchange tokens for backup reinforcers). Such rules are crucial when a small number of staff members must administer the program with a large number of clients.

Token economies are used to treat diverse problem behaviors and client populations.[6] To show how token economies function, we will describe two token economies in detail: the Community Training Center (a program for patients with chronic psychiatric disorders) and Achievement Place (a home-style program for juveniles who have been arrested for minor offenses). We also will briefly review the application of token economies to people with mental retardation, children in classrooms, and individuals and families.

The Community Training Center: A Token Economy for Patients with Chronic Psychiatric Disorders

The Community Training Center, a day treatment program for individuals previously hospitalized for chronic psychiatric disorders (predominantly schizophrenia), was developed by Michael Spiegler and Haig Agigian at the Palo Alto (California) Veterans Administration Hospital.[7] The goal of the program was to prepare the patients, called *trainees,* for independent living in the community. The trainees had been hospitalized for an average of more than 8 years. Most trainees were male, and their average age was 45. They lacked the self-care, home management, interpersonal, and community interaction skills necessary to live independent lives. To treat these behavioral deficits, the Community Training Center was run as a school, with classes in which the skills were taught. Examples of the classes were social communication, problem solving, money management, health and hygiene, social customs, and current events.

For the most part, trainees had little desire to learn the skills taught. They were frightened of independent living and had grown accustomed, through years of hospitalization, to acting dependently. To motivate the trainees to develop independent living skills, a token economy, named the *credit system,* was set up.

CREDITS AND CREDIT CARDS

The units of exchange in the credit system were points called *credits.* Each day, trainees received a new *credit card,* on which all credit transactions were recorded (see Figure 8-1). Trainees filled out their own credit cards, and to prevent cheating, staff members validated transactions (see Fig-

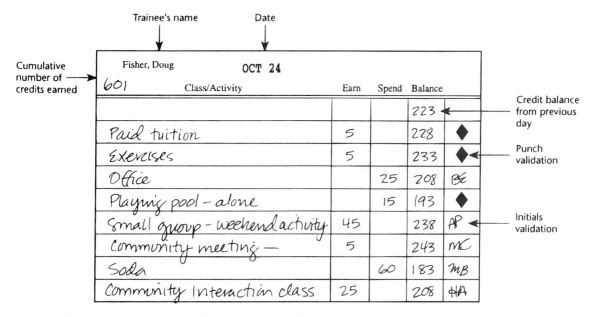

Figure 8-1 Example of a credit card used by trainees in the Community Training Center credit system (token economy)
SOURCE: Adapted from Spiegler & Agigian, 1977, p. 119.

ure 8-1). For example, trainees recorded what they had done to earn credits (such as attending a class) and the number of credits they had earned. Trainees' recording transactions themselves made the contingency between their behaviors and the reinforcers salient. It also gave the trainees practice in self-reinforcement, which is important for independent living.

EARNING CREDITS

Trainees earned credits for learning skills, which were assessed by written and oral quizzes and behavioral tests (such as role-playing). Trainees also earned credits for doing homework, which was an integral part of many classes. Most homework assignments involved practicing skills in the community (for instance, taking a friend out to lunch).

The procedures for administering credits during classes were based on four principles, which are important in all token economies. First, the criteria for earning credits were clearly defined. Second, the staff made trainees aware of the criteria (as by posting them in the classroom). Third, staff members awarded credits as soon as possible after a target behavior was performed. Fourth, the program paired earning credits with social reinforcers (such as praise from the instructor and other class members).

Generally, each target behavior resulted in earning a specified number of credits. Occasionally, however, the staff individualized the credit values for trainees, depending on the relative difficulty of that behavior for the trainee. For example, trainees who rarely spoke to other people received substantially more credits for commenting on another trainee's performance in class than did trainees who had little difficulty speaking up.

BACKUP REINFORCERS

Trainees spent their credits on a variety of backup reinforcers that fell into two categories: reinforcing activities and tangible reinforcers. During the design of the credit system, trainees were interviewed to determine potential reinforcers. Trainees also were observed for several weeks to assess how they spent their time during the day. Activities in which they engaged frequently became potential backup reinforcers, consistent with the Premack principle.

Table 8-1 lists examples of reinforcing activities that trainees could purchase with credits, along with their costs. Notice that the credit costs reflect the relative therapeutic benefit of activities. The more beneficial an activity, the lower its cost was, which encouraged trainees to spend credits on more beneficial activities. For example, activities with other people (such as playing table games) provide opportunities to practice social communication skills, and trainees paid less for social activities than for solitary activities. For instance, table games cost 10 credits per hour while reading cost 15 credits per hour and just sitting cost 25 credits per hour.

The Reinforcement Room was a large area in which trainees could engage in various pleasurable activities, such as playing pool, darts, and pinball; watching television; listening to music; and reading magazines. These reinforcers could be purchased in two ways. Trainees could spend their credits for specific activities, or they could purchase a block of time in the Reinforcement Room and engage in whatever activities they chose during that period.

The Crediteria was a store where trainees used their credits to purchase a variety of tangible reinforcers (such as drinks, snacks, toiletries, and

Table 8-1 Examples of reinforcing activities and their credit costs at the Community Training Center
SOURCE: Adapted from Spiegler & Agigian, 1977, p. 127.

Activity	Credit Cost
Travel club	10/hour
Photography	10/hour
Short films	10/hour
Feature films	50/film
Pool	
Playing alone	15/game
Playing with 1 or 2 others	10/game
Playing with 3 others	5/game
Ping-pong	
Singles	10/game
Doubles	5/game
Bowling	10/hour
Table games	10/hour
Ceramics	10/hour
Cooking	10/hour
Reading	15/hour
Sitting	25/hour

hobby items). Posters advertising items sold in the Crediteria were displayed around the Community Training Center. The posters encouraged trainees to spend their credits. In a token economy, exchanging tokens for backup reinforcers is important because it reinforces the adaptive behaviors for which the tokens were earned.

DECELERATING MALADAPTIVE BEHAVIORS

The major function of the credit system was to accelerate adaptive social and daily living skills by reinforcing them, initially with credits and later with backup reinforcers. Trainees' maladaptive behaviors were treated primarily by reinforcing competing adaptive behaviors.

Maladaptive behaviors sometimes were decelerated directly by having trainees pay credits for engaging in them (in other words, response cost). Table 8-2 lists examples of undesirable behaviors for which trainees paid credits. Notice that the credit costs for engaging in maladaptive behaviors are considerably higher than the credit costs for engaging in reinforcing activities listed in Table 8-1. The high credit cost for the undesirable behaviors discouraged trainees from performing them. For instance, missing class and sleeping in class, which were the most expensive undesirable behaviors, were rarely purchased—which means that trainees rarely engaged in these behaviors.

EVALUATION OF THE COMMUNITY TRAINING CENTER PROGRAM

A number of studies have demonstrated the effectiveness of the Community Training Center program.[8] One experiment compared a sample of graduates from the program with a sample of patients not in the program. The two groups were matched for age, diagnosis, length of hospitalization, type of hospital treatment, and time spent in the community. The groups were compared on eight different indices of personal adjustment. As Figure 8-2 shows, the Community Training Center graduates had significantly higher functioning on all but one of the outcome variables.

Table 8-2 Examples of undesirable behaviors and the average number of credits trainees at the Community Training Center paid to engage in them
SOURCE: Adapted from Spiegler & Agigian, 1977, p. 132.

Undesirable Behavior	Average Credit Cost
Sleeping in class	75
Smoking in class	50
Leaving class early (unexcused)	50
Cutting class	100
Being late to class	15
Coming to class without having done the homework	50
Pacing in class	20
Having an unbalanced credit card	10
Making a mess (for example, flicking ashes on the floor)	25
Begging	20

Figure 8-2 Comparison of personal adjustment between Community Training Center graduates and a comparable sample of outpatients. The Community Training Center graduates showed higher functioning than the comparison out-patients on all but the last index of personal adjustment.

SOURCE: Data from Spiegler & Agigian, 1977.

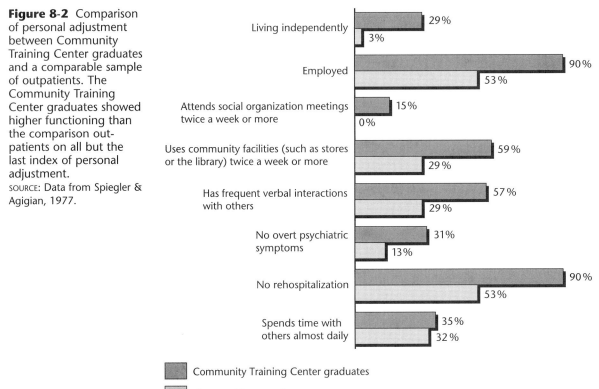

Community Training Center graduates

Comparable outpatients

Rehospitalization is a critical measure of the effectiveness of treatment for previously hospitalized patients. The Community Training Center program resulted in consistently lower rehospitalization rates than comparable programs. For example, during the first 2 years of the Community Training Center, the rehospitalization rate was 11%; during the comparable period for the previous day's treatment program, the rate was 73%. In another comparison, during a 6-month period, the Community Training Center rehospitalization rate was 5%, in contrast to 22% and 31% for two programs using different forms of treatment.

Achievement Place: A Token Economy for Juveniles in Trouble with the Law

Achievement Place is the prototype of the *teaching family model* for rehabilitating juveniles in trouble with the law. Established in 1967 in Lawrence, Kansas, under the direction of Elery Phillips, Montrose Wolf, and Dean Fixsen,[9] Achievement Place has inspired more than 200 other programs.[10] A token economy is central to the operation of Achievement Place. To illustrate its use, we will describe the original program for boys. (Most of the teaching family programs have been for boys.[11])

Achievement Place served as a residence for six to eight boys, 10 to 16 years of age, from lower socioeconomic backgrounds. The courts had referred the boys for committing minor crimes, such as petty theft and fighting. Achievement Place was set up in a large house in the boys' community. It was run by two *teaching parents,* a married couple trained in behavior therapy.[12]

At Achievement Place, the boys earned points for appropriate social behaviors (such as using proper manners), academic performance (for example, good study behaviors), and daily living behaviors (for instance, personal hygiene). They lost points for inappropriate behaviors in these areas. Table 8-3 lists some of the behaviors for which points were earned or lost, and Table 8-4 lists examples of backup reinforcers at Achievement Place.

The token economy was divided into three systems or levels. Initially, the boys were placed on a *daily system,* in which the points they earned were exchangeable each day for backup reinforcers. This arrangement helped them learn how the token economy worked. After boys became familiar with the token economy, they were switched to a *weekly system,* in which the points they earned were exchanged for backup reinforcers once a week. For example, a boy could purchase snacks and television

Table 8-3 Examples of behaviors for which boys at Achievement Place earned or lost points
SOURCE : Phillips, 1968, p. 215.

Behaviors That Earned Points	Points
Watching news on television or reading the newspaper	300 per day
Cleaning and maintaining neatness in one's room	500 per day
Keeping neat and clean	500 per day
Reading books	5 to 10 per page
Aiding houseparents in various household tasks	20 to 1000 per task
Doing dishes	500 to 1000 per meal
Being well dressed for an evening meal	100 to 500 per meal
Doing homework	500 per day
Obtaining desirable grades on school report cards	500 to 1000 per grade
Turning out lights when not in use	25 per light

Behaviors That Lost Points	Points
Failing grades on the report card	500 to 1000 per grade
Speaking aggressively	20 to 50 per response
Forgetting to wash hands before meals	100 to 300 per meal
Arguing	300 per response
Disobeying	100 to 1000 per response
Being late	10 per minute
Displaying poor manners	50 to 100 per response
Engaging in poor posture	50 to 100 per response
Using poor grammar	20 to 50 per response
Stealing, lying, or cheating	10,000 per response

Table 8-4 Privileges that could be earned with points on the daily and weekly point systems at Achievement Place

SOURCE: Adapted from Phillips, Phillips, Fixsen, & Wolf, 1971, p. 46.

Privilege	Price in Points	
	Daily System	Weekly System
Hobbies and games	400	3000
Snacks	150	1000
Television	50	1000
Allowance (per $1)	300	2000
Permission to leave Achievement Place (home, downtown, sports events)	NA	3000
Bonds (savings for gifts, special clothing, etc.)	150	1000
Special privileges	NA	Variable

NA = not available.

time for the entire week. Table 8-4 shows a comparison of the points needed to purchase different privileges on the daily and weekly systems. Most boys were on the weekly system for the 9 to 12 months they typically lived at Achievement Place. Because ample opportunities to earn points existed, the boys usually could buy all the privileges they wanted.

The final level in the token economy, the *merit system,* was reserved for boys who were ready to leave Achievement Place in the near future. Under the merit system, a boy would not earn or lose points, and he would not have to pay points for any backup reinforcers—as long as he continued to demonstrate a high level of appropriate social, academic, and daily living behaviors. Instead, the teaching parents merely praised the boy for appropriate behaviors. The merit system prepared boys for returning to their home environments, where no point system existed.[13]

A DAY AT ACHIEVEMENT PLACE

A typical weekday at Achievement Place began when the boys arose at about 6:30 A.M., washed and dressed, and cleaned their rooms. Morning chores were followed by breakfast, and then the boys were off to school.

Each day one boy served as *manager,* paying points to hold this prestigious position. As one of his responsibilities, the manager assigned cleanup jobs, supervised their completion, and awarded points to other boys for doing the jobs. The manager earned points according to how well the boys performed the household chores.[14]

Academic achievement was a major goal of the program. Each boy attended the same school in which he had been enrolled before coming to Achievement Place. The teachers and school administrators worked closely with the teaching parents, providing them with systematic feedback about each boy's school performance through daily or weekly report cards. The boys earned or lost points based on how well they were doing at school.[15]

After school, the boys returned to Achievement Place, had a snack (purchased with points), and then began their homework or other point-earning activities, such as chores around the house. Later they spent time in various recreational activities (such as bike riding or playing games), for which they paid points.

After dinner, a "family conference" was held. The boys and the teaching parents discussed the day's events, evaluated the manager's performance, discussed problems with the program, and decided on consequences for specific rule violations. The conferences allowed the boys to actively collaborate in their treatment program. The boys spent the rest of the evening, until bedtime at 10:30 P.M., in group or individual activities.

EVALUATION OF ACHIEVEMENT PLACE AND OTHER TEACHING FAMILY PROGRAMS

Numerous controlled studies have evaluated the effectiveness of Achievement Place and other teaching family programs.[16] These studies have shown that the programs are effective in reducing delinquent and other inappropriate behaviors (such as acting aggressively and using poor grammar) and increasing appropriate prosocial behaviors (such as being on time, completing homework, and saving money). Favorable attitudinal changes also have occurred, including increased self-esteem and optimism about having control over one's life.[17]

Unfortunately, the behavioral changes occur only while boys are in the program and for a year or so afterward.[18] This poor long-term maintenance of treatment gains is not completely surprising, however. The environment in a teaching family group home is very different from that of the home environments from which the boys came and, most important, to which they returned. Most of the boys were from home environments where they received little reinforcement for prosocial behaviors and ample reinforcement for antisocial behaviors from their peers—just the opposite of the contingencies in the teaching family home.[19] Thus, when the boys left the teaching family home, the contingencies changed; prosocial behaviors were no longer reinforced, which resulted in their eventual decline. Given the less-than-ideal home environments from which most youths in teaching family programs come, specific procedures must be used to promote long-term maintenance of treatment gains. One approach is to provide aftercare in specially developed foster homes, where prosocial behaviors continue to be reinforced and antisocial behaviors are discouraged.[20] Another approach is to give parents behavioral child management training (described later in this chapter).[21]

Token Economies for Training Individuals with Mental Retardation

Individuals institutionalized because of mental retardation display many of the same behavioral deficits as patients hospitalized for psychiatric disorders. For example, they frequently lack basic self-care and daily living skills (such as dressing appropriately and preparing simple meals). Token economies are effective in teaching such skills and motivating their consistent practice.[22] In addition to accelerating adaptive behaviors, token economies are used to decelerate various socially inappropriate behaviors (such as eating with one's fingers) and personally maladaptive behaviors (such as refusing to brush one's teeth) among institutionalized people with mental retardation.[23]

Language skills often are target behaviors for children, adolescents, and sometimes adults with mental retardation.[24] Because of the complexity of language and speech skills, token reinforcement programs for such target behaviors usually are administered individually and are likely to be part of a treatment package that includes modeling, prompting, and shaping.

Token economies are effective in increasing the quantity and quality of job-related tasks performed by individuals with mental retardation.[25] In one sophisticated token economy program, young adults with moderate mental retardation earned tokens for jobs on three levels.[26] The lowest level involved janitorial-type tasks; the middle level consisted of jobs with more responsibility (such as using machines and checking attendance); the highest level required more skill, responsibility, and independence (such as sorting and distributing mail and serving as a teacher's aide). The clients advanced through the levels by meeting specified performance criteria. The clients exchanged tokens for a variety of backup reinforcers, including favorite snacks, money, and access to pleasurable activities. The program successfully placed some of the highest-level clients into community-based jobs.

In another program, residents of a group home for adults with mental retardation received tokens for various tasks involved in running the home and for socializing with other residents and staff.[27] They also earned tokens for attending recreational activities in the community and for behaviors leading to gainful employment, such as contacting prospective employers and going on job interviews. Once residents were working in the community, their employers were asked to participate in the token economy program. The employers provided the staff with feedback about residents' performance on the job so that the residents could receive tokens for appropriate on-the-job behaviors.[28]

Token Economies in the Classroom

Token economies have been applied in preschool, elementary, and secondary classrooms at various educational levels (special education, remedial, and mainstream). These programs, which teachers rate as highly acceptable interventions,[29] have focused on classroom conduct and academic performance.

CLASSROOM CONDUCT

Token economies have modified a variety of undesirable behaviors that interfere with classroom learning, including problems associated with attention deficit hyperactivity disorder.[30] Examples are aggressive behaviors toward other students, talking out of turn, being out of one's seat, disregarding teachers' instructions, throwing objects, destroying property, and disturbing other students.[31] Three basic strategies are used to treat classroom conduct problems: (1) earning tokens for engaging in competing acceleration target behaviors, (2) losing tokens for performing inappropriate behaviors, and (3) both earning and losing tokens. Earning and losing tokens appear to be equally effective in modifying classroom conduct and academic behaviors.[32] Token economies also have been used in classrooms specifically to promote adaptive target behaviors, such as helping others.[33]

Backup reinforcers in classroom token economies have included tangible reinforcers (such as toys, snacks, and school supplies) and attractive activities (such as extended recess time and field trips). As children get older, in-class backup reinforcers become less potent than reinforcers available at home (such as playing video games or talking on the telephone). When this occurs, the students can exchange tokens earned at school for backup reinforcers at home.[34]

ACADEMIC PERFORMANCE

The ultimate purpose of decreasing disruptive classroom behaviors is to enhance students' academic performance. However, attention and proper conduct in the classroom are necessary but not sufficient conditions for promoting academic skills.[35] Thus, token economies also are used to *directly* increase learning of academic skills. The programs employ the same basic strategies used to treat classroom conduct problems.

Token economies have successfully improved children's academic performance in basic subject areas, such as arithmetic, reading, and spelling, as well as in more complex skills, such as creative writing.[36] These programs not only have increased students' skill levels but also have been associated with higher grades and fewer suspensions from school.[37]

One illustrative program was designed to increase writing skills.[38] Elementary school students earned points for the number of different adjectives, verbs, and beginnings of sentences they wrote in stories. The class was divided into two teams, and a group contingency was employed. Backup reinforcers included candy and early recess. As Figure 8-3 shows, an increase in the number of different sentence parts (such as adjectives) occurred when, and only when, points were given for the specific sentence parts. For example, the average number of adjectives used increased

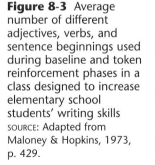

Figure 8-3 Average number of different adjectives, verbs, and sentence beginnings used during baseline and token reinforcement phases in a class designed to increase elementary school students' writing skills
SOURCE: Adapted from Maloney & Hopkins, 1973, p. 429.

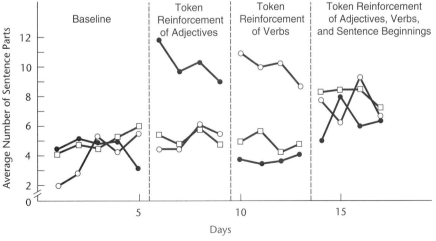

during the 4 days that adjectives were reinforced with points, but not on the following 4 days when only verbs were reinforced. When all three sentence parts were reinforced, an increase in each sentence part was observed. Moreover, people who were unfamiliar with the procedures used in the class rated the stories written during the token reinforcement days as more creative than those written during the baseline period, when no token reinforcers were administered.

Token Economies for Individuals

Token economies are used for individuals and small groups (such as families) as well as with large groups of clients. Individual token economies most often are employed with children for such problems as stuttering, use of inappropriate table manners, reading difficulties, and poor attention to schoolwork.[39] In one case, a single-parent father used a token economy to increase his 14-year-old son's completing household chores, which had been an area of constant conflict between them.[40] The simple token economy reduced conflict and helped improve their relationship. In another application, a home token economy was set up for a 6-year-old boy to treat three persistent problems: getting out of bed at night, eating only certain foods (such as pizza), and disobeying his parents' instructions.[41] The boy's parents gave stickers to the boy for proper behaviors (see Photo 8-1), and he exchanged them for tangible reinforcers and privileges listed on a reinforcement menu. The token economy resulted in immediate and substantial improvement of each of the problem behaviors. Individual token economies occasionally are used with adults—in particular, adults with mental retardation and with senior citizens, such as in Case 8-1.

Photo 8-1 Parents can be trained to administer simple token economy programs for their children at home. Stickers, which are placed on chart, may be used as tokens and exchanged for backup reinforcers.

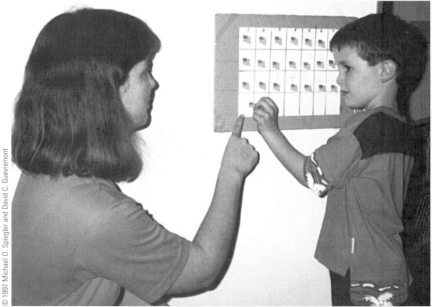

© 1997 Michael D. Spiegler and David C. Guevremont

Case 8-1

INCREASING ADHERENCE TO A MEDICAL REGIMEN WITH AN INDIVIDUAL TOKEN ECONOMY[42]

Mr. A. was an 82-year-old retired longshoreman who had suffered a massive heart attack. His physician told him to exercise, to eat foods high in potassium, and to take his medication, but he failed to follow these instructions. Mr. A.'s granddaughter, who lived with him, agreed to administer a token economy in which Mr. A. earned poker chips for walking, drinking potassium-rich orange juice, and taking his medication. He exchanged the poker chips for the privilege of choosing what he wanted for dinner at home or going out to eat at a restaurant of his choice. The token economy significantly increased each of the three target behaviors. When the tokens were temporarily withdrawn in a reversal period, the target behaviors declined to baseline levels, and reinstating the tokens immediately brought the behaviors back to the treatment level (see Figure 8-4 as an example). Instituting the token economy also appeared to improve Mr. A.'s relationship with his family by reducing arguments, especially about Mr. A.'s adherence to his medical regimen.

Figure 8-4 Number of walks per day Mr. A. took under baseline and token reinforcement conditions
SOURCE: Dapcich-Miura & Hovell, 1979.

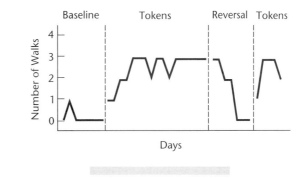

If you'd like to experience the process of setting up and being motivated by a token economy (and also receive some personal benefits), do Participation Exercise 8-1 over the next couple of weeks.

Participation Exercise 8-1

MORE THAN A TOKEN GESTURE: DESIGNING AND IMPLEMENTING A TOKEN ECONOMY

A good way to learn how token economies work is to design and participate in one yourself. This Participation Exercise provides directions for setting up a simple token economy to motivate you to do those everyday chores that you'd rather not do.

Part I: Selecting Behaviors to Change

Step 1: Make a list of four chores that you "must" do but dislike doing. Depending on your tastes and tolerances, such chores might include doing laundry, ironing, making your bed, cleaning the bathroom, paying bills, writing letters, shopping for food, and taking out the garbage. Write the four chores you have chosen in the first column on Work Sheets 8-1, 8-3, and 8-4.*

Part II: Establishing a Baseline

Step 2: To assess whether the token economy increases the chores you do, you need to know how often you did the chores before the token economy was instituted. In other words, you need to record a baseline. Over 5 consecutive days, place a check mark in the middle column on Work Sheet 8-1 each time you do one of the chores. At the end of the 5 days, add the number of check marks for each chore and write the sum in the last column of Work Sheet 8-1.

Part III: Setting Up the Token Economy

Now you are ready to set up your token economy.

Step 3: Rank order the four chores from most unpleasant to least unpleasant for you.

Step 4: On Work Sheet 8-2,† write the four chores, in rank order, in column A. Column B contains the points you will receive for doing each of the chores. Note that the more unpleasant a chore, the higher the number of points you will earn for doing it (from most to least unpleasant: 40, 30, 20, and 10).

Part IV: Identifying Backup Reinforcers

You will exchange the points you earn for backup reinforcers, which will be simple activities that meet the following three requirements.

1. You find engaging in the activity for relatively brief periods of time enjoyable.

2. You engage in the activity frequently (at least several times per week).

3. *You are willing to temporarily give up the activities you've included as backup reinforcers* (if you do not earn them). The reason is that during the time your token economy is in effect, you will be able to engage in the backup reinforcing activities only when you have performed your chores. (For example, if you consider jogging an essential part of your life and won't give it up, do not make jogging a backup reinforcer.)

Your backup reinforcing activities might include listening to music, talking on the telephone, watching TV, reading for pleasure, surfing the Internet, checking your e-mail, having a cup of coffee with friends, and exercising. Any activity that you enjoy, that would reinforce doing your chores, and that can be done in a relatively brief period is fine.

Step 5: Choose four activities that meet the three requirements just described.

Step 6: Rank order the four activities from most enjoyable to least enjoyable.

---

*You will find these work sheets in your Student Resource Materials.
†You will find this work sheet in your Student Resource Materials.

Step 7: Write the four activities, in rank order, on Work Sheet 8-2, column C. Column D lists the points that each backup reinforcer will cost you. As you can see, the more enjoyable an activity is, the higher is the cost (from most to least enjoyable: 25, 20, 10, and 5).

Part V: Implementing the Token Economy

You now are ready to start your token economy. Begin on the same day of the week on which you started your baseline and continue the token economy for 5 consecutive days.

Step 8: Each time you complete one of your chores, place a check mark in the second column of Work Sheet 8-3 next to the chore. Then, write the number of points earned for doing that chore (refer to Work Sheet 8-2, column B) in the Points Earned column of Work Sheet 8-5.*

Step 9: Each time you engage in one of the backup reinforcing activities, record the number of points spent in the Points Spent column of Work Sheet 8-5.

Maintain a running balance in the Point Balance column of Work Sheet 8-5 by adding points earned and subtracting points spent, as you do (or should do!) with your check book.

While your token economy is in effect, you may engage in the reinforcing activities *only* after purchasing them with points. If you violate this rule, the token economy will not accelerate your doing the chores.

Part VI: Evaluating the Token Economy

Step 10: At the end of the 5 days in which your token economy was in effect, add up the number of check marks for each chore in the middle column of Work Sheet 8-3. Record the sums in the last column of Work Sheet 8-3.

Now you can compare the frequencies of doing chores during the baseline period (Work Sheet 8-1) and during the token economy period (Work Sheet 8-3). If the token economy was effective, you should have done more chores during the token economy period than during the baseline period. If this did not occur, you may have to increase the point values earned for each chore or select more enjoyable backup reinforcers.

If your token economy appears to have been effective in increasing the chores you do, you may want to provide further evidence for its efficacy by introducing a reversal period. For another 5-day period (beginning on the same day of the week), discontinue the token economy. However, continue to record the number of times you do each chore by placing check marks in the middle column on Work Sheet 8-4. At the end of the 5-day reversal period, add up the number of times you did each chore. Record the sums in the last column on Work Sheet 8-4. Because the token economy was not in effect during the reversal period, you would expect your frequency of doing chores to be lower during the reversal period than during the token economy period.

Finally, if you would like to do your chores more than you have in the past, you can reinstate the token economy after your reversal period. Eventually, you may be able to discontinue the token economy if doing your chores begin to

---

*You will find this work sheet in your Student Resource Materials.

be naturally reinforced (such as by your roommate's comments on your neater room or your appreciating the fresher odors in the kitchen when you take out the garbage regularly).

◆

Token Economy in Perspective

Since the first major token economy was developed some 40 years ago,[43] numerous token economies have been implemented to treat diverse target behaviors, ranging from simple self-care skills to complex problems that develop in marital relations. Clients of all ages—from children to elderly individuals—with a wide range of intellectual capacities have been treated. Token economies have been used in many different settings—in homes, classrooms, group living situations, hospitals, outpatient facilities, and work environments.

The effectiveness of token economies has been evaluated systematically with reversal and multiple baseline studies.[44] The general finding is that clients consistently perform target behaviors *only* when they are receiving tokens for engaging in them. On one hand, these reliable findings provide impressive evidence that the token economy is responsible for changes in clients' target behaviors. On the other hand, the rapid loss of treatment gains typically observed when token reinforcement is discontinued is a major limitation of token economies.

Clients enter token economy programs because they have a deficit of adaptive behaviors and/or an excess of maladaptive behaviors. In their natural environments, adaptive behaviors were not reinforced or maladaptive behaviors were reinforced. The token economy reverses these contingencies, which often results in impressive (sometimes immediate) changes. However, when clients leave the token economy and return to their previous home environments, the contingencies usually revert to their pretreatment state—that is, the conditions that had been instrumental in maintaining the clients' presenting problems.

The most obvious solution to this dilemma is to keep clients in the token program. Occasionally, this solution is viable, as when a token economy is instituted in a client's natural environment. For example, two token economies to promote safety in open-pit mines were continued for more than 11 years.[45]

In most cases, however, token economies are only temporary treatment procedures. The key to long-term maintenance of treatment gains is for clients to be reinforced in their natural environments for the same behaviors that were reinforced in the token economy. Sometimes it is possible to change the environment to which clients return after leaving a token program. For instance, parents can be trained to reinforce their child's adaptive behaviors. Alternatively, clients can go to a different environment, such as a specialized foster home in which the foster parents are trained in behavior therapy procedures.

The reinforcers used in token economies usually are different from those the clients typically receive in their everyday lives. Accordingly, therapists must make provisions to shift to reinforcers that are actually available in the client's natural environment. Toward this end, social reinforcers such as praise are generally administered along with tokens. Further, the use of tokens may be withdrawn gradually while clients are still in the token economy. This allows natural reinforcers (such as feeling good after completing a task) to assume an increasingly important role in maintaining the adaptive behaviors. Tokens can be withdrawn gradually by having clients move through levels within the token economy, such as the daily, weekly, and merit systems at Achievement Place.[46] Clients also may be reinforced with tokens on an intermittent reinforcement schedule.[47]

Critics have voiced ethical and humanitarian objections to token economies. For example, token economies have been described as demeaning, especially for adults. The argument is that token reinforcement is appropriate for children but not for adults, who are supposed to be "above" receiving tokens for behaving appropriately. Interestingly, the same people who think token reinforcement is inappropriate for adults often forget that they participate in a large-scale token economy every time they make a monetary transaction. The token economy also has been mistakenly viewed as a form of bribery (an argument we rebutted in Chapter 6, page 137).

In fact, the evidence indicates that token economies enhance clients' dignity by increasing their self-esteem, self-respect, pride, and sense of worth. Consider the following evaluation of an early token economy at a psychiatric hospital. "The program's most notable contribution to patient life is the lessening of staff control and putting the burden of responsibility, and thus more self-respect, on the patient."[48] Or consider the comment of a highly intelligent 40-year-old trainee at the Community Training Center. The man approached the program director and, with obvious pride in what he had accomplished in his classes, said, "Doctor, I earned 120 credits today."[49] These words sound very much like a sales executive's telling her husband at dinner, "I earned a bonus today for closing the deal," or a college student's telling his roommate, "I got an *A* on the paper I worked so hard on."

CALVIN AND HOBBES copyright 1986 Watterson. Dist. by UNIVERSAL PRESS SYNDICATE. Reprinted with permission. All rights reserved.

Another common positive side effect of token economies is that once clients' behaviors improve and become more prosocial, their relationships with family members and other people in their lives improve (as in the individual token economies described earlier).

CONTINGENCY CONTRACT

A **contingency contract** is a written agreement that specifies the relationship between target behaviors and their consequences for a particular client. The essential components of a contingency contract are clear, unambiguous statements of (1) the target behaviors, (2) the consequences

Figure 8-5 Contingency contract with individual contingencies for each target behavior used with a 15-year-old boy
© 2002 Michael D. Spiegler and David C. Guevremont

Effective dates: From : 2-10-02   To : 3-9-02

Jerry agrees to:
1. Go to school each day

His parents agree to:
Reward: Give Jerry $10 spending money per week (on Sunday)

Penalty: Subtract $2 from a possible $10 for each school day that Jerry fails to attend

2. Arrive home each day after school by 4 p.m. to check in with his parents

Reward: Allow Jerry to stay out until 10 p.m. on Saturday night

Penalty: Subtract 1 hour from a 10 p.m. curfew on Saturday for each day Jerry fails to check in by 4 p.m.

3. Come home each day no later than 6 p.m. to have dinner with the family

Reward: Allow Jerry to play video games for 45 minutes

Penalty: Lose access to video games for the day

Bonus: Each time Jerry goes 4 weeks with fewer than six infractions, his parents will give him money to purchase one compact disk (maximum of $18 per purchase).

Penalty: Each time Jerry has more than six infractions, he will be grounded (remain in the house and not be able to watch television, talk on the telephone, or use the computer) for the entire day on Saturday.

I, Jerry Michaelson, agree to the terms of the above contract.

_____
Signature   Date

I, Mrs. Michaelson, agree to the terms of the above contract.

_____
Signature   Date

I, Mr. Michaelson, agree to the terms of the above contract.

_____
Signature   Date

for performing (or failing to perform) them, and (3) the precise contingency between each target behavior and its consequences (for example, "If the client does X for 3 consecutive days, then the client will receive Y").[50]

The contract in Figure 8-5 illustrates other features of contingency contracts. They specify the responsibilities of the client and the other people involved in the therapy, each of whom signs the contract. With deceleration target behaviors, contracts can include both reinforcement and negative consequences. For clients who cannot read, the contract can consist of pictures, such as Figure 8-6.

Rather than being a treatment itself, a contingency contract is used to formalize a treatment plan. For example, contingency contracts were part of an effective substance abuse treatment program for adolescents and young adults.[51] Clients contracted to engage in specific overt behaviors that competed with drug abuse, such as attending school, complying with an early curfew, and notifying their families of their whereabouts when they were not at home, school, or work. The contracts specified the participation of the client, family members, and the therapist and were reviewed weekly. Family members administered immediate and delayed reinforcers.

Using contingency contracts to formalize treatment plans has a number of benefits. Contingency contracts minimize disagreements about the conditions of the plan. The contract is the final authority, which underscores the importance of stating the terms of the contract unambiguously. Signing the contract increases the commitment of the people involved to fulfill their roles as stated in the contract. The process of designing a contingency contract makes clients active participants in therapy. When the people participating in the contract are having difficulty in their relationship (for example, child and parents, spouses), jointly developing a contingency contract may benefit the relationship by providing structure for their interactions and opportunities to practice cooperating and negotiating.

Contingency contracts are used as part of treatment plans for clients of all ages.[52] Examples of behaviors treated include disruptive classroom behaviors,[53] school attendance,[54] school and homework performance,[55] antisocial behaviors,[56] sibling cooperation,[57] studying,[58] physical exercise,[59]

Figure 8-6 Pictorial contingency contract showing the target behavior and the reinforcer

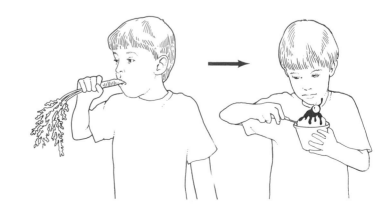

smoking,[60] overeating,[61] undereating,[62] problem drinking,[63] and marital discord.[64] Contingency contracts sometimes are used to increase compliance with behavior therapy homework assignments, such as getting parents who physically abuse their children to practice using positive reinforcement procedures with their children.[65] Relatively few studies have examined the essential features of contingency contracts.[66] It is clear, however, that specifying the contingency between the target behavior and the consequence is essential.[67]

BEHAVIORAL CHILD MANAGEMENT TRAINING

One third of all referrals of children for psychotherapy involve so-called "misbehavior" and "discipline" problems.[68] They include noncompliance with parental requests and rules, and disruptive behaviors (such as aggressive acts, oppositional behaviors, and temper tantrums). When these behaviors occur occasionally, as they do with most children, they are considered normal ("growing pains" or "just a stage"). However, when the noncompliant and disruptive behaviors are frequent, long-lasting, or intense, parents appropriately may seek professional assistance.

One approach to dealing with children's noncompliant and disruptive behaviors is for the child to receive individual psychotherapy. However, around 1960 it became clear that traditional psychotherapy with children exhibiting such problems was largely ineffective.[69] The reason may be because the problem does not reside within the child, as is assumed in traditional psychotherapy. The problem is with the parent–child interactions. In fact, parents who seek help for their child's noncompliant and disruptive behaviors interact differently with their child than parents who are not reporting such problems. Specifically, extensive observations have revealed that parents who are experiencing difficulty with their children's problem behaviors (1) give more vague and inconsistent instructions; (2) use more negative, threatening, and angry warnings in an attempt to modify the child's behaviors; (3) administer inconsistent and ineffective consequences for undesirable behaviors; and (4) provide fewer positive consequences for their child's prosocial, desirable behaviors.[70]

Courtesy of Gerald Patterson

Gerald Patterson

Courtesy of Rex Forehand

Rex Forehand

These observations led two prominent behavior therapists—Gerald Patterson[71] at the Oregon Social Learning Center and Rex Forehand[72] at the University of Georgia—to develop *behavioral child management training* (also known as *behavioral parent training*).[73] **Behavioral child management training** teaches parents behavior therapy procedures to manage their children's behavioral problems effectively.

The primary goals of behavioral child management training are to increase parents' use of (1) clear, direct, and age-appropriate instructions to their children; (2) positive consequences for prosocial, desirable child behaviors; and (3) consistent and appropriate negative consequences for children's noncompliant and disruptive behaviors. Positive reinforcement, including differential reinforcement, and time out from positive reinforcement are the major therapy procedures that therapists teach parents. They may also teach parents to use contingency contracts, home token economies, and response cost.[74]

Parents initially learn to notice and reinforce their children's desirable behaviors. Therapists teach them to use a variety of reinforcers, including enthusiastic praise (for instance, "What a great job. You came the first time I called!"), physical affection (a hug, for example), and the provision of privileges (such as staying up 15 minutes past bedtime). Next, parents are taught how to differentially reinforce behaviors that compete with serious undesirable behaviors (such as hitting siblings) and to ignore minor undesirable behaviors (such as whining). Parents learn to give clear-cut instructions calmly and to refrain from angry, indirect negative instructions (such as "Wait until your father gets home!"). They also learn to use time out in a consistent manner.

Planned activity scheduling is another procedure taught in behavioral child management training.[75] Parents learn to change settings events in anticipation of their children's behavior problems to prevent the problems from occurring in the first place.[76] A common strategy is to provide children with an active task that they enjoy and that is appropriate for the situation. In the case of a child who is disruptive while waiting in a doctor's office, for example, parents might bring some of the child's favorite games or toys to the doctor's office. Planned activity scheduling has been most extensively employed with and is an effective treatment for families whose members have developmental disabilities[77] and parents who abuse their children,[78] as well as with families whose children have everyday behavior problems.[79]

Behavioral child management training is conducted with a single family or in small groups containing 4 to 10 sets of parents. Parents rehearse the behavior therapy procedures in the training sessions and receive feedback from the therapist. The practice involves role-playing, with the therapist or another parent playing the role of the child. Occasionally, parents will practice with their own child during training sessions.[80] Homework between sessions is an integral part of the training.[81] For example, parents may be asked to self-monitor and self-reinforce their use of the behavioral skills they have learned.

Behavioral child management training has been applied effectively to a variety of child behavior problems, including noncompliance with instructions and rules,[82] oppositional behaviors,[83] disruptive behaviors,[84] aggressive behaviors,[85] fighting and stealing,[86] childhood sleep problems,[87] eating behavior of undernourished children with cystic fibrosis,[88] and completion of homework.[89] The training has been successful with parents who physically abuse their children[90] and parents with mild mental retardation.[91] Behavioral child management training is more effective when administered by trained mental health practitioners than when parents learn the procedures by following exercises in a workbook.[92]

Behavioral child management training is effective in changing children's noncompliant and disruptive behaviors. In one study children whose parents received the behavioral training showed a 63% reduction in problem behaviors in comparison to a 17% reduction for children whose parents received a nonbehavioral (control) treatment.[93] Another study demonstrated that behavioral child management training was more effective than the typical, eclectic treatment offered by community mental health clinics for children with disruptive behavior problems.[94]

Behavioral child management training can result not only in children's becoming compliant with their parents' instructions but also in their becoming more compliant than children who have no significant behavior problems.[95] Besides changing children's behaviors, behavioral child management training modifies parents' interactions with their children[96] and may reduce parents' stress.[97]

Following successful behavioral child management training, transfer to other settings (such as from home to school)[98] and generalization to non-treated behaviors[99] may or may not occur. Additional specific interventions to promote transfer and generalization may be required. Interestingly, the training sometimes decreases the problem behaviors of untreated siblings.[100]

The positive effects of behavioral child management training are consistently maintained over time, as demonstrated in follow-up studies ranging from 4 to 10 years after the training.[101] The major factor that interferes with successful training is parents who are coping with significant problems of their own. These may be personal problems, such as depression or other serious psychological disorders, or familial problems, such as financial hardship and unsafe living conditions. Such problems are likely to interfere with parents' effectively learning and implementing behavioral child management skills.[102]

SUMMARY

1. A token economy is a system for motivating clients to perform desirable behaviors and to refrain from performing undesirable behaviors; clients earn token reinforcers for the former and lose them for the latter. Tokens can be tangible, such as poker chips, or symbolic, such as points. Clients exchange tokens for backup reinforcers. Token economies most often are used for groups of clients.

2. The basic elements of a token economy are (1) a list of target behaviors and the number of tokens clients can earn or lose for performing each, (2) a list of backup reinforcers and the token cost of each, (3) the type of token used, and (4) specific procedures and rules for running the token economy.

3. The Community Training Center, a day treatment program for individuals previously hospitalized for chronic psychiatric disorders, employed a token economy to motivate learning social and daily living skills needed for independent living. The Community Training Center was run as a school in which the skills were taught in classes. The program was shown to be superior to other comparable day treatment programs.

4. Achievement Place was a home-style, residential rehabilitation program for juveniles in trouble with the law that employed a token economy. Points were earned for appropriate social behaviors, academic performance, and daily living behaviors; points were lost for inappropriate behaviors. The program was effective while the clients were in treatment and up to a year afterward.

5. Token economies have been applied to teach self-care and daily living skills to clients with mental retardation and to modify classroom conduct and academic performance in schoolchildren.

6. Token economies have been used with both individuals and small groups, such as families.

7. Evidence from reversal and multiple baseline studies clearly shows that token economies can modify clients' behaviors. However, treatment gains often decline rapidly when token reinforcement is discontinued unless specific procedures to foster durability of change are instituted. Such procedures include gradually withdrawing tokens while increasing natural reinforcers, using intermittent reinforcement, and establishing the same reinforcement contingencies used in the token program in the environment to which clients return.

8. A contingency contract is a written agreement that specifies the relationship between target behaviors and their consequences for a particular client.

9. Behavioral child management training involves teaching parents behavior therapy procedures to manage their children's behavior problems effectively. The major therapy procedures taught are positive reinforcement, differential reinforcement, time out from positive reinforcement, and planned activity scheduling.

Reference Notes

1. For example, Franco, Galanter, Castaneda, & Paterson, 1995.
2. Barry, 1958; Maconochie, 1848.
3. Kaestle, 1973; Lancaster, 1805.
4. For example, Ulman & Klem, 1975.
5. Ayllon & Azrin, 1968.
6. Kazdin, 1977c; Milan, 1987.
7. Spiegler & Agigian, 1977.
8. Spiegler & Agigian, 1977.
9. Phillips, 1968.
10. Braukmann & Wolf, 1987.
11. Compare with Minkin, Braukmann, Minkin, Timbers, Timbers, Fixsen, Phillips, & Wolf, 1976; Timbers, Timbers, Fixsen, Phillips, & Wolf, 1973.
12. Fixsen, Phillips, Phillips, & Wolf, 1976; Phillips, Phillips, Fixsen, & Wolf, 1971.
13. Phillips, Phillips, Fixsen, & Wolf, 1971.
14. Phillips, Phillips, Wolf, & Fixsen, 1973.
15. Bailey, Wolf, & Phillips, 1970.
16. Braukmann, Wolf, & Kirigin Ramp, 1985; Fixsen, Phillips, Phillips, & Wolf, 1976; Kirigin [Ramp], Braukmann, Atwater, & Wolf, 1982; Maloney, Fixsen, & Phillips, 1981.

17. Eitzen, 1975.
18. For example, Bailey, Timbers, Phillips, & Wolf, 1971; Phillips, 1968.
19. Compare with Wilson & Herrnstein, 1985.
20. For example, Jones & Timbers, 1983; Meadowcroft, Hawkins, Trout, Grealish, & Stark, 1982.
21. Reid, Eddy, Bank, & Fetrow, 1994.
22. For example, Girardeau & Spradlin, 1964; Horner & Keilitz, 1975; Hunt, Fitzhugh, & Fitzhugh, 1968; Spradlin & Girardeau, 1966.
23. For example, Peniston, 1975.
24. For example, Baer & Guess, 1971, 1973; Brickes & Brickes, 1970; Guess, 1969; Guess & Baer, 1973; MacCubrey, 1971; Schumaker & Sherman, 1970.
25. For example, Hunt & Zimmerman, 1969; Zimmerman, Stuckey, Garlick, & Miller, 1969.
26. Welch & Gist, 1974.
27. Asylum on the front porch, 1974; Clark, Bussone, & Kivitz, 1974; Clark, Kivitz, & Rosen, 1972; Wilkie, Kivitz, Clark, Byer, & Cohen, 1968.
28. Clark, Bussone, & Kivitz, 1974.

29. McGoey & DuPaul, 2000.
30. McGoey & DuPaul, 2000; Reid, 1999; Roberts, White, & McLaughlin, 1997.
31. Cavalier, Ferretti, & Hodges, 1997; McGoey & DuPaul, 2000.
32. Sullivan & O'Leary, 1990.
33. Anderson & Katsiyannis, 1997; Cook, 1999.
34. Kelley, 1990.
35. For example, Ferritor, Buckholdt, Hamblin, & Smith, 1972; Harris & Sherman, 1974. See also O'Leary, 1972; Winett & Winkler, 1972.
36. For example, Ayllon & Roberts, 1974; Chadwick & Day, 1971; Dalton, Rubino, & Hislop, 1973; Glynn, 1970; Knapczyk & Livingston, 1973; Lahey & Drabman, 1974; Maloney & Hopkins, 1973; McGinnis, Friman, & Carlyon, 1999; McLaughlin, 1982; Wilson & McReynolds, 1973.
37. For example, Bushell, 1978; Heaton & Safer, 1982.
38. Maloney & Hopkins, 1973.
39. Gannon, Harmon, & Williams, 1997; Heward, Dardig, & Rossett, 1979; Ingham & Andrews, 1973; Jason, 1985; Moore & Callias, 1987.
40. Strauss, 1986.
41. Heward, Dardig, & Rossett, 1979.
42. Dapcich-Miura & Hovell, 1979.
43. Ayllon & Azrin, 1965, 1968.
44. For example, Glynn, 1990.
45. Fox, Hopkins, & Anger, 1987.
46. For example, Paul & Lentz, 1977; Phillips, Phillips, Fixsen, & Wolf, 1971.
47. For example, Rosen & Rosen, 1983.
48. Atthowe & Krasner, 1968, p. 41.
49. Spiegler, 1983.
50. See DeRisi & Butz, 1975; Hall & Hall, 1982; O'Banion & Whaley, 1981.
51. Azrin, McMahon, Donohue, Besalel, Lapinski, Kogan, Acierno, & Galloway, 1994.
52. Kazdin, 1994.
53. White-Blackburn, Semb, & Semb, 1977.
54. Vaal, 1973.
55. Kahle & Kelley, 1994; Newstrom, McLaughlin, & Sweeney, 1999.
56. Stuart, 1971; Stuart & Lott, 1972.
57. Guevremont, 1987.
58. Bristol & Sloane, 1974.
59. Wysocki, Hall, Iwata, & Riordan, 1979.
60. Spring, Sipich, Trimble, & Goeckner, 1978.
61. Mann, 1972.
62. Donahue, Thevenin, & Runyon, 1997.

63. Miller, 1972.
64. Jacobson & Margolin, 1979; Stuart, 1969.
65. Wolfe & Sandler, 1981.
66. Kazdin, 1994.
67. Spring, Sipich, Trimble, & Goeckner, 1978.
68. Forehand & McMahon, 1981.
69. Levitt, 1957, 1963.
70. For example, Patterson, 1982; Patterson, Reid, & Dishion, 1992.
71. Patterson, 1982.
72. Forehand & McMahon, 1981.
73. Wells, 1994.
74. Barkley, Guevremont, Anastopolous, & Fletcher, 1992; Robin & Foster, 1989.
75. O'Reilly & Dillenburger, 1997.
76. Bigelow & Lutzker, 1998; Close, 2000.
77. Lutzker & Steed, 1998.
78. Bigelow & Lutzker, 1998; Close, 2000.
79. Lutzker, Huynen, & Bigelow, 1998.
80. Greene, Kamps, Wyble, & Ellis, 1999.
81. For example, Barkley, 1989; Wells, Griest, & Forehand, 1980.
82. For example, Long, Forehand, Wierson, & Morgan, 1993.
83. For example, Powers & Roberts, 1995; Webster-Stratton, Kolpacoff, & Hollingsworth, 1988.
84. For example, Powers, Singer, Stevens, & Sowers, 1992.
85. For example, Patterson, Chamberlain, & Reid, 1982.
86. For example, Reid, Hinjosa-Rivera, & Loeber, 1980.
87. For example, Wolfson, Lacks, & Futterman, 1992.
88. For example, Stark, Knapp, Bowen, Powers, Jelalian, Evans, Passero, Mulvihill, & Hovell, 1993; Stark, Powers, Jelalian, Rape, & Miller, 1994.
89. For example, Anesko & O'Leary, 1982.
90. Lundquist & Hansen, 1998; Wolfe & Wekerle, 1993.
91. Bakken, Miltenberger, & Schauss, 1993.
92. Sanders, Markie-Dadds, Tully, & Bor, 2000.
93. Patterson, Chamberlain, & Reid, 1982.
94. Taylor, Schmidt, Pepler, & Hodgins, 1998.
95. Forehand & King, 1977; Wells & Egan, 1988.
96. For example, Peed, Roberts, & Forehand, 1977.
97. Danforth, 1998.
98. For example, Breiner & Forehand, 1981.
99. Brestan, Eyberg, Boggs, & Algina, 1997.

100. For example, Humphreys, Forehand, McMahon, & Roberts, 1978; Patterson, 1974.

101. For example, Baum & Forehand, 1981; Forehand & Long, 1988; Patterson & Reid, 1973.

102. Forehand & Long, 1988; Wahler & Graves, 1983; Wells, 1994.

Brief/Graduated Exposure Therapy

When something makes us anxious or fearful, the last thing we want to do is to expose ourselves to it. But often that is the best way to reduce the anxiety or fear—the common wisdom of getting back on the horse that has just thrown you. **Exposure therapies** are used to treat anxiety, fear, and other intense negative emotional reactions (such as anger) by exposing clients—under carefully controlled and safe conditions—to the situations or events that create the negative emotion.

We will use the terms *anxiety* and *fear* interchangeably to refer to intense, inappropriate, and maladaptive reactions that are characterized by uneasiness, dread about future events, a variety of physical responses (such as muscle tension, increased heart rate, and sweating), and avoidance of the feared events.* (The term *anxiety* comes from the Latin *anxius,* which means constriction or strangulation.) Anxiety is inappropriate when its intensity is disproportionate to the actual situation, and it is maladaptive when it interferes with normal, everyday functioning. Anxiety-related disorders are the most prevalent psychological problem in the United States, affecting an estimated 24 million adults[1] and 5 million children and adolescents.[2]

Some strong fears are realistic and adaptive, such as the fear of walking alone at night in high-crime neighborhoods. Further, mild anxiety can be adaptive when it motivates us to act. For example, most students require some anxiety about an upcoming exam to get them to study. The goal of exposure therapies is to reduce the client's anxiety to a level that allows the client to function effectively and feel comfortable.

There are two basic models of exposure therapy: brief/graduated and prolonged/intense. **Brief/graduated exposure therapy** exposes the client to a threatening event (1) for a short period (ranging from a few seconds to a few minutes) and (2) incrementally, beginning with aspects of the event that produce minimal anxiety and progressing to more anxiety-evoking aspects. Graduated exposure is a prime example of the stepwise progression that characterizes many behavior therapy procedures. **Prolonged/intense exposure therapy** exposes the client to the threatening event (1) for a lengthy period (10 to 15 minutes at a minimum and sometimes more than an hour), and (2) from the outset, the client is exposed to aspects of the event that elicit intense anxiety.

The *mode of exposure* in both models can occur in four basic ways that fall on a continuum, as shown in Figure 9-1. At one end is *in vivo exposure*—actually encountering the event (such as taking a flight, in the case of fear of flying). At the other end is *imaginal exposure*—vividly imagining the event, as one does in a daydream (for example, visualizing taking a flight). Close to the in vivo end of the continuum, *virtual reality* technology now allows clients to be exposed to anxiety-evoking events

*Early theorists made a distinction between fear and anxiety. *Fear* referred to apprehension concerning a tangible or realistic event, whereas *anxiety* referred to apprehension about something intangible or unrealistic. Some theorists have considered fear to be emotional and anxiety to be cognitive in nature (for example, Beck & Emery, 1985). In general, behavior therapists have not found it useful to distinguish between the two concepts (for example, Rachman, 1990), which is the position we have adopted in this book.

Figure 9-1 The continuum on which modes of exposure fall in exposure therapy

Basic modes: IN VIVO   IMAGINAL

Variations: Virtual reality   Verbal and visual depictions

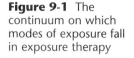

through interactional computer simulations that appear almost real.[3] Toward the imaginal end, clients can listen to detailed *verbal descriptions*[4] or view *visual* (video)[5] *depictions* of anxiety-evoking events.

The exposure also can be either *therapist-directed* in therapy sessions or *self-managed* by the client as a homework assignment. Finally, exposure therapies may use additional procedures to augment the exposure, such as the following:

1. *Competing response:* During exposure, the client may engage in a behavior that competes with anxiety, such as relaxing muscles while visualizing an anxiety-evoking event.

2. *Response prevention:* During treatment, the client may be kept from engaging in the maladaptive avoidance or escape behaviors he or she typically uses to reduce anxiety, such as not speaking in public because of a fear of stuttering.

3. *Exaggerated scenes:* To heighten the intensity or vividness of imaginal exposure, the depiction of the event may be exaggerated. For example, a therapist might ask a client who is afraid of snakes to imagine being in a pit with hundreds of snakes.

If the variety of models, modes, and other procedures that make up exposure therapies is slightly overwhelming, have no fear. You will be gradually exposed to examples of exposure therapy procedures that mix and match these components; in context, their use will become clear. Choosing the particular components of exposure therapy for a client is like ordering a hot fudge sundae with coffee rather than vanilla ice cream, pecans instead of walnuts, holding the cherry, and adding marshmallow sauce. You get a hot fudge sundae, but it is created with your unique preferences in mind.

So let's see what exposure therapy looks like in practice (you can have the sundae later). We begin with the brief/graduated model (which includes systematic desensitization and in vivo exposure therapy) because they were the first to be developed; in the next chapter we turn to the prolonged/intense model (in vivo flooding, imaginal flooding, and implosive therapy).

STANDARD SYSTEMATIC DESENSITIZATION

Systematic desensitization, developed by Joseph Wolpe 50 years ago, was the first major behavior therapy.[6] In **systematic desensitization,** the client imagines successively more anxiety-arousing situations while engaging in a behavior that competes with anxiety (such as muscle relax-

Courtesy of Joseph Wolpe

Joseph Wolpe

ation). The client gradually (systematically) becomes less sensitive (desensitized) to the situations. The therapy involves three steps:

1. The therapist teaches the client a response that competes with anxiety.
2. The specific events that cause anxiety are ordered in terms of the amount of anxiety they engender.
3. The client repeatedly visualizes the anxiety-evoking events, in order of increasing anxiety, while performing the competing response.

Muscle Relaxation as a Competing Response to Anxiety

Deep muscle relaxation is the most frequently used competing response in systematic desensitization. Consider that people are not likely to feel anxious and relaxed at the same time. In fact, muscle relaxation counters some of the physiological components of anxiety, including increased muscle tension, heart rate, blood pressure, and breathing.

Training in **progressive relaxation** involves relaxing various skeletal muscle groups: arms, face, neck, shoulders, chest, abdomen, and legs. (Progressive relaxation used in systematic desensitization is an abbreviated version of Edmund Jacobson's original procedures, which required as much as 200 hours of training.[7]) Clients first learn to differentiate relaxation from tension by tensing and then releasing each set of muscles (see Photo 9-1), and later to induce relaxation without tensing their muscles.[8] While the client is sitting or reclining comfortably, the therapist guides the client through the relaxation process. Clients are asked to practice progressive relaxation at home, often with a prerecorded tape of the relaxation instructions. The following is an excerpt from relaxation instructions:

Photo 9-1 Client being taught deep muscle relaxation. The client (reclining) is tensing his lower arm muscles before relaxing them.

© 1997 Michael D. Spiegler and David C. Guevremont

Close your eyes, settle back comfortably. . . . Let's start with your left hand. I want you to clench your left hand into a fist, clench it very tightly and study those tensions, hold it . . . (5-second pause) and now release the tension. Relax your left hand and let it rest comfortably. Just let it relax . . . (15-second pause). Once again now, clench your left hand . . . clench it very tightly, study those tensions . . . (5-second pause) and now release the tension. Relax your hand and once again note the very pleasant contrast between tension and relaxation.

Progressive relaxation training alone can be effective in treating anxiety disorders and in some cases is as effective as exposure therapy.[9] Progressive relaxation also is used to treat a host of psychological and physical problems, including asthma, eczema (skin inflammation), headaches, hypertension, pain, side effects of chemotherapy, postsurgical distress, and insomnia.[10]

Constructing an Anxiety Hierarchy

An **anxiety hierarchy** is a list of events that elicit anxiety, ordered in terms of increasing levels of anxiety. When clients are not clear about what is making them anxious, they may complete a self-report inventory known as a **fear survey schedule,** which provides a list of stimuli that evoke anxiety in many adults (see Table 9-1).[11] Fear survey schedules for children include events youngsters often find fear provoking, such as being in the dark and being in a fight.[12] To construct the scenes in the hierarchy, the therapist questions the client about the details of the specific situations that elicit anxiety.

The anxiety-evoking events are ordered from least to most anxiety producing. This process often uses the **Subjective Units of Discomfort scale.** The units of this scale, called **SUDs,** range from 0 to 100 (sometimes 0 to 10). Zero represents no anxiety; 100 represents the highest level of anxiety that the client can imagine.[13] As the word *subjective* implies, SUDs are specific to each individual. Two people who report experiencing the same SUDs levels are not necessarily experiencing equivalent degrees of discomfort, and comparisons between them is meaningless. However, the same person's SUDs levels can be compared at various times and in different situations. For example, if a client reported experiencing 60 SUDs last week and 40 SUDs today in the same situation, then it is safe to conclude that the client is less anxious today. Comparisons of a client's SUDs levels often are used as measures of change in therapy. To see for yourself the usefulness of SUDs, do Participation Exercise 9-1 over the next few days.

Participation Exercise 9-1

DAILY SUDsing

Choose a regularly occurring (at least daily) situation or experience in your life in which you generally feel uncomfortable. Whenever the situation occurs, rate

Table 9-1 Portion of a fear survey schedule

SOURCE: Developed by Spiegler & Liebert, 1970

Instructions: The items in this questionnaire are objects, experiences, or ideas that may cause fear, anxiety, or other unpleasant feelings. Using the scale below, write the appropriate number after each item to describe the degree to which the item causes you to feel fear, anxiety, or other unpleasant feelings.

1 = Not at all
2 = A little
3 = A moderate amount
4 = Much
5 = Very much

1. Open wounds	18. Cats	34. Going blind
2. Being alone	19. Being watched while working	35. Drowning
3. Public speaking		36. Examinations
4. Falling	20. Dirt	37. Cancer
5. Automobiles	21. Dogs	38. Fog
6. Being teased	22. Sick people	39. Being lost
7. Dentists	23. Fire	40. Police
8. Thunder	24. Mice	41. Talking on the telephone
9. Failure	25. Blood	
10. High places	26. Enclosed places	42. Death of a loved one
11. Receiving injections	27. Flying in airplanes	
12. Strangers	28. Darkness	43. Pain
13. Feeling angry	29. Lightning	44. Suicide
14. Insects	30. Doctors	45. War
15. Sudden noises	31. Losing control	46. Going insane
16. Crowds	32. Making mistakes	47. Violence
17. Large open spaces	33. Older people	48. Psychologists

your SUDs level (1–100), and record it on Work Sheet 9-1* along with a brief description of (1) your feelings and thoughts and (2) what is happening at the time. Record a minimum of 10 instances of the situation you have chosen. Figure 9-2 shows a portion of a work sheet for a student who monitored her SUDs levels when she spoke up in her history class.

After collecting your series of SUDs ratings, graph the ratings to provide an overall picture of how your level of discomfort varied. To account for the variations, consult your work sheet for particular circumstances that may have changed your level of discomfort.

*You will find this work sheet in your Student Resource Materials.

Figure 9-2 A portion of a work sheet of SUDs levels, feelings and thoughts, and descriptions of what was happening each time a woman spoke up in her history class (Participation Exercise 9-1)

Situation: Speaking up in history class			
Date	**SUDs**	**Feelings and thoughts**	**What is happening**
9/4	80	Scared to death; I'm going to sound dumb	Professor asks our reasons for taking course
9/6	—		Didn't do anything
9/9	75	This is hard; butterflies	Answering questions from reading
9/11	70	Nervous; here I go again— better say something worthwhile	Joining discussion

Anxiety hierarchies often are made up of events that share a common theme (see Table 9-2). For instance, fear of evaluation might include fear of speaking in public, being interviewed, and taking tests. When a client is anxious about more than one class of situations, multiple hierarchies are constructed. Anxiety hierarchies are individualized for each client; even if two clients include the same general events in a hierarchy, they would not necessarily assign the same rank-ordering and SUDs levels to them. Participation Exercise 9-2 describes one way that SUDs are used to construct an anxiety hierarchy.

Participation Exercise 9-2

CONSTRUCTING AN ANXIETY HIERARCHY USING SUDs*

From Table 9-3 choose a situation in which you could easily imagine yourself feeling anxious. Alternatively, choose a situation that actually makes you anxious. Then, complete the following steps in order:

*This Participation Exercise can be done before you continue reading or later, but you should read it now.

Table 9-2 Examples
of anxiety hierarchies

Item	SUDs	Item	SUDs
DEATH		FLYING	
19. Death of a close friend or loved one	100	20. Plane is flying in rough weather	100
18. Death of strangers in a dramatic fashion	85	19. Plane touching down on runway	95
17. Watching horror movies	80	18. Pilot turns on seatbelt sign and announces turbulence ahead	90
16. Seeing others in dangerous situations	75		
15. Hearing about a fatal and especially gruesome disease	70	17. Plane is banking	85
		16. Plane is descending for landing	80
14. Being around guns	60	15. Announcement of preparation for final descent and landing	75
13. Swimming in the ocean at night	55		
12. Riding as a passenger in a car on the highway	50	14. Plane is taking off	65
		13. Plane is taxiing to the runway	60
11. Flying in an airplane	48	12. Plane is climbing to cruising altitude	55
10. Driving a car on the highway	45		
9. Thoughts of fire	43	11. Plane is cruising in good weather	50
8. Climbing on high objects	40		
7. Being alone in a house at night	38	10. Sitting down and fastening seatbelt	45
6. Thinking about auto crashes	35	9. Announcement that the plane is ready for boarding	40
5. Thoughts of earthquakes	25		
4. Thinking of witches and ghosts	20	8. Boarding the plane	35
		7. Waiting to be boarded	30
3. Swimming in a pool at night	15	6. Checking in at the airport	25
		5. Driving to the airport	22
2. Seeing a snake	10	4. Calling the airport to find out if the flight is on time	20
1. Hearing a siren	5		
		3. Packing for the trip	15
		2. Purchasing ticket 10 days before flight	10
		1. Making reservations 3 weeks before flight	5

1. Assume the role of a person who is experiencing anxiety related to the situation you chose.

2. Write eight brief descriptions of scenes related to the situation that would cause you to experience varying levels of anxiety. Be sure you include

Table 9-3 Situations to be role-played for constructing anxiety hierarchies (Participation Exercise 9-2)

1. You receive a letter in your mailbox instructing you to make an appointment with the dean before the end of the week to discuss "concerns" about your academic standing. You know that you have not been doing as well as you would like in your classes, but you didn't know your academic standing was in jeopardy.

2. You have a dentist appointment next week to have several cavities filled. You always have hated going to the dentist, and you have put off this visit for months.

3. You got into an automobile accident with your parents' car after borrowing it for the weekend. The accident was your fault, and the damages are estimated at $2800. You have not yet told your parents, but you are supposed to return the car in an hour.

4. You have a final exam in 2 days. The exam is in your most difficult subject this semester. You need a high grade on the exam to pass the course. You haven't started studying for the exam yet, and you have two other final exams before the one you are dreading most.

5. You have to give an oral presentation in one of your classes in 2 days. You have always had difficulty speaking in public, and this is a particularly large class. One-third of your grade is based on this oral presentation.

one scene that would elicit very high anxiety and one that would elicit very little anxiety.

3. Assign SUDs to each scene (using a scale of 1 to 100).

4. Write the numbers 8 through 1 in descending order on a sheet of paper. List the scenes from lowest anxiety (SUDs) to highest anxiety (SUDs), with number 1 being lowest.

5. Optimally, the six scenes between your lowest and highest will be approximately spaced at even intervals of SUDs levels. For example, if your lowest scene was rated 5 and your highest 95, then the six intermediate scenes should be *roughly* 15 SUDs apart. If you find that you have large gaps, fill them in with additional scenes that you would assign intermediate SUDs levels.

You have now constructed a rudimentary anxiety hierarchy that could be used in systematic desensitization.

◆

The Desensitization Process

Desensitizing anxiety-evoking events begins as soon as the client has learned progressive relaxation (or another competing response) and has constructed an anxiety hierarchy. The therapist instructs the client, who is seated or reclining comfortably, to relax all of his or her muscles. The therapist then describes scenes from the anxiety hierarchy for the client to imagine, starting with the lowest item on the hierarchy. The scenes are described in detail and are specific to the client. For example, "initially greeting a date" might be elaborated as follows:

> You arrive at your date's apartment and knock on the door. There is no immediate answer and waiting seems endless. Finally, your date opens the door, smiles, and says, "Hi!"

The client imagines each scene for about 15 seconds at a time. Whenever the client experiences anxiety or discomfort, the client signals the therapist, usually by raising a finger. When this occurs, the therapist instructs the client to "stop visualizing the scene and just continue relaxing." The result is that the client visualizes anxiety-evoking scenes *only when relaxed*. The aim is for relaxation to replace the tension previously associated with the scene. Each scene in the hierarchy is presented repeatedly until the client reports little or no discomfort. Then, the next highest scene in the hierarchy is visualized. Case 9-1 illustrates the desensitization process.

THE FAR SIDE®   By GARY LARSON

© 1987 FarWorks, Inc. All Rights Reserved/Dist. by Creators Syndicate

"Now relax. ... Just like last week, I'm going to hold the cape up for the count of 10. ... When you start getting angry, I'll put it down."

SYSTEMATIC DESENSITIZATION FOR SEVERE
Case 9-1 ## TEST ANXIETY[14]

A 24-year-old female art student entered therapy complaining of severe test anxiety that had caused her to fail a number of tests. When she discussed her anxiety with the therapist, the therapist discovered that other situations also made her anxious. Accordingly, the client and therapist constructed four different anxiety hierarchies: taking tests, witnessing discord between other people, being scrutinized by others, and being devalued by others.

The desensitization process began with the therapist instructing the client to become deeply relaxed. Then, the therapist said:

I am now going to ask you to imagine a number of scenes. You will imagine them clearly and they will generally interfere little, if at all, with your state of relaxation. If, however, at any time you feel disturbed or worried and want to attract my attention, you will be able to do so by raising your left index finger. First I want you to imagine that you are standing at a familiar street corner on a pleasant morning watching the traffic go by. You see cars, motorcycles, trucks, bicycles, people, and traffic lights; and you can hear the sounds associated with all these things. *(Pause about 15 sec.)* Now stop imagining that scene and give all your attention once again to relaxing. If the scene you imagined disturbed you even in the slightest degree, I want you to raise your left index finger *now. (Client does not raise finger.)* Now imagine that you are at home studying in the evening. It is the 20th of May, exactly a month before your examination. *(Pause of 5 sec.)* Now stop imagining the scene. Go on relaxing. *(Pause of 10 sec.)* Now imagine the same scene again—a month before your examination. *(Pause of 5 sec.)* Stop imagining the scene and just think of your muscles. Let go, and enjoy your state of calm. *(Pause of 15 sec.)* Now again imagine that you are studying at home a month before your examination. *(Pause of 5 sec.)* Stop the scene, and now think of nothing but your own body. *(Pause of 5 sec.)* If you felt any disturbance whatsoever to the last scene raise your finger. *(Client does not raise finger.)* If the amount of disturbance decreased from the first presentation to the third, do nothing, otherwise again raise your finger. *(Client does not raise finger.)* Just keep on relaxing. *(Pause of 15 sec.)* Imagine that you are sitting on a bench at a bus stop and across the road are two strange men whose voices are raised in an argument. *(Pause of 10 sec.)* Stop imagining the scene and just relax. *(Pause of 10 sec.)* Now again imagine the scene of these two men arguing across the road. *(Pause of 10 sec.)* Stop the scene and relax. Now I am going to count up to 5 and you will open your eyes, feeling very calm and refreshed.

A total of 17 sessions were required for the client to report no anxiety while visualizing the highest scene in each hierarchy. Afterward, the client successfully passed a series of examinations, which demonstrated that the anxiety reduction transferred from the imagined scenes to the actual situations.

Three features of Case 9-1 are typical of systematic desensitization. First, before presenting scenes the therapist assessed if the client was deeply relaxed by presenting a neutral scene—one not expected to elicit anxiety—and observing if the client experienced anxiety. Second, scenes from more than one hierarchy were visualized in the same session. Third, the therapy was relatively brief.

Essential and Facilitative Components of Systematic Desensitization

Therapies usually have both essential and facilitative components. An *essential component* is an element that is necessary for the therapy to be effective; the therapy will not work without it. A *facilitative component* is an element that is not always necessary but that may enhance the therapy's effectiveness and efficiency. Researchers isolate the essential components of a therapy by systematically omitting components and then comparing the abbreviated treatment with the full treatment.[15] If an abbreviated treatment is shown to be as effective as the complete one, then the missing component is not essential.

The three major components of systematic desensitization are (1) *repeated safe exposure* to anxiety-evoking situations (2) in a *gradual manner* (3) while engaging in a *competing response.* It turns out that clients need not be exposed to the anxiety scenes gradually. In fact, desensitization can be effective when the client is exposed to the highest items in the hierarchy first[16] or only to the highest items.[17] Research also has demonstrated that desensitization with and without relaxation training can be equally effective.[18] The essential component in systematic desensitization is *repeated exposure to anxiety-evoking situations without the client experiencing any negative consequences.*[19]

The studies that have isolated the essential and facilitative components of systematic desensitization were carried out with mild to moderately anxious volunteers rather than actual clients and in research rather than clinical settings. Accordingly, it is important to exercise caution in generalizing from these analogue studies to clinical practice. The facilitative components—gradual exposure and a competing response—are more likely to be beneficial when the client's anxiety is severe. For example, in a study with cancer patients, both gradual exposure and relaxation were *necessary* to alleviate nausea that patients experienced in anticipation of chemotherapy.[20] One effect of the facilitative components of desensitization may be to render the therapy more acceptable to clients (less disturbing), which in turn may motivate clients to participate more in the treatment and to remain in therapy.

VARIATIONS OF STANDARD SYSTEMATIC DESENSITIZATION

The standard systematic desensitization procedures just described are still widely used. Since Wolpe developed them, a number of variations have been devised, and we will look at five: competing responses other than muscle relaxation, target behaviors other than anxiety, group treatment, a coping model of systematic desensitization, and interoceptive exposure.

Other Competing Responses

Deep muscle relaxation is not always the most appropriate competing response. Some clients, especially young children but also some adults, have difficulty learning progressive relaxation. **Emotive imagery** employs pleasant thoughts to counter anxiety and often is used with children.[21] It was part of the treatment of Paul's school-phobic behavior in Case 4-1. Other examples of competing responses include eating, listening to music, behaving assertively, and becoming sexually aroused.

Humor and laughter can compete with anxiety.[22] Indeed, research in psychology and medicine has demonstrated the effectiveness of humor and laughter in treating a wide array of problems,[23] including coping with AIDS.[24] One advantage that humor and laughter have over progressive relaxation is that the client does not have to learn the response. Thus, with laughter as the competing response, it is possible to carry out "crisis" desensitization in a single session, as Case 9-2 illustrates.

Case 9-2

ONE-SESSION SYSTEMATIC DESENSITIZATION FOR FEAR OF HUMILIATION[25]

A 20-year-old woman contacted a behavior therapist with a pressing problem. She was distressed about having to attend a banquet that evening because she feared that she might be embarrassed by her former boyfriend and his new girlfriend. The client and the therapist constructed an anxiety hierarchy of humiliating situations that might arise at the banquet. The scenes were presented to the client with details that elicited laughter. In one scene, for example, the client pictured herself sitting at the banquet and seeing her old flame enter the room. In describing the scene, the therapist added that the man was dressed in tights. The client found the recast scenes quite humorous, and she completed the hierarchy in a single therapy session. Several hours later, she attended the banquet and experienced only minor discomfort.

Other Target Behaviors

Anxiety or fear is, by far, the most frequent problem treated by systematic desensitization. However, systematic desensitization as a general model of treatment is applicable to a variety of problems. Examples include anger,[26] asthmatic attacks,[27] insomnia,[28] motion sickness,[29] night-mares,[30] problem drinking,[31] sleepwalking,[32] speech disorders,[33] body image disturbances,[34] and even racial prejudice.[35] Case 9-3 illustrates the application of systematic desensitization to the treatment of anger, using laughter as a competing response. The woman's anger was intense and sometimes resulted in her physically abusing her child and husband.

Case 9-3

SYSTEMATIC DESENSITIZATION FOR ANGER WITH LAUGHTER AS THE COMPETING RESPONSE[36]

A 22-year-old woman referred herself for treatment because of her reported inability to control her extreme anger toward her husband and 3-year-old son. She described her son as "a very active child whose almost constant misbehavior appeared to be attempts to antagonize his mother and gain her attention." Behavioral observations of the mother and child supported this description. The client reported that she generally reacted to her son's misbehavior by "screaming at the top of her voice, jumping up and down, smashing things, and physically attacking [him]." She said she could not control these responses. The client also reported that, when angry, she screamed at her husband and berated him, and she occasionally physically assaulted him. At the time of her self-referral, the client indicated that she had been contemplating suicide because "my temper makes everyone, including me, miserable."

After seven sessions of systematic desensitization using relaxation as the competing response, little progress was made. Because of the strength of the client's anger responses, she was able to imagine only the most innocuous scenes involving her son or husband without experiencing anger. At this point, it was decided to try laughter as a competing response. When the client signaled that a scene evoked anger, the therapist introduced and emphasized humorous aspects of the situation—generally in the form of slapstick comedy—such as in the following scene.

As you're driving to the supermarket, little Pascal the Rascal begins to get restless. Suddenly he drops from his position on the ceiling and trampolines off the rear seat onto the rear view mirror. From this precarious position, he amuses himself by flashing obscene gestures at shocked pedestrians. As you begin to turn into the supermarket . . ., Pascal alights from his perch and lands with both feet on the accelerator. As the car careens through the parking lot, you hear Pascal observe, "Hmm, . . . 25–80 in 2 sec . . . not bad." But . . . your main concern is the two elderly . . . women that you're bearing down upon. [They are] . . . limping toward the door of the supermarket clutching their little bargain coupons. One, who is clutching a prayer book in the other hand, turns and, upon seeing your car approaching at 70 mph, utters a string of profanities, throws her coupons into the air, and lays a strip of Neolite as she sprints out of the way and does a swan dive into a nearby [ditch]. The other . . . nimbly eludes your car and takes refuge in a nearby shopping cart, which picks up speed as it rolls downhill across the parking lot.

The client reacted to the scenes with laughter and amusement, and rarely reported experiencing anger to any of the scenes in the hierarchy. Importantly, she reported major reductions in the frequency and intensity of her anger responses to her son and husband as well as an increased ability to remain calm in situations that previously had infuriated her. The client's self-reports were confirmed by relatives and behavioral observations of playroom interactions with her son before and after treatment. Moreover, the client reported that she no longer experienced depressive episodes and suicidal thoughts.

Group Systematic Desensitization

Groups of clients can be treated using systematic desensitization by making slight modifications in the standard procedures.[37] Progressive relaxation is simultaneously taught to the entire group. When the clients share a common problem (such as public speaking anxiety), a **group hierarchy** is constructed, which combines information from each client.[38] When a group hierarchy is not appropriate, individual hierarchies are used; the hierarchy items are written on cards to which each client refers during desensitization. When one of the clients signals that he or she is experiencing anxiety, the scene is terminated and then repeated for all group members. (Although this procedure is inefficient for some group members, it does not decrease the effectiveness of the treatment.) Compared with individually administered desensitization, group desensitization requires less therapist time, and sharing similar problems and solutions can be beneficial for clients.

Coping Desensitization

Courtesy of Marvin R. Goldfried

Marvin Goldfried

In standard desensitization, anxiety associated with specific events is replaced with a competing response to the events. In **coping desensitization,** a variation developed by Marvin Goldfried, it is the *bodily sensations* of anxiety (rather than anxiety related to a particular class of events) that are replaced with a *coping* response.[39] The sensations are used to cue the client to engage in a coping response, such as muscle relaxation. For example, when a client signals that a scene is producing anxiety, the therapist instructs the client to "stay in the scene and use relaxation to cope with the anxiety"—rather than terminating the scene and just relaxing, as in standard desensitization. In addition, the client continues visualizing the anxiety-evoking scene while thinking, "I'm handling things; I don't have to be anxious," or similar thoughts.

In addition to the difference in the desensitization process, the other major difference between coping and standard desensitization concerns the anxiety hierarchy. The hierarchy items need not have a common theme, as they often have in standard desensitization. Because sensations generally associated with anxiety are desensitized, rather than specific anxiety-producing events, the hierarchy items only must result in increasing levels of anxiety. This feature makes coping desensitization applicable to nonspecific anxiety (generalized anxiety disorder).[40]

Coping desensitization is a prime example of the self-control approach that is part of many behavior therapies.[41] First, clients practice reducing their anxiety while visualizing anxiety-evoking scenes by imagining themselves actively coping with the situation, such as by relaxing their muscles. Then, they use anxiety sensations as reminders to use coping skills whenever they experience sensations of anxiety in their daily lives.

Although few studies have evaluated the effectiveness of coping desensitization, it appears to be at least as effective as standard desensitization in reducing anxiety.[42] Some evidence exists that the coping skills generalize to unrelated anxiety-evoking events other than the ones specifically treated in therapy.[43]

Anxiety Management Training, originally developed by Richard Suinn and Frank Richardson,[44] is a variant of coping desensitization in which clients learn to use feelings of anxiety as cues to begin relaxing or to use emotive imagery. Anxiety Management Training is highly structured and brief (six to eight sessions)[45] and does not employ an anxiety hierarchy. Whereas Anxiety Management Training usually is used to treat anxiety disorders,[46] recent research also has demonstrated its efficacy in treating anger, including anger associated with "road rage."[47]

Interoceptive Exposure for Panic Attacks

Panic disorder is an anxiety disorder characterized by repeated, unexpected and sudden attacks of intense apprehension and terror, which are accompanied by physical symptoms, such as shortness of breath, dizziness, heart palpitations, and chest pain. Clients with panic disorder are hypersensitive to bodily sensations that can trigger a panic attack (for example, misinterpreting mild chest pain as a heart attack). David Barlow and his colleagues have developed a specific treatment package for panic attacks.[48] The novel treatment component is **interoceptive exposure** in which the somatic sensations associated with panic attacks are artificially induced while the client visualizes panic-evoking events. (*Interoceptors* are specialized nerve receptors that respond to sensations in internal organs.) For example, increased heart rate and dizziness can be artificially induced by rapid stair climbing and spinning in a chair. During the interoceptive exposure, clients cope with their anxiety by using cognitive restructuring in which they view the situation and sensations as less threatening (see Chapter 12 for details). Finally, clients are taught to use *breathing retraining,* which involves deep, slow, and steady inhaling and exhaling to combat the hyperventilation (abnormally fast or deep respiration) associated with panic attacks.

This treatment package has been found to be highly effective in treating panic disorder as well as social phobia and generalized anxiety disorder.[49] It also has been found to be at least as effective as medication[50] and significantly more effective than medication alone for long-term maintenance.[51]

SYSTEMATIC DESENSITIZATION IN PERSPECTIVE

Despite having been developed 50 years ago, systematic desensitization remains a highly effective and efficient treatment that still is practiced.[52] The general model of treatment provided by systematic desensitization for anxiety also is useful for treating a variety of problems that are maintained by other maladaptive emotional reactions, such as anger.

Systematic desensitization is not applicable to all clients or types of anxiety. For example, young children experience difficulty carrying out the procedures.[53] Techniques more suitable for children include emotive imagery, in vivo exposure (covered later in this chapter), flooding (see Chapter 10), and modeling therapy (see Chapter 11).

When anxiety is maintained by a skill deficit, systematic desensitization is not the appropriate treatment.[54] For instance, people with dating anxiety often do not know how to act appropriately while on a date. The anxiety may be a by-product of the skill deficit rather than the primary maintaining condition of the problem. Thus, the appropriate treatment is skills training (see Chapter 11). When both a skill deficit and anxiety are maintaining conditions of a problem, therapy must address both.

Systematic desensitization is an acceptable treatment to clients. It is relatively "painless" because clients are gradually and symbolically exposed to anxiety-evoking situations. Further, clients control the process by proceeding at their own pace and terminating exposure when they begin to feel anxious.

Efficiency of Systematic Desensitization

Systematic desensitization is efficient in three ways. First, exposure to problematic situations in one's imagination is less time consuming (for both client and therapist) than in vivo exposure, which involves venturing to the actual anxiety-provoking situations. And clients do transfer the anxiety reduction they experience with imagined scenes to the real-life situations. Second, compared with traditional psychotherapies that treat anxiety-related problems, systematic desensitization requires relatively few sessions. Third, the procedures can be adapted for groups of clients.

Desensitization can be automated by using tape-recorded instructions,[55] written instructions,[56] or computer programs.[57] Self-managed desensitization obviously reduces the amount of time therapists need to spend with clients. In some instances, such procedures can be as effective as therapist-directed treatment.[58] However, self-administered desensitization is used infrequently because it has limitations, especially for clients who are extremely anxious or who have problems following the standard procedures (such as difficulty visualizing scenes).[59] A therapist can modify standard procedures to handle unexpected problems that arise (as in Case 9-3, where the therapist introduced humorous scenes) and can provide support and encouragement.[60]

Effectiveness of Systematic Desensitization

There is no doubt that systematic desensitization is an effective procedure for treating a variety of anxiety-related problems. The findings of hundreds of studies assessing the effectiveness of systematic desensitization over the past 40 years are overwhelmingly positive.[61] As early as 1969, a review of the controlled outcome studies of systematic desensitization concluded that "for the first time in the history of psychological treatments, a specific treatment . . . reliably produced measurable benefits for clients across a broad range of distressing problems in which anxiety was of fundamental importance."[62] Seven years and many studies later, another comprehensive review concluded, "Systematic desensitization is demonstrably more effective than both no treatment and every psychotherapy variant with which it has so far been compared."[63] Moreover, the treatment effects are relatively durable. For example, one study found that 70 clients with dental phobias still were maintaining regular dental checkups between 1 and 4 years after being treated by systematic desensitization.[64]

The primary source of evidence for the effectiveness of systematic desensitization comes from experiments. Case 9-4 presents a classic analogue experiment by Gordon Paul illustrating the type of study that has provided evidence for the efficacy of systematic desensitization.

Case 9-4

EFFECTIVENESS OF SYSTEMATIC DESENSITIZATION IN TREATING PUBLIC SPEAKING ANXIETY: A CLASSIC EXPERIMENTAL TEST[65]

Volunteers from a public speaking class first were given a comprehensive pretreatment assessment consisting of self-report, physiological, and overt behavioral measures of public speaking anxiety. The self-report measures asked the students to rate the amount of anxiety they experienced in various public speaking situations. The physiological measures were pulse rate and palm sweat. As the participants gave 4-minute impromptu speeches, observers in the audience noted whether a sample of overt indications of public speaking anxiety were present or absent in 30-second intervals (see Figure 9-3).

The participants were randomly assigned to one of four conditions: (1) standard systematic desensitization, (2) insight-oriented psychotherapy, (3) an attention-placebo control group, or (4) a no-treatment control group. Insight-oriented psychotherapy involved a dialogue between therapist and participant that emphasized gaining self-understanding about the origins of the participants' public speaking anxiety. Participants in the attention-placebo control condition were given what they thought was a fast-acting tranquilizer; actually the capsule contained sodium bicarbonate, an inert substance. This group was included to control for the possible beneficial effects of interacting with the therapist and participants' positive expectations of improvement. Treatment and attention-placebo participants attended five sessions over 6 weeks. Participants in the no-treatment control condition just had their public-speaking anxiety assessed at the same time as the participants in the other conditions. The purpose of the no-treatment control condition was to determine whether changes would take place without any treatment or therapist contact.

Figure 9-3 Part of the checklist observers used to rate participants' overt indications of anxiety while giving a speech (Case 9-4)
SOURCE: Adapted from Paul, 1966, p. 109.

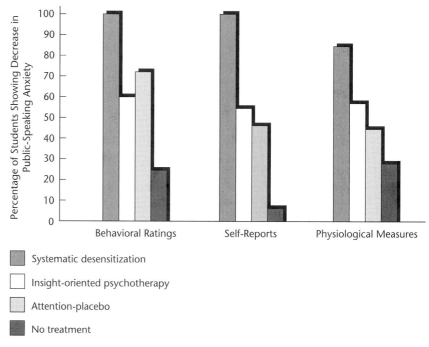

TIMED BEHAVIORAL CHECKLIST
FOR PERFORMANCE ANXIETY

Rater_____ Name_____

Date_____ Speech No. _____ I.D. _____

Behavior observed	Interval								Sum
	1	2	3	4	5	6	7	8	
1. Paces									
2. Sways									
3. Shuffles feet									
4. Arms rigid									
5. Hand tremors									
6. No eye contact									
7. Moistens lips									
8. Swallows									
9. Clears throat									
10. Perspires (face, hands)									
11. Voice quivers									

Comments: Grand total

Figure 9-4 Percentage of students showing a decrease in anxiety immediately after treatment (Case 9-4)
SOURCE: Data from Paul, 1966.

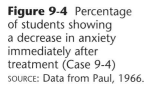

Systematic desensitization

Insight-oriented psychotherapy

Attention-placebo

No treatment

After the last session, the self-report, physiological, and overt behavioral measures were administered again. The results, shown in Figure 9-4, revealed a clear superiority of systematic desensitization over insight-oriented therapy and the two control conditions. Follow-up assessments based on the participants' self-reports 6 weeks[66] and 2 years[67] after therapy indicated the same pattern of results.

This classic experiment has been criticized on two counts. One criticism is that five sessions is hardly enough time for insight-oriented therapy to be effective. An adequate therapist–client relationship, which is crucial in insight-oriented therapy, cannot be built in five sessions.[68] Still, the greater *efficiency* of systematic desensitization may be sufficient grounds for concluding that it is a superior treatment.

The other criticism of the study concerned symptom substitution, a general criticism that psychoanalysts in the 1950s and 1960s made of behavior therapy.[69] *Symptom substitution* refers to the notion that treating behaviors—rather than their so-called "underlying causes"—will result in another maladaptive behavior (symptom) replacing (substituting for) the treated behavior. A hypothetical example would be a client's developing a fear of undressing in locker rooms after successfully being desensitized to a fear of public speaking. A psychoanalyst might argue that this occurred because the underlying cause of the public speaking, such as an unconscious conflict about exposing oneself in public places, was not treated. Although the client no longer was afraid of speaking in public, the unconscious conflict still existed, and it manifested itself in another symptom, fear of undressing in locker rooms.

The symptom substitution criticism of behavior therapy is fallacious for two reasons. First, it is based on the *mistaken* premise that behavior therapy treats symptoms (problem behaviors).[70] As you know, behavior therapy *directly* treats the maintaining conditions—which are the *causes*—of problem behaviors (symptoms). Second, and most important, there is no empirical support for symptom substitution's occurring in behavior therapy.[71]* For example, in Paul's experiment (Case 9-4), evidence for symptom substitution was specifically sought, but not found. None of the participants developed any maladaptive substitute behaviors.

IN VIVO EXPOSURE THERAPY

In vivo exposure therapy (or **in vivo exposure,** for short) essentially is systematic desensitization in which the client is exposed to the actual feared event (rather than imagining it). The exposure is brief and graduated, and the client has the option of terminating the exposure if it becomes too uncomfortable. As an example, for a 6-year-old girl who was afraid to be at school without her mother, the amount of time she spent

---

*Symptom substitution is not the same as negative side effects, which pose potential problems for all types of therapy (Kazdin & Wilson, 1978).

in class alone was gradually increased until she could be in the classroom without her mother for the entire school day.[72]

Muscle relaxation often is used to compete with anxiety, although complete deep muscle relaxation is not possible because the client is using a variety of muscles during the in vivo exposure.[73] However, it is possible for clients to relax all muscles that are not essential to the behaviors being performed and to tense required muscles only as much as is needed. This procedure is known as **differential relaxation.**[74] For example, standing requires some tension in the neck, back, and leg muscles, but facial, arm, chest, and abdominal muscles do not have to be tensed. (Participation Exercise 14-1 will teach you differential relaxation to reduce muscle tension associated with your everyday activities.) Other competing responses used for in vivo exposure therapy include pleasant images, laughter, and sexual arousal. Sometimes simply the *therapist's presence*—which is reassuring and calming to the client—competes with anxiety. Case 9-5 illustrates the basic procedures of in vivo exposure.

Case 9-5

FEAR OF LEAVING HOSPITAL GROUNDS TREATED BY IN VIVO EXPOSURE[75]

A 36-year-old man, who had been hospitalized for 7 years for a serious psychiatric disorder, was intensely afraid of venturing outside the hospital. Spending increasing amounts of time outside the hospital grounds was established as an acceleration target behavior.

After several relaxation sessions in the office, the relaxation sessions were continued while the patient was seated in an automobile. Each week the automobile was driven by the therapist closer to the gate of the hospital grounds, and then farther and farther away from the hospital, until a five-mile drive took place during the third session in the car. During each trip outside the hospital, the patient was let out of the car for increasing lengths of time, going from one minute to a half-hour in three weeks. Concomitant with therapy sessions outside the hospital grounds, the patient was encouraged to go on trips with other patients. By the seventh week, the patient had been to a country fair in the neighboring state, an art show across the river, a local fireman's carnival, and a fishing trip. The art show was the only trip on which the therapist accompanied the patient, and even then, he was alone for half the two-hour show. After the seventh session it was no longer necessary to encourage the patient to go out on day passes, since he signed up for passes and outside activities on his own. At the end of seven in vivo [exposure] . . . sessions, the patient felt comfortable enough to venture outside the hospital without the support of the therapist [or other patients].

Case 9-5 is a "textbook case" of in vivo exposure. Exposure was graduated both *spatially,* by increasing the distance the patient ventured from the hospital, and *temporally,* by increasing the time he spent outside the car. Differential relaxation was employed as a competing response to the client's anxiety.

In an unusual application of in vivo exposure to anorexia nervosa, a 24-year-old man was treated for his pronounced anxiety related to consuming high-fat/high-calorie foods.[76] At the time of treatment, the client reported that in the past year he had lost approximately 100 pounds through diet and exercise. The anxiety hierarchy consisted of foods that made the client anxious and that he routinely avoided, ranging from a plain bagel to pizza and cookies. The client brought foods from the hierarchy to the therapy session. He ate the food with the support of the therapist, which served as a competing response for the client's anxiety. By the 10th session, the client was able to consume as many as 2500 calories a day. By the end of treatment (34th session), he had integrated more foods into his diet and no longer had an intense fear of high-calorie foods.

A related application of in vivo exposure therapy involved a 13-year-old girl who was treated for fear of choking on food.[77] Foods were arranged in the anxiety hierarchy from the easiest to eat (for example, crackers) to the most difficult to eat (for example, raw vegetables). After 14 sessions, the client demonstrated substantially reduced self-reported, observer-rated, and parent-reported anxiety. In addition, she increased her eating rate and bite size as well as the variety of foods she was willing to eat.

Case 9-6 further illustrates the variety of psychological problems to which in vivo exposure is applicable.

Case 9-6

RELIGIOUS-RELATED OBSESSIONS AND COMPULSIONS TREATED BY IN VIVO EXPOSURE[78]

A 36-year-old man had a 14-year history of religious-related obsessions and compulsions. They centered around the belief that he was "damned to hell" because he had not behaved in a religiously proper way. Before beginning exposure therapy, the client had been unsuccessfully treated with clomipramine, a standard medication used to treat obsessive-compulsive disorder. Typically, he spent more than 8 hours a day preoccupied with intrusive thoughts and obsessional doubts about his religious shortcomings, which, not surprisingly, seriously interfered with his life.

The client was exposed in vivo to a hierarchy of situations that evoked obsessional thoughts about sin and damnation, such as purposely making "wrong number" telephone calls and telling tasteless jokes. He also was exposed imaginally to images of the feared consequences of his actions in the hierarchy situations. Following fifteen 90-minute sessions over the course of 8 weeks, the client's symptoms decreased significantly.

Self-Managed In Vivo Exposure

The case of the man treated for his fear of leaving the hospital grounds (see Case 9-5) illustrates two forms of in vivo exposure. Initially, the therapist was present to guide the patient through the exposure, which is **therapist-directed exposure.**[79] Later, the patient engaged in the exposure procedures on his own, following the therapist's directions, which is **self-managed exposure.**[80]

Self-managed in vivo exposure was part of a treatment package used with a 28-year-old teacher suffering from *body dysmorphic disorder*[81] (preoccupation with a perceived physical defect that is not noticeable to others[82]). The teacher was convinced that she had a "bad" complexion. Her repeated checking of her face in the mirror for blemishes significantly interfered with her work and home life. Self-managed in vivo exposure involved the client's gradually applying less makeup and getting physically closer to people at work when she talked to them. After the 11th session, the therapist instructed her to wear no makeup at all and to expose herself to a broader range of people by going to stores and restaurants. By the end of the treatment, she was spending no time checking for physical defects (in contrast to 4 hours a day before treatment).

Self-managed exposure clearly is more efficient than therapist-directed exposure. Moreover, clients may be less likely to drop out of therapy when they fully control their own exposure.[83] Self-managed treatment at home can be implemented through the use of treatment manuals written for clients and with the assistance of family members.[84] The therapist may make occasional home visits to ensure that the client is carrying out the exposure correctly.[85] It even is possible for clients to carry out self-managed in vivo exposure with guidance from the therapist via telephone calls.[86] Telephone-administered therapy has obvious advantages for clients who are housebound or who live far from available therapists. Case 9-7 is an unusual example of self-managed in vivo exposure that illustrates the flexibility of the procedure.

SELF-MANAGED IN VIVO EXPOSURE FOR FEAR OF DOGS[87]

Case 9-7

A man sought the help of a behavior therapist to deal with his overwhelming fear of dogs. Between the first and second therapy sessions, a fortuitous incident occurred. A friend told the client that his dog had just had puppies, and he jokingly asked the client if he wanted one of them. After consulting with his therapist, the client decided to take one of the dogs because he believed he could tolerate a *puppy* in his home.

The situation contained all the essential ingredients for self-managed in vivo exposure. The client would be exposed to a dog that gradually became larger. Moreover, his exposure to the dog would be in the context of happy interactions with his children and the accompanying pleasure would serve as a competing response to his anxiety about dogs. After 6 months of raising the puppy, the client no longer reported any fear of dogs.

In Case 9-7, the client initiated in vivo exposure with a therapist's advice. Sometimes people successfully deal with their fears completely on their own by engaging in an *informal* self-managed in vivo exposure process. Case 9-8 is an example.

Case 9-8

SELF-INITIATED AND SELF-MANAGED IN VIVO EXPOSURE FOR SEPARATION ANXIETY IN A 5-YEAR-OLD BOY[88]

During the first week of school, 5-year-old Robin insisted that his parent come into the classroom and remain with him. Each time his parent prepared to leave, Robin clung to the parent and cried. Eventually, the teacher, Mrs. Mort, had to help physically separate Robin from his parent and urge the parent to exit the room quickly.

Mrs. Mort suggested to Robin's parents that they attempt to leave him just inside the classroom door. On Monday of the second week of school, Robin's father walked Robin into the classroom and told him that he was going to leave after Robin had signed in. Robin protested, but not as much as in the previous week.

A week and a half after school had begun, Robin spontaneously "took charge" of the in vivo exposure. Robin told his father, "You don't have to come into the room with me. You can just walk me to the door." Several days later, Robin told his mother that she could leave him just inside the entrance to the school, which was a short distance from his classroom. After another 3 days, Robin indicated that he would say goodbye right before entering the school. Finally, in the middle of the third week of school, Robin said that it was "okay" to drop him off at the end of the walk that led to the front door of the school, which is the point where most parents left their children. Thereafter, Robin was able to leave his parent each morning with little or no visible signs of distress. A 3-year follow-up revealed that the problem had not recurred.

After some initial interventions made by his teacher and parents, Robin spontaneously assumed responsibility for overcoming his separation anxiety. He progressed through an implicit anxiety hierarchy at a pace that was comfortable for him. Robin also may have benefited from other children's modeling being dropped off for school without their parents' remaining with them. The case is noteworthy because the self-initiated and self-managed therapy was done by a 5-year-old.

SELF-MANAGED IN VIVO EXPOSURE IN THE TREATMENT OF SEXUAL DYSFUNCTIONS

Self-managed in vivo exposure is especially useful when the therapist's presence is inappropriate, such as in the treatment of sexual dysfunctions.[89] *Sexual dysfunctions* include diminished sexual desire, problems achieving orgasm, and pain during intercourse. Couples, rather than individuals, are treated because sexual dysfunctions are viewed in the context of a sexual relationship and not as a problem of one of the partners.[90]

Anxiety often is a primary maintaining condition of sexual dysfunctions, and in vivo exposure typically is part of a treatment package for such problems. At home, the couple is instructed to engage in physical intimacies gradually. Increasingly more anxiety-producing sexual behaviors form an anxiety hierarchy. For example, at the bottom of the hierarchy might be holding hands, and at the top might be sexual intercourse. The couple's physical intimacies produce sexual arousal (often mild at first), which competes with the anxiety. The couple proceeds up the hierarchy, stopping whenever one partner begins to experience anxiety and his or her sexual arousal starts to diminish. Only when both partners feel comfortable engaging in a particular sexual behavior is the next step in the hierarchy attempted. Sexual performance, including intercourse and orgasm, is not a goal of the treatment. Couples are instructed to follow the rule that pleasurable physical contact alone is the goal of each in vivo exposure session. In such a *nondemand situation,* couples learn to enjoy sexual activity by gradually coming to feel comfortable and sexually aroused.

IN VIVO EXPOSURE THERAPY IN PERSPECTIVE

In vivo exposure, like systematic desensitization, is a versatile procedure that can be applied to many different anxiety-related disorders.[91] For example, in vivo exposure is at least as effective as medication in treating clients with panic attacks.[92] It is superior to other psychological interventions and behavior therapies (including educational information-based approaches, social support, cognitive restructuring, and relaxation training) in reducing anxiety associated with social phobias.[93]

In vivo exposure can reduce both overt behavioral and cognitive components of anxiety. For instance, clients treated by in vivo exposure therapy for public speaking anxiety showed fewer overt behavioral components of anxiety (such as pacing while talking) and reported fewer cognitive components of anxiety (such as worrying about others' negative evaluations of them).[94]

In vivo exposure has three advantages over systematic desensitization. First, in vivo exposure can be effective for clients who have difficulty imagining scenes, which occasionally occurs with adults and often with young children.[95] Second, avoidance behaviors can be monitored directly with in vivo exposure; this is not possible with systematic desensitization because the therapist does not have access to the client's mental images.[96] Third, in some instances in vivo exposure is more effective than systematic desensitization; because the therapy takes place directly in the anxiety-evoking situation, the need for transfer from the imagined to the actual situation is eliminated.

In vivo exposure has three limitations. First, because in vivo exposure involves going to the actual environment where the client's anxiety occurs, considerable therapist time is required. For instance, two therapists were required to implement the in vivo exposure with Paul in Case 4-1. Self-managed in vivo exposure is one way to deal with the problem of inordinate demands on therapists' time. A second limitation is that in vivo exposure is not feasible with certain anxiety-evoking events (for example, natural disasters such as earthquakes). Third, some clients cannot tolerate being in the actual threatening situation, even when exposure is graduated and the client is engaging in a competing response. Imaginal exposure in systematic desensitization may be all that the client can tolerate, at least initially. A promising strategy for dealing with children's resistance to in vivo exposure incorporates behavioral child management training.[97] The parents are taught to use child management techniques (such as prompting and shaping) to facilitate their children's exposure to anxiety-evoking situations.

EXPOSURE THERAPY THROUGH VIRTUAL REALITY

Reaping the advantages of in vivo exposure without its disadvantages may seem like having one's cake and eating it too. In fact, this may be possible by exposing clients to anxiety-evoking stimuli through computer-generated virtual reality technology.[98] Clients wear a head-mounted display that provides a computer-generated view of a virtual reality environment (see Photo 9-2).[99] Electromagnetic sensors placed on the head and arm monitor the client's movements so that the client is able to "interact" with objects in the virtual environment. For example, in a study in which clients were treated for fear of flying, the virtual reality scenes placed clients in a window seat of a commercial airliner. As clients moved their heads, they were able to look out the window or inside to empty

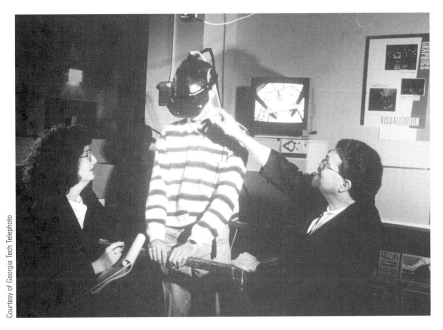

Photo 9-2 Client with fear of heights undergoing exposure therapy using virtual reality technology

Courtesy of Georgia Tech Telephoto

seats. Clients were gradually exposed to increasingly anxiety-evoking scenes and sensations, including sitting on a plane with engines off, sitting on a plane with engines on, taxiing, takeoff, smooth flight, a thunderstorm with turbulence, and landing.

As is implied by the term *virtual reality,* what clients experience is about as real as if they were in the actual situation, as the following incident illustrates.[100] When the procedures were used to treat fear of heights, one of the virtual reality scenes was an open elevator door with only space below. Not even the therapists, who exposed themselves to this virtual reality scene before it was used with clients, were willing to "walk off the elevator into midair" without being prompted to do so and being reassured that it was perfectly safe.[101]

Barbara Rothbaum and Larry Hodges pioneered exposure therapy through virtual reality, which has been used to treat phobias, including fear of flying[102] fears of heights,[103] fear of spiders,[104] and claustrophobia (fear of enclosed spaces).[105] At present, evaluation of exposure therapy through virtual reality is just barely a reality, with two controlled studies indicating its effectiveness in significantly reducing clients' fears compared with wait-list control groups.[106] However, its potential benefits are exciting to consider. These benefits include the ability to expose clients to anxiety-evoking situations that they could not be exposed to in vivo (such as earthquakes) and the savings in time compared with in vivo exposure.

◆ In Theory 9-1

WHY DOES BRIEF/GRADUATED EXPOSURE THERAPY WORK?

Why does brief/graduated exposure reduce anxiety? A number of theoretical explanations have been advanced, and we will describe the five most common.

Counterconditioning

Wolpe's original theory involved a *counterconditioning process* in which an adaptive response (feeling relaxed, for example) is substituted for a maladaptive response (such as anxiety) to a threatening stimulus.[107] To understand this process, it is helpful to first see how anxiety may develop according to a classical conditioning model of learning. Anxiety develops when a neutral event (a conditioned stimulus), one that does not elicit anxiety, is associated with an event that causes anxiety (an unconditioned stimulus). Consider the simple example diagrammed in Figure 9-5. You *speak up in class* (conditioned stimulus) and *students laugh at you* (unconditioned stimulus). This establishes an association between speaking in class and feeling embarrassed or humiliated. Being laughed at is likely to make you anxious. Subsequently, speaking in class may make you anxious.

Brief/graduated exposure counters this conditioning by associating the anxiety-evoking event with relaxation or another anxiety-competing response (see Figure 9-6). One problem with the counterconditioning explanation is that brief/graduated exposure without a competing response can be effective.

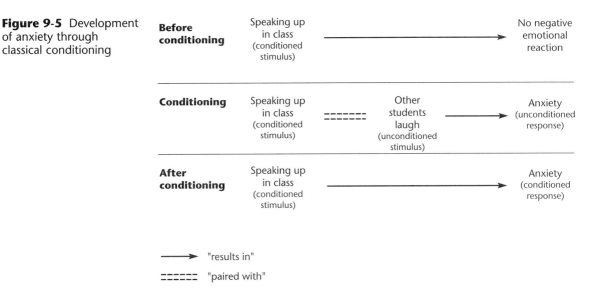

Figure 9-5 Development of anxiety through classical conditioning

"results in"

"paired with"

Reciprocal Inhibition

Wolpe's theory included a more basic, neurophysiological explanation. Our physical emotional responses associated with anxiety (for example, increased heart rate and sweating) are largely controlled by the autonomic nervous system, which is divided into two branches: sympathetic and parasympathetic. The physical symptoms of anxiety are primarily sympathetic functions, whereas relaxation generally is associated with parasympathetic functions. At any given moment, either the sympathetic or the parasympathetic system predominates. Thus, during brief/graduated exposure therapy, the client's anxiety is *inhibited* by a *reciprocal* or opposite physiological response, relaxation. This process is known as *reciprocal inhibition*. One potential problem with this explanation is that sympathetic activity and parasympathetic activity are only partly independent because both branches of the autonomic nervous system always are active to some degree.

Extinction

Another explanation of how brief/graduated exposure works suggests that extinction is the basic underlying mechanism.[108] The extinction explanation, like Wolpe's counterconditioning explanation, assumes that anxiety develops by classical conditioning. Extinction involves terminating reinforcement. In classical conditioning, *reinforcement* specifically refers to the pairing of the conditioned stimulus and the unconditioned stimulus. This pairing is broken in brief/graduated exposure when the client is repeatedly exposed to the conditioned stimulus (speaking in class) *in the absence* of the unconditioned stimulus (being laughed at).

Cognitive Factors

Cognitive theories deal with changes in the client's thinking, which may occur in at least three different ways. One explanation is that the safe exposure to anxiety-arousing situations may result in clients' *thinking about the situations more*

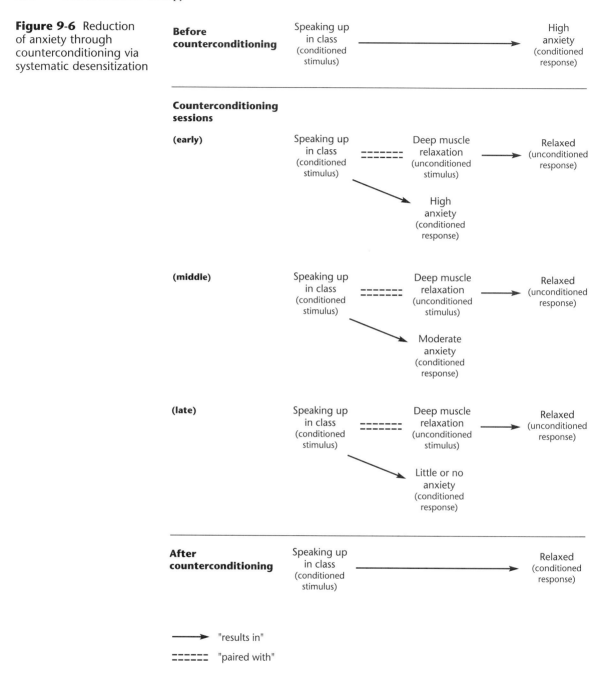

Figure 9-6 Reduction of anxiety through counterconditioning via systematic desensitization

realistically.[109] Realistic thinking renders the situations less threatening. Brief/graduated exposure is used to treat anxiety that is unreal- istic in the sense of being inappro- priate and exaggerated. Relaxation, or another competing response, may help clients focus and think more objectively about their anxiety, which allows them to see it as unrealistic.[110]

A second cognitive explanation suggests that brief/graduated exposure leads clients to *expect that they will be less anxious* than they had assumed they would be when exposed to anxiety-evoking events. This change in expectation occurs because clients' levels of anxiety are reduced. This explanation is consistent with the finding that when people are led to believe that they are less afraid (as through false feedback), they actually feel less afraid.[111]

A third cognitive explanation holds that brief/graduated exposure may *strengthen clients' beliefs that they are capable of coping with their anxiety.*[112] This belief would be expected to develop from clients' repeated successes during treatment— that is, they repeatedly are exposed (either imaginally or in vivo) to anxiety-provoking situations without experiencing negative consequences, including feeling anxious.

Nonspecific Factors

Finally, the effects of brief/graduated exposure may be explained by *nonspecific factors,* which are elements that are part of therapy in general but not part of the specific therapy. The attention a therapist gives the client is a generic nonspecific factor. Research studies have controlled for therapist attention to assess its effect on therapy outcome. This is done by comparing clients who receive brief/graduated exposure with clients in an attention-control condition, in which clients spend time with the therapist but receive no therapy. These studies indicate that nonspecific factors such as therapist attention can play a role in the success of brief/graduated exposure.[113] However, the studies also show that nonspecific factors alone do not account for the effectiveness of the therapy.[114]

Obviously, there are many answers to the question, Why does brief/graduated exposure therapy work? We have presented the most prominent theoretical explanations; a variety of other explanations have been proposed, including those based on shaping and modeling.[115]

In the next chapter, we turn to the other model of exposure therapy, prolonged/intense. The extinction, cognitive, and nonspecific factors explanations of brief/graduated exposure therapies just described also explain why prolonged/intense exposure therapies work.

◆ ## ALL THINGS CONSIDERED: BRIEF/GRADUATED EXPOSURE THERAPY

The first exposure therapies to be developed were brief and graduated, starting with imaginal exposure (systematic desensitization) and later introducing in vivo exposure procedures. These early exposure therapies all employed a competing response for anxiety, usually muscle relaxation. In more recent applications of brief/graduated exposure, a competing response sometimes is not included, which is legitimate given that a competing response is not an essential component of the treatment.[116]

Increasingly imaginal and in vivo exposure are being combined for clients,[117] which is consistent with a general trend in behavior therapy to use treatment packages to enhance therapy effectiveness and bring about change more quickly. Another trend in imaginal exposure therapies has been to supplement visualization of anxiety-evoking scenes with their verbal descriptions during imaginal exposure and for the descriptions to be audio taped and used during homework practice.[118]

The results from hundreds of studies evaluating brief/graduated exposure therapies clearly indicate that they are effective treatments for a variety of anxiety and related disorders. Justifiably, then, relatively few outcome studies of these therapies have been done in recent years. However, brief/graduated exposure therapies are still widely used in clinical practice.[119] Indeed, there even has been a trend toward using a graduated exposure component in exposure therapies that are more consistent with the prolonged/intense model (the topic of the next chapter).[120]

When exposure is brief and graduated, clients experience little or no distress. Accordingly, clients find brief/graduated exposure more acceptable than prolonged/intense exposure, and they are more likely to undergo and less likely to drop out of brief/graduated exposure therapies.

SUMMARY

1. Exposure therapies are used to treat anxiety, fear, and other intense negative emotional responses by exposing clients to the events that create negative emotions.

2. There are two models of exposure therapy. With brief/graduated exposure, the client is gradually exposed to increasingly threatening events for a short period. With prolonged/intense exposure, the client is exposed all at once to highly threatening events for a lengthy period. In both models, the client can be exposed to the threatening events imaginally or in vivo. The exposure can be therapist-directed or self-managed by the client. Procedures that may be used to augment exposure include a competing response to anxiety, response prevention, and exaggerated scenes.

3. In systematic desensitization, the client is exposed imaginally to successively more anxiety-arousing situations while engaging in a response that competes with anxiety. First, the client learns the competing response, most often progressive relaxation. Second, the client and therapist construct an anxiety hierarchy, which is a list of events ordered in terms of increasing levels of anxiety they elicit. Clients may use the Subjective Units of Discomfort (SUDs) scale to rate their discomfort. Third, the client visualizes the anxiety-evoking events in the hierarchy, beginning at the low end, while performing the competing response. If the client experiences anxiety while visualizing a scene, the client stops visualizing it and relaxes.

4. The essential component of systematic desensitization is repeated exposure to anxiety-evoking situations without experiencing any

negative consequences. Gradual exposure and a competing response are facilitative components.

5. Variations of systematic desensitization include competing responses other than muscle relaxation (such as pleasant thoughts and laughter), target behaviors other than anxiety (such as anger), group desensitization, and coping desensitization, in which clients use bodily sensations of anxiety as cues to relax and otherwise cope with an anxiety-evoking event. Interoceptive exposure is a treatment package that artificially induces the bodily sensations the client experiences while gradually visualizing panic-inducing events.

6. With in vivo exposure therapy, clients are exposed to the actual feared events. The competing response is usually differential relaxation, which involves clients' relaxing all nonessential muscles. The exposure is brief and graduated. In vivo exposure can be therapist-directed or self-managed. Self-managed exposure is efficient and useful when it is impractical or inappropriate for the therapist to be present, such as in the treatment of sexual dysfunctions.

7. In vivo exposure is a versatile procedure that sometimes is superior to systematic desensitization. Its limitations include the extensive amount of therapist time required, its not being applicable to some anxiety-evoking events, and the inability of some clients to tolerate being in the actual threatening situation.

8. Exposing clients to anxiety-producing stimuli through computer-generated virtual reality technology is a promising new method of treatment.

9. Brief/graduated exposure can be explained in terms of learning (counterconditioning and extinction), physiological processes (reciprocal inhibition), cognitive variables, and nonspecific factors. The learning explanations are predicated on anxiety being developed and maintained through classical conditioning.

10. Recent trends in brief/gradual exposure therapy include not using a competing response, combining imaginal and in vivo exposure, and including verbal descriptions of scenes the client is visualizing. Brief/gradual exposure therapies clearly have been demonstrated to be effective, and clients consider them to be acceptable treatments.

REFERENCE NOTES

1. Landers, 1990.
2. Wilson, O'Leary, & Nathan, 1992.
3. For example, Rothbaum & Hodges, 1999; Rothbaum, Hodges, Smith, Lee, & Price, 2000.
4. For example, Fecteau & Nicki, 1999; Tolin & Foa, 1999.
5. For example, Coldwell, Getz, Milgrom, Prall, Spadafora, & Ramsay, 1998; Schwartz, Houlihan, Krueger, & Simon, 1997; Tolin & Foa, 1999.
6. Wolpe, 1958.
7. Jacobson, 1929.
8. Compare with Lucic, Steffen, Harrigan, & Stuebing, 1991.
9. Bernstein, Borkovec, & Hazlett-Stevens, 2000; Lukins, Davan, & Drummond, 1997; Öst & Breitholz, 2000; Öst, Westling, & Hellstrom, 1993.
10. For example, Bernstein, Borkovec, & Hazlett-Stevens, 2000; de L. Horne, Taylor, & Varigos,

1999; Jorgensen & Carey, 1994; Means, Lichstein, Eppereson, & Johnson, 2000; Spector, Carey, Jorgensen, Meisler, & Carnrike, 1993.
11. For example, Geer, 1965; Spiegler & Liebert, 1970; Wolpe & Lang, 1964.
12. McCathie & Spence, 1991; Ollendick, 1983; Ramirez & Kratochwill, 1990; Scherer & Nakamura, 1968.
13. Wolpe & Lazarus, 1966; see also Spiegler & Agigian, 1977, p. 100.
14. Wolpe & Lazarus, 1966, quotation from p. 81.
15. Lang, 1969.
16. For example, Krapfl, 1967; Richardson & Suinn, 1973.
17. For example, Goldfried & Davison, 1994; Walker, Hedberg, Clement, & Wright, 1981.
18. For example, Miller & Nawas, 1970; Nawas, Welsch, & Fishman, 1970.
19. Bandura, 1969; Lang, 1969.
20. Morrow, 1986.
21. Lazarus & Abramovitz, 1962.
22. Nevo & Shapira, 1988.
23. Cousins, 1979, 1989.
24. Seligson & Peterson, 1992.
25. Ventis, 1973.
26. For example, Rimm, DeGroot, Boord, Heiman, & Dillow, 1971.
27. For example, Moore, 1965.
28. For example, Steinmark & Borkovec, 1974.
29. Saunders, 1976.
30. For example, Shorkey & Himle, 1974.
31. For example, Hedberg & Campbell, 1974.
32. For example, Meyer, 1975.
33. For example, Walton & Mather, 1963.
34. Fisher & Thompson, 1994.
35. For example, Cotharin & Mikulas, 1975.
36. Smith, 1973; quotations from pp. 577–578.
37. For example, Anton, 1976; Lazarus, 1961; Paul & Shannon, 1966; Taylor, 1971.
38. For example, Spiegler, Cooley, Marshall, Prince, Puckett, & Skenazy, 1976.
39. Goldfried, 1971.
40. Borkovec & Costello, 1993; Borkovec & Mathews, 1988; Borkovec & Whisman, 1996.
41. For example, Borkovec & Costello, 1993; Borkovec & Whisman, 1996.
42. Spiegler, Cooley, Marshall, Prince, Puckett, & Skenazy, 1976.
43. Borkovec & Mathews, 1988.
44. Suinn & Richardson, 1971.
45. Suinn, 2001.
46. Suinn, 2001; Thom, Sartory, & Johren, 2000.
47. Deffenbacker, Filetti, Lynch, & Dahlen, 2000; Deffenbacker, Huff, Lynch, Oetting, & Salvatore, 2000.
48. Barlow, 1988.
49. Barlow, 1993; Barlow & Cerney, 1988; Barlow, Craske, Cerney, & Klosko, 1989; Barlow, Gorman, Shear, & Woods, 2000; Brown, Antony, & Barlow, 1995; Carter & Barlow, 1993, 1995; Gould & Otto, 1995; Gould, Otto, & Pollack, in press; Stuart, Treat, & Wade, 2000.
50. Otto, Pollack, Sachs, Reiter, Meltzer-Brody, & Rosenbaum, 1993; Pollack, Otto, Kaspi, Hammerness, & Rosenbaum, 1994.
51. Barlow, Gorman, Shear, & Woods, 2000; Otto & Gould, 1995; Otto, Gould, & Pollack, 1994.
52. Guevremont & Spiegler, 1990; Spiegler & Guevremont, 2002.
53. For example, Silverman & Rabian, 1994.
54. Compare with Kirkland & Hollandsworth, 1980.
55. For example, Donner & Guerney, 1969; Evans & Kellam, 1973; Lang, Melamed, & Hart, 1970.
56. For example, Rosen, Glasgow, & Barrera, 1976.
57. For example, Bornas, Fullana, Tortella-Feliu, Llabrés, J., & de la Banda, 2001; Chandler, Burck, & Sampson, 1986.
58. For example, Evans & Kellam, 1973; Rosen, Glasgow, & Barrera, 1976.
59. For example, Bernstein & Borkovec, 1973; Bernstein, Borkovec, & Hazlett-Stevens, 2000; Carlson & Bernstein, 1995; Marquis, Morgan, & Piaget, 1971.
60. For example, Goldfried & Davison, 1994; Walker, Hedberg, Clement, & Wright, 1981.
61. For example, Kazdin & Wilcoxon, 1976; Kazdin & Wilson, 1978; Masters, Burish, Hollon, & Rimm, 1987.
62. Paul, 1969b, p. 159.
63. Leitenberg, 1976, p. 131.
64. Liddell, DiFazio, Blackwood, & Ackerman, 1994.
65. Paul, 1966.
66. Paul, 1966.
67. Paul, 1967.
68. Strupp, 1966.
69. Cahoon, 1968; Ullmann & Krasner, 1965.
70. For example, Sahakian & Charlesworth, 1994.
71. For example, Bandura, 1969; Kazdin & Wilson, 1978; Sloane, Staples, Cristol, Yorkston, & Whipple, 1975.

72. Hagopian & Slifer, 1993.
73. For example, McCarthy & Craig, 1995; McGlynn, Moore, Rose, & Lazarte, 1995.
74. Goldfried & Davison, 1994.
75. Weidner, 1970; quotation from p. 80.
76. Boutelle, 1998.
77. Chorpita, Vitali, & Barlow, 1997.
78. Abramowitz, 2001.
79. Williams, Dooseman, & Kleifield, 1984.
80. For example, Fecteau & Nicki, 1999; Marks, 1978.
81. Neziroglu & Yaryura-Tobias, 1993.
82. Thompson, 1992.
83. For example, Barlow, O'Brien, & Last, 1984; Jannoun, Munby, Catalan, & Gelder, 1980.
84. Barlow, O'Brien, & Last, 1984; Mathews, Teasdale, Munby, Johnston, & Shaw, 1977; Munby & Johnston, 1980.
85. For example, Mathews, Gelder, & Johnston, 1981; Mathews, Teasdale, Munby, Johnston, & Shaw, 1977.
86. Lovell, Fullalove, Garvey, & Brooker, 2000; McNamee, O'Sullivan, Lelliott, & Marks, 1989; Swinson, Fergus, Cox, & Wickwire, 1995.
87. Goldfried & Davison, 1994.
88. From the author's (MDS) clinical files.
89. Masters & Johnson, 1970.
90. For example, Kaplan, 1974, 1975; Masters & Johnson, 1970; Wolpe & Lazarus, 1966.
91. For example, Antony, McCabe, Leeuw, Sano, & Swinson, 2001; Boutelle, 1998; Chambless, 1985; Chorpita, Vitali, & Barlow, 1997; de Jong, Vorage, & van den Hout, 2000; Dyck & Spinhoven, 1997; Franklin, Abramowitz, Kozak, Levitt, & Foa, 2000; Hill, 1989; Kearney & Silverman, 1999; Marks, 1978, 1987; McGlynn & Cornell, 1985; Menzies & Clarke, 1993; Sturges & Sturges, 1998.
92. Clum, Clum, & Surls, 1993.
93. Donohue, Van Hasselt, & Hersen, 1994.
94. Newman, Hofmann, Trabert, Roth, & Taylor, 1994.
95. Hill, 1989; Morris & Kratochwill, 1983; Ollendick & Cerny, 1981.
96. Chambless, 1985.
97. Silverman, Kurtines, Ginsburg, Weems, Lumpkin, & Carmichael, 1999; Silverman, Kurtines, Ginsburg, Weems, Rabian, & Serafini, 1999.
98. North, North, & Coble, 1998; Rothbaum, Hodges, Kooper, Opdyke, Williford, & North, 1995a, 1995b; Vincelli & Molinari, 1998.
99. Hodges, Rothbaum, Kooper, Opdyke, Meyer, De Graff, & Williford, 1994.
100. Hodges, Rothbaum, Kooper, Opdyke, Meyer, De Graff, & Williford, 1994; Kalawsky, 1993; Rothbaum, Hodges, Kooper, Opdyke, Williford, & North, 1995b.
101. Hodges, Rothbaum, Kooper, Opdyke, Meyer, De Graff, & Williford, 1994.
102. Rothbaum, Hodges, Smith, Lee, & Price, 2000; Smith, Rothbaum, & Hodges, 1999.
103. Rothbaum & Hodges, 1999; Rothbaum, Hodges, Kooper, Opdyke, Williford, & North, 1995b.
104. Carlin, Hoffman, & Weghorst, 1997.
105. Botella, Baños, Perpiña, Villa, Alcañiz, & Rey, 1998.
106. Rothbaum, Hodges, Kooper, Opdyke, Williford, & North, 1995b.
107. Wolpe, 1958.
108. Kazdin & Wilcoxon, 1976.
109. For example, Borkovec & Whisman, 1996.
110. Beck, 1976.
111. Lick, 1975; Valins & Ray, 1967
112. Bandura, 1977a, 1978, 1984.
113. Compare with Strupp, 1995.
114. Kazdin & Wilcoxon, 1976.
115. Kazdin & Wilcoxon, 1976.
116. de Jong, Vorage, & van den Hout, 2000.
117. For example, Abramowitz, 2001; Tolin & Foa, 1999.
118. For example, Fecteau & Nicki, 1999; Tolin & Foa, 1999.
119. Spiegler & Guevremont, 2002.
120. For example, Tolin & Foa, 1999.

Prolonged/Intense Exposure Therapy

We introduced exposure therapy in the previous chapter by likening it to getting back on the horse that has thrown you. In fact, brief/graduated exposure is more like getting back on an old mare, whereas prolonged/intense exposure is more like mounting a wild stallion. Brief/graduated exposure minimizes clients' anxiety during treatment by presenting clients with small doses of anxiety-evoking stimuli that gradually become more intense. In contrast, prolonged/intense exposure *maximizes* clients' anxiety with large doses of anxiety-evoking stimuli that are intense from the outset. Because prolonged/intense exposure therapies reduce anxiety by initially increasing it, they are sometimes called **anxiety-induction therapies.** In a sense, these therapies fight anxiety with anxiety.

Most prolonged/intense exposure therapies fall in the category of **flooding,** which consists of exposure to stimuli that elicit high levels of anxiety[1] for a prolonged period (sometimes for more than an hour).[2] Although the client experiences high levels of anxiety during exposure, the feared negative consequences do not actually occur—a characteristic of all exposure therapies. The exposure in flooding can occur in vivo or imaginally.

Before looking at flooding and its variants, consider the following case of informal self-managed flooding. You will see that the exposure did not last long, but it was very intense. And it was highly effective and long lasting.

Case 10-1

DEBUGGING A COCKROACH PHOBIA: A CASE OF INFORMAL SELF-MANAGED FLOODING[3]

Occasionally, people inadvertently find themselves in circumstances that are analogous to flooding and can use it to overcome a strong and even long-standing fear. This occurred to V. W., a world-famous entomologist (insect specialist), when, as a graduate student, he was given a lab assignment to draw blood from a cockroach. This seemingly innocuous task for someone who was about to embark on a career studying insects created tremendous anxiety for V. W. Although he had been fascinated with insects from an early age, he detested cockroaches. His aversion to cockroaches began when he first encountered them in his home as a child. Although his repulsion to and avoidance of cockroaches had persisted into adulthood, it had not generalized to other insects.

To complete his lab assignment, V. W. had to go with other students in his class to an underground passageway and secure a specimen from the thousands of cockroaches that could be found there. He went to the passageway feeling intensely anxious. As his classmates nonchalantly picked up cockroaches and returned to the lab, V. W. stood there frozen, not knowing what he would do. At that moment, V. W. realized that if he could not complete this lab assignment, he would have to drop out of graduate school. Although he was terrified, he reached out and grabbed a cockroach. Almost immediately his anxiety began to diminish. By the time he reached the lab holding his cockroach, the anxiety was completely gone. More than 50 years later, V. W. has remained free of his former intense aversion to cockroaches.

In Vivo Flooding

In vivo flooding involves prolonged/intense exposure to *actual* anxiety-producing stimuli. It is used to treat an array of problems, including phobias,[4] obsessive-compulsive disorder,[5] posttraumatic stress disorder,[6] anorexia nervosa,[7] and body dysmorphic disorder.[8] Case 10-2 illustrates the basic procedures of in vivo flooding, including the essential component: *exposure to a highly aversive situation long enough for the client's discomfort to peak and then start to decline.* [9] In the case description, you will see that before the therapy began, the therapist explained in vivo flooding to the client, including telling her that the treatment would cause some discomfort.

Case 10-2 ## Fear of Riding on Escalators Treated by In Vivo Flooding[10]

The patient was a 24-year-old female student with an intense fear . . . of escalators. She had developed this phobia about 7 years previously. She had ascended an escalator with some of her immediate family with relative ease, but had expressed fear of descending because of the apparent height. The relatives had jokingly forced her on to the escalator, and ever since she had experienced an aversion toward escalators, always taking the stairs or the elevator. . . . On one occasion she had unexpectedly come upon an escalator while shopping, and had become so overwhelmed with anxiety that it was only with great difficulty that she had prevented herself from vomiting. Whenever she was in the company of anyone who proposed riding an escalator to another floor, she would experience a quickening of the pulse and would bluntly refuse. Before [entering therapy] . . ., she had made some unsuccessful attempts to overcome the fear by attempting, in the company of friends, to get on to an escalator. On those occasions when she could bring herself to stand at the foot of the escalator, she would not step on [because she feared] . . . that by holding on to the hand rail she would be pulled downward and so miss her step.

At the single session during which the history of the disorder was obtained, the in vivo flooding procedure was explained to the patient. She was told that the technique had been successfully employed in the treatment of numerous phobias and was almost certain to work in her case. She was also informed that she would experience some emotional distress but was assured that [the therapist] would be with her throughout the experience to ensure no resulting adverse effects. [The therapist] then arranged to meet her at a large department store with four levels of escalators. Initially, the patient manifested an intense anxiety reaction when requested to approach the escalator, and it was only through much coaxing, reassurance, and [mild] physical [prompting] from [the therapist] that she finally stepped on to it. She then threatened to vomit and seemed at the verge of tears, all the time clinging tightly to [the therapist's] shirt. Getting on to the second flight of the escalator was much easier, but she still manifested the same signs of anxiety. After 27 minutes of riding up and down the escalator, she was approaching it with increasing readiness and reported a dramatic decrease in anxiety. She was then instructed to ride the escalator alone, and did so with relative ease. When she felt that there was no need for further treatment the session was terminated, after 29 minutes. Six months later the patient reported that she still experienced no anxiety on escalators except on rare occasions when descending.

The woman in Case 10-2 clearly was motivated to rid herself of her intense fear. Before seeking therapy, she was unsuccessful in her attempts to overcome her fear on her own (unlike V. W. in Case 10-1). The woman experienced considerable initial anxiety during the flooding procedure, followed by a rapid decrease in anxiety. Although flooding occasionally can involve just a few sessions of intense exposure, as in Case 10-2, typically more sessions are required.

The description of the development and maintenance of the patient's fear of riding on escalators in Case 10-2 is worth noting. Her intense fear began with a single, traumatic experience. From that time on, she avoided going on escalators, which reduced her fear and reinforced her avoidance behaviors. This sequence of events is consistent with the two-factor learning theory described in In Theory 10-1.

In Theory 10-1

THE TWO-FACTOR LEARNING THEORY OF THE DEVELOPMENT AND MAINTENANCE OF FEAR

The two-factor learning theory of how debilitating fear develops and is maintained involves both classical and operant conditioning.[11] Fear initially develops through classical conditioning (see Figure 9-5, page 229). A neutral event (conditioned stimulus)—one that does not elicit fear—is associated with a threatening event (unconditioned stimulus), which elicits fear. Because of the association between the conditioned and unconditioned stimuli, the previously neutral event now causes the person to feel fearful. For instance, a person who previously had no fear of being in an automobile may develop an intense fear of driving in cars after being in an automobile accident. Being in an accident naturally results in fear; and through the association of being in a car and having an accident, just being in a car comes to elicit fear. Once the person's fear has developed, it is maintained through operant conditioning; the person learns to engage in a fear-reducing response whenever he or she is faced with the fear-evoking event. Usually, this response involves avoiding or escaping from the fear-evoking event. The response continues and is strengthened because it is negatively reinforced—that is, it terminates the unpleasant experience of fear. For example, when a person who is afraid of driving in cars refuses an offer of a ride, the person's fear declines because the threatening situation is avoided. On one hand, the avoidance behavior serves the function of keeping the individual from feeling fearful. On the other hand, the behavior is maladaptive because the person never learns that driving in a car can be safe, which is important in our car-dependent world. Fortunately, exposure therapy can create such learning.

In vivo flooding often includes **response prevention,** in which clients are specifically prevented from engaging in their typical maladaptive anxiety-reducing responses. (Response prevention sometimes is used with in vivo exposure.[12]) Consider how flooding with response prevention is employed to treat *bulimia nervosa,* a disorder in which the person first binges (consumes large quantities of food) and then purges the food, usually by inducing vomiting. The client is instructed to binge eat (exposure) but is not allowed to induce vomiting (response prevention).[13]

Response prevention is an essential component of in vivo flooding for *obsessive-compulsive disorder,* in which a person is preoccupied (obsessed) with particular anxiety-evoking events and alleviates the resulting anxiety by performing maladaptive ritualistic behaviors (compulsions).[14] As you will see in Case 10-3, response prevention involves keeping the person from performing the ritualistic behaviors.

Case 10-3

HOME TREATMENT OF OBSESSIVE-COMPULSIVE BEHAVIORS BY IN VIVO FLOODING[15]

A 45-year-old divorced woman suffered from an obsessive-compulsive disorder that consisted of washing and cleaning rituals whenever she came in contact with objects that she thought might be even remotely associated with death. For example, holding a newspaper article about someone who had been killed would make her intensely anxious. The disorder first occurred when the client was 15 years old, at the time of her mother's death.

When the client entered treatment, she was to be remarried in 2 weeks. She was experiencing panic attacks and heart palpitations related to her fear of contamination almost daily. As time passed, the number of objects she considered potentially contaminated increased. Because her fiancé was a widower, he became a "carrier" of contamination by association with his dead wife. The client did not think she could deal with marriage in her present condition. In vivo flooding was indicated because the client wanted to alleviate her problem within 2 weeks and because her high motivation for treatment allowed her to undergo the discomfort of an anxiety-induction therapy.

The patient chose to be treated in her home environment, but the in vivo flooding began in a hospital mortuary. There the client and the therapist became "contaminated" by handling a corpse, which made the client intensely anxious. Later, the therapist and the client completely "contaminated" the client's apartment with objects associated with death (such as a newspaper photograph of a man shot to death in the street). Response prevention was instituted by the therapist's instructing the client to refrain from engaging in her typical rituals of washing and cleansing, which would reduce the anxiety she was experiencing during flooding. That evening and the next morning, she successfully resisted engaging in her rituals. During daily hour-long therapy sessions, the therapist gave her various "contaminated" objects while encouraging her not to resort to her rituals and praising her for complying. By the third day of flooding, she had not performed the rituals. However, when the client's fiancé brought some groceries from his house to her apartment, the client was unable to touch them, fearing that they were contaminated by association with his deceased wife. She called the therapist, and over the phone, the therapist guided her through a flooding session that consisted of "contaminating" her entire apartment by placing the groceries throughout the apartment.

After 12 days of therapy, the client reported that she had made considerable progress with her problem, and she was married the next day. Although she continued to have periodic episodes of tension over the next 8 months, she no longer felt the urge to engage in her compulsive rituals.

This case clearly illustrates one of the common characteristics of behavior therapy—namely, brevity. In this instance the client engaged in many hours of flooding, but the entire therapy was accomplished within 12 days. The therapist directed each of the in vivo flooding sessions, including one by telephone. The therapist's presence and guidance no doubt makes it easier for clients to undergo in vivo flooding. In contrast to self-managed in vivo exposure therapy (described in Chapter 9), in which the exposure is brief and gradual, self-managed in vivo flooding is especially difficult for clients. Nonetheless, it is occasionally employed successfully, such as in the treatment of social phobias where the therapist's presence in the client's actual social circumstances is impractical.[16]

Case 10-3 provides an example of a relatively severe obsessive-compulsive disorder. The woman's anxiety was intense, as evidenced by her panic attacks. Moreover, her obsession was extensive because virtually any object she touched in the course of the day could potentially be associated with death. Given the level of her anxiety, it is not hard to understand how difficult the prolonged/intense exposure of flooding might have been for the woman. Like most clients who decide to undergo in vivo flooding, she was highly motivated to alleviate her problem behaviors.

Medication frequently is prescribed for obsessive-compulsive disorder. However, for several reasons, in vivo flooding appears to be a superior treatment. In vivo flooding can be as effective as the antidepressant medication (for example, Prozac) that is used to treat obsessive-compulsive disorder, and clients may view it as more effective than medication.[17] The findings of one study, for example, showed that when clients received both medication (Luvox) and flooding, they were less likely to need medication 1 year after treatment had ended than when clients were treated with medication alone.[18] Interestingly, both a lower relapse rate and a lower dropout rate have been reported for in vivo flooding in comparison with medication-based treatments.[19] Studies have shown actual changes in brain chemistry for clients with obsessive-compulsive disorder treated with in vivo flooding.[20] Specifically, clients underwent a positron emission tomography (PET) scan before and after 10 weeks of in vivo flooding. Changes in glucose metabolic rates (which are reliable indicators of neural activity) were assessed in the brain regions (caudate nucleus) believed to be involved in obsessive-compulsive disorder. Only clients who showed significant reductions in obsessive-compulsive behaviors after in vivo flooding showed significant changes in glucose metabolic rates. These results are comparable to brain activity changes associated with successful treatment of obsessive-compulsive disorder with medication (such as Prozac).

In vivo flooding with response prevention also is used to treat body dysmorphic disorder. In one treatment study, clients went to public places where perceived bodily imperfections could potentially be easily observed by others.[21] The clients were asked to make eye contact with others, talk to strangers, and ask salespeople for assistance. Further, they were instructed to refrain from using any tactics that would minimize their perceived flaws, such as wearing special clothing or makeup. (Compare this prolonged/intense exposure and response prevention with the brief/gradual in vivo exposure treatment of body dysmorphic disorder described in Chapter 9, page 224.) Additionally, half the clients in the study also received specific training in dealing with relapses, including information about the nature of relapse, self-managed exposure exercises, and a contingency contract specifying that they attend emergency sessions with the therapist to address relapse. All the clients in the study showed a significant reduction in body dysmorphic perceptions and in avoidance of situations that had previously triggered intense anxiety (such as being seen in public). Those who participated in the relapse prevention component were better at managing minor relapses that occurred over time and had significantly lower self-reported depression and anxiety.

IMAGINAL FLOODING

Imaginal flooding follows the same basic principles and procedures used with in vivo flooding except that exposure occurs in the client's imagination. One advantage of imaginal exposure is that there are no restrictions on the nature of the anxiety-evoking situations that can be treated. This feature has proved useful in the application of imaginal flooding to help victims of traumatic experiences, such as natural disasters and physical assault. Such people may suffer from *posttraumatic stress disorder,* which is characterized by (1) highly disturbing recurrent recollections of the event (such as nightmares and flashbacks), (2) avoiding any stimuli associated with the event (for example, refusing to drive in a car after being in a serious automobile accident), and (3) a variety of distressing symptoms, including anxiety, depression, and an inability to concentrate.

In vivo exposure to the actual traumatic events (such as a rape or a tornado) generally is not possible or is inappropriate for ethical reasons.[22] Imaginal flooding is well suited for re-creating the circumstances of the trauma safely—that is, without the actual aversive consequences occurring.[23] Imaginal flooding was first used to treat posttraumatic stress disorder in Vietnam War veterans.[24] It now is being applied to other traumas, such as rape[25] and war-related traumas in civilians,[26] as Case 10-4 illustrates.

Case 10-4

Treatment of an Adolescent's Posttraumatic Stress Disorder by Imaginal Flooding[27]

A 14-year-old Lebanese boy was referred for evaluation by his school principal because of academic and behavioral problems. Six months earlier, the client had been abducted in Beirut by the Lebanese militia for 2 days. At the time of the evaluation, the client was experiencing anxiety related to recollections of his traumatic experience. He also reported avoiding the area where he had been abducted, having difficulty concentrating and remembering information, and being depressed. The client had not experienced these problems before he was abducted.

The therapist described the pros and cons of imaginal flooding and systematic desensitization, and the client and his parents chose flooding. Before therapy began, a number of direct self-report inventories (of general anxiety and depression) and cognitive measures (of memory and concentration) were administered. The client also was given a 12-step behavioral avoidance test that included leaving his home, walking to the area of his abduction, entering a store, making a purchase, and walking home by another route. During the test, two assistants unobtrusively observed the client through a store window and by following the client at a distance. Finally, during flooding, the client reported his level of discomfort using a 10-point SUDs scale.

The client was asked to imagine the four different scenes described in Table 10-1. Flooding was applied to each scene in succession—in other words, after one scene no longer induced anxiety, the client was exposed to the next scene. The client was asked to imagine the scenes in detail, which included what he saw, heard, thought, and felt (such as the location of the abduction, the voices of the abductors, thoughts he had of being executed, and discomfort caused by the blindfold). Each of the six therapy sessions involved 60 minutes of flooding, which was preceded and followed by 10 minutes of relaxation exercises.

Scenes 1, 2, and 4 were each successfully treated (reduced to zero SUDs) in the course of a single therapy session, and scene 3 required three sessions to achieve the same results. The client's anxiety and depression decreased, and his memory and concentration increased. This improvement was evident immediately after treatment and was maintained at a 4-month follow-up. Also, immediately after treatment and at the 4-month

Table 10-1 Scenes used in imaginal flooding for a 14-year-old boy with posttraumatic stress disorder (Case 10-4)
SOURCE: Saigh, 1987, p. 148.

Scene Number	Content
1	Approaching the area where the abduction occurred, being stopped, forced into a car at gunpoint, blindfolded, and driven away
2	Walking into a building while blindfolded, being questioned and accused, and listening to the militia argue over the merits of his execution
3	Being interrogated, responding, receiving repeated blows to the head and body, and experiencing intermittent periods of isolation
4	Learning that he was going to be released and not trusting the militia to keep its word

follow-up, the client completed all 12 steps of the behavioral avoidance test, compared with only 4 steps before therapy.

Because the area in Beirut where the client had been abducted remained a dangerous locale, he generally continued to avoid going there. However, after the termination of therapy, he did visit the area several times out of necessity. He reported that he experienced no abnormal anxiety on these occasions. Finally, the client expressed satisfaction with the flooding treatment, and he commented that the success of the therapy was adequate compensation for the discomfort he experienced during the flooding sessions.

Case 10-4 illustrates all the basic elements of imaginal flooding. Clients' clear and detailed visualization of scenes are critical factors in how effective the imaginal flooding is. Accordingly, the client was asked to use multiple senses to experience both the stimuli surrounding the anxiety-evoking situations and his responses to the situations. Exposure to these cues was both prolonged (60 minutes) and intense (highly anxiety-inducing).

Deep muscle relaxation sometimes is induced before and after a flooding session. This practice may at first seem paradoxical, given that the purpose of flooding is to induce high levels of anxiety. The relaxation is *not* a competing response to anxiety, as in systematic desensitization. Rather, relaxation is used before flooding to enhance the client's ability to imagine scenes vividly and after flooding to allow the client to return quickly to a normal level of arousal. Additionally, relaxation training teaches clients that they have control over their emotions and provides a coping skill they can use outside therapy.[28]

Another means of enhancing the vividness of traumatic scenes in imaginal flooding is to have clients verbally describe, in detail and in the present tense, the scenes they are imagining.[29] Consistent with flooding, this is done for prolonged periods, sometimes with the therapist prompting the client about omitted details.

Implosive Therapy

Implosive therapy is an imaginal prolonged/intense exposure therapy developed by Thomas Stampfl and Donald Levis.[30] Three procedures during scene presentation make implosive therapy different from other imaginal flooding treatments: (1) the use of hypothesized anxiety-producing cues, (2) the exaggeration of scenes to heighten anxiety, and (3) the elaboration of scenes as they are presented. These differences are highlighted in Table 10-2.

Based on the client's problem and personal characteristics, the therapist adds hypothesized cues to the client's description of the threatening situation (such as who is there and what is happening).[31] With bulimia, for example, the therapist may incorporate cues of striving for perfection and fear of abandonment, which are associated with the disorder.[32] Other hypothesized cues are based on *psychoanalytic* interpretations. For instance, the therapist might speculate that a man with a dental phobia also would fear castration (according to psychoanalytic theory, tooth extraction symbolizes castration). The hypothesized cues are assumed to be relevant for the client if the client shows strong emotional responses when the therapist introduces them.[33]

The scenes are exaggerated, sometimes with fantasy-like details, to heighten the client's anxiety. The following is an example of an exaggerated scene a therapist used with a client who was afraid of flying insects:

> Insects are flying around your head. First there is one, then a few, then dozens. They just keep flying around you, more and more of them, until you are surrounded by hundreds of flying insects. They are getting bigger and bigger by the moment. Huge bugs, the size of birds, are flying so close to you that you can feel the vibrations of their wings against your skin. And now they begin to touch your skin, to bite you while moving up from your ankles and legs to your groin. Now they are boring into you and flying into your mouth and down your esophagus. You can feel them tearing up your insides.

For each scene, the therapist begins by describing what appear to be the salient cues (actual and hypothesized) that make the client anxious. Then, the therapist questions the client about his or her reactions ("How

Courtesy of the University of Wisconsin, Milwaukee

Thomas Stampfl

Courtesy of Donald Levis

Donald Levis

Table 10-2 Differences between the scenes in implosive therapy and imaginal flooding

	Implosive Therapy	Imaginal Flooding
CUES INCORPORATED IN SCENE	Client-reported cues and therapist-hypothesized cues	Client-reported cues only
DESCRIPTION OF SCENE	Exaggeration of reported scenes	Actual reported scenes (unexaggerated)
CONSTRUCTION OF SCENE	Scenes evolve as they are presented	Scenes constructed before they are presented

does that make you feel?" "What are you thinking?"). Based on the client's feedback, the therapist can further refine and embellish the scene. Case 10-5 illustrates how hypothesized cues are presented and tested as well as how role-playing is used during scene presentation.

EXCERPT FROM AN IMPLOSIVE THERAPY SESSION[34]

Case 10-5

A young college professor reported first experiencing intense anxiety attacks shortly after she and her husband moved to another city. The move furthered her husband's career, but it interfered with the client's professional development. The client's anxiety appeared to be elicited by the situational cues of being in the presence of other people and the imagined cues of being unable to speak, losing control, and fainting. In addition, the therapist hypothesized that the client was afraid of her own unexpressed anger toward her husband. To test this hypothesis, the therapist presented a relevant scene for the client to imagine and assessed her reaction to it.

THERAPIST: . . . See yourself getting up in the morning. Your husband has gone to work. Another day faces you sitting around the apartment doing nothing but wasting time. You really feel bored, unproductive. What is going through your mind?

CLIENT: I need to find a job. I have to do something with my life.

THERAPIST: That's right. You don't want to waste your time. This morning you set out to find a job. You go down to the employment bureau. See yourself there. You're filling out forms. But no jobs are available for you. Next, you look through the want ad section of the newspaper, but nothing in your area is advertised. You already tried the colleges in the area but they are not hiring. How do you feel?

CLIENT: Depressed.

THERAPIST: That's right. Feel the depression. You had a good teaching job. People liked you. You had friends. But you moved and your life has become worthless, empty, and unproductive. You now think about your husband. He likes his job. He is moving up the ladder of success. How do you feel?

CLIENT: I feel angry.

THERAPIST: Try to feel the anger toward your husband.

CLIENT: No, it is not his fault. We both agreed to the move.

THERAPIST: Whether it is his fault or not, try to imagine that all he is really concerned about is his work and his needs. Your needs and aspirations are not important. See him, get a clear image. Ask him to go back to his former job so you can return to your old job. Verbalize it.

CLIENT: "Can we go back to [couple's former residence]?"

THERAPIST: Put some feeling into the request.

CLIENT: "Can we?"

THERAPIST: He looks at you in a cold, rejecting manner. "No. You agreed to come here. I am making more money. You will find something here. Stop feeling sorry for yourself." Feel that concern. Try and communicate to him so he will understand.

CLIENT: "Please. I can't stand it here."

THERAPIST: "Stop acting like a baby. Grow up." How do you feel?

CLIENT: Mad.

THERAPIST: Tell him off, express your anger. Tell him you hate him.

CLIENT: "I hate you."

THERAPIST: Say it with feeling.

CLIENT: "I hate you. I hate you. I hate you."

After this scene, the client was asked to imagine being back in high school, a period when she had felt alone and rejected (note the psychoanalytic emphasis on the past). At that time, she had not felt any anger toward her peers who rejected her. A series of scenes involving rejection in high school were described to the client. The therapist augmented successive scenes with new material provided by the client. Eventually, the client was able to feel considerable anger and hostility toward the people who had rejected her. The therapist continued to present each scene, with embellishments, until the client experienced a high degree of upset (anxiety, anger, and depression) and the negative feelings began to diminish.

Much of the evidence for the effectiveness of implosive therapy comes from case studies rather than controlled experiments.[35] Although there is research evidence indicating that implosive therapy can reduce anxiety,[36] many of the studies contain methodological flaws.[37] Some studies indicate that implosive therapy is not more effective than control conditions.[38] Moreover, implosive therapy generally has not been shown to be superior to other therapies, such as systematic desensitization.[39] In sum, no definitive statements about the effectiveness of implosive therapy can be made.

Incorporating psychoanalytic themes and exploring past events clearly is inconsistent with the theory and practice of behavior therapy and is highly controversial.[40] As it turns out, implosive therapy with little or no psychoanalytic imagery can be successful.[41]

Eye Movement Desensitization and Reprocessing

Eye movement desensitization and reprocessing (EMDR) is a relatively new and controversial exposure-based treatment that Francine Shapiro developed to treat upsetting memories and thoughts about traumatic experiences (such as a sexual assault, robbery at gun point, and combat-related trauma).[42] EMDR is a hybrid imaginal exposure therapy in that it does not fit cleanly into either the prolonged/intense or the brief/graduated model. Although clients visualize anxiety-evoking scenes for relatively brief periods, the scenes often engender intense anxiety. The treatment consists of three basic phases that involve (1) assessment and preparation, (2) imaginal flooding, and (3) cognitive restructuring.

In the *assessment and preparation* phase, clients (1) identify a traumatic image (memory) that results in anxiety or distress, (2) identify the bodily sensations associated with the anxiety (such as tension in the chest), (3) assess the level of anxiety they are experiencing using a 0 to 10 SUDs scale, (4) identify a maladaptive belief that is strongly associated with the event (for example, in the case of a rape image, "I should have run away" or "I am totally powerless"), and (5) think of an adaptive belief that would alleviate the distress associated with the traumatic event (for instance, "I did the best I could" or "I have options") and rate how personally believable the adaptive belief is on a 1 to 7 scale.

Next, in the *imaginal flooding* phase, the client visualizes the traumatic image while verbalizing the maladaptive belief and concentrating on his or her physical sensations associated with the trauma. During this process, the client is asked to visually track the therapist's index finger as it is moved rapidly and rhythmically back and forth across the client's line of vision (from left to right, twice per second, 12 to 24 times). (Shapiro theorizes that the eye movements produce a neurological effect—similar to the rapid eye movements associated with intense dreaming—that facilitates the processing of emotionally charged, stress-related material.[43]) After the eye movements, the client is instructed (1) to block out the experience momentarily and take a deep breath and (2) to report what he or she is imagining, thinking, and feeling and rate the experience using SUDs.

When the client's SUDs rating has been reduced to 0 or 1, the client is ready for the final phase of treatment, which essentially involves *cognitive restructuring* (described in detail in Chapter 12). The client again is asked to imagine the traumatic image (which now elicits little, if any, anxiety) but this time while thinking about the adaptive belief. The aim is to associate the traumatic image with the adaptive belief so that the image no longer results in tension and maladaptive thinking. The believability of the adaptive belief and the client's anxiety level are reassessed at this time. If the client now can generally accept the adaptive belief as valid and experiences little anxiety, therapy is terminated. If either criterion has not been met, then additional exposure with eye movements is required.

Following Shapiro's first published account of EMDR in 1989,[44] a slew of reports about the procedure and testimonials about its success appeared in both the professional and popular literature.[45] Many suggested that EMDR results in rapid and dramatic improvement (such as complete elimination of symptoms in a single session[46]) in trauma-based anxiety problems.[47] Unfortunately, these claims are misleading[48] because most of the evidence for the effectiveness of EMDR comes from studies that have serious methodological flaws, including drawing broad conclusions about the efficacy of EMDR on the basis of case study findings,[49] using poorly specified and vaguely defined treatment procedures, employing multiple treatments without isolating the specific contribution of EMDR,[50] and conducting outcome studies without appropriate control groups.[51] Moreover, the vast majority of outcome studies attesting to EMDR's efficacy have predominantly relied on self-report measures or therapist's subjective evaluations of success.[52] When appropriate control conditions and more objective measures of treatment outcomes have been employed, the results have been far less favorable,[53] although some studies support the efficacy of EMDR.[54] The general finding is that EMDR results in changes primarily in self-report measures and not in overt behaviors (such as avoidance behaviors).[55] There is little evidence that the treatment effects transfer outside of therapy and are maintained over time.[56]

When EMDR is compared directly with EMDR without the eye movement component or to standard imaginal flooding, there is no evidence that eye movements are necessary.[57]* In general, controlled outcome studies have failed to support the efficacy of the techniques beyond that of its imaginal flooding component.[58]

Thus, except for the addition of eye movements, EMDR is a treatment package consisting of variants of imaginal flooding and cognitive restructuring. In contrast to the documented efficacy of these two therapy components, at present the effectiveness of EMDR has not been demonstrated according to the standards of empirical validation typically required of behavior therapy procedures.[59]

In Theory 10-2

ETHICAL QUESTIONS ABOUT THE USE OF POORLY VALIDATED TREATMENTS

Implosive therapy and eye movement desensitization and reprocessing—two exposure therapies that are variants of standard imaginal flooding—have, at best, marginal empirical validity. In both cases, claims for the effectiveness of the treatments rest heavily on case studies that do not provide acceptable evidence of treatment effectiveness (see Chapter 4). And many of the experimental studies that have evaluated their efficacy have serious methodological flaws. Thus, neither implosive therapy nor EMDR meet the established standards of empirical validation in behavior therapy.

We have included these therapies because, despite little definitive evidence for their effectiveness, they are used. Whereas implosive therapy probably is employed infrequently today,[60] EMDR has become increasingly popular since its inception about 15 years ago. A fair number of therapists who use EMDR in their clinical practice (many of whom, incidentally, would not classify themselves as *behavior therapists*) believe the treatment is highly effective. But these impressions are not supported by controlled research evidence.

This state-of-affairs raises an important ethical question: Does a

---

*It is possible that eye movements might be a *facilitative* component, serving to make the flooding more effective or efficient for some clients (just as gradual exposure and a competing response are facilitative components of systematic desensitization). For example, following the therapist's hand movements may help clients focus their attention on the scenes they are imagining. Further, a therapist may be able to detect a client's wandering attention by noting that the client is not tracking hand movements (Agigian, 1996). These and other possible functions of the eye movement component of EMDR hopefully will be elucidated by future research.

pressing clinical need for treatment for a psychological disorder justify employing untested therapies or those that have been tested but for which there is little empirical support? Consider Shapiro's statement in the preface of her 1995 book on EMDR:

> The unfortunate split between the clinical community, which finds EMDR highly successful, and the academic and research community, which demands further study of EMDR before it is used on clients, is essentially a false dichotomy.

Naturally, all clinicians would prefer to have their tools verified by research. However, the pressing daily need to treat their clients' suffering comes first, and clinical practice simply cannot wait for the research to catch up.[61]

What do you think about the points Shapiro raises? We will return to the general issue we are raising here in Chapter 16. For now, keep the issue in mind as you continue to learn about behavior therapy procedures.

◆ ALL THINGS CONSIDERED: PROLONGED/INTENSE EXPOSURE THERAPY

Prolonged/intense exposure therapy commonly is used to treat anxiety-related disorders, including phobias,[62] obsessive-compulsive disorder,[63] posttraumatic stress disorder,[64] and agoraphobia.[65] Other problems treated include bulimia,[66] complaints of cardiac-like symptoms,[67] psychogenic urinary retention,[68] and agitated depression.[69]

Outcome studies indicate that flooding, in vivo and imaginal, is an effective treatment. Although some studies have found in vivo flooding to have more striking results,[70] no general statement can be made about the superiority of one variant over the other.[71] In specific cases, one form of presentation may be superior (for example, imaginal flooding when the threatening event cannot be reproduced).[72] In vivo and imaginal flooding sometimes are combined, as for clients with intense social phobias[73] and with severe trauma-based anxiety.[74] The use of imaginal flooding prior to in vivo flooding may actually facilitate subsequent in vivo exposure for clients who initially are unable to tolerate in vivo exposure to threatening situations.[75] Studies comparing the efficacy of flooding with that of systematic desensitization also have not found either of these two exposure therapies to be clearly superior.[76] Flooding is an efficient means of reducing clients' anxiety, often in a relatively brief time (as you saw in Cases 10-2 and 10-3). Group treatment using imaginal flooding for anxiety-based problems is an effective and efficient alternative to individual treatment.[77]

One major drawback of flooding is the discomfort it produces.[78] In one study, clients were treated for test anxiety with flooding, modeling, or systematic desensitization.[79] Nearly all the clients who had received modeling and about half who had received desensitization indicated satisfaction with their treatments. In contrast, clients who had undergone flooding said they would not recommend the treatment because of the discomfort they had experienced—even though the flooding had significantly reduced their anxiety! Moreover, clients may be more likely to refuse to enter therapy or drop out of therapy that involves flooding, compared with less upsetting exposure therapies.[80]

In an effort to make flooding more palatable for clients, prolonged exposure that includes response prevention occasionally is presented *gradually*.[81] In other words, the client is exposed to increasingly more anxiety-evoking events, rather than the very highest anxiety-evoking events initially. However, the exposure is for a prolonged period and is terminated only when the client's anxiety begins to diminish.

Some therapists have considered the possibility that flooding might be made less aversive for clients if the exposure occurred in the presence of and assisted by a family member.[82] Three studies have systematically examined this possibility, and only one demonstrated additional benefits of family-assisted exposure beyond those achieved with therapist-directed or self-managed exposure.[83] When the relationship between the client and the relative is marked by conflict or overdependence, the relative's assistance may even diminish the effectiveness of the therapy.[84] Despite procedures aimed at making prolonged/intense exposure more tolerable, the fact remains that clients often experience discomfort. As a consequence, clients may not elect such treatment, even though it may be the treatment of choice for their problems.

With prolonged/intense exposure, there is a *potential* danger that clients will become even more anxious or fearful than before therapy as a result of the treatment. This possibility exists because prolonged/intense exposure therapies induce anxiety in order to reduce it. Fortunately, there is no evidence that serious negative side effects occur. In a survey of behavior therapists who had used prolonged/intense exposure therapies, serious negative side effects were reported in only 0.26% of the clients treated (9 out of 3493).[85] The major exception to this general finding is the use of prolonged/intense exposure therapy for posttraumatic stress disorder with clients who have a history of other serious psychiatric disorders.[86] In such cases, the chances of being retraumatized, of increased anxiety, and of other adverse reactions to the treatment are substantially increased.[87]

The major ethical or humanitarian objection to prolonged/intense exposure therapy is that it increases clients' anxiety. The question is: Should already traumatized clients, such as victims of rape or incest, be subjected to therapy procedures that further disturb them?[88] Such treatment runs counter to the ethical principle "First, do no harm." However, the following two caveats should be kept in mind. First, clients have prior knowledge about the process of prolonged/intense exposure therapy, and they consent to undergo the temporarily stressful treatment. Second, discomfort often is a necessary part of psychotherapy; for example, many psychotherapies require clients to confront disturbing events in their lives.

Ultimately, the decision to use prolonged/intense exposure therapy should be based on a cost-benefit analysis of the discomfort associated with the treatment and its practical advantages. For example, sometimes prolonged/intense exposure can bring about a marked reduction in anxiety in a few sessions and occasionally in a single session, which is generally quicker than brief/graduated exposure.[89] More rapid treatment has obvious practical, ethical, and humanitarian advantages for distressed clients. In some cases, only a limited time may be available for treatment (such as in Case 10-3, where the woman wanted relief from her obsessive-compulsive disorder before getting married in 2 weeks).[90]

Another factor that enters into the choice of therapy is that clients differ in their tolerance for discomfort.[91] Some clients find that getting the treatment over with quickly compensates for the brief distress they experience. For example, the teenage boy who was treated for recurring disturbing thoughts about his abduction (see Case 10-4) reported that the success of his treatment was adequate compensation for the unpleasantness he experienced during the flooding sessions.

◆   **ALL THINGS CONSIDERED: EXPOSURE THERAPY**

A variety of exposure therapies exists. All share the common procedural element of *exposure to anxiety-evoking stimuli without actual negative consequences occurring.* Exposure therapies differ with respect to the basic model into which they fit (brief/graduated or prolonged/intense), the mode of exposure (ranging from in vivo to imaginal), whether the exposure is therapist-directed or self-managed, and whether additional features are employed (such as a competing response, response prevention, and exaggerated scenes).

Systematic desensitization, the parent of exposure therapies, is a tried-and-true treatment that is broadly applicable. Because exposure is imaginal, the nature of the anxiety-evoking events is limited only by the client's imagination. Because the exposure is brief, graduated, and imaginal, systematic desensitization is the least distressing exposure therapy. Systematic desensitization also has the practical advantage that it can be implemented in a therapist's office.

In vivo exposure shares with systematic desensitization the advantages associated with brief/graduated exposure without the potential limitation of clients' inability to imagine scenes clearly. Exposure to the actual situations is likely to be more upsetting, but the treatment may be quicker and may transfer more readily to actual situations in the client's life. Therapist-directed in vivo exposure is costly in terms of therapists' time, but self-managed in vivo exposure, when viable, is highly cost-effective.[92] In vivo exposure now is recognized as one of the critical components in the treatment of agoraphobia. Agoraphobia involves intense fear and avoidance of public places or situations from which escape might be difficult should the individual experience incapacitating anticipated panic-like symptoms.

In vivo flooding can rapidly reduce fear, and it often is used to treat agoraphobia. It is the treatment of choice for obsessive-compulsive disorder,[93] and research has shown long-term maintenance for at least 5 years.[94] The studies that provide strong support for the effectiveness of in vivo exposure for obsessive-compulsive disorder predominantly have examined Caucasian clients. More recently, studies have included African-American clients and have obtained the same results.[95]

In vivo flooding is applicable to a wide range of clients, including elderly individuals.[96] In vivo flooding, rather than imaginal flooding, is more commonly used with children (as young as 4 years old).[97] Two potential limitations of in vivo flooding are that clients must be willing to subject themselves to the discomfort of prolonged/intense exposure to the actual threatening event and that therapist assistance generally is necessary, which is not always practical.

Imaginal flooding also can result in rapid reduction of fear and shares with systematic desensitization the advantages of imaginal exposure. Imaginal flooding does involve discomfort for the client, although usually to a lesser degree than in vivo flooding.

As these brief evaluations of specific exposure therapies indicate, each is a viable treatment for some clients and some anxiety-related disorders. None, however, is useful in all cases. A similar conclusion can be drawn if we examine the relative merits of the two basic dimensions of exposure: imaginal versus in vivo and brief/graduated versus prolonged/intense.

Although some behavior therapists believe that exposure in vivo generally is superior to imaginal exposure,[98] there is reason to question this broad conclusion.[99] Many of the investigations that indicate that exposure in vivo is more effective than imaginal exposure are analogue studies in which the problems treated are mild.[100] When studies using only clinical samples (actual clients with serious anxiety-related problems) are examined, it appears that exposure in vivo has no clear-cut, general superiority to imaginal exposure. This is true when in vivo exposure is compared with systematic desensitization[101] and when in vivo flooding is compared with imaginal flooding.[102]

When the actual feared events cannot be reproduced, imaginal exposure must be used. For instance, a client who repeatedly checks to see that the front door is locked may fear that an intruder will enter the house. Although such a scenario can be created easily in the client's imagination, actually producing these events would be impractical and unethical. Imaginal flooding has been shown to be superior to in vivo flooding in preventing relapse for clients with obsessive-compulsive disorder who compulsively check.[103] The safest conclusion that can be drawn about imaginal versus in vivo exposure is that both are useful and effective procedures.

The decision to employ brief/graduated or prolonged/intense exposure depends, in part, on the psychological disorder being treated, as there is no general superiority of either model.[104] For instance, in vivo exposure (brief/graduated) is particularly useful with agoraphobia, whereas imaginal flooding (prolonged/intense) is the treatment of choice for posttraumatic stress disorder.[105] In the case of obsessive-compulsive disorder, both types of exposure may be warranted because they affect different aspects of the disorder. Brief/graduated exposure reduces anxiety and avoidance behaviors, whereas prolonged/intense exposure reduces ritualistic acts.[106]

Other factors likely to influence the decision about the optimal model of exposure include the severity of the complaint and the client's preference. The actual decision about which exposure therapy to employ is a joint one, drawing on the behavior therapist's knowledge and experience and the client's predilection. In some cases, the therapist clearly can recommend one exposure therapy based on research findings regarding its relative effectiveness with the particular disorder. The therapist describes to the client the procedures of each potentially beneficial therapy, as well as its pros and cons. For example, both systematic desensitization and flooding may alleviate a client's fear of flying. Desensitization is likely to take longer and be less "painful," whereas the reverse is true for flooding. With exposure therapies, the issue of how much discomfort the client is willing to endure must be considered in addition to factors of effectiveness and efficiency.

As a group, exposure therapies appear to be the single most potent behavior therapy for anxiety-related disorders[107] and can have long-lasting effects. This conclusion does not mean that exposure alone always is sufficient. Indeed, with severe and multifaceted disorders, the use of more than one type of therapy often is required. When a client's anxiety is maintained by multiple maintaining conditions, separate therapies may be required to deal with each. For example, social anxiety often is maintained by a combination of subjective feelings of anxiety, avoidance of social situations, negative attitudes about social interactions, and social skills deficits. Subjective feelings and avoidance behaviors are treated optimally by exposure therapy, negative attitudes by cognitive restructuring (see Chapter 12), and skills deficits by social skills training (see Chapter 11).

◆   **In Theory 10-3**

EXPOSURE THERAPIES OR THERAPY?

All exposure therapies share the common element of exposing clients to feared or otherwise negative events in order to reduce clients' adverse reactions to the events. Beyond that core element, the components of a specific application of exposure therapy vary considerably. For example, a given treatment may involve imaginal exposure, in vivo exposure, or a variant of the two basic modes; the exposure may be therapist-directed, self-managed, or both; a wide array of competing responses can be used or none at all; response prevention may or may not be employed. On the most basic level, the exposure may be brief/graduated, prolonged/intense, or a hybrid of the two models. More than any other category of behavior therapy, exposure therapy mixes and matches approaches and procedures. In terms of treating individual clients, this practice clearly allows clients' treatment plans to be individualized to meet their specific problems and personal preferences. In research, the practice requires behavior therapists to specify in considerable detail the specific components that make up the exposure therapy being studied. Unfortunately, all too often this is not done.

Behavior therapists have been notoriously inconsistent in their use of terms to describe exposure therapies, with the exception of systematic desensitization. In some cases the same term is used to designate more than one therapy, as Table 10-3 shows. The inconsistency leads to confusion about the specific therapy procedures being employed. At the same time, it may reflect the current state of affairs— namely, a genuine overlap among exposure therapies.

To begin with, all of the exposure therapies share common theoretical explanations (see In Theory 9-1). Further, although the major exposure therapies we have described seem to differ in a variety of procedural aspects, in fact, they may have more similarities than differences.

A simple example is that implosive therapy actually is a specialized form of imaginal flooding, which may account for the frequent use of the term *implosive (flooding) therapy* to indicate implosive therapy.[108]

Consider a more complex example of overlapping procedures. Whichever form of flooding clients receive—in vivo or imaginal—they often also receive the other form. With in vivo flooding, clients know about the nature of the exposure in advance. Thus, it is likely that before an in vivo flooding session, clients think about (imagine) the exposure procedure, including the events to be presented; this process approximates imaginal flooding.[109]

Likewise, imaginal flooding may involve in vivo flooding. Therapists may recommend that clients engage in self-managed in vivo flooding at home.[110] Even without this suggestion, clients may naturally engage in flooding as they encounter the threatening stimuli during the course of their daily activities.[111]

Another instance of procedural overlap is the use of competing responses. Only in brief/graduated exposure therapies do clients specifically engage in behaviors that compete with anxiety (most often muscle relaxation). In prolonged/

Table 10-3 Common terms used to designate exposure therapies

Most Common Term	Other Terms
Systematic desensitization	Desensitization
In vivo exposure	In vivo desensitization Graduated exposure Graded exposure Exposure
In vivo flooding	Flooding In vivo exposure Exposure Response prevention In vivo exposure with response prevention Rapid exposure
Imaginal flooding	Flooding In vitro flooding Fantasy flooding
Implosive therapy	Implosion Implosive (flooding) therapy Flooding

intense exposure therapies, however, the presence and support of the therapist may serve a similar function. It also is possible that clients spontaneously employ coping responses (such as using reassuring self-instructions) that compete with the high levels of anxiety encountered in prolonged/intense exposure.

The similarities among exposure therapies raise the question of whether it would be more fruitful to classify such procedures as *exposure therapy with variations than as different exposure therapies*. Uncovering the similarities may increase our understanding of the fundamental nature of exposure as a treatment and help account for the effectiveness of seemingly different exposure procedures. Such efforts are consistent with the trend toward integrating psychotherapies (about which we will comment further in Chapter 16).[112]

SUMMARY

1. Prolonged/intense exposure therapies, generally called flooding, expose clients for extended periods to anxiety-evoking stimuli that, from the outset, are intense. Exposure is continued until the client's anxiety peaks and then begins to decline.

2. In flooding, the exposure can be in vivo or imaginal. It often involves response prevention, in which clients remain exposed to the anxiety-evoking stimuli for a prolonged period without engaging in their typical maladaptive anxiety-reducing behaviors. In vivo flooding is a treatment of choice for obsessive-compulsive disorder and entails clients' engaging in anxiety-evoking behaviors without engaging in their typical compulsive rituals.

3. Imaginal flooding makes it possible to expose clients to any anxiety-evoking event. It can be used to treat posttraumatic stress disorder, for which it would be impractical and unethical to use in vivo flooding.

4. The development and maintenance of fear that often is treated by exposure therapies can be explained by a two-factor learning theory. Fear is initially learned by association of a neutral event with one that elicits fear (classical conditioning). Then, anxiety-reducing responses (avoidance) that follow are maintained through negative reinforcement (operant conditioning).

5. Both in vivo and imaginal flooding are effective treatments. Because of the discomfort caused by prolonged/intense exposure therapies, clients may not choose these treatments, despite their effectiveness.

6. Implosive therapy involves imaginal prolonged/intense exposure in which the scenes the client visualizes are exaggerated and elaborated on with hypothesized cues (often psychoanalytically based) related to the client's fear. Implosive therapy generally has not proved superior to other exposure therapies.

7. Eye movement desensitization and reprocessing (EMDR) is a relatively new and controversial variant of exposure-based therapy that essentially involves imaginal flooding (including rapid, rhythmic eye movements) and cognitive restructuring. Currently, the effectiveness of EMDR has not been demonstrated definitively.

8. The fact that both implosive therapy and EMDR have marginal validity raises the ethical issue of whether behavior therapies that have not met the standards of empirical validation typically required of behavior therapy procedures should be used with clients.

9. Each of the major exposure therapies is a viable treatment for some clients and some anxiety-related problems; none is useful in all cases.

10. Although exposure therapies differ in a variety of procedural aspects, they overlap sufficiently to raise the question of whether they should be considered variations of a single therapy.

REFERENCE NOTES

1. For example, Agras, Kazdin, & Wilson, 1979; Chambless, Foa, Groves, & Goldstein, 1982.
2. Malleson, 1959.
3. From the author's (MDS) clinical files, 1992.
4. For example, de Jong, Vorage, & van den Hout, 2000.
5. For example, Roth & Fonagy, 1997.
6. For example, Tolin & Foa, 1999.
7. Boutelle, 1998.
8. For example, McKay, 1999; McKay, Todaro, Neziroglu, Campisi, Moritz, & Yaryura-Tobias, 1997.
9. For example, Kozak, Foa, & Steketee, 1988.
10. Nesbitt, 1973, pp. 405–406.
11. Mowrer, 1960; Solomon, 1964.
12. Franklin, Abramowitz, Kozak, Levitt, & Foa, 2000.
13. For example, Leitenberg, 1993; Leitenberg, Gross, Peterson, & Rosen, 1984; Wilson, Rossiter, Kliefield, & Lindholm, 1986.
14. For example, Abramowitz, 1996; Calamari, Faber, Hitsman, & Poppe, 1994; Steketee, 1994; Van Oppen, De Hann, Van Balkom, Spinhoven, Hoogduin, & Van Dyck, 1995; Walker, Freeman, & Christensen, 1994.
15. Meyer, Robertson, & Tatlow, 1975.
16. Scholing & Emmelkamp, 1993a, 1993b.
17. For example, Van Balkom, Van Oppen, Vermeulen, Van Dyck, Nauta, & Vorst, 1994.
18. Cottraux, Mollard, Bouvard, & Marks, 1993.
19. Stanley & Turner, 1995.
20. Baxter, Schwartz, Bergman, Szuba, Guze, Mazziotta, Akazraju, Selin, Ferng, Munford, & Phelps, 1992; Schwartz, Stoessel, Baxter, Martin, & Phelps, 1996.
21. McKay, 1999.
22. Compare with Tolin & Foa, 1999.
23. For example, Frueh, 1995.
24. Foa & Rothbaum, 1989; Frueh, Turner, & Beidel, 1995.
25. For example, Foa, Rothbaum, Riggs, & Murdock, 1991.
26. For example, Saigh, 1986, 1987.
27. Saigh, 1987.
28. Keane, Fairbank, Caddell, & Zimering, 1989.
29. Rothbaum, Meadows, Resick, & Foy, 2000.
30. Levis, 1980; Stampfl, 1961; Stampfl & Levis, 1967, 1973.
31. Stampfl, 1970.
32. Johnson, Corrigan, & Mayo, 1987.
33. Levis, 1980; Levis & Malloy, 1982.
34. Levis, 1980; quoted therapeutic dialogue from pp. 125–126.
35. Saper, Blank, & Chapman, 1995.
36. Hogan & Kirchner, 1967; Levis & Carrera, 1967; Stampfl, 1966.
37. Morganstern, 1973.
38. For example, Hodgson & Rachman, 1970; Willis & Edwards, 1969.
39. For example, Borkovec, 1970, 1972; Mealiea & Nawas, 1971.

40. Levis, 1988.
41. Hogan, 1968, 1969.
42. Shapiro, 1989a, 1989b, 1995.
43. Shapiro, 1995; compare with Rosen, 1995.
44. Shapiro, 1989a, 1989b.
45. Bouhenie & Moore, 2000; Cowley, 1994; Oldenburg, 1994; Stone, 1994.
46. Cocco & Sharpe, 1993.
47. For example, Forbes, Creamer, & Rycroft, 1994; Kleinknecht, 1993; Sanderson & Carpenter, 1992; compare with Jacobson, Mulick, & Schwartz, 1995.
48. Bouhenie & Moore, 2000.
49. Bouhenie & Moore, 2000.
50. For example, De Jong, Andrea, & Muris, 1997.
51. For example, Herbert & Mueser, 1992; Kleinknecht & Morgan, 1992; Lohr, Kleinknecht, Conley, Dal Cerro, Schmidt, & Sonntag, 1992; Marquis, 1991.
52. For example, De Jong, Andrea, & Muris, 1997; Feske & Goldstein, 1997; Kleinknecht & Morgan, 1992; Lipke & Botkin, 1992; Marquis, 1991; McCann, 1992; Muris, Meckelbach, Holdrinet, & Sijsenaar, 1998; Puk, 1991; Shapiro, 1989a; Wolpe & Abrams, 1991.
53. For example, Acierno, Hersen, Van Hasselt, Tremont, & Meuser, 1994; Acierno, Tremont, Last, & Montgomery, 1994; Boudewyns, Stwertka, Hyer, Albrecht, & Sperr, 1993; Goldstein, de Beurs, Chambless, & Wilson, 2000; Montgomery, 1993; Renfrey & Spates, 1994.
54. For example, Carlson, Chemtob, Rusnak, Hedlund, & Muraoka, 1998; Rothbaum, 1997; Wilson, Becker, & Tinker, 1997.
55. For example, Muris, Meckelbach, Holdrinet, & Sijsenaar, 1998.
56. For example, Devilly, Spence, & Rapee, 1998; Feske & Goldstein, 1997.
57. For example, Acierno, Tremont, Last, & Montgomery, 1994; Boudewyns, Stwertka, Hyer, Albrecht, & Sperr, 1993; Devilly, Spence, & Rapee, 1998; Feske & Goldstein, 1997; Pitman, Orr, Altman, Longpre, Poire, & Lasko, 1993; Renfrey & Spates, 1994; Rosen, 1996; Sanderson & Carpenter, 1992.
58. For example, Acierno, Hersen, Van Hasselt, & Meuser, 1994; Bouhenie & Moore, 2000; Claude, Tolin, van der Kolk, & Pitman, 2000; Keane, 1998; Lohr, Lilienfeld, Tolin, & Hebert, 1999; Lohr, Tolin, & Lilienfeld, 1998; Marafiote, 1993; Page & Crino, 1993; Vaughan, Armstrong, Gold, O'Connor, Jenneke, & Tarrier, 1994.
59. For example, Acierno, Hersen, Van Hasselt, Tremont, & Meuser, 1994; Lohr, Tolin, & Montgomery, 1996; Meichenbaum, 1994.
60. Spiegler & Guevremont, 2002.
61. Shapiro, 1995, p. x.
62. For example, Butler, 1985; Stravynski & Greenberg, 1989; Yule, Sacks, & Hersov, 1974.
63. Abramowitz, 1996; Steketee, 1994; Van Balkom, Van Oppen, Vermeulen, Van Dyck, Nauta, & Vorst, 1994.
64. For example, Meichenbaum, 1994; Otto, Penava, Pollock, & Smoller, 1995.
65. Chambless, 1985; Swinson & Kuch, 1989; Trull, Nietzel, & Main, 1988.
66. For example, Leitenberg, Gross, Peterson, & Rosen, 1984; Schmidt, 1989.
67. For example, Stambaugh, 1977.
68. Glasgow, 1975; Lamontagne & Marks, 1973.
69. Hannie & Adams, 1974.
70. For example, Emmelkamp & Wessels, 1975; Watson, Mullet, & Pillay, 1973.
71. James, 1986.
72. For example, Saigh, 1986, 1987.
73. For example, Turner, Beidel, & Jacob, 1994.
74. Richards, Lovell, & Marks, 1994.
75. Steketee, 1994.
76. For example, Boulougouris, Marks, & Marset, 1971; De Moor, 1970; Horne & Matson, 1977; Strahley, 1965; Suarez, McCutcheon, & Adams, 1976.
77. Fals-Stewart, Marks, & Schafer, 1993; Steketee, 1994.
78. Cox, Fergus, & Swinson, 1994.
79. Horne & Matson, 1977.
80. For example, Greyson, Foa, & Steketee, 1985; Richard, 1995; Smith, Marcus, & Eldredge, 1994.
81. For example, Ollendick, Hagopian, & King, 1997; Öst, Westling, & Hellstrom, 1993; Tarrier, Pilgrim, Sommerfield, Faragher, Reynolds, Graham, & Barrowclough, 1999; Tolin & Foa, 1999.
82. For example, Emmelkamp, De Haan, & Hoogduin, 1990; Mehta, 1990.
83. Steketee & Lam, 1993.
84. Emmelkamp, De Haan, & Hoogduin, 1990.
85. Shipley & Boudewyns, 1980.
86. Meichenbaum, 1994.

87. For example, Allen & Bloom, 1994; Pitman, Altman, Greenwald, Longpre, Macklin, Poire, & Steketee, 1991.

88. Kilpatrick & Best, 1984.

89. For example, Marshall, Gauthier, Christie, Currie, & Gordon, 1977; Nesbitt, 1973; Rychtarik, Silverman, Landingham, & Prue, 1984; Yule, Sacks, & Hersov, 1974.

90. For example, Rychtarik, Silverman, Landingham, & Prue, 1984.

91. For example, Rothbaum, Meadows, Resick, & Foy, 2000.

92. For example, Van Oppen, De Hann, Van Balkom, Spinhoven, Hoogduin, & Van Dyck, 1995.

93. DeRubeis & Crits-Christoph, 1998; Roth & Fonagy, 1997; Rowa, Antony, & Swinson, 2000.

94. McKay, 1997; Rowa, Antony, & Swinson, 2000.

95. For example, Williams, Chambless, & Steketee, 1998.

96. Beck & Stanley, 1997; Calamari, Faber, Hitsman, & Poppe, 1994.

97. Ollendick, Hagopian, & King, 1997.

98. Emmelkamp, 1982; Jansson & Öst, 1982; Mavissakalian & Barlow, 1981; Wilson, 1982.

99. James, 1985, 1986.

100. For example, Emmelkamp & Wessels, 1975; Rabavilas, Boulougouris, & Stefanis, 1976.

101. James, 1985.

102. James, 1986.

103. Foa, Steketee, Turner, & Fischer, 1980.

104. For example, Öst, Brandenberg, & Alm, 1997.

105. For example, Chambless, Foa, Groves, & Goldstein, 1982; Glynn, Eth, Randolph, Foy, Urbaitis, Boxer, Paz, Leong, Firman, Salk, Katzman, & Crothers, 1999; Keane, Fairbank, Caddell, & Zimering, 1989; compare with Tolin & Foa, 1999.

106. Foa, Rothbaum, & Kozak, 1989.

107. For example, Berman, Weems, Silverman, & Kurtines, 2000; Trull, Nietzel, & Main, 1988.

108. For example, Keane, Fairbank, Caddell, & Zimering, 1989; Levis, 1993; Levis & Hare, 1977.

109. Marshall, Gauthier, & Gordon, 1979.

110. Barlow, O'Brien, & Last, 1984; Mathews, Teasdale, Munby, Johnston, & Shaw, 1977.

111. For example, Mathews, Johnston, Lancashire, Munby, Shaw, & Gelder, 1976.

112. For example, Arkowitz, 1992a, 1992b, 1995; Goldfried, 1995; Goldfried, Castonguay, & Safran, 1992; Goldfried, Wiser, & Raue, 1992.

Chapter 11

Modeling Therapy and Skills Training

Just shy of 4 months after two hijacked airliners were deliberately crashed into the World Trade Center in New York on September 11, 2001, 15-year-old Charles Bishop intentionally flew a stolen small private plane into a bank building in Tampa, Florida. He carried a note in which he expressed sympathy for Osama bin Laden. Although the reasons for Bishop's suicidal act are unknown, there is no doubt where he got the idea for ending his life as he did. In the same vein, ever since two students at Columbine High School in Colorado went on a shooting rampage, there have been other shootings as well as numerous plots by teenagers to murder students and teachers in their own schools.

Learning by observing and then imitating other people's behaviors is a pervasive part of our lives. Fortunately, most of the time such learning and imitation is prosocial. We learn language, attitudes and values, preferences, standards for how to act, mannerisms, emotional responses, and countless skills by observing others. We borrow many of our habits, such as verbal expressions and body language, from others with whom we identify, such as our parents or older siblings. Think about some of your own mannerisms, favorite expressions, and even your general ways of dealing with everyday situations. Do these behaviors remind you of anyone you know?

Modeling can play a role in the development and maintenance of psychological and physical disorders. For example, the aggression people have observed in their families of origin correlates with the amount and type of aggression in their own marriages.[1] Similarly, how we experience pain seems to be influenced by how significant people in our lives have dealt with pain.[2] There is even evidence that observing mass media depictions of suicide, actual or fictional, may lead to imitation; suicide rates typically rise following such media presentations.[3]

The same fundamental processes of modeling that can result in problem behaviors have been harnessed to alleviate them. **Modeling therapies** are procedures in which clients observe a person demonstrate a behavior that they can learn.

Do What I Do: Basics of Modeling

The basic ingredients for modeling are simple: a **model** who engages in a behavior and an **observer** who attends to the model. Observing a model provides two pieces of information: (1) what the model did and (2) what happened to the model as a result of the model's actions. The consequences of a model's behaviors—known as **vicarious consequences**—are important because they indicate the consequences observers are likely to receive for imitating the model. **Vicarious reinforcement** occurs when the consequences of the model's behaviors *increase* the likelihood that observers will imitate the model. With **vicarious negative consequences,** the consequences of the model's acts *decrease* the likelihood that observers will imitate the model. Consider whether you'd be more or less likely to speak up in class if your professor praised (vicarious reinforcement) or ridiculed (vicarious negative consequences) other students who spoke up in class.[4]

Up to this point in our discussion, *imitation* has not been defined because it is a common term that we use in everyday language. Formally, *imitation* refers to a person's behaving like a model who has been observed. Although imitation can be the result of observing a model, it may not be. For imitation to occur certain conditions must be met, as In Theory 11-1 describes.

In Theory 11-1

THREE STAGES OF OBSERVATIONAL LEARNING

Observational learning is the process by which people are influenced by observing someone's behaviors. The process involves three sequential stages, illustrated in Figure 11-1.[5] Assuring that each of these stages occurs is crucial for the success of modeling therapy.

The first stage is *exposure* to (observation of) the model's behaviors. The second stage is *acquisition* of (learning) the model's behaviors. Acquisition requires that the observer pay attention to and remember what the model does. The third and final stage of observational learning is *acceptance* of the model's behaviors as a guide for the observer's own actions.

Four types of acceptance are possible. Table 11-1 contains everyday examples of the possible outcomes in the acceptance stage. Acceptance can involve imitation or counterimitation, and it can be either specific or general. *Imitation* involves behaving *like* the model, and *counterimitation* involves behaving *differently* from the model. In *specific imitation,* the observer engages in the *same* behavior as the model; in other words, the observer copies the model. In *specific counterimitation,* the observer does *exactly the opposite* of what the model did. In *general imitation,* the observer behaves *similarly* (but not in precisely the same way) to the model. In *general counterimitation,* the observer behaves *differently* (but not in the directly opposite manner) from the model. Finally, an observer may be

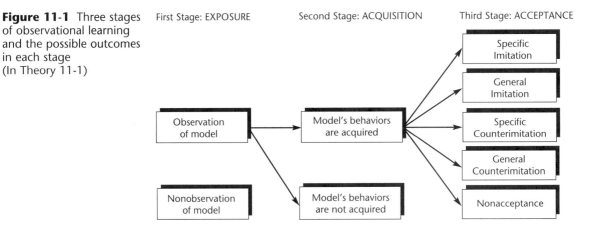

Figure 11-1 Three stages of observational learning and the possible outcomes in each stage (In Theory 11-1)

Table 11-1 Examples of the five possible outcomes in the acceptance stage of observational learning (In Theory 11-1)

Modeled Behavior: Miri observes her roommate's frequently making charitable donations	
Acceptance Outcome	*Example of Miri's Behaviors*
SPECIFIC IMITATION	Miri puts coins in a beggar's cup.
GENERAL IMITATION	Miri shares her belongings with her friends.
SPECIFIC COUNTERIMITATION	Miri walks past the beggar without putting coins in the cup.
GENERAL COUNTERIMITATION	Miri does not share her belongings with her friends.
NONACCEPTANCE	Miri is unaffected by observing her roommate's donating behaviors.

exposed to a model and remember what the model did but may not be influenced by the model; this is called *nonacceptance.*

Exposure and acquisition are necessary but not sufficient conditions for modeling to influence an observer. The observer also must accept the model's behaviors as a guide for his or her own behaviors. The form of acceptance is largely determined by the vicarious consequences that occur. Vicarious reinforcement is most likely to result in imitation, whereas vicarious negative consequences are most likely to result in counterimitation.

Two types of models exist. A model who is actually present ("in the flesh") is known as a **live model;** a model who is observed indirectly is called a **symbolic model.** We often are exposed to symbolic models on television, in books and movies, and through oral descriptions (such as when we are told about what someone has done). Myths and fairy tales are rich, time-honored sources of culturally shared symbolic models.[6] Hansel and Gretel are models of courage, and Beauty (in "Beauty and the Beast") is a model of compassion. A common form of symbolic modeling is **covert modeling,** in which people *imagine* someone's, including themselves, engaging in a behavior they wish to perform.[7] For instance, a child might imagine how a favorite cartoon character would handle a difficult or feared situation.[8]

Modeling serves five functions for observers—teaching, prompting, motivating, reducing anxiety, and discouraging—which Table 11-2 describes.[9] Modeling therapies often serve multiple functions. Social skills training, for example, involves teaching, prompting, and motivating clients to engage in socially adaptive behaviors. Although the discouraging function of modeling has potential for treating deceleration target behaviors in behavior therapy,[10] it is rarely used.[11]

Table 11-2 Five functions of modeling

Function	Description	Example
TEACH	Observer learns a new behavior by observing a model	Children's learning language by hearing adults speak
PROMPT	Observer is cued (reminded) to perform a behavior after observing a model engage in the behavior	People's laughing when they hear other people laugh, as with laugh tracks on TV sitcoms
MOTIVATE	Observing a model's behavior and the favorable consequences it receives (vicarious reinforcement) serves as an incentive for an observer to engage in the same behavior	Students' volunteering to read aloud when they observe other students' reading aloud and the teacher's responding favorably
REDUCE ANXIETY	Observing a model safely engage in an anxiety-evoking behavior reduces an observer's anxiety	People's overcoming their anxiety about going swimming by watching other people who are enjoying swimming
DISCOURAGE	Observing a model's behavior and the unfavorable consequences it receives (vicarious negative consequences) decreases the likelihood that the observer will imitate the model's behavior	Children who see peers punished for hitting others are less likely to engage in the same or even a similar behavior

Self-Modeling

Similarity between the model and the observer tends to enhance imitation.[12] With children, for example, peer models tend to be more effective than adult models.[13] Similarity is maximized by **self-modeling,** in which clients serve as their own models of adaptive functioning.[14] Covert self-modeling, in which clients imagine themselves performing the target behavior, is the simplest application. Video self-modeling therapy, developed by Peter Dowrick,[15] has clients view videos of their own performance of acceleration target behaviors.* Outside of therapy, video self-

*To make a self-modeling video, the client must be able to perform either (1) the target behavior under *some* conditions or (2) each of the components of the target behavior. When a client has difficulty performing the target behavior in a particular problematic situation, the client is taped in a nonproblematic situation, and this portrayal is superimposed on scenes of the problematic situation; in the final version, it appears that modeling is used in sports instruction (such as in skiing, tennis, and golf) to teach and motivate students. As one student pilot commented while watching a video of his landings, "I can see what I did right and what I did wrong, but mostly I can see that I *did* it."[16] The standard procedures used in self-modeling therapy are illustrated in Case 11-1.

Case 11-1

MODIFYING INAPPROPRIATE SOCIAL BEHAVIORS BY SELF-MODELING[17]

Ten-year-old Chuck, a resident of a treatment center for patients with bronchial asthma, spent most of his time alone. His peers rebuffed his attempts to interact with them by calling him "boob" and "baby." Chuck would respond by retreating to his room and having a temper tantrum. He also displayed inappropriate behaviors with adults, such as giggling constantly, attempting to tickle them, and jumping on to their laps during interviews.

To deal with these problems, a self-modeling video was prepared. Chuck and two other boys enthusiastically agreed to take part in a "television film." In one self-modeling sequence, Chuck appropriately approached the two boys who were playing a game and asked if he could play with them; in another sequence, Chuck came into an adult's office and seated himself in a chair (rather than on the adult's lap).

After Chuck viewed the self-modeling tape daily for 4 weeks, the frequency of Chuck's socially appropriate behaviors in his daily interactions increased substantially. After treatment ended, Chuck maintained his appropriate social behaviors for the remaining 6 months that he was at the center. It is noteworthy that many of the reports of Chuck's improved behaviors came from staff members who were unaware that Chuck had undergone the self-modeling treatment.

Self-modeling therapy has been applied to clients across the age spectrum for such diverse problems as skills deficits,[18] verbal responses of children with autism,[19] selective mutism,[20] stuttering,[21] tic disorders,[22] aggressive behaviors,[23] hyperactivity,[24] problematic classroom behavior,[25] depression,[26] anxiety in an adult with posttraumatic stress disorder,[27] sexual unresponsiveness,[28] inappropriate sexual behaviors,[29] and, with elderly clients, performing physical exercise[30] and hearing impairment.[31] Self-modeling can create rapid changes in a target behavior, sometimes requiring as little as 12 minutes of self-observation to achieve clinically significant effects.[32]

the client is performing the target behavior in the problematic situation (for example, Dowrick, 1991; Dowrick & Hood, 1978; Dowrick & Raeburn, 1977). When the client can perform only the individual components of the behavior, a video is made of the client performing each component separately; then the video is edited to make it appear that the client is performing the components in sequence (Dowrick, 1994).

The Nature of Modeling Therapy

Modeling procedures generally are combined with other behavior therapies, such as reinforcement, prompting, shaping, in vivo exposure, and **behavior rehearsal,** in which clients practice performing an acceleration target behavior and coping skills. Although modeling often is part of a treatment package, it can be highly effective by itself. Case 11-2 provides an example of how powerful even casual observation of a model can be in influencing a person's behaviors.

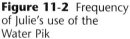

Case 11-2 ## Accelerating a Prescribed Oral Hygiene Practice Through Modeling[33]

Julie was a 25-year-old married woman who recently had had oral surgery for serious, progressive gum disease. The dentist reminded Julie to use her Water Pik, a device that squirts water to clean between the teeth. She had bought a Water Pik months before her surgery, but she had never used it. The dentist warned that if she did not use the Water Pik daily, her gum condition would regress.

   Several months after Julie's surgery, her husband, Art, became concerned because Julie was not using the Water Pik, and he mentioned this to her. Julie said she would start using it. Another month passed, and the Water Pik remained unused. Art became increasingly concerned and began to remind her to use the Water Pik. Julie became annoyed at Art's "playing parent" and told him to stop worrying about *her* teeth.

   At this point Art called the dentist. The dentist suggested that Art use the Water Pik himself on a daily basis and record the times that his wife used it to see if his modeling made a difference. The results of Art's modeling were striking. As Figure 11-2 shows, Julie had not used the Water Pik

Figure 11-2 Frequency of Julie's use of the Water Pik

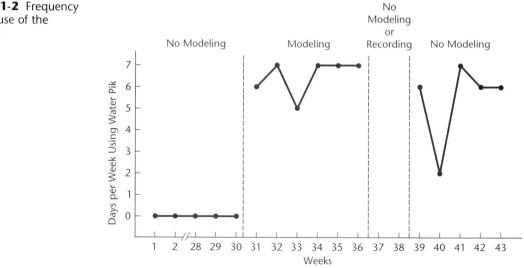

once in the 30 weeks before Art's modeling. During the first week of modeling, Julie used the Water Pik 6 of 7 days; the next week she used it every day; after a drop to 5 times in the third week, she used the Water Pik every day for the next 3 weeks.

No modeling or recording took place during the next 2 weeks because Art was out of town on business. The day he returned from his trip, he called the dentist to report on the success of the dentist's advice. The dentist suggested that Art discontinue his modeling and just continue to record how often Julie used the Water Pik. During the next 5 weeks, Julie used the Water Pik an average of 5 times per week (see Figure 11-2). This was a vast improvement from her baseline rate (zero). Moreover, the outcome of the informal modeling therapy was clinically significant because 5 times a week was sufficient to keep her gums healthy.

In the preceding case, modeling was the sole treatment. Art merely performed the target behavior, which Julie could observe. No prompting to pay attention to the modeling or reinforcement for imitating was used, as often is done. This is a clear demonstration of the potency of modeling alone.

The case also illustrates the subtleness of modeling, which can be advantageous when clients resist direct instructions from others to change their behaviors. Julie did not use the Water Pik when Art reminded her; in fact, Art's prompts probably made Julie more resistant to using the Water Pik. Children often resist parents' telling them what to do ("Mother, I'd rather do it myself!") but will respond to more subtle prompts. For example, parents' bringing their own plates and silverware to the sink after a meal may be more effective in getting their children to do so than reminding them each time.

Modeling therapies have been used primarily for two broad classes of problems—skills deficits and fears—and we will describe a variety of modeling therapy procedures to deal with them.

SKILLS TRAINING

Deficits in skills often are maintaining conditions of clients' problems. To perform a skill, a person must (1) know what to do, (2) be proficient at the skill, (3) know when it is appropriate to use the skill, and (4) be adequately motivated to perform the skill. Each of these conditions are prerequisites, which are antecedents in the ABC model (see Chapter 3). Skills deficits, then, consist of deficiencies in one or more of these four components, which are described in Table 11-3.

Skills training refers to treatment packages designed to overcome clients' skills deficits.[34] Along with modeling, skills training may include direct instruction, prompting, shaping, reinforcement, behavior rehearsal, role-playing, and corrective feedback.[35] Modeling is a key component of skills training because direct instruction often is insufficient to communicate the subtleties of performing complex skills, and prompting and

Table 11-3 Types of skills deficits

Type	Description	Example
KNOWLEDGE	Client does not know how to perform the skill	A college student who has never learned to use email
PROFICIENCY	Client is not competent at performing the skill because of inadequate practice	Psychiatric patient who has been hospitalized for many years is not used to managing money
DISCRIMINATION	Client does not know the conditions (time and place) in which it is appropriate to perform the skill	Student who initiates conversations with classmates while the professor is lecturing
MOTIVATION	Client does not have adequate incentives to perform the skill	Nursing home resident who has no desire or reason to engage in self-care skills

shaping alone may be insufficient.[36] The client may need to "see" the behavior performed.[37] The major components of skills training are illustrated in the following excerpt from a social skills training session with a high school student who was having difficulty calling for dates.

THERAPIST: Suppose you wanted to ask Cornelia to attend a dance at school. What might you say?

CLIENT: Well, I'm not exactly sure. I guess I'd just ask her if she wanted to go.

THERAPIST: Why don't you pretend that you are calling Cornelia and actually say what you might say on the phone to her?

CLIENT: OK, but don't expect much.

THERAPIST: Remember, we are only practicing. Just give it a try. [prompting]

CLIENT: "Hello, Cornelia, this is Clint. How y'all doin'? Listen, if you've got nothing better to do, would you want to go to the dance with me?" [role-playing]

THERAPIST: That's a reasonable start. [feedback, shaping] Let's see if you can do even better. For one thing, you don't want to make it sound like going to the dance with you is a last resort. [direct instruction] Let me demonstrate one possible way you might continue the conversation after you've said hello. Listen, and see if you can hear a difference. [prompting] "There's a dance at school next Saturday, and I'd like to take you if you're not busy." [modeling]

CLIENT: Yeah, I can hear the difference.

THERAPIST: Why don't you try to say something like that.

CLIENT: "I saw a sign about the dance next weekend at the gym, and I was wondering if you'd like to go with me." [behavior rehearsal]

THERAPIST: Very good. That's much better. Just a straightforward statement of what you'd like. [reinforcement, feedback]

Figure 11-3 General procedures for skills training
SOURCE: © Michael D. Spiegler and David C. Guevremont

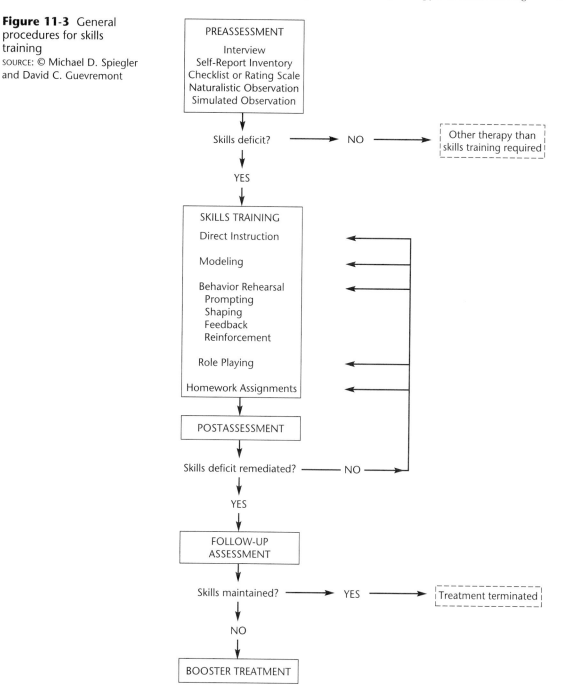

The general procedures for skills training are presented in a flowchart in Figure 11-3. The sequence begins with an assessment of the problem, which often includes behavioral observations in the client's natural environment or in a role-playing situation. Once it is determined that the problem is being maintained by a skills deficit and the components (knowledge, proficiency, discrimination, or motivation) that are lacking have been identified, skills training is instituted. When further assessment reveals that the client is performing the relevant skills successfully, training ends. If follow-up assessments indicate that the skills have not been maintained, then booster treatments may be necessary.[38]

One of the earliest applications of skills training was to ameliorate the enormous skills deficits associated with autistic disorder.[39] Language skills are a prime example, and modeling is a critical component in teaching such children to speak. However, unlike most children who learn to imitate in the course of normal development by being reinforced for imitating the behaviors of others, children with autistic disorder usually do not. The ability to imitate is a social skill called **generalized imitation,**[40] and if it is not learned naturally, it can be specifically taught. This is done by initially reinforcing *any* behavior the child imitates, whether or not it is an adaptive behavior, so that the child learns to imitate. Once generalized imitation is established, modeling can be used to teach children with autistic disorder the host of adaptive behaviors they have never learned to perform (see Photo 11-1).

Other groups of clients who may suffer from major skills deficits and have benefited from skills training include clients with mental retardation,[41] learning disabilities,[42] and head injuries.[43] Skills training has been employed to alleviate a wide array of skills deficits, including cognitive,[44] problem-solving,[45] self-appraisal,[46] stress management,[47] academic,[48]

Photo 11-1 Modeling is a key component in language training for children with autistic disorder. The therapist models the correct mouth and tongue positions and the sound for the child to imitate.

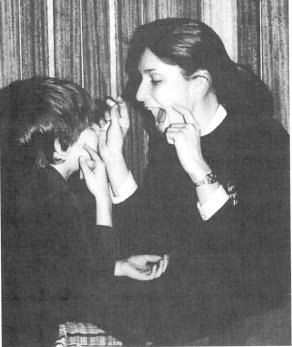

SOURCE: Courtesy of the Eden Institute

consumer,[49] employment,[50] and child management skills.[51] We will illustrate basic skills training by examining treatment packages used to teach children skills for preventing abduction and sexual abuse.

Preventing Abduction and Sexual Abuse Through Skills Training

Child abduction is a serious problem in the United States and other countries. Only 10% to 17% of abductors use force to lure their victims.[52] Typically, the abductor attempts to develop a relationship with the child or to verbally entice the child, and children usually are unskilled at quickly resisting abductors' inducements.[53]

Skills training interventions for teaching children to protect themselves from abduction have been spearheaded by Cheryl Poche.[54] In one of her studies, three preschool children, who appeared susceptible to abduction, were taught abduction prevention skills.[55] Potential susceptibility was assessed by having an adult male role-play an abductor who approached the child and asked the child to leave the preschool with him. The "abductor" used three strategies commonly employed to lure children, which are described in Table 11-4.

The children were taught an appropriate response to each of the three common lures through modeling, behavior rehearsal, feedback, and

Photo 11-2 In child-abduction prevention training, children practice self-protection skills (such as yelling "No" and running away) in response to an adult who role-plays an abductor.

© 1997 Michael D. Spiegler and David C. Guevremont

	Type of Lure	Definition	Role-Played Scenario
Table 11-4 Lures used in naturalistic role-played assessment of children's ability to avoid abduction SOURCE: Based on Poche, Brouwer, & Seraringen, 1981.	SIMPLE	Simple request to go with the "abductor"	"Abductor" approaches child, says "Hello" or "Hi, there," and engages in small talk (for example, saying "Nice day, isn't it?"). Then "abductor" says, "Would you like to go for a walk?"
	AUTHORITY	Request with the implication that an authority figure (such as a parent or teacher) approves	After small talk, "abductor" says, "Would you like to go with me for a walk? Your teacher won't mind."
	INCENTIVE	Request with the promise of an incentive	After small talk, "abductor" says, "I've got a nice surprise in my car. Would you like to see it?"

social reinforcement. (A fully appropriate response was succinctly telling the "abductor" that he or she will not go with him [for example, saying, "No, I have to ask my teacher"] and running away within 3 seconds.) Before training, the appropriateness of the children's responses, based on a rating from 0 to 6, was near 0. After training, the appropriateness was near 6, and the responses transferred to a different setting in the community. A 12-week follow-up for the two children who remained at the preschool demonstrated that the treatment effects were maintained.

The same treatment components were incorporated in a 20-minute interactive video in which child models demonstrated two safety rules: (1) saying, "No, I have to go ask my teacher [or parent]," and then (2) quickly running to the teacher (or parent). After each enticement scene, the narrator asked viewers if the child had done and said the right things.[56] After a pause, the narrator praised appropriate responses and corrected inappropriate ones by saying, "If you said _____, you're right, good listening! If you said _____, then I've fooled you. Watch again."[57] The video also provided an opportunity for behavior rehearsal of what children who had viewed the video had learned. For children aged 5 to 7, the combination of viewing the video and behavior rehearsal was more effective than only viewing the video; this indicates that direct practice is important in teaching children to protect themselves from potential abductors.

In a skills training program developed by Sandy Wurtele, children as young as 4 years old learned to discriminate between situations in which it is appropriate and inappropriate for "bigger people" to touch children's "private parts," as well as what to say and do if an adult tried to abuse them.[58] The program effectively increased children's knowledge of sexual abuse and skills for protecting themselves from abuse without upsetting the children,[59] which is an important consideration given the frightening nature of sexual abuse.[60]

Similar skills training packages have been used to prevent sexual abuse among adult woman with mental retardation.[61] Research evaluating these treatment packages demonstrated not only that these women can learn protective skills but also that they are able to use them when they encounter inappropriate sexual advances.[62] The latter finding was ascertained by having adult male assistants, whom the clients did not know, make inappropriate sexual solicitations toward the women while other assistants unobtrusively observed the women's responses.

SOCIAL SKILLS TRAINING

Social skills, the interpersonal competencies necessary to successfully interact with others, are essential for normal living. Their absence is correlated with a host of adjustment problems throughout the life span.[63] For example, in childhood and adolescence, social skills deficits are associated with social isolation, poor academic achievement, and delinquency;[64] in adulthood, social skills deficits are associated with depression, social anxiety, and schizophrenia.[65] Not surprisingly, many clients treated in psychotherapy have social skills deficits.

Skills training has been extensively used to teach social skills to both children[66] and adults,[67] including specific social interaction skills related to social isolation,[68] couple relationships,[69] and sexual behaviors.[70] We will illustrate the nature of skills training by focusing on basic social skills training, including assertion training.[71]

Social Skills Training with Children and Adolescents

Children who exhibit low levels of social interaction with peers are prime candidates for social skills training. Film modeling has proved effective with nursery school children.[72] One such modeling film, 23 minutes in length,

> portrayed a sequence of 11 scenes in which children interacted in a nursery school setting. In each of these episodes, a child is shown first observing the interaction of others and then joining in the social activities, with reinforcing consequences ensuing. The other children, for example, offer him play material, talk to him, smile, and generally respond in a positive manner to his advances into the activity. The scenes [are] graduated on a dimension of threat in terms of the vigor of the social activity and the size of the group. The initial scenes involve very calm activities such as sharing a book or toy while two children are seated at a table. In the terminal scenes, as many as six children are shown gleefully tossing play equipment around the room.[73]

Viewing such modeling films once or twice has been sufficient to increase children's social interactions to a normal level, and these gains have been maintained over time.[74] Film modeling is highly efficient, compared with other procedures such as shaping.[75] Live peer modeling also is effective in increasing social interaction with children.[76] In one case, two sixth-grade boys with poor social skills were taught to conduct social skills training with two kindergarten boys with low rates of peer interaction.[77] Not only did the kindergarten boys show an increase in positive social interactions with peers following the intervention, but so did the sixth-grade trainers. The latter finding illustrates the potential reciprocal effects of live modeling; by modeling a behavior, the model may become more competent at the behavior. A familiar example of this phenomenon is parents' overcoming their own fears by modeling non-fearful behaviors for their children.

Poor social interaction skills are a serious handicap for adolescents, for whom socializing is so important. Case 11-3 illustrates the use of social skills training for this problem.

SOCIAL SKILLS TRAINING WITH A YOUNG ADOLESCENT[78]

Case 11-3

Fourteen-year-old Sherman interacted with children who were 5 to 8 years younger. He had no friends his own age and especially was reluctant to interact with his classmates. He had difficulty engaging in even simple conversations with peers.

Social skills training for Sherman was conducted twice weekly for 20 to 30 minutes. The training focused on four conversational skills: (1) asking appropriate questions, (2) making positive or acknowledging comments, (3) maintaining appropriate eye contact, and (4) acting in a warm and friendly manner. For each skill, the therapist provided Sherman with a rationale for learning it and modeled each component of the behaviors. Then, Sherman rehearsed each of the skills with the therapist. After demonstrating proficiency in the skills with the therapist, Sherman practiced them with peers of both sexes for 10 minutes at a time. The therapist prompted Sherman to use the four conversational skills and gave him feedback on their use. Sherman also practiced his new conversational skills at home and at school.

Whereas Sherman rarely engaged in the four targeted social skills before therapy, after social skills training he showed significant increases in each conversational skill. To assess the social validity of Sherman's behavior changes, 10 peers who attended a different school rated videos of Sherman's conversations before and after training. The peer ratings consistently indicated that Sherman's social skills had improved considerably. Ratings made by Sherman's parents and teachers after training also indicated significant improvements in Sherman's overall social adjustment, ability to make friends, ease of interacting with peers, and involvement in extracurricular activities. In a telephone call 16 months after treatment, the therapist learned that Sherman's improved social skills and peer relations had been maintained. Sherman now had classmates come to his home, he had begun to date, and he was trying out for a school athletic team.

Social skills training has been beneficial with children and adolescents who engage in aggressive and disruptive behaviors. Examples include adolescents being treated for sexual offenses,[79] youths hospitalized for conduct disorder (habitual violation of others' rights),[80] juveniles who are incarcerated,[81] inner-city minority children,[82] and children with attention deficit hyperactivity disorder.[83]

Social skills training also has been successfully extended to children and adolescents with special needs. For example, children diagnosed with cancer who received social skills training reported receiving greater social support from classmates and teachers.[84] Likewise, adolescents with language and hearing disabilities benefited from social skills training and then were able to use self-control strategies (such as self-reinforcement) to maintain their use of the newly acquired skills.[85]

Social skills training is not just appropriate for children and adolescents. For example, elderly people have benefited from training in specific social skills,[86] such as conversational skills to decrease feelings of loneliness and the fundamentals of reinforcement and extinction to influence people in their lives.[87] Another population for which social skills training has been applied is adults with schizophrenia.

Social Skills Training for Adults with Schizophrenia

Social skills deficits and social withdrawal are hallmarks of schizophrenia.[88] Even when disabling symptoms such as hallucinations and delusions are absent (usually as a result of medication), significant social impairment often continues to be problematic.[89] Moreover, the rate of relapse and rehospitalization is higher for clients who are socially isolated and who cannot function effectively within the community.[90]

The goals of social skills training for clients with schizophrenia are (1) to increase social interactions, (2) to teach the specific social skills needed to function in the community (such as talking to neighbors), and (3) to reduce stress by teaching clients to cope with problematic social situations that arise in their daily lives.[91]

The specific skills taught depend on the severity of the client's social deficits. For clients with the most severe deficits, social communication skills might include basic nonverbal behaviors, such as appropriate eye contact, facial expressions, posture, and proximity to others. Clients who are able to perform basic skills are trained in holding conversations, behaving assertively, interviewing for a job, asking for a date, and general social problem solving that can be applied to any interpersonal problem in daily living.[92] As with other applications of social skills training, the primary components are modeling, behavior rehearsal, feedback, and reinforcement.

Social skills training has been effective in teaching clients with schizophrenia social skills, as assessed through role-playing. Although clients often transfer the skills from therapy sessions to their hospital living setting, transfer outside the hospital is a major challenge.[93] This is illustrated by the findings of a study evaluating an intensive social skills training program for clients with schizophrenia.[94] The clients were taught conversational skills 4 days a week, in 20- to 30-minute sessions. The clients' rehearsal of these skills was videotaped, and while they watched themselves on the video, they received feedback from the therapist about their performance. The clients were in an ongoing token economy and earned tokens for participating in the training. Although the social skills training resulted in significant increases in appropriate conversational skills during the training sessions, the skills did not transfer spontaneously to other situations or people.

To promote transfer, the clients were given (1) homework assignments to practice the conversational skills on the hospital unit, (2) prompts to do the homework assignments, and (3) positive reinforcers when the target behaviors were performed. These procedures significantly increased clients' use of the conversational skills in different settings and with people other than the trainers, and the skills were maintained 3 months after the training had ended.

In addition to improving social competence of clients with schizophrenia, social skills training appears to reduce social anxiety and improve hospital discharge rates.[95] Social skills training also has a moderate influence on reducing the probability of relapse in comparison with other forms of psychological treatment (such as family education and family therapy), particularly within the first 3 to 6 months after treatment has terminated.[96]

Teaching clients general problem-solving skills that can be applied to diverse social situations may enhance the durability of behavior changes following social skills training. First, clients learn to identify when they are experiencing stress from an interpersonal problem; then, to generate and evaluate potential solutions; and finally, to select an active and socially acceptable plan to alleviate the problem. In one intensive 6-month social problem-solving training program, clients with schizophrenia received 12 hours of training a week.[97] After the training, the clients showed better social functioning, lower relapse rates, and a greater subjective quality of life than clients in a comparison treatment program who received occupational therapy.

Skills training relying heavily on modeling also has been used to teach clients with schizophrenia daily living skills, such as personal hygiene, self-care, job finding, self-administration of medication, personal recreation skills, food preparation, vocational skills, home maintenance, use of public transportation, and management of personal finances.[98]

Assertive behaviors are actions that secure and maintain what one is entitled to in an interpersonal situation without infringing on the rights of others.* Assertive behaviors are one of the critical components of social skills that clients with schizophrenia are taught. For instance, besides using the right words to ask for a service, obtaining it may require making one's request definitive and repeating the request a number of times. Further, acting assertively is especially important for clients with schizophrenia because their rights are particularly vulnerable to abuse by

---

Assertive behavior has been variously and vaguely defined and even been equated with socially adaptive behavior. Our definition is an attempt to combine widely accepted but restrictive definitions (for example, Alberti & Emmons, 2001; Lazarus, 1971; Wolpe, 1990).

others. Deficits in assertive behaviors certainly are not restricted to clients with schizophrenia. Indeed, the ability to act assertively is an essential basic social skill that many people lack,[99] and we will discuss assertion training shortly.

Promoting Transfer and Generalization in Social Skills Training

Transfer and generalization of social skills is not always a natural outcome of social skills training. In fact, improved social interactions often occur only in the settings and with the people with whom social skills training was conducted.[100] This is especially true for clients with significant handicapping conditions,[101] as in the case of people with schizophrenia. Accordingly, active strategies to promote transfer and generalization may be an essential component of social skills training. The following are strategies that are used for this purpose: (1) a sufficient number and variety of examples during training,[102] (2) intermittent reinforcement during training so that skills taught become more resistant to extinction,[103] (3) common physical and social stimuli between the training setting and the client's natural environment,[104] (4) prompts in the natural environment,[105] (5) natural reinforcers, such as praise,[106] (6) exposure to opportunities to practice newly acquired skills,[107] and (7) self-control skills (for example, self-monitoring and problem solving) to apply to novel social situations.[108]

The importance of using specific transfer strategies is illustrated in a study of social skills training for preschool children with hearing impairments who exhibited low rates of peer interactions.[109] Initially, social skills training occurred in the context of playing a narrow range of games with a small number of the same peers. The training resulted in increased rates of appropriate social interactions, but only in the specific classroom setting in which training had occurred and with the same peers. The children then received training with many different peers, in the presence of different teachers, and using a wider array of play activities. Additionally, the rate of teacher praise was faded and delivered intermittently. After these new strategies were incorporated into social skills training, the children began showing increased rates of appropriate social interactions, which also occurred in a classroom other than the one in which the training took place.

A peer transfer and generalization component is part of the Social Effectiveness Therapy for Children program, which specifically was designed to enhance social skills and decrease social anxiety in children with social phobia (who typically have significant social skills deficits).[110] The program is based on a successful multifaceted treatment program used to treat adults with social phobia.[111] It includes child and parent education about the nature of social phobia in children, social skills training (such as learning to greet others and joining groups of peers), and weekly in vivo exposure exercises (for example, reading aloud in front of a group of peers). In the peer transfer and generalization component, the children join a group of unfamiliar peers who are not anxious in a 90-minute group activity (such as bowling and a pizza party). The activity allows clients to practice the social skills they have learned in a naturalistic setting. The peers are recruited through newspaper advertisements and are screened for good social skills, the absence of significant social anxiety, and a desire to help children with social phobia. Different peers are used throughout the 12-week training program, and they serve as positive role models for the clients.

Research evaluating the treatment program showed that it resulted in significant improvements in social skills, reduced social anxiety, and increased social interaction (compared with a control group that received study skills training). Moreover, after treatment, 67% of the children in the program compared with 5% in the control group no longer met the criteria for social phobia, and their treatment gains were maintained at a 6-month follow-up.

ASSERTION TRAINING

Deficits in assertive behaviors are extremely common and, in some cases, can result in dire consequences, such not being forthright about wanting to practice safer sex.[112] Assertive behaviors fall into several categories that are relatively distinct (see Table 11-5).[113] Assertive behaviors are, for the most part, situation specific, which has three important implications.[114] First, we cannot characterize a *person* as assertive or unassertive. We can, however, say that a person's *behavior* in a particular situation or class of situations is assertive or unassertive. And it is no doubt the case that some people generally act assertively or unassertively in a majority of situations. Second, training in one type of assertive behavior may not generalize to other types.[115] Third, assertive behaviors are not always appropriate or adaptive.[116] How appropriate they are is determined by the consequences, for oneself and others, of being assertive in the particular situation.[117] For example, if a waiter overcharges you by a small amount, you can act assertively and bring it to the waiter's attention. If you are in

Table 11-5 Five relatively distinct types of assertive behavior

Type of Assertive Behavior	Example
ASKING FOR WHAT YOU ARE ENTITLED TO	Correcting the mistake when you receive incorrect change
STANDING UP FOR YOUR RIGHTS	Objecting when a person steps ahead of you in line
REFUSING UNREASONABLE REQUESTS	Saying no when a friend asks to borrow money you can't spare
EXPRESSING OPINIONS AND FEELINGS (EVEN WHEN THEY ARE UNPOPULAR OR NEGATIVE)	Voicing your conservative views in a group of liberals
EXPRESSING DESIRES AND REQUESTS	Telling your sexual partner what you enjoy

a rush, however, you may decide to pay the higher amount, which would be an unassertive but appropriate response under the circumstances.

The appropriateness of acting assertively varies in different cultures. Whereas assertive behavior generally is considered admirable in Western countries, Chinese cultures, for example, value compliance with tradition, which may run counter to acting assertively. Moreover, even in cultures that do consider asserting one's rights socially desirable (such as mainstream United States), fostering assertive behaviors should not be considered a goal for all people. This caveat is consistent with the practice in behavior therapy to provide individualized treatment and for clients to set their own treatment goals. Thus, if a behavior therapist thinks that a client would benefit from behaving more assertively in certain situations but the client does not or just is not interested in acting more assertively, assertive training would not be part of the client's treatment program.

Assertive and aggressive behaviors are not the same. Although assertive and aggressive behaviors may result in the same end—obtaining what one wants or is entitled to—they differ in the *means* by which they accomplish the goal.[118] Assertive behaviors achieve the goal without violating others' rights, whereas aggressive behaviors do so at someone else's expense. Table 11-6 compares examples of assertive, aggressive, and unassertive responses.

Assessing Assertive Behavior Deficits

Clients' deficits in assertive behaviors are assessed by a variety of methods, including interviews, direct self-report inventories, self-monitoring, systematic naturalistic observations, and simulated observations, including role-playing.[119] Assessment provides information about the specific details of the client's assertive skills deficits as well as the type(s) of skills

Table 11-6 Comparison of assertive, aggressive, and unassertive responses to common situations

Situation	Assertive Response	Aggressive Response	Unassertive Response
You don't drink alcohol. At a party someone offers you a drink.	**"No, thank you."**	"No! I don't want any alcohol; just get it away from me."	"Oh . . . thanks but . . . I guess it won't hurt me."
You are rushing off to class and don't want to be late. A friend stops you and asks you to help move furniture in his room right then.	**"Sorry, I'm on my way to class. If you still need help this evening, let me know."**	"You must be kidding! I'm on my way to class. Find someone else."	"Well, I'm on my way to class, but I guess I could give you a hand for just a few minutes."

Figure 11-4 Item on the Conflict Resolution Inventory

SOURCE: McFall & Lillesand, 1971, p. 315.

A person *you do not know very well* is going home for the weekend. He or she has some books that are due at the library and asks if you would take them back so they won't be overdue. From where you live, it is a 25-minute walk to the library, the books are heavy, and you hadn't planned on going near the library that weekend.

_____ 1. I would *refuse* and would not feel uncomfortable about doing so.

_____ 2. I would *refuse* but would feel uncomfortable doing so.

_____ 3. I would *not refuse* even though I might prefer to, but would feel uncomfortable because I didn't.

_____ 4. I would *not refuse* even though I might prefer to, but would not feel particularly uncomfortable because I didn't.

_____ 5. I would *not refuse*, because it seems to be a reasonable request.

deficit the client has (knowledge, proficiency, discrimination, or motivation), which is crucial for selecting the most appropriate treatment.

Two types of direct self-report inventories are used to assess deficits in assertive behavior. With one type, clients rate the degree to which they engage in various assertive behaviors (see Participation Exercise 11-1).[120] The second type of self-report inventory has clients indicate how they would respond to a situation (described in writing) by choosing one of several responses. Figure 11-4 shows an item from the Conflict Resolution Inventory[121] that measures one type of assertive behavior, refusing unreasonable requests.

Participation Exercise 11-1

ASSESSING YOUR ASSERTIVE BEHAVIORS BY A DIRECT SELF-REPORT INVENTORY*

In this Participation Exercise, you will respond to a brief self-report inventory for assessing assertive behaviors.[122] List the numbers 1 to 13 on a sheet of paper. Read each item, and write the number from the following scale that best describes your typical behavior (there are no right or wrong answers).

0 = Never
1 = Rarely
2 = Sometimes
3 = Usually
4 = Always

1. When someone is unfair to me, I call it to the person's attention.
2. When I am not receiving service to which I am entitled, I ask for it.
3. I speak up when someone steps ahead of me in line.

*You should do this Participation Exercise before you continue reading.

4. When a salesperson tries to sell me something that I do not want, I tell the salesperson I am not interested.
5. I freely speak up when I am in a group.
6. If a person has borrowed something from me (such as money or a book) and is late in returning it, I say something to the person.
7. I express my positive feelings to others.
8. I express my negative feelings to others.
9. If food I have ordered in a restaurant is served improperly, I ask to have it corrected.
10. I return merchandise that I find to be defective.
11. I refuse unreasonable requests made of me.
12. I compliment and praise others.
13. If someone is disturbing me, I say something to the person.

Your responses to this inventory may make you aware of how you deal with various situations that call for assertive behaviors. The higher the scale score for an item, the more assertive you tend to be in the particular situation described. However, it is not appropriate to add the scores to obtain a total assertiveness score because the items are related to different situations and assertive behaviors are situation specific.

◆

Complete assessment of assertive behavior deficits usually requires behavioral observations. If feasible, systematic naturalistic observations are made of the client in the situations in which the client is having difficulty behaving assertively. Simulated observations are more typical, however, because they are easier to arrange. Generally, the simulated observations involve the client's role-playing responses to hypothetical situations that call for assertive behaviors.

Behavioral observations, either naturalistic or simulated, make it possible to assess the stylistic components of the client's attempts to act assertively, such as voice tone and body posture (see Table 11-7), which are critical components of effective assertive behaviors.[123]

Assertion Training Procedures

Assertion training refers to the specific social skills training procedures used to teach clients how and when to behave assertively. Modeling is especially valuable in teaching assertive behaviors because stylistic components that are difficult to describe verbally can be modeled for the client (for example, appropriate volume and expression to show confidence).

Homework assignments are routinely part of assertion training and proceed in a stepwise progression, as in graduated exposure (see Table 11-8). Feedback on the client's performance both in the therapy sessions and for homework assignments is an important aspect of the training. The therapist reinforces the client for acting assertively but not for obtaining a favorable outcome. The reason is that the outcome of an assertive behavior rarely is totally in the client's control (for instance, securing a day off from work may depend on the availability of other workers). Accordingly, clients are taught, through modeling and behavior rehearsal, how to react

Table 11-7 Physical and vocal stylistic components of assertive, unassertive, and aggressive behaviors

Stylistic Component	Assertive Behavior	Unassertive Behavior	Aggressive Behavior
EYE CONTACT	**Looking at person while talking**	Looking away from person while talking	Intently staring at person while talking
FACIAL EXPRESSION	**Appropriate to message**	Sheepish or expressionless	Hostile no matter what the message is
GESTURES	**Moderate; appropriate to message**	None or inappropriate to message	Excessive; overenthusiastic
BODY POSTURE	**Erect; at an appropriate distance; leaning slightly toward the person**	Slouched; a bit too far from the person; leaning away from the person	Erect; either too close or too far from person; exaggerated leaning in either direction
VOICE QUALITY	**Firm (confident); appropriate volume; appropriate expression**	Apologetic; whisper; monotone	Overzealous; shouting; "soapbox" speech

and cope when their appropriate assertive responses fail to obtain the desired outcomes.

Modeling assertive behavior can be covert,[124] as in the case of a 7-year-old girl who had been sexually abused and responded with emotional outbursts and sexually inappropriate behaviors whenever she felt taken advantage of.[125] The therapist asked the girl to visualize scenes in which a peer model similar to the girl constructively dealt with her negative feelings, such as by saying something to a teacher who treated her unfairly. Table 11-9 has examples of typical scenes used in covert modeling of assertive behaviors. Covert modeling may be supplemented with **covert behavior rehearsal,** which involves clients' imagining themselves performing target behaviors. We often do this informally to rehearse how we are going to act. For example, right before going to see a professor about getting an extension on a paper, you might mentally rehearse making the request.

Hundreds of studies have demonstrated the efficacy of assertion training for clients with diverse problems and across the age spectrum.[126]* For example, assertion training is being used increasingly to prevent HIV

---

*Research on assertion training has decreased significantly over the past 20 years. This may be due, in part, to deficits in assertive behavior not being classified as a disorder in the *Diagnostic and Statistical Manual of Mental Disorders* (American Psychiatric Association, 1987, 1994, 2000a), which generally is necessary for research funding. It certainly is not due to clients' no longer having assertive behavior skills deficits.

Table 11-8 Hierarchy of assertive behaviors practiced by a client having difficulty with refusing unreasonable requests (in descending order)

9. Refusing an unreasonable request from a close friend when the request is very important to the friend

8. Refusing an unreasonable request from a close friend when the request is moderately important to the friend

7. Refusing an unreasonable request from an acquaintance when the request is very important to the acquaintance

6. Refusing an unreasonable request from an acquaintance when the request is moderately important to the acquaintance

5. Refusing an unreasonable request from a close friend when the request is relatively unimportant to the friend

4. Refusing an unreasonable request from an acquaintance when the request is relatively unimportant to the acquaintance

3. Refusing an unreasonable request from a stranger when the request is very important to the stranger

2. Refusing an unreasonable request from a stranger when the request is moderately important to the stranger

1. Refusing an unreasonable request from a stranger when the request is relatively unimportant to the stranger

NOTE: The rank ordering is an individual matter and will vary from client to client.

Table 11-9 Covert modeling scenes used to accelerate assertive behaviors

Situation	Modeled Assertive Behavior	Vicarious Reinforcement
A woman is eating in a restaurant with friends. She orders a salad and tells the waiter to put the dressing on the side. When the salad arrives, it has the dressing directly on it.	The woman immediately turns to the waiter and says, "I asked for my salad with the dressing on the side. Please bring me another salad without dressing and the dressing in a separate dish."	A few minutes later the waiter returns with the salad correctly prepared and says that he is very sorry for the error and hopes that the woman enjoys the salad.
A man who is trying to stop smoking is at a party where most people are smoking. The host offers him a cigarette.	The man says, "No, thanks. But I would like something to eat."	The host replies, "Sure thing. The food is in the dining room."

infection among vulnerable populations, including women who are chronically hospitalized for schizophrenia and depression,[127] inner city low-income African-American men[128] and women,[129] people with mental retardation,[130] and high-risk adolescents such as those with other sexually transmitted diseases[131] and those with poor heterosocial skills (the social behaviors necessary for initiating, maintaining, and terminating social and sexual relationships with persons of the opposite sex).[132] These applications have been effective in reducing the risk of contracting HIV as assessed by such measures as the number of sexual partners, the number of sexual contacts with strangers, and the use of condoms.

Research also has been directed at identifying the components of optimal assertive behavior. For example, people are considered competent and likable if their assertive response is empathic[133] and complimentary.[134] An example would be, "You guys are doing a great job given how shorthanded you are; I just hope you'll be able to have my car fixed by the end of the day."

Assertion training is a "popular" therapy. It frequently is used in conjunction with other behavior therapies, such as cognitive therapy (which we will cover in Chapter 12).[135] Although clearly a behavior therapy, assertion training also has been incorporated into many different kinds of psychotherapy (such as Gestalt therapy). Assertion training also has been a hot topic in "pop" psychology for many years. Consider the large number of books on the subject written for the general public, including "treatises . . . on the technique of how, when and why to say no; what to say no to; and why you should not feel guilty in saying no."[136]

◆

Participation Exercise 11-2

ASSERTION TRAINING FOR REFUSING UNREASONABLE REQUESTS*

In this Participation Exercise, you will engage in assertion training consisting of symbolic modeling, behavior rehearsal, and feedback to teach you to appropriately refuse unreasonable requests. Table 11-10 contains four hypothetical situations in which requests are made in a letter. For each, read the letter, keeping in mind the particular situation. Assume that you have received the letter and write an appropriate reply. If the request is unreasonable, refuse the request; if the request is reasonable, agree to it.

Here are some general guidelines for writing an *appropriate* refusal to an unreasonable request:

1. Be polite.
2. Be direct; say what you mean. If you mean that you *don't want* to do something, say that directly (and politely) instead of saying that you are not sure whether you can do it. The former reply would be honest and unambiguous, whereas the latter would be dishonest and ambiguous.
3. Do not apologize excessively. It might, however, be appropriate to wish the writer luck in obtaining a positive response from others.
4. Tailor the letter to the degree of unreasonableness of the request. For example, a mildly unreasonable request should be responded to with mild refusal, such as "Sorry, but I won't be able to help you out."
5. Consider your relationship, present and future, with the writer. If it is important to you, you may want to tone down your reply.
6. In *some* cases it may be appropriate to compromise, which, in effect, would render the request more reasonable so that you feel comfortable doing part of what the writer requested.

*This Participation Exercise can be done before you continue reading or later.

7. Remember: You are entitled to refuse others' unreasonable requests—and even reasonable ones.

After you have replied to the first letter, look at Table 11-11 and read the modeled reply along with the explanation, which will give you feedback on what you have written. Your reply need not match the modeled reply, but it

Table 11-10 Hypothetical situations and letters requiring responses (Participation Exercise 11-2)

Situation	Letter to Respond to

1. You are invited to a party by a student who was in a class you took during the summer. She asks you to pick up someone you don't know, which will mean your driving 30 miles out of your way.	Dear Classmate,
	
	    How's it going? We're having a little party at my house next Thursday, and I'd like you to come. My cousin was coming, but he's having trouble getting a ride down. Do you think you can give him a lift? He lives about 45 minutes out of town so I've enclosed a map. See you on Thursday.
	
	              Regards,
	              Classmate

2. A CD company you recently joined has sent you four CDs you never ordered. In fact, you promptly returned the order card stating that you didn't want any CDs sent.	Dear CD Club Member,
	
	    We have, up to this time, sent you four CDs for a total of $59.80. We have not received any payment. Please send full payment immediately, plus shipping and handling costs, as indicated on the enclosed bill.
	
	              Thank you,
	              President,
	              Ripoff Recordings, Inc.

3. You receive a letter asking for a contribution to a religious group you have never heard of.	Dear Neighbor,
	
	    In order for our organization to grow and to build new places of worship, it is essential that we receive financial backing from people like you. Please open your heart and send your check today. Return this card with your contribution so that we can continue sending you news and information about our ministry.
	
	              Most sincerely,
	              President,
	              United Affluent Church

4. A close friend writes you asking if you would pick up an important package for him at the local post office, which you pass every day, and pay the delivery charge.	Dear Friend,
	
	    I won't be in the city until some time next week, but I'm expecting an important package to arrive at the main post office. I would really appreciate it if you could pick it up for me and pay the delivery charge. It should only be a few dollars. I'll pay you when I get back.
	
	              Thanks,
	              Your friend

Table 11-11 Model letters for refusing unreasonable requests, with explanations (Participation Exercise 11-2)

Model Letter	Explanatory Note
1. Dear Classmate, Thanks for the invitation to the party. I'll sure be there, but I really won't be able to pick up your cousin. Thirty miles is just too far for me to go out of my way. I'm looking forward to seeing you at the party.	Polite and friendly; states what you will and will not do; ends on an upbeat note
2. Dear President: I did not order the four CDs you have sent. I promptly returned the order card and checked off that I did not want the CDs. Therefore, I refuse to pay for them, although I will return them at your company's expense.	Clearly explains situation; categorically says no; adds a compromise that demonstrates good faith
3. Dear President, I am not interested in your organization or in receiving any further news or information from you.	Very brief, formal reply, appropriate for the impersonal form letter received; unequivocally states your position
4. Dear Friend, I'll be glad to pick up the package for you. Give me a call when you get back in town, and we'll arrange for you to pick it up.	*Reasonable* request in this case

should contain the same basic elements. Repeat the process for each situation and letter. To benefit from the feedback provided in Table 11-11, refer to the modeled reply after writing each letter and before writing the next letter.

◆

VICARIOUS EXTINCTION: REDUCING FEAR BY MODELING

Fear or anxiety is maintained by the anticipation of negative consequences (such as expecting to be turned down when asking for a date) and by skills deficits (such as not knowing how to ask for a date). Modeling can treat both of these maintaining conditions simultaneously when a model demonstrates the anxiety-evoking behaviors without incurring negative consequences, a process known as **vicarious extinction.**

Vicarious extinction typically employs a **coping model**—a model who is initially fearful and incompetent and who gradually becomes more comfortable and skilled performing an anxiety-evoking behavior.[137] Coping models are appropriate for clients who are fearful and incompetent themselves (which enhances the similarity of the model and the observer). In contrast, a **mastery model** is an expert who shows no fear and is competent from the outset.[138] Mastery models are more suitable for precise skill development, such as learning to physically defend oneself from sexual assault.[139]

Live Modeling to Reduce Fear

Live models have been used to treat a variety of fear and anxiety-related disorders, such as specific phobias (for example, fear of small animals),[140] test anxiety,[141] social phobia,[142] and obsessive-compulsive disorder.[143] Case 11-4 is an unusual application of parental modeling and in vivo exposure to reduce a child's fear of dental treatment.

Case 11-4

PLANNED AND UNPLANNED TREATMENT OF FEAR OF DENTAL PROCEDURES BY PARENTAL MODELING AND IN VIVO EXPOSURE[144]

Four-year-old S. Z. needed restorative dental work, but she was intensely afraid of the dentist. In the six attempted visits to the dentist, S. Z. would "scream, cry, shake violently as [she] walked to the dentist, was short of breath and would adamantly refuse to cooperate." S. Z.'s mother reported that she too was terrified of dentists, and she believed that her daughter had learned to fear dentists from her.[145] Although S. Z.'s mother did not want to be treated for her own fear, she did agree to serve as a model for her daughter.

In the first five weekly visits to the dentist's office, S. Z. and her mother viewed a video depicting various dental procedures (modeling) and spent time in the office with no dental procedures being performed (in vivo exposure). During the sixth visit, the therapist and the mother both modeled experiencing a 1-minute dental checkup. Playing the role of coping models, they exhibited initial hesitancy; then, they cooperated with the dental procedures and commented that it "wasn't that bad at all." The mother had been instructed ahead of time to act as if she were unafraid and cooperate with the dentist while the procedures were being done, which she was able to do despite her own fear. During the seventh session, S. Z. received dental treatment while her mother provided reassurance.

The eighth and final session served as a posttherapy assessment. The dentist performed two procedures on S. Z. under local anesthesia. S. Z. sat by herself in the chair and showed no overt signs of fear. Before therapy and during the final session, S. Z.'s mother used a 100-point SUDs-like scale to rate her daughter on 10 dentistry-related behaviors, which ranged from "telling S. Z. about an appointment" to "the dentist's using the drill." During the final session, the average SUDs rating was 6, compared with 78 before therapy. Over the next 6 months, S. Z. received considerable dental treatment. At a 6-month follow-up, S. Z.'s average SUDs rating was 3. A 1-year telephone follow-up with both the mother and the dentist indicated that S. Z. continued to display little or no fear of dental procedures.

S. Z.'s mother was not specifically treated for her fear of dental procedures. However, she had participated in S. Z.'s in vivo exposure procedures and her modeling for S. Z. resulted in both self-modeling and behavior rehearsal for her. Apparently, this indirect therapy was sufficient to almost eliminate her own fear. The mother's pretherapy, posttherapy, and 6-month follow-up average SUDs ratings were 54, 3, and 7, respectively. A year later, the mother and her dentist reported that she was experiencing very little fear about dental visits.

In **participant modeling,** the therapist models the fear-evoking behavior for the client and then encourages and physically guides the client's practicing the behavior. Developed by Brunhilde Ritter,[146] participant modeling combines modeling, prompting, behavior rehearsal, and in vivo exposure. Participant modeling also is known as *contact desensitization*[147] and as *guided participation*,[148] for reasons that will become apparent shortly. The three basic steps in participant modeling are as follows:

1. *Modeling:* The therapist first models the fear-evoking behavior for the client.
2. *Prompting, Behavior Rehearsal,* and *In Vivo Exposure:* The therapist verbally prompts the client to imitate the behavior she or he has just modeled. The therapist physically prompts the client to perform the behavior (such as by actually holding a client's hand while petting a dog). The physical contact between the therapist and client also reassures and calms the client, and these feelings compete with fear.
3. *Fading Prompts:* The therapist gradually withdraws the verbal and physical prompts. The client begins to perform the behavior with the therapist present but without physical contact, and finally without the therapist present.

The behaviors that are modeled and practiced are arranged in a hierarchy. The treatment proceeds from the least to the most threatening behaviors. The rate of exposure is determined by the client's fear level, as in in vivo exposure therapy. Case 11-5 illustrates the basic steps in participant modeling.

Case 11-5
FEAR OF CROSSING STREETS TREATED BY PARTICIPANT MODELING[149]

Mrs. S. was a 49-year-old widow who for 10 years had been intensely afraid of crossing streets. Her fear had caused her to withdraw from social contacts almost completely, and her resulting despair had led her to attempt suicide. Participant modeling proceeded as follows:

> A low-traffic location in which a narrow street intersected with a moderately wide street was chosen. The counselor walked across the narrow street for about one minute while Mrs. S. watched. Then the counselor firmly placed her arm around Mrs. S.'s waist and walked across with her. This was repeated . . . until Mrs. S. reported she was

fairly comfortable at performing the task. . . . Street crossing was then continued while physical contact between counselor and Mrs. S. was gradually reduced until the counselor only lightly touched the back of Mrs. S.'s arm . . . [and] walked slightly behind her. Contact was then eliminated completely, with the counselor first walking alongside Mrs. S. as the street was crossed and then slightly behind her. The counselor subsequently followed Mrs. S. approximately three-fourths of the way across the street and allowed her to go the remaining distance alone. Gradually the counselor reduced the distance she accompanied Mrs. S. until eventually Mrs. S. was able to cross the street entirely alone.

These procedures then were applied on increasingly wider and busier streets, and Mrs. S. was given more responsibility for her therapy, including planning and carrying out her own homework assignments. She had set four specific goals for therapy, including independently crossing the four streets of a busy intersection. She accomplished all four goals in less than 7 weeks.

Participant modeling has been used to treat a variety of anxiety-related problems, including small animal phobias,[150] fear of dental treatment,[151] public speaking anxiety,[152] fear of water,[153] and agoraphobia.[154] Participant modeling has been shown to be superior to live modeling,[155] film modeling,[156] and in vivo exposure.[157] The potency of participant modeling may be due to the integration of modeling, behavior rehearsal, and in vivo exposure. Clients' fears are reduced both by what they "see" and by what they do.[158]

Film/Video Modeling to Reduce Fear

Fear of medical and dental procedures can have far-reaching consequences because it can keep people from seeking regular health checkups and obtaining necessary treatment. Film/video modeling has been highly successful in reducing such fear and avoidance behaviors. One survey indicated that 37% of all pediatric hospitals in the United States used film/video modeling to prepare children for hospitalization and surgery.[159] We will describe film/video modeling therapies for reducing fear of surgery and related medical procedures. Parallel modeling therapies have proven effective in reducing fear of dentistry in children and adults.[160]

Barbara Melamed spearheaded the use of films to reduce children's anxiety about hospitalization and medical procedures with *Ethan Has an Operation,* a 16-minute modeling film depicting the experiences of a 7-year-old boy who has been hospitalized for a hernia operation (see Photo 11-3).[161]

This film . . . consists of 15 scenes showing various events that most children encounter when hospitalized for elective surgery from the time of admission to the time of discharge including a child's

Photo 11-3 Scene from the film *Ethan Has an Operation,* showing Ethan in the operating room as the surgeon inserts an intravenous needle

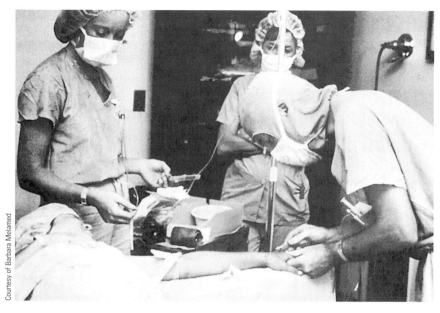

Courtesy of Barbara Melamed

orientation to the hospital ward and medical personnel such as the surgeon and anesthesiologist; having a blood test and exposure to standard hospital equipment; separation from the mother; and scenes in the operating and recovery rooms. In addition to explanations of the hospital procedures provided by the medical staff, various scenes are narrated by the child, who describes his feelings and concerns that he had at each stage of the hospital experience. Both the child's behavior and verbal remarks exemplify the behavior of a coping model so that while he exhibits some anxiety and apprehension, he is able to overcome his initial fears and complete each event in a successful and nonanxious manner.[162]

Compared with children who viewed a control film (depicting a boy on a nature trip), children who viewed *Ethan Has an Operation* had less postoperative anxiety and fewer conduct problems at home.[163]

Another film was developed to minimize children's fear of receiving injections.[164] In this 18-minute film, at the moment of the injection, a close-up of the child's upper body and face shows the child's wincing, exclaiming "Ouch," and frowning, which is a realistic reaction to the injection. Children (ages 4 to 9) viewed the film in their homes 36 hours before receiving their preoperative injections. These children, who had seen realistic coping models, were compared with children who saw the same basic film, except that the patient-models in the film did not show any signs of pain or discomfort. Such behavior is unrealistic because injections do hurt. Another group of children saw no movie at all. Children who had seen the realistic film (some pain) indicated experiencing the least pain when they received their injections; those who had viewed the unrealistic film (no pain) reported experiencing the most pain.[165]

Modeling films also have been combined with other behavior therapies to reduce children's fears of medical procedures. For example, a 12-minute modeling film, *Joy Gets a Bone Marrow and Spinal Tap,* was part of a treatment package for reducing the distress of children with cancer (ages 3 to 7) undergoing two very painful treatments: bone marrow aspirations and spinal taps.[166] The model in the film is a 6-year-old leukemia patient who comes to the clinic for treatment.

> She describes her thoughts and feelings. . . . As a coping model, Joy admits she is scared about the procedures, exhibits some signs of distress, but then copes effectively. . . . Joy explains *why* she has to have the procedures and she illustrates *what* happens at each point in the procedures.[167]

The treatment package successfully reduced the distress for each of the children in the study.

Modeling films to treat adults' fear and distress *during* medical procedures also are beneficial.[168] Sexual anxiety in women is yet another target behavior that has been treated with video modeling.[169]

◆   **In Theory 11-2**

SELF-EFFICACY AS A GENERAL EXPLANATION OF THE EFFECTS OF BEHAVIOR THERAPY

When we are confronted with a difficult or frightening task, we usually have a "sense" of the chances of successfully performing it. **Perceived self-efficacy** refers to the belief that one can be successful at a task.[170] The self-efficacy is *perceived* because it depends totally on how the individual views his or her chances of success, independent of the external odds. A person can have high perceived self-efficacy for an impossible task, such as swimming across the Pacific Ocean, and low self-efficacy for a relatively easy task, such as swimming across a pool.

According to Bandura's theory of perceived self-efficacy, people's level of self-efficacy determines (1) whether they will attempt a task, (2) the effort they will expend to complete the task, and (3) the time they will spend on the task.[171] The stronger one's perceived self-efficacy, the more vigorous and persistent one tends to be in the face of obstacles and setbacks.[172] Self-efficacy is situation specific—it varies with the particular task.[173] For example, people's self-efficacy expectations about their ability to stop smoking predict success in smoking cessation but not in remaining on a diet.[174]

Bandura has speculated that modeling and other behavior therapies (as well as other forms of psychotherapy) are effective because they create and strengthen a client's perceived self-efficacy.[175] Recall that one of the proposed theoretical explanations of exposure therapies is that they heighten clients' beliefs that they are capable of handling their anxiety (see In Theory 9-1, page 228).

Self-efficacy is strengthened by information provided by the following four sources:

Table 11-12 Examples of behavior therapies that provide clients with each of the four sources of self-efficacy (numbers in parentheses refer to chapters in which the therapies are discussed) (In Theory 11-2)

Self-Efficacy Source	Behavior Therapies
PERFORMANCE ACCOMPLISHMENTS	In vivo exposure (9) In vivo flooding (10) Reinforcement therapy (6) Behavior rehearsal (11) Participant modeling (11) Stress inoculation training (13) Problem-solving therapy (13)
VICARIOUS EXPERIENCE	Modeling therapy (11)
VERBAL PERSUASION	Rational emotive behavior therapy (12) Cognitive therapy (12) Self-instructional training (13)
EMOTIONAL AROUSAL	Systematic desensitization (9) Relaxation training (9) Imaginal flooding (10) Implosive therapy (10)

NOTE: The sources of self-efficacy categories are not mutually exclusive; for a given therapy, self-efficacy may come from more than one source

1. *Performance accomplishments:* Direct experience in succeeding at a task may be the most powerful source of self-efficacy.

2. *Vicarious experience:* Observing models succeed at tasks helps clients believe that they themselves can succeed.

3. *Verbal persuasion:* Telling or logically proving to clients that they can succeed is the most common source of self-efficacy in verbal psychotherapies and also plays a role in behavior therapies, especially cognitive-behavioral therapies (as you will see in Chapters 12 and 13).

4. *Emotional arousal:* Their levels of emotional arousal is one factor that people use to judge their self-efficacy. Generally, high arousal is associated with anxiety and doubt and hence low self-efficacy; low arousal tends to be associated with calm and confidence and hence high self-efficacy. Therapies that lower clients' arousal levels (such as relaxation training) can enhance clients' perceived self-efficacy.

Table 11-12 presents examples of behavior therapies that provide clients with each of the four sources of self-efficacy.

Storytelling to Reduce Fear and Other Negative Emotions

Storytelling is another form of symbolic modeling used to treat fear. For example, a puppet show depicting a teddy bear going through a typical hospital visit has been shown to be as effective as films, including *Ethan Has an Operation,* which is considered a benchmark.[176] Many commercially available books and pamphlets describing various diagnostic and treatment procedures, such as those found in physicians' offices, include modeling in that they describe the experiences of actual or hypothetical patients (see Figure 11-5).

Uncle Lightfoot is an 85-page book designed to reduce children's fear of the dark.[177] A young boy, Michael, who is afraid of the dark visits his Uncle Lightfoot who teaches him fun games to play in the dark (see Figure 11-6). As a coping model, Michael learns to deal with progressively more threatening situations in the dark. The games have been adapted so that children can engage in behavior rehearsal with their parents after reading the book.

Covert modeling can be used to treat anxiety-related problems, such as social anxiety,[178] specific phobias,[179] anxiety anticipatory to surgery,[180] and obsessive-compulsive disorder.[181] Covert modeling implicitly is part of storytelling because the observer imagines the character's actions. Parents and teachers frequently use stories, rather than direct instructions, to influence children's behaviors and emotions.[182] Modeling can be more effective than instructions because modeling provides *suggestions* rather than directives, which puts children "in charge" of their own behaviors.

Bob Knight and Associates, 1969.

With Joe and the nurse, Tim drove to a room and met a doctor there
Who wore a mask upon his face and a funny cap to hide his hair.

The doctor let him breathe through it and that was quite a treat,
He felt just like an astronaut and drifted off to sleep.

Figure 11-5 Pages from *My Tonsillectomy Coloring Book,* which uses modeling to reduce children's anxiety about their impending tonsillectomies

Figure 11-6 Picture from *Uncle Lightfoot,* a story book that uses modeling to reduce children's fear of the dark

Coffman, 1980.

For instance, an 8-year-old girl confided in her father that she was intimidated by a bully at school. Rather than directly suggest how she might handle the situation, the father wisely chose to give her vicarious advice by telling her a story about the way he had handled a bully when he had been a child.[183] In the same vein, to reduce children's fears in the wake of the September 11, 2001, terrorist attacks in New York and Washington, parents have been advised to expose their children to stories that depict similar-age models coping with fear. For young children, "Sesame Street" produced a segment in which Elmo is a coping model who deals with his fear after a fire in his neighborhood.

◆ ALL THINGS CONSIDERED: MODELING THERAPY AND SKILLS TRAINING

Modeling is effective in reducing skills deficits and treating fear and anxiety-related disorders.[184] Although early research consisted mostly of analogue studies (for example, studies of college students afraid of snakes),[185] more recent controlled experiments have dealt with clinical populations and serious problems. Overall, modeling therapies have been found to be at least as effective as other behavior therapies with which they have been compared. For a number of specific applications, such as in reducing children's fears,[186] modeling procedures have been shown to be more effective.[187]

Modeling therapies are very efficient. Significant changes sometimes are obtained in one or two brief sessions.[188] One reason may be that modeling simultaneously teaches clients adaptive behaviors, prompts their performance, motivates their practice, and reduces anxiety about performing the behaviors. Symbolic modeling is highly cost-effective. Once produced, modeling films/videos and books do not require therapists' time. For example, modeling videos to reduce fear of dental procedures now are routinely shown in some dentists' offices. The major limitation of standard symbolic modeling presentations is that they are aimed at the "average" client, which means that they are not individualized. However, present technology makes it possible to customize symbolic modeling relatively easily. For instance, individualized modeling videos can be made using video recorders,[189] and written stories can be customized with a word processor by changing a few significant phrases (such as names of people and locations). Symbolic modeling also can be supplemented with individualized live modeling, in which case the live modeling may not have to be as extensive and time consuming because the client has already been exposed to symbolic modeling.

Modeling therapies easily can be implemented in naturalistic settings by nonprofessional behavior change agents, which is another way in which modeling therapies are efficient. In one application, social skills training for preschoolers with low levels of peer social interaction consisted of modeling and prompting by teachers' aides, followed by behavior rehearsal.[190] The training significantly increased the children's social interactions in a short time.

Modeling can be highly cost-effective in another way. **Natural models**—people in clients' everyday environments who exhibit behaviors that clients need to learn and practice—are abundantly available, and clients can observe them on their own.[191] For example, a client who is fearful of speaking to people at social gatherings could go to a large party and observe how people speak to one another and what happens when they do (vicarious consequences). Parents and teachers naturally serve as models for children and adolescents, which should be used to therapeutic advantage. For instance, children who give up easily when tasks are difficult could benefit from observing adults in their lives who model appropriately coping with frustration.[192] Although the use of natural models is a potentially potent and efficient form of modeling therapy, the extent to which behavior therapists instruct clients to observe appropriate natural models is unknown.

Modeling is an acceptable therapy to clients. It is subtle and unintrusive. Modeling indirectly influences clients merely by presenting an example of how one might behave, which may result in clients' feeling more in control of their behavior changes. This is important because behavior change is more effective when people believe that they are personally responsible for the change.

Skills training increases clients' personal freedom by providing them with alternative ways of behaving. This is equally true for the child with mental retardation who learns to ask for assistance and for the business executive who learns appropriate assertive behaviors to use in complex social interactions. In fact, competency-based treatments that involve skills training can enhance self-efficacy, independent functioning, and the overall quality of life even for clients with serious, chronic psychiatric disorders.[193]

Modeling is inherent to many behavior therapies. For example, modeling is part of in vivo exposure and in vivo flooding when the therapist demonstrates the desired behavior for the client (such as walking out of the house in the case of agoraphobia).[194] The therapist's modeling not only prompts the target behavior but also shows the client that no harm comes from performing it. Modeling also is a component of many cognitive-behavioral therapies (which you will read about in Chapters 12 and 13).

Besides being a treatment modality, modeling is used to teach therapy skills to therapists and nonprofessional change agents, including clients themselves.[195] For example, modeling is an essential component in behavioral child management training (as you saw in Chapter 8).[196] The therapist first models a behavior management procedure, such as shaping. Then, parents practice shaping their children's behaviors and receive feedback from the therapist. Similar procedures are used to teach family members to care for elderly relatives with physical and psychological impairments.[197] Modeling also has potential for encouraging clients to seek therapy[198] and in preparing clients for psychotherapy.[199]

SUMMARY

1. Modeling requires two people: a model who demonstrates a behavior and an observer who attends to what the model does. Live models are actually present, and symbolic models are observed indirectly, as on TV. Observing a model provides information about what the model does as well as the consequences of the model's actions, which are called vicarious consequences (vicarious reinforcement or vicarious negative consequences).

2. Observational learning is the process by which people are influenced by observing a model's behaviors. It involves three stages: exposure to the model, acquisition of the model's behaviors, and acceptance of the model's behaviors as a guide for one's own actions. The observer can be influenced by the model in four ways: specific imitation, specific counterimitation, general imitation, and general counterimitation.

3. Modeling serves five functions for observers: teaching, prompting, motivating, reducing anxiety, and discouraging.

4. Self-modeling, in which clients serve as their own models (on a video or in their imagination), maximizes observer–model similarity, which enhances imitation.

5. Modeling generally is part of a treatment package, which often includes behavior rehearsal. However, modeling can be effective by itself.

6. Skills deficits can involve deficiencies in knowledge, proficiency, discrimination, and motivation. Skills training is a treatment package that may include modeling, direct instruction, prompting, shaping, reinforcement, behavior rehearsal, role-playing, and corrective feedback. Occasionally, clients, such as children with autistic disorder, may have to be taught generalized imitation—the ability to imitate—before skills training using modeling can be implemented.

7. Social skills training, employing modeling films/videos and live modeling, often is used to increase social interactions. It is an important component in the treatment of clients with schizophrenia, in which the major goals are to increase social interactions, to teach skills needed for functioning in the community, and to reduce stress by teaching clients how to cope with problematic social situations.

8. Specific procedures often must be used to promote transfer and generalization of skills learned in social skills training.

9. Assertive behaviors are actions that secure and maintain what one is entitled to in an interpersonal situation without infringing on the rights of others. Assertive behaviors are situation specific.

10. Assertion training begins by assessing the specific details of the client's assertive skills deficit and the type(s) of skill deficit the client has. Live or symbolic modeling and behavior rehearsal are the primary components of assertion training.

11. Vicarious extinction involves reducing fear or anxiety by having a client observe a model's performing the feared behavior without the model incurring negative consequences. A coping model is initially fearful and incompetent and then gradually becomes comfortable and competent performing the feared behavior. A mastery model shows no fear and is competent from the outset. Coping models are more appropriate for reducing fear.

12. In participant modeling, the therapist models the anxiety-evoking behaviors for the client, then verbally and physically prompts the client to perform the behaviors, and finally fades the prompts.

13. Film/video modeling has been used to treat fear of medical procedures in both children and adults. Storytelling is another form of symbolic modeling used to reduce fear and other negative emotions in children.

14. Perceived self-efficacy is the belief that one will be successful at a task. Modeling and other therapies may be effective because they increase clients' self-efficacy through performance accomplishments, vicarious experiences, verbal persuasion, and emotional arousal.

15. Modeling therapies are effective and efficient treatments for skills deficits and for anxiety-related disorders. They simultaneously teach clients adaptive behaviors, prompt performance, motivate practice, and reduce anxiety about performing the threatening behaviors. Modeling is a subtle and unintrusive therapy and is acceptable to clients. It is a component of many behavior therapies because therapists often model adaptive behaviors. Modeling also is used to train therapists and other change agents.

REFERENCE NOTES

1. Kalmuss, 1984.
2. Craig, 1986.
3. Gould & Shaffer, 1986; Lester, 1987; Ostroff & Boyd, 1987; compare with Wasserman, 1984.
4. Compare with Strain, Shores, & Kerr, 1976; Wilson, Robertson, Herlong, & Haynes, 1979.
5. Liebert & Spiegler, 1994.
6. For example, Bly, 1990; Campbell, 1988; Constantino, Malgady, & Rogler, 1986.

7. Kazdin, 1973, 1974a, 1974b, 1974c.

8. Kendall, Chu, Pimentel, & Choudhury, 2000.

9. Bandura, 1971, 1977b.

10. Kazdin, 1979; Rosenthal & Steffek, 1991.

11. Compare with Kellam, 1969; Maeda, 1985; Olson & Roberts, 1987; Owusu-Bempah & Howitt, 1985; Rosenthal, Linehan, Kelley, Rosenthal, Theobald, & Davis, 1978; Rosenthal, Rosenthal, & Chang, 1977; Wickramasekera, 1976.

12. Bandura, 1986b.

13. For example, Barry & Overmann, 1977; Hicks, 1965; Kazdin, 1974b; Kornhaber & Schroeder, 1975; Rosekrans, 1967.

14. Meharg & Woltersdorf, 1990.

15. Dowrick, 1991, 1994.

16. Simmons, 1993, p. 161, emphasis in original.

17. Creer & Miklich, 1970.

18. Dowrick, 1979, 1983, 1986.

19. Buggey, Toombs, Gardener, & Cervetti, 1999.

20. Dowrick & Hood, 1978; Kehle, Madaus, Baratta, & Bray, 1998; Kehle, Owen, & Cressy, 1990; Pigott & Gonzales, 1987.

21. Bray & Kehle, 1998, 2001; Hosford, 1974.

22. Clarke, Bray, Kehle, & Truscott, 2001.

23. Dowrick, 1978.

24. Davis, 1979; Dowrick & Raeburn, 1977; Kehle, Clark, Jenson, & Wampold, 1986.

25. Bray & Kehle, 1998; Clare, Jenson, Kehle, & Bray, 2000; Possell, Kehle, Mcloughlin, & Bray, 1999.

26. Kahn, Kehle, Jenson, & Clark, 1990; Prince & Dowrick, 1984.

27. Schwartz, Houlihan, Krueger, & Simon, 1997.

28. Hosford & Brown, 1975.

29. Dowrick & Ward, 1997.

30. Neef, Bill-Harvey, Shade, Iezzi, & DeLorenzo, 1995.

31. Andersson, Melin, Scott, & Lindberg, 1995.

32. Dowrick & Raeburn, 1995.

33. From the author's (MDS) clinical files.

34. O'Donohue & Krasner, 1995a, 1995b.

35. For example, Corrigan, Schade, & Liberman, 1992; Hansen, MacMillan, & Shawchuck, 1990; Matson, Bamburg, Smalls, & Smiroldo, 1997; Matson, Smalls, Hampff, Smiroldo, & Anderson, 1998; Miltenberger, 2000; Taras, Matson, & Leary, 1988.

36. For example, Charlop & Milstein, 1989; Gambrill, 1995a.

37. For example, Star, 1986.

38. For example, Baggs & Spence, 1990.

39. For example, Charlop & Milstein, 1989; Charlop, Schreibman, & Tryon, 1983; Egel, Richman, & Koegel, 1981; Lovaas, 1977, 1987.

40. Metz, 1965.

41. For example, Goldstein & Mousetis, 1989; Rietveld, 1983.

42. For example, Rivera & Smith, 1988; Smith & Lovitt, 1975.

43. For example, Foxx, Martella, & Marchand-Martella, 1989.

44. Newman & Haaga, 1995.

45. O'Donohue & Noll, 1995.

46. Szymanski & O'Donohue, 1995.

47. Pierce, 1995.

48. Vargas & Shanley, 1995.

49. Haring, Breen, Weiner, Kennedy, & Bednerah, 1995.

50. Rusch, Hughes, & Wilson, 1995.

51. Barclay & Houts, 1995.

52. Groth, 1980.

53. For example, Poche, Brouwer, & Swearingen, 1981.

54. Miltenberger & Thiesse-Duffy, 1988; Poche, Brouwer, & Swearingen, 1981; Poche, Yoder, & Miltenberger, 1988.

55. Poche, Brouwer, & Swearingen, 1981.

56. Poche, Yoder, & Miltenberger, 1988.

57. Poche, Yoder, & Miltenberger, 1988, p. 255.

58. Wurtele, Currier, Gillispie, & Franklin, 1991.

59. Wurtele, 1990; Wurtele, Currier, Gillispie, & Franklin, 1991; Wurtele, Marrs, & Miller-Perrin, 1987.

60. For example, Brazelton, 1987.

61. Lumley, Miltenberger, Long, Rapp, & Roberts, 1998; Miltenberger, Roberts, Ellingson, Galensky, Rapp, Long, & Lumley, 1999.

62. Miltenberger, Roberts, Ellingson, Galensky, Rapp, Long, & Lumley, 1999.

63. Frame & Matson, 1987.

64. Matson, Sevin, & Box, 1995.

65. Gambrill, 1995b; Trower, 1995.

66. Matson, Sevin, & Box, 1995.

67. Trower, 1995.

68. Gambrill, 1995b.

69. Gottman & Rushe, 1995.

70. Gold, Letourneau, & O'Donohue, 1995.

71. Gambrill, 1995a.

72. Ballard & Crooks, 1984; O'Connor, 1969; Rao, Moely, & Lockman, 1987.

73. O'Connor, 1969, p. 18.

74. O'Connor, 1969; Rao, Moely, & Lockman, 1987.
75. O'Connor, 1969.
76. For example, Star, 1986.
77. Gumpel & Frank, 1999.
78. Franco, Christoff, Crimmins, & Kelly, 1983.
79. For example, Graves, Openshaw, & Adams, 1992.
80. For example, Foxx, Faw, & Weber, 1991.
81. For example, Cunliffe, 1992.
82. For example, Middleton & Cartledge, 1995.
83. For example, Guevremont, 1990; Posavac, Sheridan, & Posavac, 1999.
84. Varni, Katz, Colegrove, & Dolgin, 1993.
85. Rasing, Coninx, Duker, & Van Den Hurk, 1994.
86. Gambrill, 1985; Garland, 1985.
87. Carstensen & Fisher, 1991.
88. Bellack, Morrison, Wixted, & Mueser, 1990; Spiegler & Agigian, 1977; Trower, 1995.
89. Emmelkamp, 1994.
90. For example, Bellack & Mueser, 1994.
91. For example, Liberman, Vaccaro, & Corrigan, 1995.
92. For example, Liberman, Wallace, Blackwell, Eckman, Vaccaro, & Kuehnel, 1993.
93. Emmelkamp, 1994.
94. Wong, Martinez-Diaz, Massel, Edelstein, Wiegand, Bowen, & Liberman, 1993.
95. For example, Benton & Schroeder, 1990.
96. For example, Bellack & Mueser, 1994; Benton & Schroeder, 1990.
97. Liberman, Wallace, Blackwell, & Vaccaro, 1993.
98. For example, Bellack & Mueser, 1994; Liberman, Kopelowicz, & Young, 1994; Spiegler & Agigian, 1977.
99. Alberti & Emmons, 2001.
100. Herring & Northup, 1998; Miller & Cole, 1998.
101. Ducharme & Holborn, 1997; Huang & Cuvo, 1997; Pollard, 1998.
102. For example, Beidel & Turner, 1998; Beidel, Turner, & Morris, 2000; Ducharme & Holborn, 1997.
103. For example, Ducharme & Holborn, 1997.
104. For example, Griffiths, Feldman, & Tough, 1997.
105. For example, Coyne, Faul, & Gross, 2000; Herring & Northup, 1998.
106. For example, Coyne, Faul, & Gross, 2000; Griffiths, Feldman, & Tough, 1997; Herring & Northup, 1998.
107. For example, Beidel & Turner, 1998; Beidel, Turner, & Morris, 2000.
108. For example, Griffiths, Feldman, & Tough, 1997.
109. Ducharme & Holborn, 1997.
110. Beidel & Turner, 1998; Beidel, Turner, & Morris, 2000.
111. Heimberg, 2001; Turk, Coles, & Heimberg, 2002; Turner, Beidel, & Cooley-Quille, 1997.
112. Kelly, St. Lawrence, Hood, & Brasfield, 1989; Powell, 1996.
113. For example, Bucell, 1979.
114. For example, Frisch & Froberg, 1987; Gambrill, 1995a; Lazarus, 1973.
115. Lazarus, 1973; Schroeder & Black, 1985.
116. Gambrill, 1995a.
117. Wilson & Gallois, 1993.
118. Alberti & Emmons, 2001; Gambrill, 1995a.
119. Blumberg, Hovell, Werner, Kelley, Sipan, Burkham, & Hoffstetter, 1997; Gambrill, 1995a; St. Lawrence, 1987.
120. For example, Gambrill & Richey, 1975; Rathus, 1973.
121. McFall & Lillesand, 1971.
122. Alberti & Emmons, 2001.
123. For example, Eisler, Hersen, & Miller, 1973; Hersen, Eisler, Miller, Johnson, & Pinkston, 1973; McFall & Lillesand, 1971; Prince, 1975.
124. For example, Alberti & Emmons, 2001; Hersen, Kazdin, Bellack, & Turner, 1979; Kazdin, 1974d, 1976; Maeda, 1985; Rosenthal & Reese, 1976.
125. Krop & Burgess, 1993b.
126. Gambrill, 1995a.
127. Weinhardt, Carey, Carey, & Verdecias, 1998.
128. Kalichman, Cherry, & Browne-Sperling, 1999.
129. Carey, Braaten, Maisto, Gleason, Forsyth, Durant, & Jaworski, 2000.
130. Miltenberger, Roberts, Ellingson, Galensky, Rapp, Long, & Lumley, 1999.
131. Metzler, Biglan, Noell, Ary, & Ochs, 2000.
132. Nangle & Hansen, 1998.
133. Kern, 1982; Kern, Cavell, & Beck, 1985; Romano & Bellack, 1980; Woolfolk & Dever, 1979.
134. Levin & Gross, 1984; St. Lawrence, Hansen, Cutts, Tisdelle, & Irish, 1985.
135. Ball, Kearney, Wilhelm, Dewhurst-Savellis, & Barton, 2000.
136. Franks & Wilson, 1976, p. 148.
137. Meichenbaum, 1971.
138. Bandura, 1986b.

139. Ozer & Bandura, 1990.
140. For example, Öst, 1989.
141. For example, Sarason, 1975.
142. For example, Mattick & Peters, 1988.
143. For example, Silverman, 1986; Thyer, 1985.
144. Klesges, Malott, & Ugland, 1984; quotation from p. 161.
145. Milgrom, Mancl, King, & Weinstein, 1995.
146. Ritter, 1968a, 1968b.
147. Ritter, 1968a, 1968b, 1969a, 1969b, 1969c.
148. Bandura, 1976; Bandura, Jeffery, & Gajdos, 1975; Bandura, Jeffery, & Wright, 1974; Blanchard, 1970.
149. Ritter, 1969a; quotation from pp. 170–171.
150. For example, Ladouceur, 1983; Minor, Leone, & Baldwin, 1984; Öst, Ferebee, & Furmark, 1997.
151. Klingman, Melamed, Cuthbert, & Hermecz, 1984.
152. Altmaier, Leary, Halpern, & Sellers, 1985.
153. Downs, Rosenthal, & Lichstein, 1988; Menzies & Clarke, 1993; Osborn, 1986.
154. For example, Williams & Zane, 1989.
155. Menzies & Clarke, 1993; Öst, Ferebee, & Furmark, 1997.
156. For example, Downs, Rosenthal, & Lichstein, 1988; Klingman, Melamed, Cuthbert, & Hermecz, 1984; Öst, Ferebee, & Furmark, 1997.
157. Williams, Dooseman, & Kleifield, 1984; Williams, Turner, & Peer, 1985; Williams & Zane, 1989.
158. Bandura, 1986b.
159. Peterson & Ridley-Johnson, 1980.
160. Kleinknecht & Bernstein, 1979; Klorman, Hilpert, Michael, LaGana, & Sveen, 1980; Melamed, 1979; Melamed, Hawes, Helby, & Glick, 1975; Melamed, Weinstein, Hawes, & Katkin-Borland, 1975.
161. Melamed & Siegel, 1975.
162. Melamed & Siegel, 1975, p. 514.
163. Melamed & Siegel, 1975.
164. Vernon, 1974.
165. Vernon, 1974.
166. Jay, Elliott, Ozolins, Olson, & Pruitt, 1985.
167. Jay, Elliott, Ozolins, Olson, & Pruitt, 1985, p. 516.
168. Allen, Danforth, & Drabman, 1989; Shipley, Butt, & Horwitz, 1979; Shipley, Butt, Horwitz, & Farbry, 1978.
169. Nemetz, Craig, & Reith, 1978; Wincze & Caird, 1976.

170. Bandura, 1997, 2001.
171. Bandura, 1977a, 1986b, 1989, 1997, 2001; Schwarzer, 1992.
172. Cervone & Peake, 1986.
173. Cervone & Scott, 1995.
174. For example, Haaga, 1990.
175. Bandura, 1984.
176. Peterson, Schultheis, Ridley-Johnson, Miller, & Tracy, 1984.
177. Mikulas & Coffman, 1989; Mikulas, Coffman, Dayton, Frayne, & Maier, 1985.
178. Dawe & Hart, 1986.
179. Cautela, 1993; Jackson & Francey, 1985.
180. A. J. Kearney, 1993.
181. Hay, Hay, & Nelson, 1977.
182. Compare with Swaggart, Gagnon, Bock, Earles, Quinn, Myles, & Simpson, 1995.
183. Author's (MDS) clinical files.
184. Bandura, 1986b; Rachman & Wilson, 1980.
185. For example, Thelen, Fry, Fehrenbach, & Frautschi, 1979.
186. Graziano, DeGiovanni, & Garcia, 1979; Ollendick, 1979.
187. Rachman & Wilson, 1980.
188. For example, Allen, Danforth, & Drabman, 1989; Dowrick & Raeburn, 1995; Rao, Moely, & Lockman, 1987; Spiegler, Liebert, McMains, & Fernandez, 1969.
189. For example, Charlop & Milstein, 1989; Dowrick, 1991.
190. Storey, Danko, Ashworth, & Strain, 1994.
191. Spiegler, 1970.
192. Braswell & Kendall, 2001.
193. Hunter, 1995.
194. For example, Mattick & Peters, 1988; Silverman, 1986; Thyer, 1985.
195. Altmaier & Bernstein, 1981; Brown, Kratochwill, & Bergan, 1982; Duley, Cancelli, Kratochwill, Bergan, & Meredith, 1983.
196. For example, Ducharme, Pontes, Guger, Crozier, Lucas, & Popynick, 1994; Ducharme & Popynick, 1993; Minor, Minor, & Williams, 1983; Webster-Stratton, 1981a, 1981b, 1982a, 1982b, 1984.
197. Pinkston, Linsk, & Young, 1988.
198. Park & Williams, 1986.
199. For example, Day & Reznikoff, 1980; Doster, 1972; Truax, Shapiro, & Wargo, 1968; Weinstein, 1988.

Chapter 12

Cognitive-Behavioral Therapy: Cognitive Restructuring

Michael stood at the top of the expert ski slope contemplating his fate. "Do you think I can make it?" Michael asked Daryl, his ski instructor. Daryl smiled and matter-of-factly said, "Whether you think you can, or whether you think you can't, you're right."

The way we think about events in our lives exerts a powerful and pervasive influence on how we act and feel.[1] *Cognitions* are thoughts—including beliefs, assumptions, expectations, attributions, and attitudes. *Cognitive-behavioral therapy* changes cognitions that are the maintaining conditions of a wide array of psychological disorders and problems. Cognitive-behavioral therapy has proliferated during the past 20 years[2] and is at the forefront of behavior therapy.[3]

THE NATURE OF COGNITIVE-BEHAVIORAL THERAPY

Clients' cognitions are modified in two ways: cognitively and behaviorally. Cognitions are modified *directly* when clients change their maladaptive thoughts and *indirectly* when clients change their overt actions. Changing what we do overtly in order to change what we think is the time-honored strategy for attitude change.[4] For example, arguing *for* a political position with which you *disagree* is likely to dispose you more favorably toward the position. The emphasis on cognitive (direct) versus overt behavioral (indirect) change varies in different cognitive-behavioral therapies; however, most include both cognitive and behavioral components, hence the hyphenated name.[5]

Cognitive-behavioral therapies fit into two basic models.* **Cognitive restructuring therapy,** one model, teaches clients to change distorted and erroneous cognitions that are maintaining their problem behaviors. **Cognitive restructuring** involves recognizing maladaptive cognitions and substituting more adaptive cognitions for them.[6] Cognitive restructuring is used when clients' problems are maintained by an *excess* of *maladaptive* thoughts.

*Our conceptualization of two models of cognitive-behavioral therapy is consistent with Kendall and Braswell's (1985) distinction between cognitive distortions and deficits, and it shares commonalities with the categories of mechanisms used to change cognitions proposed by Ross (1977) and Hollon and Beck (1986).

Table 12-1 Two models of cognitive-behavioral therapy

	Cognitive Restructuring	Cognitive-Behavioral Coping Skills
FOCUS OF THERAPY	Excess of maladaptive cognitions	Deficit of adaptive cognitions
GOAL OF THERAPY	Substituting adaptive cognitions for maladaptive cognitions	Using cognitive-behavioral coping skills
EXAMPLES OF THERAPIES	Thought stopping Rational emotive behavior therapy Cognitive therapy	Self-instructional training Problem-solving therapy/ training Stress inoculation training Cognitive-behavioral couple therapy

Cognitive-behavioral coping skills therapy, the other model, teaches clients adaptive responses—both cognitive and overt behavioral—to deal effectively with difficult situations. When clients act adaptively, they begin to think differently about troublesome situations. This model is appropriate for problems that are maintained by a *deficit* in *adaptive* cognitions. Table 12-1 summarizes the two models. Cognitive restructuring therapy is covered in this chapter, and cognitive-behavioral coping skills therapy is the topic of Chapter 13.

Operationalizing Cognitions: Making Private Thoughts Public

Behavior therapists pride themselves on dealing with concrete, observable phenomena. How, then, do they handle such abstract, amorphous phenomena as thoughts, beliefs, and attitudes? You may discover the answer to this dilemma by taking just a minute to complete Participation Exercise 12-1 before reading further.

◆

Participation Exercise 12-1

THINKING ABOUT THINKING

Identify a problem that you must solve or deal with in the near future. The problem can be a major one, such as having to make a decision that will influence your future in a significant way, or it can be a minor one, such as deciding what you should do this weekend. The only requirement is that the problem be detailed enough so that you can easily spend several minutes thinking about it.

Once you have chosen a problem, think about it for a minute. As you think about the problem, *be aware of your thoughts, particularly the form they take.* "Listen" to yourself thinking. After doing this for a minute, continue reading.

◆

What form did your thoughts take? They probably included words, phrases, and perhaps full sentences. Much of our thinking involves the explicit use of language (see In Theory 12-1). Capitalizing on this fact, behavior therapists generally operationally define cognitions as **self-talk,** what people say to themselves when they are thinking. If you want to know what someone is thinking, the question that is likely to be most productive is *"What are you saying to yourself?"* Cognitions also consist of sensory images (including visual, auditory, and tactile), but the focus in cognitive-behavioral therapy is on inner, verbal language.[7]

We often are not aware of our inner speech; that is, we do not think about our thinking. Thinking is a habitual, automatic process that goes on even when we are not specifically engaged in mental endeavors, such as when we are exercising and eating.

Only after clients can identify what they are saying to themselves can they change the cognitions that are maintaining their problems. Thus, the first step in cognitive-restructuring therapy is for clients to become aware of their self-talk, especially before, during, and after their problem behaviors occur.

This chapter is devoted primarily to two cognitive-behavioral therapies that make extensive use of cognitive restructuring: *rational emotive behavior therapy* and *cognitive therapy*. We also briefly describe *thought stopping,*

◆   **In Theory 12-1**

TALKING TO YOURSELF ISN'T NECESSARILY CRAZY

The world is such and such or so-and-so only because we tell ourselves that is the way it is. . . . You talk to yourself. You're not unique at that. Every one of us does that. We carry on internal talk. . . . In fact we maintain our world with our internal talk.[8]

Thus does cultural anthropologist and author Carlos Castaneda suggest the salience of "inner speech" in our lives. More specifically, inner speech has been described as the

> soundless, mental speech, arising at the instant we think about something, plan or solve problems in our mind, recall books read or conversations heard, read and write silently.

In all such instances, we think and remember with the aid of words which we articulate to ourselves. Inner speech is nothing but speech to oneself, or concealed verbalization, which is instrumental in the logical processing of sensory data, in their realization and comprehension within a definite system of concepts and judgments. The elements of inner speech are found in all our conscious perceptions, actions, and emotional experiences, where they manifest themselves as verbal sets, instructions to oneself, or as verbal interpretations of sensations and perceptions. This renders inner speech a rather important and universal mechanism.[9]

a simple technique that employs cognitive restructuring to reduce upsetting thoughts. However, first things first—that is, assessing cognitions, the initial step in cognitive restructuring therapy.

Assessing Cognitions

Four basic methods are used to assess clients' cognitions: interview, self-recording, direct self-report inventory, and think-aloud procedures. Each method elicits clients' self-reports of their cognitions, which is the only way to gain direct information about another's thoughts. The methods differ along five dimensions: (1) timing (for example, retrospective, concurrent), (2) degree of structure (for example, open-ended, forced choice), (3) mode of response (for example, written, oral), (4) nature of the stimulus (for example, written scenario, simulated situation), and (5) source of evaluation (for example, by the client, by the therapist).[10] Later in this chapter we illustrate the application of interview techniques and self-recording. Here we describe the use of self-report inventories and think-aloud procedures.

Direct self-report inventories for assessing cognitions consist of common self-statements related to a particular problem area.[11] Clients indicate how often they make each self-statement.[12] For example, the Social Interaction Self-Statement Test, developed by Carol Glass, lists 15 positive and 15 negative self-statements about problematic heterosocial dating interactions (see Table 12-2).[13] Adults rate each statement on a 5-point scale to indicate how frequently they have had each thought. Children's cognitions also can be assessed with self-report inventories. For instance, the Children's Negative Affectivity Self-Statement Questionnaire assesses maladaptive thoughts associated with anxiety.[14] Standardized self-report inventories are efficient methods for initial screening purposes. They give the therapist a general idea about the type of thoughts the client is having. Specific, individualized assessment requires other methods of assessing cognitions.

Think-aloud approaches require clients to verbalize their thoughts (usually by talking into a tape recorder) while engaging in a simulated task or role-playing situation.[15] The Articulated Thoughts in Simulated Situations method, developed by Gerald Davison, is an example of a think-aloud procedure.[16] Clients listen to audio taped scenarios designed to

Table 12-2 Examples of items on the Social Interaction Self-Statement Test (rated on a 5-point scale from "Hardly Ever" to "Very Often")

I hope I don't make a fool of myself.
She/he probably won't be interested in me.
This will be a good opportunity.
It would crush me if she/he didn't respond to me.
This is an awkward situation but I can handle it.
Maybe we'll hit it off real well.
What I say will probably sound stupid.

elicit different cognitions. A social criticism scenario, for instance, describes a person's overhearing two acquaintances talking about him or her in negative terms (such as ridiculing the person's choice of clothes). The therapist asks clients to imagine themselves in the situation and to "tune in" to their thoughts. Every 30 seconds, a tone prompts clients to say their thoughts aloud into a microphone. The therapist assures clients that there are no good or bad or right or wrong thoughts and encourages them to verbalize their thoughts without concern about whether their thoughts seem appropriate.

Think-aloud approaches to cognitive assessment have five distinct advantages over direct self-report inventories.[17] First, think-aloud approaches have an open-ended response format so that clients do not have to make forced choices from a predetermined and limited array of responses. Second, think-aloud approaches tap clients' cognitions immediately following the simulated situation, which eliminates the problems associated with retrospective reporting, such as forgetting.[18] Third, think-aloud approaches can be customized for each client. Fourth, audio taped simulated presentations of stressful stimuli may more readily elicit genuine emotional responses than written stimuli, resulting in a more realistic sampling of potentially maladaptive cognitions. Finally, children as young as 9 are able to respond to think-aloud approaches in the assessment of cognitions.[19]

Think-aloud procedures are designed for simulated situations rather than actual situations. Talking into a tape recorder while engaging in everyday activities usually is not practical. Thus, an important potential limitation of think-aloud approaches is that they may miss highly relevant but low-frequency thoughts that are likely to occur only in vivo.

THOUGHT STOPPING

Thought stopping is designed to decrease the frequency and duration of persistent, disturbing thoughts by interrupting them and substituting pleasant thoughts for them.[20] Examples of the problems treated with thought stopping are obsessive ruminations (such as constantly worrying about being contaminated by germs), depressive ideas (for example, "Nothing seems to go right"), and self-deprecating thoughts (for instance, "I'm just not good at anything"). Thought stopping involves two phases: (1) first interrupting the disturbing thoughts and (2) then focusing on a competing adaptive thought.*

In the first phase, whenever disturbing thoughts occur, the client says, "Stop!" The word is said with a sharp, jolting expression, as if warning of imminent danger. Initially, clients say "Stop!" aloud; after they are doing this consistently, they switch to saying "Stop!" silently to themselves. Although saying "Stop!" usually is the interrupting stimulus, another

---

*Thought stopping should not be confused with *thought suppression,* which involves deliberate attempts *not* to think about something. Unlike thought stopping, thought suppression can result in either an immediate or delayed increase of the thoughts (Zeitlin, Netten, & Hodder, 1995).

appropriate stimulus could be used, such as a loud noise or an image of a stop sign.[21]

Therapists sometimes introduce thought stopping to clients with a dramatic demonstration of its effect. The therapist asks the client to concentrate on the disturbing thought and to signal the therapist (such as by raising a finger) when the thought is clear. At that moment, the therapist shouts, "Stop!" The client is then asked, "What happened?" Typically, clients report that they were startled and that the disturbing thought vanished.

Although "Stop!" momentarily eliminates intrusive thoughts, the thoughts may reappear quickly if the person does not start thinking about something else. (As you know, trying *not to think* about something almost guarantees your thinking about it.) Thus, in the second phase of thought stopping, immediately after saying "Stop!" the client focuses on a prepared thought that competes with the disturbing thought, as is illustrated in Case 12-1. Therapists assist clients in selecting one or more adaptive competing thoughts that can be used in the second phase of thought stopping.

ELIMINATING JEALOUSY BY THOUGHT STOPPING[22]

Case 12-1

A 27-year-old man, K. F., discovered that the woman he was living with had had a brief affair a week before they had moved in together. After an initial period of feeling intensely hurt and angry, K. F. resolved to forget the incident. He wanted the relationship to continue, and he believed the woman's feelings for him had not changed. However, K. F. frequently thought about the woman's affair and became extremely upset whenever he imagined her being sexually intimate with the other man. These thoughts not only were disturbing but also prevented him from concentrating on whatever he was doing at the time.

Several years previously, K. F. had learned thought stopping as part of the treatment for another problem. Recalling the procedure, he applied thought stopping to his jealous thoughts. Whenever he began ruminating about the woman's affair, he yelled "Stop!" to himself and then imagined one of two prearranged pleasant thoughts. One involved the woman's acting lovingly toward him. The other was completely unrelated to the woman or the relationship; it concerned his playing a good game of tennis, which was a source of personal satisfaction. Both pleasant thoughts successfully kept him from thinking of the woman's affair.

Before thought stopping, the distressing thoughts had lasted from several minutes to as long as an hour and had occurred on the average of 10 times a day. Thought stopping immediately reduced the duration of the intrusive thoughts to only a few seconds, and the frequency of the intrusive thoughts gradually declined. By the end of the second week, the thoughts occurred about 5 times per week; after a month, they occurred no more than once a week. Three months after K. F. initiated thought stopping, he was completely free of the disturbing thoughts, and they did not return during the 2-year span of his relationship with the woman.

The substitute thoughts that K. F. used in Case 12-1 were completely different from his jealous thoughts. Another technique, called **imagery rescripting,** has the client modify the disturbing thought, image, or belief so that it is more tolerable and even pleasant.[23] For example, a client who experienced the frightful thought of falling from a height and hearing his bones breaking as he hit the ground rescripted the thought to an image of hitting the ground and bouncing up in the air in a cartoon-like humorous manner. Another client who had been sexually abused as a child rescripted intrusive images of the abuse by creating a new scenario in which she visualized herself today entering the scene to help the "child." Imagery rescripting may be particularly helpful for clients who experience recurrent distressing thoughts related to prior traumatic experiences, such as sexual victimization.[24]

Thought Stopping in Perspective

Thought stopping is a simple, straightforward procedure used to treat intrusive, disturbing thoughts. Such thoughts not only upset the individual but also result in a variety of serious problems that thought stopping has been successful in treating, including anxiety,[25] compulsive behaviors,[26] headaches,[27] excessive masturbation,[28] physical aggression,[29] and self-injurious behaviors.[30]

Clients can quickly learn and easily apply thought stopping on their own with little or no supervision from a therapist. As illustrated in Case 12-1, thought stopping, like other cognitive-behavioral therapies, gives clients self-control skills that they can generalize to other problems.[31]

Thought stopping usually is part of a treatment package.[32] It is used relatively frequently, which seems to indicate that it is effective.[33] However, little controlled research has been done to validate its effectiveness.[34] Further, it is difficult to draw conclusions from the few existing outcome studies because the effects of thought stopping cannot be isolated from the other treatments with which it is combined or because the studies contain methodological weaknesses.[35] Despite the lack of definitive evidence for its efficacy, no risks appear to be associated with clients' using thought stopping. In the light of the issues raised in In Theory 10-2 (page 249), consider the following question. Given the rather innocuous nature of thought stopping, do you see any problems with its being used despite the paucity of empirical studies evaluating its efficacy?

RATIONAL EMOTIVE BEHAVIOR THERAPY

Rational emotive behavior therapy[36] **(REBT)** is a well-known treatment that primarily employs cognitive restructuring to change the irrational thoughts that cause psychological problems such as anxiety, depression, anger, and guilt.[37] Albert Ellis designed REBT more than 40 years ago.[38] The procedures follow from Ellis' theory of how psychological disorders develop and are maintained. Before reading about his theory, take 2 minutes to complete Participation Exercise 12-2, which will help you understand Ellis' theory.

Courtesy of Albert Ellis, Institute for Rational-Emotive Therapy

Albert Ellis

Participation Exercise 12-2	**WHAT ARE YOU MAD ABOUT?**

First, get a paper and pen. Then read the following scenario and picture yourself in the situation described—in other words, role-play it in your mind *as if it were happening to you.*

> You are taking out a special friend for a birthday celebration that you want to be especially nice. You have made a reservation at a fancy restaurant and have dressed up for the occasion. When you arrive at the restaurant, you give your name to the hostess, who goes to check the reservation book to see which table you've been assigned. As you are waiting, your friend remarks, with obvious appreciation, how elegant the restaurant is. When the hostess returns, she tells you that she cannot find your reservation, that they are fully booked for the evening, and that it will not be possible to seat you. Not surprisingly, you are mad!

Now write brief answers to the following two questions.

1. What has made you mad?
2. What are you saying to yourself?

The Rational Emotive Theory of Psychological Disorders

According to Ellis' rational emotive theory, psychological problems—negative emotions and maladaptive behaviors—are maintained by the *interpretations* people make of events in their lives. This is the fundamental assumption on which REBT and other cognitive restructuring therapies are based. The Greek Stoic philosopher Epictetus succinctly stated it 2000 years ago, saying that *people are disturbed not by things, but by the views they take of them.*

What is striking about this simple idea is that most people implicitly disagree with it. Generally, people believe that "things" cause negative emotions. When someone takes the parking spot we are about to pull into, we get angry *because* someone took "our" spot. (In Participation Exercise 12-2 that you just completed, did you answer the question "What made you mad?" by attributing your upset to the situation or the hostess?) In contrast, Ellis' theory holds that our *beliefs* about the event, not the event itself, are what make us angry. The sequence always is the same: (1) Some event activates (2) an irrational belief that results in (3) negative consequences (negative emotions as well as maladaptive behaviors). In the parking spot example, our anger is likely to be the *direct* result of irrational beliefs such as "That was *my* parking spot," "It's not fair," and "That so-and-so *made* me late for my appointment." (In Participation 12-2, was your self-talk related to similar beliefs?)

Psychological problems are maintained by irrational beliefs that come from faulty reasoning or logical errors, such as absolute thinking, over-generalizing, and catastrophizing.[39] *Absolute thinking* is viewing an event in an all-or-none, black-or-white fashion, such as "I must *always* do well" and "Others should treat me considerately and precisely in the manner I would like to be treated." *Overgeneralization* is drawing the conclusion that all instances of a situation will turn out a particular way because one or two did. For example, after having delivered one poor lecture, a professor told himself, "I'll never be a good lecturer." *Catastrophizing* involves seeing minor situations as disastrous. For instance, a woman who received a low grade on a quiz told herself, "This is the end of my college career."

Ellis has found that two themes often run through the irrational ideas that lead to psychological problems: personal worthlessness and a sense of duty. *Personal worthlessness* is a specific form of overgeneralization associated with failure. For example, a business executive decides that she is "a total failure" because she was unable to get all her work done by the end of the day.

To appreciate the second theme, *before* you continue reading, write down three things you *have* to do this week.

A *sense of duty,* the second theme in irrational ideas, is evident in the use of the words *must, have to, should,* and *ought to* in speech and thoughts. Ellis colorfully has called the use of these words *musturbation.*[40] Musturbatory statements are irrational because, in fact, there are only a few behaviors that people *must* do. Consider what happens when you are physically ill and unable to attend to normal activities, such as the three things you *have* to do this week. At such times, all the tasks you *had* to get done do not, in fact, get done—yet somehow you survive, and the consequences rarely are catastrophic.

Insisting that you *must* do something is abdicating personal choice. It often may be convenient to blame an external source for what is actually a personal choice. When Juanita responds, "I *have* to study," to her friends' invitation to go out for the evening, her friends readily accept her reason. However, they are likely to find it difficult to accept "I *want* to study." How can Juanita want to study and not want to go out with her friends? Something must be wrong with her! In fact, Juanita may want to go out with her friends, but she wants to study even more—most likely because of the negative consequences of not studying, such as failing an exam the next day. Yet, however disagreeable those consequences, she still has the choice to study or go out with her friends.

Although irrational beliefs play an important role in maintaining psychological disorders, they are not the only maintaining conditions. Psychological disorders also are influenced by a complex interaction of biological, developmental, and environmental factors.[41] By changing clients' irrational beliefs, cognitive restructuring therapies modify an important—albeit not the only—class of maintaining conditions.

◆ ▨▨▨▨▨▨▨▨▨▨▨▨▨▨▨▨▨▨▨▨▨▨▨▨▨▨▨▨▨▨▨▨▨▨▨▨▨▨▨

Participation Exercise 12-3

KICKING THE MUSTURBATION HABIT*

Most people are unaware that they frequently use the words *must, have to, should,* and *ought to.* For example, students tell teachers, "I can't take the exam

*You will need to do this Participation Exercise later.

on Friday because I *have* to go home for a wedding"; teachers inform students, "You *must* turn in your papers by Friday." Countless times each day people speak as if the world would end if they did not do one thing or another.

The purpose of this Participation Exercise is to make you aware of your own musturbation and to give you practice in the REBT technique of disputing irrational thoughts and substituting rational thoughts for them. Divide a lined sheet of paper into three equal columns, labeling the first column *Musturbatory Thoughts,* the second column *Rational Rebuttals,* and the third column *Rational Thoughts.*

Over the course of the next few days, write down examples of your use of the words *must, should, have to,* and *ought to* in your speech and thoughts. Record them in the first column of the work sheet you have prepared, skipping several lines between each. Because we generally are oblivious to our musturbatory thoughts, ask friends to point out your use of *must*-type words.

When you have a minimum of 10 musturbatory statements, write a brief rebuttal of each in the second column of your work sheet. The rebuttal should explain why the statement is irrational. Finally, write a rational statement in the third column as an alternative to the irrational, musturbatory statement. The rational statement should reflect your taking responsibility for directing your actions. It should state what you *want* or *choose* to do rather than what you believe you must do. Part of a student's work sheet is shown in Figure 12-1 to give you examples of possible rebuttals and rational thoughts.

Figure 12-1 Excerpts from a student's work sheet used in Participation Exercise 12-3

Musturbatory Thoughts	Rational Rebuttals	Rational Thoughts
I can't go to class because I have to study for next period.	I could go to class if I chose to. I just feel it's important to be well prepared for the exam.	I would rather miss class than risk not being prepared.
I must clean up my room before my parents visit this weekend.	My parents are going to be upset with a messy room, but they won't disown me if my room is a mess.	I'd like to get my room neat before my parents get here.
I have to get home in time to see my favorite TV program.	I sure do enjoy my favorite TV show, but my life won't end if I miss an episode.	I hope I can get home in time for my favorite TV show.

The Process of Rational Emotive Behavior Therapy

The aim of REBT is to modify irrational beliefs, which is accomplished through three major procedures: (1) identifying thoughts based on irrational beliefs, (2) challenging the irrational beliefs, and (3) replacing thoughts based on irrational beliefs with thoughts based on rational beliefs.

First, to identify thoughts based on irrational beliefs, clients are asked about the specific self-statements they make when they feel upset (for example, depressed) or when they are engaging in maladaptive behaviors. As with other cognitive restructuring therapies, clients may have to learn to attend to their self-talk, such as by writing down their self-talk whenever their problems occur.

Once the client's self-talk associated with the problem has been identified, the therapist teaches the client to challenge irrational statements by stating why they are irrational.[42] For example,

CLIENT: I feel awful because May wouldn't go out with me. I don't seem to attract women that I am attracted to.

THERAPIST: That doesn't make any sense. You are blowing up the situation, overgeneralizing. I'm sure you don't feel great being turned down, but it's not the end of the world. And it certainly does not follow that just because May isn't interested in going out with you that you are not attractive to other women you like.

Active disputing of irrational beliefs is the key element that distinguishes REBT from other cognitive restructuring therapies.[43] As much as 90% of the therapy session may involve the therapist's challenging the rationality of the client's thoughts and debunking the client's myths about how the world "should be."[44]

Finally, the client learns to substitute rational thoughts for irrational thoughts. In the previous example, the therapist might suggest that the client tell himself, "I'm disappointed that May wouldn't go out with me, but she is not the last woman in the world." Table 12-3 presents an example of the changes in clients' thinking and emotional reactions that are expected over the course of REBT.

Table 12-3 Example of how the client's self-talk about the causal sequence of events leads to emotional reactions and how the resulting emotional reactions change in REBT

	Situation	Client's Self-Talk About Situation	Client's Emotional Reaction
BEFORE THERAPY	Failed course	(Unaware of or not focusing on self-talk)	Angry, depressed
DURING THERAPY	Failed course	1. "This is horrible." 2. "My parents will hit the roof." 3. "I am just plain stupid."	Angry, depressed
AFTER THERAPY	Failed course	1. "This sure won't help my average." 2. "My parents aren't going to be pleased, but they'll get over it." 3. "It's not the end of the world; I can make up the course."	Upset, disappointed

Case 12-2 presents part of an initial REBT session and illustrates many of the principles and procedures employed in REBT.

TREATMENT OF DEPRESSION BY RATIONAL EMOTIVE
Case 12-2 BEHAVIOR THERAPY[45]

The client was a college student in his second semester at a highly competitive university. He had not found high school particularly challenging, and he earned high grades with little effort. He described himself as apathetic and depressed. The dialogue that follows is an excerpt from the first REBT session. It is annotated with comments about the process and procedures.

THERAPIST: How long have you had these feelings of depression?

CLIENT: Ever since the beginning of this quarter, I think.

THERAPIST: Can you tell me what is bothering you?

CLIENT: Everything is . . . I don't know . . . a bunch of shit. I don't seem to care about anything anymore. I don't even care about school anymore, and that used to mean a lot to me.

THERAPIST: How are you doing in school, grade-wise?

Therapist (T) asks about possible activating events.

CLIENT: Lousy. This quarter I've studied a total of two hours.

THERAPIST: Let's see. Fall quarter was your first at Stanford? How were your grades then?

CLIENT: Shitty; had a 2.3 average. *C* average. And I worked hard, too. I feel like shoving the whole thing.

THERAPIST: Maybe this is part of what is getting you down. . . . What does that make you, in your eyes?

T inquires about interpretations of external events.

CLIENT: I'm a failure. . . . I'll never get accepted to a decent medical school with grades like that. I'll probably end up pumping gas in Salinas . . . that's all I'm good for. I feel worthless.

Client (C) draws an illogical conclusion.

THERAPIST: Sounds like you've been saying to yourself, "I'm a failure . . . I'm worthless" on account of your *C* average last quarter. That would be enough to depress anybody.

T introduces idea of self-talk.

CLIENT: It's true. I've got to do well and I'm not.

THERAPIST: So, you believe that in order for you to consider yourself a worthwhile person, you've got to succeed at something . . . like making *A*'s at Stanford?

Musturbation and absolute thinking.

T makes C's irrational belief explicit.

CLIENT: A person's got to be good at something to be worth a damn. School was the only thing I was ever much good at in the first place.

THERAPIST: I'd like to point out that you're competing against some of the best students in the country, and they don't care very much about grading on a curve there. An average performance among outstanding people isn't really average, after all, is it?

CLIENT: I know what you are getting at, but that doesn't help too much. Any decent medical school requires at least a *B+* average, and I've got to get into medical school. That's been my goal ever since I was a kid.

THERAPIST: Now, wait a minute! You say you *have* to go to medical school. Sounds like you think not going to medical school is against the law. Is that so?

CLIENT: Well, not exactly. You know what I mean.

THERAPIST: I'm not sure. Do you really mean that you want very much to go to medical school? Because that is very different from believing that you *must* go to medical school. If you think you have to go to medical school, you are going to treat it like it's a life-or-death thing, which it isn't. But you believe that it is, and that is likely to be a major reason why you're depressed.

CLIENT: I can see your point, but even if I agreed with you, there's my family. . . . All my life my parents have been telling me that the whole family is counting on my being a doctor.

THERAPIST: OK, but that is their belief. Does it have to be yours?

CLIENT: I just can't let them down.

THERAPIST: What would happen if you did?

CLIENT: They'd be hurt and disappointed. Sometimes I almost think they wouldn't like me any more. That would be awful!

THERAPIST: Well, the worst possible thing that could happen if you don't go to medical school is that your father and mother wouldn't like you, and might even reject you. You aren't even sure this would happen. But, even if they did, does it follow that it would be awful? Could you prove that, logically, I mean?

C confirms the irrational belief.

T introduces rational ideas to counter C's irrational ideas.

More musturbation.

T challenges the irrationality of C's "have to" and suggests the rational alternative "want to."

T explains that irrational beliefs maintain depression.

A possible origin of C's irrational beliefs is revealed.

T disputes C's illogical assumption

Catastrophizing.

T points out the lack of evidence.

T models logical analysis of thoughts and beliefs.

CLIENT: It's lousy when your own family rejects you.

THERAPIST: I still can't see the logical connection between their rejecting you and things being awful or even lousy. I would agree that it wouldn't exactly be a pleasant state of affairs. You are equating rejection with catastrophe, and I'd like you to try and convince me one follows from the other.

T continues to challenge C's illogical thoughts.

CLIENT: They wouldn't even want me around . . . like I was a worthless shit. And that would be rotten.

THERAPIST: Well, there you go again, telling yourself that because they would reject you, which means they wouldn't want you around, you are a worthless shit. Again, I don't see the logic.

CLIENT: It would make me feel that way.

THERAPIST: No, I emphatically disagree . . . it's *you* who would make you feel that way. By saying those same things to yourself.

T directly confronts C's idea and introduces the basic premise of REBT.

CLIENT: But I believe it's true.

THERAPIST: I'm still waiting for some logical basis for your belief that rejection means you are worthless, or not going to medical school means you're a shit.

CLIENT: OK, I agree about the medical school bit. I don't *have* to go. But about my parents . . . that's heavy. . . . I was thinking . . . where would I go over the holidays? But I don't spend that much time at home anyway, come to think of it. But, there is money . . . this place is damned expensive and I don't have a scholarship. If they cut off funds, that would be a disaster.

C begins to think rationally.

THERAPIST: There you go again . . . catastrophizing. Prove to me that it would be a disaster.

CLIENT: Well, maybe I was exaggerating a bit. It would be tough, though I suppose I could apply for support, or get a job maybe. In fact, I know I could. But then it would take longer to get through school, and that would be shitty.

THERAPIST: Now you are beginning to make a lot of sense. I agree that it would be shitty . . . but certainly not terrible.

CLIENT: You know, for the first time in weeks I think I feel a little better. Kind of like there is a load off my mind. Is that possible?

THERAPIST: I don't see why not, but I'm wondering what would happen if you'd start feeling depressed tonight or tomorrow . . . how would you deal with it?

At this point, the therapist suggested that the client rehearse identifying and challenging his irrational ideas.

You can see many of the characteristics of REBT in the therapist–client dialogue in Case 12-2. The therapist actively challenges the client's irrational thoughts and models this process for the client. The therapist's style is confrontational, almost argumentative. The client's task is to learn to identify and dispute irrational thoughts and beliefs and then to substitute rational thoughts for them. The client first rehearses these skills in the therapy sessions and then is asked to use them at home, which is what the therapist was leading up to at the end of the dialogue in Case 12-2. Besides practicing identifying and disputing irrational beliefs, clients in REBT engage in a variety of homework assignments, including overt behavior rehearsal of skills learned in therapy sessions (such as appropriate assertive behaviors), keeping mood diaries, and reading material related to REBT principles.[46]

Rational Emotive Education

Rational emotive behavior therapy is used primarily with adults, who are more practiced at reasoning verbally. The basic format of disputing irrational beliefs is not as well suited for children, especially young children.[47] A few cases using standard REBT with children have been reported, but its effectiveness was not evaluated.[48]

Rational emotive education is an adaptation of REBT for children and adolescents.[49] The curriculum includes (1) identifying emotions and differentiating them from thoughts; (2) learning how thoughts, rather than situations, influence emotions; (3) recognizing rational and irrational thoughts; and (4) dealing with common difficult situations (such as being teased) by using these concepts and skills. Children learn experientially, as through the Expression Guessing Game, which involves trying to guess the emotions pantomimed by other children. By playing the game, children discover for themselves that the most reliable way to know what other people are feeling is to ask them. Such user-friendly formats for children increasingly are being used in cognitive-behavioral approaches.[50]

A small number of studies have indicated that rational emotive education can reduce children's irrational thoughts and anxiety. However, the results of these studies are limited because they are based solely on self-report measures.[51] Generally, self-report measures need to be corroborated by observations made by others. Further, rational emotive education has not always been shown to be superior to no-treatment control conditions.[52] Rational emotive education does not appear to be effective for treating children with serious psychological disorders. Potentially, rational emotive education could prevent psychological disorders;[53] however, longitudinal studies have not been carried out to evaluate this possibility.[54]

◆

Participation Exercise 12-4

I THINK, THEREFORE I FEEL: MAKING THE CONNECTION*

Identifying the cognitions that are associated with our emotions and recognizing how our thoughts may influence the way we feel are essential goals of REBT and rational emotive education. This Participation Exercise can help you become more aware of how your thoughts influence your emotions. Over the next few days, whenever you experience a strong emotion (positive or negative), reflect on what you are thinking at the moment—in other words, what you are saying to yourself. Immediately write the emotion and the associated cognitions on an index card or sheet of paper you carry with you. Divide the card into two columns: the first column for the *emotion* you are experiencing and the second for your *cognitions* at the time.

After you have collected a sample of different emotions and associated cognitions, consider the following questions: (1) What did you learn from this exercise? (2) Did you find yourself becoming more aware of your self-talk? (3) What were the basic differences between your cognitions associated with positive emotions and your cognitions associated with negative emotions? (4) Did your emotions seem to come from your thoughts or vice versa? Your answers to these questions can give you some insight into the basic assumptions and practices of REBT and cognitive restructuring therapies in general.

◆

Rational Emotive Behavior Therapy in Perspective

Rational emotive behavior therapy is popular among therapists and clients for a number of reasons. Its focus on rationality makes sense! Ellis' theory of the development and maintenance of psychological problems is easy to understand. Further, the "direct, persuasive, and authoritative approach . . . conforms to culturally sanctioned doctor–patient roles."[55] The notoriety of REBT has been enhanced by self-help books based on the REBT approach, many of which have been written by Albert Ellis.[56] Ellis, an outspoken advocate of REBT, draws attention because of his colorful personality, which could be described as inspired and charismatic.[57]

Potentially, REBT could be used to treat any problem maintained by irrational beliefs.[58] Problems that have been treated include stress, generalized anxiety, agoraphobia and other phobias, unassertive behaviors, obsessions, anger, depression, antisocial behaviors, headaches, stuttering, sexual dysfunctions, obesity, Type A behaviors, and chronic fatigue syndrome.[59]

REBT has been applied to diverse client populations. For clients with strong religious beliefs, REBT can capitalize on those convictions to chal-

*You will need to do this Participation Exercise later.

lenge clients' irrational beliefs and reinforce the use of adaptive thoughts.[60] For example, a client who is thinking, "I just have to get my job back," might be reminded of the reflections in the biblical book of Ecclesiastes, "For everything there is a season . . . a time to keep, and a time to cast away." Self-defeating beliefs about mathematical ability in African-American high school students have been changed by REBT.[61] Components of REBT have been successfully employed in the treatment of Puerto Rican adolescents with depression.[62] REBT has been used with elderly clients, who may become vulnerable to irrational thoughts and beliefs related to aging.[63] Common irrational beliefs that elderly clients hold include "I must do as well as I previously did when I was younger or else I am an inadequate person," "Other people must treat me kindly and fairly especially because of my age," and "I should have the good health I used to have and not be ill and disabled." Although variations of REBT have been devised for children and adolescents,[64] REBT is more suitable for adults.

The reliance on direct confrontation of clients' beliefs is likely to be ineffective for a number of disorders, including substance dependence, paraphilias, panic disorder, anorexia and bulimia, and obsessive-compulsive disorder.[65] In fact, there is evidence that confrontation in therapy generally is associated with clients' noncompliance with treatment procedures.[66] REBT also may be less effective with clients from cultures that eschew direct confrontation (such as Native American and Japanese).

Despite proponents' enthusiastic claims for the clinical efficacy of REBT, empirical support is only modest.[67] Many of the studies evaluating the effectiveness of REBT were poorly designed, so their findings are inconclusive.[68] One major methodological weakness has been a failure to operationally define REBT.[69] Thus, it is unclear which specific therapy procedures were used in different studies. In general, REBT has been found to be superior to no-treatment and wait-list control groups,[70] but often REBT is only equivalent to or less effective than other behavior therapies (such as exposure therapies and progressive relaxation). Finally, few long-term follow-up studies exist.

No systematic process research has been conducted to identify the essential components of REBT, which leaves important questions unanswered.[71] For example, is strong confrontation of the client's irrational beliefs a necessary component? Would the therapy work as well with a gentler exploration of the client's irrational beliefs rather than direct confrontation?[72] These are crucial questions to answer because some clients and therapists feel uncomfortable with REBT's "tough-minded," confrontational approach.[73]

COGNITIVE THERAPY

Cognitive therapy is another cognitive restructuring therapy that emphasizes empirically testing the validity of maladaptive beliefs. Aaron Beck[74] conceived of cognitive therapy in the early 1960s, at the same time Ellis was developing REBT. Apparently, Beck and Ellis created their theories and therapy techniques independently.[75] Both therapies rest on the

Courtesy of the University of Pennsylvania Medical Center

Aaron Beck

fundamental assumption that psychological disorders are maintained by distorted cognitions, and the therapies share the goal of modifying these cognitions. Both involve challenging distorted, irrational beliefs, but the strategies they use to do this differ. Cognitive therapy has the client view beliefs as tentative hypotheses; the client then tests the validity of these hypotheses by gathering evidence that refutes (or supports) them.[76] In contrast, REBT primarily relies on direct instruction, persuasion, and logical disputation to challenge distorted beliefs. Table 12-4 summarizes the major differences between REBT and cognitive therapy.

Cognitive therapy evolved from Beck's research on the distorted thinking of clients who were depressed,[77] and treating depression has been its primary focus. More recently, the scope of cognitive therapy has been widened to include anxiety disorders,[78] including panic attacks[79] and panic disorder,[80] phobias,[81] and obsessive-compulsive disorder;[82] personality disorders;[83] marital distress;[84] anger;[85] suicidal behaviors;[86] anorexia;[87] bulimia;[88] obesity;[89] and schizophrenia.[90]

The Cognitive Therapy Theory of Psychological Disorders

Beck's theory of the development and maintenance of psychological disorders shares the same fundamental premises as Ellis' theory. Differences emerge in the specific concepts each theory employs. To begin with, Beck refers to maladaptive (irrational) cognitions as **automatic thoughts,** a term that emphasizes how clients experience their distorted thinking.[91] Specifically, clients report that their distorted thoughts arise as if they were a reflex, without prior reflection or reasoning. Automatic thoughts seem totally plausible and valid to the client, which may help explain their powerful influence on emotions and actions. According to Beck's

Table 12-4 Major differences between REBT and cognitive therapy

	Rational Emotive Behavior Therapy	Cognitive Therapy
APPROACH	Deductive	Inductive
BASIS OF APPROACH	Rationality	Empirical evidence
PROCEDURE	Instruction, persuasion, disputation	Empirical hypothesis testing
MECHANISM	Primarily cognitive restructuring	Combination of cognitive restructuring and overt behavioral interventions
ROLE OF THERAPIST	Model of rational thinking (recognizing and disputing irrational beliefs)	Coinvestigator seeking empirical test of client's beliefs
STYLE OF THERAPIST	Confrontational	Collaborative
ROLE OF HOMEWORK	Practice disputing irrational beliefs and cognitive restructuring	Gather evidence to establish validity of beliefs

theory, psychological disorders occur when people perceive the world as threatening.

> When this happens, there is a functional impairment in normal cognitive processing: Perceptions and interpretations of events become highly selective, egocentric, and rigid. The person has a decreased ability to "turn off" distorted thinking . . . to concentrate, recall, or reason. Corrective functions, which allow reality testing and refinement of global conceptualizations, are weakened.[92]

Thus, the person makes systematic errors in reasoning. For example, children who are anxious tend to misinterpret benign situations as hostile,[93] and adults with panic disorder make catastrophic interpretations of their physical sensations (such as increased heart rate meaning a heart attack).[94] Beck has identified six common *cognitive distortions* or logical errors that frequently are found in the thoughts of people experiencing psychological distress; these cognitive distortions are listed in Table 12-5. Not surprisingly, there is some overlap with the common forms of

Table 12-5 Cognitive distortions associated with psychological disorders
SOURCE: Beck & Weishaar, 1989.

Cognitive Distortion	Definition	Example
ARBITRARY INFERENCE	Drawing conclusions without sufficient evidence, or when the evidence is actually contradictory	Believing that you have been laid off from a job because of personal incompetence, although the company has gone out of business
OVERGENERALIZATION	Drawing a general conclusion on the basis of a single incident	Concluding that you will never succeed after failing on the first attempt
SELECTIVE ABSTRACTION	Attending to a detail while ignoring the total context	Feeling rejected because a friend who was rushing to catch a bus did not stop to talk
PERSONALIZATION	Erroneously attributing an external event to yourself	Thinking that people who are laughing are laughing at you
POLARIZED (DICHOTOMOUS) THINKING	Thinking in extremes, in a black-or-white or all-or-none fashion	Believing that you are a pauper after having lost your wallet
MAGNIFICATION OR MINIMIZATION	Viewing something as far more or less important than it is	Thinking that you are a poor writer after getting back a paper with several corrections or thinking that you are a great writer after getting back a paper with dozens of corrections

irrationality Ellis has identified. You may note in Table 12-5 that overlap also exists among the different types of cognitive distortions, so that distorted thoughts may be examples of more than one type of cognitive distortion.

The Process of Cognitive Therapy

The goals of cognitive therapy are to (1) correct clients' faulty information processing, (2) modify clients' dysfunctional beliefs that maintain maladaptive behaviors and emotions, and (3) provide clients with the skills and experiences that create adaptive thinking.[95] The therapist and client collaborate to identify the client's dysfunctional beliefs and challenge their validity. Cognitive therapy requires clients' active participation, including homework assignments that are considered an integral part of the treatment. Compliance with and the quality of homework assignments have been found to be positively correlated with the effectiveness of cognitive therapy.[96]

Because collaboration between the client and therapist is a key element in cognitive therapy, establishing a good therapeutic relationship is considered a prerequisite for effective treatment.[97] Toward this end, cognitive therapists focus on clients' ways of viewing the world, which includes understanding their cognitive distortions.[98]

Cognitive therapists help clients recognize dysfunctional beliefs through a *Socratic dialogue.* They ask clients a series of easily answerable questions that lead clients to recognize dysfunctional beliefs and automatic thoughts for themselves—rather than directly pointing out such beliefs, as REBT therapists do.

The therapist asks the client to view automatic thoughts as *hypotheses* that are subject to empirical verification rather than as "the way things are" (established facts). The therapist and client design homework assignments that serve as investigations to test these hypotheses, a process Beck calls **collaborative empiricism.**[99] For instance, a woman believed that a co-worker she found attractive disliked her because he did not talk to her. The therapist suggested that the woman check out the validity of this *hypothesis* by observing how frequently the man interacted with other women in the office. Much to her surprise, she found that the man rarely spoke to any of the women. Thus, her dysfunctional belief, which was based on arbitrary inference and personalization, was refuted with empirical evidence.

Notice that both cognitive therapy and REBT attempt to change faulty thinking, but they employ different strategies. Cognitive therapy uses *empirical* disputation based on observations of actual events to challenge faulty thinking. In contrast, REBT uses *rational* disputation, focusing directly on the illogical nature of the beliefs.

Once clients in cognitive therapy learn to challenge the validity of their dysfunctional beliefs, they are taught to replace them with adaptive beliefs. The woman in our previous example came to see the man she was attracted to as "uninterested in women in general." This view not only was more accurate but also was more adaptive in that it allowed her to feel better about herself.

Sometimes testing the validity of a dysfunctional belief reveals that the belief is valid—that it is consistent with what actually is occurring. This would have been the case if the woman had discovered that the man was interacting with other women in the office, excluding only her. In such instances, the client is helped to view the situation in a way that fits the data but does not lead to maladaptive reactions. For example, the woman might have changed her thoughts to "The man doesn't know what he is missing by not paying attention to me. It's his loss, not mine."

The specific techniques used in cognitive therapy to change clients' dysfunctional thinking fall into two categories: cognitive interventions and overt behavioral interventions.

Cognitive Interventions

Cognitive interventions, which are based on cognitive restructuring, change clients' cognitions directly. For example, to dispel unrealistic fear, the therapist and the client would *analyze faulty logic* the client is using, and the therapist might *provide relevant information* about what makes the fear unrealistic (for instance, people rarely are hurt riding elevators).

Clients are asked to keep records of their automatic thoughts during the course of the day, including such information as the situation in which the thought occurs, their emotions at the time, the logical errors they are making, and rational responses to the situation.[100] An example of such a record, sometimes called a *three-column technique,* can be seen in Figure 12-2.

Generating alternative interpretations is a crucial aspect of cognitive restructuring. For example, a student who is anxious about being one of the last to finish exams could counter the thought "I must be stupid" with more adaptive thoughts, such as "I knew the material well and had a lot to say" and "Writing well-organized answers takes time." The therapist first models generating nonthreatening interpretations of anxiety-evoking events, and then the client rehearses this skill.

Figure 12-2 Example of a client's use of a three-column technique

Situations	Automatic Thoughts	Logical Errors
Wearing new outfit for first time	People are going to laugh at me.	No evidence
Giving an oral report in class	I froze last time, and I'll freeze again.	Overgeneralization
	I'll die if I don't do well.	Magnification
Family moved away	They just don't want to be around me anymore.	Personalization
Rejected by date	My life is ruined.	Magnification
Getting a B on a paper	I just have no grasp of the material in this course.	Polarized thinking

Reattribution of responsibility is helpful when clients believe they have more control over potentially negative outcomes than they actually do. A young man who was highly anxious about an upcoming date feared that the woman would not have a good time. Through Socratic dialogue, the therapist helped the man accept that he could plan the evening and enjoy it himself, but he had no control over the woman's feelings.

Decatastrophizing is a specific form of reattribution that is useful when clients anticipate dire consequences, which is common in anxiety disorders. Through Socratic dialogue, the therapist guides the client to see the absurdity of highly unlikely consequences and to entertain more probable, noncatastrophic outcomes. For example, a headache is much more likely to be caused by fatigue, hunger, or stress than by a brain tumor.

Overt Behavioral Interventions

Besides changing clients' cognitions directly, cognitive therapy changes clients' overt behaviors, which indirectly modifies their cognitions and emotions. In general, the more severe the clients' disorders and cognitive distortions, the more reliance is put on overt behavioral interventions, at least at the beginning of therapy. For example, clients with severe depression generally have little interest in engaging in Socratic dialogues and generating alternative interpretations. From their perspective, "Everything is hopeless, so what's the use?" Further, their reasoning abilities may be too impaired to benefit from direct cognitive interventions. Thus, changing their overt behaviors may be the better strategy.[101]

Many different techniques are used in cognitive therapy to change overt behaviors, most of which are not unique to cognitive therapy. For example, in vivo exposure might be used for clients who have specific fears. Social skills training, including assertion training, is appropriate when clients' appraisal of their ineptness is accurate. For instance, when a client checked out his belief that "whenever I make a simple suggestion to my wife, she gets upset," he found that it was accurate. The client and therapist role-played how the client made "simple suggestions" to his wife, and it became clear that his suggestions were more like commands. Accordingly, the client learned and then practiced more adaptive ways of making suggestions to his wife.

Three particular overt behavioral interventions commonly are used in cognitive therapy: activity schedule, mastery and pleasure rating, and graded task assignment.

ACTIVITY SCHEDULE

An **activity schedule** is used to plan a client's daily activities and is particularly useful for clients who are anxious or depressed. The client and therapist schedule activities for most hours of each day (see Figure 12-3). An activity schedule gives a sense of direction and control to clients who are anxious. It counteracts feelings of disorganization and being overwhelmed and serves to distract clients from anxiety-evoking thoughts. Clients who are depressed often are inactive and have difficulty doing even the simplest tasks. An activity schedule provides a structure that encourages clients to engage in active behaviors throughout the day.

Figure 12-3 Portion of an activity schedule for 45-year-old man suffering from depression

	Monday	Tuesday	Wednesday
8–9	Get out of bed, get dressed	Get out of bed, get dressed	Get out of bed, get dressed
9–10	Clean bathrooms	Do grocery shopping	Vacuum house
10–11	Go to museum	↓	Go to library
11–12	Exercise	Exercise	Exercise or take walk
12–1	Lunch	Lunch with friend	Lunch
1–2	Do therapy homework	↓	Clean bedrooms
2–3	Do laundry	Clean living room	Pay bills
3–4	Housework	Visit with mother	Attend therapy
4–5	Read newspaper	Read newspaper	Read newspaper
5–6	Fix dinner	Go out to dinner	Fix dinner
6–7	Eat dinner with family	Do therapy homework	Eat dinner with family
7–8	Clean kitchen	Take walk	
8–9	Watch TV, read novel	Work on computer	Watch TV, read novel
9–11	↓	Read novel	↓

MASTERY AND PLEASURE RATING

Clients suffering from depression and anxiety not only need to be active but also need to feel satisfaction and pleasure from what they are doing. The **mastery and pleasure rating** technique provides clients with feedback about the satisfaction and pleasure they actually are experiencing. *Mastery* refers to a sense of accomplishment (not perfection), and *pleasure* refers to feelings of enjoyment or satisfaction while performing a task. Clients rate each activity on their activity schedule for mastery and for pleasure using a 0 to 5 rating scale (with 0 representing no mastery/pleasure and 5 representing maximum mastery/pleasure).[102] Using a rating scale encourages clients to recognize *partial* successes and *small* pleasures. Mastery and pleasure rating is especially useful for depression because it penetrates clients' "'blindness' . . . to situations in which they are successful and their readiness to forget situations that do bring them some satisfaction."[103] The same clients who make statements such as, "I can't do anything right, and nothing gives me pleasure," often rate specific activities with scale scores higher than zero.

GRADED TASK ASSIGNMENT

A **graded task assignment** encourages a client to perform small sequential steps that lead to a goal. It is a specialized shaping technique that allows the client to progress toward a goal with minimal stress. Case 12-3 illustrates the impact that graded task assignments can have on a client whose activity level is minimal. The therapist was Aaron Beck.

Case 12-3

USING GRADED TASK ASSIGNMENTS TO ACCELERATE WALKING IN A CLIENT WITH SEVERE DEPRESSION[104]

The patient was a 52-year-old man who had spent over a year in a hospital without moving away from his bed. He had many trials of antidepressant medications without any improvement. I saw him for only one visit. At this time, the patient was sitting in a chair next to his bed. After preliminary introductions and general social interchanges, the interview proceeded thus:

THERAPIST: I understand that you haven't moved away from your bedside for a long time. Why is that?

PATIENT: I can't walk.

THERAPIST: Why is that? . . . Are your legs paralyzed?

PATIENT: (irritated) Of course not! I just don't have the energy.

THERAPIST: What would happen if you tried to walk?

PATIENT: I'd fall on my face, I guess.

THERAPIST: What would you say if I told you that you were capable of walking any place in the hospital?

PATIENT: I'd say you were crazy.

THERAPIST: How about testing that out?

PATIENT: What's that?

THERAPIST: Whether I'm crazy.

PATIENT: Please don't bother me.

THERAPIST: You said you don't think you could walk. Many depressed people believe that, but when they try it they find they do better than they expected.

PATIENT: I *know* I can't walk.

THERAPIST: Do you think you could walk a few steps?

PATIENT: No, my legs would cave in.

THERAPIST: I'll bet you can walk from here to the door (about 5 yards).

PATIENT: What happens if I can't do it?

THERAPIST: I'll catch you.

PATIENT: I'm really too weak to do it.

THERAPIST: Suppose I hold your arm. (The patient then took a few steps supported by the therapist. He continued to walk beyond the prescribed five yards—without further assistance. He then walked back to his chair, unassisted.)

THERAPIST: You did better than you expected.

PATIENT: I guess so.

THERAPIST: How about walking down to the end of the corridor (about 20 yards)?

PATIENT: I know I don't have the strength to walk that far.

THERAPIST: How far do you think you can walk?

PATIENT: Maybe to the next room (about 10 yards).

The patient easily walked to the next room and then continued to the end of the corridor. [I] . . . continued to propose specific goals and to elicit the patient's responses to the goals. After successful completion of each task, a greater distance was proposed.

Within 45 minutes, the patient was able to walk freely around the ward. He was thereby able to [reinforce] . . . himself for his increased activity by being able to obtain a soda from the vending machine. Later, when he extended the range of his activities, he was able to walk to different points in the hospital and gain satisfaction from various recreational activities. Within a few days, he was playing Ping-Pong and going to the hospital snack bar and, in less than a week, he was able to walk around the hospital grounds and enjoy seeing the flowers, shrubs, and trees. Another [natural reinforcer] . . . was the favorable response he received from members of the hospital staff and from the other patients. The patient began to speak about himself in positive terms and to make concrete plans for leaving the hospital permanently—a goal he reached in a month.

The graded task assignments helped the patient become more active and provided him with immediate success experiences. The assignments also served as informal investigations to test his hypothesis that he was too weak to walk. When the man's experiences indicated that his belief about himself was invalid, he was able to view himself differently. In turn, this new perspective allowed him to attempt new behaviors that were consistent with the belief that he was healthy and capable of functioning.

Cognitive Therapy for Anxiety-Related Disorders

Next to depression, cognitive therapy has been applied most frequently to anxiety-related disorders. Although exposure therapies often are considered the treatment of choice for obsessive-compulsive disorder, cognitive therapy can be used to challenge and replace obsessive thoughts such as the need to be perfect, exaggerated views of one's responsibility, and magical thinking (for example, "It is dangerous to step on the cracks on the sidewalk").[105] Posttraumatic stress disorder is another anxiety-related disorder for which cognitive therapy is employed with such diverse traumatic precipitants as war[106] and sexual assault.[107] Victims of sexual assault often perceive the world as dangerous and themselves as incapable of coping with stress. Cognitive therapy is well suited to addressing victims' maladaptive automatic thoughts related to fear (for example, "That man is going to attack me"), guilt and shame (for example, "I could have stopped it"), anger and rage (for example, "Why me?"), and sadness (for example, "I'll never be the same again"). Cognitive therapy has been shown to be as effective as imaginal exposure in treating posttraumatic stress disorder.[108] Cognitive therapy combined with exposure therapies is an effective treatment for social phobia and can be as effective as medication that is often prescribed for social phobia.[109] In treating clients with generalized anxiety disorder, cognitive therapy has been found to be as effective as relaxation training.[110]

Irritable bowel syndrome is a stress-related disorder that results in abdominal pain and discomfort associated with altered bowel function, including constipation and diarrhea. It is not caused by a specific organic condition, and psychological events, such as stress and anxiety, can contribute significantly to the symptoms. The general goal of cognitive therapy is to help clients reconceptualize their bowel-related symptoms.[111] Clients are taught to shift their view that their symptoms are all-encompassing and constitute an uncontrollable medical condition to the belief that the symptoms are subject to their mood and are therefore controllable. Other applications of cognitive therapy in stress management have been with gay men who are HIV-infected[112] and with women in treatment for early-stage breast cancer.[113]

Cognitive Therapy for Schizophrenic Delusions and Hallucinations

Delusions and hallucinations are the hallmark of schizophrenia. Recently, cognitive therapists have accepted the challenge of treating delusions and hallucinations,[114] which often are very disturbing to the person experiencing them (as well as others) and seriously impair the person's functioning.

Delusions are blatantly false beliefs people steadfastly hold despite contrary evidence (for example, a client's believing that she is Joan of Arc). Cognitive therapy for schizophrenic delusions involves the same basic steps used with depression and anxiety. First, cognitive distortions are identified; then, evidence for their validity is sought; and finally, adaptive cognitions are substituted for the distorted cognitions. A few special procedures and precautions are required, however, because of the nature and severity of schizophrenic delusions and the fragility of the clients. For example, the client–therapist relationship is especially important because clients must trust their therapist if they are to talk about delusions that are frightening, threatening, and bizarre.[115] The therapist avoids directly challenging schizophrenic delusions because such confrontation often meets with negative reactions.[116] This is especially likely with *paranoid delusions,* which involve thoughts that people are following, plotting against, and wanting to harm the client.

To help identify specific delusional beliefs, the therapist asks the client to keep a daily log of his or her delusions. The log includes an indication of the client's strength of conviction that the delusion is true, which may be rated on a 0% to 100% scale.

Treatment of delusions proceeds in a stepwise fashion.[117] Initially, the focus is on beliefs having the lowest conviction ratings. As the client begins to feel more comfortable in therapy, more strongly held delusions are addressed.[118] Therapists encourage clients to consider alternative interpretations of events.[119] For instance, a 22-year-old man believed that a "haggly witch" followed him around wherever he went.[120] Considering alternative interpretations of his delusion (such as "Maybe I just have a wild imagination") dramatically decreased the frequency and strength of his delusions, as well as his need for medication (Thorazine) to control his delusional thoughts.

The client and therapist collaborate to evaluate empirically the evidence on which clients base their delusions.[121] For example, a client believed that to avoid being physically attacked, he had to get angry and shout back at hallucinated voices he was "hearing."[122] The client agreed to refrain from becoming angry and shouting back at the voices and just to observe whether he was attacked. When the client discovered that he was not attacked, he was greatly relieved and became much less concerned about his safety. Such empirical investigations are useful because they allow clients to draw their own conclusions about the validity of their delusions.[123]

Hallucinations, the other core symptom of schizophrenia, are false sensory perceptions that people experience as real. Auditory hallucinations, which usually involve hearing nonexistent voices that are very disturbing, may be the most frequently observed symptom of schizophrenia, occurring in more than 60% of cases. An example of a schizophrenic auditory hallucination might be a client's hearing a voice that instructs him to do penance by cutting himself. According to the prevailing theoretical explanation of auditory hallucinations,[124] they arise from the client's thoughts, which are obviously internal, but the client attributes them to an external source. And what clients believe the source to be influences how distressing the voices are (for example, the condemnation of God is likely to be more distressing than the condemnation of a preacher). On the basis of these formulations, cognitive therapy for auditory hallucinations involves challenging the interpretations and content of hallucinatory voices.[125]

To challenge clients' interpretations of the source of their voices, clients are asked to generate as many alternative explanations for their voices as possible and to rate the alternatives in terms of their believability (0% to 100%). Next, the evidence for each alternative explanation is examined, which may include homework assignments involving collaborative empiricism. In addition to these steps, which parallel standard cognitive therapy procedures, special techniques applicable to schizophrenic hallucinations are included. Clients are educated about the nature of hallucinations, stressors that tend to trigger them, and the prevalence of hallucinatory experiences in the general population. Therapists help clients examine the advantages (such as increased attention from hospital staff) as well as the disadvantages of hearing voices.

Clients frequently use what voices say as "evidence" to support the source of the voices (for example, "It must be the CIA who has been telling me what to do; only the CIA could know so much about me"). If disconfirmatory evidence for the content can be found, then the source may be discredited. Thus, it also is necessary to challenge the content of the hallucinations, which involves the same basic procedures employed to challenge the client's interpretations of them.

The preliminary analysis of the efficacy of cognitive therapy in treating auditory hallucinations that was carried out with 10 clients provided encouraging results.[126] Over a period of a week, the percentage of clients experiencing no auditory hallucinations increased from 0% to 50%, clients experiencing minimal distress increased from 10% to 80%, and clients experiencing minimal impairment increased from 30% to 90%, as assessed by the Psychotic Symptom Rating Scale.[127]

The treatment of delusional beliefs and auditory hallucinations of clients with schizophrenia is an exciting new application of cognitive therapy. It would be premature, however, to draw any conclusions about its efficacy because few controlled studies have been conducted at this time.

Schema-Focused Cognitive Therapy

So far, we have seen the application of cognitive therapy to changing clients' discrete cognitive distortions that are maintaining conditions of their psychological disorders. In recent years, this traditional strategy has been extended to address the needs of clients with longstanding psychological problems, such as personality disorders. Such problems tend to be maintained primarily by maladaptive schemas. A **schema** is a broad, pervasive, cognitive theme about oneself, others, and the world.[128] Schemas often stem from childhood experiences and are further developed throughout one's lifetime. For example, a girl who received little nurturing, empathy, or protection from her parents had, as an adult, an "emotional deprivation" schema.[129] It involved an exaggerated theme of not being cared for or understood by others, even in light of contradictory evidence, and it pervaded the client's view of the world.

In contrast to a discrete cognitive distortion, a schema serves as a template to process a wide range of experiences, is self-perpetuating, and is far more irrefutable and rigid, which makes it extremely resistant to change. Table 12-6 lists five broad-based schemas that have been tentatively identified as core cognitive structures of clients with chronic and resistant forms of psychological problems.[130]

Although schemas are long-standing, they are triggered by present experiences. A client's "abandonment" schema that developed in childhood may be triggered when his wife goes out of town for a business meeting. Once activated, schemas generate significant psychological distress, including depression, anxiety, feelings of intense loneliness, interpersonal conflicts, and addictive behaviors.

Table 12-6 Broad-based schemas that have been tentatively identified as core cognitive structures of clients with chronic and resistant forms of psychological problems
SOURCE: Young, 1994.

Schema	Description
ABANDONMENT/ INSTABILITY	The perceived instability or unreliability of others for support and stable, trustworthy relationships
MISTRUST/ABUSE	The expectation that others will intentionally hurt, abuse, humiliate, cheat, or manipulate you
EMOTIONAL DEPRIVATION	The expectation that others will not adequately meet your desire for emotional support, including nurturance, empathy, and protection
DEFECTIVENESS/SHAME	The feeling that you are defective, inferior, bad, or unlovable, which results in hypersensitivity to criticism, rejection, and blame as well as self-consciousness about perceived flaws
SOCIAL ISOLATION/ ALIENATION	The feeling that you are isolated from the rest of the world, different from others, and unconnected to any group or community

The assessment phase of schema-focused cognitive therapy involves four steps: (1) schema identification, (2) schema activation, (3) schema conceptualization, and (4) schema education. Schemas are identified from information gathered in a variety of ways, including self-report inventories,[131] interviews, and clients' self-recorded observations at home, such as filling out the Schema Identification Worksheet (see Figure 12-4).[132] From the data obtained, the therapist searches for the underlying themes around which the client's automatic thoughts are organized.[133]

Once a client's specific schemas have been identified, the therapist intentionally activates them through imagery or role-playing (which

Figure 12-4 Example of an entry on the Schema Identification Worksheet

Situation	Mood Intensity (1–10)	Automatic thought	Underlying assumption	Schema
Was not invited to Julie's party	depressed (7)	There's something wrong with me. I'm abnormal.	If I were normal, I'd be popular.	Defectiveness/ Shame
	depressed (5)	No one likes me. I'm the class outcast.	She didn't invite me because she doesn't like me.	Social Isolation/ Alienation

might involve a painful childhood experience associated with the schema). The purpose of schema activation is to identify those schemas that elicit strong emotional responses. Those that do are considered critical schemas for the client and are dealt with during the change phase of therapy.

Next, the therapist formulates a schema conceptualization for the client. This includes the specific schemas impacting the client's life experiences, the situational cues that activate the schemas, and the specific cognitions, emotions, and actions the client displays when the schemas are activated. Finally, the therapist explains the schema conceptualization to the client, and the therapist and client formulate a treatment plan.

Schema-focused cognitive therapy employs the same basic cognitive and overt behavioral change techniques used in traditional cognitive therapy, but they may be modified for dealing with schemas. For instance, *life review* is a cognitive exercise in which therapists ask clients to provide evidence from their lives that supports and contradicts their schemas. This helps clients see how their schemas distort their perceptions and begins a process of distancing themselves from their schemas, rather than identifying with them. A graded task assignment in which clients gradually perform new behaviors that contradict their schemas is an example of an overt behavioral technique used in schema-focused cognitive therapy.

Experiential and interpersonal change techniques also are part of schema-focused cognitive therapy. *Schema dialogue* is an experiential technique. Clients role-play both the "voice" of the schema and the "voice" of their own healthy responses to the schema, while moving back and forth between two chairs, confronting and refuting the schema. Experiential techniques may be the most effective interventions in schema-focused cognitive therapy.[134]

Interpersonal change techniques are used because clients treated with schema-focused cognitive therapy often have core interpersonal problems, including difficulty establishing a relationship with the therapist. With *limited reparenting*, for example, the therapist provides a therapeutic relationship that counteracts maladaptive schemas. In the case of a client with a "rejection" schema who experienced extreme criticism as a child, the therapist would be as accepting as possible and praise the client frequently.[135]

Schema-focused cognitive therapy differs from traditional cognitive therapy in four important respects: (1) a greater use of the client–therapist relationship as a change vehicle, (2) the exploration of the earliest expression (often in childhood) of a schema to understand the nature of its current expression, (3) a greater emphasis on emotions and the use of experiential change strategies, and (4) a longer course of treatment. The schema-focused approach has demonstrated its effectiveness in treating personality disorders, substance dependence, clients with histories of childhood abuse, eating disorders, and chronic pain, as well as in preventing relapse in depression and anxiety disorders.[136] However, conclusions about the relative effectiveness of schema-focused versus traditional cognitive therapy await controlled, clinical outcome studies.

Adaptations of Cognitive Therapy to Diverse Populations

Cognitive therapy primarily has been used with adults who are not hospitalized. However, increasingly, it is being adapted to other populations, including hospitalized clients[137] and elderly clients.[138] Adaptations of cognitive therapy for children have been particularly innovative.[139] For example, the Adolescent Coping with Depression program[140] uses popular cartoon strip characters (such as "Garfield") to illustrate how negative thoughts contribute to depression and how positive thoughts can improve mood. This therapy program has been modified to be relevant for African-American adolescents.[141] Cognitive therapy has been adapted for Turkish children with test anxiety; the adaptation involves listening to stories in which characters learned to replace negative thoughts with positive thoughts about test taking.[142]

A large-scale cognitive therapy program was developed for children aged 10 to 13 to prevent depression and related difficulties in school (such as conduct problems, low achievement, and poor peer relations). At-risk children were taught to identify inaccurate and overly pessimistic beliefs and then to replace them with more accurate and optimistic thoughts. The program resulted in significant reductions in depression and improvements in classroom behaviors, which were maintained at a 6-month follow-up.[143]

Cognitive therapy, like all therapies, is most effective when it is tailored to the particular characteristics of the client.[144] For example, a creative adaptation of cognitive therapy for religious clients treated for depression employed religious rationales for the therapy procedures and religious arguments to counter clients' irrational beliefs (similar to the use of REBT for religious clients described earlier in the chapter).[145] The religious-oriented cognitive therapy was more effective than standard cognitive therapy for this population.

◆

Participation Exercise 12-5

TURNING YOUR THINKING UPSIDE DOWN: COGNITIVE RESTRUCTURING*

You can use cognitive restructuring to cope with difficult or stressful situations in your daily life. In this Participation Exercise you will read brief descriptions of everyday situations followed by examples of negative self-statements someone faced with the situations might make. These self-statements are maladaptive because they present the consequences of the situation as so terrible that nothing can be done to cope with them. In fact, the situation may be unfortunate, but it is not necessarily disastrous.

Your task is to think of self-statements that are more positive, optimistic, and adaptive. The self-statements also must be realistic. For example, if your new car is stolen, it would be unrealistic to think, "I didn't need the car," because that is not likely to be true.

*This Participation Exercise can be done before you continue reading or later.

For each situation and negative self-statement, write two possible alternative self-statements that are positive, optimistic, adaptive, and realistic. Then compare your self-statements with the examples given in your Student Resource Materials.

Situation	Negative Self-Statements
1. Having to hand in a long, difficult assignment the next day	1. "There is just no way I can get this work done for tomorrow."
2. Getting into an automobile accident	2. "Oh no, my father will kill me."
3. Being asked to dance but not being a skillful dancer	3. "I can't dance; I'll make a fool of myself."
4. Losing your job	4. "I'll never get another job."
5. Moving to a new home, away from family and friends	5. "Everything I care about is left behind."
6. Having a roommate with whom you don't get along	6. "We'll never get along. What a horrible year this is going to be!"
7. Breaking up with the person you are in love with	7. "She (or he) was everything to me . . . my whole life. I have nothing else to live for."

◆

Cognitive Therapy in Perspective

Beck's studies of the distorted thinking of depressed clients led him to develop cognitive therapy 40 years ago.[146] Subsequently, it has become clear that distorted thinking also is associated with many other psychological disorders, and the general principles of cognitive therapy appear to be adaptable to a variety of disorders. Specialized cognitive therapy procedures have been designed to treat anxiety,[147] obsessive-compulsive disorder,[148] personality disorders,[149] marital distress,[150] and recently, schizophrenic delusions and hallucinations.[151] In some cases, such as in the treatment of sexual dysfunctions[152] and obesity,[153] therapists have employed cognitive therapy along with other behavior therapy treatments to deal with clients' cognitive distortions that are contributing to their problems.

The most substantial body of research on the efficacy of cognitive therapy involves the treatment of depression. Cognitive therapy clearly is an effective treatment for depression.[154] Although most of the controlled studies have been conducted with women, cognitive therapy appears to be equally effective with men suffering from depression.[155] The quality of studies has been especially high (in contrast to outcome research on REBT),[156] and many of the studies have been carried out with true clinical populations. The specific interventions are well defined, so clinicians using cognitive therapy and researchers evaluating it are employing standard procedures (which is not the case with REBT[157]). Moreover, clients rate cognitive therapy as a highly useful treatment for depression.[158]

Overall, it appears that cognitive therapy is an effective treatment for acute episodes of major depression[159] and is less effective for chronic depression.[160] Successful cognitive therapy for chronic depression may require more sessions and repetition, narrowing the focus to one or two pivotal problems, and enriching mastery and pleasure exercises.[161] Cognitive therapy also has been used to treat bipolar disorder, which is characterized by mood fluctuations between depression and manic states.[162]

It is especially noteworthy that cognitive therapy has been shown to be at least as effective in treating depression as medication, even in severe cases.[163] Medication, the most common treatment for depression, has major drawbacks, including possible physical and psychological negative side effects. Moreover, cognitive therapy is a more cost-effective treatment than medication; for example, Prozac alone may result in 33% higher expected costs than individual cognitive therapy.[164]

Cognitive therapy also may prevent the recurrence of depression to a greater degree than other treatments.[165] It is possible that cognitive therapy (1) sensitizes clients to the types of cognitions associated with depression and (2) provides them with coping skills to neutralize potential depression-evoking events (such as substituting adaptive thoughts for automatic thoughts).

Evidence from one large-scale, multisite study carried out by the National Institute of Mental Health has called into question whether cognitive therapy is more effective for depression than other forms of treatment.[166] However, the study has a number of methodological flaws.[167] For example, poor adherence to cognitive therapy procedures by some of the therapists[168] may have contributed to the results. Additionally, cognitive therapy may be more effective than other therapies in particular circumstances (for example, with clients who have certain characteristics, such as those who possess some coping skills).[169] Further research is needed to clarify this issue.[170]

The efficacy of cognitive therapy in treating depression and a host of other psychological disorders has strong empirical support based on hundreds of methodologically sound studies. However, most of these studies are carried out in research settings (such as hospitals) where the clients have been recruited (as through a newspaper advertisement). In contrast, the vast majority of clients treated with cognitive therapy have sought therapy, rather than enrolling in a treatment study, and the therapy occurs in community-based settings. Because there are essential differences between these two groups of clients, it is important to ascertain whether cognitive therapy is effective for self-referred, community-setting clients. Recent evidence indicates that it is effective in community settings for both depression and panic disorder.[171]

Cognitive therapy is a versatile treatment. Although typically implemented individually, cognitive therapy is effective in a group format,[172] which has been shown to be as effective as individual treatment.[173] Cognitive therapy has been efficiently and effectively used to treat depression in patients with multiple sclerosis.[174] Telephone-administered cognitive therapy is well suited to clients with physical illnesses and impairments as well as to elderly clients who cannot travel for therapy sessions.

Cognitive therapy integrates a variety of cognitive and overt behavioral interventions[175] and emphasizes a self-control approach.[176] Hypothesis-testing skills to examine one's beliefs and between-session practice of skills are two self-control components of cognitive therapy that are associated with its effectiveness.[177]

Cognitive therapy is popular with clients and therapists for some of the same reasons that REBT is—namely, it makes sense, and it is based on a theory that is easy to understand. In addition, some clients like cognitive therapy because participating in collaborative empiricism and Socratic dialogue allows them to discover the distortions in their thinking for themselves. Indeed, clients report feeling more control over their thoughts and feelings and greater insight into their problems after completing cognitive therapy.[178]

◆ ALL THINGS CONSIDERED: COGNITIVE RESTRUCTURING THERAPY

The order in which we have presented the three cognitive restructuring therapies—thought stopping, rational emotive behavior therapy, and cognitive therapy—parallels the increasing complexity of the procedures they employ. That order also parallels the increasing reliance on behavioral interventions in these therapies: Thought stopping is exclusively a cognitive technique, REBT is more cognitive than behavioral, and cognitive therapy clearly employs both cognitive and behavioral interventions.

Whereas the application of thought stopping is restricted to intrusive thoughts, REBT and cognitive therapy treat a wide range of problems and overlap in some of their specific procedures. Although REBT and cognitive therapy share the goal of promoting adaptive thought processes, they take two different approaches to attaining it: rational disputation versus collaborative empiricism. Using rational disputation in REBT, the therapist makes the client aware of dysfunctional thoughts through verbal persuasion; it is a "tell me" approach. The focus of collaborative empiricism in cognitive therapy is on the client's self-discovery of dysfunctional thinking through empirical hypothesis testing; it is a "show me" approach. Individual clients differ in their preferences for one of these two distinctive strategies, which is a reason for having both therapies available to clients. Cognitive therapy and REBT both require clients to reason using better logic or data, so they are likely to exclude clients who have limited cognitive abilities due to intellectual and communication deficits (such as severe mental retardation or serious brain damage).

Cognitive restructuring is a core procedure in thought stopping, REBT, and cognitive therapy. It also is a component of the cognitive-behavioral coping skills therapies about which you will read in Chapter 13. Changing our interpretations of life events can have a powerful effect on our overt behaviors, our emotions, and our overall life satisfaction and happiness.[179]

♦   **In Theory 12-2**

CONSTRUCTIVISM: ALL IN THE EYE OF THE BEHOLDER

The philosophical basis of cognitive restructuring is known as *constructivism*, which holds that people make (construct) their own realities (what is real and meaningful to them).[180] The interpretations we place on events—rather than the events themselves—determine the meaning of events. This idea applies both to external events (such as what other people do in relation to us) and to internal events (such as how we are feeling physically).

To appreciate the usefulness of constructivism, consider how frequently the same event has different meanings for different people. On an unusually hot day in October, some people complain about the heat, while others rejoice about getting a few more days of summer weather. As another example, there often are wide discrepancies among eyewitness accounts of accidents and crimes.[181]

Clients construct the irrational thoughts that maintain their negative emotions and maladaptive behaviors. By the same token, they can reconstruct their thoughts—

view situations differently—so that their cognitions lead to positive feelings and adaptive behaviors.

This process is illustrated by the case of M. H., a 44-year-old woman who had decided to leave her job at the end of the year, which was 4 months away.[182] She had been intensely unhappy at work because her supervisor, Wanda, seemed to be criticizing her constantly. Although M. H. felt good about her decision to leave, she increasingly found going to the office aversive. She dreaded the morning commute, felt "on edge" all day, and was relieved when she left work each day.

M. H.'s therapist suggested that she *reframe* (cognitively reconstrue) her interactions with Wanda in such a way that M. H. would come to view them positively. Specifically, the therapist suggested viewing Wanda's criticisms as validating M. H.'s decision to leave her job. M. H. expanded on this general reframe on her own. Each time Wanda criticized her, M. H. told herself something like "That was

CALVIN AND HOBBES copyright 1986 Watterson. Dist. by UNIVERSAL PRESS SYNDICATE. Reprinted with permission. All rights reserved.

really nice of Wanda to show me, once again, how good my decision was." Initially, such self-talk just made her chuckle or smile. By the second week, M. H. was viewing Wanda as her ally rather than her enemy. On one occasion, she told herself, "How wonderful it is to have a friend like Wanda who repeatedly reminds me of the wis-dom of my decision to leave." Within 3 weeks, M. H. no longer dreaded going to work, remained relaxed while on the job, and left work feeling good. In essence, M. H.'s work situation had changed for her. As a result, she was able to finish out the year with relatively little stress in her reconstrued work situation.

SUMMARY

1. Cognitive-behavioral therapy changes cognitions that are maintaining conditions of psychological disorders in two ways. Cognitions are modified directly, by cognitive restructuring, and indirectly, by changing overt behaviors.

2. Cognitive-behavioral therapy consists of two basic models. Cognitive restructuring therapy teaches clients to change distorted and erroneous cognitions that are maintaining their problem behaviors and to substitute more adaptive cognitions. Cognitive-behavioral coping skills therapy teaches clients adaptive responses—both cognitive and overt behavioral—to deal effectively with difficult situations they encounter.

3. Cognitions are operationally defined as self-talk. Four basic methods are used to assess clients' cognitions: interview, self-recording, self-report inventory, and think-aloud procedures.

4. Thought stopping decreases the frequency and duration of disturbing thoughts by interrupting them and substituting adaptive competing thoughts.

5. Rational emotive behavior therapy (REBT) employs cognitive restructuring to change irrational thoughts. Ellis' rational emotive theory holds that it is beliefs about events in our lives, rather than the events themselves, that maintain psychological problems.

6. Maladaptive thoughts are illogical because they result from logical errors in thinking, including absolute thinking, overgeneralizing, and catastrophizing. Two themes are common in irrational ideas that lead to psychological problems: personal worthlessness and a sense of duty.

7. REBT identifies thoughts based on irrational beliefs, challenges the irrational beliefs, and substitutes thoughts based on rational beliefs. The therapist challenges the rationality of the client's thoughts, debunks the client's myths about how the world "should be," and persuades the client to recognize irrational thoughts and to think rationally.

8. REBT is used primarily with adults. Rational emotive education is an adaptation of REBT principles and procedures for children and adolescents.

9. Cognitive therapy is similar to REBT. Both assume that psychological disorders are maintained by distorted cognitions, and both use cognitive restructuring as a major technique. However, cognitive therapy emphasizes empirical hypothesis testing as a means of changing existing beliefs—rather than disputation and persuasion, as in REBT.

10. The goals of cognitive therapy are to correct faulty information processing, to modify dysfunctional beliefs, and to provide skills and experiences that create adaptive thinking. Cognitive therapy involves a collaborative effort between the client and therapist. Clients are taught to view automatic thoughts (maladaptive cognitions) as hypotheses subject to empirical validation, rather than as established facts. Clients test out the hypotheses in homework assignments in which they make observations to refute (or confirm) the hypotheses.

11. Cognitive therapy procedures that directly change clients' cognitions include analyzing faulty logic, obtaining accurate information, self-recording automatic thoughts, generating alternative interpretations of events, reattributing responsibility about negative outcomes, and decatastrophizing.

12. Cognitive therapy procedures that indirectly change clients' cognitions and emotions by changing overt behaviors include activity schedule, mastery and pleasure rating, and graded task assignment.

13. Treating schizophrenic delusions and hallucinations with cognitive therapy involves the same basic procedures employed with other problems along with special considerations and procedures due to the severity of the cognitive distortions and the fragility of the clients.

14. Some clients problems are maintained less by discrete, maladaptive cognitions and more by maladaptive schemas, which are broad and pervasive cognitive themes about oneself, others, and the world. Schemas often stem from childhood experiences and are developed throughout one's lifetime. Schema-based cognitive therapy employs specialized assessment procedures and then traditional cognitive therapy treatment procedures to change schemas.

15. Although cognitive therapy primarily has been used with adults who are not hospitalized, it also had been adapted for hospitalized clients, older adults, and children and adolescents. It has been tailored for clients with particular characteristics, such as those with strong religious beliefs.

16. Cognitive restructuring is based on constructivism, the philosophical position that people make their own realities. The interpretations we place on events—rather than the events themselves—determine the meaning of events.

REFERENCE NOTES

1. For example, Lazarus & Folkman, 1984.
2. Craighead, 1990b.
3. Cottraux, 1990; Goldfried, Greenberg, & Marmar, 1990; Spiegler & Guevremont, 2002
4. Festinger, 1957; Kelly, 1955.
5. Bandura, 1986a.
6. For example, Hartl & Frost, 1999; Reinecke, 2000; Rudd, Joiner, & Rajab, 2001.
7. Beidel & Turner, 1986; Beutler & Guest, 1989.
8. Castaneda, 1972, pp. 218–219.
9. Sokolov, 1972, p. 1.
10. Blankstein & Segal, 2001; Glass & Arnkoff, 1997.
11. Glass & Arnkoff, 1997.
12. Glass & Arnkoff, 1989.
13. Glass, Merluzzi, Biever, & Larsen, 1982.
14. Ronan, Kendall, & Rowe, 1994.
15. For example, Craighead, Kimball, & Rehak, 1979; Genest & Turk, 1981; White, Davison, Haaga, & White, 1992.
16. For example, Davison, Navarre, & Vogel, 1995; White, Davison, Haaga, & White, 1992.
17. Davison, Vogel, & Coffman, 1997.
18. Davison, Navarre, & Vogel, 1995.
19. Lodge, Tripp, & Harte, 2000.
20. Wolpe, 1958; compare with Ellis, 1989b.
21. For example, Kenny, Mowbray, & Lalani, 1978.
22. Author's (MDS) clinical files.
23. Rusch, Grunert, Mendelsohn, & Smucker, 2000.
24. Smucker, Dancu, Foa, & Niederee, 1995.
25. Upper, 1993.
26. A. B. Kearney, 1993.
27. Dewhurst, 1993.
28. Krop & Burgess, 1993a.
29. Groden, 1993.
30. Jurgela, 1993.
31. Newman & Haaga, 1995.
32. For example, Broder, 2000; Lerner, Franklin, Meadows, Hembree, & Foa, 1998.
33. Freeman & Simon, 1989; Gordon, 1983; Guevremont & Spiegler, 1990; Spiegler & Guevremont, 2002.
34. Tryon, 1979.
35. For example, Armstrong & Rimm, 1974; Hackmann & McLean, 1975; Kenny, Mowbray, & Lalani, 1978; Rimm, Saunders, & Westel, 1975; Stern, Lipsedge, & Marks, 1973.
36. Ellis, 1993, 1995, 1999.
37. Ellis & Dryden, 1993.
38. Ellis, 1962, 1994a; Hansen, 2001.
39. Bernard & DiGiuseppe, 1989; Ellis & Bernard, 1985.
40. Ellis & Dryden, 1987.
41. Beck & Weishaar, 1989; Ellis, 1989a.
42. Ellis, 1970.
43. Ellis & Bernard, 1985.
44. Ellis, 1989a; Kopec, Beal, & DiGiuseppe, 1994; Lazarus, 1989b.
45. Rimm & Masters, 1979; dialogue is quoted from pp. 385–387; annotations are original to this text.
46. Broder, 2000.
47. For example, DiGiuseppe, 1981; Kendall, 1987b.
48. For example, Ellis, 1959; Ellis & Bernard, 1983.
49. Bernard & Joyce, 1984; Knaus, 1974, 1985; Knaus & Eyman, 1974; Knaus & Haberstroh, 1993; Knaus & McKeever, 1977; Knaus & Wessler, 1976; Omizo, Cubberly, & Omizo, 1985; Omizo, Lo, & Williams, 1986; Vernon, 1983; Zionts, 1983.
50. Braswell & Kendall, 2001; Friedberg, Crosby, Friedberg, Rutter, & Knight, 2000; Kendall, 2000.
51. Gossette & O'Brien, 1993.
52. Gossette & O'Brien, 1993.
53. Joyce, 1995.
54. Haaga & Davison, 1989a.
55. Mahoney, Lyddon, & Alford, 1989, p. 87.
56. For example, Burns, 1980; Dyer, 1977; Ellis & Harper, 1975.
57. Mahoney, Lyddon, & Alford, 1989.
58. For example, Dryden & Hill, 1993; Ellis, 1994b, 1994c, 1994d, 1994e.
59. Abrams & Ellis, 1994; Alvarez, 1997; Balter & Unger, 1997; Greaves, 1997; Haaga & Davison, 1989a; Rieckert & Moller, 2000; Scholing & Emmelkamp, 1993a, 1993b.
60. Nielsen, 2001; Robb, 2001.
61. Shannon & Allen, 1998.
62. Rossello & Bernal, 1999.
63. Dryden & Ellis, 2001; Ellis, 1999.
64. Bernard, 1990; Flanagan, Povall, Dellino, & Byrne, 1998.
65. Lazarus, 1989b.
66. Meichenbaum, 1991; Patterson & Forgatch, 1985.

67. Franks, 1995; Haaga & Davison, 1989a, 1989b; Hollon & Beck, 1986; Mahoney, Lyddon, & Alford, 1989.

68. Solomon & Haaga, 1995.

69. Haaga & Davison, 1989a, 1989b, 1993; Haaga, Dryden, & Dancey, 1991; Kendall, Haaga, Ellis, Bernard, DiGiuseppe, & Kassinove, 1995.

70. Lyons & Woods, 1991.

71. Haaga & Davison, 1993.

72. Compare with Goldfried, 1988; Goldfried, Decenteceo, & Weinberg, 1974; Haaga & Davison, 1989a.

73. Weinrach, 1995.

74. Beck, 1963, 1976.

75. Bernard & DiGiuseppe, 1989.

76. Hollon & Beck, 1986.

77. Beck, 1967, 1976.

78. For example, Alford, Freeman, Beck, & Wright, 1990; Beck, 1988; Beck & Emery, 1985; Freeman & Simon, 1989.

79. Laberge, Gauthier, Cote, Plamondon, & Cormier, 1993.

80. Schmidt & Woolaway-Bickel, 2000.

81. Brown, Heimberg, & Juster, 1995.

82. Van Oppen, De Haan, Van Balkom, Spinhoven, Hoogduin, & Van Dyck, 1995.

83. Beck & Freeman, 1989; Young, 1990.

84. Baucom & Epstein, 1990; Beck, 1988; Dattilio & Padesky, 1990; Epstein & Baucom, 1989.

85. Deffenbacher, Dahlen, Lynch, Morris, & Gowensmith, 2000.

86. Beck, 1967; Freeman & White, 1989; Reinecke, 2000; Rudd, Joiner, & Rajab, 2001.

87. Edgette & Prout, 1989; Simon, 1994; Weishaar, 1996.

88. Leitenberg & Rosen, 1988; Leung, Waller, & Thomas, 2000.

89. Kramer & Stalker, 1989.

90. Alford & Beck, 1994; Bentall, Haddock, & Slade, 1994; Gumley & Power, 2000; McNally, 1994.

91. Beck, 1976.

92. Beck & Weishaar, 1989, p. 23.

93. Bell-Dolan, 1995.

94. Otto & Gould, 1995.

95. Beck & Weishaar, 1989.

96. Addis & Jacobson, 2000; Burns & Sprangler, 2000; Schmidt & Woolaway-Bickel, 2000.

97. Beck & Emery, 1985; Beck & Freeman, 1989.

98. Burns & Nolen-Hoeksema, 1992.

99. Beck & Weishaar, 1989.

100. For example, Beck, Wright, Newman, & Liese, 1993; Foa & Rothbaum, 1998.

101. Bowers, 1989.

102. Beck, Rush, Shaw, & Emery, 1979.

103. Beck, 1976, p. 272.

104. Beck, 1976, pp. 284–286.

105. Freeston, Leger, & Ladouceur, 2001; Hartl & Frost, 1999.

106. Chemtob, Novaco, Hamada, & Gross, 1997.

107. Foa & Rothbaum, 1998.

108. Tarrier, Sommerfield, Pilgrim, & Faragher, 2000.

109. Coles, Hart, & Heimberg, 2001; Otto, Pollack, Gould, Worthington, McArdle, & Rosenbaum, 2000.

110. Öst & Breitholz, 2000.

111. Toner, Segal, Emmott, & Myran, 2000; Vollmer & Blanchard, 1998.

112. Antoni, Kumar, Ironson, Cruess, Lutgendorf, Klimas, Fletcher, & Scheiderman, 2000.

113. Antoni, Lehman, Kilbourn, Boyers, Culver, Alferi, Yount, McGregor, Arena, Harris, Price, & Carver, 2001.

114. Alford & Beck, 1994; Bentall, Haddock, & Slade, 1994; McNally, 1994; Morrison & Renton, 2001.

115. Alford & Correia, 1994; Perris, 1989.

116. Alford & Correia, 1994.

117. Alford & Beck, 1997.

118. Alford & Beck, 1994.

119. Alford & Correia, 1994; Himadi, Osteen, & Crawford, 1993.

120. Alford, 1986.

121. Chadwick & Lowe, 1990.

122. Tarrier, 1992.

123. Alford & Beck, 1994.

124. For example, Morrison, 1998.

125. Morrison & Renton, 2001.

126. Morrison, Renton, Williams, & Dunn, 1999.

127. Haddock, McCarron, Tarrier, & Faragher, 1999.

128. McGinn & Young, 1996.

129. DeRubeis, Tang, & Beck, 2001.

130. Young, 1994.

131. For example, Schmidt, Joiner, Young, & Telch, 1995.

132. Tinch & Frieberg, 1998.

133. Persons, 1989.

134. McGinn & Young, 1996.

135. McGinn & Young, 1996.

136. McGinn, Young, & Sanderson, 1995; Young, Beck, & Weinberger, 1993.

137. Bowers, 1989; Thase & Wright, 1991.

138. Glanz, 1989.
139. DiGiuseppe, 1989.
140. Clarke, Hawkins, Murphy, Sheeber, Lewinsohn, & Seeley, 1995; Lewinsohn & Rohde, 1993.
141. Lewinsohn, Clarke, & Rohde, 1994.
142. Aydin & Yerin, 1994.
143. Jaycox, Reivich, Gillham, & Seligman, 1994.
144. Lewinsohn, Clarke, & Rohde, 1994; Vallis, Howes, & Standage, 2000.
145. Propst, Ostrom, Watkins, Dean, & Mashburn, 1992.
146. Beck, 1967; Beck, Rush, Shaw, & Emery, 1979.
147. Hollon & Beck, 1994; Otto & Gould, 1995.
148. van Oppen & Arntz, 1994; van Oppen, de Hann, van Balkom, Spinhoven, Hoogduin, & van Dyck, 1995.
149. Beck & Freeman, 1989.
150. Abrahms, 1983; Baucom & Epstein, 1990; Beck, 1988; Dattilio & Padesky, 1990; Epstein, 1983.
151. Alford & Beck, 1994; Alford & Correia, 1994; Morrison, Renton, Williams, & Dunn, 1999.
152. McCarthy, 1989.
153. Kramer & Stalker, 1989.
154. For example, Lewinsohn, Clarke, & Rohde, 1994; Pace & Dixon, 1993; Scott, Scott, Tacchi, & Jones, 1994; Shapiro, Rees, Barkham, Hardy, Reynolds, & Startup, 1995; Teasdale, Segal, & Williams, 1995.
155. Thase, Reynolds, Frank, Simons, McGeary, Fasiczka, Garamoni, Jennings, & Kupfer, 1994.
156. For example, Shapiro, Rees, Barkham, Hardy, Reynolds, & Startup, 1995.
157. Haaga & Davison, 1993; Kendall, Haaga, Ellis, Bernard, DiGiuseppe, & Kassinove, 1995.
158. For example, Friedberg, Viglione, Stinson, Beal, Fidaleo, & Celeste, 1999.
159. Antonuccio, Danton, & DeNelsky, 1995; Beckham & Watkins, 1989; Blackburn, 1988; Dobson, 1989; Hollon & Beck, 1986; Perris, 1989; Thase, Bowler, & Harden, 1991; Thase, Simons, Cahalane, & McGeary, 1991.
160. Sanderson, Beck, & McGinn, 1994; Thase, Reynolds, Frank, Simons, Garamoni, McGeary, Harden, Fasiczka, & Cahalane, 1994.
161. Thase, 1994.
162. Lam, Bright, Jones, Hayward, Schuck, Chisholm, & Sham, 2000.
163. Antonuccio, Danton, & DeNelsky, 1995; Antonuccio, Thomas, & Danton, 1997.
164. Antonuccio, Thomas, & Danton, 1997.
165. Elkin, Shea, Watkins, Imber, Sotsky, Collins, Glass, Pilkonis, Leber, Docherty, Fiester, & Parloff, 1989; Hollon & Beck, 1986; Hollon, Shelton, & Davis, 1993; Shea, 1990; Teasdale, Segal, & Williams, 1995; compare with Otto, Pava, & Sprich-Buckminster, 1995.
166. Elkin, Shea, Watkins, Imber, Sotsky, Collins, Glass, Pilkonis, Leber, Docherty, Fiester, & Parloff, 1989.
167. Otto, Pava, & Sprich-Buckminster, 1995.
168. Hollon, Shelton, & Loosen, 1991.
169. Beckham & Watkins, 1989; Shea, 1990.
170. Thase, 1994.
171. Penava, Otto, Maki, & Pollack, 1998; Persons, Bostrom, & Bertagnolli, 1999; Stuart, Treat, & Wade, 2000.
172. For example, Deffenbacher, Dahlen, Lynch, Morris, & Gowensmith, 2000; Oei & Shuttlewood, 1997.
173. Vollmer & Blanchard, 1998.
174. Mohr, Likosky, Bertagnolli, Goodkin, Van Der Wende, Dwyer, & Dick, 2000.
175. Hollon & Beck, 1994.
176. Newman & Haaga, 1995; O'Leary & Rathus, 1993.
177. Robins & Hayes, 1993.
178. O'Leary & Rathus, 1993.
179. For example, Csikszentmihalyi, 1990; Csikszentmihalyi & Csikszentmihalyi, 1988.
180. Neimeyer, 2000; Neimeyer & Raskin, 2000, 2001.
181. Loftus, 1979.
182. From the author's (MDS) clinical files.

Cognitive-Behavioral Therapy: Coping Skills

◆ **ALL THINGS CONSIDERED: COGNITIVE-BEHAVIORAL COPING**
   SKILLS THERAPY
◆ **ALL THINGS CONSIDERED: COGNITIVE-BEHAVIORAL THERAPY**
SUMMARY
REFERENCE NOTES

As you know from reading Chapter 12, cognitive restructuring therapy changes distorted and erroneous cognitions, which means that it is appropriate for problems maintained by an *excess of maladaptive thoughts*. In contrast, cognitive-behavioral coping skills therapy—the other model of cognitive-behavioral therapy—is used to treat problems that are maintained by a *deficit of adaptive cognitions*. Here, the focus is not so much on what clients are thinking as on what they are not thinking. As with cognitive restructuring therapy, cognitive-behavioral coping skills therapy changes both clients' cognitions and overt behaviors. We will discuss four cognitive-behavioral coping skills therapies: self-instructional training, problem-solving therapy/training, stress inoculation training, and cognitive-behavioral couple therapy.

Self-Instructional Training

The odds of surviving ejecting from a jet fighter at 47,000 feet (nearly 9 miles above Earth), where the temperature, not counting the windchill, is 70 degrees below zero are not favorable, to say the least. As horrific as that experience was for William Rankin, it was nothing compared to the next 40 minutes, in which he fell through a thunderstorm with turbulence that could have disintegrated his abandoned F8U Crusader. Rankin may well owe his surviving these tandem events to his self-talk while plummeting to Earth, such as *"Hang on! You might make it yet. You're thinking. You're conscious. You know what's going on. Just ride out this free fall and you've got it made."*[1]

Every day, in much less dramatic circumstances, when we are confronted with difficult situations, we tell ourselves what to do, what to think, and how to feel. "Go to the cleaners first because it may close early and then stop by the bank on the way home." "Concentrate. I studied hard for this test, and I know this material." "Keep your eye on the ball, racket back, step in, follow through." Such directed self-talk is known as *self-instructions*. Self-instructions serve six different functions, which are described in Table 13-1, and they can be phrased in a variety of ways, as you can see in Table 13-2.

Table 13-1 Functions of self-instructions

Function	Example
PREPARING CLIENT TO USE SELF-INSTRUCTIONS	"Remember to use the self-instructions while you're working on the test."
FOCUSING ATTENTION	"Concentrate. Don't let your mind wander."
GUIDING BEHAVIOR	"All right. Now, check your answer one more time before going on."
PROVIDING ENCOURAGEMENT	"So far, so good. Keep on trying."
EVALUATING PERFORMANCE	"Good work. I got another one right."
REDUCING ANXIETY	"Stay calm. Just relax. I'm doing fine."

Table 13-2 Forms of self-instructions

Form	Example
IMPERATIVE	"Sit and relax for a moment."
FIRST PERSON	"I'd better sit and relax for a moment."
SECOND PERSON	"You need to sit and relax for a moment."
NAME	"Megan, sit and relax for a moment."

Courtesy of the University of Waterloo, Ontario, Canada

Donald Meichenbaum

Donald Meichenbaum developed **self-instructional training** to teach people to instruct themselves to cope effectively with difficult situations.[2] It has been used to treat a wide array of problems, ranging from deficits in academic skills of children[3] to the bizarre thoughts and speech of clients with schizophrenia.[4]

Self-instructional training was first used to treat children's impulsive behaviors.[5] Children who act impulsively do not think before acting, which has undesirable consequences for both them and others. The general goal of self-instructional training for impulsive behaviors is to teach children to think and plan before acting—to "stop, look, and listen" (see Figure 13-1). Five steps are involved.

1. *Cognitive modeling.* An adult model performs a task while verbalizing aloud a deliberate strategy. As an example, while demonstrating a line copying task, the model said aloud,

> OK, what is it I have to do? . . . copy the picture with the different lines. . . . go slowly and carefully. OK, draw the line down, down, good; then to the right, that's it; now down some more and to the left. Good, I'm doing fine so far.[6]

2. *Cognitive participant modeling.* The child performs the task as the model verbalizes the instructions aloud.

3. *Overt self-instructions.* The child performs the task while verbalizing the instructions aloud.

4. *Fading of overt self-instructions.* The child performs the task while whispering the instructions.

Figure 13-1 Pictures used to encourage and remind children to employ self-instructions to reduce impulsive behaviors
SOURCE: Palkes, Stewart, & Kahana, 1968, p. 819.

5. *Covert self-instructions.* Finally, the child performs the task while saying the instructions to herself or himself.

The child first practices these steps with brief, simple tasks (such as tracing lines) and then with lengthier and more complex tasks (such as solving math problems).[7] With young children, the therapy may be presented as a game, with pictorial prompts to remind the child to use self-instructions (see Figure 13-2). Case 13-1 illustrates self-instructional training with a preschool boy.

Figure 13-2 Cue cards for prompting children to use self-instructions to solve problems
SOURCE: Camp, B. W., & Bash, M. A. S. *Think Aloud: Increasing cognitive and social skills—A problem-solving program for children (Primary Level).* Champaign, IL, Research Press, 1981. Reprinted by permission.

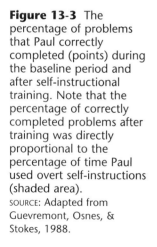

Case 13-1

Improving a Preschooler's Academic Skills Through Self-Instructional Training[8]

Five-year-old Paul attended a preschool for children with conduct and learning problems. Although he was bright and capable of doing his schoolwork, Paul often did not complete his assignments. During work periods, he spent considerable time looking around the classroom and daydreaming. As time was running out, he would rush to complete his work, particularly when recess was the next activity.

The therapist met with Paul three times a week for 20 to 30 minutes in a room adjacent to his classroom. The therapist taught Paul to use four specific self-instructions: (1) "What do I have to do first?" (problem definition); (2) "Circle all the words that begin with *bl*" (attention focusing and response guidance); (3) "Did I find all the words on the line?" (self-evaluation and error correction); and (4) "Good job. I found all of them" (self-reinforcement). The therapist taught these self-instructions sequentially; only after Paul was using a self-instruction correctly was he taught the next one.

Two types of recordings of Paul's behaviors were made to assess the effectiveness of the self-instructional training. First, videos of Paul during work periods provided a measure of the time he spent paying attention to his work. Second, a small microphone connected to a tape recorder was attached to Paul's work desk to record self-instructions that Paul spoke aloud.

The average percentage of time Paul paid attention to his work increased from 31% before self-instructional training to 72% after training. The improved attention was reflected in an increase in the percentage of problems Paul correctly completed each day, from an average of 32% before training to an average of 79% after training. As Figure 13-3

Figure 13-3 The percentage of problems that Paul correctly completed (points) during the baseline period and after self-instructional training. Note that the percentage of correctly completed problems after training was directly proportional to the percentage of time Paul used overt self-instructions (shaded area).

SOURCE: Adapted from Guevremont, Osnes, & Stokes, 1988.

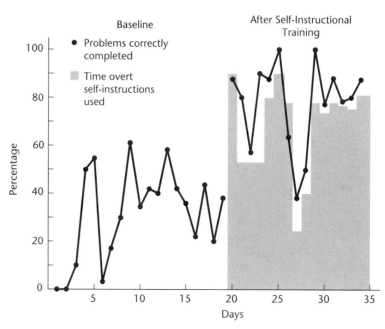

shows, Paul correctly completed significantly more problems when he used overt self-instructions. The fewer self-instructions Paul used, the fewer problems he solved correctly. Thus, the use of self-instructions was associated with both increased attention to and quality of his school-work.

Both overt and covert self-instructions have advantages. Overt self-instructions can be monitored by others, as you just saw in Case 13-1. Further, overt self-instructions are likely to increase clients' attention to self-instructions because clients actually hear them aloud. Covert self-instructions have two advantages. They do not disturb others, and clients are not embarrassed by others' hearing their self-instructions.

Enhancing the Effects of Self-Instructional Training

A number of factors appear to enhance the effectiveness of self-instructional training for academic problems. Children who are more actively involved in their training (for instance, children who help to generate the self-instructions they use) show greater improvements than children who are passive recipients of training. Not surprisingly, a good relationship with the therapist is associated with better performance.[9] Involving natural change agents (such as parents and teachers) in the training[10] and increasing the number of training sessions[11] also appear to result in greater improvements in children's academic and social behaviors.

Various procedures are used to help clients transfer their self-instructional training from the therapy to the classroom setting. These procedures include making training materials (such as work sheets) similar to those the children will use in the classroom[12] and arranging training situations to simulate normal classroom conditions, such as conducting self-instructional training in the presence of other children.[13]

Generalization to different tasks is influenced by the types of self-instructions children are taught. General conceptual instructions that children can apply to many tasks (for instance, "I must go slowly and be careful") result in greater generalization than task-specific instructions (such as "I have to circle the pictures that are the same").[14]

◆

Participation Exercise 13-1

BEING YOUR OWN BOSS: USING SELF-INSTRUCTIONS*

Using self-instructions can help you deal with many difficulties you encounter in your daily life. They can guide your behavior, reduce your anxiety, focus your attention, and encourage you.

*You should do this Participation Exercise before you continue reading.

For each of the following situations, write a self-instruction that you might find useful. When you have finished, compare your self-instructions with the examples in your Student Resource Materials.

1. It is Friday evening. You feel overwhelmed with all the studying and assignments you are supposed to complete by Monday.

2. You are tired during a long drive at night. You find that you are having trouble concentrating on driving. Several times you had to quickly steer the car back into your lane as the car wandered into the other lane.

3. You are hurriedly packing for an overnight trip and don't want to forget your essential clothes.

4. You are on a diet, which involves not eating desserts. When you go out with friends after a movie and everyone is ordering pie or ice cream, your resolve is starting to weaken.

5. You are in the last mile of a 5-mile run. You are getting very tired and feel like quitting. However, another part of you wants to complete the 5 miles.

6. You are driving in an unfamiliar area. You stop for directions. The person tells you, "Make a right at the next traffic light. Go about a mile to a stop sign and turn left. Then, in a half mile or so, the road ends. Go left there. The restaurant is down about a quarter of a mile on the right."

7. You are about to go into a job interview. You feel confident and relaxed. In fact, you realize you are too relaxed and not at all "psyched" for the interview.

8. You want to ask a classmate for a date. You have gone to the phone, but you are not sure what to say.

◆

Self-Instructional Training in Perspective

Self-instructional training has been used for more than 30 years for a wide array of problems, including impulsive behaviors,[15] schizophrenic behaviors,[16] social withdrawal,[17] anxiety (for example, test,[18] speech,[19] and social anxiety[20]), children's fears,[21] anger,[22] personality disorders,[23] obesity,[24] bulimia,[25] poor body image,[26] and pain,[27] as well as deficits in assertive behaviors,[28] problem solving,[29] leisure skills,[30] creativity,[31] and cognitive and motor performance of children and adults with sustained brain injuries.[32]

Although self-instructional training is employed more often with children, it also is used with adolescents and adults. For example, adolescents who frequently acted aggressively and displayed angry outbursts were taught coping self-instructions to deal with conflicts.[33] They learned self-instructions to *prepare* to act (for instance, "I'm not going to take it personally"), to *guide* their behaviors during conflicts (such as "I've got to keep in control"), and to *evaluate* their actions afterward (for example, "I handled that pretty well").

Self-instructional training has been used to guide job-related tasks of adults with all levels of mental retardation.[34] The training has resulted in significant improvements in work-related on-task behaviors,[35] accuracy of performance,[36] completion of tasks,[37] and punctuality.[38] These findings are impressive because they indicate that cognitive-behavioral coping skills therapy can be applied successfully to improve the quality of life of individuals with significant intellectual impairment.

Although a large number of studies have been conducted to evaluate the efficacy of self-instructional training, the findings have been inconsistent. Whereas self-instructional training has been consistently effective in improving performance on highly specific tasks, applications to complex problems have been less successful. Overall, self-instructional training is moderately effective when it is applied to narrowly focused problems that are maintained solely by inadequate self-instructions regarding how to proceed with a task. Self-instructional training is less effective as a treatment for broader problems that are likely to be maintained by more than deficits in adaptive cognitions, such as social anxiety. With such problems, self-instructional training can be useful when employed as one of several components of a treatment package.[39] Indeed, one advantage of self-instructional training is that it easily can be integrated with other treatments.[40]

Research evaluating self-instructional training has four limitations. First, because it is impossible to assess clients' use of covert self-instructions directly, it often is difficult to determine the extent to which clients use self-instructions. Second, self-instructional training generally is part of a treatment package,[41] and the specific effects of the self-instruction component may not be studied. Third, much of the research consists of analogue studies in which nonclinical problems are treated (for example, mild anxiety among college students).[42] Thus, not enough is known about the effectiveness of self-instructional training with clinical problems. Fourth, few long-term follow-up assessments have been conducted; thus, the durability of the effects of self-instructional training is unknown. These research problems are not an indictment of self-instructional training, but they make it difficult to draw definitive conclusions about the therapy's efficacy.

PROBLEM-SOLVING THERAPY/TRAINING

Problems are a ubiquitous part of life, and problem solving is a broadly useful skill for coping with many of life's difficulties.[43] Moreover, inadequate problem solving is associated with a host of psychological problems.[44]

In the present context, *problem solving* refers to a systematic process by which a person (1) generates a variety of potentially effective solutions to a problem, (2) judiciously chooses the best of these solutions, and (3) implements and evaluates the chosen solution. Like reinforcement, problem solving was not invented by behavior therapists. Behavior therapists, however, have refined problem-solving procedures and adapted them to treating and preventing psychological problems.

Problem-solving therapy is the application of problem solving to difficulties for which a client has specifically sought treatment. With adults, it is used to treat a variety of problems, including stress,[45] depression,[46] agoraphobia,[47] eating disorders,[48] smoking,[49] habitual gambling,[50] marital discord,[51] child abuse,[52] and living skills of patients with schizophrenia and depression.[53] Problem solving also has helped with difficulties families face in caring for relatives with schizophrenia[54] and cancer.[55] With children and adolescents, applications include anxiety,[56] migraine headaches,[57] obesity,[58] aggressive behaviors,[59] anger,[60] habitual gambling,[61] assertive social behaviors,[62] classroom behaviors,[63] school adjustment,[64] and parent and adolescent conflicts.[65]

Because problem solving is a broadly applicable coping skill, problem-solving therapy often serves a dual purpose. First, it treats the immediate problems for which clients seek treatment. Second, it prepares clients to deal with future problems on their own, which may help prevent psychological disorders from developing.[66]

Problem-solving training, in contrast to *therapy,* serves only the second function. It teaches problem-solving skills as a general coping strategy for dealing with problems that may arise in the course of daily life. The training often is provided for populations who have been identified as being at risk for developing psychological disorders (such as adolescents who have difficulties controlling anger) or at risk for relapsing (such as adults with chronic schizophrenia).[67] Prevention-oriented problem-solving training sometimes is incorporated into regular classroom curricula so that all children learn problem-solving skills.[68] Most of our discussion of the problem-solving method is applicable to both problem-solving therapy and problem-solving training.

Basic Procedures

Courtesy of Thomas D'Zurilla

Thomas D'Zurilla

Problem-solving therapy, which has been spearheaded by Thomas D'Zurilla,[69] divides the problem-solving process into stages or steps.[70] The basic seven stages are (1) adopting a problem-solving orientation, (2) defining the problem, (3) setting goals, (4) generating alternative solutions, (5) choosing the best solution, (6) implementing the solution, and (7) evaluating its effects (see Figure 13-4). The successful completion of each stage depends on skills and information learned in previous stages. Accordingly, if clients encounter difficulty in later stages, they may have to return to previous stages (as indicated by the dashed lines in Figure 13-4).

STAGE 1: ADOPTING A PROBLEM-SOLVING ORIENTATION

Adopting a problem-solving orientation is a crucial stage of problem solving and may, in fact, determine the outcome of the subsequent stages.[71] Clearly, it is necessary to recognize that a problem exists before one can attempt to solve it. For example, people who lose their jobs easily recognize that they will be facing a (financial) problem. However, if a person views a dilemma as unsolvable, he or she may not consider the dilemma a "problem," in the sense that it might be amendable to problem solving. Additionally, when individuals develop exaggerated or maladaptive reactions to difficult or unchangeable situations (such as the death of a loved one), they are less likely to recognize that a potentially solvable problem exists. In these cases, it is their reaction to the situation that is the problem, not the situation itself.

Adopting a problem-solving orientation requires understanding that (1) it is essential to identify problems when they occur so that appropriate

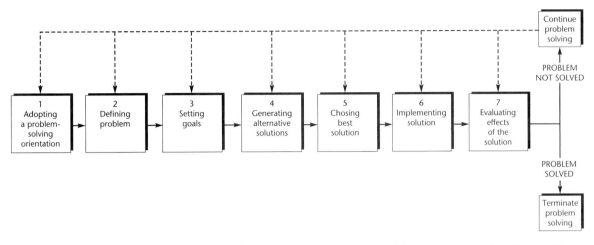

Figure 13-4 Schematic representation of the seven stages of problem-solving therapy/training. Dashed lines indicate the possibility that difficulties at one stage may necessitate returning to a prior stage.

action can be taken; (2) problems are a normal part of life, and people can learn to cope with them; and (3) effective problem solving involves carefully assessing alternative courses of action.

STAGE 2: DEFINING THE PROBLEM

In the second stage, the therapist helps the client precisely define the problem so that specific solutions can be generated. It would be difficult, for example, to generate solutions for the vaguely defined problem: "My roommate and I can't get along." In contrast, "My roommate likes to go to sleep early and wake up early, and I prefer just the opposite schedule" does lend itself to concrete solutions (see Figure 13-5).

STAGE 3: SETTING GOALS

To set goals, the client must answer the question, "What must happen so that I no longer have the problem?" The goals can focus on the (1) problem situation, (2) reactions to the problem situation, or (3) both.[72] *Situation-focused goals* are aimed at changing the problem situation itself (such as getting out of debt). *Reaction-focused goals* are aimed at changing one's emotional, cognitive, and overt behavioral reactions to the problem situation (such as feeling worthless because one is in debt). The nature of the problem—that is, how it is defined—determines the type of goal that is appropriate. For example, when the situation cannot be changed, only a reaction-focused goal is possible. The client's goals guide the generation of solutions in the fourth stage.

STAGE 4: GENERATING ALTERNATIVE SOLUTIONS

In the fourth stage, the client is taught to generate solutions (courses of action) that might solve the problem. The objective is to come up with as

Figure 13-5 Sample problem-solving work sheet

Problem-Solving Work Sheet

1. *Define the problem, including important details*:

   Background: My roommate likes to go to bed early and wake up early in the morning. I like to stay up late and sleep in. We are good friends but don't get a lot of time to talk or socialize because of our different schedules. Also, I have to limit myself to quiet activities in the evening because she has gone to bed. I would like to have other friends over in the evening, but this wouldn't be fair to my roommate. In the morning while I'm still sleeping, my roommate's getting up so early frequently wakes me up, and then I have trouble getting back to sleep.

   Specific problem situation: Our different schedules are beginning to interfere with our friendship and cause inconveniences for both of us. I would like to be able to socialize with friends in the evening and sleep in without being awakened by my roommate.

2. *Set specific goals (What must happen so that I no longer have the problem?)*: I have to be able to socialize with friends in the evening because I really enjoy doing this and not be awakened in the morning while my roommate prepares to leave the house.

3. *Generate alternative solutions (brainstorm)*:

4. *Chose best solution:*
   (+ + = very good; + = good;
   0 = neutral; – – = poor; – – = very poor)

a. Just put up with the situation for the rest of the semester.

   a. ___– –___

b. Make plans to go over to other friends' places during the evening.

   b. ___+___

c. Move out of the apartment completely.

   c. ___–___

d. Ask some friends what they think I should do.

   d. ___–___

e. Rearrange the house a bit so that we don't interfere with each other in the morning and evening.

   e. ___+ +___

f. Start going to bed early and getting up early like my roommate.

   f. ___– –___

g. Take turns so that one day I follow her schedule and the next day she follows mine.

   g. ___+___

many alternative solutions as possible to maximize the chances of finding a successful one (see Figure 13-5). Clients are encouraged to use *brainstorming,* a procedure in which any possible solution is entertained, no matter how impractical or outlandish it might appear. Although the "wild" ideas may not be viable themselves, they may lead to usable solutions by directing the client's attention in a new direction. To draw on the previous example, "murdering your roommate" clearly is not a viable solution, but its intended effect—eliminating the roommate—might lead to a more workable solution, such as moving out. Brainstorming counters the narrow, rigid thinking that clients in therapy often exhibit and may reveal solutions that clients might otherwise miss.

Brainstorming is a general strategy that is employed in different stages of problem solving.[73] For example, brainstorming can be used to generate alternative goals in the third stage and to identify different consequences of a particular solution in the fifth stage.

STAGE 5: CHOOSING THE BEST SOLUTION

In the fifth stage, the client chooses the best solution *from among the alternatives generated* in the fourth stage. This choice is made by examining the potential consequences of each course of action: what is likely to happen in the short and long run, for the client and for other people. Using a rating scale to evaluate the alternative solutions is helpful, as in the example in Figure 13-5.

STAGE 6: IMPLEMENTING THE SOLUTION

In the sixth stage, the client implements the solution chosen in the previous stage. In one sense, this is the most critical stage because the best solutions will solve the problem only if they are implemented effectively. This means that the client must have the requisite skills and opportunity to implement the solution and also be motivated to do so.

STAGE 7: EVALUATING THE EFFECTIVENESS OF THE CHOSEN SOLUTION

Finally, once the implemented solution has had time to take effect, the client evaluates how successful it has been. If the problem has been resolved, therapy is terminated. If the problem still exists, then the client repeats one or more of the previous stages. First, the client would choose another solution (Stage 5). If no acceptable alternatives remain, more solutions must be generated (Stage 4). Sometimes the difficulty lies in how the problem was defined (Stage 2) or in the goals that were selected (Stage 3), and it is necessary to return to those stages.

Teaching Problem-Solving Skills to Clients

A variety of behavior therapy procedures are used to teach clients problem solving, including modeling, prompting, self-instructions, shaping, and reinforcement.[74] In the early stages, the therapist may employ *cognitive modeling* to demonstrate the problem-solving process. For example, the therapist might brainstorm aloud about a hypothetical problem to illustrate this uninhibited, open-ended procedure, as in the following cognitive-modeling scenario.

> How am I going to get my thesis finished by the June deadline? I could put in more hours, which would mean giving up my daily jogging and watching television . . . even sleeping. Don't evaluate; just come up with ideas. I could hire an assistant to do some of the literature search. Maybe I could get an English grad student to help with my writing. Of course, I could buy a thesis from one of those companies that sells them . . . or I could bribe the dean.

During the fourth stage, the therapist *prompts* the client to use brainstorming and *reinforces* the client's ideas, both practical and outrageous. If the client has difficulty with brainstorming, the procedure may need to be *shaped*. The therapist also teaches and encourages the client to *self-reinforce* appropriate problem-solving behaviors. In the final stage, the therapist may have to use other behavior therapy procedures to facilitate the client's actions. For example, if the client feels anxious or inhibited in asking a friend for help, systematic desensitization and assertion training might be employed.

Problem-Solving Therapy/Training for Children

George Spivack and Myrna Shure were among the first to apply problem-solving training with children.[75] Problem-solving therapy/training, with minor procedural differences, is the same for both adults and children.[76] For example, hypothetical problem scenarios, such as those in Table 13-3, are used to teach problem-solving skills for interpersonal difficulties and aggressive behaviors.

Problem-solving therapy/training has been used with preschoolers,[77] preadolescents,[78] and adolescents,[79] both individually and in group formats.[80] Problem-solving therapy is especially suitable for adolescents who resist unilateral adult decision and rule making.[81] For example, incorporating family problem-solving therapy into a traditional behavioral child management training program resulted in increased cooperation and compliance on the part of an adolescent boy who was defiant with adults.[82] Case 13-2 illustrates the use of problem-solving therapy with a preadolescent.

Table 13-3 Hypothetical problem scenarios used to teach problem-solving skills to boys	You just get in from recess on a very hot day. You are standing in line to get a drink of water. A bunch of other kids are in line in front of you. After a 5-minute wait you are finally next in line. Just as you are about to have your turn, another boy in your class cuts in front of you.
	You notice that some kids in your neighborhood are playing basketball. You think one of them goes to the same school as you, but you are not sure who the others are. You would like to play with them, but you are not sure they will let you.
	After school, you notice some of your classmates smoking cigarettes behind the school building. They call you over and ask you if you want a cigarette. You don't really want to smoke, but you don't want them to dislike you either.
	When you arrive at school, another boy in your class begins to laugh at you and tease you about the haircut you just had. You tell him to stop it, but he continues anyway. Soon several other kids begin to tease you also.

Case 13-2   REDUCING AGGRESSIVE AND DISRUPTIVE BEHAVIORS IN A PREADOLESCENT BOY USING PROBLEM-SOLVING THERAPY[83]

Eleven-year-old Carl was referred for treatment by his teacher because of his aggressive and disruptive classroom behaviors and poor relationships with his classmates. Carl frequently drew attention to himself by engaging in a variety of inappropriate behaviors, such as burping loudly, humming, and leaving his seat. Carl wanted to have friends, but he was shunned by his classmates, who found his behaviors rude and obnoxious. When faced with a conflict with his teacher or classmates, Carl often acted aggressively—threatening others, yelling obscenities, or storming out of the room. The therapist spoke with Carl's teacher about the specific types of situations that Carl handled ineffectively, and brief scenarios about each problem situation were constructed (similar to those in Table 13-3).

Carl and the therapist met for a total of 18 half-hour sessions over 12 weeks in a private room at Carl's school. The therapist explained the rationale and benefits of "stopping and thinking" before acting, as well as how the therapy could help Carl get along better with his peers and teacher. Carl was taught to think of as many solutions to the problem scenarios as he could. Next, Carl learned to select the best solutions, those that were both realistic and most likely to result in positive, or at least neutral, consequences. If Carl evaluated a solution unrealistically (for example, "If I hit him, he won't bother me anymore"), the therapist reminded him of what the consequences actually were likely to be. Finally, Carl and the therapist discussed how he would implement the chosen solutions and assess their effectiveness.

In later sessions, Carl and the therapist role-played situations that might occur as Carl attempted the solutions. For example, when Carl had decided that he would ask another boy in his class to play with him at recess, the therapist assumed the role of the boy and Carl practiced what he would actually say and do. The therapist provided Carl with feedback about how he was presenting himself and modeled alternative approaches when Carl had difficulty.

Carl learned each of the problem-solving skills, as evidenced by his applying them to the problem scenarios. More importantly, he was able to use the skills to change his behaviors at school. After problem-solving therapy had begun, his disruptive classroom behaviors decreased significantly. Before problem-solving therapy, Carl engaged in disruptive behaviors an average of 30% of the time; at the end of therapy, this fell to 15%.

Problem-Solving Therapy/Training in Perspective

Problem solving has been applied to diverse problems and populations. It has its strongest empirical support in the treatment of adult depression[84] and as a maintenance strategy following behavioral weight-control programs.[85] Problem-solving therapy can help clients solve immediate problems and provide clients with skills for solving future problems—which exemplifies the self-control approach in behavior therapy. It is especially beneficial for problems that involve conflict or require a decision, such as deciding whether to have a baby, to change jobs, or to drop out of school. Problem-solving therapy also is useful for more serious problems, such as depression, including depressed mood in elderly clients.[86] Deficits in problem-solving skills have been linked to hopelessness and suicide risk,[87] and problem-solving therapy might be employed to help clients contemplating suicide consider alternatives to ending their lives.

Some of the factors that appear to be important in effective problem-solving interventions are (1) a positive client–therapist relationship, (2) individualized procedures, (3) the therapist's modeling problem-solving skills, (4) the client's doing homework assignments, and (5) the client's learning specific means of implementing solutions.[88]

The effectiveness of problem-solving therapy/training depends on three sequential outcomes: (1) learning problem-solving skills, (2) applying them to real-life problems, and (3) benefiting from their application—that is, actually solving problems. To evaluate the first outcome, clients' problem-solving skills are assessed before and after therapy/training, often using hypothetical problems. Clients' responses to the problems are recorded and later rated by the therapist. Table 13-4 contains abbreviated scoring guidelines for rating children's problem-solving skills based on their responses to problem scenarios (such as those in Table 13-3, page 354). Alternatively, problem-solving ability can be assessed by paper-and-pencil measures, such as the Social Problem-Solving Inventory,[89] which

Table 13-4 Abbreviated guidelines for rating children's problem-solving skills

SOURCE: Adapted from Guevremont & Foster, 1992.

1. *Number of Solutions*
   Solutions are considered separate only if they differ in a significant way. For example, telling the teacher, telling the principal, and telling the playground supervisor all would be considered one solution—that is, telling an authority.

2. *Effectiveness of Solutions*
   The characteristics of an effective solution are that it (1) is nonaggressive, (2) is likely to resolve the problem, and (3) does not result in adverse effects for the child or others. Ratings are as follows:

   1–2 Physical aggression
   3–4 Verbal aggression
     5 Nonaggressive but passive and unlikely to resolve problem
   6–7 Nonaggressive, prosocial, and active attempt to solve problem

3. *Sophistication of Planning*
   Ratings from 1 to 7 are based on the number of the following categories the child's problem-solving skills demonstrate.

   1. Sensitivity to possible consequences
   2. Anticipation of obstacles
   3. Reference to social rules
   4. Goal setting
   5. Amount of detail
   6. Realistic
   7. Sequential

also has a Spanish version.[90] The evidence is clear that adults and children can learn problem-solving skills, often very quickly.[91]

Do clients apply and benefit from problem-solving therapy/training? Controlled studies have not consistently found a relationship between children's acquisition of problem-solving skills and their behavioral adjustment.[92] Although children do learn problem-solving skills, changes in their problems at home and in school may not be clinically significant. Studies with adults have obtained similar findings.

What accounts for the disappointing general finding that clients do not consistently apply problem-solving skills they have learned to deal with actual problems in their lives? One possibility is that clients may not view difficulties in daily living as problems. This may be true particularly in cases in which reaction-focused goals are appropriate. One solution may be additional Stage 1 training in viewing life difficulties, including both situations and reactions to situations, as problems that can be solved or dealt with. Interestingly, one study found that a negative problem orientation was a strong predictor of depression and anxiety in adults.[93] *Negative problem orientation* refers to the general tendency (1) to appraise a problem as a threat, (2) to doubt one's own problem-solving ability, (3) to expect negative problem-solving outcomes, and (4) to show a low tolerance for frustration when confronted with a problem.

Another reason why clients fail to apply problem-solving techniques consistently may be that they lack the specific skills required to implement solutions. For instance, clients may not have the requisite knowledge and proficiency to competently perform the behaviors specified by the solution. This would be the case for a client who decided to confront her boss about unfair treatment but who did not have the appropriate assertive skills to carry out this course of action. Or clients may simply lack the motivation necessary to implement the solution, perhaps because it seems like too much effort.

Traditionally, problem-solving therapy/training has emphasized helping clients generate alternative solutions and selecting the optimal one. However, to get clients to apply problem-solving skills in their daily lives, more attention may need to be paid to adopting a problem-solving orientation and implementing solutions (Stages 1 and 6).

◆

Participation Exercise 13-2

SOLUTIONS, SOLUTIONS, AND MORE SOLUTIONS: PRACTICING PROBLEM SOLVING*

Solving problems can be fun if you view the process as a challenge. In this Participation Exercise, you will practice two stages of problem solving: generating alternative solutions and choosing the best solution.

Begin by reading the description of Situation 1 and follow the directions for generating solutions and selecting the best solution.

*This Participation Exercise can be done before you continue reading or later.

Situation 1. Although the weather report predicts rain, you are skeptical and walk to the library without a raincoat or umbrella. When it is time to come home, it is pouring. You live five blocks from the library and will get soaked walking home. *What could you do?*

Think of as many *different* solutions to the problem as you can. You are interested in *quantity,* not quality. Brainstorm: List any and all solutions, no matter how impractical or "far out" they appear. Of course, don't omit practical or conventional solutions. Even if you find what seems to be the most obvious or optimal solution, don't stop thinking of additional solutions. Write down your alternative solutions.

When you have a sizable list of solutions, rate the overall potential consequences of each. Consider (1) how successful you expect the solution to be and (2) the consequences of the solution for you and others. Using the following scale, write the appropriate rating next to each solution.

> 5 = very good
> 4 = good
> 3 = neutral
> 2 = poor
> 1 = very poor

Next, look at all the solutions you've rated *5* (very good), or *4* (good) if none is rated *5.* (If you have rated none of your solutions *4* or *5,* generate some additional solutions.) From among those solutions, choose the best one—that is, the one you think would result in the most satisfactory consequences.

Now repeat the same steps for Situation 2 and then Situation 3. When you have finished, continue reading the Participation Exercise.

Situation 2. You have a final exam Friday morning. A friend has lost her class notes and asks to borrow yours. You expect it will take a full day to go over the notes, and you plan to do that on Wednesday. You tell your friend that she can have the notes on Thursday morning. However, by Thursday morning you have not yet looked at your notes. You need to spend much of Thursday reviewing the notes, but you have promised your friend that she could have them Thursday morning. *What could you do?*

Situation 3. You are treating a friend to dinner. When it comes time to pay the check, you discover that you left your wallet at home. *What could you do?*

Consider what you have learned by doing this Participation Exercise. Did brainstorming help you generate solutions? Were you surprised by the number of different solutions possible for each of the problems? Can you identify any "mental blocks," such as rigid thinking, that impeded your generating alternative solutions? How well do you think the process of selecting the best solution worked? Finally, you may find it enlightening to compare your alternative solutions with someone else who did this Participation Exercise.

◆

STRESS INOCULATION TRAINING

People experience many life events—both large and small—as stressful. We have little control over many potentially stress-evoking events, ranging from earthquakes and serious illness to academic examinations and flat tires. However, we can control how we *view* and *cope* with such events. *Stress* broadly refers to an array of negative psychological reactions, including anxiety, anger, frustration, and depression, and a variety of physical ailments, including headaches, insomnia, fatigue, ulcers, and hypertension.[94]*

Basic Procedures

Meichenbaum, the creator of self-instructional training, developed **stress inoculation training** to help clients cope with stress-evoking events. Clients learn coping skills and then practice using them while being exposed to stress-evoking events.[95] The therapy is divided into three phases: (1) conceptualization, (2) coping skills acquisition, and (3) application.

PHASE 1: CONCEPTUALIZATION

The first phase of stress inoculation training is educational. The therapist explains to the client that events themselves do not cause negative emotional reactions, such as anxiety or anger; rather, the negative reactions arise from how we perceive these events. Clients are told that they can learn coping skills that will allow them to reconceptualize and deal with potentially stress-evoking events without becoming emotionally upset. Clients are encouraged to view coping as a simple, five-step process:

1. *Preparing* for the potentially stress-evoking event
2. *Confronting and coping with* the event
3. *Dealing with temporary difficulties* in coping
4. *Assessing one's performance* in coping with the event
5. *Reinforcing oneself* for successful coping

PHASE 2: COPING SKILLS ACQUISITION

In the second phase of stress inoculation training, the client learns and rehearses coping strategies. Although the specific coping skills depend on the nature of the client's problem, four general coping skills are employed most often: differential relaxation, cognitive restructuring, problem-solving self-instructions, and self-reinforcement/self-efficacy self-instructions.

Most clients who have stress-related problems experience muscle tension, which *differential relaxation* can alleviate. Similarly, clients generally

---

*In everyday usage, people use the term *stress* to refer both to *events* that result in adverse reactions and to the *reactions* themselves. This dualism is regrettable because it perpetuates the idea that events themselves cause adverse reactions. This idea is counter not only to cognitive-behavioral theorizing but also to the prevailing scientific conceptualization of stress (for example, Lazarus & Folkman, 1984).

Table 13-5 Examples of task-oriented problem-solving self-instructions used in stress inoculation training
SOURCE : Based on Meichenbaum & Deffenbacher, 1988.

Viewing the stressful situation as a problem

This is not the end of the world, just a problem to be solved.

It's okay to feel discouraged, but just remember that you can deal with this problem

Orienting to the stressful situation as a problem

Just think about what I can do about it.

Focus on the information I need to gather.

Breaking the stressful situation into smaller units

What are the steps I need to do?

How can I break this thing down so I can tackle one piece at a time?

Problem solving

Set up a plan of action. What is the first thing to do?

What's my goal? What would I like to happen?

have negative thoughts about potentially stress-evoking events and about their ability to cope with them. Clients can use *cognitive restructuring* to deal with negative thoughts. Examples of coping self-statements that clients might use are "This anxiety is a reminder to use my relaxation"; "Look for the positives, and don't assume the worst"; "I have a right to get annoyed, but I can keep the lid on"; and "When the pain increases, I can switch to a different coping strategy."

Clients whose problems are being maintained, in part, by not knowing how to approach and solve problems can benefit from *task-oriented problem-solving self-instructions*. As the examples in Table 13-5 illustrate, these self-instructions put the problem in perspective and focus the client's attention on concrete problem-solving steps.

Clients will continue to perform coping skills only if they are reinforced. Natural consequences, such as accomplishing goals, cannot be relied on to maintain coping skills, especially when the client is first beginning to apply coping skills and may not be successful. Thus, clients are taught individualized *self-reinforcement/self-efficacy self-instructions*, such as the examples in Table 13-6.

Table 13-6 Self-reinforcement/self-efficacy self-instructions used in stress inoculation training

Keep it up. You're doing great.

Hang in there. You're coping well.

I'm getting better and better at this.

That wasn't as bad as I expected. Next time it will be even easier.

I'm not doing as well as I would like, but I do feel good that I am continuing to try.

In addition to these general coping skills that are applicable to diverse problems, clients also may be taught coping skills that are tailored to specific problems. For fear, the client might learn to gather accurate information about threatening events. For chronic pain, the client might learn to use self-distracting thoughts.

PHASE 3: APPLICATION

In the first two phases of stress inoculation training, clients develop adaptive ways of viewing potentially stress-evoking events and learn coping skills to deal with them. In the third phase, clients apply their new outlooks and coping behaviors. Initially, this is done in therapy sessions through visualizing and role-playing potentially stress-evoking scenes. For example, a client who experiences panic attacks might be asked to visualize having an attack and coping with it (a variation of coping desensitization; see Chapter 9). Imagining the panic attack can be made more realistic by inducing hyperventilation, a common symptom in panic attacks,[96] as in interoceptive exposure (see Chapter 9). *Hyperventilation* is abnormally fast or deep respiration in which excessive amounts of air are taken in, causing tingling in the extremities, buzzing in the ears, and sometimes fainting. It can be induced by sustained blowing into a balloon.

A single session of stress inoculation training was used to help African-American children (average age 12 years) cope with pain associated with sickle cell anemia (a disease that is limited to the African-American population). The cognitive coping skills taught included relaxation, emotive imagery, and calming self-instructions. The therapist first described and modeled each skill for the clients. The clients then practiced each skill until they were proficient at it. Next, clients practiced the newly acquired coping skills while experiencing two trials of low-intensity laboratory-induced pain; the pain was created through the use of a pressure stimulator, in which a dull plastic edge is applied at a continuous pressure to a finger to gradually produce a dull, aching pain. The clients were given homework assignments involving daily practice of the skills along with audio taped instructions about how to perform the skills. The therapist also telephoned clients once during the week after treatment to prompt them to practice using their coping skills. In comparison to children in a standard care control group, those receiving stress inoculation training had lower levels of negative thinking and were less likely to report pain during the pain stimulation trials after treatment.[97]

For children who frequently engage in aggressive behaviors, anger coping programs (based on the work of John Lochman) include stress inoculation training as a component.[98] First the therapist teaches coping skills to the children in groups. Then, while other children taunt and tease the client for 30-second periods, each client practices implementing anger control strategies. Clients are given feedback on their performance and reinforced for using appropriate coping skills.

In the preceding examples, the simulated stress-evoking events with which clients practiced coping closely resembled the events the clients were expected to encounter in their daily lives. However, the simulated

THE FAR SIDE®   By GARY LARSON

stressors need not be the same as the actual events because clients usually are taught *general* coping skills applicable to a wide range of potentially stress-evoking events (which parallels coping desensitization procedures).

When clients have become proficient in applying coping skills to simulated stress-evoking events during therapy sessions, the therapist gives them homework assignments that gradually expose them to increasingly more stress-evoking events in real life. The therapist also trains clients in **relapse prevention,** which consists of specific procedures for handling the inevitable setbacks that occur in coping with real-life stress-evoking events.[99] For example, clients learn to view inevitable failures and setbacks as "learning experiences." The client and the therapist identify high-risk situations—those in which relapses are most likely—and rehearse coping with them. Relapse prevention is a specialized application of stress inoculation training that you will read about in more detail in Chapter 15.

Case 13-3 illustrates an innovative application of stress inoculation training to a serious problem that 4 years of psychoanalytic therapy (three times per week) had not successfully treated.

Case 13-3

Eliminating a Self-Mutilating Behavior Through Stress Inoculation Training[100]

Donna was a 32-year-old mother of two children who was hospitalized because of a severe self-mutilating behavior consisting of "savagely scratching the left side of her face, resulting in an extensive, deep and frequently bleeding scar." Donna had a 15-year history of self-mutilation.

Stress inoculation training was the major component of the treatment package that was designed for the client. During the educational phase, Donna kept a daily written log of (1) situations in which she felt the urge to scratch, (2) duration of the urges, (3) thoughts and feelings prior to and during scratching, and (4) thoughts and feelings after scratching. From this information, three situations that triggered her scratching emerged: looking at herself in the mirror; thinking about the scar on her face; and thinking about her estranged husband, who often had humiliated her because of the scratching. The increased tension she felt in these situations was relieved only by vigorous scratching, lasting a few minutes to several hours.

Donna was taught four coping skills: (1) muscle relaxation, (2) self-instructions, (3) covert sensitization, and (4) self-administered physically aversive consequences (slapping the hand that she used to scratch herself). She rehearsed these skills as she looked at herself in a mirror and as she visualized herself with her husband.

After six sessions over a 2-week period, Donna's scratching had declined and she went home for a visit. During the visit, she was unable to cope with a provocative encounter with her husband and reverted to scratching. After another six sessions of therapy, Donna again made a home visit. This time she was able to apply her coping skills to an anxiety-provoking incident involving her husband. This success experience was a turning point for Donna. Thereafter, she reported needing to rely on only two of the coping skills—relaxation and self-instructions—and expressed confidence in her ability to cope.

After 18 sessions, Donna was no longer scratching herself. She was discharged from the hospital and continued to keep a daily log. One year after therapy her scratching had not recurred, and she reported that she no longer had the urge to scratch and that her scar had healed. Further, she had held a full-time job for 6 months and had divorced her husband.

Case 13-3 illustrates how the successful treatment of one problem can have positive effects on other problems a client is experiencing. This is an advantage of treating one or two target behaviors at a time. After Donna's scratching had been eliminated, she was able to work full-time, which her self-mutilating behavior previously had precluded. Additionally, she was able to put her family life in order.

STRESS
INOCULATION
TRAINING:
PARALLELS WITH
BIOLOGICAL
IMMUNIZATION

Stress inoculation training is a behavioral analogue to *biological immunization*—such as a measles vaccination—in which disease-causing microorganisms are introduced into the body at doses too small to produce the physical symptoms of the disease. The body's immune system releases antibodies that fight off or neutralize the microorganisms. The antibodies remain in the system and are available to combat disease-causing microorganisms in the future, which strengthens the body's immune system.

Ernest Poser[101] first proposed the idea of psychologically immunizing people to stress-evoking events that result in maladaptive behaviors. *Behavioral immunology* involves exposing people to stress-evoking events in small doses and under safe conditions before they encounter the full-blown events in real life. Presumably, individuals preexposed to minor stress-evoking events develop, *on their own*, coping strategies that they can employ with future stress-evoking events.

Stress inoculation training does not rely on clients' devising their own coping skills. Instead, clients are directly taught a variety of coping skills that they rehearse while being exposed to controlled doses of stress-evoking events. Coping skills can be thought of as "psychological antibodies" that increase one's resistance to stress. The goal is for clients to be able to activate these stress-fighting coping skills as they encounter real-life stressors.

Stress Inoculation Training in Perspective

Stress inoculation training has been used to treat and prevent a wide array of problems in adults. The three most common problems have been anxiety,[102] anger,[103] and pain.[104] Specific problems treated include fear of flying,[105] presurgical anxiety,[106] coping with dental examinations,[107] reducing stress in cancer patients,[108] trauma (such as from terrorist attacks),[109] and child abuse by adults.[110] Stress inoculation training can be applied with groups of clients as well as individually.[111] Although stress inoculation training most often has been used with adults, it occasionally has been applied with children and adolescents, such as for dealing with aggressive behaviors[112] and refusal to attend school.[113] Unfortunately, controlled research on stress inoculation training applications to the problems of children and adolescents is lacking.[114]

Stress inoculation training recently has been used to treat posttraumatic stress disorder, especially with female victims of sexual and physical assault.[115] In one intensive treatment program involving nine biweekly individual sessions, therapists taught clients a variety of coping skills, including progressive relaxation, differential relaxation, thought stopping, cognitive restructuring, self-instructions, and covert modeling.[116] Clients practiced applying their coping skills to manage assault-related anxiety that arose during their daily activities. Stress inoculation training significantly reduced posttraumatic stress disorder symptoms and depression compared with clients in a wait-list control group, and clients maintained these gains at a 12-month follow-up. Stress inoculation training can be as effective as exposure therapy, which is the most frequently used treatment for posttraumatic stress disorder. Further, women who have been sexually assaulted consider stress inoculation training a palatable treatment.[117] Preliminary evidence also indicates that stress inoculation training is effective in treating posttraumatic stress disorder with 8- to 10-year-old girls and boys who were sexually abused.[118]

The stress inoculation model has potential for preparing people to deal with almost any stress-inducing event. For example, it may be useful for adolescents with gay, lesbian, and bisexual orientations who experience significant stress related to others' negative attitudes about homosexuality (homophobia); accepting one's sexual identity; disclosing one's sexual orientation to others; and developing relationships, both sexual and friendship based.[119]

Most controlled research studies evaluating stress inoculation training have indicated that it is an effective treatment.[120] Some studies have yielded impressive results; one investigation found stress inoculation training to be superior to medication in reducing symptoms of anxiety, depression, and subjective feelings of distress in adults.[121] Moreover, in a 3-year follow-up, patients given stress inoculation training had significantly fewer hospital readmissions than did patients treated with medication alone. Long-term treatment effects of stress inoculation training also have been found for the treatment of dental phobia.[122] Of clients who had received stress inoculation training, 70% were still going for regular dental checkups 1 to 4 years after treatment.

The essential treatment component in stress inoculation training appears to be *learning coping skills*. In a complex analysis of the treatment components of stress inoculation training for pain, for example, the complete training was compared with each phase alone, with all the possible pairs of phases, and with no treatment.[123] Although the complete package was superior to any of the partial treatments, the most substantial contribution to the effectiveness of stress inoculation training was the acquisition of coping skills. Another study contrasted coping skills alone, exposure to a stress-evoking event alone, and both coping skills and exposure for the treatment of pain.[124] Whereas exposure alone had little effect on pain tolerance, coping skills alone significantly increased pain tolerance (with the combined treatment's being even more effective). Because both of these investigations were analogue studies, it remains to be seen whether the findings hold in clinical studies.

If acquiring coping skills is essential to the success of stress inoculation training, then clients who experience difficulty learning new skills may not be suitable for stress inoculation training. One such population would be clients with limited or compromised cognitive abilities, such as people with traumatic brain injuries.[125]

Stress inoculation training has not been as extensively evaluated as other cognitive-behavioral therapies.[126] One possible reason is that stress inoculation training is a treatment package consisting of components that have been evaluated independently, including relaxation training, cognitive restructuring, and self-instructions. It is tempting to assume that combining therapies that are known to be effective will produce an even more potent treatment than any single therapy. However, it is possible that a component may be more effective alone than in combination with other therapies. Whether the whole is even equal to one of its parts is an empirical question that research must answer.

COGNITIVE-BEHAVIORAL COUPLE THERAPY

Problems in couple relationships—in or out of marriage, between same- or opposite-sex partners—are among the most frequent reasons that adults seek psychological assistance. Because couple relationships are complex and multifaceted, therapy generally involves treatment packages that address different aspects of couples' difficulties. The three basic components of cognitive-behavioral couple therapy are (1) training in communication and problem-solving skills, (2) increasing positive behavior exchanges, and (3) training in cognitive restructuring. The various approaches to cognitive-behavioral couple therapy differ in the emphasis they place on each of these components.

Training in Communication and Problem-Solving Skills

Communication is the basis for any interpersonal relationship, and poor communication is a common denominator among distressed couples.[127] Communication skills emphasized in cognitive-behavioral couple therapy include listening, restating what the other has said, expressing feelings directly, making requests, giving feedback, and arranging regular times to talk. Distressed couples also tend to have poor problem-solving skills. Both communication and problem-solving skills are taught to couples using standard skills training procedures (see Chapter 11).

Increasing Positive Behavior Exchanges

Distressed partners often do not feel especially loving toward one another, and not surprisingly, this is reflected in the negative ways they interact (for example, using sarcasm and doing things the other person dislikes). Accordingly, a general goal of cognitive-behavioral couple therapy is to increase partners' *positive behavior exchanges*.[128] One way to accomplish this goal is through the **caring-days technique,** developed by Richard Stuart, in which partners act *as if* they cared for each other.[129] The therapist instructs partners to perform small, specific, positive behaviors for each other (consistent with *My Fair Lady*'s Eliza Doolittle's request of Professor Higgins, "If you're in love, show me"). Each partner is asked to answer the question, "What would you like your partner to do that would show you that he or she cares for you?" and compile a list of these *caring behaviors*. The therapist instructs each partner to perform a minimum number of caring behaviors from his or her partner's list, even if his

Figure 13-6 Record of each partner's caring behaviors

Caring Behaviors Record

Week of June 16

Sandy does for Shelly	Su	Mo	Tu	We	Th	Fr	Sa
Ask how I'm feeling.		✓		✓	✓		
Play Scrabble with me.	✓	✓					
Do the dishes.		✓	✓		✓	✓	✓
Make me a cup of coffee.	✓		✓		✓		
Kiss me when I leave or come home.		✓	✓	✓		✓	
Put the cap on the tooth paste.	✓		✓	✓	✓		✓
Turn lights off.	✓		✓	✓	✓		
Compliment me.	✓		✓	✓	✓	✓	
Say "good night" before going to sleep.	✓	✓				✓	✓
Say "good morning," when I first wake up.						✓	✓

Shelly does for Sandy	Su	Mo	Tu	We	Th	Fr	Sa
Kiss me spontaneously.			✓		✓		✓
Call me at work to say hello.			✓	✓		✓	
Compliment my appearance.			✓	✓		✓	✓
Flush the toilet after using it.			✓	✓		✓	✓
Leave/send me short, loving notes.	✓	✓		✓			
Thank me for something I did.	✓	✓		✓			
Laugh at my jokes.	✓				✓	✓	✓
Keep your dresser neat.	✓		✓	✓			
Ask how my day went.		✓		✓		✓	

or her partner has not done so. The partners keep records of their performing the caring behaviors, such as the record in Figure 13-6.

Another way to increase positive behavior exchanges is through the Catch Your Partner Doing Something Nice technique.[130] Each partner notices and acknowledges one pleasing behavior performed by the other each day. Contingency contracts also are employed to promote positive behavior exchanges and implement broader behavior changes in the relationship.[131]

Training in Cognitive Restructuring

Discrepancies in partners' cognitions about aspects of their relationship often play a role in creating and maintaining couple problems. The discrepancies may be in (1) *perceptions* about what has occurred, (2) *attributions* about why a partner did something, (3) *expectations* about how

Table 13-7 Common cognitive discrepancies held by distressed couples

Discrepancy	Description	Example
PERCEPTIONS	Partners "see" things differently	PAT: "We haven't talked in months." CHRIS: "We talked just last week."
ATTRIBUTIONS	One partner wrongly infers the cause of other's behavior	PAT: "I've been waiting for a half hour. You just wanted to keep me waiting." CHRIS: "I'm late because I had a flat tire on the way here."
EXPECTATIONS	Partners anticipate different outcomes	PAT: "I was looking forward to making love tonight." CHRIS: "I was hoping to watch TV and just drift off to sleep."
ASSUMPTIONS	Partners hold different assumptions	PAT: "*You* are supposed to take care of the kids." CHRIS: "Taking care of *our* children is *our* responsibility."

Neil Jacobson

Andrew Christensen

Courtesy of Virginia Rutter

Courtesy of Andrew Christensen, UCLA

things will be, and (4) *assumptions* about how things are or should be (see Table 13-7).[132] To deal with these discrepancies, couples use cognitive restructuring and other cognitive-behavioral therapy procedures. Couples are taught first to evaluate how valid or reasonable their cognitions are and then to modify biased or unrealistic thoughts by substituting more appropriate and adaptive ones.

Integrative Behavioral Couple Therapy and the Goal of Acceptance

Cognitive-behavioral couple therapy traditionally has focused on changing those behaviors of each partner that are most upsetting to the other partner.[133] In contrast, Neil Jacobson and Andrew Christensen's **integrative behavioral couple therapy** establishes an alternative goal for distressed couples—namely, *acceptance of one's partner's upsetting behaviors*.[134]* In couple therapy, emotional acceptance is sometimes the only realistic goal. In some cases, partners are not willing to change particular behaviors that upset their partner, such as giving up a job that requires working nights or sleeping late in the morning. In other cases, a partner may be willing to change, but achieving the change may be extremely difficult and take a long time, as in overcoming long-standing emotional inhibitions or modifying habitual ways of behaving. And in some instances partners have limitations that are unchangeable, such as when physical conditions preclude engaging in particular activities that the other partner enjoys. Finally, partners will always have differences, which

*Acceptance should not be confused with the *acceptability* of behavior therapy procedures to clients and therapists, one of the criteria of treatment effectiveness (see Chapter 4).

implies that acceptance may be a fundamental requirement for long-term maintenance of satisfaction in a couple relationship.[135] At the risk of stating the obvious, when domestic violence is one of the presenting problems in couple therapy, acceptance is not a viable goal.

It is important to note that acceptance as a goal in the present context does not mean resignation to a troubled relationship as it is. Accepting one's partner's limitations or "unacceptable characteristics" can be a vehicle for promoting greater closeness and intimacy, which does change the nature of the relationship. Moreover, when acceptance is the goal of couple therapy there is an absence of pressure to change, and, paradoxically, the absence of pressure may create change.[136]

Acceptance as a goal in couple therapy is not a new idea. Until recently, however, concrete methods for promoting acceptance have not been available.[137] To promote acceptance, integrative behavioral couple therapy uses four strategies:

1. *Empathic joining* refers to the partners' learning to understand and appreciate each other's experience of emotional pain within the relationship, without introducing anger or blame. Empathic joining requires careful listening to one's partner's description of what he or she is experiencing, not judging the experience, and attempting to view the experience from the partner's perspective. The therapist helps the couple understand that the way they view and react to their differences—not the mere fact that they have differences (which is inevitable)—is primarily responsible for their interpersonal distress.[138]

2. *Detachment* fosters acceptance through the partners' distancing themselves from their conflicts. The partners are encouraged to talk and think about their difficulties as an "it"—something external to each of them rather than part of them.[139] The "it" becomes a painful, common enemy that they share and cope with together rather than a problem that one partner creates or something that one does to the other. Couples may feel less upset when talking about "it," even though the problem itself has not been resolved.

3. *Tolerance building* involves learning ways to become less upset by one's partner's behaviors. Through cognitive restructuring, partners come to view the other's so-called negative behaviors positively. For example, "moody" might be reconstrued as "thoughtful," "picky" as "careful," and "scatterbrained" as "free-wheeling." To effectively engage in such cognitive restructuring, the couple must understand that most behaviors are not inherently negative or positive. "Positive" and "negative" are evaluations we place on behaviors. Moreover, often the very behaviors that partners view as disturbing when they are experiencing conflict in their relationship are the same behaviors they found attractive in the past, particularly during courtship.[140] For instance, when they were dating, a man may have found a woman's willingness to do things on the spur of the moment refreshing. Several years into their marriage, however, the husband may complain that his wife is unpredictable and seems to change her mind all the time.

4. *Self-care* consists of each partner's developing ways to derive satisfaction and personal fulfillment independent of the relationship. This

promotes less dependence on one another for these basic life needs. Couples are asked to facilitate each other's engaging in self-care activities.

At first glance, the idea of promoting acceptance in distressed couples may not seem particularly behavioral. On closer inspection, it turns out to be well grounded in behavior therapy principles and procedures.[141] In addition to using specific cognitive-behavioral procedures (such as cognitive restructuring) to foster acceptance, the general approach is action-oriented. Partners engage in specific behaviors to develop acceptance. This active approach differs from traditional views of acceptance as passive resignation. Further, cognitive-behavioral couple therapy is highly individualized. For example, treatment is guided by an assessment of the maintaining conditions of the particular couple's conflicts rather than by a priori assumptions about what generally leads to conflicts in couples.

Cognitive-Behavioral Couple Therapy in Perspective

A number of well-controlled studies have demonstrated that cognitive-behavioral couple therapy can effectively reduce couples' distress.[142] Further, for married couples it has been found to alleviate depression.[143] This is an important finding because almost half the clients who seek treatment for depression have marital difficulties.[144] Cognitive-behavioral couple therapy also has shown particular promise in treating substance abuse.[145]

Unfortunately, cognitive-behavioral couple therapy is effective for only about two thirds of couples treated; of these couples, only about two thirds maintain their improvement over a 1- to 2-year period.[146] The net result is that less than half the couples treated with cognitive-behavioral couple therapy maintain the benefits after therapy. This sobering statistic was the impetus for developing the more durable goal of acceptance for couple therapy.[147] The results of one recent study indicate that couples receiving integrative behavioral couple therapy reported greater increases in marital satisfaction than couples receiving traditional cognitive-behavioral couple therapy.[148]

Couple relationship problems are difficult to treat because of their complex, multifaceted nature and because, over time, patterns of maladaptive interactions have been mutually reinforced. One way around this inevitable hurdle is to prevent such patterns from developing in the first place.[149] Toward this end, Howard Markman has developed a *prevention and relationship enhancement program* that parallels cognitive-behavioral couple therapy.[150] This preventive approach teaches couples specific skills that are associated with successful relationships, before they develop problems. The skills include communication, problem solving, negotiation of roles and responsibilities, and clarification of values and expectations related to sexuality and intimacy desires. The relationship-enhancement skills training approach has led to improved relationship satisfaction and positive perceptions of partners, lower levels of couple violence, and lower rates of separation.[151]

◆ ALL THINGS CONSIDERED: COGNITIVE-BEHAVIORAL COPING SKILLS THERAPY

Cognitive-behavioral coping skills therapies are used to treat a wide array of problem behaviors. In contrast to cognitive restructuring therapies (see Chapter 12), which are most applicable to adults, cognitive-behavioral coping skills therapies also are suitable for children and adolescents.

In general, the effectiveness of cognitive-behavioral coping skills therapy is well documented by research, especially for emotional problems such as anxiety and depression. However, the complexity of cognitive-behavioral coping skills therapy poses problems for evaluating its effectiveness. The therapy always involves a treatment package, and often the specific contributions of the various components are not assessed. Further, the specific components employed can vary from study to study, even though the same name is used to designate the therapy in each study. These variations may account, in part, for occasional discrepant findings of research evaluating cognitive-behavioral coping skills therapies.

The self-control nature of cognitive-behavioral coping skills therapies requires clients to accept major responsibility for the success of treatment, especially in the transfer of the coping skills to their everyday lives. Whereas the general findings are that clients can and do learn the coping skills, clients often fail to implement the coping skills on their own when the skills are needed.[152] This is true for employing self-instructions, problem-solving strategies, and coping skills learned and practiced in stress inoculation training, which is a major limitation of cognitive-behavioral coping skills therapies that needs to be addressed.

Cognitive-behavioral coping skills therapies have been used with ethnic minority and culturally diverse clients,[153] including those with gay, lesbian, and bisexual orientations.[154] The emphasis on self-control may be especially well suited for cultures that consider it shameful and embarrassing to seek help from others for personal problems.

Therapies that teach clients coping skills serve two functions. First, they enable clients to deal with the problems for which they have sought therapy. Second, clients may be able to apply the coping skills to future problems in their lives. For example, this is essential in treating *borderline personality disorder,* which is characterized by repeated unstable relationships, extreme mood changes, a negative self-image, and impulsive and often self-destructive behaviors. People with this debilitating disorder appear to have one crisis after another in their lives. Marsha Linehan developed *dialectical behavior therapy* specifically to treat borderline personality disorder.* One of its components is teaching clients cognitive-behavioral coping skills, including problem solving, relaxation, cognitive restructuring, and the use of assertive behaviors for dealing effectively with stress-evoking events.[155]

---

*Dialectical behavior therapy is rooted in a nonbehavioral "worldview" that incorporates Eastern spiritual philosophy and psychoanalytic concepts. However, it does include specific behavior therapy components, such as skills training and in vivo exposure.

◆ ALL THINGS CONSIDERED: COGNITIVE-BEHAVIORAL THERAPY

We conclude our discussion of cognitive-behavioral therapy, begun in Chapter 12, with some general comments on its current status. In 1968, a group of prominent behavior therapists suggested that "current [behavior therapy] procedures should be modified and new procedures developed to capitalize upon the human organism's unique capacity for cognitive control."[156] Clearly, this recommendation was heeded. Over the next decade, cognitive-behavioral therapy developed, with only minor opposition from those who believed that behavior therapy should deal only with overt behaviors.[157] By 1980, cognitive-behavioral therapy constituted a subfield of behavior therapy,[158] and today it is at the forefront of behavior therapy.[159] The cognitive-behavioral *Zeitgeist* (German for "spirit of the times") within behavior therapy parallels the "cognitive revolution" in psychology.[160] Bandura has argued that *all* behavior therapies are most usefully viewed as cognitive-behavioral:

> The field of psychological change is not well served by false dichotomies that there exist pure cognitive and pure [overt] behavioral treatments. One would be hard pressed to find a "behavioral" method that does not rely, at least in part, on cognitive conveyance [mediation], or a "cognitive" method that is devoid of any performance [overt behavioral] elements.[161]

To benefit from cognitive restructuring therapies (see Chapter 12), clients must possess the requisite cognitive skills, such as the ability to use language and to think abstractly. These abilities are linked to cognitive development,[162] which is one reason that cognitive restructuring therapies are more suitable for adults than children and adolescents.

In contrast, cognitive-behavioral coping skills therapies have been effective with children and adolescents, as well as clients with severe intellectual deficits. Because the treatment procedures are largely self-administered, successful treatment by cognitive-behavioral coping skills therapy requires clients to have relatively high motivation to change their behaviors. For instance, youngsters who are referred by adults for treatment of aggressive or impulsive behaviors generally have little motivation to change their behaviors. After all, it is the adults who want these children to behave differently. Thus, children may be capable of learning self-instructions and problem-solving skills, but they often cannot be relied on to apply them in their natural environments without additional interventions, such as prompting and reinforcement.[163]

SUMMARY

1. Cognitive-behavioral coping skills therapy treats problems that are maintained by a deficit of adaptive cognitions by changing both cognitions and overt behaviors.
2. In self-instructional training, clients learn to instruct themselves to cope effectively with difficult situations. Self-instructions serve

six functions: preparing clients to use self-instructions, focusing attention, guiding behavior, providing encouragement, evaluating performance, and reducing anxiety.

3. The five steps of self-instructional training are cognitive modeling, cognitive participant modeling, overt self-instructions, fading of overt self-instructions, and covert self-instructions.

4. Self-instructional training can be moderately effective when it is applied to narrowly focused problems that are maintained solely by inadequate task-related self-instructions. It is less effective as a treatment for broader problems that are maintained by more than just cognitive deficits.

5. Problem-solving therapy/training teaches clients a systematic strategy for approaching problems. Problem-solving therapy serves the dual purpose of treating clients' immediate problems and preparing clients to deal with future problems on their own. Problem-solving training teaches problem-solving skills as a general coping strategy for dealing with problems that arise in the course of daily life.

6. The seven stages of problem solving are adopting a problem-solving orientation, defining the problem, selecting goals, generating alternative solutions, choosing the best solution, implementing the best solution, and evaluating its effects. Problem-solving skills are taught to clients through cognitive modeling, prompting, self-instructions, and reinforcement.

7. Children and adults can learn problem-solving skills, often quickly. However, clients all too often do not apply the skills in their everyday lives.

8. Stress inoculation training helps clients cope with stress by teaching them coping skills and then having clients practice the skills while they are exposed to stress-evoking events. Stress inoculation training consists of three phases: conceptualization, coping skills acquisition, and application. Anxiety, anger, and pain are the most frequently treated problems. The essential component is learning coping skills.

9. Stress inoculation training is a behavioral analogue of biological immunization. The coping skills clients learn can be considered "psychological antibodies" that increase a person's resistance to potentially stress-evoking events.

10. The three basic components of cognitive-behavioral couple therapy are training in communication and problem-solving skills, increasing positive behavior exchanges, and training in cognitive restructuring. The usual goal of cognitive-behavioral couple therapy is for each partner to change behaviors that are problematic for the other. Integrative behavioral couple therapy employs the alternative goal of accepting each other's behaviors. A preventive approach to the problem of couple distress teaches couples specific skills that are associated with successful relationships.

REFERENCE NOTES

1. Rankin, 1960.
2. Meichenbaum & Goodman, 1971.
3. For example, Camp & Bash, 1981; Camp, Blom, Herbert, & Van Doorwick, 1977; Spivack & Shure, 1974.
4. For example, Meichenbaum & Cameron, 1973; Meyers, Mercatoris, & Sirota, 1976.
5. For example, Guevremont, Tishelman, & Hull, 1985.
6. Meichenbaum & Goodman, 1971, p. 117.
7. Meichenbaum, 1977.
8. Guevremont, Osnes, & Stokes, 1988.
9. Kendall & Braswell, 1985.
10. For example, Guevremont, Tishelman, & Hull, 1985.
11. For example, Lochman, 1985; Lochman & Curry, 1986a.
12. For example, Bryant & Budd, 1982; Guevremont, Osnes, & Stokes, 1988.
13. Burgio, Whitman, & Johnson, 1980.
14. For example, Kendall & Wilcox, 1980; Schleser, Meyers, & Cohen, 1981.
15. For example, Kendall & Finch, 1978; Meichenbaum & Goodman, 1971.
16. Bentall, Higson, & Lowe, 1987; Meichenbaum & Cameron, 1973; Meyers, Mercatoris, & Sirota, 1976.
17. Combs & Lahey, 1981.
18. For example, Holroyd, 1976; McCordick, Kaplan, Finn, & Smith, 1979.
19. For example, Cradock, Cotler, & Jason, 1978; Meichenbaum, Gilmore, & Fedoravicius, 1971.
20. For example, Glass, Gottman, & Shmurak, 1976.
21. Kendall, 1994; Ollendick, Hagopian, & King, 1997.
22. For example, Camp, Blom, Herbert, & Van Doorwick, 1977; Foreman, 1980.
23. Overhoser & Fine, 1994.
24. For example, Dunkel & Glaros, 1978.
25. For example, Kettlewell, Mizes, & Wasylyshyn, 1992.
26. Cash & Lavallee, 1997.
27. Gil, Carson, Sedway, Porter, Schaeffer, & Orringer, 2000.
28. For example, Carmody, 1978; Craighead, 1979; Jacobs & Cochran, 1982; Kaplan, 1982; Kazdin & Mascitelli, 1982.
29. For example, Labouvie-Vief & Gonda, 1976; Meichenbaum, 1974.
30. Keogh, Faw, Whitman, & Reid, 1984.
31. Meichenbaum, 1975.
32. O'Callaghan & Couvadelli, 1998; Suzman, Morris, Morris, & Milan, 1997.
33. Ecton & Feindler, 1990.
34. Rusch, Hughes, & Wilson, 1995.
35. For example, Rusch, Morgan, Martin, Riva, & Agran, 1985.
36. For example, Hughes & Rusch, 1989.
37. For example, Rusch, Martin, Lagomarcino, & White, 1987.
38. For example, Sowers, Rusch, Connis, & Cummings, 1980.
39. For example, Kendall & Wilcox, 1980; Lochman & Curry, 1986a; Woodward & Jones, 1980.
40. For example, Ollendick, Hagopian, & King, 1997.
41. For example, Guevremont, Osnes, & Stokes, 1988.
42. For example, Denney, Sullivan, & Thiry, 1977; Goren, 1975.
43. For example, D'Zurilla & Chang, 1995.
44. For example, Asarnow & Callan, 1985; Biggam & Power, 1999; Doerfler, Mullins, Griffin, Siegel, & Richards, 1984; D'Zurilla, Chang, Nottingham, & Faccini, 1998; D'Zurilla & Nezu, 1982; Frye & Goodman, 2000; Kant, D'Zurilla, & Maydeu-Olivares, 1997; Lochman & Curry, 1986b; McCabe, Blankstein, & Mills, 1999; Nezu & D'Zurilla, 1989; Rudd, Joiner, & Rajab, 2001; Sayers, Bellack, Wade, Bennett, & Fong, 1995.
45. For example, Meichenbaum & Jaremko, 1982.
46. For example, Arean, Perri, Nezu, Schein, Christopher, & Joseph, 1993; Nezu, Nezu, & Perri, 1989.
47. Kleiner, Marshall, & Spevack, 1987.
48. Black, 1987; Johnson, Corrigan, & Mayo, 1987.
49. Shaffer, Beck, & Boothroyd, 1983.
50. Bujold, Ladouceur, Sylvain, & Boisvert, 1994.
51. Jacobson, 1991; Jacobson & Margolin, 1979; O'Leary & Turkewitz, 1978.
52. Dawson, De Armas, McGrath, & Kelly, 1986; MacMillan, Guevremont, & Hansen, 1989.
53. Hansen, St. Lawrence, & Christoff, 1985.
54. Falloon & Coverdale, 1994.
55. Varni, La Greca, & Spirito, 2000.
56. For example, Kendall & Gerow, 1995.

57. For example, Lascelles, Cunningham, McGrath, & Sullivan, 1989.
58. Braet & Winckel, 2000.
59. For example, Kazdin, Esveldt-Dawson, French, & Unis, 1987.
60. Lochman & Curry, 1986a; Lochman, Nelson, & Sims, 1981.
61. Bujold, Ladouceur, Sylvain, & Boisvert, 1994.
62. Feindler, Ecton, Kingsley, & Dubey, 1986; Feindler, Marriott, & Iwata, 1984.
63. Frisby, 1990.
64. Shure & Spivack, 1980; Spivack & Shure, 1974.
65. Robin & Foster, 1989.
66. For example, Kendall & Gerow, 1995.
67. Tarrier, Kinney, McCarthy, Humphreys, Wittkowski, & Morris, 2000.
68. Weisenberg, Gesten, Carnike, Toro, Rapkin, Davidson, & Cowen, 1981.
69. For example, D'Zurilla, 1986; D'Zurilla & Goldfried, 1971; D'Zurilla & Sheedy, 1991.
70. For example, D'Zurilla & Goldfried, 1971; Spivack & Shure, 1974.
71. D'Zurilla & Nezu, 2001.
72. Nezu, Nezu, D'Zurilla, & Rothenberg, 1996.
73. Nezu, Nezu, D'Zurilla, & Rothenberg, 1996.
74. Nezu, Nezu, D'Zurilla, & Rothenberg, 1996; Nezu, Nezu, & Houts, 1993; Watson & Kramer, 1995.
75. Spivack & Shure, 1974.
76. Braswell & Kendall, 2001.
77. For example, Sharp, 1981; Spivack & Shure, 1974.
78. For example, Giebink, Stover, & Fahl, 1968; Kazdin, Esveldt-Dawson, French, & Unis, 1987; Weisenberg, Gesten, Carnike, Toro, Rapkin, Davidson, & Cowen, 1981; Yu, Harris, Solovitz, & Franklin, 1986.
79. Feindler, Marriott, & Iwata, 1984.
80. Feindler, Ecton, Kingsley, & Dubey, 1986.
81. Grothberg, Feindler, White, & Stutman, 1991; Robin & Foster, 1989.
82. Nangle, Carr-Nangle, & Hansen, 1994.
83. Adapted from Guevremont & Foster, 1992.
84. D'Zurilla & Nezu, 2001.
85. D'Zurilla & Nezu, 1999.
86. Arean, Perri, Nezu, Schein, Christopher, & Joseph, 1993.
87. D'Zurilla, Chang, Nottingham, & Faccini, 1998; Rudd, Joiner, & Rajab, 2001.
88. Nezu, Nezu, D'Zurilla, & Rothenberg, 1996; Nezu, Nezu, & Houts, 1993.
89. Maydeu-Olivares & D'Zurilla, 1997.
90. Maydeu-Olivares, Rodriguez-Fornells, Gomez-Benito, & D'Zurilla, 2000.
91. For example, D'Zurilla & Nezu, 1982; Sharp, 1981; Shure & Spivack, 1980; Spivack & Shure, 1974; Weisenberg, Gesten, Carnike, Toro, Rapkin, Davidson, & Cowen, 1981; Yu, Harris, Solovitz, & Franklin, 1986.
92. Yu, Harris, Solovitz, & Franklin, 1986; compare with D'Zurilla & Maschka, 1988.
93. McCabe, Blankstein, & Mills, 1999.
94. Cofer & Appley, 1964; Lazarus & Folkman, 1984.
95. Meichenbaum, 1977, 1985.
96. Barlow & Cerney, 1988.
97. Gil, Wilson, Edens, Workman, Ready, Sedway, Redding-Lallinger, & Daeschner, 1997.
98. Lochman, in press; Lochman & Lenhart, 1993; Lochman, Whidby, & FitzGerald, 2000; Nelson & Finch, 2000.
99. Marlatt & Gordon, 1985.
100. Kaminer & Shahar, 1987; quotation from p. 289.
101. Poser, 1970; Poser & King, 1975; Spiegler, 1980.
102. Meichenbaum & Cameron, 1972; Suinn, 2001.
103. Novaco, 1975, 1977a, 1977b; Suinn, 2001.
104. Turk, 1975, 1976.
105. Meichenbaum & Deffenbacher, 1988.
106. For example, Wells, Howard, Nowlin, & Vargas, 1986.
107. For example, Getka & Glass, 1992; Liddell, Di Fazio, Blackwood, & Ackerman, 1994; Moses & Hollandsworth, 1985; Siegel & Peterson, 1980.
108. Elsesser, Van Berkel, Sartory, Biermann-Göcke, & Öhl, 1994.
109. Meichenbaum & Deffenbacher, 1988.
110. Meichenbaum & Deffenbacher, 1988.
111. For example, Lochman, in press; Lochman & Lenhart, 1993; Lochman, Whidby, & FitzGerald, 2000; Meichenbaum & Deffenbacher, 1988; Nelson & Finch, 2000.
112. For example, Feindler, Ecton, Kingsley, & Dubey, 1986; Feindler, Marriott, & Iwata, 1984; Lochman & Curry, 1986a; Lochman, Nelson, & Sims, 1981.
113. King, Tonge, Heyne, Pritchard, Rollings, Young, Myerson, & Ollendick, 1998.
114. Maag & Kotlash, 1994.
115. Foa & Rothbaum, 1998; Rothbaum, Meadows, Resick, & Foy, 2000.

116. Foa, Dancu, Hembree, Jaycox, Meadows, & Street, 1999.
117. Meadows & Foa, 1998; Muran & DiGiuseppe, 2000.
118. Farrell, Hains, & Davies, 1998.
119. Safren, Hollander, Hart, & Heimberg, 2001.
120. Meichenbaum, 1985; Meichenbaum & Deffenbacher, 1988.
121. Meichenbaum & Deffenbacher, 1988.
122. Liddell, Di Fazio, Blackwood, & Ackerman, 1994.
123. Vallis, 1984.
124. Horan, Hackett, Buchanan, Stone, & Stone, 1977.
125. Aeschleman & Imes, 1999.
126. For example, Maag & Kotlash, 1994.
127. For example, Geiss & O'Leary, 1981.
128. For example, Jacobson & Margolin, 1979; Patterson & Reid, 1970.
129. Stuart, 1969, 1980.
130. O'Farrell & Fals-Stewart, 2000.
131. Baucom & Epstein, 1990; Jacobson & Margolin, 1979; O'Farrell & Fals-Stewart, 2000; Stuart, 1969, 1980.
132. Baucom & Epstein, 1990; Beck, 1989.
133. For example, Stuart, 1980.
134. Christensen, Jacobson, & Babcock, 1995; Jacobson, 1991, 1992, 1993; Jacobson & Christensen, 1996.
135. Waller & Spiegler, 1997.
136. Jacobson, Christensen, Prince, Cordova, & Eldridge, 2000.
137. Waller & Spiegler, 1997.
138. Compare with Waller & Spiegler, 1997.
139. Compare with White, 1989, 1995.
140. Waller & Spiegler, 1997.
141. Jacobson, 1992.
142. Baucom & Hoffman, 1986; Baucom, Shoham, Mueser, Daiuto, & Stickle, 1998; Hahlweg & Markman, 1988; Jacobson, 1989.
143. For example, Baucom, Shoham, Mueser, Daiuto, & Stickle, 1998; Beach & O'Leary, 1992.
144. Beach, Whisman, & O'Leary, 1994.
145. Epstein & McCrady, 1998; O'Farrell & Fals-Stewart, 2000.
146. Christensen, Jacobson, & Babcock, 1995.
147. Christensen, Jacobson, & Babcock, 1995.
148. Jacobson, Christensen, Prince, Cordova, & Eldridge, 2000.
149. Jacobson & Addis, 1993; Sullivan & Bradbury, 1996.
150. Markman, Floyd, Stanley, & Lewis, 1986; Markman, Renick, Floyd, Stanley, & Clements, 1993.
151. Hahlweg & Markman, 1988; Markman, Floyd, Stanley, & Storaasli, 1988; Markman, Renick, Floyd, Stanley, & Clements, 1993; Stanley, Markman, St. Peters, & Leber, 1995.
152. For example, Peterson, Crowson, Saldana, & Holdridge, 1999.
153. Hansen, Zamboanga, & Sedlar, 2000; Paniagua, 1998.
154. Safren, Hollander, Hart, & Heimberg, 2001.
155. Linehan, 1993a, 1993b; Linehan, Armstrong, Suarez, Allmon, & Heard, 1991; Linehan, Heard, & Armstrong, 1993; Linehan & Schmidt, 1995.
156. Davison, D'Zurilla, Goldfried, Paul, & Valins, 1968.
157. For example, Ledwidge, 1978, 1979; Locke, 1979; Mahoney & Kazdin, 1979; Meichenbaum, 1979; Zettle & Hayes, 1982.
158. Spiegler, 1983.
159. Kendall, 1987b; Spiegler & Guevremont, 2002.
160. Dember, 1974.
161. Bandura, 1986a, p. 14.
162. Bernard & Joyce, 1984; Morris & Cohen, 1982; Schleser, Meyers, & Cohen, 1981.
163. For example, Kendall, 1993.

PART III

BROADER APPLICATIONS AND ISSUES

Now that you have digested the appetizers (basic principles) and the main course (behavior therapies), it's time for dessert. Dessert is supposed to be a treat, and we hope that what we have prepared will be one for you. It consists of a sample of the applications of behavior therapy principles and procedures to issues of health. Chapter 14 describes how behavior therapy procedures are employed to treat and prevent medical disorders. Chapter 15 discusses the role that behavior therapy can play in treating psychological disorders whose primary features are physical problems. You will be familiar with most of the behavior therapy procedures described in Chapters 14 and 15, but their applications will be new. The applications illustrate the versatility and breadth of behavior therapy principles and procedures and serve as a review of previous material.

Then, having finished dessert, it is time to sit back and reflect on your elaborate dinner. In place of coffee or tea, in the final chapter we offer the chef's selection of the hearty strengths and tempting challenges to behavior therapy, seasoned with some spicy controversies surrounding its future.

Chapter 14 **Applications to Behavioral Medicine**

Chapter 15 **Applications to Psychological Disorders with Primary Physical Characteristics**

Chapter 16 **Contemporary Behavior Therapy in Perspective: Strengths, Challenges, and Controversies**

Applications to Behavioral Medicine

The application of behavioral principles and procedures to physical health and illness burgeoned in the last two decades of the 20th century and is a flourishing endeavor in the new millennium. Much of this work is subsumed under the interdisciplinary field known as *behavioral medicine.* The field applies behavioral science, including behavior therapy, to the assessment, treatment, management, rehabilitation, and prevention of physical disease and related behavioral reactions to physical dysfunction.[1]

Behavior therapy serves four functions in dealing with medical disorders: (1) treating medical disorders; (2) increasing adherence to medical treatments, such as taking medication; (3) helping patients cope with treatments and illness; and (4) preventing medical disorders. Table 14-1 describes and gives examples of these four functions. In discussing each function, we present representative examples of the medical disorders with which behavior therapy deals. They further illustrate the versatility of behavior therapy.

TREATMENT OF MEDICAL DISORDERS

Behavior therapy can add to existing medical treatments in three ways. First, behavior therapy can be combined with medical treatments (for example, both relaxation training and medication can be employed to control high blood pressure). Second, behavior therapy may be more desirable than medical treatments that are associated with risk (such as with surgery) or with undesirable side effects (such as with medication). Third, behavior therapy can play an especially important role in cases for which no viable medical treatments exist (as for certain types of chronic

Table 14-1 Functions of behavior therapy in dealing with medical disorders

Function	Description	Example
TREATMENT	Correct or alleviate a medical condition and the pain and suffering associated with it	Relaxation training to lower blood pressure in patients with essential hypertension
ADHERENCE	Increase patients' following prescribed medical treatments (such as medication, diet, and exercise)	Taking medication at the same time each day so that it will come under stimulus control
COPING	Reduce anxiety, discomfort, and distress associated with medical procedures	Self-instructional training to decrease the anxiety associated with dental work
PREVENTION	Reduce the risk of developing disease, including motivating people to engage in healthful behaviors	Assertion training to promote safer sexual practices (such as refusing to engage in unprotected sex)

pain). We will illustrate the use of behavior therapy to treat medical disorders by describing its application to three medical problems: essential hypertension, chronic pain, and medically unexplained symptoms.

Essential Hypertension

Cardiovascular disease is the leading cause of death in the United States, claiming about 1 million lives annually.[2] Affecting approximately 15% of the population, high blood pressure is a major contributor to cardiovascular disorders, including heart attacks and strokes, as well as to other physical disorders, such as kidney failure.[3] *Essential hypertension* is chronic high blood pressure with no physical cause that can be treated directly. For convenience, we will shorten the term *essential hypertension* to *hypertension.*

Despite the well-known health hazards of hypertension, providing patients with basic medical information about reducing blood pressure frequently is insufficient to lead to significant reductions.[4] Hypertension most often is treated with medication. Although antihypertensive medication generally is effective in lowering blood pressure, its extended use may actually increase the risk of cardiovascular disease. Further, it is estimated that up to 50% of patients stop taking medication within a year of diagnosis, and a smaller percentage do not take enough medication to control their hypertension.[5] Thus, there is a need for nonpharmacological treatments.

Both relaxation training and biofeedback sometimes are employed by themselves to treat mild or moderate hypertension. Typically, relaxation or biofeedback is used in conjunction with medication, in which case it often is possible to lower the drug dosage. Relaxation and biofeedback directly influence blood pressure, in contrast to other nonpharmacological treatments, such as diet and exercise, that indirectly change contributory conditions.

RELAXATION TRAINING

Edmund Jacobson, the father of relaxation training, pioneered its use to reduce hypertension.[6] Patients may be taught progressive relaxation by a behavior therapist or given instructions (such as on an audio tape) by a physician and practice the skills at home.[7] (Meditation, which is not a behavior therapy, is the other technique for inducing relaxation and also is used to treat hypertension.[8])

There are two approaches to using relaxation to lower blood pressure. One is to set aside one or two 15- to 30-minute periods each day to induce progressive relaxation.[9] It is assumed that the relaxed state achieved during these periods will transfer to the remainder of patients' daily activities. The other approach employs differential relaxation as a coping skill, as in coping desensitization (see Chapter 9). The patient is taught to rapidly relax all nonessential muscles (those not being used to perform ongoing behaviors) and to tense essential muscles only as much as needed to perform ongoing behaviors. The patient then learns to use environmental cues typically associated with rising blood pressure (for example,

Visual Image Presentations

Edmund Jacobson

being in a stressful situation) to prompt the use of differential relaxation.[10] Clients often employ both approaches.[11]

Differential relaxation is a highly useful skill that can help anyone cope with everyday stress-evoking events. Participation Exercise 14-1 can teach you differential relaxation. Although learning differential relaxation will require a number of days of practice, reading the Participation Exercise now will give you a more complete understanding of the technique.

◆

**Participation
Exercise 14-1**

PROGRESSIVELY MAKING A DIFFERENCE IN YOUR LIFE WITH PROGRESSIVE AND DIFFERENTIAL RELAXATION

Differential relaxation allows us to get rid of excess muscle tension as we engage in our normal behaviors. Learning differential relaxation requires that you first learn progressive relaxation and then practice relaxing your nonessential muscles during the course of everyday activities.

Part I: Preparation

You will need a comfortable firm surface where you can lie down, such as on a rug, a mat, or a firm bed. The practice location should be free of distractions. Turn off the phone, tell roommates you'll be busy for about an hour, place a "Do Not Disturb" sign on your door, and so on. If you are interrupted, just resume where you left off. Open this book to Table 14-2, and place the book close to where you will be lying down, as you will need to refer to the table for the specific relaxation instructions for each muscle group.

Part II: Learning Progressive Relaxation

You will learn progressive relaxation in two phases. In the first phase, you will tense each muscle group before relaxing it. This procedure will make you aware of the sensations associated with muscle tension. Then, whenever you experience these sensations, you will know that you need to apply differential relaxation. In the second phase of training, you will relax your muscles without first deliberately tensing them, which simulates your using differential relaxation in everyday situations.

PHASE 1: TENSION AND RELAXATION

Before you begin, remember two things. First, during your practice, *concentrate on the sensations of tension and relaxation* and try not to let your mind wander to other thoughts. Second, *do not fall asleep* while practicing. (However, once you learn progressive relaxation, you will be able to use it to help you fall asleep.)

Loosen tight clothing; remove your shoes and any articles of clothing or jewelry that might interfere with the relaxation exercises. Lie flat on your back with your legs slightly apart and your arms at your sides. Adjust your body so that you are comfortable. To remove visual distractions, keep your eyes lightly shut, except to read the relaxation instructions.

Table 14-2 Tensing instructions for learning progressive relaxation (Participation Exercise 14-1)

Part A: 16 Muscle Groups	
Muscle Group	Tensing Instructions
A1. Dominant hand and forearm (right hand if you're right-handed)	A1. Make a tight fist.
A2. Dominant biceps	A2. Push your elbow down against the floor (or bed), and simultaneously pull the elbow inward toward your body.
A3. Nondominant hand and forearm	A3. Follow instruction A1.
A4. Nondominant biceps	A4. Follow instruction A2.
A5. Upper part of face (forehead and scalp)	A5. Lift your eyebrows as high as you can. (Alternative: make an exaggerated frown.)[a]
A6. Central part of face (upper cheeks and nose)	A6. Squint your eyes tightly, and simultaneously wrinkle up your nose.
A7. Lower part of face (jaw and lower part of cheeks)	A7. Clench your teeth together, and pull the corners of your mouth back. *Caution:* Do not clench your teeth very hard—just enough to feel tension in your jaw and cheeks.
A8. Neck and throat	A8. Pull your chin down toward your chest, and simultaneously try to keep your chin from touching your chest. (You should feel a small amount of trembling or shaking in your neck.) (Alternative: Press your head against the floor or bed.)[a]
A9. Chest, shoulders, and upper back	A9. Take a deep breath and hold it; at the same time pull your shoulders back as if you were trying to make your shoulder blades touch each other. (Alternative: Pull your shoulders upward as if you were trying to touch your shoulder blades to your ears. It may help to imagine that puppet strings are attached to your shoulders, which are being pulled upward.)[a]

[a]Use the alternative tensing strategy only when the first one presented does not create tension in the appropriate muscle group.

(continued)

Table 14-2 *(continued)*

Part A: 16 Muscle Groups (continued)	
Muscle Group	*Tensing Instructions*
A10. Abdomen	A10. Make your stomach hard, as if you were bracing before being hit in the stomach. (Alternatives: Pull your stomach in as far as it will go. Or push your stomach out as far as it will go.)[a]
A11. Dominant thigh (upper leg)	A11. Keeping your leg straight, lift it a few inches off the floor.
A12. Dominant calf (lower leg)	A12. Pull your toes upward toward your head (without moving your legs).
A13. Dominant foot	A13. Point your toes downward, turn your foot inward, and curl your toes downward (as if you were burying them in the sand). *Caution:* Do not tense these muscles very hard or very long—just enough to feel the tightness under your arch and the ball of your foot for about three to five seconds. (You may also feel some tension in your calf.)
A14. Nondominant thigh	A14. Follow instruction A11.
A15. Nondominant calf	A15. Follow instruction A12.
A16. Nondominant foot	A16. Follow instruction A13.

Part B: 7 Muscle Groups	
Muscle Group	*Tensing Instructions*
B1. Dominant hand, forearm, and biceps	B1. Hold your arm out in front of you with your elbow bent at about 45 degrees while making a fist. (Alternative: Leave your arm supported on the floor or bed. Bend your arm at the elbow [about 45 degrees], make a fist, and press your elbow down or in toward your body.)[a]
B2. Nondominant hand, forearm, and biceps	B2. Follow instruction B1.

[a]Use the alternative tensing strategy only when the first one presented does not create tension in the appropriate muscle group.

Table 14-2 *(continued)*

Part B: 7 Muscle Groups *(continued)*	
Muscle Group	*Tensing Instructions*
B3. Face	B3. At the same time, raise your eyebrows (or frown), squint your eyes, wrinkle your nose, bite down, and pull the corners of your mouth back.[b]
B4. Neck and throat	B4. Follow instruction A8.
B5. Chest, shoulders, upper back, and abdomen	B5. Take a deep breath and hold it, pull your shoulder blades back and together, and make your stomach hard (or pull it in or push it out).
B6. Dominant thigh, calf, and foot	B6. Lift your leg up a few inches off the floor or bed, point your toes downward, and turn your foot inward.
B7. Nondominant thigh, calf, and foot	B7. Follow instruction B6.

Part C: 4 Muscle Groups	
Muscle Group	*Tensing Instructions*
C1. Both hands, forearms, and biceps	C1. Follow instruction B1 for both sides simultaneously.
C2. Face, throat, and neck	C2. Follow instructions B3 and A8 simultaneously.
C3. Chest, shoulders, back, and abdomen	C3. Follow instruction B5.
C4. Both thighs, calves, and feet	C4. Follow instruction B6 for both sides simultaneously.

[b]This procedure may be a bit difficult at first, but a few practice sessions will make simultaneous tensing of all the facial muscles relatively easy.

When you are ready to begin, take a few deep breaths. Start with the first of the 16 muscle groups (instruction A1 in Table 14-2, Part A). *Tense those muscles for about 5 seconds* (you may wish to count to yourself, "one-thousand-one, one-thousand-two," and so on). Tense the muscles tightly, but do *not* strain them. You should definitely feel the tension, but it should not hurt. As you tense the muscles, concentrate on the physical sensations you experience.

After 5 seconds of tensing, say "relax" or "calm" to yourself and *gradually* relax the muscles you have just tensed. *Make your muscles loose; smooth them out.* Continue relaxing your muscles for at least 30 seconds until they feel totally relaxed. As you relax, pay attention to the sensations of relaxation, *noting the difference between the sensations of relaxation and tension.*

Now repeat the tension-relaxation sequence for the same muscle group (instruction A1).

After you have tensed and relaxed the first muscle group (instruction A1) *twice,* proceed to the next muscle group (instruction A2) and go through the tension-relaxation sequence twice. Continue until you have gone through all of the 16 muscle groups (instructions A1 through A16). This should take about 45 minutes at first and less time as you become familiar with the tensing procedures and proficient at relaxing your muscles.

After you have tensed and relaxed each of the 16 muscle groups twice, remain in a relaxed state for several minutes. If you feel tension in any of your muscles during this period, try to relax that tension away by making your muscles loose and smooth.

To end the practice session, slowly count backward from 4 to 1, following these instructions for each number:

- At *4* begin to move your legs and feet.
- At *3* move your arms and hands.
- At *2* move your head and neck.
- At *1* open your eyes.

When you reach *1, you should feel relaxed and calm, as if you had just awakened from a restful sleep.* Sit up slowly. When you are ready, stand up.

Devote at least three practice sessions to tensing and relaxing each of the 16 muscle groups (instructions A1 through A16) and more if you still are feeling tension in any of your muscles at the end of a session.

Next, follow the instructions just outlined for the seven muscle groups (instructions B1 through B7 in Table 14-2, Part B) for at least two sessions. Finally, spend at least two sessions tensing and relaxing each of the four muscle groups (instructions C1 through C4 in Table 14-2, Part C).

PHASE 2: RELAXATION ONLY

In this phase of training, you will just relax your muscles (without any initial tensing). Begin with the first muscle group (A1), and relax those muscles as deeply as you can. Even when you think your muscles are completely relaxed, it is always possible to relax them a bit more. Proceed through each of the 16 muscle groups (instructions A1 through A16), relaxing each for at least 60 seconds until they are completely relaxed. When you have relaxed all of the 16 muscle groups, follow the same procedure described earlier for concluding the practice session. Remember: Now you are *only relaxing* your muscles; do *not* tense them first.

Spend a minimum of two sessions relaxing each of the 16 muscle groups, then at least two sessions relaxing each of the 7 muscle groups, and finally at least two sessions relaxing each of the 4 muscle groups. Many people find that a few muscle groups are especially hard to relax, so you may need to spend more time practicing relaxing "troublesome" muscles.

Part III: Differential Relaxation

When you have completed the two phases of progressive relaxation training, you are ready to apply these skills to differential relaxation. In the course of your everyday activities, whenever you experience tension in your nonessential muscles (those not being used to perform your present activity), relax them. In addition, relax any excess tension in your essential muscles; these muscles should have the minimum tension required to perform the activity.

You can use differential relaxation at almost any time, such as while driving your car, eating a meal, standing in line, or sitting in class. Use muscle tension as a signal to relax. You may find it helpful to say the self-instruction "relax" or "calm" at the first sign of muscle tension and then proceed to relax the muscles. It is likely that you will discover that you experience more tension in some of your muscles than others, and you may want to devote some additional practice with these specific muscles following the instructions for phase 2.

◆

BIOFEEDBACK

Biofeedback provides information (feedback) about a physiological function, such as blood pressure, to help the person modify that function. The individual is "hooked up" to electromechanical equipment, such as a polygraph, that records physiological functions and provides the individual with information about them (see Photo 14-1). For example, a tone or visual display on a computer screen might be used to indicate that blood pressure is below a pre-established level.[12] Patients being treated for hypertension are instructed to keep their blood pressure below this level. Patients report using a variety of strategies to accomplish this goal, such as visualizing pleasant images. Once patients have learned to lower their blood pressure by using biofeedback, they then need to learn to achieve the same outcome without biofeedback. This involves becoming attuned

Photo 14-1 In biofeedback training, electrodes attached to the client transmit information about a physiological function, such as muscle tension, to electromechanical equipment that provides the client with feedback about a physiological state.

© 1997 Michael D. Spiegler and David C. Guevremont

to the sensations associated with both lower and higher blood pressure during biofeedback training, and then using these sensations as cues to modulate their blood pressure, employing the same strategies they used during biofeedback training.

BEHAVIORAL TREATMENT OF HYPERTENSION IN PERSPECTIVE

Relaxation training has been successful in reducing blood pressure.[13] In one series of studies, relaxation training resulted in reductions in blood pressure that persisted throughout the day and also were evident in the evening.[14] The reductions obtained in the clinic transferred to patients' work environments[15] and were maintained in both settings at a 15-month follow-up.[16] The more home practice patients engage in, the more effective the treatment tends to be.[17]

Not all studies have found relaxation training to be effective, however.[18] Although some studies have reported long-term benefits,[19] others have not.[20] The lack of change in some studies may be attributable to poor compliance with home relaxation practice. Relaxation training appears to be maximally effective when the patient practices at home at least twice a day for 15 to 20 minutes and has booster sessions of relaxation training with a therapist at follow-up appointments.[21] Although patients may report that they practice relaxation on their own, two studies—one treating hypertension and the other treating anxiety—have documented that patients actually practice less than they say they do.[22] Later in this chapter we will discuss the general issue of adherence to medical treatments.

Biofeedback has had modest success in lowering blood pressure,[23] with some studies revealing favorable outcomes[24] and others, unfavorable outcomes.[25] The conflicting results are due, in part, to wide variations in the procedures employed in different studies. The failures may be attributable partially to poor transfer to the patients' natural environments, where biofeedback equipment is unavailable.[26]

An advantage of relaxation training over biofeedback is that the former does not require elaborate, expensive equipment. Combining relaxation and biofeedback does not seem to enhance treatment effectiveness.[27] What may be more critical than the specific treatment (relaxation or biofeedback) are such factors as the way the treatment is individualized for patients, the frequency with which the skills are practiced, how well the skills are learned, and patients' expectations about the efficacy of the treatment.[28]

Although both relaxation and biofeedback are capable of lowering *some* patients' blood pressure, often the magnitude of the change is not sufficient to benefit patients' hypertension. Clearly, individuals differ in their abilities to use relaxation[29] and biofeedback.[30] It is important to remember that the results of controlled experiments always represent the *average for a group* of people. Thus, it is possible that some patients in an experiment may experience clinically significant changes as a result of relaxation or biofeedback although the average change of the group is not clinically significant.

Medication, the most common treatment for essential hypertension, typically results in a 10% to 30% reduction in blood pressure.[31] In contrast, nonpharmacological treatments, such as relaxation and biofeedback, typically yield less than a 10% reduction.[32] However, relaxation and biofeedback remain useful adjuncts to pharmacological treatment. First, they work well for *some* patients. Second, even limited effectiveness may be beneficial for patients who cannot tolerate hypertensive medication, such as some pregnant women and elderly individuals.[33]

Chronic Pain

Pain is the most common problem that patients present to physicians, as well as the most frequently cited cause of disability. A distinction usually is made between acute and chronic pain. *Acute pain* is the result of bodily trauma and disappears when the injury heals. Acute pain generally is adaptive in that it signals bodily damage (as when the pain from touching a hot object alerts you to pull your hand away). *Chronic pain* occurs after an injury has healed or when no trauma exists. Pain is considered chronic if it lasts for at least 6 months.[34] In the United States, more than 75 million people suffer from chronic pain, and chronic pain results in the loss of 550 million work days and in pain-related disability payments of well over $100 billion annually.[35]

Medication is by far the most common treatment for pain, but medication has a number of limitations, especially for chronic pain. First, medication may not fully alleviate patients' pain. Second, many drugs lose their effectiveness over time. Third, long-term use of pain medication may lower people's tolerance for mild forms of pain. Fourth, drugs frequently have undesirable side effects (such as drowsiness). Fifth, more potent pain medications may result in physical and psychological dependence.[36] Thus, alternatives to medication are important in the treatment of chronic pain.

Behavioral treatment of chronic pain has two goals: (1) to reduce the patient's subjective discomfort (for example, decreasing the intensity or frequency of headaches) or, when this is not possible, (2) to increase the patient's tolerance for pain through coping strategies that minimize life disruptions.

PAIN AS BEHAVIOR

How pain is viewed makes a difference. We usually think of pain in terms of the subjective experience of intense discomfort. Behavior therapists have found it more useful to view pain as a *behavior* because behaviors can be readily assessed and changed.[37] **Pain behaviors** are overt behaviors that generally indicate a person is experiencing pain—for example, grimacing and saying "Ouch!" In contrast, **well behaviors** are overt behaviors that typically indicate that a person is not experiencing pain, such as smiling and saying, "I feel good today." Well behaviors compete with pain behaviors. Table 14-3 lists common examples of both pain behaviors and well behaviors.

Table 14-3 Examples of pain behaviors and well behaviors

Pain Behaviors	Well Behaviors
Moaning, screaming	Laughing, singing
Grimacing, wincing	Smiling
Talking about the uncomfortable or unbearable sensations	Talking about feeling good
Moving in a guarded, unnatural manner indicating discomfort (for example, limping)	Moving spontaneously, in an unrestricted manner
Reclining or sitting in order to ease pain	Standing or walking
Restricting activities that might result in pain	Engaging in activities that might result in pain
Requesting and taking pain medication	Refusing pain medication
Requesting help moving	Moving by oneself
Using crutches, cane, walker, or wheelchair	Walking without support

Pain behaviors, like any other behaviors, are maintained by their antecedents and consequences. A simple example illustrates this conceptualization:

> Vinny is playing a rough game of football with his friends, and his body is becoming badly bruised. However, he does not complain. He continues to play as if nothing hurt. If he did complain, his friends might call him a weakling.
>
> The minute Vinny gets home, the story changes. He slumps into a chair, "unable" to move. He tells his mother that he hurts all over, and she offers to help him upstairs and bring him his dinner in bed.

Clearly, the antecedents and consequences in the two situations are different, and it is easy to see how they influenced Vinny's pain behaviors.

The behavioral conceptualization of pain does not ignore the physical sensation of discomfort caused by the stimulation of pain receptors. The physical sensations of pain are one of the maintaining antecedents of pain behaviors, albeit antecedents that are not amenable to change directly through behavior therapy. In contrast, situational factors (as with Vinny) and a person's ability to cope with discomfort can be changed by behavior therapy.

The consequences of exhibiting pain behaviors often are important maintaining conditions.[38] Significant consequences include (1) social reinforcers, notably attention and sympathy; (2) avoidance of responsibilities (for example, missing work); (3) financial compensation (for instance, disability payments); and (4) receipt of pain medication. Just how closely pain behaviors can be associated with social attention is illustrated by the case of a 47-year-old man with chronic lower back pain.

CALVIN AND HOBBES copyright 1988 Watterson. Dist. by UNIVERSAL PRESS SYNDICATE. Reprinted with permission. All rights reserved.

Looking at Figure 14-1, you can see that the number of pain behaviors the man exhibited clearly varied with the presence or absence of attention from the hospital staff.

CHANGING THE CONSEQUENCES OF PAIN BEHAVIORS

One behavioral approach to the treatment of pain is to change the consequences maintaining patients' pain behaviors. The prototype for this approach was developed by Wilbert Fordyce and his colleagues at the University of Washington Pain Clinic.[39] The program begins in the hospital and later is extended to the patient's home environment.

The first step in the University of Washington Pain Clinic program is to assess the factors maintaining a patient's pain behaviors. Often, the

Figure 14-1 Effects of professional staff attention on the pain behaviors of a 47-year-old man with chronic lower back pain
SOURCE: Adapted from Fordyce, 1976, p. 89.

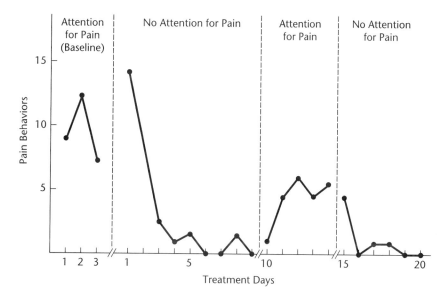

patient is being reinforced for pain behaviors but not for well behaviors.[40] When this is the case, treatment involves reversing the contingencies: Reinforcers are administered for well behaviors and withheld for pain behaviors.

The most common reinforcer for pain behaviors is attention from others. Thus, a major focus of the treatment program involves encouraging *everyone* who comes in contact with the patient to ignore or respond matter-of-factly to the patient's pain behaviors in order to extinguish them. At the same time, people are asked to reinforce—as with praise and attention—instances of the patient's well behaviors.

Rest is another reinforcing consequence of pain. Accordingly, rest is made a consequence of activity rather than pain behaviors. First, the amount of activity the patient can tolerate without experiencing pain, known as the *pain threshold,* is assessed. Then, the initial amount of activity that the patient is required to do is set below the patient's pain threshold. When this criterion is reached, the patient is allowed to rest before going on to the next activity. The hospital staff gives the patient attention and praise for completing the activity criterion. As the patient's pain threshold rises, the criteria for rest are gradually increased.

Receiving medication also results in a variety of reinforcing consequences. Positive reinforcers include the pleasant side effects of pain medication, such as feeling "high," and attention from the person administering the medication. Negative reinforcers include relief from discomfort and not having to fulfill unpleasant responsibilities (such as household chores).

Pain medication typically is administered on an as-needed basis. In contrast, during the treatment program, access to medication is made *time contingent* rather than pain contingent. Patients are given medication at fixed time intervals, whether or not they request it. Over the course of treatment, the medication dosage is gradually reduced (and eventually eliminated in many cases).

After a course of hospital treatment, the patient's therapy continues at home. Systematic procedures are established to ensure that the decrease in pain behaviors transfers from the hospital to the patient's home environment and is maintained over time. The patient's spouse, other family members, and close friends are asked to participate in the treatment and are trained in the procedures. For example, family and friends learn to withhold reinforcers for the patient's pain behaviors and to administer reinforcers for the patient's well behaviors.

Although the family and friends' assistance may be reinforced by their observing the patient's progress, that may not be sufficient to maintain their efforts over an extended period. Accordingly, procedures are established to ensure that the therapeutic endeavors of family and friends are adequately reinforced. For example, patients are instructed to explicitly thank family members for their help.

Part of the program also deals with reestablishing previously reinforcing activities in patients' lives. These activities, which often are natural reinforcers, are made contingent on well behaviors. As an example, suppose a woman's walking, bending, and lifting increased in the hospital. If the patient had enjoyed shopping, then she would be allowed to go shopping only if she walked to the store. If having friends over had been a favorite activity, the patient would be permitted to entertain only if she did some of the preparatory housework.

TREATMENT PACKAGES FOR CHRONIC PAIN

Because pain is a multifaceted behavior, treatment packages generally are more effective than single treatments. In one study, for example, clients who were taught and practiced coping skills along with changing the consequences of pain showed better pain management than clients who only had the consequences of pain changed.[41] The components of treatment packages for pain include changing the maintaining consequences of pain behaviors, cognitive-behavioral coping skills therapy, relaxation training, and biofeedback (as well as nonbehavioral treatments such as medication, physical therapy, and exercise).[42]

Relaxation training and biofeedback are widely applied behavior therapies for treating and preventing chronic headaches.[43] For tension headaches, relaxation training and electromyographic (muscle tone) biofeedback appear to be equally effective.[44] For migraine headaches in adults, the combination of relaxation training and thermal (skin temperature) biofeedback results in larger reductions in migraine activity than either treatment alone.[45] Thermal biofeedback may be the treatment of choice for children's migraine headaches.[46] Biofeedback equipment that resembles a computer game has been developed for children and adolescents, and it may increase patients' motivation to undergo and remain in the treatment.[47]

Adding behavioral child management training to biofeedback for the treatment of migraine headaches has reduced headache frequency in children significantly more than biofeedback alone.[48] The parents were instructed to (1) praise their child's use of coping skills during headaches, (2) encourage normal activity during headaches (for example, attending school and performing daily chores), (3) remove attention for pain-related behaviors (for instance, not asking how much the headache hurts), (4) administer pain medication only as prescribed and not on request, (5) treat headaches that require reduction of normal activity as an illness (for example, the child must remain in bed), and (6) recruit others (such as teachers) to follow the same guidelines.

More than 100 empirical studies have demonstrated the effectiveness of relaxation training and biofeedback for both migraine and tension headaches. The studies have obtained an average of 50% reduction in headaches compared with 5% improvement for clients in wait-list control groups and 15% improvement for clients receiving a placebo medication.[49] Biofeedback and relaxation training also can be effective when self-administered with minimal therapist contact.[50]

Biofeedback-assisted relaxation may be superior to self-relaxation (10 to 15 minutes of relaxing each day while thinking peaceful thoughts) for reducing both headaches and medication usage.[51] Cognitive therapy and other cognitive-behavioral therapies for migraine headaches do not appear to enhance the effectiveness of biofeedback-assisted relaxation training alone.[52] Biofeedback-assisted relaxation appears to change important physiological functions associated with headaches, such as cerebral blood flow velocity.[53]

In contrast to the poor long-term maintenance obtained with medication alone for headaches, follow-up studies indicate that behavioral treatments maintain their effectiveness for at least as long as 3 years.[54] Further, behavioral treatments for headaches are associated with positive side effects, such as reduction in anxiety and depression, which do not occur with medication.[55]

Cognitive-behavioral coping skills treatment packages that have included relaxation techniques and cognitive restructuring are effective treatments for managing pain associated with rheumatic diseases.[56] Juvenile rheumatoid arthritis, a chronic and recurrent pain condition, has been treated successfully with relaxation training, breathing exercises, and emotive imagery.[57] Cognitive-behavioral treatment packages incorporating cognitive restructuring, relaxation training, and emotive imagery have been effective in reducing pain from fibromyalgia, a chronic pain condition characterized by aching, stiffness, and abnormal tenderness at multiple sites in the body.[58]

Some cognitive-behavioral coping skills treatment packages have been very brief. An example is a single-session stress inoculation training program employed to help African-American children cope with pain associated with sickle cell anemia, which was described in Chapter 13 (page 361).[59] In another program involving three 45-minute therapy sessions, African-American adults with sickle cell anemia learned calming self-instructions through modeling and behavior rehearsal to cope with pain.[60] The treatment package also included relaxation training and self-distraction techniques. Sixty-seven patients were assigned either to the cognitive-behavioral coping skills training group or to a control group that received disease education. At a 3-month follow-up, patients who had participated in the coping skills treatment reported significantly less pain and more attempts to cope with pain than patients in the control group. Moreover, on days when they experienced pain, patients receiving the cognitive-behavioral treatment required fewer contacts with health care professionals than patients in the control group.

Learning differential relaxation allows patients to employ muscle relaxation to cope with pain during the course of their daily activities.[61] Often, there are identifiable antecedents to pain that people can use as cues to begin differential relaxation. For example, stress-evoking situations and anxiety often precipitate and exacerbate pain associated with existing medical conditions, such as the uncomfortable itchiness associated with eczema (skin inflammation) or the physical discomfort associated with menopause, both of which have been successfully treated with relaxation.[62] To identify situations in which patients are particularly vulnerable to headaches, patients learn to monitor their headaches; they record in a *pain diary* such information as the circumstances in which the pain occurs, what they are doing and thinking at the time, and the consequences of the pain.[63]

In many cases of chronic pain, living with pain, rather than reducing it, is the most realistic goal of therapy. Cognitive-behavioral coping skills therapy can help patients achieve this goal. An example is Dennis Turk's stress inoculation treatment for pain that combines relaxation, breathing exercises, attention diversion, and emotive imagery.[64] These procedures are similar to the Lamaze method of natural childbirth.[65]

BEHAVIORAL TREATMENT OF CHRONIC PAIN IN PERSPECTIVE

Although behavior therapy procedures have been used to treat a variety of pain conditions, most research has focused on headaches and lower back pain. Generally, behavioral treatment of chronic pain has been successful.[66] In the majority of cases, however, patients experience a *reduction* in pain, rather than a complete remission of their pain.[67] The improvement often is substantial enough that patients can resume normal activities despite their still experiencing some physical discomfort. In the case of headaches, treatment gains have been maintained for 1 to 4 years without any specific maintenance procedures.[68] An indirect measure of the effectiveness of behavioral treatments for pain is that most pain clinics employ behavior therapy procedures as part of the treatment packages offered to patients.

Turning to specific treatments, changing maintaining consequences of pain behaviors has been shown to be effective in a number of studies.[69] However, its application has been narrow. It has been applied exclusively to pain associated with physical activity (particularly chronic lower back pain), and it has focused on increasing exercise and activity and decreasing medication usage while ignoring emotional and cognitive aspects of pain.[70] Another potential limitation of the consequential approach concerns transfer to and long-term maintenance in the client's natural environment.[71] The ultimate success of the treatment may depend on instituting specific procedures to foster transfer and maintenance (such as family members' continuing appropriate contingencies), which has not always been done.

Both relaxation training and biofeedback can be effective in treating headaches.[72] Cognitive-behavioral coping skills approaches also have been successful in treating a variety of types of pain.[73] Treatment outcomes with patients suffering from chronic pain appear to be enhanced when patients are given detailed information about when and how to use coping skills[74] and when coping skills are individualized.[75]

To summarize, four major behavioral interventions have been used to treat chronic pain: changing maintaining consequences, relaxation training, biofeedback, and cognitive-behavioral coping skills therapy. At present, no basis for choosing one treatment over another exists because no treatment has been shown to be consistently superior.[76] This state of affairs is not necessarily bad because individual patients differ widely in their responses to the treatments, which means that there is a need for a variety of effective procedures.[77] Moreover, treatment packages consisting of a combination of the four therapies generally are effective.[78]

Medically Unexplained Symptoms

Medically unexplained symptoms refer to physical complaints for which a physiological cause cannot be found and that do not fit the criteria for a known psychological disorder (for example, heart palpitations that are secondary to panic disorder). The symptoms are chronic and result in decreased activity, social behavior, and work performance. Medically unexplained symptoms are very common. According to some studies, physical complaints such as fatigue, backache, headache, dizziness, chest pain, and abdominal pain have no demonstrable organic cause in more than 75% of cases.[79] Because the symptoms persist and are unexplained, patients often engage in a continual and costly search for the "correct" diagnosis, which results in multiple diagnostic tests and hospitalizations.

Cognitive-behavioral therapies have had some success in treating medically unexplained symptoms by providing additional treatment to patients' ongoing medical treatment, replacing medical treatments associated with invasive procedures or negative side effects, and offering treatment where no effective medical treatment exists. The cognitive-behavioral interventions used include relaxation training, biofeedback, cognitive restructuring, problem-solving training, assertion training, and collaborative empiricism exercises.[80] We will illustrate the application of cognitive-behavioral therapies to treating medically unexplained symptoms for chronic fatigue syndrome, noncardiac chest pain, and fibromyalgia syndrome.

Chronic fatigue syndrome is characterized by disabling fatigue lasting more than 6 months and resulting in a 50% reduction in daily activity. Cognitive-behavioral interventions have resulted in reduced emotional distress, increased activity level, and increased functional abilities (such as daily self-care behaviors).[81] These interventions appear to be more beneficial than medical treatments alone.[82]

Noncardiac chest pain is persistent chest pain without any identifiable cardiac etiology. The benefits of cognitive-behavioral treatments for this condition include decreased or cessation of chest pain, increased activity, reduced emotional distress, and decreased use of medications.[83] However, studies have yet to demonstrate that the cognitive-behavioral interventions are superior to other treatments and attention-placebo controls.[84]

Fibromyalgia syndrome is a musculoskeletal condition of diffuse pain of at least 3 months' duration. There is increased pain sensitivity in multiple tender points throughout the body and often stiffness in muscles and connective tissue. Certain forms of fibromyalgia have no identifiable physiological cause. The effects of cognitive-behavioral interventions for fibromyalgia have included reduced pain and emotional distress, as well as improved self-efficacy beliefs and quality of life.[85] However, these changes have not exceeded those obtained from less costly, education-only interventions.[86]

The treatment of medically unexplained symptoms is an exciting new application of cognitive-behavioral therapies. At present, the research findings appear to support the conclusion that the interventions are promising, but further research is required to demonstrate clear-cut efficacy.[87]

ADHERENCE TO MEDICAL REGIMENS

Patients' failure to follow medical advice—for example, to take medication or do rehabilitative exercises—is a major problem for the medical profession.[88] In fact, nonadherence in general may occur as frequently as 50% of the time[89] and 87% of the time with pediatric patients.[90] The most effective treatment is worthless if patients do not avail themselves of it. Early research on increasing adherence to medical regimens attempted to identify patient characteristics associated with nonadherence, such as educational level and personality traits. However, it appears that there is little or no relationship between patient characteristics and nonadherence.[91] It is more useful to view adherence as a *behavior,* rather than a trait,[92] and to develop procedures for accelerating specific adherence behaviors, such as employing frequent, immediate, and meaningful positive reinforcement to enhance parental adherence to their children's health care needs.[93]

With many medical regimens, the immediate consequences of "following the doctor's orders" at best are weak because the benefits are usually delayed. At worst, complying with medical regimens may be distinctly aversive, such as taking bad-tasting medicine and engaging in exhausting physical rehabilitation exercises. In contrast, patients readily adhere to medical regimens that have immediate benefits, such as taking pain medication.

Adherence can occur only *if the patient first remembers and then is sufficiently motivated* to follow the prescribed treatment. Prompting is used to help patients remember to perform treatment-related behaviors, and reinforcement is employed to provide motivation.

We will illustrate behavioral interventions for increasing adherence to three important aspects of medical treatment: taking medication, engaging in health-related behaviors (such as following a prescribed diet), and keeping medical appointments.

Taking Medication

Physicians frequently prescribe regular doses of medication for an extended time, ranging from a week to years (as for essential hypertension, epilepsy, and diabetes). Stimulus control procedures are used to prompt patients to take medication. Environmental prompts may be as simple as special labels on medicine bottles, such as a picture of a clock on which the times the medication needs to be taken are circled.[94] A more sophisticated prompting device is a portable timer and pill dispenser that sounds a tone when a pill should be taken.[95] The tone continues until a knob is turned that releases a pill into the patient's hand. The advent of handheld computers could facilitate elaborate prompting of medical regimens that could include explicit step-by-step directions for carrying out the procedures.[96]

Naturalistic stimulus control can be used to tailor a medication schedule to the patient's daily routine so that regularly occurring activities serve as cues for taking medication. This might involve taking medications at the same time each day,[97] with meals, or right before leaving the house in the morning.[98]

Merely remembering to take medication often is not sufficient to ensure adherence. Accordingly, stimulus control procedures generally are

Photo 14-2 Patient using a simple stimulus control device that prompts taking daily medication

© 1997 Michael D. Spiegler and David C. Guevremont

supplemented with reinforcement. For example, in one study, the combination of telephone reminders and lottery tickets as reinforcers increased taking anticonvulsive medication an average of 43%.[99] Another example involved employing a token system to increase using an inhaler three times a day for an 8- and a 10-year-old with asthma.[100]

Although prompting and reinforcement can be effective in obtaining adherence to taking medication, when these procedures are discontinued the adherence may not persist.[101] Adherence is more likely to be maintained if self-control skills are added to stimulus control and reinforcement procedures. As an example, one program taught patients with high blood pressure to use stimulus control procedures (for example, to associate pill taking with breakfast) and self-monitoring (of the medication taken and blood pressure).[102] Additionally, every 2 weeks the patients' blood pressure was checked. When their blood pressure was below a set criterion, patients were given a $4 credit toward the purchase of blood pressure recording equipment. Six months after the intervention, patients' medication adherence (assessed by random urine samples) was 80%, compared with 39% for patients who were not in the program.

Another strategy is to make the consequences of nonadherence unattractive. An example was the use of response cost for failure to take doses of Antabuse (a drug used in the treatment of alcohol dependence).[103] The patients, who had chronic drinking problems, left "security deposits" with their therapist, and they forfeited between $5 and $10 for each missed dose during the 3-month treatment contract. The patients missed only 8% of the scheduled clinic visits and were abstinent on 95% of the treatment days.

Engaging in Health-Related Behaviors

Besides prescribing medication, physicians instruct patients to perform various health-related behaviors, such as maintaining a prescribed diet, engaging in regular exercise, and monitoring indicators of bodily function (such as blood glucose level). However, physicians' instructions alone are not likely to change patients' health-related behaviors.[104] Getting children and adolescents to engage consistently in necessary medical procedures is especially difficult, particularly when multiple behaviors are required.[105] For instance, people with diabetes may have to engage in a variety of health care routines, including maintaining dietary restrictions, self-injecting insulin, testing their urine, and taking care of their feet (because of the increased vulnerability to infections from poor circulation in the extremities). Prompting in the form of visual cues generally has a minimal effect on adherence;[106] however, written prompts have been shown to increase self-monitoring of blood glucose levels.[107]

More elaborate prompting involving a 56-step checklist for glucose monitoring was successful with a woman who had serious memory impairment.[108] The patient was verbally prompted to read each instruction, perform it, and check it off before going to the next step. She was praised for correctly performing each step and given corrective feedback for errors. After 90% accuracy was achieved, the prompts and feedback were faded. Whereas before the intervention the patient's accuracy was as low as 40%, after the intervention her accuracy was consistently at or above 90%.

Self-monitoring may be an effective intervention for increasing adherence to simple regimens, such as engaging in a single exercise.[109] However, self-monitoring is likely to be ineffective for complex regimens, such as those required for diabetes.[110]

Reinforcement results in the most consistent adherence to health-related behaviors.[111] Token economy programs have been used to increase compliance with prescribed medical regimens for children with diabetes[112] and children on hemodialysis (a blood purification procedure).[113] The successful use of a token economy with an 82-year-old man to obtain adherence to diet, exercise, and taking medication after a massive heart attack was described in Case 8-1 (page 198). Contingency contracts have proved useful with children and adolescents, as well as with adults. In a program for children and adolescents with hemophilia (a disorder in which blood will not clot), for example, the use of contingency contracts with token reinforcers resulted in 81% to 90% adherence to exercise and diet over 6 months.[114] Other procedures that enhance adherence to prescribed dietary and exercise regimens are self-monitoring, stimulus control, and relapse prevention procedures.[115]

When low adherence is maintained by a skill deficit in the prescribed medical procedure, modeling can increase adherence.[116] For example, parents of children with hemophilia were taught to administer a difficult emergency treatment for bleeding (factor replacement therapy).[117] A nurse practitioner demonstrated the procedure and then gave parents feedback as they rehearsed it. The parents' skill level increased from 15% before the intervention to 92% during the intervention and 97% at follow-up. Modeling also has been helpful in teaching social and coping skills to overcome social barriers to adherence that children and adolescents experience (such as being called "sicky" when abstaining from sports in school).[118] Behavioral child management training for parents is another strategy for enhancing children's adherence to medical regimens, such as prescribed diets for children with cystic fibrosis.[119]

Keeping Medical Appointments

Keeping scheduled medical appointments is crucial for obtaining medical care and treatment. Telephone calls[120] and mailed reminders[121] are simple, relatively low-cost prompts, but they are not always successful.[122] As with the other targets of adherence, reinforcement generally is the most effective strategy to get people to keep medical appointments. For example, in a treatment program for heroin dependence, clients were given the privilege of taking their methadone (a drug used to treat heroin dependence) at home over the weekend if they made weekly clinic visits. This intervention increased the percentage of appointments kept from 45% to 89%.[123] In a pediatric clinic, the number of appointments that were kept was increased by including parking passes with mailed reminders;[124] the passes allowed parents to park adjacent to the clinic, which saved them time. Similarly, whereas keeping follow-up appointments at a family practice center was unaffected by reminder cards, offering free or reduced-rate appointments significantly increased appointments kept.[125]

COPING WITH MEDICAL/DENTAL PROCEDURES AND ILLNESS

Medical procedures, hospitalization, and even routine visits to the doctor or dentist produce significant stress and anxiety in many individuals. People fear pain, unfamiliar instrumentation and surroundings, separation from loved ones, and receiving a serious diagnosis. Children are particularly vulnerable to these fears.

As you saw in Chapter 11, modeling therapy is used to prepare children and adults for medical treatments. Another strategy is to teach patients coping skills to actively reduce their anxiety and discomfort as they prepare for and undergo treatments. Using coping skills also can facilitate medical procedures (such as lying still during a lumbar puncture) and aid in the recovery process. Specifically, coping skills (1) improve patients' cooperation before, during, and after surgery; (2) reduce the amount of postoperative analgesic medications required; (3) speed recovery and reduce time spent in the hospital; and (4) reduce the amount of time and support patients require from others during recovery.[126]

To cope with painful medical procedures—such as those typically associated with cancer treatment—children have been taught cognitive-behavioral coping skills, such as progressive relaxation, breathing exercises, emotive/distracting imagery, and the use of positive self-statements.[127] A type of desensitization, in which children's preferred activities (such as playing a video game) are paired with stimuli associated with invasive medical procedures, has lowered the distress of children who must repeatedly undergo such procedures.[128] Treatment packages usually are employed and tend to be more effective than single therapies.[129]

Medical procedures need not be painful to cause distress. For example, magnetic resonance imaging (MRI) used for diagnostic purposes may cause claustrophobia (fear of enclosed spaces) because patients are placed in a narrow tube and must remain motionless for extended periods. One approach to reducing such anxiety is to administer a pleasant fragrance during the MRI procedure, which may serve to distract or relax the patient.[130] Another approach used with children is to dispense token reinforcers for lying still during the MRI procedure.[131] After the procedure, the children exchange the tokens for backup reinforcers.

In a related application, a stimulus control procedure called *behavioral momentum compliance training,* along with differential reinforcement and extinction, was used to keep 22-month-old Aaron still while he was undergoing a medical procedure.[132] **Behavioral momentum compliance training** is used to get a client to comply with a low-probability request—one with which the client is not likely to comply—by preceding it with a series of high-probability requests—those with which the client is likely to comply. In this case, Aaron's mother first made a series of high-probability requests of Aaron (such as "Touch your head," "Say 'Mom,'" and "Blow Mom a kiss") and praised him for compliance with each request. Immediately after the series of high-probability requests, Aaron's mother told him, "Hold still," which was a low-probability request. The treatment package resulted in a significant increase in Aaron's holding still, from 44% to 78%.

Parents' participation in interventions aimed at reducing their children's stress related to medical procedures is beneficial. Pediatric cancer patients undergoing venipuncture, for example, cried significantly less when their parents prompted and reinforced (with praise and token reinforcers) their children's use of a breathing distraction technique.[133] Parents' participation not only is helpful to their children but also can vicariously reduce parents' anxiety.[134] Parents whose children are seriously ill and undergoing medical procedures often experience high levels of stress, which may cause or exacerbate their children's anxiety. In contrast, parents who are calm and effectively deal with their own stress are better able to help their children, including serving as coping models for them.

Various programs have been developed to directly treat parents' anxiety about their children's illnesses. For instance, parents whose children underwent painful bone marrow aspirations or lumbar punctures for leukemia were given stress inoculation training to deal with their own anxiety.[135] The training consisted of three brief (15-minute) training sequences: (1) exposure to a modeling film that provided information and examples of coping behaviors, (2) instruction in using coping-oriented self-statements to counter catastrophic self-statements, and (3) relaxation training (including home practice). Other parents received no direct intervention for their own anxiety but participated in their children's cognitive-behavioral treatment. The parents who received stress inoculation training reported lower anxiety and used more positive self-statements than parents who only participated in their children's treatment. As another example, a problem-solving training program has been developed specifically for parents whose children are diagnosed with cancer and who are at increased risk for significant emotional distress.[136]

Various treatments have been found to be effective in helping children and adults cope with stress associated with dental visits.[137] For instance, low-income preschool children who had no previous dental treatment benefited from learning to employ relaxation, breathing exercises, and coping words (such as *calm* and *nice*).[138] The children also were given descriptive information regarding the dental procedures and the sights, sounds, and physical sensations they would experience. These interventions reduced the children's disruptive behaviors, anxiety and discomfort, and physiological arousal, and they also increased children's cooperation.

Adults with true dental phobias are so anxious about dental procedures that they will not see a dentist even though they may need treatment. Systematic desensitization can be helpful in such cases.[139] In one study, a single-session treatment package consisting of systematic desensitization and stress inoculation training was compared with antianxiety medication (benzodiazepine) and a no-treatment control condition. Both active treatments reduced clients' anxiety during dental procedures significantly more than the control condition. However, at a 2-month follow-up, the clients treated with medication showed a return to pretreatment levels of anxiety, whereas the clients who received the behavioral intervention maintained their treatment gains. Most important, 70% of the clients receiving the behavioral treatment, compared with 20% of those receiving medication, continued to obtain dental care.[140]

People experiencing medical crises, such as finding out that one requires invasive surgery, may experience significant symptoms of anxiety and depression because of unrealistic beliefs, cognitive distortions, and poor coping strategies. Cognitive-behavioral therapies, including stress inoculation training, problem-solving training, and cognitive restructuring, are particularly well suited for treating the distress surrounding medical crises.[141]

Psychological distress, such as anxiety and depression, in adults who learn that they are infected with HIV is associated with more rapid progression of AIDS. A 10-week, group cognitive-behavioral treatment package consisting of relaxation training, cognitive restructuring, assertion training, and anger management was used to assist gay men in coping with HIV. Clients receiving the intervention, in comparison with clients in a wait-list control group, showed significant decreases in depressed mood and anxiety; they also had fewer cases of herpes virus, which is common in people infected with HIV and may contribute to the progression of the disease.[142]

In addition to helping people cope with the distressing psychological ramifications of illness and medical treatments, behavior therapies have been used to reduce the negative physical side effects of medical treatments. For example, nausea and vomiting often occur with chemotherapy for cancer. These extremely noxious side effects generally begin 1 to

2 hours after the injection of the chemical and can persist as long as 24 hours.[143] Relaxation training has been successful in reducing the frequency and severity of nausea and vomiting.[144] Some patients also experience anticipatory nausea and vomiting,[145] which can be treated by systematic desensitization.[146]

The physical side effects of cancer treatment and the pain and fatigue caused by the disease itself are horrible enough. In addition, cancer patients often are demoralized by the hospital social environment, which can result in psychological disorders, including anxiety and depression.[147] Cancer patients may be deprived of social reinforcers,[148] especially patients in isolation (which may be required because chemotherapy compromises the immune system). The source of these patients' social reinforcers are limited to contact with the medical personnel who care for their needs. Accordingly, one of the few ways patients can control their social contacts is to develop symptoms that require close attention.[149] Case 14-1 describes the treatment of physical symptoms that were maintained by nurses' attention.

Case 14-1

PHYSICAL SYMPTOMS RELATED TO CANCER TREATMENT ALLEVIATED BY EXTINCTION AND DIFFERENTIAL REINFORCEMENT[150]

Two patients with acute leukemia developed symptoms for which no physical cause could be found. Patient 1, a 24-year-old man, had a deep, raspy cough that did not respond to medication. Patient 2, a 63-year-old woman, regurgitated saliva excessively. Both patients were described as outgoing, friendly, and well adjusted to their illnesses. Their symptoms developed when they were placed in restrictive isolation.

The nursing staff believed that the patients' symptoms worsened in the presence of a staff member. This belief was confirmed by a sophisticated systematic naturalistic observation procedure. The symptoms were tape recorded for 16 hours over the course of 2 days. Three-minute segments were analyzed for (1) the presence of the symptom (for example, loud, repeated exhalation of air or sounds of spitting), (2) a nurse entering (for instance, sounds of the door opening and footsteps), and (3) talking. The assessment revealed that the patients' symptoms were maintained by a nurse's presence, which served as a setting event. The symptoms were more likely to occur when a nurse was with the patients (the probabilities were .75 and .82 for Patients 1 and 2, respectively) than when the patients were alone (.25 and .18, respectively).

Treatment involved extinction and differential reinforcement of other behaviors. The nurses did not discuss the patients' symptoms with them at any time. If the symptoms continued during standard nursing procedures, the nurse finished the procedures and immediately left the room. However, if the symptom ceased or did not occur, the nurse remained in the room and talked with the patient for a minimum of 10 minutes after the medical procedures had been completed. Within 2 weeks, both patients' symptoms were eliminated.

PREVENTION OF PHYSICAL ILLNESS

Behavior therapy procedures not only have been employed in the treatment of medical disorders, but they also have been applied to preventing physical illness. Behavioral prevention programs have two major aims. One is to *educate* people about the controllable factors that cause and exacerbate illnesses and about specific behaviors that can reduce the risk of developing illnesses. The other aim is to *motivate* people to engage in preventive behaviors. We will look at behavioral prevention programs related to cardiovascular disease, women's health care, and HIV/AIDS.

Cardiovascular Disease

The Stanford Three Community Study was a multifaceted program for preventing cardiovascular disease that causes serious medical problems, such as heart attacks and strokes.[151] The groups compared in this experiment were entire communities in northern California, with populations of about 14,000. One community received a mass-media campaign, a second community received a face-to-face intensive instructional program as well as the media campaign, and a third community received no preventive interventions and served as a control group.

The 10-week intensive instruction program was given to a random sample of people who had a high risk of developing cardiovascular disease. The program was administered both individually and in groups, and the spouses of the high-risk participants were involved in the program. The behavior therapy components included (1) behavioral assessment of each person's health-related behaviors, (2) modeling of new healthful behaviors, (3) guided behavior rehearsal of the new behaviors, (4) reinforcement for performing the new behaviors, and (5) procedures to maintain the new behaviors.

Both the media campaign and the intensive instruction successfully (1) increased participants' knowledge of cardiovascular disease and the importance of risk factors; (2) decreased participants' specific high-risk behaviors, such as smoking and eating food high in cholesterol; and (3) lowered the estimated risk of participants' developing cardiovascular disease. For high-risk individuals, the combination of the media campaign and intensive instruction was more effective than the media campaign alone.

The Stanford Three Community Study became the prototype of whole-community prevention programs. Since its initial success, similar programs have been instituted in other parts of the United States and in other countries.[152]

Women's Health Care

Hypertension not only is associated with cardiovascular disease but also increases the risk of other medical problems, including complications in pregnancy. In one study, relaxation was taught to pregnant women in six weekly sessions.[153] Compared with women in a control group who received no intervention, women taught relaxation had (1) significantly lower blood pressure throughout pregnancy, (2) fewer hospital admissions for problems related to pregnancy, and (3) substantially shorter stays in the hospital.

Breast cancer, a leading cause of death in women, often is curable if detected early.[154] Regular breast self-examination is the simplest and most cost-effective means of early detection. Despite the ease of breast self-examinations, many women do not perform them. One program used biweekly postcards or phone calls to prompt women to do their breast self-examinations.[155] Initially, the women participated in a 1-hour workshop in which they learned how to examine their breasts. The procedure included placing baby oil on their fingers, palpating their breasts, and placing a sheet of tissue on their chests to absorb the oil. The women were instructed to mail the tissue they used, signed and dated, each time they performed the procedure. This provided a measure of the frequency of self-examinations. Compared with women who received no prompts, women who were prompted either by mail or telephone returned more self-examination tissues. However, the frequency of self-examinations decreased over time for both prompted and unprompted women. It is likely that providing reinforcers for breast self-examination would have increased compliance. For example, one study found that woman were more likely to perform breast self-examinations following small group education sessions when they received a silver dollar each month they had performed their breast self-examination.[156]

HIV/AIDS

Since it was first identified in 1981, acquired immune deficiency syndrome (AIDS) has become the most serious disease epidemic in the United States,[157] with infection rates rising fastest among heterosexual women.[158] As its name implies, AIDS involves a breakdown in the immune system, rendering the individual vulnerable to a host of diseases. It is caused by the human immunodeficiency virus (HIV), which is transmitted primarily through sexual contact (in semen and vaginal secretions) and direct infusion of contaminated blood (through shared hypodermic needles, blood transfusions, and childbirth).[159] According to the Joint United Nations Programme on HIV/AIDS, as of the end of 2000, more than 36 million people are estimated to be living with HIV/AIDS; in the year 2000, AIDS was responsible for the death of an estimated 3 million people. In the United States, more than three quarters of a million people have contracted AIDS over the past two decades, and almost two thirds of them have died from the disease.[160]

Because HIV infection has no known cure at present, it is a prime candidate for prevention. Fortunately, unlike many other life-threatening diseases with no known cures, the transmission of HIV is linked to specific, identifiable, and potentially changeable patterns of behavior.[161] Preventive efforts have focused on reducing high-risk activities (see Table 14-4), especially with gay men, who, in the United States, comprise more than half of the people with AIDS.[162]

Table 14-4 Behaviors that place people at high risk for AIDS and alternative low-risk behaviors

SOURCE: Adapted from Kelly & St. Lawrence, 1987, p. 9.

High-Risk Behaviors	Low-Risk Alternatives
Sexual activities that allow bloodstream exposure to seminal secretions or blood products (such as unprotected anal intercourse and oral sex)	Nonpenetrative sexual acts (such as massage and masturbation) and use of condoms
Sexual contact with multiple partners	Establishment of stable relationships
Frequenting settings where casual or anonymous sexual contacts occur (such as bathhouses and certain pornographic theaters)	Avoidance of high-risk settings and the development of social supports conducive to a nonpromiscuous lifestyle
Excessive use of chemical substances that promote behavioral/sexual disinhibition or impaired judgment	Curtailed use of chemical substances that impair judgment and produce disinhibition

Modest and cost-effective programs have attempted to encourage simple safer-sex practices, such as using condoms. For example, to increase gay bar patrons' taking free condoms, signs were posted as prompts.[163] Printed in large blue and red letters on a 1-by-2-foot poster board, the signs read: "In the State of Alaska 38 people have died from AIDS. Many more have tested positive. Condoms can reduce the spread of AIDS." Commercially printed signs regarding safer-sex practices to prevent HIV infection also were displayed in rest rooms during the intervention periods and reminded patrons that free condoms were available in the bar. The prompting intervention was evaluated by an ABAB reversal study, with baseline and prompting being reversed every 2 weeks. In three different bars, condoms were taken an average of 47% more of the time when prompts were displayed. (Of course, this does not mean that the condoms were *used* more as a result of the intervention.)

The primary thrust of behavioral AIDS prevention programs has been to change complex, high-risk sexual behavior patterns by using treatment packages based on the model developed by Jeffrey Kelly and Janet St. Lawrence.[164] Their cognitive-behavioral coping skills model begins with extensive individual assessment, including tests of knowledge of risk behaviors, self-report measures of sexual activity in the recent past, self-monitoring of current risk behaviors, and role-played tests of sexual assertiveness (for instance, refusing a proposition to engage in unsafe sex). The program is conducted in small groups and consists of four basic components:

1. *HIV risk education* involves direct instruction concerning risk factors and ways to reduce them.

2. *Cognitive-behavioral self-management* begins with participants' identifying the maintaining antecedents of their high-risk behaviors (such as setting, mood, and intoxicant use). Then, strategies for changing personal and environmental antecedents to lessen risks are taught. Participants

generate and practice self-statements emphasizing that safer practices are possible, will reduce anxiety, and are worthwhile (for example, "I can change my sex practices"; "I'll feel better if I change my sex practices"; and "I did well avoiding that high-risk situation").

3. *Assertion training* is aimed at clients' learning to refuse high-risk sexual propositions and to insist on engaging in safer sexual activities.

4. *Social skills training* teaches participants how to develop stable relationships involving a mutual commitment to healthy sexual behaviors.

In the final group session, participants identify risk reduction changes they have made during the program. This session exposes participants to multiple coping models, gives them additional ideas about how they can modify their own behaviors, and strengthens their self-efficacy for reducing high-risk behaviors in their lives.[165]

Cognitive-behavioral coping skills therapies to prevent HIV infection have been used with high-risk adolescents such as those with other sexually transmitted diseases or who have substance abuse problems[166] and those who lack the social behaviors necessary for initiating, maintaining, and terminating social and sexual relationships with persons of the opposite sex.[167] Other targeted groups include teenagers who have run away from home[168] and those living in HIV epicenters,[169] inner-city low-income men[170] and women,[171] gay and bisexual men,[172] college students,[173] adults with chronic psychiatric disorders such as schizophrenia and depression,[174] and people with mental retardation.[175] Overall, such interventions appear to reduce high-risk sexual behaviors in a variety of age groups and populations, when compared with information-oriented treatments and no treatment.[176] The most common outcome measures used in these studies are (1) number of sexual partners; (2) number of protected and unprotected occasions of oral, anal, and vaginal intercourse; (3) percentage of time condoms are used; and (4) number of sexual encounters with a high-risk partner.[177] Unfortunately, each of these measures is based on self-reports that are easily fabricated. Ideally, these self-report measures should be corroborated by other types of measures, but this is rarely possible with sexual activity.

The long-term maintenance of reductions in high-risk sexual behaviors brought about through cognitive-behavioral coping skills therapies has not yet been evaluated thoroughly. Initial studies indicate that the effects diminish over time.[178] For example, a 16-month follow-up assessment of 68 gay and bisexual men who had completed a cognitive-behavioral treatment program showed that 40% of the men had returned to unsafe sexual practices. Relapse was more common in men who were younger and who used alcohol or other drugs in conjunction with their high-risk sexual behaviors.[179]

◆ ALL THINGS CONSIDERED: BEHAVIORAL MEDICINE APPLICATIONS

Behavior therapy principles and procedures are proving useful in comprehensive health care. They are especially valuable with regard to helping patients cope with medical treatments and increasing their adherence to medical procedures. Behavior therapy also can play a role in providing alternative treatments for some medical disorders and in preventing diseases.

Medicine has traditionally focused on treatment—that is, on getting the patient well. Concern for the psychological well-being of patients in treatment has been an afterthought at best. For example, the practice of waking sleeping patients in the hospital to give them sleeping medication is more than a well-worn joke. Many people may endure inconveniences and discomfort associated with medical treatments because they subscribe to the "no pain, no gain" philosophy. More serious psychological consequences are associated with the intense discomfort and pain brought about by cancer therapy, the dread of undergoing surgery, and the hopelessness and despair caused by chronic illness and its care. Behavior therapy has begun to contribute to alleviating such problems.

Physicians have long recognized that patients' failure to follow prescribed treatment is a major impediment to providing adequate health care. However, neither physicians' skills nor medical technology is suited to changing the prevailing high rate of nonadherence. In contrast, behavior therapists have a large armamentarium of effective procedures for increasing patients' adherence behaviors.

Prevention of physical illness by promoting healthful behaviors and lifestyles also is an area in which behavior therapy procedures are beginning to make a difference. For instance, behavior therapy can influence proper diet, regular exercise, and the elimination of harmful drug habits (such as smoking and heavy drinking), all factors that directly enhance physical health. The major obstacle to implementing behavioral prevention programs is one faced by all prevention endeavors—namely, the prevailing attitude: "If it ain't broke, don't fix it." The benefits of preventive interventions may not become evident until years after the interventions are implemented. Further, because the goal of prevention is always the *absence* of disease, people may not recognize and appreciate the results of preventive interventions. Consider the fact that, as you read these words, you are unaware that you are breathing normally or that you are seeing the words clearly. In contrast, you would be aware of labored breathing if you had emphysema or of blurred vision if you had cataracts.

A final contribution made by behavior therapy to medicine is in providing alternative forms of treatment. For some medical conditions, such as certain types of chronic pain, existing medical treatments are inadequate. In other cases, existing medical treatments may be associated with potentially serious negative side effects, as with many drugs. Sometimes, the treatments themselves may be potentially life threatening, such as with certain types of medication. In such instances, behavioral treatments may be preferable, especially if they safely provide comparable results. Finally, even putting aside the negative side effects of medication, one advantage that cognitive-behavioral interventions have over drugs is that patients learn coping skills. The use of coping skills may be associated with greater long-term maintenance of treatment gains,[180] and the skills may generalize to dealing with other problems people encounter in their lives.

SUMMARY

1. The application of behavior therapy to the assessment, treatment, management, rehabilitation, and prevention of physical disease is part of behavioral medicine.
2. Behavior therapy serves four functions in dealing with medical disorders: treating medical disorders, increasing adherence to medical treatments, helping patients cope with treatments and illness, and preventing medical disorders.
3. Relaxation training and biofeedback can directly influence blood pressure, but often the magnitude of the change is not clinically significant. However, relaxation training and biofeedback can lead to a reduction in medication.
4. Pain behaviors—actions indicating that the person is experiencing sensations of pain—are accessible to assessment and treatment. Well behaviors are overt behaviors that typically indicate a person is not experiencing pain sensations.
5. One approach to treating pain involves changing the consequences that are maintaining pain behaviors. Social attention, rest, and medication are typical reinforcers for pain. Treatment involves extinction of pain behaviors and reinforcement of well behaviors. Attention and rest are made contingent on well behaviors rather than pain behaviors. Pain medication is made time contingent rather than pain contingent.
6. Cognitive-behavioral coping skills treatment packages that include relaxation training and biofeedback also are used to treat pain.
7. Behavioral treatments for pain typically result in reduction, rather than elimination, of pain. The reduction can be substantial enough for patients to resume normal activities.
8. Cognitive-behavioral therapies have been used to treat medically unexplained symptoms, such as in chronic fatigue syndrome, noncardiac chest pain, and fibromyalgia syndrome.
9. Following medical advice and engaging in health-related behaviors have been increased by means of stimulus control, reinforcement, teaching patients self-control skills, and making the consequences of nonadherence unpleasant. Reinforcement generally is the most effective technique for increasing adherence. When low adherence is maintained by skills deficits, modeling is useful.
10. A variety of strategies have been used to help patients and their families deal with the stress, discomfort, and pain associated with medical and dental procedures, hospitalization, and illness. They include teaching patients cognitive-behavioral coping skills and employing reinforcement and extinction procedures. Similar procedures also have been used to reduce the negative physical and psychological side effects of medical treatments.
11. Behavioral interventions have been used to help prevent physical illness by educating people about disease and motivating them to engage in healthful, preventive behaviors.
12. The Stanford Three Community Study was a multifaceted, large-scale prevention program that incorporated behavior therapy

procedures to reduce the risk of cardiovascular disease in three communities.

13. Behavior therapies have been applied to women's health care, including relaxation training to lower hypertension during pregnancy and prompting to increase breast self-examination.

14. Treatment programs for decreasing high-risk behaviors for HIV infection have employed education, cognitive-behavioral coping skills therapy, assertion training, and social skills training.

REFERENCE NOTES

1. Pinkerton, Hughes, & Wenrich, 1982.
2. *Information Please Almanac,* 1989.
3. Appel, Saab, & Holroyd, 1985.
4. Haaga, Davison, Williams, Dolezal, Haleblian, Rosenbaum, Dwyer, Baker, Nezami, & DeQuattro, 1994.
5. Pratt & Jones, 1995.
6. Jacobson, 1929, 1939.
7. Agras, 1981; Brauer, Norlick, Nelson, Farquhar, & Agras, 1979; Lehrer, 1982; McGrady, 1994; McGrady, Olson, & Kroon, 1995.
8. For example, Carrington, 1977.
9. For example, Benson, 1975.
10. For example, Patel, 1977.
11. Appel, Saab, & Holroyd, 1985; McGrady, Olson, & Kroon, 1995.
12. For example, Kristt & Engel, 1975; Tursky, Shapiro, & Schwartz, 1972; Wittrock & Blanchard, 1992.
13. For example, Beiman, Israel, & Johnson, 1978; Haaga, Davison, Williams, Dolezal, Haleblian, Rosenbaum, Dwyer, Baker, Nezami, & DeQuattro, 1994; Rici & Lawrence, 1979; Taylor, Farquhar, Nelson, & Agras, 1977.
14. Agras, Taylor, Kraemer, Allen, & Schneider, 1980.
15. Southam, Agras, Taylor, & Kraemer, 1982.
16. Agras, Southam, & Taylor, 1983; Lynch, Birk, Weaver, Gohara, Leighton, Repka, & Walsh, 1992; Manne, Jacobsen, Gorfinkle, Gerstein, & Redd, 1993.
17. For example, Wittrock, Blanchard, & McCoy, 1988; compare with Hoelscher, Lichstein, Fischer, & Hegarty, 1987.
18. For example, Cottier, Shapiro, & Julius, 1984; Jacob, Shapiro, Reeves, Johnson, McDonald, & Coburn, 1986.
19. Jacobson, 1978.

20. For example, Agras, Taylor, Kraemer, Southam, & Schneider, 1987; Jacob, Wing, & Shapiro, 1987.
21. McGrady, Olson, & Kroon, 1995.
22. Hoelscher, Lichstein, & Rosenthal, 1984; Taylor, Agras, Schneider, & Allen, 1983.
23. Pickering, 1982.
24. For example, Blanchard, Young, & Haynes, 1975; McGrady, Olson, & Kroon, 1995.
25. For example, Elder & Eustis, 1975.
26. Goldstein, Shapiro, Thananopavarn, & Sambhi, 1982.
27. Pinkerton, Hughes, & Wenrich, 1982; Walsh, Dale, & Anderson, 1977.
28. Bradley & Hughes, 1979; Pinkerton, Hughes, & Wenrich, 1982; Wittrock, Blanchard, & McCoy, 1988.
29. Carlson & Bernstein, 1995; Edinger & Jacobsen, 1982.
30. Miller, 1978.
31. Kaplan, 1983.
32. Appel, Saab, & Holroyd, 1985.
33. McGrady, Olson, & Kroon, 1995.
34. Black, 1975.
35. Bonica, 1986; Osterweis, Mechanic, & Kleinman, 1987.
36. Agras, 1981; Brauer, Norlick, Nelson, Farquhar, & Agras, 1979; Lehrer, 1982; McGrady, 1994; McGrady, Olson, & Kroon, 1995.
37. Compare with Kaplan, 1990.
38. Fordyce, 1976.
39. Fordyce, 1976, 1988.
40. Block, Kremer, & Gaylor, 1980; Cairns & Pasino, 1977; Doleys, Crocker, & Patton, 1982; Flor, Kerns, & Turk, 1987.
41. Kole-Snijders, Vlaeyen, Rutten-van Molken, Heuts, van Eek, & van Breukelen, 1999.
42. Turk & Meichenbaum, 1989; Turk & Rudy, 1995.

43. Blanchard, 1992; Holroyd & Penzien, 1994.
44. Andrasik & Blanchard, 1987.
45. Holroyd & Penzien, 1994.
46. Andrasik, Larsson, & Grazzi, 2002; Blanchard, 1992.
47. Andrasik, Larsson, & Grazzi, 2002.
48. Allen & Shriver, 1998.
49. Holroyd & Penzien, 1994; McGrady, Andrasik, Davies, Striefel, Wickramasekera, Baskin, Penzien, & Tietjen, 1999; Penzien & Holroyd, 1994.
50. Larsson & Andrasik, 2002; McGrady, Andrasik, Davies, Striefel, Wickramasekera, Baskin, Penzien, & Tietjen, 1999.
51. McGrady, Wauquier, McNeil, & Gerard, 1994.
52. Compas, Haaga, Keefe, Leitenberg, & Williams, 1998.
53. Wauquier, McGrady, Aloe, Klausner, & Collins, 1995.
54. Lake & Pingel, 1988.
55. Blanchard, 1992; Nicholson & Blanchard, 1993.
56. Compas, Haaga, Keefe, Leitenberg, & Williams, 1998.
57. Varni, La Greca, & Spirito, 2000.
58. Mason, Goolkasian, & McCain, 1998.
59. Gil, Wilson, Edens, Workman, Ready, Sedway, Redding-Lallinger, & Daeschner, 1997.
60. Gil, Carson, Sedway, Porter, Schaeffer, & Orringer, 2000.
61. Linton, 1982; Linton & Melin, 1983.
62. de L. Horne, Taylor, & Varigos, 1999; Wijma, Melin, Nedstrand, & Hammar, 1997.
63. For example, Peterson & Tremblay, 1999.
64. Meichenbaum & Turk, 1976; Turk, 1975, 1976; Turk & Genest, 1979; Turk, Meichenbaum, & Genest, 1983.
65. Lamaze, 1970.
66. For example, Blanchard, 1987; Carey, 1994; Rokke & al'Absi, 1992.
67. For example, Feuerstein & Gainer, 1982.
68. Blanchard, 1987.
69. Anderson, Cole, Gullickson, Hudgens, & Roberts, 1977; Cairns, Thomas, Mooney, & Pau, 1976; Fordyce, 1976; Fordyce, Fowler, & DeLateur, 1968; Fordyce, Fowler, Lehmann, DeLateur, Sand, & Trieschmann, 1973; Fordyce & Steger, 1979; Kerns, Turk, Holzman, & Rudy, 1986; Roberts, 1979; Turner, 1982.
70. Schmidt, Gierlings, & Peters, 1989.
71. Cairns & Pasino, 1977; Dolce, Doleys, Raczynski, Lossie, Poole, & Smith, 1986; Doleys, Crocker, & Patton, 1982.
72. For example, Blanchard, 1987; Blanchard, Applebaum, Radnitz, Morrill, Michultka, Kirsch, Guarnieri, Hillhouse, Evans, Jaccard, & Barron, 1990.
73. Anderson, Lawrence, & Olson, 1981; Blanchard, 1987; Holroyd, Andrasik, & Westbrook, 1977; Reeves, 1976; Steger & Harper, 1977; Turk & Meichenbaum, 1989; Turk, Meichenbaum, & Genest, 1983; Turk & Rudy, 1995.
74. James, Thorn, & Williams, 1993.
75. For example, Osman, Barrios, Osman, Schnekloth, & Troutman, 1994; Rokke & al'Absi, 1992.
76. For example, Blanchard, Theobald, Williamson, Silver, & Brown, 1978; Silver, Blanchard, Williamson, Theobald, & Brown, 1979.
77. For example, Blanchard, Andrasik, Neff, Arena, Ahles, Jurish, Pallmeyer, Saunders, Teders, Barron, & Rodichok, 1982.
78. For example, Anderson, Lawrence, & Olson, 1981; Follick, 1979; Steger & Harper, 1977; Turner & Clancy, 1988; Turner, Heinrich, McCreary, & Dawson, 1979.
79. For example, Katon & Walker, 1998; Kroenke & Mangelsdorf, 1989.
80. Nezu, Nezu, & Lombardo, 2001.
81. For example, Bertagnolli & Morris, 1997; Deale, Chalder, Marks, & Wessely, 1997.
82. Nezu, Nezu, & Lombardo, 2001.
83. For example, Nezu, Nezu, & Lombardo, 2001; Potts & Bass, 1995; Van Peski-Oosterbaan, Spinhoven, Van der Does, Brushke, & Rooijmans, 1999.
84. Nezu, Nezu, & Lombardo, 2001.
85. For example, Buckelew, Conway, Parker, Deuser, Read, Witty, Hewett, Minor, Johnson, Van Male, McIntosh, Nigh, & Kay, 1998; Nicassio, Radojevic, Weisman, Shuman, Kim, Schoenfeld-Smith, & Krall, 1997.
86. Nezu, Nezu, & Lombardo, 2001.
87. Nezu, Nezu, & Lombardo, 2001.
88. For example, Gentry, 1971; Haynes, Taylor, & Sackett, 1979; Meichenbaum & Turk, 1987; Zifferblatt, 1975.
89. For example, Gillum & Barsky, 1974; Pratt & Jones, 1995; Sackett & Snow, 1979.
90. Varni, La Greca, & Spirito, 2000.
91. Marston, 1970; Sackett & Haynes, 1976.

92. For example, Kasl, 1975; Zifferblatt, 1975.
93. Allen & Warzak, 2000.
94. Lima, Nazarian, Charney, & Lahti, 1976.
95. Azrin & Powell, 1969.
96. Newman, Kenardy, Herman, & Taylor, 1996, 1997a.
97. Azrin & Teichner, 1998.
98. Compare with Skinner & Vaughan, 1983.
99. Masek, 1982.
100. Da Costa, Rapoff, & Goldstein, 1997.
101. For example, Masek, 1982.
102. Haynes, Sackett, Gibson, Taylor, Hackett, Roberts, & Johnson, 1976.
103. Bigelow, Strickler, Liebson, & Griffiths, 1976.
104. Orleans, 2000.
105. LaGreca, 1988.
106. For example, Lowe & Lutzker, 1979; compare with Lima, Nazarian, Charney, & Lahti, 1976.
107. Wagner, 1998.
108. Wong, Seroka, & Ogisi, 2000.
109. For example, LaGreca & Ottinger, 1979; Waggoner & LeLieuvre, 1981.
110. Epstein, Beck, Figueroa, Farkas, Kazdin, Daneman, & Becker, 1981.
111. Epstein, Beck, Figueroa, Farkas, Kazdin, Daneman, & Becker, 1981.
112. Lowe & Lutzker, 1979.
113. Magrab & Papadopoulou, 1977.
114. Greenan, Powell, & Varni, 1984.
115. For example, Brownell & Cohen, 1995; Dubbert, 1992.
116. For example, Gilbert, Johnson, Spillar, McCallum, Silverstein, & Rosenbloom, 1982.
117. Sergis-Deavenport & Varni, 1982, 1983.
118. Follansbee, LaGreca, & Citrin, 1983; Gross, Johnson, Wildman, & Mullett, 1981.
119. Stark, Knapp, Bowen, Powers, Jelalian, Evans, Passero, Mulvihill, & Hovell, 1993.
120. For example, Turner & Vernon, 1976.
121. For example, Nazarian, Mechaber, Charney, & Coulter, 1974.
122. For example, Barkin & Duncan, 1975; Kidd & Euphrat, 1971.
123. Stitzer, Bigelow, Lawrence, Cohen, D'Lugoff, & Hawthorne, 1977.
124. Friman, Finney, Rapoff, & Christophersen, 1985.
125. Rice & Lutzker, 1984.
126. de L. Horne, Vatmanidis, & Careri, 1994.

127. Dahlquist, Gil, Armstrong, Ginsberg, & Jones, 1985; Jay, Elliott, Katz, & Siegel, 1987; Katz, Kellerman, & Ellenberg, 1987; Manne, Redd, Jacobsen, Gorfinkle, Schorr, & Rabkin, 1990; Peterson & Shigetomi, 1981; Rains, 1995.
128. Slifer, Babbitt, & Cataldo, 1995.
129. For example, Peterson & Shigetomi, 1981.
130. Redd, Manne, Peters, Jacobsen, & Schmidt, 1994.
131. Slifer, Cataldo, Cataldo, Llorente, & Gerson, 1993.
132. McComas, Wacker, & Cooper, 1998.
133. Manne, Bakeman, Jacobsen, Gorfinkle, & Redd, 1994.
134. For example, Manne, Redd, Jacobsen, Gorfinkle, Schorr, & Rabkin, 1990; Peterson & Shigetomi, 1981.
135. Jay & Elliott, 1990.
136. Varni, La Greca, & Spirito, 2000.
137. For example, Nocella & Kaplan, 1982.
138. Siegel & Peterson, 1980.
139. For example, Gatchel, 1980.
140. Thom, Sartory, & Johren, 2000.
141. DiTomasso, Martin, & Kovnat, 2000.
142. Lutgendorf, Starr, McCabe, Antoni, Ironson, Klimas, Fletcher, Kumar, Schneiderman, & Cleven, 1997.
143. Redd & Andrykowski, 1982.
144. Burish & Lyles, 1979; Burish, Shartner, & Lyles, 1981; Compas, Haaga, Keefe, Leitenberg, & Williams, 1998; Lyles, Burish, Krozely, & Oldham, 1982.
145. Morrow & Morrell, 1982.
146. Morrow, Asbury, Hammon, Dobkin, Caruso, Pandya, & Rosenthal, 1992; Morrow & Morrell, 1982.
147. Cullen, Fox, & Isom, 1976; Holand, Plumb, Yates, Harris, Tuttolomondo, Holmes, & Holland, 1977.
148. Agras, 1976.
149. Redd, 1980.
150. Redd, 1980.
151. Farquhar, 1978; Maccoby, Farquhar, Wood, & Alexander, 1977; Meyer, Nash, McAlister, Maccoby, & Farquhar, 1980.
152. Farquhar, Maccoby, & Solomon, 1984.
153. Little, Hayworth, Benson, Hall, Beard, Dewhurst, & Priest, 1984.
154. Jansen, 1987.

155. Mayer & Frederiksen, 1986.
156. Solomon, Flynn, Worden, Mickey, Skelly, Geller, Peluso, & Webster, 1998.
157. Kelly & St. Lawrence, 1987.
158. Centers for Disease Control and Prevention, 1994.
159. Hall, 1988.
160. National Center for HIV, STD and TB Prevention, 2001.
161. Kelly & St. Lawrence, 1988a.
162. National Center for HIV, STD and TB Prevention, 2001.
163. Honnen & Kleinke, 1990.
164. Kelly, St. Lawrence, Hood, & Brasfield, 1989.
165. McKusick, Wiley, Coates, & Morin, 1986.
166. Metzler, Biglan, Noell, Ary, & Ochs, 2000; St. Lawrence, Brasfield, Jefferson, Alleyne, O'Bannon, & Shirley, 1995; St. Lawrence, Jefferson, Alleyne, & Brasfield, 1995.
167. Nangle & Hansen, 1998.
168. Rotheram-Borus, Koopman, Haignere, & Davies, 1991.
169. Walter & Vaughan, 1993.
170. Kalichman, Cherry, & Browne-Sperling, 1999.
171. For example, Carey, Braaten, Maisto, Gleason, Forsyth, Durant, & Jaworski, 2000; Hobfoll, Jackson, Lavin, Britton, & Shepherd, 1994; Kelly, Murphy, Washington, Wilson, Koob, Davis, Lepezma, & Davantes, 1994.
172. For example, Kelly, St. Lawrence, Hood, & Brasfield, 1989.
173. For example, Sikkema, Winett, & Lombard, 1995.
174. Kalichman, Sikkema, Kelly, & Bulto, 1995; Weinhardt, Carey, Carey, & Verdecias, 1998.
175. Miltenberger, Roberts, Ellingson, Galensky, Rapp, Long, & Lumley, 1999.
176. For example, Carey, Braaten, Maisto, Gleason, Forsyth, Durant, & Jaworski, 2000; Metzler, Biglan, Noell, Ary, & Ochs, 2000; St. Lawrence, Brasfield, Jefferson, Alleyne, O'Bannon, & Shirley, 1995; St. Lawrence, Jefferson, Alleyne, & Brasfield, 1995; Weinhardt, Carey, Carey, & Verdecias, 1998.
177. For example, Carey, Braaten, Maisto, Gleason, Forsyth, Durant, & Jaworski, 2000; Chesney, 1994; Kalichman, Carey, & Johnson, 1996; Kelly & Murphy, 1992; Metzler, Biglan, Noell, Ary, & Ochs, 2000.
178. Kalichman, Carey, & Johnson, 1996.
179. Kelly, St. Lawrence, Hood, & Brasfield, 1989.
180. For example, Otto & Gould, 1995; Otto, Gould, & Pollack, 1994.

Chapter 15

Applications to Psychological Disorders with Primary Physical Characteristics

In addition to its contribution to behavioral medicine described in the previous chapter, behavior therapy plays an important role in the treatment of a variety of psychological disorders whose primary feature is a physical problem. We will illustrate this application of behavior therapy for enuresis, tics and nervous habits, insomnia, bulimia nervosa, and addictive behaviors.

The distinction between these psychological disorders and the medical problems discussed in Chapter 14 is based on the way they are classified in the health professions.[1] For example, whereas essential hypertension and pain are considered medical disorders, insomnia and bulimia nervosa are viewed as psychological disorders. This distinction is, admittedly, somewhat arbitrary and artificial. Both psychological disorders with primary physical characteristics and medical disorders increasingly are being viewed in terms of an interplay of physical and psychological factors.[2] Psychological factors are both antecedents and consequences of physical problems, which creates a vicious cycle (see Figure 15-1). Once the cycle begins, reciprocal determinism develops; thus, it is not useful to ask, "Which is causing which?" For example, worrying interferes with falling asleep, and the resulting fatigue over an extended period may affect one's job performance; poor job performance may cause additional worry that makes sleeping even more difficult.

ENURESIS

Enuresis is the inability of people beyond the age of 5 to voluntarily control urination, when no known physical cause is involved. Enuresis most frequently occurs during sleep, so treatment efforts have focused on *nocturnal enuresis,* or bedwetting. It is a common problem among children, occurring in approximately 15% to 20% of all 5-year-olds, 5% of 10-year-olds, and 2% of 12- to 14-year-olds.[3] Nocturnal enuresis is more prevalent in boys than in girls.[4]

Urination is the natural response to tension in the bladder as it fills up. Normally, bladder tension wakes us when we are sleeping, and we get out of bed and go to the bathroom. The problem in enuresis is that bladder tension does not wake the person. Traditional verbal psychotherapy

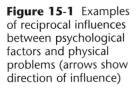

Figure 15-1 Examples of reciprocal influences between psychological factors and physical problems (arrows show direction of influence)

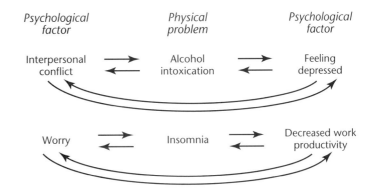

Psychological factor	*Physical problem*	*Psychological factor*
Interpersonal conflict	Alcohol intoxication	Feeling depressed
Worry	Insomnia	Decreased work productivity

generally has been unsuccessful in treating enuresis.[5] In contrast, two behavior therapy procedures—the urine alarm and dry-bed training—have proved to be highly effective.

Urine Alarm

A **urine alarm** is a device that sounds an alarm to wake the child when the child begins to urinate. The original urine alarm was the bell-and-pad method in which urine that contacts a special pad under the bed sheet completes an electrical circuit that sounds an alarm (see Figure 15-2).[6] Through repeated associations between the alarm and bladder tension, bladder tension alone becomes the stimulus that awakens the child before urination starts.

Although the bell-and-pad apparatus still is available, a more convenient device generally is used today. It consists of a moisture-sensitive switching system; the sensor end goes inside the client's underpants and is connected to a small alarm that unobtrusively is attached to the client's outer clothing, such as pajamas. This device, which can be purchased over the counter in pharmacies, also is applicable to diurnal (daytime) enuresis, which affects approximately 1% of children over the age of 5.[7]

The urine alarm is very easy to use. It has been employed for 65 years, and it continues to be effective with 70% to 80% of clients.[8] It has been shown to be superior to medication (specifically, imipramine)[9] and traditional psychotherapy.[10] The relapse rate after 6 months has been about 33%, and the predominant reason for relapse has been poor compliance

Figure 15-2 Bell-and-pad apparatus used to treat nocturnal enuresis

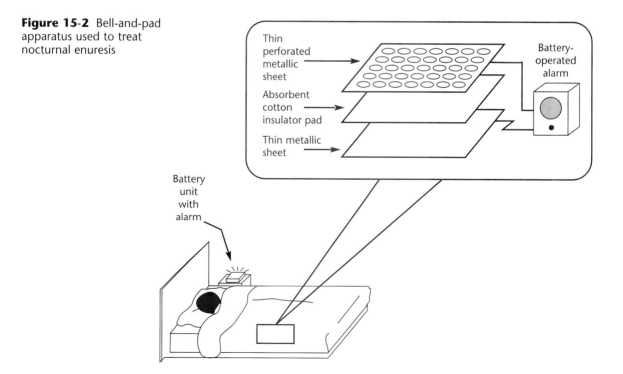

Thin perforated metallic sheet

Absorbent cotton insulator pad

Thin metallic sheet

Battery-operated alarm

Battery unit with alarm

with the procedures.[11] The urine alarm has been used alone and as part of treatment packages.[12] Interestingly, the urine alarm tends to be as effective alone as when it is combined with other behavioral treatments.[13]

Dry-Bed Training

Dry-bed training, developed by Nathan Azrin and his associates,[14] is a comprehensive treatment package that employs shaping and overcorrection to teach children the behaviors required to keep the bed dry throughout the night. Table 15-1 outlines the steps involved in dry-bed training. These procedures illustrate the detail and precision inherent in many behavior therapy procedures.

Treatment begins with a night of intensive training. The child is awakened every hour to urinate if necessary and to be praised for having a dry bed. When an accident occurs, the child goes through a two-phase overcorrection procedure. First comes *cleanliness training,* a form of restitution in which the client changes the wet nightclothes and sheets. Second, there is repeated *positive practice,* which consists of (1) the child lying in bed for a count of 50, then (2) hurrying to the bathroom and attempting to urinate, and finally, (3) returning to bed. In addition, during the day the child practices retaining urine in the bladder by using **retention control training.**[15] This procedure involves shaping the retention of increasingly greater amounts of urine (created by frequently drinking favorite beverages) for increasingly longer periods.

Parents can be trained to implement dry-bed training in about an hour and a half,[16] and the child is made largely responsible for carrying out the dry-bed training procedures. For example, the therapist first teaches the procedures to the child, who then explains them to the parents and requests their help in carrying them out.[17] The emphasis in dry-bed training is on the child's developing self-control skills and being reinforced for accomplishments. When accidents occur, the child assumes the responsibility of correcting them by cleaning up and then by practicing the behaviors required to prevent accidents in the future.

Table 15-1 Protocol for dry-bed training with parents as trainers for a 6-year-old boy
SOURCE: Based on Azrin & Thienes, 1978.

I. *Training day*
   A. Afternoon
      1. Child encouraged to drink favorite beverage to increase urination
      2. Child requested to attempt urination every half hour
         a. If child feels urge to urinate, he is asked to wait for increasingly longer periods of time
         b. If child *has* to urinate, he is asked to lie in bed as if asleep, then jump up and go to the bathroom (role-playing what he should do at night); his behavior is then reinforced with a beverage and praise
      3. Child motivated to work at dry beds
         a. Parents and child review inconveniences caused by bed-wetting
         b. Parents contract with child for reinforcers to be given after first dry night and after a specified series of dry nights
         c. Child specifies whom he'd like to tell that he is keeping dry
         d. Child is given a chart to mark his progress

(continued)

Table 15-1 *(continued)*

    B. One hour before bedtime with parents watching
       1. Child informed of all phases of procedures
       2. Child role-plays cleanliness training (to be used if bed-wetting occurs)
          a. Child required to put on own pajamas
          b. Child required to remove sheets and put them back on
       3. Child role-plays positive practice in toileting (to be used if bed-wetting occurs)
          a. Child lies down in bed as if asleep (lights out)
          b. Child counts to 50
          c. Child arises and hurries to bathroom where he tries to urinate
          d. Child returns to bed
          e. Steps a–d repeated 20 times with parents counting
    C. At bedtime
       1. Child tells parents instructions on accident correction and nighttime awakenings
       2. Child continues to drink fluids
       3. Parents talk to child about reinforcers and express confidence in child
       4. Parents comment on dryness of sheets
       5. Child retires for the night
    D. Hourly awakenings by parents until 1 A.M.
       1. If child is dry
          a. Minimal prompt (light touching) used to awaken (stronger prompt used if child doesn't wake)
          b. Child asked if he needs to urinate
             i. If he can wait another hour
                (a) Parents praise his urinary control
                (b) Child returns to bed
             ii. If he must urinate
                (a) Child goes to bathroom
                (b) Parents praise him for correct toileting
                (c) Child returns to bed
          c. Child feels sheets and comments on their dryness
          d. Parents praise child for having dry bed
          e. Child given fluids (discontinued after 11 P.M.)
          f. Child returns to sleep
       2. When an accident has occurred
          a. Parent awakens child and reprimands him for wetting
          b. Parent directs child to bathroom to finish urinating
          c. Child given cleanliness training
             i. Child changes pajamas
             ii. Child removes wet sheets and places them in laundry basket
             iii. Child obtains clean sheets and remakes bed
          d. Positive practice in correct toileting (20 times) performed immediately after cleanliness training
          e. Child reminded that positive practice is necessary before going to bed the next evening
    E. Parents check child half hour earlier than normal waking the next morning
       1. If bed is wet, steps under IIB (below) implemented

  II. *Posttraining (after training day)*
    A. If bed dry in the morning
       1. Parents point out to child half hour before his usual bedtime that he does not have to practice (because bed was dry that morning) and so he can do what he wants in the half hour before going to bed

(continued)

Table 15-1 *(continued)*

2. Parents point out child's chart that shows his progress toward reinforcers
3. Parents tell visitors to the home how child is keeping his bed dry
4. Parents remark on child's success at least three times a day

B. If bed wet in the morning
1. Parents wake child half hour earlier, prompt him to check his sheets, and ask him to say what he should do
2. Child required to change bed and pajamas
3. Child engages in positive practice in correct toileting (20 times)
4. Child engages in positive practice (20 times) half hour before bed that night
5. Child marks chart and is told "We will try again tomorrow"
6. Parents tell visitors to the home that the child is learning to keep his bed dry

---

Dry-bed training eliminates enuresis more quickly and results in longer-lasting effects than the urine alarm.[18]* The results of one study with 44 children between the ages of 3 and 15 (average age of 7) illustrate the rapidity and long-lasting effectiveness of dry-bed training.[19] As Figure 15-3 shows, before dry-bed training the children were wetting their beds

Photo 15-1 As part of dry-bed training, the child is responsible for changing bedding after accidents

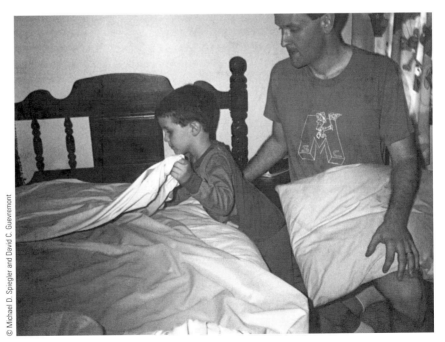

© Michael D. Spiegler and David C. Guevremont

*The more rapid and more long-lasting effects of dry-bed training notwithstanding, the percentage of clients who have been successfully treated for enuresis is higher for the urine alarm (Rushton, 1989), perhaps because it is much easier to implement and therefore more likely to be used.

Figure 15-3 Bed-
wetting by 44 children
with enuresis after office
instruction in dry-bed
training
SOURCE: Adapted from Azrin,
Thienes-Hontos, & Besalel-
Azrin, 1979, p. 18.

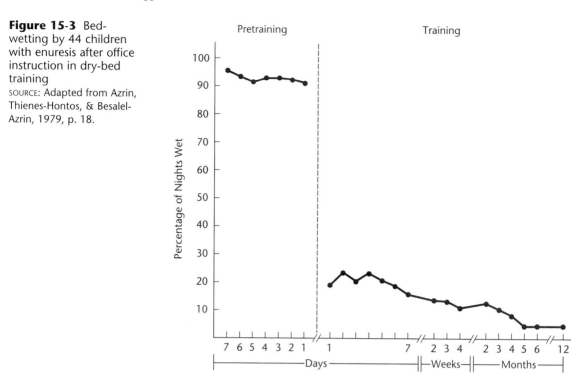

an average of 92% of the nights. On the first day after the intensive training, bedwetting was reduced to 18%. At a 5-month follow-up, bedwetting
was occurring on only 4% of the nights, a level that was maintained 1
year later.

Dry-bed training occasionally is used for adults, and one study revealed
that 8 of 9 clients who had had enuresis most of their lives remained continent at a 6-year follow-up.[20]

Dry-Pants Method

The principles of dry-bed training have been extended to normal daytime
toilet training with impressive results.[21] In the course of normal development, most children learn to use the toilet over a period of several months;
parental attempts to hasten the process generally have little effect.[22] Several methods of intensive reinforcement training have been moderately
successful in reducing training time to approximately 1 month.[23] In
contrast, using the **dry-pants method** (the daytime version of dry-bed
training), children ranging in age from 20 to 36 months have been toilet-
trained in an average of 4 hours, and the average is 2 hours for children
older than 26 months.[24]

A simplified variation of the dry-pants method was used to toilet-train
John, a 21-year-old man with profound mental retardation who lived in a
residential facility.[25] Over the years, the many previous attempts to toilet-
train John had failed. Throughout the day, John was given large amounts

of liquid and was taken to the bathroom every 30 minutes. An alarm system was attached to the inside of the toilet bowl and was activated by a small amount of urine. When the alarm sounded, a staff member praised John and gave him an edible reinforcer. John also wore a dry-pants alarm that signaled toileting accidents. When an accident occurred, a staff member took John to a private area, mildly reprimanded him (for example, "No, don't wet your pants"), and then withdrew social attention as John's clothing was changed and for an additional 10 minutes thereafter. The intervention resulted in a significant increase in appropriate urinations and a reduction in toileting accidents. At a 3-month follow-up, John was completely continent.

TIC DISORDERS AND NERVOUS HABITS

A *tic* is a recurring, sudden, rapid movement or vocalization. Examples of *motor tics* are repetitive neck jerking, shoulder twitching, facial grimacing, and slapping oneself. Examples of *vocal tics* are repetitive throat clearing, snorting, and grunting. Although tics are largely involuntary, people can suppress them for varying lengths of time. Tics usually begin in childhood, are three times more common in males, and are exacerbated by stress. Children and adolescents who exhibit tics are viewed negatively by their peers,[26] and adults' social and occupational functioning may be impaired because of social ostracism and anxiety about exhibiting tics in the presence of others. In severe cases, tics may directly interfere with a person's daily functioning, as when eye blinking makes reading difficult. *Tourette's disorder* is the most serious tic disorder, involving multiple motor and vocal tics (which sometimes include uttering obscenities).[27]

Medication is the most common treatment for tics, but its use is problematic. In the case of Tourette's disorder, for example, the frequency of tics is only reduced about 50%,[28] and unwanted side effects have been noted in about 80% of clients taking medication.[29] Further, only about 20% to 30% of clients continue taking medication on a long-term basis.[30] Clearly, alternative treatments are needed. The major behavioral treatments for tics are massed negative practice, changing maintaining consequences, relaxation training, self-monitoring, and habit reversal.

Massed negative practice, the most frequently used behavioral treatment for tics, has the client deliberately perform the tic as rapidly as possible. This is done for a set time (for example, 30 minutes), with short rest periods (for instance, 1 minute of rest for each 4 minutes of performing the tic).[31] Negative practice has been moderately successful in reducing the frequency of tics for some people,[32] with an average reduction of about 60%.[33]

Changing the maintaining consequences of tics is the second most frequently employed behavior therapy. Differential reinforcement[34] is effective in reducing tics in children by itself[35] and when combined with other therapies.[36] Consequential deceleration therapies, including contingent electric shock[37] and time out from positive reinforcement,[38] also can reduce tic frequency. However, the treatment effects with deceleration therapies may not transfer from the specific therapy setting to the client's natural environment, may be only temporary,[39] and clearly are less preferable than reinforcement procedures.

Using progressive relaxation is consistently effective in decreasing tics *while* the clients are relaxing.[40] However, the tics tend to return shortly after relaxation sessions terminate.[41]

Self-monitoring can be an effective treatment for tics.[42] Although self-monitoring typically is an assessment procedure (see Chapter 5), it is sometimes specifically used to modify a target behavior. Self-monitoring makes clients more aware of their tics, which is necessary for effective treatment.

In sum, massed negative practice, changing maintaining consequences, relaxation training, and self-monitoring all are moderately effective treatments for tics. To increase their effectiveness, various combinations of these treatments generally are used.

Habit Reversal for Tics

Habit reversal, by far the most effective treatment package for tics, was developed by Azrin and his colleagues.[43] Habit reversal incorporates four components: (1) awareness training, (2) competing response training, (3) relaxation training, and (4) reinforcement. Awareness training and competing response training seem to be the critical components.[44]

Awareness training, which includes self-monitoring, involves extensive self-assessment to ensure that the client is aware of the frequency and severity of the tics, their environmental antecedents, and the individual responses that make up the tics. Clients and family members keep a record of when, how often, where, and with whom tics occur. Clients are asked to observe their tics by looking in a mirror or videotaping themselves, because knowing the specific responses involved is necessary to control tics. Clients also practice detecting the first signs of tics so that they will be able to stop the tics early in their sequence.

In *competing response training,* clients practice performing a response that competes with the tic, can be sustained for several minutes, is compatible with everyday activities, and is inconspicuous to others.[45] Table 15-2 provides examples of competing responses for various kinds of tics.[46]

Clients are taught progressive relaxation and are instructed to practice it daily. Additionally, they are taught to use differential relaxation in their daily lives whenever they feel anxious or emit a tic (as in coping desensitization; see Chapter 9).

Family members are asked to praise the client when they observe that the client is tic free or shows a significant reduction in tics. Clients compile a list of the negative consequences of emitting tics (such as embarrassment and inconvenience) and the positive consequences of eliminating tics. They write the list on a card that they carry with them and periodically refer to as reminders of the benefits of engaging in habit reversal procedures. Children are given specific reinforcers for completing therapy assignments and reducing tics below a predetermined goal level.

Habit reversal consistently has been shown to be highly effective in treating tics,[47] reducing tics by about 90%, compared with 50% to 60%

Table 15-2 Competing responses for tics used in habit reversal

SOURCE: Based on Azrin & Peterson, 1988b.

Tics	Competing Responses
HEAD JERK	Isometric contraction of neck flexor muscles: pull chin down and in, head in, eyes forward
SHOULDER SHRUG	Isometric contraction of shoulder depressor muscles: push elbow toward hip
HEAD SHAKE	Slow isometric contraction of neck muscles with eyes forward until head can be held perfectly still
ARM JERK	Push hand down on thigh or stomach and push elbow in toward hip
LEG JERK	If sitting, place feet on floor and push down; if standing, lock knees
EYE BLINK	Systematic, soft blinking at rate of one blink every 3–5 seconds; frequent downward glance every 5–10 seconds
ORAL VOCAL TICS	Continuous slow, rhythmic breathing through nose with mouth closed
NASAL VOCAL TICS	Continuous slow, rhythmic breathing through mouth

with medication.[48] Habit reversal also has been used to treat a variety of other problems, including eczema (skin inflammation),[49] temporo-mandibular disorders (which involve pain in the jaw and surrounding structures),[50] and overeating,[51] as well as problems that can be loosely categorized as nervous habits.[52] Habit reversal generally has been found to be superior to other treatments for these problems and is preferable to aversive treatments that sometimes are used to treat them.

Habit Reversal for Nervous Habits

We will illustrate the use of habit reversal for nervous habits with tri-chotillomania (hair pulling)[53] and stuttering.[54] Other nervous habits treated by habit reversal include thumb sucking,[55] finger nail biting,[56] and bruxism (teeth grinding).[57]

   As an example of how habit reversal is used to treat chronic trichotil-lomania, consider the treatment employed with three 12-year-olds (two girls and one boy).[58] During awareness training, the clients learned to detect their hair pulling, first by describing what hair felt like between their fingers and then by actually feeling their hair between their fingers without actually pulling out hair. In competing response training, each client identified several behaviors that were incompatible with hair pulling (such as crossing one's arms and sitting on one's hands). The therapist instructed the clients to use these behaviors every time they became aware of pulling out their hair or of having an urge to do so. The clients simulated hair pulling and engaged in the competing response for 1 minute, which was repeated 12 to 15 times. The therapist taught the clients' parents first to prompt their child to engage in a competing response when they observed their child pulling out hair and then to praise the child for performing the competing response. Habit reversal resulted in significant reductions in hair pulling with all three clients.

Stuttering affects nearly 1% of adults and 5% to 10% of children;[59] stuttering is the most prevalent maladaptive habit in individuals with mental retardation, occurring in up to 32% of that population.[60] The standard procedures for habit reversal are used to treat stuttering. The most common competing response employed for stuttering is *regulated breathing exercises* that consist of relaxing, slowly inhaling deeply through the nose, and slowly exhaling through the mouth. Habit reversal not only decreases stuttering but also can increase the naturalness of speech, including the rate of speech (which often is slow and labored in people who stutter).[61]

One downside of habit reversal is that it generally requires considerable time—from the client, the therapist, and family members (when they participate in the treatment). However, this is not always the case. In one study, five boys between the ages of 5 and 11 received a single session of habit reversal training in their homes for stuttering.[62] During awareness training, each child and his parents practiced together identifying the occurrences of stuttering from videotaped speech samples of the child, which were made ahead of time. Both the child and his parents learned and practiced regulated breathing exercises as the competing response. The child learned to stop speaking when he began to stutter and begin regulated breathing. Parents provided social support and praise when their son applied habit reversal procedures. Habit reversal resulted in significant reductions in stuttering in four of the five children, and three of the children maintained these gains for up to 9 months. The parents found habit reversal to be an acceptable treatment.

Although habit reversal often is a sufficient treatment for decreasing clients' maladaptive habits, it sometimes needs to be augmented with additional procedures to achieve the desired outcome. For example, when habit reversal only minimally reduced a 6-year-old girl's hair pulling and thumb sucking, differential reinforcement and response cost were added, which resulted in near zero levels of both deceleration target behaviors.[63] Similarly, adding response cost to habit reversal resulted in further reductions in a 14-year-old boy's disruptive outbursts during athletic events.[64] Brief booster training sessions also can enhance long-term maintenance of treatment gains following habit reversal training.[65]

INSOMNIA

Insomnia refers to difficulties in falling or staying asleep, which cause personal distress and affect one's daytime performance, mood, and general psychological well-being.[66] Insomnia includes sleep disturbances that are not directly caused by a medical condition or the effects of drugs. It is estimated that 15% to 20% of adults suffer from chronic insomnia and that 30% to 40% experience occasional or transient insomnia.[67] Sedatives or other sleep-inducing drugs are the most common treatment for adult insomnia. Sedating drugs—usually antihistamines—also are widely prescribed for infant and childhood sleep difficulties.[68] A number of potential problems are associated with using sleep medications, including a deterioration in daytime functioning, "rebound insomnia" (greater difficulty sleeping after using sleep medication), psychological and physiological dependence on the drug, and financial expense.[69] Given the high prevalence of sleep problems among both children and adults and the disadvantages of using drug therapy, psychological treatments play an important role in the treatment of chronic sleep problems. Behavior therapies are among the most effective psychological treatments.[70]

Infant and Childhood Sleep Problems

Sleep problems in infants and young children (up to age 6) usually involve refusal to go to bed, difficulty in settling down and falling asleep, and nighttime awakening and crying. Such sleep disturbances are chronic problems for 15% to 35% of children under the age of 5.[71] Not surprisingly, parents typically respond to their child's sleep problems with some form of attention, which can reinforce the sleep disturbance. When parental attention is the primary maintaining condition of infant and toddler sleep disturbances, extinction is the treatment of choice.[72]

In the standard application of extinction for infant sleep problems, parents refrain from attending to their child after placing the child in bed (as you may recall from Case 7-1, page 147). Attention is withheld if the child refuses to get into bed or to go to sleep and if the child wakes up and cries during the night. This simple procedure is highly effective in decreasing children's refusal to go to bed or sleep and the frequency and duration of awakenings; it also improves children's general sleep quality. The improvements have been shown to last at least as long as 2 years after the treatment ends.[73] A major advantage of extinction is that it is simple for parents to learn. In addition, extinction, along with changing setting events (which we describe in the next section), has been effective in preventing infant sleep problems.[74]

Despite the demonstrated effectiveness of extinction for infant sleep problems, some parents are unwilling to use it because, understandably, they are upset by their child's crying and sleep problems and they feel compelled to provide comfort. The occurrence of extinction bursts—the temporary, initial increase in the target behavior that is common with extinction (such as increased crying when the child is put to bed)—is another factor that makes extinction unacceptable as a treatment to some parents.[75] Moreover, some critics have argued that extinction is unethical because it damages the parent–child relationship, such as by decreasing the infant's security.[76] In fact, the empirical evidence suggests just the opposite. Studies reveal that infants treated by extinction appear to be more secure and exhibit fewer negative emotions (such as crying) than do untreated infants with sleep problems and infants without sleep problems.[77]

Because change agents will use a therapy only if it is acceptable to them, behavior therapists have modified extinction procedures to render them more palatable for parents. The simplest modification allows parents to make a specified number of brief, time-limited checks on their child if the child cries after having been put to bed (for instance, looking in on the child for 15 seconds or less, no more often than once every 20 minutes).[78]

Graduated extinction is a more complex modification that involves either gradually increasing the time the parent ignores the child's bed-time crying[79] or gradually decreasing the time the parent spends attending to the child when the child awakens during the night.[80] The increments are individualized for each family. Parents tend to find modified extinction procedures more acceptable,[81] but they generally are less effective than standard extinction procedures.[82]

When the sleep disturbances of children clearly are not being maintained by parental attention, alternative interventions are needed. Such is the case with *sleep terrors,* which involve episodes of a child's awakening screaming with diffuse fear and agitation. The child has no recollection of dreaming and does not remember the incident in the morning. It is difficult to comfort a child who has had a sleep terror. It is estimated that between 1% and 6% of children have sleep terrors,[83] and the exact causes are unknown. Sleep terrors in children are not believed to be triggered or maintained by parental attention, but they possibly are maintained by a disruption in the sleep cycle.

Scheduled awakenings are an effective behavioral intervention for sleep terrors. For a given child, sleep terrors occur at about the same time each night (usually occurring in the first third of the child's sleep period). Parents are instructed to awaken the child approximately 30 minutes before the anticipated sleep terror episode. The parent lightly touches or moves the child until his or her eyes are open, and then the child is allowed to fall back asleep. Scheduled awakenings are carried out until the child achieves a specified number of nights without experiencing a sleep terror episode. Scheduled awakenings have resulted in significant reductions in children's sleep terrors.[84]

Adult Insomnia

Adult insomnia is maintained primarily by three antecedent conditions: inappropriate setting events for sleeping, excessive muscle tension, and excessive worry. Three behavior therapies are used to change these maintaining conditions: changing setting events, progressive relaxation training, and cognitive restructuring, respectively.

CHANGING SETTING EVENTS

Some people have difficulty falling asleep because, for them, being in bed has strong associations with a host of activities other than sleeping, such as reading, watching TV, snacking, talking on the phone, studying, and worrying about not being able to fall asleep. Modifying setting events can be effective when insomnia is maintained by such non–sleep-related setting events.

Procedures for adjusting setting events to treat insomnia, developed by Richard Bootzin,[85] establish a client's bed as a clear-cut cue for sleeping and *only* for sleeping. Clients are instructed to adhere to three basic rules.[86]

1. Get into bed *only* when you are sleepy.

2. Use your bed *only* for sleeping. (The one exception is for sexual behavior, but only if you feel relaxed or sleepy afterward. If sex leaves you wide awake, engage in it somewhere other than the bed in which you sleep.)

3. If you cannot fall asleep within 15 minutes, get out of bed and go into another room. Return to bed when you are sleepy. If you still cannot fall asleep, repeat this step. (It does not seem to matter what you do when you get out of bed, as long as the activity is not stimulating.)

In addition to these rules that establish appropriate setting events, clients also are asked to follow two other rules that promote good sleep habits.

4. Get up at the same time every morning, regardless of what time you go to bed. (This routine allows you to establish a regular sleep rhythm.)

5. Do not take naps. (Napping can disrupt the regular sleep rhythm and makes it harder to fall asleep at night.)

These procedures are highly effective in treating sleep-onset insomnia.[87] They consistently have been shown to be superior to no treatment and placebo control conditions in decreasing *sleep-onset latency,* the time it takes to fall asleep.

Modifying setting events has been an effective treatment for older adults who often experience sleep-onset problems and frequent nighttime awakenings.[88] In one study with adults aged 47 to 76, changing setting events was combined with *sleep education,* which provides clients with information about behaviors that facilitate sleep (such as daily exercise) and behaviors that interfere with sleep (such as consuming alcohol before retiring).[89] This treatment package was compared with sleep education alone, sleep education plus relaxation training, and a no-treatment control group.

Interestingly, all the clients, including those in the control group, showed improvement on self-report measures immediately after treatment, including the number of nighttime awakenings, feelings of depression, and feelings of being refreshed on awakening. Because clients in the control group also reported these improvements, it was not possible to conclude that any of the treatments were responsible for the positive changes. However, at a 2-year follow-up, clients who had been taught to alter setting events reported shorter sleep-onset latencies and had the highest ratings of sleep quality. It is noteworthy that these clients were still using the setting events intervention. Two factors may have accounted for the long-lasting effects: Changing setting events was easy to implement, and the new, appropriate setting events became a natural part of the clients' lives. These factors also may explain why, in general, modifying setting events consistently is the single most effective treatment for adult insomnia.[90]

Many everyday behaviors besides falling asleep are maintained by setting events, which means that they can be influenced by altering setting events. Studying is one such behavior that you easily can bring under stimulus control.

◆

Participation Exercise 15-1

MODIFYING SETTING EVENTS TO ENHANCE STUDYING*

Studying is maintained by a host of setting events, including the time of day, the physical setting, and the presence of other students. If your study habits are being maintained by inappropriate setting events, modifying these events may increase the efficiency and effectiveness of your studying.

Using the rules for treating insomnia described earlier as models, make a list of rules to establish setting events that will prompt you to study and will make studying more productive, including increasing concentration and decreasing distractions. Consider the following situational factors and how differences in them affect your studying.

1. *When* you study. This includes the days of the week, the time of day, and the length of study sessions and breaks. What time parameters are optimal for you?

2. *Where* you study. This includes the general location (for instance, at home or at the library) and the specific physical setup (for example, at a desk or on your bed). What factors facilitate your studying (such as ample light and optimal temperature) and inhibit your studying (such as noise and interruptions)?

3. *With whom* you study. Do you study more efficiently by collaborating with one or more other students or by yourself? If you study by yourself, is your studying facilitated by others' studying around you (such as in a study lounge) or by being alone?

After you have compiled your rules, refer to your Student Resource Materials for examples of possible rules. Finally, you might want to follow your rules and see if they affect your studying. If some of your inefficient or ineffective study habits are maintained by setting events, appropriately modifying the events will make a difference.

◆

RELAXATION TRAINING

People who have problems sleeping often report being "all keyed up" and "tense" before going to bed. When insomnia is maintained by muscle tension, training in progressive relaxation is the treatment of choice. Once clients have learned progressive relaxation, they use the relaxation skills when they get into bed to go to sleep. Clients using progressive relaxation in systematic desensitization sometimes get so relaxed that they fall asleep while visualizing scenes. Although this interferes with systematic desensitization, it is precisely the desired outcome for clients who have difficulty falling asleep.

To decrease sleep-onset latency, progressive relaxation consistently has been found to be superior to no treatment[91] but only inconsistently superior to placebo conditions.[92] Clients who receive relaxation training may

*This Participation Exercise can be done before you continue reading or later.

not routinely show improvements in their daytime functioning (for example, alertness during the day).[93] However, relaxation training may serve as a daytime coping skill for dealing with daily stressors,[94] which is beneficial because many clients with chronic insomnia report high levels of daytime anxiety. Finally, relaxation training can facilitate clients' attempts to stop using sleep medications.[95]

The effectiveness of relaxation training for insomnia can be enhanced by (1) greater individualization of treatment, (2) a larger number of treatment sessions,[96] and (3) increased practice in relaxation exercises between therapy sessions.[97] Standard progressive relaxation training appears to be as effective as electromyographic (muscle tone) biofeedback-assisted relaxation training, particularly for clients with sleep-onset problems. Thus, the additional cost of using biofeedback appears to be unwarranted.[98]

COGNITIVE RESTRUCTURING

Worry that can interfere with sleep can be about anything, including work, interpersonal problems, illness, and even sleep difficulties themselves. We will focus on this last problem to illustrate the use of cognitive restructuring to deal with worry that interferes with sleep.

When excessive worry about not sleeping and about the possible negative effects of sleep loss is a maintaining antecedent of sleep problems, cognitive restructuring may be the treatment of choice. Typically, the worry is the result of faulty or distorted beliefs about sleeping, involving one of the following themes: exaggerated ideas about the negative consequences of sleep loss (for instance, "If I don't get a good night's sleep, I'll flunk my exam tomorrow"), unrealistic expectations about what constitutes acceptable sleep requirements (such as "I can't function on less than 9 hours of sleep"), and beliefs about not having control over one's sleeping (for example, "I'm 'wired' by the time I get to bed, and with my schedule, I can't do anything about it"). A client's specific sleep-related cognitions can be assessed initially with a direct self-report inventory, such as the Personal Beliefs and Attitudes About Sleep inventory that asks clients to rate the degree to which they have a number of common thoughts about sleep problems (see Table 15-3 for sample items).[99]

Table 15-3 Items from the Personal Beliefs and Attitudes About Sleep inventory rated on a scale ranging from *strongly agree* to *strongly disagree*
SOURCE: Adapted from Sloan, Hauris, Bootzin, Morin, Stevenson, & Shapiro, 1993.

I am worried that if I go for one or two nights without sleep, I may have a "nervous breakdown."

After a poor night's sleep, I know that it will interfere with my daily activities the next day.

I feel that insomnia is basically the result of aging and there isn't much that can be done about this problem.

My sleep is getting worse all the time, and I don't believe anyone can help.

When I sleep poorly on one night, I know that it will disturb my sleep schedule for the whole week.

Cognitive restructuring for insomnia involves three steps: (1) identifying unrealistic, maladaptive sleep-related cognitions; (2) challenging the validity of these cognitions; and (3) replacing unrealistic, maladaptive cognitions with realistic, adaptive ones. For example, "If I don't fall asleep soon, I won't be able to function tomorrow" might be more realistically and adaptively restructured as "I may be tired tomorrow, but I'll still be able to function. And what I don't get done tomorrow, I can do the next day after a good night's sleep." Note that the adaptive thoughts realistically acknowledge that sleep loss may have some negative consequences, but not the catastrophic consequences predicted by the maladaptive thoughts. With a more realistic outlook, worry about loss of sleep will diminish, which, in turn, will make it more likely that the person will sleep better.

Cognitive restructuring for insomnia has been shown to be effective compared with no-treatment control conditions.[100] Although cognitive restructuring can be used as the sole treatment for insomnia, it generally is part of a treatment package.[101]

TREATMENT PACKAGES FOR ADULT INSOMNIA

As an example of a treatment package for insomnia, we will describe a structured cognitive-behavioral intervention for adults who had suffered from insomnia for an average of more than 11 years.[102] Therapy was conducted individually and typically required 8 to 10 therapy sessions. Besides cognitive restructuring and setting events interventions, the other two major components in the treatment package were sleep education and sleep restriction. *Sleep restriction* involves limiting the time spent in bed to the actual time a client usually sleeps. For example, if a client typically spends 10 hours in bed but sleeps only 5 hours, the client would be instructed to stay in bed for only 5 hours, no matter how much of that time the client is asleep. Clients also kept a *sleep diary* that included such information as bedtime, arising time, daytime naps, frequency of night awakenings, sleep quality (rated on a 5-point scale), and medication intake. Figure 15-4 shows an excerpt from a sleep diary. Finally, therapists offered clients who were using sleep medication a withdrawal plan to decrease or eliminate drug use.

This cognitive-behavioral treatment package significantly reduced clients' sleep-onset latency, awakenings after sleep onset, and early morning awakenings. Significant reductions in clients' use of sleep medication also occurred; the number of clients who had habitually used sleep medication decreased by 54% by the end of therapy. Similar results have been obtained using short-term cognitive-behavioral therapy for older adults (average age of 67) suffering from insomnia.[103]

Cognitive-behavioral treatment packages also have been administered in small groups (five to seven clients). One such treatment package for clients whose insomnia was related to chronic pain combined sleep education (which included specific information about pain-related sleep problems), changing setting events, relaxation training, and cognitive restructuring.[104] The treatment was administered in seven 2-hour weekly sessions. Compared with a wait-list control condition, the treatment

Figure 15-4 Excerpt from a sleep diary

Day/date:	Monday, 2/14
Naps	11:15 a.m. – 12:05 p.m. (50 min.) 3:30 – 4:00 p.m. (30 min.)
Medication Intake	None
Bedtime	10:30 p.m.
Nighttime Awakenings	12:50 a.m. 3:35 a.m.
Sleep Quality (5-point rating)	2
Arising Time	7:10 a.m.

Day/date:	Tuesday, 2/15
Naps	11:30 a.m. – 12:15 p.m. (45 min.)
Medication Intake	Sominex—2 pills at 10:30 p.m.
Bedtime	11:20 p.m.
Nighttime Awakenings	1:20 a.m. 4:10 a.m.
Sleep Quality (5-point rating)	2
Arising Time	7:45 a.m.

package improved clients' self-reports of sleep-onset latency, the number of awakenings after falling asleep, and sleep quality and also reduced movement during sleep (as measured by a monitor, worn on the wrist, which continuously recorded movement).

Although the efficacy of a variety of cognitive-behavioral interventions for treating insomnia have been well documented in controlled studies conducted in research settings,[105] it is important to know if these interventions can be effectively delivered in clinics where most clients receive help. This question was addressed by examining the results of 47 cases of clients who were treated for insomnia in a sleep clinic.[106] (This study is an example of using a series of case studies to provide evidence of the effectiveness of an intervention.) The treatments included sleep restriction, modification of setting events, relaxation training, cognitive therapy, and sleep education. On average, clients undergoing the clinic-based treatment showed a 65% reduction in sleep latency, 46% decrease in awakenings each night, 48% reduction in time awake after sleep onset, and 13% increase in total sleep time. These data are comparable to results obtained in research settings. Total sleep time was the outcome measure least affected by the treatment, improving only 13%. This is not surprising because sleep restriction and modification of setting events (such as getting out of bed if one does not fall asleep in 15 minutes) may initially decrease sleep time (in order to eventually increase sleep time). Fortunately, there is evidence that after cognitive-behavioral interventions, total sleep time eventually increases.

Treatment packages for insomnia may be more effective than single therapies, especially when a client's sleeping problems result from more than one category of maintaining conditions. For example, changing setting events and relaxation training have been shown to be more effective than changing setting events alone.[107] To decrease dependence on sleep medication, treatment packages that combine medication-tapering schedules and cognitive-behavioral procedures have proved successful.[108] Although treatment packages for insomnia are effective, research has not yet suggested which specific combinations of therapies are optimal and which clients are likely to benefit most from treatment packages rather than single therapies.[109]

BULIMIA NERVOSA

Bulimia nervosa is a serious eating disorder characterized by binge eating and purging.[110] Clients with bulimia nervosa typically are preoccupied with their body image and weight. *Binge eating* involves consuming large quantities of food in a brief period. The person then *purges* what has been eaten, most often by self-induced vomiting and also through the abuse of laxatives and diuretics. Purging prevents the person from gaining weight following binge eating episodes. Generally, people suffering from *bulimia* (the shortened term for the disorder) maintain a normal weight because of their purging. Bulimia affects 1% to 3% of women (it is rare in men), primarily in industrialized countries, and typically begins in late adolescence or early adulthood. Recurrent purging after binge eating can result in serious medical problems, especially loss of body fluids and electrolytes, as well as damage to the esophagus and teeth caused by stomach acid that is regurgitated.[111]

The behavioral treatment of bulimia generally consists of a comprehensive cognitive-behavioral treatment package that is a rich integration of both behavioral and cognitive procedures.[112] It can be implemented in as few as 20 sessions, individually or in groups. Therapy begins by providing the client with information about bulimia, nutrition, and weight regulation.[113] A combination of the following eight behavior therapy procedures then is used:

1. *Self-monitoring.* Self-monitoring of binge eating and purging episodes and the circumstances surrounding them is the clients' first task and continues throughout the treatment. Clients also record their daily food and liquid intake and sometimes the type of food and the time and place of eating. The self-monitoring records help identify maintaining conditions of binge/purge episodes and provide a continuous measure of change.

2. *Changing setting events.* The therapist teaches the client to adjust setting events related to eating, such as eating at specified times, eating in a particular location, and buying only foods that the client is less likely to

binge on. The aim of these procedures is for the client to develop habits of eating three normal meals a day plus planned snacks.

3. *Activity scheduling.* The client learns to schedule pleasurable between-meal activities that reduce the likelihood of binge eating. Such competing behaviors include doing moderate exercise and engaging in work that holds the client's attention.

4. *Cognitive restructuring.* Clients are trained to identify and alter their dysfunctional thoughts and attitudes about eating, food, and body image. People suffering from bulimia typically have rigid and perfectionist attitudes regarding their body shape and weight, eating, and dieting (for example, "I'll never be happy until I am thin").[114]

5. *Collaborative empiricism.* Clients engage in empirical hypothesis testing designed to challenge their dysfunctional beliefs and thoughts. For example, a client who erroneously believed that she weighed well above normal for her height could check a current table of normal weight ranges.

6. *Problem solving.* Clients learn problem-solving skills to help them cope with stress-evoking events that have been associated with binge eating. Clients are encouraged to anticipate these events so that they can solve problems before binge eating is imminent.[115]

7. *Flooding with response prevention.* Binge eating and the threat of gaining weight typically evoke a great deal of anxiety in clients with bulimia. Purging reduces the anxiety, which negatively reinforces purging. Flooding is used to break this vicious cycle.[116] In the presence of the therapist, clients are encouraged to eat the foods on which they typically binge (often high-caloric, sweet, and soft-textured foods that can be rapidly swallowed). After this exposure, clients are instructed not to vomit (response prevention). The flooding session is terminated only when the strong urge to purge dissipates. Although flooding can be effective, it does not appear to be a necessary treatment component.[117] In some cases, flooding may make the treatment package less effective[118] because clients are reluctant to participate in the unpleasant flooding procedures.[119]

8. *Relapse prevention.* Bulimia tends to occur in cycles[120] and is characterized by relapses.[121] Thus, preparing clients for the possibility that the bulimic behaviors will return in the future is important.[122] Accordingly, clients identify high-risk situations for binge eating and rehearse coping strategies that can be used if the situations occur. This may include recruiting and using social support from family and friends. (We will describe relapse prevention more fully later in the chapter.)

The comprehensive cognitive-behavioral treatment package we have just described generally is considered the treatment of choice for bulimia.[123] Well-controlled studies support its efficacy, showing an average reduction in clients' binge eating ranging from 93% to 73% and an average reduction in purging ranging from 94% to 77%.[124] For clients who do not experience significant changes in their binge eating habits after a standard number of sessions, additional therapy sessions have proved beneficial.[125]

The cognitive-behavioral treatment package consistently is superior to traditional verbal/interpersonal psychotherapies[126] and antidepressant medication (which has been used to treat depression related to bulimia).[127] Compared with medication, the treatment package is more effective in reducing clients' binge eating and purging frequency, feelings of depression, and attitudes about eating in general.[128] The treatment package often results in more rapid changes in clients' binge eating and purging behaviors than alternative treatments.[129] Additionally, cognitive-behavioral interventions for bulimia can be administered successfully through cost-effective self-help formats.[130]

In addition to significantly reducing binge eating and purging, the cognitive-behavioral treatment package consistently improves clients' beliefs and attitudes about their body and weight.[131] Further, most studies show significant improvements in self-esteem, depression, and social functioning.[132]

Long-term maintenance of treatment gains have been found in some,[133] but not all,[134] studies. Cognitive interventions that target clients' maladaptive cognitions that maintain binge eating and purging may be especially important in fostering long-term maintenance of treatment gains.[135]

ADDICTIVE BEHAVIORS

Addictive behaviors result in immediate, highly pleasurable consequences and in delayed negative consequences. The immediate pleasurable consequences are so powerful that they override the delayed negative consequences.[136] Consider college students who are drinking heavily at a party and feeling uninhibited, relaxed, and "high." Their drinking behavior is not influenced by the consequences that will occur the next day, such as a horrendous hangover and missed classes. The longer-term harmful effects to one's health, interpersonal relations, and job performance associated with alcohol abuse are even further removed from the immediate pleasure experienced while drinking. The same holds true for other forms of substance abuse, as well as other behaviors that have an addictive quality, such as gambling and overeating.[137] In a nutshell, then, the major obstacle to treating addictive behaviors is that the immediate consequences are so reinforcing that clients strongly resist modifying them.

Alcohol abuse, cigarette smoking, and the use of illicit drugs (such as cocaine and heroin) are the most common addictive behaviors treated by behavior therapy. Aversion therapy, cue exposure, and consequential therapies are among the behavior therapies used.

Aversion therapy pairs an addictive behavior with an aversive stimulus (such as nausea) to "discourage" the client from engaging in the behavior in the future (see Chapter 7). For example, **rapid smoking** is an aversion therapy that requires clients (1) to smoke at the rate of one puff every 6 seconds, (2) to inhale normally, and (3) to continue smoking rapidly until they cannot tolerate it anymore. In some cases, the aversion created by rapid smoking can have long-lasting effects in decreasing smoking.[138] However, such results have not been obtained consistently.[139] Further, rapid smoking can cause temporary cardiovascular stress, which makes the procedure unsuitable for anyone who is at risk for cardiovascular disease.[140] Accordingly, rapid smoking is employed infrequently.

In **cue exposure,** the client is exposed to cues associated with the addictive behavior but is prevented from engaging in the actual addictive behavior, which is similar to response prevention. For example, a client with a drinking problem might spend time in a bar. There, the client would experience the visual (such as seeing other people drinking), auditory (such as hearing people order drinks), and olfactory (such as smelling alcohol) cues associated with drinking. However, the client would refrain from drinking alcohol. Cue exposure by itself can be effective in reducing clients' cravings for the addictive substance.[141] However, it is more effective when clients use specific coping skills, such as differential relaxation, to deal with their cravings.[142] In essence, clients learn to substitute coping responses for their habitual addictive behaviors when they encounter the salient cues that previously have prompted the addictive behaviors.

One approach to using consequential therapy for substance abuse gives clients potent reinforcers for abstaining from taking the drug.[143] In a controlled study of 70 outpatients who were dependent on cocaine, reinforcing cocaine-free urinalyses with vouchers exchangeable for retail items resulted in abstinence during treatment and at a 1-year follow-up.[144] Similarly, for clients who were dependent on marijuana, the combination of learning coping skills to deal with urges and avoid high-risk situations and receiving vouchers for retail items contingent on abstinence from marijuana led to significantly greater abstinence than just learning coping skills.[145]

Photo 15-2 In cue exposure, a client is exposed to cues associated with an addictive behavior, but the client refrains from engaging in the addictive behavior. Here, the client (at the far right) interacts with others who are drinking in a bar, but he himself does not drink.

© Michael D. Spiegler and David C. Guevremont

A second consequential approach for drug abuse is to reinforce clients when they engage in behaviors that compete with drug-abusing behaviors. In one study, clients attending a methadone clinic for opiate dependence earned up to $15 each week in vouchers for goods and services contingent on their completing specific tasks that competed with drug-abusing behaviors (such as applying for a job and receiving vocational training). The program resulted in significant reductions in illicit drug use.[146]

A third consequential approach to reduce addictive behaviors is response cost. An example is the case you read about in Chapter 7 (pages 151–152) of the African-American client whose abuse of amphetamines was eliminated by the threat of having $50 checks sent to the Ku Klux Klan each time he used the drug.[147]

The problem with each of these singular behavior therapy approaches is that they may be effective only in the short run. All too often, clients *relapse*—that is, revert to their addictive behaviors—after therapy has ended. This is not surprising because the maintaining conditions of addictive behaviors typically consist of ubiquitous everyday situational cues related to the addictive behavior (such as readily available alcohol at parties and in restaurants) and powerful immediate reinforcers for engaging in the addictive behavior (such as feelings of euphoria from drugs). Clearly, changing these maintaining conditions on a long-term basis is difficult. Relapse prevention provides an alternative strategy.[148]

Relapse Prevention

Alan Marlatt and his colleagues[149] developed an approach to preventing the recurrence of addictive behaviors *after* the behaviors have been eliminated successfully. Central to their relapse prevention model is the distinction between a lapse and a relapse. A *lapse* is a single, isolated violation of abstinence, which does not necessarily lead to a *relapse*, which is a full-blown return to the addictive behavior (that is, to pretreatment levels of substance abuse). Therapists teach clients to view a lapse as an error and as an opportunity for additional learning.

Marlatt's model of relapse prevention provides clients with the cognitive-behavioral coping skills necessary to prevent lapses from escalating into relapses. It consists of four components: (1) identifying high-risk situations, (2) learning coping skills, (3) practicing coping skills, and (4) creating a lifestyle balance. The first three components essentially are a form of stress inoculation training.

IDENTIFYING HIGH-RISK SITUATIONS

Relapses are most likely to occur in high-risk situations. Almost three fourths of all relapses of addictive behaviors are associated with (1) negative emotional states (35%), including frustration, anxiety, depression, anger, and loneliness; (2) social pressure (20%), such as being coaxed to go to a bar; and (3) interpersonal conflicts (16%), such as arguments with a spouse.[150] Clients must become aware of the specific situations that are most likely to trigger their relapse episodes so that they will be prepared to deal with them.

LEARNING COPING SKILLS

The ability to engage in effective coping responses when faced with a high-risk situation decreases the probability of a relapse. Further, successful coping with one high-risk situation tends to increase one's self-efficacy (belief that one can succeed) about being able to cope with other high-risk situations.[151]

The cognitive-behavioral coping skills that clients are taught include (1) *assertive behaviors* to help clients deal with social pressures to engage in addictive behaviors, (2) *relaxation and stress management* to reduce tension and discomfort associated with negative emotional states, (3) *social and communication skills* to manage interpersonal conflicts, (4) *problem-solving skills* to deal effectively with problems in their daily lives, and (5) *cognitive restructuring* to change maladaptive addictive-related cognitions (see Table 15-4, which describes the four types of cognitions most often associated with addictive behaviors[152]).

PRACTICING COPING SKILLS

Once clients have learned coping skills, they practice them in simulated high-risk situations. For example, the therapist and client might role-play a scenario in which a friend asks the client to go out drinking, and the client responds with an appropriately assertive refusal. The two aims of this behavior rehearsal are for the client (1) to learn to recognize high-risk situations and then (2) to "automatically" engage in well-rehearsed coping skills rather than "automatically" reverting to habitual addictive behaviors.

Table 15-4 Cognitions associated with addictive behaviors
SOURCE: Based on Liese, 1994.

Cognitions	Descriptions	Examples
ANTICIPATORY BELIEFS	Expectation of a positive result from engaging in an addictive behavior	"They'll think I'm pretty cool if I get high with them."
RELIEF-ORIENTED BELIEFS	Expectation of reduced discomfort from engaging in an addictive behavior	"I need a cigarette so I can relax."
FACILITATING BELIEFS	Client's giving himself or herself permission to engage in an addictive behavior	"It's only pot. It's not like I'm doing drugs."
AUTOMATIC THOUGHTS	Brief, repetitive, spontaneous mental images related to an addictive behavior that result in urges or cravings	Imagining sipping a cold beer while socializing with friends

CREATING A LIFESTYLE BALANCE

A common trigger of addictive behaviors occurs when clients perceive that there is an imbalance in their lives between their obligations (what they "should" do, such as go to work) and their desires (what they want to do, such as play golf).[153] The obvious solution is to increase clients' access to their desires. However, in the case of clients recovering from addictive habits, their most salient desires are likely to involve addictive behaviors. For instance, a client might think, "I deserve a drink for all the work I did today."

Accordingly, clients are encouraged to develop a lifestyle balance between obligations and desires. First, they self-monitor their obligations and desires daily to identify the degree and nature of the imbalance. Then, where imbalances exist, clients use an activity schedule to increase activities that are both enjoyable and adaptive. The process can be viewed as relearning joy or "rejoyment."[154]

EFFICACY OF RELAPSE PREVENTION FOR ADDICTIVE BEHAVIORS

Cognitive-behavioral relapse prevention has been used as part of the treatment of different types of substance abuse, including alcohol,[155] nicotine,[156] cocaine,[157] marijuana,[158] and opiates.[159] Relapse prevention typically is part of a treatment package. For example, it has been combined with pharmacological treatment,[160] with the Alcoholics Anonymous Twelve-Step Recovery program,[161] and with behavioral couple therapy (when alcohol abuse is present).[162] Relapse prevention also is used for other types of problems, such as to prevent high-risk sexual activity (for HIV infection)[163] and to treat erectile dysfunction (problems with obtaining and maintaining an erection)[164] and child molestation.[165]

The evidence regarding the efficacy of relapse prevention for addictive behaviors is mixed.[166] Some studies show relapse prevention to be more effective than alternative treatments and no-treatment control conditions. For example, clients receiving transdermal (through the skin) nicotine replacement patches plus relapse prevention training had higher rates of smoking cessation than clients who received only the pharmacological intervention.[167] Other studies indicate that relapse prevention is at least equally as effective as alternative therapy approaches.[168] Some studies suggest that the benefits of relapse prevention are most evident with cigarette smoking and with more severe drug abuse.[169]

Thus far, the strongest evidence for the effectiveness of relapse prevention is in the treatment of the abuse of alcohol and multiple drugs.[170] In addition to promoting long-term maintenance, relapse prevention may decrease the severity of relapses.[171] Finally, relapse prevention may be effective in the treatment of alcohol abuse when it is self-administered, as through a guided self-help approach that includes self-monitoring, goal setting, and brief readings and homework assignments.[172]

Positive findings regarding the efficacy of relapse prevention must be viewed cautiously. Some of the relevant studies contain methodological weaknesses, such as not employing control groups[173] and evaluating relapse prevention in the context of a larger treatment package,[174] which clouds the specific contribution of the relapse prevention component. Further, some studies are less supportive of the superiority of relapse prevention compared with other treatments, particularly for cigarette smoking.[175] Taken together, the cumulative evidence to date indicates that the efficacy of relapse prevention for addictive behaviors is promising but remains inconclusive.

◆ ALL THINGS CONSIDERED: APPLICATIONS OF BEHAVIOR THERAPY TO PSYCHOLOGICAL DISORDERS WITH PRIMARY PHYSICAL CHARACTERISTICS

Behavior therapy for psychological disorders with primary physical characteristics provides psychological treatment alternatives to traditional medical interventions that are more intrusive and have serious negative side effects. The predominant use of sedatives or other sleep-inducing drugs to treat insomnia is a prime example. Prolonged use of sleep medication may actually interfere with sleeping, can lead to diminished daytime functioning, and often results in psychological and physical dependence on the drug.

The effectiveness of behavior therapy in treating psychological disorders with primary physical characteristics varies considerably with the particular disorder (as is the case with medical disorders). The disorders we discussed—enuresis, tics and nervous habits, insomnia, bulimia, and addictive behaviors—roughly fall on a continuum ranging from narrow impact to broad impact on a person's life. For instance, nocturnal enuresis is limited to one's sleeping time, whereas addictive behaviors generally interfere with almost every sphere of one's life. In general, the narrower the impact of the problem, the easier it is to treat. Behavior therapy interventions for enuresis and tics and nervous habits tend to have a high rate of success, whereas interventions for bulimia and addictive behaviors are less effective.

Although the problems we discussed in this chapter are classified as psychological rather than medical, their physical aspects can have serious medical implications. To begin with, the role of physical factors must be assessed because they may need to be treated directly. For example, bedwetting can be caused by medication the client is currently taking (such as diuretics) and general medical conditions (such as diabetes); sleep difficulties can result from drug use (for instance, use of amphetamines) and medical conditions (for instance, hyperthyroidism). Additionally, comprehensive treatment often includes both behavior therapy and medical interventions. With bulimia, for instance, electrolyte imbalances and serious loss of tooth enamel are two consequences of purging that require medical attention.

Compared with medical conditions, psychological disorders with primary physical characteristics are more likely to be associated with guilt, embarrassment, and shame and to be clouded in secrecy. This is true for all the problems you read about in this chapter, with the exception of insomnia. For example, people often try to hide or disguise bedwetting, binge eating and purging, and tics. Accordingly, treating clients with these disorders requires an especially good client–therapist relationship. The client must trust the therapist sufficiently to reveal embarrassing behaviors. Also, the therapist must trust the client to be honest and straightforward. In the case of bulimia, for instance, the therapist must be able to rely on clients' accurately self-monitoring binge eating and purging episodes because clients engage in these behaviors privately.

Many of the behavior therapy interventions employed with psychological disorders with primary physical characteristics involve self-control techniques. For example, habit reversal for tic disorders teaches clients to "catch" their maladaptive behaviors early in their sequence and counter them with competing responses. Gaining self-control over so-called involuntary physical disabilities (such as tics) is likely to increase clients' self-efficacy about their ability to modify them, and enhanced self-efficacy may be one of the factors responsible for the success of habit reversal for tics.

The use of treatment packages is another common element in the behavior therapy treatment of psychological disorders with primary physical characteristics. Dry-bed training for enuresis, habit reversal for tics, cognitive-behavioral treatment packages for bulimia, and relapse prevention for addictive behaviors all involve a multifaceted approach.

It is fitting that we conclude our presentation of behavior therapy interventions for psychological disorders with primary physical characteristics by discussing relapse prevention. Relapse prevention initially was developed for treating substance abuse. However, both the specific procedures and the general principles of relapse prevention increasingly are being applied to other problems, such as preventing the recurrence of high-risk sexual behaviors, bipolar disorder,[176] and nervous habits.[177] Many psychological problems involve long-standing habitual behavior patterns that require continued management and coping. Relapse prevention potentially offers a means of achieving such long-term maintenance.

SUMMARY

1. Behavior therapy treats a variety of psychological disorders whose primary feature is a physical problem. Psychological factors and physical problems influence each other reciprocally.

2. The urine alarm is an efficient and effective treatment for nocturnal enuresis. An alarm is activated when urine contacts a special pad under the child's bed sheet or in the child's underpants. Through repeated pairings of the alarm and bladder tension, bladder tension alone comes to awaken the child before urination starts.

3. Dry-bed training is a highly effective treatment package for nocturnal enuresis that uses shaping and overcorrection to teach children the behaviors required to keep their beds dry throughout the night. The dry-pants method is an extension of dry-bed training that is used for normal daytime toilet training.

4. Behavioral treatments for tics include massed negative practice, changing maintaining consequences, relaxation training, and self-monitoring. Habit reversal, the most effective treatment, incorporates four components: awareness training, relaxation training, competing response training, and reinforcement. Awareness training and competing response training are the critical components. Habit reversal also is used to treat nervous habits such as hair pulling and stuttering.

5. When sleep problems in infants and children are maintained by parental attention, extinction, involving withholding attention for nighttime crying, is a simple, effective treatment. Modified forms of extinction are more acceptable to parents but somewhat less effective. Sleep terrors, which are not maintained by attention, can be treated by scheduled awakenings before the onset of a sleep terror episode.

6. For adult insomnia, changing setting events establishes a client's being in bed as a clear-cut cue only for sleeping. Relaxation training helps clients reduce muscle tension associated with insomnia before going to bed. Cognitive restructuring reduces worry, such as about sleeping, by identifying, challenging, and replacing maladaptive beliefs with adaptive cognitions.

7. Treatment packages involving changing setting events, relaxation training, cognitive restructuring, sleep restriction, and sleep education for insomnia are appropriate when a client's sleeping problems are the result of multiple maintaining conditions.

8. The treatment of choice for bulimia nervosa is a comprehensive cognitive-behavioral treatment package that includes self-monitoring, changing setting events, activity scheduling, cognitive restructuring, collaborative empiricism, problem solving, flooding with response prevention, and relapse prevention. The treatment package reduces binge eating and purging and improves self-image, depression, and social functioning.

9. Behavioral treatments of addictive behaviors include aversion therapy, cue exposure, and consequential therapies. Aversion therapy pairs the addictive behavior with an aversive stimulus to discourage engaging in it. Cue exposure involves exposing the client to cues associated with the addictive behavior and preventing the client from engaging in the addictive behavior. Consequential therapies include administering reinforcers for abstaining from addictive behaviors and for behaviors that compete with addictive behaviors, as well as response cost for engaging in addictive behaviors.

10. Relapse prevention is a cognitive-behavioral treatment package that prepares clients who have completed treatment for addictive behaviors to deal with future relapses. Clients identify high-risk situations, develop coping skills, practice the coping skills before they are needed, and develop a lifestyle that balances obligations and desires. Relapse prevention also may prove to be a general procedure for increasing the long-term maintenance of treatment gains with diverse problem behaviors.

REFERENCE NOTES

1. American Psychiatric Association, 1994; World Health Organization, 1992.

2. Friedman, Sobel, Myers, Caudill, & Benson, 1995; Schell, 1996.

3. Lovibond & Coote, 1970; Oppel, Harper, & Rider, 1968; Yates, 1970.

4. American Psychiatric Association, 1994.

5. For example, Deleon & Mandell, 1966; Werry & Cohrssen, 1965; Yates, 1970.

6. Mowrer & Mowrer, 1938.

7. Friman & Vollmer, 1995.

8. Deleon & Sacks, 1972; Doleys, 1977; Houts, Berman, & Abramson, 1994; Mowrer & Mowrer, 1938; Rushton, 1989; Walker, Milling, & Bonner, 1988.

9. Wagner, Johnson, Walker, Carter, & Witner, 1982.

10. Novick, 1966; Werry & Cohrssen, 1965.

11. Deleon & Sacks, 1972; Doleys, 1977.

12. Azrin, Sneed, & Foxx, 1973; Houts, Peterson, & Whelan, 1986.

13. Houts, Berman, & Abramson, 1994.

14. Azrin, Sneed, & Foxx, 1973.

15. Kimmel & Kimmel, 1970; Paschalis, Kimmel, & Kimmel, 1972.

16. Azrin, Thienes-Hontos, & Besalel-Azrin, 1979.

17. Azrin, Thienes-Hontos, & Besalel-Azrin, 1979.

18. Azrin, Sneed, & Foxx, 1974.

19. Azrin, Thienes-Hontos, & Besalel-Azrin, 1979.

20. Van Son, Van Heesch, Mulder, & Van Londen, 1995.

21. Foxx & Azrin, 1973a, 1973b.

22. For example, Madsen, Hoffman, Thomas, Karopsak, & Madsen, 1969.

23. For example, Madsen, 1965; Madsen, Hoffman, Thomas, Karopsak, & Madsen, 1969; Mahoney, Van Wagenen, & Meyerson, 1971; Pumroy & Pumroy, 1965.

24. Foxx & Azrin, 1973a.

25. Wilder, Higbeen, Williams, & Nachtwey, 1997.

26. Boudjouk, Woods, Miltenberger, & Long, 2000; Long, Woods, Miltenberger, Fuqua, & Boudjouk, 1999.

27. American Psychiatric Association, 1994; Bauer & Shea, 1984; Cohen, Leckman, & Shaywitz, 1984.

28. Peterson & Azrin, 1993; Ross & Moldofsky, 1978; Shapiro & Shapiro, 1984; Shapiro, Shapiro, Fulop, Hubbard, Mandeli, Nordlie, & Phillips, 1989.

29. Shapiro & Shapiro, 1984.

30. Cohen, Leckman, & Shaywitz, 1984.

31. Yates, 1958.

32. For example, Browning & Stover, 1971; Clark, 1966; Storms, 1985.

33. Azrin & Peterson, 1988a; Turpin, 1983.

34. For example, Browning & Stover, 1971; Doleys & Kurtz, 1974; Miller, 1970; Schulman, 1974; Tophoff, 1973; Varni, Boyd, & Cataldo, 1978; Wagaman, Miltenberger, & Woods, 1995.

35. Wagaman, Miltenberger, & Williams, 1995.

36. Azrin & Peterson, 1988a.

37. For example, Barr, Lovibond, & Katsaros, 1972; Clark, 1966.

38. For example, Canavan & Powell, 1981; Lahey, McNees, & McNees, 1973; Varni, Boyd, & Cataldo, 1978.

39. For example, Barr, Lovibond, & Katsaros, 1972; Canavan & Powell, 1981; Lahey, McNees, & McNees, 1973.

40. For example, Franco, 1981; Friedman, 1980.

41. Peterson & Azrin, 1990.

42. For example, Billings, 1978; Hutzell, Platzek, & Logue, 1974; Thomas, Abrams, & Johnson, 1971.

43. Azrin & Nunn, 1973; Long & Miltenberger, 1998.

44. Miltenberger, Fuqua, & McKinley, 1985.

45. Carr, 1995.

46. See Carr, 1995.

47. Azrin & Peterson, 1988a, 1988b, 1990; Finney, Rapoff, Hall, & Christopherson, 1983; Peterson & Azrin, 1993.

48. Peterson & Azrin, 1993.

49. de L. Horne, White, & Varigos, 1989.

50. Peterson, Dixon, Talcott, & Kelleher, 1993.

51. Nunn, Newton, & Faucher, 1992.

52. Miltenberger & Fuqua, 1985; Miltenberger, Fuqua, & Woods, 1998; Peterson, Campise, & Azrin, 1994; Woods & Miltenberger, 1995.

53. Fleming, 1984; Friman, Finney, & Christophersen, 1984; Friman & O'Connor, 1984; Lerner, Franklin, Meadows, Hembree, & Foa,

1998; Tarnowski, Rosen, McGrath, & Drabman, 1987.

54. For example, Wagaman, Miltenberger, & Arndorfer, 1993; Wagaman, Miltenberger, & Woods, 1995.

55. Azrin, Nunn, & Frantz-Renshaw, 1980; Christensen & Sanders, 1987; Long, Miltenberger, & Rapp, 1999; Rapp, Miltenberger, Galensky, Roberts, & Ellingson, 1999; Woods, Murray, Fuqua, Seif, Boyer, & Siah, 1999.

56. Long, Miltenberger, Ellingson, & Ott, 1999.

57. Bebko & Lennox, 1988; Miltenberger, Fuqua, & Woods, 1998.

58. Rapp, Miltenberger, Long, Elliott, & Lumley, 1998.

59. Elliott, Miltenberger, Rapp, Long, & McDonald, 1998.

60. Long, Miltenberger, & Rapp, 1998.

61. de Kinkelder & Boelens, 1998.

62. Elliott, Miltenberger, Rapp, Long, & McDonald, 1998.

63. Long, Miltenberger, & Rapp, 1999.

64. Allen, 1998.

65. Elliott, Miltenberger, Rapp, Long, & McDonald, 1998; Rapp, Miltenberger, Galensky, Roberts, & Ellingson, 1999.

66. For example, Murtagh & Greenwood, 1995; Sloan & Shapiro, 1993.

67. For example, Murtagh & Greenwood, 1995.

68. For example, France & Hudson, 1993.

69. For example, Murtagh & Greenwood, 1995.

70. Lichstein & Riedel, 1994.

71. For example, Blampied & France, 1993; France & Hudson, 1993.

72. For example, Didden, Curfs, Sikkema, & de Moor, 1998; France & Hudson, 1990, 1993; Williams, 1959.

73. For example, France & Hudson, 1990.

74. For example, Ashbaugh & Peck, 1998; Wolfson, Lacks, & Futterman, 1992.

75. France & Hudson, 1990, 1993.

76. France, 1992.

77. France, 1992.

78. For example, Pritchard & Appleton, 1988.

79. For example, Durand & Mindell, 1990; Rolider & Van Houten, 1984.

80. For example, Lawton, France, & Blampied, 1991.

81. For example, Hall & Nathan, 1992.

82. For example, Lawton, France, & Blampied, 1991.

83. American Psychiatric Association, 2000a.

84. Durand & Mindell, 1999; Johnson & Lerner, 1985; Rickert & Johnson, 1988.

85. Bootzin, 1972; Bootzin, Epstein, & Wood, 1991.

86. Bootzin & Engle-Friedman, 1987; France & Hudson, 1990.

87. Bootzin & Perlis, 1992; Espie, Lindsay, Brooks, Hood, & Turvey, 1989; Lichstein & Riedel, 1994; Puder, Lacks, Bertelson, & Storandt, 1983.

88. Backhaus, Hohagen, Voderholzer, & Riemann, 2001; Booztin & Epstein, 2000; Engle-Friedman, Bootzin, Hazlewood, & Tsao, 1992; King, Dudley, Melvin, Pallant, & Morawetz, 2001; Lichstein, Wilson, & Johnson, 2000; Morin & Azrin, 1987, 1988; Reidel & Lichstein, 2000.

89. Engle-Friedman, Bootzin, Hazlewood, & Tsao, 1992.

90. Lichstein & Riedel, 1994.

91. Nicassio, Boylan, & McCabe, 1982.

92. Lacks, Bertelson, Gans, & Kunkel, 1983; Nicassio, Boylan, & McCabe, 1982.

93. Means, Lichstein, Epperson, & Johnson, 2000.

94. Bootzin & Perlis, 1992.

95. Lichstein, Peterson, Riedel, Means, Epperson, & Aguillard, 1999.

96. Carlson & Hoyle, 1993.

97. Lichstein, 1988; Lichstein & Riedel, 1994.

98. Bootzin & Perlis, 1992; Borkovec, Grayson, & O'Brien, 1979; Hauri, 1981.

99. Sloan, Hauris, Bootzin, Morin, Stevenson, & Shapiro, 1993.

100. Morin, 1993; Morin, Kowatch, Barry, & Walton, 1993.

101. For example, Jacobs, Benson, & Friedman, 1993; Lichstein & Riedel, 1994.

102. Morin, Stone, McDonald, & Jones, 1994.

103. Morin, Kowatch, Barry, & Walton, 1993.

104. Currie, Wilson, Pontefract, & deLaplante, 2000.

105. Morin, Culvert, & Schwartz, 1994; Murtagh & Greenwood, 1995.

106. Perlis, Aloia, Millikan, Boehmler, Smith, Greenblatt, & Giles, 2000.

107. Jacobs, Rosenberg, Friedman, Matheson, Peavy, Domar, & Benson, 1993.

108. Morin, Stone, McDonald, & Jones, 1994.
109. Lacks & Morin, 1992; Murtagh & Greenwood, 1995.
110. American Psychiatric Association, 1994.
111. American Psychiatric Association, 1994.
112. Smith, Marcus, & Eldredge, 1994.
113. Olmsted, Davis, Rockert, Irvine, Eagle, & Garner, 1991.
114. For example, Heatherton & Baumeister, 1991.
115. Smith, Marcus, & Eldredge, 1994.
116. Kennedy, Katz, Neitzert, Ralevski, & Mendlowitz, 1995; Leitenberg, 1993.
117. Wilson, Eldredge, Smith, & Niles, 1991.
118. Agras, Schneider, Arnow, Raeburn, & Telch, 1989.
119. Smith, Marcus, & Eldredge, 1994; Sturmey, 1992.
120. Keller, Herzog, Lavori, Bradburn, & Mahoney, 1992.
121. Mitchell, Pyle, Hatsukami, Goff, Glotter, & Harper, 1989.
122. Wilson, Loeb, Walsh, Labouvie, Petkova, Liu, & Waternaux, 1999.
123. Agras, 1993; American Psychiatric Association, 2000b; Fairburn, Marcus, & Wilson, 1993; Latner & Wilson, 2000; Mitchell, Raymond, & Specker, 1993.
124. Wilson & Fairburn, 1993, 1998.
125. Eldridge, Agras, Arnow, Telch, Bell, Castonguay, & Marnell, 1997.
126. Agras, Walsh, Fairburn, Wilson, & Kraemer, 2000; DeAngelis, 2002; Kirkley, Schneider, Agras, & Bachman, 1985.
127. Leitenberg, Rosen, Wolf, Vara, Detzer, & Srebnik, 1994; Wilson & Fairburn, 1993.
128. Whital, Agras, & Gould, 1999.
129. Wilson, Loeb, Walsh, Labouvie, Petkova, Liu, & Waternaux, 1999.
130. Carter & Fairburn, 1998; Fairburn, 1995; Wilson, Vitousek, & Loeb, 2000.
131. For example, Garner, Rockert, Davis, Garner, Olmsted, & Eagle, 1993.
132. For example, DeAnglis, 2002; Fairburn, Peveler, Jones, Hope, & Doll, 1993; Whital, Agras, & Gould, 1999.
133. For example, Fairburn, Jones, Peveler, Hope, & O'Connor, 1993.
134. For example, Agras, Telch, Arnow, Eldredge, & Marnell, 1997; Agras, Walsh, Fairburn, Wilson, & Kraemer, 2000; Eldridge, Agras, Arnow,

135. Telch, Bell, Castonguay, & Marnell, 1997; Thackwray, Smith, Bodfish, & Meyers, 1993.
135. Thackwray, Smith, Bodfish, & Meyers, 1993; compare with Wolf & Crowther, 1992.
136. Spiegler, 1983.
137. For example, Marlatt & Barrett, 1994.
138. Lichtenstein, Harris, Birchler, Wahl, & Schmahl, 1973; Lichtenstein & Rodrigues, 1977.
139. Lando, 1975; Raw & Russell, 1980; Sutherland, Amit, Golden, & Rosenberger, 1975.
140. Dawley & Dillenkoffer, 1975; Hauser, 1974; Horan, Hackett, Nicholas, Linberg, Stone, & Lukaski, 1977; Lichtenstein & Glasgow, 1977; Poole, Sanson-Fisher, German, & Harker, 1980.
141. For example, Lee & Oei, 1993; Monti, Abrams, Kadden, & Cooney, 1989.
142. For example, Monti, Rohsenow, Rubonis, Niaura, Sirota, Colby, Goddard, & Abrams, 1993.
143. For example, Higgins, Budney, Bickel, Foerg, Donham, & Badger, 1994; Petry, Martin, Cooney, & Kranzier, 2000; Shaner, Eckman, & Roberts, 1994.
144. Higgins, Wong, Badger, Ogden, & Dantona, 2000.
145. Budney, Higgins, Radonovich, & Novy, 2000.
146. Iguchi, Belding, Morral, Lamb, & Husband, 1997.
147. Boudin, 1972.
148. Marlatt, 1982; Marlatt & Barrett, 1994; Marlatt & Gordon, 1985.
149. Marlatt & Gordon, 1985.
150. Marlatt & Barrett, 1994.
151. Marlatt & Barrett, 1994.
152. Liese, 1994.
153. Collier & Marlatt, 1995; Marlatt & Tapert, 1993.
154. Collier & Marlatt, 1995.
155. For example, Peterson & Lowe, 1992; Sobell, Sobell, & Leo, 2000; Somers & Marlatt, 1992.
156. For example, Dooley & Halford, 1992; Gruder, Mermelstein, Kirkendol, Hedeker, Wong, Schreckengost, Warnecke, Burzette, & Miller, 1993.
157. For example, Carroll, Rounsaville, & Gawin, 1991; Maude-Griffen, Hohenstein, Humfleet, Reilly, Tusel, & Hall, 1998; Rohsenow, Monti, Martin, Michalec, & Abrams, 2000; Wallace, 1992.

158. For example, Stephens, Roffman, & Simpson, 1994.

159. For example, Chang, Carroll, Behr, & Kosten, 1992.

160. For example, Irvin, Bowers, Dunn, & Wang, 1999; O'Farrell, 1994; O'Farrell, Cutter, Choquette, Floyd, & Bayog, 1992.

161. For example, Minneker-Hugel, Unland, & Buchkremer, 1992.

162. Wells, Peterson, Gainey, Hawkins, & Catalano, 1994.

163. For example, Corrigan, Thompson, & Malow, 1992.

164. McCarthy, 2001.

165. Gillies, Hashmall, Hilton, & Webster, 1992.

166. For example, Carroll, 1996; Hollon & Beck, 1994.

167. Minneker-Hugel, Unland, & Buchkremer, 1992.

168. For example, Carroll, Rounsaville, & Gawin, 1991; Ouimette, Finney, & Moos, 1997; Wells, Peterson, Gainey, Hawkins, & Catalano, 1994.

169. Carroll, 1996; Carroll, Rounsaville, & Gawin, 1991.

170. Irvin, Bowers, Dunn, & Wang, 1999.

171. Carroll, 1996; Wells, Peterson, Gainey, Hawkins, & Catalano, 1994.

172. Sobell & Sobell, 2000; Sobell, Sobell, & Leo, 2000.

173. For example, Mazur & Michael, 1992.

174. For eample, Chang, Carroll, Behr, & Kosten, 1992.

175. Brown, Lichtenstein, McIntyre, & Harrington-Kostur, 1984; Carmody, 1992; Irvin, Bowers, Dunn, & Wang, 1999; Minneker-Hugel, Unland, & Buchkremer, 1992; Ockene, Emmons, Mermelstein, Perkins, Bonollo, Voorhees, & Hollis, 2000.

176. For example, Lam, Bright, Jones, Hayward, Schuck, Chisholm, & Sham, 2000.

177. For example, Lerner, Franklin, Meadows, Hembree, & Foa, 1998.

Chapter 16

Contemporary Behavior Therapy in Perspective: Strengths, Challenges, and Controversies

Having come this far in the book, you know what behavior therapy is and have seen the wide range of assessment and therapy procedures it employs, as well as the broad spectrum of problems it treats. What, then, is left for this last chapter? We have chosen three topics. First, we think it is important to review the major strengths of contemporary behavior therapy. However, so as not to just rest on the laurels of the field, we then suggest some critical challenges that we believe behavior therapists must meet in the future. Finally, we comment on three current controversies that involve a change in the identity of the field of behavior therapy. In essence, then, this chapter covers where behavior therapy is, where it should be going, and where it may end up.

MAJOR STRENGTHS OF BEHAVIOR THERAPY

What do you consider the major strengths of behavior therapy? Before reading further, take a moment to jot them down.

We have chosen to highlight five strengths of behavior therapy: (1) precision in specifying goals, target behaviors, and procedures; (2) effectiveness and accountability; (3) efficiency; (4) breadth and complexity of applications; and (5) ethical practices.

Precision in Specifying Goals, Target Behaviors, and Therapy Procedures

In behavior therapy, goals are very specific and target behaviors are defined in unambiguous, measurable terms, which provides both the client and the therapist with explicit criteria for evaluating the therapy's success. Thus, it is clear how well the therapy is working and when it can be terminated. In contrast, many types of psychotherapy employ goals that are implicit and vaguely defined (for example, "gaining insight" about one's problems), and selecting specific targets of treatment is not considered a critical part of therapy. In such cases, the criteria of progress and success often amount to the therapist's subjective opinions.

The therapy procedures used in behavior therapy also are precisely specified. (See the procedures for dry-bed training in Table 15-1 [page 417] for a prime example.) This practice has four benefits. First, many therapists can use the specific therapy procedures that have been found to be effective. Second, behavior therapists can explain to clients exactly what the therapy will entail. This allows clients to give informed consent about treatment. Third, detailed descriptions of therapy procedures are invaluable in training behavior therapists. Finally, independent researchers can test the efficacy of behavioral interventions because the procedures are clearly specified. In contrast, when procedures are loosely defined, different studies may be evaluating treatments that may be called by the same name but actually differ in significant respects. The emphasis in behavior therapy on precision in specifying goals, target behaviors, and therapy procedures is consistent with contemporary managed health care requirements.[1] Clearly defined and measurable goals and target behaviors make it possible to determine whether therapy needs to be continued.[2] Detailing therapy procedures provides a check on the appropriateness and quality of the treatment being offered.

Effectiveness and Accountability

The bottom line for any psychotherapy is its success, which is measured in terms of *change*. The question is: How much has the client changed with respect to the goals of therapy? Because the goals in behavior therapy are specific, clear-cut, and measurable, the success of treatment is easy to determine for an *individual* client.* In contrast, making statements about the *general* effectiveness of behavior therapy is a complex task. Determining the effectiveness of a particular behavior therapy requires asking a series of qualifying questions, including For what target behavior? For which client population? and In what context? Further, the effectiveness of therapy must be evaluated vis-à-vis alternatives, such as other forms of treatment as well as placebo effects and no treatment. People with psychological disorders sometimes improve without the benefit of psychotherapy, a phenomenon known as *spontaneous remission.* Spontaneous remission does not occur simply because time passes. Rather, positive changes in the person's life (such as a change of job or improved marital relations) comprise the major factor that accounts for spontaneous remission. In assessing the effectiveness of therapy, it is important to determine whether the rate of improvement for a particular treatment is significantly greater than the rate of spontaneous remission.

Even when carefully qualified questions are asked, a host of practical, methodological, and ethical problems may hinder research efforts.[3] For one thing, researchers use multiple criteria to assess the effectiveness of therapy: the meaningfulness of change, transfer and generalization of change, maintenance of change over time, and the acceptability of the therapy. To their credit, behavior therapists are increasingly examining the effectiveness of their treatments in terms of each of these criteria.[4] And the research ethic of behavior therapists has had an impact beyond behavior therapy: It has encouraged proponents of other forms of psychotherapy to conduct outcome research.[5] Behavior therapy arguably has the broadest and strongest empirical base among psychotherapies.[6]† Further, a number of behavior therapy procedures currently are the *treatments of choice* (best available treatments) for some specific problem areas (for example, exposure as a treatment for anxiety disorders).[7] Today, managed care organizations dictate the treatments that are acceptable

*Strictly speaking, the fact that a client's goals have been met does not mean the therapy caused the change. It always is possible that some other factors occurring at the same time as the therapy (such as changes in home or work life) were responsible. Controlled research, such as a single-subject reversal or multiple baseline study, is necessary to draw more definitive conclusions about the effectiveness of therapy procedures for an individual client.

†The *overall* strong empirical support for behavior therapies notwithstanding, there are a relatively small number of behavior therapies that have marginal empirical support, as we have alluded to in previous chapters and as we discuss later in this chapter.

for particular disorders and therefore the treatments for which therapists can be reimbursed. Because of their strong empirical support, many behavior therapies are among the most frequently "approved" treatments.[8]

It is noteworthy that behavior therapy fares well in comparison to drug therapy, which is the treatment most frequently employed for psychological disorders. Despite the effectiveness of many drug treatments, behavior therapy is a desirable form of treatment because (1) pharmacological therapies may not be useful for situational or life adjustment problems (which constitute about half of all referrals for therapy), (2) behavior therapy works just as well as drug treatments for many disorders and may reduce relapse, (3) many clients eschew drug therapies, (4) a significant minority of clients do not respond favorably to drug treatments, and (5) many clients cannot tolerate medications because of undesirable side effects.[9]

The existence of a strong empirical base for the effectiveness of behavior therapy procedures stems from the commitment behavior therapists have to evaluating the treatment procedures scientifically. Moreover, not only have behavior therapists accepted the difficult challenge of conducting psychotherapy outcome studies, but they also have been loud and stringent critics of their own research.[10]

Efficiency

The efficiency of a therapy is another important factor in assessing its value. Efficient therapies are those that (1) achieve the goals of therapy quickly and (2) are cost-effective for both therapists and clients, in terms of time and money.

Behavior therapy often brings about change relatively quickly, especially compared with traditional verbal psychotherapies. This is attributable to two factors. First, many behavior therapy techniques act quickly because they directly change the present maintaining conditions of the target behavior. Occasionally, the target behavior is altered almost immediately (as when powerful reinforcers are completely eliminated for a maladaptive behavior and provided exclusively for alternative, adaptive behaviors).

A second factor responsible for change in a relatively short time is that behavior therapy does not only take place during therapy *sessions*. Clients in behavior therapy often do most of their therapeutic work outside the therapy sessions. For example, for every hour in a therapy session, a client might do 4 hours of homework assignments. If the therapy involved 20 weekly, hour-long sessions, then the total amount of therapy would be 100 hours, not 20.[11] Interestingly, over the course of 2 years of once-a-week therapy sessions, a client in verbal psychotherapy might spend an equivalent number of hours. However, the client in behavior therapy would have received help more than a year and a half earlier. Besides shortening the duration of therapy, homework assignments are cost-effective because the therapist is not needed. Similarly, therapists' time is saved when nonprofessional change agents—such as parents, teachers, friends, and spouses—are trained to implement therapy procedures in clients' natural environments. Directing behavior therapy procedures by telephone[12] and through portable, palmtop (handheld) and home computers (as we describe later) is another means of making treatment more cost-effective.

In addition to valuing effective therapies, managed health care providers, whose bottom line is financial, are interested in their clients' receiving brief, cost-effective treatment.[13] Fortunately, behavior therapists are equipped to provide effective short-term therapies, even for serious problems.[14] Nonetheless, the health care industry's search for briefer therapies undoubtedly will force behavior therapists to look even more carefully at essential and facilitative components of various therapies and to reduce treatments to their core elements.[15]

Breadth and Complexity of Applications

Behavior therapy is broadly applied, serving clients of all ages and with various cultural backgrounds who exhibit the gamut of psychological disorders.[16] Behavior therapy is appropriate for meeting the needs of certain groups of clients for whom traditional verbal psychotherapy has been ineffective, including infants, young children, elderly individuals,[17] people with low intelligence, and people who cannot speak.[18] Clients who cannot afford expensive, long-term therapy have benefited from relatively efficient and therefore less costly behavior therapy interventions. Behavior therapy has made inroads in the treatment of disorders that are relatively unresponsive to other forms of psychological treatment, such as schizophrenia, attention deficit hyperactivity disorder, and a number of disorders characterized by physical problems, such as pain, enuresis, and tic disorders. Finally, behavior therapy is implemented in settings where traditional psychotherapy is not typically employed, including the home, schools, and industry.

An early criticism of behavior therapy was that it dealt only with simple problems. From your reading about behavior therapy, it should be clear that contemporary behavior therapy is used to treat many *complex* problems. Behavioral treatment of psychological trauma, depression, chronic pain, and couple relationship problems are but a few examples.

The wide breadth of applications of behavior therapy notwithstanding, in some cases behavior therapy is not the optimal or even an effective form of treatment.[19] For instance, some clients are not receptive to the general behavioral approach, including how behavior therapy is conducted. Consider two of the defining themes of behavior therapy, its active nature and emphasis on the present. Some people prefer to talk about a problem and learn about its possible origin rather than to develop coping skills and practice them in their daily lives in order to change the current maintaining conditions of their problems.[20] As another example, behavior therapists *teach* and *give advice*. The directive style inherent in behavior therapy may not sit well with clients who prefer to act independently and who resist being told what to do (even when the therapist presents advice as an alternative or suggestion).[21] Clearly, behavior therapy does not work for all people. It is not a panacea, despite its arguably being the most widely applicable form of therapy.

Ethical Practices in Behavior Therapy

Our discussion of ethical issues in the practice of behavior therapy throughout the book has focused on the concerns critics most frequently voice: in particular, depriving clients of their rights and harming clients. We believe that one strength of behavior therapy is that its practices specifically serve to *protect* clients' rights.

The scientific approach that is a hallmark of behavior therapy contributes to ethical practices in a number of ways. The detailed specification of goals and target behaviors make the process of evaluating the success of therapy clear to all parties involved. This practice also minimizes the chances that therapy will continue longer than necessary. Psychotherapy sometimes is prolonged because clients are overly dependent on their therapists. Although this dependence may be inappropriate, it is not unethical. In contrast, it is unethical for therapists to prolong therapy because of *their* dependence on clients. Therapists are vulnerable to this pitfall because their clients provide them with potent reinforcers, including the satisfaction of helping others and, of course, money. Again, the practice of continually evaluating clients' progress in behavior therapy provides a partial safeguard against therapists' inappropriately prolonging treatment. Additionally, behavior therapists usually employ empirically tested therapy procedures, ensuring that clients receive effective treatment. Finally, treatment with behavior therapies is relatively brief compared with many other psychotherapies. Alleviating psychological distress as quickly as possible is certainly an ethical practice.

Collaboration between therapist and client—an essential element of behavior therapy—also serves to protect clients' rights. In consultation with the therapist, clients decide on the goals for treatment. The therapist provides clients with detailed information about the specific therapy procedures that are appropriate for their particular problems, and clients participate in choosing the therapy procedures that will be employed.[22] Clients are active participants in the therapy process, including being responsible for carrying out aspects of the therapy on their own. Such involvement decreases the chances that clients will become victims of ethical violations.

In Chapter 2, we commented on the heightened scrutiny with regard to ethical issues that behavior therapy received in its formative years. It is worth noting that this heightened scrutiny may have been a blessing in disguise. By alerting behavior therapists to potential ethical violations, the early scrutiny may have contributed to the sensitivity to clients' welfare inherent in the practice of behavior therapy.

CHALLENGES

The strengths of behavior therapy notwithstanding, behavior therapy currently faces a number of challenges. Again, before you continue reading, you might find it instructive to think of significant challenges that you believe exist.

We will highlight six challenges: (1) enhancing durability of change, (2) preventing psychological disorders and problems, (3) treating culturally diverse clients, (4) providing behavior therapy for elderly clients, (5) employing technology in behavior therapy, and (6) promoting widespread use of empirically supported behavior therapies.

Enhancing Durability of Change

Ideally, changes that occur in a client's problems as a result of behavior therapy will endure over time. However, this goal, which behavior therapy shares with all psychotherapies, is not easily attained.[23] A major reason is that treatment focuses on initiating change in clients' behaviors, and the process of *initiating* change and the process of *maintaining* change often are different. In some cases, changes brought about through therapy do endure; however, often it is necessary to introduce specific strategies to promote long-term maintenance of change. This can be done in the course of therapy or after the therapy itself has ended.

WITHIN THERAPY INTERVENTIONS TO ENHANCE
DURABILITY OF CHANGE

Two broad strategies are employed *during* behavior therapy to foster durability of treatment gains: (1) providing clients with self-control coping skills and (2) structuring clients' natural environments. Teaching clients self-control coping skills is the easier and more frequently used strategy. The aim is for clients to use the coping skills to handle any recurrences of the problem in the future. Problem solving, self-instructions, cognitive restructuring, and muscle relaxation are examples of such self-control coping skills that might be appropriate. Central to the success of this approach is clients' understanding that behavior therapy is an educational enterprise designed to help them cope more adaptively with their problems rather than to "cure" them of their ills.[24]

The second strategy for promoting durability of treatment gains during behavior therapy is to ensure that the client's natural environment will provide the necessary antecedents and consequences to maintain the new adaptive behaviors developed in therapy. This strategy is more complicated and requires more time than teaching clients coping skills. First, clients may need to institute setting events in their natural environments, which will support the changes achieved during therapy. Second, significant people in the clients' lives may need to be trained to continue treatment procedures begun in therapy. For instance, therapists may teach parents to apply in the home the same reinforcement contingencies that are being used with their children in therapy to promote adaptive behaviors.

Even with such deliberate strategies to promote long-term maintenance, durability of treatment gains is not guaranteed. It is impossible to anticipate all the future life events that may interfere with clients' dealing effectively with problems treated in therapy. Further, the less related a client's future problems are to the problems that treatment specifically focused on, the less likely it is that the treatment gains will endure. Finally, if problems do not recur for some time after therapy has been terminated, it is likely that the client will have lost proficiency in the coping skills learned in therapy and may not remember to apply them.

Despite these obstacles, behavior therapies promote long-term maintenance as well as or better than most other therapies. (It is not possible to say this definitively because long-term maintenance data are unavailable for many other therapies.) With some disorders, both immediate effectiveness and long-term effectiveness of behavioral interventions are very impressive. For example, outcome studies of cognitive-behavioral treatment of panic disorder indicate not only that panic attacks are eliminated in more than 80% of clients immediately after treatment (which is as good or better than existing drug therapies) but also that these clients remain free of panic attacks for at least 2 years.[25]

Nonetheless, in many cases long-term maintenance of treatment gains in behavior therapy is far from optimal in an absolute sense.[26] In other words, even if behavior therapy does as well as or better than other treatments, the extent of long-term maintenance may be less than desirable. For example, only about half the couples treated by cognitive-behavioral couple therapy retain the benefits after 2 years.[27]

POSTTHERAPY INTERVENTIONS TO ENHANCE DURABILITY OF CHANGE

To enhance long-term maintenance of treatment gains, behavior therapists increasingly are relying on posttherapy interventions. Relapse prevention is the most comprehensive posttherapy approach for promoting long-term maintenance. It was originally developed for preventing substance abuse relapses (see Chapter 15). Clients learn to identify high-risk situations for relapse, develop specific coping skills to use in these situations, practice the skills, and develop a balanced lifestyle between demands and desires to decrease the need for the previous maladaptive behaviors.

A second approach to enhancing the durability of change is to offer clients booster sessions after therapy has ended. In essence, therapists give clients one or more brief refresher sessions. For example, booster sessions commonly are employed after aversion therapy because the treatment effects tend to deteriorate over time but can be renewed with periodic booster sessions (see Chapter 7).[28] This may be because substance-related disorders and paraphilias, the problems treated by aversion therapy, are highly resistant to change. Other problems that are difficult to treat, such as obsessive-compulsive disorder, often require booster sessions.[29]

A third, recently proposed approach for fostering lasting change would provide *maintenance treatment* for extended periods after therapy has terminated—even for the remainder of a client's life. This is a radical idea for behavior therapists because behavior therapy has a tradition of providing relatively brief treatment and the approach superficially resembles traditional long-term psychotherapy. However, maintenance treatment is different from traditional long-term psychotherapy, in which the therapy *itself*—that is, the process of initiating change—requires years to complete.

Specifically, maintenance treatment is less intense and less frequent than the initial treatment, and it is available to clients either on a regular basis (for example, once every 6 months) or on an as-needed basis, often over many years. Maintenance treatment has been suggested for such divergent populations and problems as couples experiencing difficulties in their relationship[30] and adolescents' engaging in delinquent behaviors.[31] The need for maintenance treatment in many cases stems from the sobering fact that

> no matter how potent the technology, after treatment ends other salient life events gradually become more important in influencing the course of . . . functioning. . . . The solution cannot simply be more and better therapy technology during the active therapy phase. Rather, maintenance may be facilitated to a greater extent by creating a context for the therapist to remain a continuing presence in the lives of [clients].[32]

Maintenance treatment is an intriguing idea, albeit one that has yet to be tried and tested.

Although behavior therapy is among the most effective forms of intervention for many disorders, treatment effects often deteriorate over time.[33] Indeed, promoting the long-term maintenance of therapeutic change has been and remains the most difficult challenge for behavior therapy (as well as other psychotherapies).[34]

Preventing Psychological Disorders and Problems

The overall objective of behavior therapy is to alleviate the human suffering that results from psychological disorders. Clearly, behavior therapy has made major advances toward this goal. Behavioral principles and procedures could make an even greater contribution if they were employed more extensively to *prevent* the occurrence of psychological disorders in the first place. Some behavior therapy procedures are immediately applicable to prevention, such as stress inoculation training and problem-solving training. Others must be adapted because there are fundamental differences between treatment and prevention[35] (just as there are differences between treatment and long-term maintenance[36]).

Prevention might be especially germane to problems for which behavior therapy has been least effective. For instance, addictive behaviors, such as substance dependence, are notoriously resistant to change, largely because of the powerful immediate consequences they provide. Although behavior therapy has been among the most effective psychotherapies in treating addictive behaviors,[37] the success rate is far below that achieved with many other problems treated by behavior therapy. In some cases, continued efforts to improve interventions have made little difference.[38] Thus, it may be more fruitful to *prevent* addictive behaviors from developing in the first place. For example, prevention programs for substance abuse and dependency that target school-age children and adolescents do exist. Often, however, they merely provide information, advice, or warnings. The popular "Just Say No" campaign, for instance, is not likely to be very effective because it does not teach youngsters the assertive behaviors they require to successfully refuse drugs. In contrast, there are cognitive-behavioral programs for preventing depression that teach children and adolescents coping skills to deal with stress-evoking events that are likely to trigger depression. These programs usually are offered to groups identified as being at greater risk for developing depression, such as children from households containing significant parental conflict[39] and adolescents whose parents have depressive disorders.[40] Similar coping-skills interventions might be effective in preventing addictive behaviors in at-risk adolescents.

Prevention is unquestionably needed with problems for which no effective treatment exists. Currently, the prime example is AIDS. Although AIDS cannot be cured, it can be prevented. Behavioral interventions have shown some promise in helping prevent people from being infected with HIV (see Chapter 14).[41]

The idea of a behavioral prevention technology is not new.[42] You have read about behavioral programs developed to prevent couple relationship problems (see Chapter 13) and medical disorders (see Chapter 14), for example. However, the number of preventive efforts is very small relative to treatment efforts. Also, behavioral preventive interventions have been narrow in scope, focusing on children and adolescents[43] and principally on medical disorders and associated psychological disorders (such as fear of surgery). The potential for preventing psychological disorders and problems using behavioral interventions is great, and it is an important challenge for the future.

Treating Culturally Diverse Clients

Over the past decade, behavior therapists have become more aware of the need to be responsive to *specific* issues of ethnic and cultural diversity. Empirical evidence from a variety of sources points to this need. The United States is becoming increasingly ethnically diverse, with ethnic minorities comprising an estimated 25% of the population.[44] Yet a content analysis of articles published in the 1970s through the early 1990s in three leading behavior therapy journals revealed that only 1.3% focused on U.S. ethnic minority groups.[45] The need for more behavior therapists who are members of ethnic minority groups is documented by the finding that although the U.S. population is becoming more diverse, the demographics of students being trained in behavior therapy and faculty at behavior therapy training institutions has remained stable.[46]

Before addressing some specific issues about cultural diversity, it is important to recognize that behavior therapy is "naturally" suited to assessing and treating clients from diverse ethnic and cultural backgrounds by virtue of its basic principles. The emphasis on the role of the environment, including the client's sociocultural background and unique life circumstances, is a key element in assessing the maintaining conditions of each client's problems. Behavioral assessment procedures, including systematic naturalistic observation, self-monitoring, and physiological measures, are likely to be culturally unbiased.[47] Treatments are designed based on the unique maintaining conditions of the client's target behavior, and standard therapy procedures are tailored for each client.[48] These assets that the behavioral approach brings to the treatment of problems of diverse clients notwithstanding, many specific issues require increased attention.[49]

Race, gender, ethnicity, and sexual orientation are critical variables that can affect the course and outcome of therapy.[50] For example, some

African-American clients' distrust of European-American therapists may reflect a healthy response to the realities of racism. However, a culturally insensitive therapist may misinterpret this "cultural paranoia" as clinical paranoia. In the area of child rearing, discipline, and family privacy, there are likely to be significant differences among cultures. Unfortunately, there are no data to suggest how to modify and tailor behavioral child management training to ethnic minority families. Research is needed to provide (1) greater understanding of how different ethnic groups perceive, define, and interpret problem behaviors (for example, whether non–European-Americans view noncompliance with parental requests, a major focus of behavioral child management training, as problematic); (2) information about the acceptability of specific behavioral treatment components, such as time out from positive reinforcement, in different cultures; and (3) data on the relative efficacy of traditional behavioral child management training for ethnic minority families.[51]

Assessment methods should be chosen with the client's cultural background in mind. For instance, many Native Americans value paying attention to *actions* rather than to verbal accounts, and they believe that asking questions is rude.[52] Accordingly, a Native American client might have more confidence in systematic naturalistic observation than an interview as a means of assessment. Culturally sensitive assessment also requires that behavior therapists be aware of cultural differences in the clinical picture that is presented by clients with a particular disorder. For example, Chinese and Southeast Asian refugees in the United States suffering from depression frequently exhibit somatic complaints, such as headaches and chest pains, more than a sad mood.[53]

Providing behavior therapy interventions and a therapeutic environment that are sensitive to differences among clients of varying cultural backgrounds is challenging.[54] To begin with, clients' cultural identities impact their preferences for type of therapy and therapist style. For instance, many Asian-American clients prefer a therapist who serves as an authority figure.[55] Japanese-American women who are unaccustomed to directly communicating negative emotions or private topics with strangers, are likely to prefer indirect means of communication, such as through the use of a thought diary rather than through verbal exchanges.[56] Therapy with Hispanic clients may be more effective when the therapist allows for a period of familiarizing "small talk," which is a traditional Hispanic mode of interaction, before launching into goal-directed activities.

The particular therapy procedures chosen must take into account unique aspects of the client's general cultural identity.[57] For example, because Native Americans value action over words, they are more likely to find the collaborative empiricism of cognitive therapy (that is, actually gathering evidence for one's beliefs) more acceptable than the rational disputation of rational emotive behavior therapy. Further, the way in which the therapist individualizes standard therapy procedures for the client must be culturally sensitive. Thus, attempting to increase eye contact as part of social skills training with Navajos might be inappropriate because, in their culture, extended eye contact is viewed as an aggressive act.[58]

Effective therapy with clients from diverse backgrounds requires that the therapist become knowledgeable about as well as sensitive and open to issues such as (1) what people in the client's culture consider normal and abnormal behavior (for instance, seeing and speaking with entities from the spirit world may be regarded as normal), (2) clients' culturally based conceptions of psychological problems, (3) differences among cultures in the roles that individuals play in a family (for example, Japanese women traditionally behave unassertively), and (4) who are considered appropriate and inappropriate behavior change agents (for instance, in some Southeast Asian cultures, a woman is not permitted to be alone with a man other than her husband).[59]

Behavior therapists have begun to attend to the impact of cultural diversity as well as other forms of diversity, such as age,[60] gender,[61] and sexual orientation.[62] Most of the work so far has consisted of proposing guidelines, including recommendations of appropriate therapy techniques for clients with particular cultural and ethnic backgrounds. Regrettably, these guidelines have a number of serious flaws.[63] First, in many cases the recommended practices for different ethnic minority groups are very similar. For example, a problem-centered, present-oriented approach has been suggested as optimal for Latino,[64] Japanese-American,[65] and African-American clients.[66] Second, the recommendations often are already an integral part of the practice of behavior therapy. In the previous example, behavior therapy is a problem-centered, present-oriented approach to treatment. Thus, nothing new has been added to already established practices. Third, some of the guidelines proposed for clients with a specific ethnic background stem from cultural stereotypes.[67] A fine line exists between useful generalizations and misleading stereotypes.[68] Fourth, a number of proposed guidelines are not specific to behavior therapy, and to some extent to psychotherapy, and could apply to any professional/business dealings with people. For instance, it has been recommended that behavior therapists address Latino clients respectfully by referring to them as Señora or Señor along with their last names and maintain a humble attitude while interacting with clients.[69] Fifth, and most important, the guidelines that have been proposed thus far rest on speculation gleaned from cultural norms. It will be important in the future to develop empirically based recommendations about how behavior therapy can optimally serve diverse clients.

Providing Behavior Therapy for Elderly Clients

As with cultural minorities, the elderly population is both increasing in numbers and underserved by behavior therapists. One commentator has mused that

> if an alien were to land on Earth and survey the activities of behavior therapists . . . the alien easily could decide that behavior therapy is intended for adults aged 18 to 40. . . . Although this conclusion could be argued with, in some respects the alien's observations accurately reflect the majority of . . . [behavior therapists'] research and clinical efforts.[70]

Among the reasons for this state of affairs is that elderly clients do not have access to treatment when they are homebound. Alternatives to traditional means of accessing behavior therapy might be provided in the clients' homes, as through high-quality self-help manuals and interactive computer programs (see section on technology later in this chapter).[71]

Both general and specific guidelines are being proposed for customizing behavior therapy for elderly clients. General considerations include (1) slower pacing of treatment, (2) use of multimodal presentations (such as both visual and auditory), (3) use of modeling and behavior rehearsal, (4) use of memory aids (such as audio tapes and notebooks), and (5) interdisciplinary coordination of therapy (for example, with medical personnel).[72]

Behavior therapists have begun to examine the efficacy of behavior therapies with older adults for specific disorders, including schizophrenia,[73] depression,[74] sexual dysfunction,[75] and anxiety disorders.[76] Some specific adaptations for elderly adults have emerged from this work. For example, older adults with anxiety disorders appear to respond more favorably to exposure therapies that are brief/graduated rather than to those that are prolonged/intense. Additionally, for older adults with musculoskeletal conditions (such as arthritis), competing responses other than progressive relaxation (in which muscle tensing may be painful) are more appropriate (for example, listening to relaxing music and emotive imagery).[77]

Research clearly has demonstrated that older adults suffering from depression respond well to brief cognitive-behavioral interventions with little alteration of the basic procedures.[78] However, in introducing the therapy to older adults, it may be necessary to dispel prevalent myths about elderly people and psychological disorders and their treatment. These myths include that (1) therapy is only for "crazy" people, (2) medical professionals can "fix" all problems, (3) depression is a normal part of aging, and (4) elderly people are too old to change.[79]

Most nursing homes for the elderly have a small number of staff members who must care for a large number of residents. This poses major problems for dealing with disruptive behaviors that elderly residents with dementia often exhibit. The typical solution is to use psychotropic medications as "chemical restraints," but this practice has come under increased scrutiny.[80] Behavior therapy interventions may provide an alternative means of reducing disruptive behaviors. In an initial study, six nursing home residents, whose mean age was 80 and who suffered from dementia and schizophrenia, were treated for behaviors that the staff thought interfered most with the residents' functioning (such as verbally disruptive behaviors and demanding or combative behaviors).[81] The treatment consisted of modeling of appropriate alternative behaviors, covert behavior rehearsal, and reinforcement. In addition, the residents' medication dosage was reduced. The residents improved in their overall functioning, and staff reports of disruptive behaviors declined. Despite the reduction in medication, the residents exhibited no significant deterioration in their behaviors.

Helping family caregivers of elderly people is another arena in which behavior therapy could prove beneficial.[82] For example, the emotional stress of caregivers has been reduced when they have been taught cognitive-behavioral coping skills to manage their own distressing thoughts and actions or to deal with the problem behaviors of their care recipients.[83]

Employing Technology in Behavior Therapy

Behavior therapy has incorporated simple technology. Some examples you have read about include mechanical devices for recording behaviors (see Chapter 5), a battery-operated apparatus for individually administering response cost to students in a classroom (see Chapter 7), the Self-Injurious Behavior Inhibiting System for automatically delivering shock when a client engages in self-injurious behaviors (see Chapter 7), and the use of video modeling (see Chapter 11). Occasionally, more sophisticated and costly technology is used, such as biofeedback for hypertension and pain (see Chapter 14) and virtual reality for exposure therapy (see Chapter 9).

For the most part, however, behavior therapy has not made extensive use of technology. In one way, this is a virtue. Technology often makes procedures complicated and costly, whereas simplicity has distinct advantages in therapy. All other things being equal, the simpler the therapy procedures are, the more likely they are to work, especially when clients administer treatment procedures themselves.

Nonetheless, there are ways in which behavior therapy could use existing and future technology, especially technology that is readily accessible and relatively inexpensive.[84] For example, clients could use home computers with modems to transmit information to the therapist. At the beginning of therapy, clients could transmit completed assessment forms, such as direct self-report inventories. During therapy, clients could keep the therapist informed of the outcome of ongoing homework assignments, such as self-monitoring and practicing coping skills. This would allow therapists to provide feedback and modify assignments before the next therapy session, which, in some cases, might reduce the number of therapy sessions required.

Palmtop computers have recently been employed in the treatment of anxiety.[85] In the case of panic disorder, the palmtop computer, which clients carry with them at all times, serves three purposes: (1) prompting clients to self-monitor the frequency and severity of their panic attacks; (2) prompting them to perform homework assignments; and (3) guiding clients through in vivo exposure, cognitive restructuring, and breathing exercises.[86] In one study, both clients in a traditional 12-session cognitive-behavioral therapy program and those involved in the computer-assisted therapy showed significant reductions in panic attacks. Neither treatment was superior, and clients found both treatments equally acceptable. However, the computer-assisted intervention was more cost-effective, which means that if these findings are replicated, the computer-assisted treatment might be preferable.

An interactive video program has been developed to teach behavioral child management and parenting skills to teenage parents or parents-to-be.[87] The program teaches the skills through modeling, quizzing, behavior rehearsal, and feedback for both correct and incorrect choice of solutions to problem situations that are presented. The program is customized in two ways. The parents control the pace of the lessons, and their success with each unit determines the content of the next unit. In comparison with a control group, parents who received the training scored significantly higher at a 2-month follow-up on measures of parenting knowledge, belief in the greater effectiveness of positive parenting practices (for example, use of positive reinforcement) than coercive parenting strategies (for example, spanking), and application of adaptive parenting skills to hypothetical problem situations.

Another example of an interactive, computer-based behavior therapy program was designed to reduce the alcohol consumption of clients who drank heavily. The behavioral self-control training package consisted of goal setting, self-monitoring, self-reinforcement, stimulus control procedures, coping skills training, and relapse prevention.[88] The computer program provided clients with interactive lessons to teach them the therapy skills; it also allowed clients to enter data related to their drinking behavior, which was automatically transformed into graphic presentations. Clients participated in eight sessions over a 10-week period with sessions lasting between 15 and 45 minutes. In comparison with a wait-list control group, clients who participated in the computer-based treatment significantly reduced their drinking and maintained the reduction at a 12-month follow-up.

As the preceding examples suggest, the use of computer-assisted therapy may be a promising way to enhance the cost-effectiveness of therapies by reducing therapist contact-time with the client. Moreover, computer-assisted behavior therapy (1) can provide standardized therapy procedures and facilitate dissemination of empirically supported treatments; (2) may be useful for reaching a wide audience of clients with limited English proficiency because the computer programs can be translated into any language; (3) allows clients to control the pace of their treatment; (4) affords clients privacy, which may increase the acceptability of therapy to some clients; and (5) may increase the accessibility of treatment to clients who are unable to engage in face-to-face behavior therapy (such as clients who do not have access to transportation, live in isolated areas where behavior therapists are not available, or for health reasons, cannot leave home). Disadvantages of computer-assisted behavior therapy include (1) the absence of a face-to-face therapeutic relationship, which is an important element of traditional behavior therapy; (2) reduced ability to individualize therapy; (3) potentially greater difficulties in monitoring clients' compliance with prescribed treatment procedures; and (4) the potential violation of confidentiality of computer-based treatment, especially as it involves Internet-based programs and communication.[89]

Promoting Widespread Use of Empirically Supported Behavior Therapies

The final challenge we propose for the future is related to the demonstrated effectiveness of many behavior therapies, which, as we discussed earlier in this chapter, is a major strength of the field. In fact, for a large array of problems and client populations, a majority of the psychotherapies that have been deemed *empirically supported* are behavior therapies.[90] Nonetheless, mental health practitioners in general have not widely adopted these treatment methods.[91] (We will explore the reasons this may occur shortly.) The result is that a large number of clients do not receive treatments with demonstrated efficacy.

Consider a few examples of the underutilization of empirically supported behavior therapies. Although interoceptive exposure therapy (see Chapter 9) is the treatment of choice for panic disorder, most clients with panic disorder do not receive this treatment.[92] Similarly, although cognitive-behavioral approaches are among the treatments of choice for bulimia nervosa, they have not been widely implemented.[93] And despite evidence that 70% of children with enuresis are successfully treated by urine alarm systems (the highest success rate of any treatment for enuresis), less than 5% of primary care physicians recommend it.[94] The list of poorly utilized empirically validated treatments could be extended. Clearly, increasing the use of effective behavior therapies is a priority. After all, the most effective treatments are only effective if they are used.

What accounts for this state of affairs? To begin with, therapists who are not behaviorally oriented may choose, on theoretical or ideological grounds, not to employ empirically validated behavior therapies. For example, from a psychoanalyst's perspective, it is necessary to explore clients' unconscious memories that are presumed to be at the root of clients' problems, which, of course, behavior therapies do not do.

A second explanation stems from the fact that many nonbehavioral clinicians were not trained to value an empirical approach in treating clients[95] and to use empirically supported procedures.[96] (In contrast, as you know from the basic tenets of behavior therapy we first discussed in Chapter 1, behavior therapists value the empirical approach highly.) The majority of practicing psychotherapists classify themselves as *eclectic,* which means that they use a variety of therapy techniques from a number of different theoretical approaches. Eclectic psychotherapists choose the therapy techniques they employ for each client based on their intuition and clinical experience regarding the particular client and the client's disorder. (Bear in mind that a psychotherapist's experience is not empirical evidence because it is not based on controlled studies that can be independently replicated.) Obviously, the eclectic psychotherapists' approach is quite different from the behavior therapists' approach of choosing treatments that have been empirically supported for a particular disorder.

Finally, practicing clinicians may not be aware of or may not have access to empirically supported behavior therapies. Behavior therapists have recently begun to address this last problem by focusing on the dissemination of effective treatments.[97]

One way to increase the dissemination of empirically established behavior therapies is through treatment manuals.[98] Treatment manuals generally focus on the treatment of specific disorders and provide detailed session-by-session guidelines and procedures for clinicians to follow. The treatments are time limited, often involving fewer than 15 sessions. The manuals usually include easy-to-use outcome measures.[99] Treatment manuals have evolved from research protocols used in controlled research studies. The standard research protocols ensure that all the clinicians providing the treatment adhere to specific session-by-session guidelines so that all the clients in a study receive the same treatment. When the efficacy of the therapy being evaluated is well documented, a manual is developed for general clinical use.

Treatment manuals have a number of advantages. Therapists who have not otherwise been trained to conduct a therapy procedure can use the manual to implement it. The structured nature of treatment manuals is particularly beneficial to novice clinicians because it keeps them focused on specific goals and active strategies.[100] Using behavior therapy treatment manuals is consistent with behavior therapists' valuing cost-effective, relatively brief, empirically validated procedures.[101] These also are qualities of therapies that are valued by managed care organizations.[102]

The major criticism of employing treatment manuals is that adhering to the standard procedures they prescribe is contrary to the behavioral models' emphasis on tailoring treatment for each client's unique problems.[103] For example, clients with milder forms of a disorder may get "too much therapy" if the full session-by-session manual guidelines are followed, which clearly is not cost-effective.[104]

Those in favor of treatment manuals note that clinicians do not have to implement treatment in the precise standardized fashion that is necessary in controlled experimental studies. The specific, step-by-step treatment techniques in behavior therapy treatment manuals can be individualized, incorporating the therapist's clinical judgment, flexibility, and sensitivity to the unique needs of clients.[105] The challenge is to be able to modify empirically established behavior therapy treatment protocols with individual clients while still maintaining the elements of the treatment that are essential for its being effective.

CURRENT CONTROVERSIES

Despite the diversity of procedures used in behavior therapy, there is cohesiveness to the field. All behavior therapies share a set of common themes and characteristics (first described in Chapter 1), which make them members of a single family of psychotherapy. Recently, three related controversial developments have arisen that threaten the integrity and identity of behavior therapy. First, behavior therapy is becoming less pure as it incorporates therapy procedures from other types of psychotherapy. Second, despite the traditional scientific ethic of behavior therapy, some relatively new therapies have been accepted as mainstream behavior therapies without adequate empirical validation. Third, behavior therapy research is shifting from the study of therapy—that is, how we treat disorders—to the study of the nature of psychological disorders.

In discussing each of these developments, we not only describe the basic issues but also present our personal opinions about them. We have chosen to depart from the generally neutral stance we have assumed throughout the book regarding controversial issues for two reasons. First, we want to stimulate debate on the issues, and debate often is sparked by advocating a strong position. Second, we do have definite opinions and concerns about these issues, which may affect the future of behavior therapy, and we would like to share them with you.

Effects of Psychotherapy Integration

In the search for optimal treatments for their clients, behavior therapists are increasingly going beyond behavioral interventions and incorporating interventions from *nonbehavioral* forms of treatment into behavior therapy treatment plans. This practice is consistent with a general trend toward *psychotherapy integration,* which involves using treatment strategies from two or more different general orientations to therapy.[106] An early example of integration in behavior therapy was implosive therapy, which melded psychoanalytic theory with behavioral procedures (see Chapter 10).

The use of medication along with behavior therapy (for example, in the treatment of anxiety,[107] hypertension,[108] and attention deficit disorders[109]) is the most common form of integration in behavior therapy. Combining medication with behavior therapy is an example of *technical eclecticism,* which involves using a variety of different treatment procedures that are based on different theoretical orientations (in the present example, the biological and behavioral models), each of which has proven efficacy for a particular disorder.[110] Another example of technical eclecticism is Arnold Lazarus's *multimodal therapy,* which combines effective nonbehavioral interventions with effective behavioral interventions.[111] It is noteworthy that the multimodal therapist remains firmly rooted in the basic tenets of the behavioral approach to therapy while using some nonbehavioral treatment procedures.[112]

The merits of integration and eclecticism are the subject of debate among behavior therapists.[113] Central to the debate is the issue of the integrity of behavior therapy. *At some point, integrating nonbehavioral treatment procedures into behavior therapy renders the treatment something other than behavior therapy.* The precise point at which this change occurs is difficult to define (just as it is not easy to specify how much milk must be added to coffee for it no longer to be coffee).

In recent years, behavior therapists have become increasingly more interested in nonbehavioral approaches.[114] For instance, over the past few years, the number of presentations on nonbehavioral approaches to therapy at the annual meeting of the Association for Advancement of Behavior Therapy has increased.[115] This trend means that the practice of behavior therapy as it has been known for the past 50 years—and as we have presented it in this book—is becoming diluted.

We believe that the challenge of psychotherapy integration for behavior therapists is to incorporate nonbehavioral treatments without violating the fundamental tenets of the behavioral approach, which would preserve the integrity of the field. Whether this can be done remains to be seen.

Premature Acceptance of Therapies

Another threat to the integrity of the field is the premature acceptance of therapy procedures that have not met the accepted standards of empirical validation in behavior therapy. This practice seems to be a growing trend over the past 10 years and threatens to erode the scientific ethic of behavior therapy.

Recently, a handful of treatment procedures have been accepted as viable, mainstream behavior therapies despite their meager and questionable empirical support.[116] Eye movement desensitization and reprocessing (EMDR), which you read about in Chapter 10, is a prime example. It has been the subject of widespread controversy in the behavior therapy literature. The seemingly endless debate has taken the form of proponents of EMDR claiming, with great exuberance, that EMDR is highly effective, whereas skeptics have called for a "reduction in the distribution and marketing of EMDR until validation through replication has been achieved . . . [which would meet the] standard and reasonable practices of empirical . . . scientists that are fully consonant with the scientific credo and spirit of behavior therapy."[117] Many behavior therapists, as well as therapists of other orientations, use EMDR despite the fact that the most compelling evidence for its effectiveness comes from case studies and personal testimonials of proponents of EMDR regarding its apparent success.[118]

EMDR is not the only "suspect" treatment procedure that has been accepted into mainstream behavior therapy without supporting empirical data. Dialectical behavior therapy,[119] acceptance and commitment therapy,[120] and functional analytic psychotherapy[121] are three other well-known therapies that fit into this category and, in fact, have far less empirical support than EMDR.[122]

In instances where a poorly validated therapy is based on a theory (such as operant conditioning) that has been empirically validated, some behavior therapists have argued that this justifies using the therapy. However, it is not legitimate to conclude that a therapy is effective because empirical data support its underlying theory (just as it would be incorrect to conclude that if a therapy were effective, its guiding theoretical underpinnings were valid).[123]

Another explanation for behavior therapists' accepting a therapy "before the data are in" may be a desire to serve the immediate needs of their clients.[124] Conducting well-controlled clinical studies to validate new therapies takes years. During that time, clinicians are confronted with clients suffering from disorders for which there may be no highly effective treatments. Thus, dedicated clinicians may use treatments that have not been empirically validated but look, on theoretical grounds or based on the testimony of other clinicians, as if they *might* work.

This set of circumstances may have been the case for EMDR and dialectical behavior therapy, which were developed to treat disorders for which highly successful treatments did not exist at the time—namely, post-traumatic stress disorder and borderline personality disorder, respectively. The ethicality of such clinical practice parallels the ethical issues raised with the use of experimental medical treatments, such as those for cancer and AIDS. However, there is an important difference between treatments labeled *experimental* and those considered accepted practice, and the behavior therapies we have been discussing in this section fall into the latter category.

Behavior Therapy's Identity Crisis

The changing focus of research done by behavior therapists is a third controversial issue that relates to the identity of the field. Much of the current research deals with the nature and characteristics of psychological disorders.[125] It primarily consists of studies that examine the variables that are correlated with particular disorders (for example, the prevalence of substance abuse in clients suffering from depression).

Because *therapy* (including assessment) is the focus of behavior therapy, the shift of research from therapy to the nature of psychological disorders is altering the identity of the field. Proponents of this shift now consider *behavior therapy* to signify much more than an approach to treatment. The term has been broadened to include the general study of psychological disorders themselves.[126]

Research on the nature of psychological disorders is a worthwhile endeavor and certainly has implications for the practice of behavior therapy. However, we believe that to establish such an all-encompassing purview for behavior therapy is an overly ambitious goal. In attempting to "do it all,"[127] behavior therapy's mission becomes too broad.

Widening the purview of behavior therapy relegates behavior *therapy* (treatment) to a less prominent role in the field that bears its name. It means that behavior therapists pay less attention to developing, refining, testing, and understanding treatment and assessment. We think this trend is regrettable because the field of behavior therapy certainly has not fulfilled its fundamental mission—namely, to provide clients with effective, long-lasting treatment.

◆   ## ALL THINGS CONSIDERED: BEHAVIOR THERAPY

In its relatively brief history, behavior therapy has come a long way. It started as a new family of kids in the psychotherapy neighborhood previously populated by one dominant family, psychoanalysis. Accordingly, behavior therapy initially had a hard time gaining acceptance. When verbal taunts (such as that it treated only the simplest problems or resulted in symptom substitution) did not scare behavior therapy away, the old-timers placed seemingly impossible barriers in its path. Behavior therapists were allowed to treat only the most difficult cases, those for whom established therapies had been ineffective. Believing they were omnipotent, as youngsters often do, the new kids enthusiastically accepted the challenge. The result was some remarkable successes with so-called hopeless clients. The established family thus had no choice but to allow the new family, which by that time had grown considerably, to take up legitimate residence in the neighborhood.

At this point, the teenagers, who were no longer kids, began to fight among themselves (which was predictable now that their common external adversaries had quieted down). Some of the teenagers began to *think*—a process that most of the other teens did not trust because they could not directly observe it. The result of this infighting was an informal division into a behavioral side of the family and a cognitive-behavioral side. The cognitive-behavioral side now outnumbers the behavioral side.[128] The two sides still squabble occasionally,[129] but for the most part, they acknowledge being part of the same family—behavior therapy.[130]

The behavior therapy family has grown considerably over the past 50 years in both number and stature. Today it is the predominant cohesive family in the psychotherapy neighborhood. Whether this cohesiveness will continue remains to be seen, especially in light of recent loosening of family ties, manifest in intermarriages (integration with other therapies), degrading standards for adoption of family members (premature acceptance of therapies), and a changing family structure (loss of identity).

The stature of behavior therapy in the current practice of psychotherapy derives largely from its effectiveness, which strong empirical evidence substantiates. Nonetheless, behavior therapy is not a panacea. The effectiveness of behavior therapy in general varies with different disorders and client populations. Further, not all clients favor the behavioral approach, with its emphasis on direct, concrete solutions to psychological problems.

Looking ahead, the advent of managed health care has raised many issues regarding the future of the treatment of psychological disorders. Although it is too early to know all the implications of a predominant managed health care system, three imperatives are clear. First, accountability is essential. Therapists must specify (1) the problems being treated, (2) clear-cut goals and criteria for determining whether the goals have been met, and (3) the specific treatment procedures being employed.[131] Accountability should be an easy requirement for behavior therapists to meet because precision and measurement are essential elements of their approach. Second, the treatments used must be empirically supported for the psychological disorder being treated.[132] Fortunately, this is true for many behavior therapies.[133] Third, managed health care emphasizes short-term and cost-effective treatment. Generally, behavior therapies are relatively brief, involving fewer therapy sessions and less overall professional time than many other types of therapy.[134] Further, the emphasis on teaching clients self-control coping skills is cost-effective over time. What all this means is that behavior therapy should fare well in the era of managed health care.[135]

The commitment to empirical accountability in behavior therapy has resulted in almost continual change in the field. Behavior therapists have remained open to new ideas, examining empirical evidence to determine their merit. An early example is the wide acceptance of cognitive factors into a therapeutic approach that initially had focused exclusively on overt behaviors. The fact that behavior therapists are self-critical is another example of their open-mindedness. They have increasingly recognized and accepted the limitations of behavior therapy as challenges for the future.[136] A prime example is the recognition that procedures instituted during therapy do not ensure the durability of treatment effects. Thus, posttherapy procedures, including protracted maintenance treatment, may be necessary with some problems and client populations.

Continual assessment and responsiveness to change characterize the field of behavior therapy. For us, this quality makes being behavior therapists exciting and challenging. We hope you share our enthusiasm.

◆

Participation Exercise 16-1

DEMYTHIFYING MYTHS ABOUT CONTEMPORARY BEHAVIOR THERAPY*

You began your introduction to behavior therapy by judging whether 13 statements about behavior therapy were valid (in Participation Exercise 1-1). You learned that all the statements are predominantly false; they all are commonly held myths or misconceptions about behavior therapy. At this point, you should know *why* each of the statements is false. As a final check of your understanding of contemporary behavior therapy, read each of the 13 statements again and write specific reasons why each is false. When you have finished, compare your reasons with those in your Student Resource Materials.

1. Behavior therapy is the application of well-established laws of learning.
2. Behavior therapy directly changes symptoms of a disorder.
3. A trusting relationship between client and therapist is not necessary for behavior therapy to be effective.
4. Behavior therapy does not deal with problems of feelings, such as depression and anger.
5. Generally, little verbal interchange takes place between the therapist and client in behavior therapy.
6. The client's cooperation is not necessary for behavior therapy to be successful.
7. Most clients in behavior therapy are treated in fewer than five sessions.
8. Behavior therapy is not applicable to changing mental processes such as thoughts and beliefs.
9. Positive reinforcement works better with children than with adults.
10. Many behavior therapy procedures use painful or aversive treatments.
11. Behavior therapy primarily deals with relatively simple problems, such as phobias (for example, fear of snakes) or undesirable habits (for instance, smoking).
12. The behavior therapist determines the goals of therapy.
13. The behavior therapist primarily is responsible for the success of therapy.

◆

*This Participation Exercise can be done before you continue reading or later, but because you are now at the end of the book, we'd suggest you do it now.

Summary

1. Five major strengths of behavior therapy are its precision in specifying goals and procedures, effectiveness and accountability, efficiency, breadth and complexity of applications, and ethical practices.

2. One major challenge for behavior therapy is to design procedures that increase the durability of change when treatment ends. The two major strategies employed during behavior therapy are teaching clients self-control coping skills and ensuring that clients' natural environments provide the necessary antecedents and consequences to maintain treatment gains. Three posttherapy strategies are used to promote durability of treatment gains: relapse prevention, booster sessions, and maintenance treatment.

3. A second major challenge for behavior therapy is to develop prevention programs using behavioral principles and techniques. Prevention is especially germane to problems for which behavior therapies have been least effective or for which there is no available treatment.

4. Providing assessment and therapy procedures that are sensitive to culturally and otherwise diverse clients is a third challenge. In a number of respects, behavior therapy practices in general are sensitive to the diversity of the clients because assessment and therapy procedures are tailored to the unique needs of each client. Many suggestions have been made for providing behavior therapy for clients from specific cultural and ethnic backgrounds, but so far there is no empirical support for them.

5. Providing behavior therapy that is effective for the growing elderly population represents a fourth challenge.

6. The effective use of technology to enhance the efficiency and effectiveness of behavior therapy procedures is a fifth challenge. Interactive, computer-based programs hold promise in this regard.

7. A final challenge for behavior therapy is the promotion of widespread use of empirically supported behavior therapies. Treatment manuals are a major way in which these therapies can be widely disseminated.

8. Three controversial issues are threatening the integrity and identity of behavior therapy. First, behavior therapy is becoming less behavioral as it incorporates therapy procedures from other types of psychotherapy, a practice known as psychotherapy integration.

9. A second controversial issue is that despite the scientific ethic of behavior therapy, some relatively new treatments have gained acceptance as mainstream behavior therapies without their having adequate empirical support.

10. A third controversy concerns the shift of behavior therapy research from the study of treatment and assessment to the study of the nature of the psychological disorders, which may be stretching the purview of the field too far.

11. Because behavior therapy emphasizes accountability, has demonstrated effectiveness, and is relatively brief, the field should fare well in the era of managed health care.

REFERENCE NOTES

1. Hayes, 1995.
2. For example, Cavaliere, 1995.
3. Bergin & Strupp, 1972; Gottman & Markman, 1978; Strupp, 1978.
4. For example, Risley, 1995.
5. Goldfried & Castonguay, 1993.
6. Barlow, 1994; Goldfried & Castonguay, 1993.
7. For example, Barlow, 1994; Kendall & Chambless, 1998.
8. Addis & Carpenter, 1997; Giles, 1991; Giles, Prial, & Neims, 1993; Kendall & Chambless, 1998; Strosahl, 1995, 1996.
9. Barlow, 1994; Bergan, 1995; Strosahl, 1995.
10. Christensen, Jacobson, & Babcock, 1995; Franks, 1995; Franks, Wilson, Kendall, & Foreyt, 1990; Jacobson, 1989, 1991; Kazdin & Wilson, 1978; Paul, 1969b.
11. Compare with White, 1995.
12. For example, Lovell, Fullalove, Garvey, & Brooker, 2000.
13. For example, Barnett, 1996; Bracero, 1996; Cantor, 1995.
14. For example, Giles, 1991; Giles, Prial, & Neims, 1993.
15. Bergan, 1995; Strosahl, 1995.
16. For example, Agras & Berkowitz, 1994; Chen, 1995; Cottraux, 1993; Simos & Dimitriou, 1994.
17. For example, Beck, 1997; Dick-Siskin, 2002; Hersen & Van Hasselt, 1992; Lemsky, 1996; Malec, 1995; Nicholson & Blanchard, 1993; Wisocki, 1994.
18. For example, Cottraux, 1993.
19. Smith, Klevstrand, & Lovaas, 1995.
20. For example, Goldfried & Castonguay, 1993.
21. Gaston, Goldfried, Greenberg, Horvath, Raue, & Watson, 1995.
22. Compare with Richard, 1995.
23. For example, Barlow, 1994; Milne & Kennedy, 1993.
24. For example, Nelson & Politano, 1993.
25. Barlow, 1994.
26. For example, Chorpita, 1995; Shea, Elkin, Imber, Sotsky, Watkins, Collins, Pilkonis, Beckham, Glass, Dolan, & Parloff, 1992.
27. Christensen, Jacobson, & Babcock, 1995.
28. Rachman & Teasdale, 1969; Voegtlin, Lemere, Broz, & O'Hollaren, 1941.
29. Turner, Beidel, Spaulding, & Brown, 1995.
30. Jacobson, 1989.
31. Wolf, Braukmann, & Ramp, 1987.
32. Jacobson, 1989, p. 329.
33. Kendall, 1989.
34. Barlow, 1994; Chorpita, 1995; Shea, Elkin, Imber, Sotsky, Watkins, Collins, Pilkonis, Beckham, Glass, Dolan, & Parloff, 1992.
35. Spiegler, 1983.
36. Jacobson, 1989.
37. For example, Foreyt, 1987, 1990.
38. For example, Bennett, 1987.
39. Jaycox, Reivich, Gillham, & Seligman, 1994.
40. Clarke, Hawkins, Murphy, Sheeber, Lewinsohn, & Seeley, 1995.
41. Honnen & Kleinke, 1990; Kelly & St. Lawrence, 1988b; Kelly, St. Lawrence, Hood, & Brasfield, 1989; Roffman, Gilchrist, Stephens, & Kirkham, 1988.
42. Poser, 1970; Spiegler, 1980.
43. For example, Church, Forehand, Brown, & Holmes, 1990; Clarke, Hawkins, Murphy, Sheeber, Lewinsohn, & Seeley, 1995; Hammond & Prothow-Stith, 1991; Jaycox, Reivich, Gillham, & Seligman, 1994.
44. Iwamasa, 1997.
45. Iwamasa & Smith, 1996.
46. Neal-Barnett & Smith, 1996; Safren, 2001.
47. Paniagua, 1998.
48. For example, Hanson, Zamboanga, & Sedlar, 2000; Tanaka-Matsumi & Higginbotham, 1994; Tanaka-Matsumi, Seiden, & Lam, 1996.
49. For example, Hanson, Zamboanga, & Sedlar, 2000; Harper & Iwamasa, 2000; Paniagua, 1998.
50. Hatch, Friedman, & Paradis, 1996; Landrine & Klonoff, 1995; Paradis, Friedman, Hatch, & Ackerman, 1996.
51. Forehand & Kotchik, 1996.
52. Reyna, 1996.
53. Tanaka-Matsumi & Higginbotham, 1994.
54. Iwamasa, 1996; Martin, 1995.
55. Chen, 1995; Toyokawa & Nedate, 1996.
56. Toyokawa & Nedate, 1996.
57. Fudge, 1996; Simos & Dimitriou, 1994; Tanaka-Matsumi & Higginbotham, 1994.
58. Tanaka-Matsumi, Higginbotham, & Chang, 2002.
59. Tanaka-Matsumi, Higginbotham, & Chang, 2002; Tanaka-Matsumi & Seiden, 1994; Tanaka-Matsumi, Seiden, & Lam, 1996.

60. For example, Lemsky, 1996; Malec, 1995; McGrady, Olson, & Kroon, 1995; Nicholson & Blanchard, 1993; Zeiss & Steffen, 1996.

61. For example, McNair, 1996; Thase, Reynolds, Frank, Simons, McGeary, Fasiczka, Garamoni, Jennings, & Kupfer, 1994.

62. Chesney & Folkman, 1994; Hunter & Schaecher, 1994; Kelly & St. Lawrence, 1990; Mylott, 1994; Purcell, Campos, & Perilla, 1996; Schneiderman, Antoni, Ironson, LaPerriere, & Fletcher, 1992; Ussher, 1990.

63. Compare with Iwamasa, 1999.

64. Organista & Muñoz, 1996.

65. Toyokawa & Nedate, 1996.

66. McNair, 1996.

67. For example, Hatch, Friedman, & Paradis, 1996; McNair, 1996; Organista & Muñoz, 1996.

68. Preciado, 1999.

69. Organista & Muñoz, 1996.

70. Beck, 1997, p. 1.

71. Azar, 2002.

72. Beck, 1997; Dick-Siskin, 2002.

73. Bartels, Mueser, & Miles, 1997.

74. Beck, 1997.

75. Fisher, Swingen, & O'Donahue, 1997; Sorocco, Kasl-Godley, & Zeiss, 2002.

76. Beck & Stanley, 1997.

77. Wetherell, 2002.

78. For example, Scogin & McElreath, 1994; Teri, Curtis, Gallagher-Thompson, & Thompson, 1994; Thompson, Gallagher-Thompson, & Breckenridge, 1987.

79. Dick-Siskin, 2002.

80. Office of Inspector General, 1996.

81. Mansdorf, Calapai, Caselli, Burstein, & Dimant, 1999.

82. Coon & Thompson, 2002.

83. Gallagher-Thompson, Lovett, Rose, McKibbin, Coon, Futterman, & Thompson, 2000.

84. For example, Gale, 1996.

85. Newman, Consoli, & Taylor, 1997, 1999.

86. Newman, Kenardy, Herman, & Taylor, 1997b.

87. Lagges & Gordon, 1999.

88. Hester & Delaney, 1997.

89. Newman, Consoli, & Taylor, 1997.

90. Kendall & Chambless, 1998.

91. Persons, 1997.

92. Barlow, 1994.

93. Wilson, 1997b.

94. Rushton, 1989.

95. Date, 1996.

96. Task Force, 1995.

97. Hansen, 2001; Persons, 1995, 1997; Wilson, 1997b.

98. For example, Addis & Carpenter, 1997; Dobson & Shaw, 1989; Heimberg, 1998; Meichenbaum, 1994.

99. Eifert, Schulte, Zvolensky, Lejuez, & Lau, 1997.

100. Chambless, 1996.

101. Addis & Carpenter, 1997.

102. Eifert, Schulte, Zvolensky, Lejuez, & Lau, 1997.

103. Addis & Carpenter, 1997.

104. Eifert, Schulte, Zvolensky, Lejuez, & Lau, 1997.

105. For example, Christensen & Dobson, 2001; Eifert, Schulte, Zvolensky, Lejuez, & Lau, 1997; Martell & Hollon, 2001; Sullaway & Henry, 2001.

106. For example, Arkowitz, 1992a, 1992b, 1995; Davison, 1995; Goldfried, 1995; Goldfried, Castonguay, & Safran, 1992; Goldfried, Wiser, & Raue, 1992; Norcross & Goldfried, 1992.

107. Wilson, 1984.

108. For example, Blanchard, McCoy, Musso, Gerardi, Pallmeyer, Gerardi, Koch, Siracusa, & Andrasik, 1986.

109. For example, Satterfield, Satterfield, & Cantwell, 1981.

110. Compare with Lazarus, 1995; Lazarus & Beutler, 1993.

111. Lazarus, 1989a.

112. Lazarus, 1985, 1989a, 1989c.

113. For example, Lazarus, 1989a, 1989c; Wolpe, 1976.

114. Forsyth, 1997.

115. For example, Greenberg, 1990; Marmar, 1990.

116. Corrigan, 2001.

117. Acierno, Hersen, Van Hasselt, Tremont, & Mueser, 1994, p. 298.

118. Compare with Casti, 1989.

119. Linehan, 1993a.

120. Hayes, Strosahl, & Wilson, 1999.

121. Kohlenberg & Tsai, 1991.

122. Corrigan, 2001.

123. Corrigan, 2001.

124. Corrigan, 2001.

125. For example, Craighead, 1990a; Peterson, 1992.

126. Craighead, 1990b.

127. Craighead, 1990b.

128. Craighead, 1990b.

129. For example, Hawkins, 1997.
130. Compare with Hawkins, 1997.
131. For example, Cavaliere, 1995.
132. For example, Strosahl, 1995, 1996.
133. For example, Kendall & Chambless, 1998.
134. For example, Bergan, 1995; Strosahl, 1995.
135. For example, Giles, 1991; Giles, Prial, & Neims, 1993; compare with Cone, Alexander, Lichtszajn, & Mason, 1996.
136. Goldfried & Castonguay, 1993.

Guidelines for Choosing a Behavior Therapist*

After the decision to seek therapy has been made, an individual may feel unsure about how to choose a therapist. Persons seeking therapy often find that they have no standards to use in evaluating potential therapists. There are many competent therapists of varying theoretical persuasions. The purpose of this guide is to provide you with information that might be useful in selecting a behavior therapist. No guideline can provide strict rules for selecting the best therapist for a particular individual. We can, however, suggest questions you might ask and areas of information you might want to cover with a potential behavior therapist before you make a final decision.

What Is Behavior Therapy?

There is no single definition of behavior therapy. Although some common points of view are shared by most behavior therapists, there is a wide diversity among those persons who call themselves behavior therapists. The definition that follows is meant to give you a general idea of what behavior therapy is. It is not, however, an absolute definition. The particular behavior therapist you select may agree with some parts of it and disagree with other parts. The following definition is adapted from "Behavior Modification: Perspective on a Current Issue," published by the National Institute of Mental Health:

*The "Guidelines" were written by Marsha Linehan, Ph.D. (University of Washington, Seattle), during her tenure as Membership Chairperson of the Association for Advancement of Behavior Therapy, with a committee consisting of Richard Bootzin, Ph.D., Joseph Cautela, Ph.D., Perry London, Ph.D., Morris Perloff, Ph.D., Richard Stuart, D.S.W., and Todd Risley, Ph.D.

Behavior therapy is a particular kind of therapy that involves the application of findings from behavioral science research to help individuals change in ways they would like to change. There is an emphasis in behavior therapy on checking up on how effective the therapy is by monitoring and evaluating the individual's progress. Most behaviorally-oriented therapists believe that the current environment is most important in affecting the person's present behavior. Early life experiences, long time intrapsychic conflicts, or the individual's personality structure are considered to be of less importance than what is happening in the person's life at the present time. The procedures used in behavior therapy are generally intended to improve the individual's self-control by expanding the person's skills, abilities, and independence.

QUALIFICATIONS AND TRAINING NECESSARY FOR PARTICULAR MENTAL HEALTH PROFESSIONALS

Behavior therapy can be done by a number of different mental health professionals. Competent behavior therapists are trained in many different disciplines, and the distinction between different types of mental health professions can sometimes be confusing. Therefore, we have listed below a brief description of the training received by different types of professionals who may offer behavior therapy.

Psychiatric Social Workers

A psychiatric social worker must have a college degree, plus at least two years of graduate training in a program accredited by the Council on Social Work Education. A psychiatric social worker who is certified by the Academy of Certified Social Workers (ACSW) must have a master's or doctoral degree in Social Work (M.S.W. or D.S.W.) from a program approved by the Council on Social Work Education, two years of post-degree experience in the practice of social work, and membership in the National Association of Social Workers. In addition, the certified psychiatric social worker must pass a written exam and submit several professional references. Licensing procedures vary from state to state.

Psychologists

Psychologists usually have doctoral degrees (Ph.D., Ed.D., or Psy.D.) from graduate programs approved by the American Psychological Association. The *National Register of Health Service Providers in Psychology* lists psychologists who have a doctoral degree from a regionally accredited university, have at least two years of supervised experience in health services, one of which is postdoctoral, and are licensed or certified by the state for the independent practice of psychology. After five years of post-doctoral experience, a psychologist may apply for credentials from the American Board of Professional Psychology. This involves a review by the Board of the applicant's experience and an examination that the applicant must pass. Licensing or certification procedures vary from state to state.

Psychiatrists

A psychiatrist must have a medical degree. Although technically an individual can practice psychiatry having had four years of medical school and a one-year medical internship, most psychiatrists continue their training in a three-year residency program in psychiatry. Psychiatrists who have Board certification have had two years of post-residency experience in practicing psychiatry and must have passed an examination given by the American Board of Psychiatry and Neurology.

PRACTICAL INFORMATION ABOUT THERAPISTS

You have the right to obtain the following information about any potential therapist. This information may be obtained from the referral person, over the phone with the therapist, or at your first visit with the therapist. Although you may not feel that all this information is relevant, you will need a substantial amount of it in order to evaluate whether a particular therapist would be good for you.

Your first session with a therapist should always be a consultation. This session does not commit you to working with the therapist. The goals in the first session should be to find out whether therapy would be useful for you and whether this particular therapist is likely to be helpful to you. During this session you may want to discuss with your therapist any values which are particularly important to you. If your therapist's views are very different from yours, you may want to find a therapist more compatible with you. An important aspect of therapy for you will be the relationship between you and the therapist. This first session is a time for you to determine whether you will feel comfortable and confident working with this particular therapist.

The following are things you need to know about a prospective therapist.

Training and Qualifications

An earlier section of this guide gives a description of the qualifications and amount of training necessary for an individual to obtain a particular mental health-related degree. You should find out whether the individual therapist is licensed or certified by your state. If the person is not licensed or certified by your state, you may want to ask whether the person is being supervised by another mental health professional.

Because behavior therapists vary in types of training, there are no set rules on which professional qualifications would be best for any given person. It is common, though, for clients to want to know about the training, experience, and other professional qualifications of a potential therapist. Good therapists will not mind being asked questions about their qualifications and will freely give you any professional information which you request. If a therapist does not answer your questions, you should consult another therapist.

Fees

Many people feel uncomfortable asking about fees. However, it is important information which a good therapist will be quite willing to give a potential client. The following are financial questions you may want to cover with a therapist. This information may be obtained over the phone or during your first visit. You will want to know:

1. How much does the therapist charge per session?
2. Does the therapist charge according to income (sliding scale)?
3. Does the therapist charge for the initial session? (Since many therapists *do* charge for the initial session, you should get this information before your first visit.)
4. Is there a policy concerning vacations and missed or cancelled sessions? Is there a charge?
5. Will your health insurance cover you if you see this therapist?
6. Will the therapist want you to pay after each session, or will you be billed periodically?

Other Questions

The following are other questions you may want to ask a potential therapist:

1. How many times a week will the therapist want to see you?
2. How long will each session last?
3. How long does the therapist expect treatment to last? (Some therapists only do time-limited therapy, whereas others set no such limits.)
4. What are some of the treatment approaches likely to be used?
5. Does the therapist accept phone calls at the office or at home?
6. When your therapist is out of town or otherwise unavailable, is there someone else you can call if an emergency arises?
7. Are there any limitations on confidentiality?

QUESTIONS TO ASK WHEN DECIDING ON A THERAPIST

A behavior therapist will devote the first few sessions to assessing the extent and causes of the concerns which you have. Generally, your therapist will be asking quite specific questions about the concerns or problems causing you distress and about when and where these occur. As the assessment progresses, you can expect that you and your therapist will arrive at mutually agreeable goals for how you want to change. If you cannot agree on the goals of therapy, you should consider finding another therapist.

Once the initial goals are decided upon, you can expect the therapist to discuss with you one or more approaches for helping you reach your goals. As you continue therapy, you can expect your therapist to continually evaluate with you your progress toward these goals. If you are not progressing, or if progress is too slow, your therapist will most likely suggest modifying or changing the treatment approach. At each of these points you may want to ask yourself the following questions:

1. Do you understand what the therapist has asked you to do?
2. Do the therapist's instructions seem relevant to your objectives?
3. Do you believe that following these instructions is likely to help you make significant progress?
4. Has the therapist given you a choice of alternative therapy approaches?
5. Has the therapist explained possible side effects of the therapy?
6. Do you know what the therapist's own values are, to the extent that they are relevant to your problem?

WHAT TO DO IF YOU ARE DISSATISFIED WITH YOUR THERAPIST

Talk with Your Therapist

People often feel angry or frustrated at times about their therapy. If you do, you should discuss these concerns, dissatisfactions, and questions with the therapist. A good therapist will be open to hearing them and discussing your dissatisfactions with you.

Get a Second Opinion

If you feel that the issues and problems you have raised with your therapist are not being resolved, you may want to consider asking for a consultation with another professional. Usually the therapist you are seeing can suggest someone you can consult. If your therapist objects to your consulting another professional, you should change to another therapist who will not object.

Consider Changing Therapists

Many people feel that it is never acceptable to change therapists once therapy has begun. This is simply not true. Good therapists realize that they might not be appropriate for every person.

The most important thing you need to ask yourself when deciding to continue with a particular therapist is "Am I changing in the direction I want to change?" If you do not feel that you are improving, and if, after discussing this with your therapist, it does not appear likely to you that you will improve with this therapist, you should consult another therapist.

HOW TO GET THE NAMES OF BEHAVIOR THERAPISTS

If you don't already have the name of a therapist, you might try some of the following suggestions:

1. Ask for recommendations from your family physician, friends, and relatives.

2. Look through the Association for Advancement of Behavior Therapy [AABT] Membership Directory. AABT is not a certifying organization, and not all members listed offer behavior therapy. However, you might call persons listed in the directory to ask for a referral. Members are listed by city and state, as well as alphabetically. [You can write or call AABT, 305 Seventh Avenue, 16th Floor, New York, NY 10001, phone (800) 685-2228 or (212) 647-1890 [or find them on the Internet at www.AABT.org].

3. Call your state psychological association or district psychiatric association, and ask for a referral. You can locate your state psychological association by writing or calling the American Psychological Association, 750 First Street, N.E., Washington, DC 20002, phone (800) 374-2721 or (202) 336-5000 [or find them on the Internet at www.APA.org]. Only certified or licensed persons will be referred by these organizations. District psychiatric associations can be found by calling or writing the American Psychiatric Association, 1400 "K" Street, N.W., Washington, DC 20005, phone (202) 682-6000 [or find them on the Internet at www.psych.org].

4. Call the university psychology, social work, or medical school psychiatry departments in your area and ask for a referral. Ask to speak with someone in clinical or counseling psychology, the chairperson of the social work department, or the chairperson of the department of psychiatry.

5. Call your local community mental health clinic. The clinic may have a behavior therapist on the staff or be able to give you a referral.

6. Look in the directories of the American Psychological Association and the American Psychiatric Association. Copies of these directories should be in your public library. Members in these organizations will often be able to give you a referral.

7. Look in the *National Register of Health Service Providers in Psychology* published by the Council of National Health Service Providers in Psychology, 1120 "G" Street, N.W., Suite 330, Washington, DC 20005, phone (202) 783-7663 [or find them on the Internet at www.nationalregister.org]. Persons listed might be able to give you a referral.

8. Look in the National Association of Social Workers' *Register of Clinical Social Workers* published by the National Association of Social Workers, 750 First Street, N.E., Suite 700, Washington, DC 20002, phone (202) 408-8600 [or find them on the Internet at www.socialworkers.org]. Persons listed might be able to give you a referral.

ABA study   Single-subject reversal study consisting of three phases: baseline (A), treatment (B), and reversal (to baseline) (A).

ABAB study   Single-subject reversal study consisting of four phases: baseline (A), treatment (B), reversal (to baseline) (A), and reinstatement of treatment (B).

ABC model   Temporal sequence of antecedents, behavior, and consequences.

acceleration target behavior   Adaptive behavior that is increased in therapy.

acceptability   Measure of how palatable therapy procedures are to clients, therapists, and change agents.

activity schedule   List of the day's activities used in cognitive therapy to provide structure in clients' lives and motivate them to remain active.

adaptation period   Initial period in systematic naturalistic observation in which observations are made, but the data are not used. Its purpose is to allow the client to become accustomed to the observer's presence in order to reduce reactivity.

analogue experiment   Experiment in which the conditions of the study are similar, but not identical, to the conditions that exist in actual clinical practice.

antecedents   Events that occur or that are present before a behavior is performed.

anxiety hierarchy   List of events that elicit anxiety, ranked in order of increasing anxiety.

anxiety-induction therapy   Exposure therapy in which the client's level of anxiety is heightened initially in order to reduce it eventually.

assertion training   Specific skills training procedures used to teach assertive behaviors.

assertive behaviors   Actions that secure and maintain what one is entitled to without infringing on the rights of others.

automatic thoughts   Cognitive therapy term for maladaptive thoughts that appear to arise reflexively, without prior deliberation or reasoning.

aversion therapy   Treatment that directly decelerates a maladaptive behavior by associating it with an unpleasant stimulus.

backup reinforcer   Reinforcer that can be purchased with tokens in a token economy.

baseline   Measurement of the natural occurrence of a target behavior prior to the introduction of a treatment. It provides a standard for evaluating changes in a target behavior after a treatment has been introduced.

behavior   Anything a person does.

behavior rehearsal   Therapy procedure in which a client practices performing a target behavior.

behavioral avoidance test   Simulated observation to assess fear; clients are asked to engage in a series of steps that involve progressively more fear-inducing behaviors.

behavioral child management training   Treatment package taught to parents consisting of acceleration and deceleration behavior therapy procedures to effectively manage their children's behavioral problems.

behavioral deficit Adaptive behavior that clients are not performing often enough, long enough, or intensely enough.

behavioral excess Maladaptive behavior that clients are performing too often, for too long, or too intensely.

behavioral momentum compliance training Technique used to get a client to comply with a low-probability request—one with which the client is not likely to comply—by preceding it with a series of high-probability requests—those with which the client is likely to comply.

biofeedback Specific information clients receive about their physiological processes.

booster treatment Additional treatment after therapy has been terminated, which is designed to promote long-term maintenance of therapeutic gains.

brief/graduated exposure therapy Treatment for anxiety in which the client experiences an anxiety-evoking event for a short period and in a gradual manner.

caring-days technique Behavioral couple therapy procedure in which each partner deliberately performs behaviors that the other partner believes indicate caring.

case study Research method that provides a detailed description of what transpires during the treatment of an individual client.

checklist List of potential problem behaviors; someone who knows the client well checks those behaviors that are problematic for the client.

clinical significance Change following therapy that makes a practical difference in the client's life.

cognitive restructuring Cognitive-behavioral technique of recognizing maladaptive thoughts and replacing them with adaptive ones.

cognitive restructuring therapy Cognitive-behavioral treatment that teaches clients to substitute adaptive cognitions for the distorted, illogical, and erroneous cognitions that are maintaining their problem behaviors.

cognitive therapy Cognitive restructuring therapy that emphasizes empirically testing hypotheses about the validity of maladaptive beliefs.

cognitive-behavioral coping skills therapy Treatment that teaches clients specific cognitive and overt behavioral skills to deal effectively with difficult situations.

cognitive-behavioral therapy Treatment that changes cognitions that are the maintaining conditions of psychological disorders.

collaborative empiricism Cognitive therapy procedure in which the therapist and client work together to frame the client's irrational beliefs as hypotheses and design homework "experiments" that the client uses to test these hypotheses.

competing responses Two behaviors that cannot easily be performed simultaneously.

consequences Events that occur as a result of a behavior being performed.

consequential deceleration therapy Treatment that directly decelerates a maladaptive behavior by changing its consequences.

contingency contract Written agreement among the client, the therapist, and other change agents that specifies the relationship between target behaviors and their consequences.

continuous reinforcement schedule Schedule of reinforcement in which the target behavior is reinforced every time it is performed.

control group Clients in a therapy outcome experiment who do not receive the therapy and serve as a comparison with clients who do receive the therapy.

coping desensitization Variation of systematic desensitization in which clients use anxiety-related bodily sensations as cues to actively cope with anxiety.

coping model Model who initially experiences difficulty performing a behavior and gradually becomes competent at it.

covert behavior Behavior that cannot be directly observed in other people, such as thinking and feeling.

covert behavior rehearsal Procedure in which clients visualize their practicing performing a target behavior.

covert modeling Procedure in which clients visualize a model's behaviors.

covert sensitization Aversion therapy in which an aversive stimulus and a maladaptive target behavior are associated completely in the client's imagination.

cue exposure   Exposure therapy procedure that exposes clients to cues associated with their addictive behaviors but prevents clients from engaging in the behaviors.

dead person rule   "Never ask a client to do something a dead person can 'do'"; a rule that reminds therapists to phrase target behaviors as active, not passive.

deceleration target behavior   Maladaptive behavior that is decreased in therapy.

differential reinforcement   Indirectly decelerating a maladaptive behavior by reinforcing an alternative acceleration target behavior.

differential reinforcement of competing behaviors   Indirectly decelerating a maladaptive behavior by reinforcing acceleration target behaviors that interfere with the simultaneous performance of the deceleration target behavior.

differential reinforcement of incompatible behaviors   Indirectly decelerating a maladaptive behavior by reinforcing acceleration target behaviors that preclude the simultaneous performance of the deceleration target behavior.

differential reinforcement of low response rates   Indirectly decelerating a maladaptive behavior by reinforcing less frequent performance of the target behavior.

differential reinforcement of other behaviors   Indirectly decelerating a maladaptive behavior by reinforcing any behaviors other than the deceleration target behavior.

differential relaxation   Relaxing all muscles not essential to the behavior being performed.

direct self-report inventory   Questionnaire containing brief statements or questions requiring simple, discrete answers that clients' complete about themselves and that provide information about their problem behaviors.

dry-bed training   Treatment package for enuresis consisting of shaping and overcorrection.

dry-pants method   Daytime version of dry-bed training (*see* dry-bed training).

emotive imagery   Exposure therapy procedure in which the client uses pleasant thoughts as competing responses for anxiety.

environment   All external influences on behaviors.

experiment   Research method involving groups of clients; all the clients are handled the same way except that some clients receive the therapy being tested and others do not.

exposure therapy   Treatment for anxiety (and other negative emotional responses) that exposes clients, under carefully controlled conditions, to the situations or events that create the anxiety.

extinction   Process of withdrawing or withholding reinforcers to decrease maladaptive behaviors.

eye movement desensitization and reprocessing (EMDR)   Exposure-based treatment package for alleviating upsetting memories about traumatic experiences; its basic components are imaginal flooding, cognitive restructuring, and the induction of rapid, rhythmic eye movements.

fading   Process of gradually withdrawing prompts as the client performs the acceleration target behavior more frequently.

fear survey schedule   Direct self-report inventory containing a list of situations and objects that may elicit fear or anxiety; clients rate each on a numerical scale of severity.

flooding   Prolonged/intense in vivo or imaginal exposure to highly anxiety-evoking stimuli.

follow-up assessment (or **follow-up**)   Measurement of the client's functioning some time after therapy has been terminated to determine the durability of the treatment effects.

functional communication training   Variant of differential reinforcement that teaches clients to use acceptable ways of communicating the desire for a reinforcer as an alternative to their typical unacceptable means of communicating the same message.

generalization   Process in which changes occurring as a result of therapy change behaviors other than those that were specifically treated in therapy.

generalized imitation   The basic ability to learn by imitating others.

generalized reinforcer   Event that functions as a reinforcer for many people.

graded task assignment   Cognitive therapy shaping technique in which clients are encouraged to perform small sequential steps leading to a goal.

group contingency   Procedure in which the behaviors of a group of clients as a whole determine the consequences for each member of the group.

group hierarchy   Common anxiety hierarchy used for all the clients in group systematic desensitization.

habit reversal Treatment package for tics and nervous habits incorporating awareness training, relaxation training, competing response training, and reinforcement.

homework assignments Specific therapeutic activities that clients carry out on their own in their everyday environments.

imagery rescripting Technique used in thought stopping in which the client modifies the disturbing thought, image, or belief so that it is more tolerable and even pleasant.

implosive therapy Imaginal, prolonged/intense exposure therapy in which the client visualizes exaggerated scenes that include hypothesized stimuli related to the client's anxiety.

in vivo Term used to designate therapy procedures implemented in the client's natural environment (Latin for "in life").

in vivo exposure therapy Brief/graduated exposure to actual anxiety-evoking events.

in vivo flooding Prolonged/intense exposure to actual anxiety-evoking events.

individual contingency Procedure in which the behaviors of an individual client determine the consequences for that client.

integrative behavioral couple therapy Behavioral couple therapy that employs techniques to create acceptance of one's partner's upsetting behaviors.

intermittent reinforcement schedule Schedule of reinforcement in which only some of the occurrences of a target behavior are reinforced.

interobserver reliability Extent to which two or more observers agree on their observations of a client's behaviors.

interoceptive exposure Therapy procedure that induces physical sensations of panic attacks so that clients can practice using cognitive-behavioral coping skills to prevent panic attacks.

interrater reliability Extent to which two or more raters agree on their ratings of a client's behaviors.

live model Model who is actually present ("in the flesh").

long-term maintenance (or **maintenance**) Durability over time of changes that occur as a result of therapy.

maintaining antecedents Prerequisites and situational cues, present before a behavior is performed, that elicit or set the stage for the behavior to occur.

maintaining conditions Antecedents and consequences of a behavior that cause the behavior to be performed.

maintaining consequences Events that occur as a result of a behavior being performed and increase the likelihood that the behavior will be repeated.

maintenance *See* long-term maintenance.

massed negative practice Treatment for tics in which the client deliberately performs the tic as rapidly as possible for a set period.

mastery and pleasure rating Cognitive therapy technique in which clients rate the degree of success and enjoyment they experience in doing daily activities.

mastery model Model who, from the outset, performs a target behavior competently.

model Person who demonstrates a behavior for another person.

modeling therapies Procedures wherein a client observes a person demonstrate a behavior that the client can benefit from observing.

modes of behavior The four dimensions of behavior that are assessed and treated in behavior therapy: overt actions, cognitions, emotions, and physiological responses.

multimethod assessment Use of two or more methods to gather information about a target behavior and its maintaining conditions.

multimodal assessment Assessment of two or more of the four modes of behavior.

multiple baseline study Single-subject study in which baseline measures are obtained on two or more target behaviors; then the same therapy procedure is applied sequentially to each of the target behaviors. (In variations, the therapy is applied sequentially to the same target behavior either for two or more clients or in two or more settings.)

natural model Person in a client's natural environment who exhibits behaviors that the client can benefit from observing.

natural reinforcer A reinforcer that is readily available to clients in their natural environments.

negative reinforcement Process that occurs when the removal or avoidance of an event as a consequence of a behavior increases the likelihood that the behavior will be repeated.

negative reinforcer An event that is removed or avoided as a consequence of a behavior's being performed, which increases the likelihood that the behavior will be repeated.

noncontingent reinforcement   Variant of differential reinforcement in which the reinforcer identified as a maintaining consequence of a problem behavior is administered on a frequent fixed-interval schedule (for example, every 15 seconds) whether or not the client engages in the deceleration target behavior.

observer   In modeling therapy, the client who observes a model demonstrating a behavior.

overcorrection   Consequential deceleration therapy in which a client corrects the harmful effects of a deceleration target behavior (restitution) and then intensively practices an acceleration target behavior (positive practice).

overt behavior   Behavior that can be observed directly by other people.

participant modeling   Treatment in which the therapist models the target behavior for the client and then physically prompts the client to perform the target behavior.

perceived self-efficacy   A person's belief that he or she can master a situation or be successful at performing a task.

physically aversive consequences   Physically painful/unpleasant consequences used to decelerate a maladaptive target behavior.

planned activity scheduling   Intervention in which a behavior change agent arranges for a client to engage in an active, desirable behavior in situations that are likely to elicit a problem behavior, which reduces opportunities for the client to engage in the problem behavior.

positive reinforcement   Process by which an event that is presented as a consequence of a behavior increases the likelihood that the behavior will be repeated.

positive reinforcer   An event presented as a consequence of a behavior that increases the likelihood that the behavior will be repeated.

Premack principle   Principle stating that a higher-probability behavior will serve as a reinforcer for a lower-probability behavior.

probable maintaining conditions   The antecedents and consequences of a behavior that appear to be causing a behavior.

problem-solving therapy   Cognitive-behavioral coping skills therapy in which clients use a series of systematic steps for solving a problem for which they specifically have sought treatment.

problem-solving training   Cognitive-behavioral coping skills training to prepare people to use a series of systematic steps for dealing with problems that arise in their daily lives.

progressive relaxation   Systematically relaxing groups of skeletal muscles.

prolonged/intense exposure therapy   Treatment in which the client experiences a highly anxiety-evoking event for a lengthy period (in order to ultimately reduce the anxiety).

prompt   Cue that reminds, instructs, or guides a client to perform a behavior.

prompting   Reminding, instructing, or guiding a client to perform a behavior.

punishment   Process by which the consequence of a behavior decreases the likelihood that the behavior will be repeated.

rapid smoking   Aversion therapy procedure in which clients take one puff of a cigarette every 6 seconds, inhaling normally, and continue until they can no longer tolerate the procedure.

rating scale   List of potential problem behaviors; someone who knows the client well rates the frequency or severity of each behavior for the client.

rational emotive behavior therapy (REBT)   Cognitive restructuring therapy in which clients' irrational thoughts are directly challenged and replaced with rational thoughts.

rational emotive education   Training in which children and adolescents learn how the basic principles and procedures of rational emotive behavior therapy can be applied in their daily lives.

reactivity   Phenomenon in which people's behaviors change because they know they are being observed.

reinforcement   Process by which the consequence of a behavior increases the likelihood that the behavior will be repeated.

reinforcer   A consequence of a behavior that increases the likelihood that the behavior will be repeated.

reinforcer sampling   Procedure for making a generalized reinforcer into a reinforcer for an individual client. The client first receives the generalized reinforcer noncontingently; then, when the client comes to value it, the client receives it contingently.

reinforcing agent   A person who administers reinforcers.

relapse prevention   Procedure for promoting long-term maintenance that involves identifying situations in which clients are likely to relapse, developing skills to cope with such situations, and creating a lifestyle balance that decreases the chances of relapse.

response cost Consequential deceleration therapy in which a client's access to a valued item or privilege is removed as a consequence of performing a maladaptive behavior.

response prevention Exposure therapy procedure in which clients remain exposed to the threatening situation without engaging in their typical maladaptive anxiety-reducing responses.

retention control training Procedure used in treating enuresis that involves shaping the retention of increasingly greater amounts of urine for increasingly longer periods.

reversal phase Phase in a reversal study in which the therapy is withdrawn temporarily while the target behavior continues to be measured.

reversal study Single-subject study in which the therapy is applied to the target behavior and then is withdrawn temporarily to determine whether the therapy is causing the change in the target behavior.

role playing Assessment or therapy technique in which clients act as if they were in actual problem situations to provide the therapist with samples of how they typically behave in the situations (assessment) or to practice adaptive behaviors (therapy).

schemas Broad, pervasive cognitive themes about oneself, others, and the world, which may stem from childhood experiences and are further developed throughout one's lifetime.

self-control approach Training clients to initiate, implement, and evaluate behavior therapy procedures on their own.

self-efficacy *See* Perceived self-efficacy.

self-instructional training Cognitive-behavioral coping skills therapy that teaches clients to instruct themselves verbally (usually silently) to cope effectively with difficult situations.

self-managed exposure Exposure therapy procedure in which clients expose themselves to anxiety-evoking events on their own.

self-modeling Therapy procedure in which clients serve as their own models, by observing themselves on videotape or in their imaginations performing an acceleration target behavior.

self-recording (self-monitoring) Clients' observing and keeping records of their target behaviors.

self-reinforcement Process by which clients administer reinforcers to themselves for performing target behaviors.

self-talk What people "say" to themselves when they are thinking.

setting events Environmental conditions that elicit a behavior.

shaping Reinforcing components of a target behavior that are successively closer approximations of the complete target behavior.

simulated observation Observing a client's behaviors under conditions set up to resemble those in the client's natural environment.

single-subject study Research method that systematically compares a client's target behaviors, when they are and when they are not treated to evaluate the effectiveness of the therapy.

situation-specific Term used to indicate that behaviors are influenced by the specific environmental context in which they are performed.

skills training Treatment package—including modeling, behavior rehearsal, and reinforcement—used to teach clients skills.

social reinforcers Reinforcers consisting of attention and affirmation from other people.

social skills Interpersonal competencies needed to interact successfully with others.

social validity Therapy outcome measure that evaluates whether a client's behaviors are similar to the behaviors of individuals judged to be functioning adaptively.

stimulus control Prompts or setting events that "set the stage" for behaviors to occur.

stimulus control procedures Procedures that change behaviors by modifying prompts or setting events.

stress inoculation training Cognitive-behavioral coping skills therapy in which clients learn coping skills for dealing with stressful situations and then practice the skills while being exposed to stressors.

Subjective Units of Discomfort scale Scale clients use to rate the level of anxiety they experience in anxiety-evoking situations; usually the scale ranges from 0, representing total calm, to 100, representing the highest level of anxiety the client can imagine.

SUDs Subjective units of discomfort (*see* Subjective Units of Discomfort scale).

symbolic model Model who is observed indirectly, such as on television, in books, and in one's imagination.

systematic desensitization Brief/graduated exposure therapy in which a client imagines successively more anxiety-evoking situations while the client engages in a behavior that competes with anxiety.

systematic naturalistic observation Observation and recording of predetermined overt behaviors as the client performs them in the client's natural environment.

tangible reinforcers Material objects that serve as reinforcers.

target behavior Aspect of a client's problem that is a relatively narrow and discrete behavior that can be clearly defined and easily measured; the focus of treatment in behavior therapy.

theft reversal Overcorrection treatment for stealing that involves exaggerated restitution, wherein a client is required not only to return the stolen items to the victim but also to purchase additional similar items for the victim.

therapist-directed exposure Exposure therapy in which the therapist guides the client through the exposure.

thought stopping Cognitive-behavioral therapy procedure in which clients interrupt disturbing thoughts by saying "Stop!" (usually silently) and then substitute a prepared pleasant thought for the disturbing thought.

time out from positive reinforcement (or **time out**) Consequential deceleration therapy in which a client's access to generalized reinforcers is withdrawn for a few minutes after the client engages in a maladaptive behavior, often by placing the client in a time-out room or area.

time-out room Isolated room in which a client spends a time-out period with no access to generalized reinforcers.

token economy System for motivating clients in which they earn token reinforcers for adaptive behaviors and lose tokens for maladaptive behaviors; the tokens are exchanged for backup reinforcers.

token reinforcers Symbolic reinforcers, such as money and points, that can be exchanged for desired tangible reinforcers and reinforcing activities.

tokens In a token economy, symbolic reinforcers, such as money and points, that clients earn for performing adaptive behaviors and lose for performing maladaptive behaviors.

transfer Process in which what is learned and practiced in one setting (such as in therapy) carries over to other settings (such as at home).

treatment group Clients in a therapy outcome experiment who receive the therapy.

treatment package Treatment consisting of two or more therapy procedures.

treatment plan The specific, individualized details of how the therapy procedures will be implemented for a particular client.

urine alarm Device to treat enuresis that sounds an alarm to wake a child when the child begins to urinate; eventually the child associates bladder tension with awakening.

vicarious consequences Consequences of a model's behaviors that indicate the consequences that observers are likely to receive for imitating the model.

vicarious extinction Process by which a client's fear is reduced by observing a model perform the feared behavior without the model's incurring negative consequences.

vicarious negative consequences Consequences of a model's acts that decrease the likelihood that an observer will imitate the model.

vicarious reinforcement Consequences of a model's acts that increase the likelihood that an observer will imitate the model.

Glossary of Psychological Disorders and Problems

addictive behavior Recurrent use of substances (for example, alcohol) or engaging in other activities (for example, compulsive gambling) that involve physiological or psychological dependence and result in maladaptive consequences for the individual or others.

agoraphobia Anxiety disorder characterized by intense fear and avoidance of public places or situations from which escape might be difficult should the individual experience anticipated incapacitating panic-like symptoms (*see* panic attack).

anorexia nervosa Eating disorder characterized by distorted body image, intense fear of gaining weight, intentional reduction in food intake, and excessive exercise, resulting in dangerously low body weight.

antisocial behavior Action characterized by a blatant disregard for and violation of other people's rights.

attention deficit hyperactivity disorder (ADHD) Disorder emerging in early childhood characterized by age-inappropriate inattention and hyperactive and impulsive behaviors.

autistic disorder Developmental disorder beginning in infancy characterized by severely impaired social interaction, delayed language development and communication, and highly restrictive and repetitive patterns of behavior.

binge eating Pattern of maladaptive eating in which a person consumes excessively large quantities of food in a short period of time.

bipolar disorder Mood disorder characterized by fluctuations between depression and manic states.

body dysmorphic disorder Maladaptive preoccupation with an imagined defect or flaw in one's appearance.

borderline personality disorder Chronic and pervasive pattern of instability of interpersonal relationships, distorted self-image, poor regulation of emotions, and extreme impulsive behaviors.

bulimia nervosa Eating disorder involving recurrent episodes of uncontrolled binge eating followed by purging (through self-induced vomiting or abusing laxatives) to avoid weight gain.

chronic fatigue syndrome Pervasive fatigue lasting more than 6 months and resulting in a 50% reduction in daily activities.

chronic pain Pain occurring for a duration of at least 6 months after an injury has healed or when no trauma exists.

chronic psychiatric disorder Psychiatric disorder characterized by long-standing and severe psychological impairment in one's ability to function independently (such as schizophrenia).

compulsions Repetitive actions and ritualistic behaviors intended to suppress obsessions.

conversion disorder Physical impairment, such as paralysis or blindness, occurring in the absence of a known medical condition and associated with psychological factors.

delusions Blatantly false, maladaptive beliefs people steadfastly hold despite contrary evidence (generally associated with schizophrenia).

dementia Progressive deterioration of brain functioning characterized by deficits in memory, abstract thinking, problem solving, judgment, and motor control.

depression Mood disorder characterized by intense sadness, feelings of despair and hopelessness, inability to experience pleasure, decreased physical energy, lack of motivation, distorted thinking, and often physical complaints.

developmental disability Handicapping condition in which one or more aspects of a person's development (for instance, intellectual, language, motor) are significantly delayed in comparison with the development of others of the same age.

eating disorder Disturbed pattern of eating associated with individuals' distorted perceptions of their body shape and weight.

enuresis Recurrent involuntary bedwetting or wetting of one's clothes after age 5.

essential hypertension Chronic high blood pressure with no apparent directly treatable physical cause.

generalized anxiety disorder Anxiety disorder characterized by excessive diffuse worry, tension, apprehension, and often physical complaints.

hallucinations False sensory perceptions that people experience as real (generally associated with schizophrenia).

hypertension *See* essential hypertension.

impulsive behavior Behavior characterized by a lack of forethought about the consequences of one's actions.

insomnia Difficulties initiating and maintaining sleep.

irritable bowel syndrome Stress-related disorder that results in abdominal pain and discomfort associated with altered bowel function, including constipation and diarrhea.

mental retardation Significantly subaverage intellectual functioning accompanied by delays in everyday, adaptive functioning.

nervous habit Repetitive manipulation of objects or movement of body parts, usually occurring when a person is anxious or experiencing stress.

obesity Weighing 20% or more than the maximum appropriate weight for a person based on age, sex, height, and body build.

obsessions Persistent, unwanted intrusive thoughts.

obsessive-compulsive disorder Anxiety disorder involving unwanted, persistent intrusive thoughts (obsessions) and repetitive, ritualistic behaviors (compulsions) intended to suppress the obsessions.

oppositional behaviors Disruptive behaviors involving acting contrary to what is expected or requested by an authority figure.

pain behaviors Overt behaviors generally indicating a person is experiencing pain sensations (such as grimacing and saying "Ouch!").

panic attack Unexpected sudden occurrence of intense apprehension and terror accompanied by physical symptoms, such as shortness of breath, dizziness, heart palpitations, and chest pain.

panic disorder Anxiety disorder characterized by repeated panic attacks (*see* panic attack).

paraphilia Sexually deviant behavior in which a person is sexually aroused by socially inappropriate objects or individuals.

personality disorder Enduring, pervasive pattern of maladaptive behaviors that are inflexible and involve distress and impairment.

phobic disorder Anxiety disorder characterized by disproportionate and irrational fear of specific objects, activities, or situations, resulting in a compelling desire to avoid the feared stimuli.

posttraumatic stress disorder Anxiety disorder that emerges after experiencing a traumatic event and is characterized by emotional numbness, heightened vigilance and arousal, and the reliving of the traumatic event through mental flashbacks and nightmares.

ruminative vomiting (rumination disorder) Regurgitating and reswallowing of partially digested food, which interferes with nutritional intake and weight gain.

schizophrenia   Severe, chronic psychiatric disorder characterized by hallucinations and delusions, emotional blunting, disorganized thought and speech, social withdrawal, and bizarre actions.

selective mutism   Refusal to speak in certain social situations despite being able to speak.

self-injurious behaviors   Physically harmful behaviors (such as head banging) people deliberately inflict on themselves.

separation anxiety   Anxiety in children that involves excessive fear that harm will come to oneself or one's primary caregivers while apart from them, resulting in extreme distress when separating from primary caregivers.

sexual dysfunction   Impaired functioning in sexual relations involving diminished sexual arousal and desire, inability to achieve sexual gratification, or the experience of pain during sexual intercourse.

skills deficit   Lack of adaptive skills that impairs a person's functioning.

social anxiety   Irrational fear and avoidance of social events or situations in which one's performance might be evaluated.

social phobia   Anxiety disorder characterized by enduring irrational fear and avoidance of social events or situations in which one's performance might be evaluated.

social withdrawal   Deliberate avoidance of being in the presence of other people.

substance abuse   Recurrent substance use resulting in significant personal distress or adverse consequences.

substance dependence   Disorder involving recurrent substance use that results in a physiological or psychological need for the substance in addition to personal distress and adverse consequences.

tic disorder   Pattern of recurring, sudden, rapid involuntary motor movements or vocalizations.

Tourette's disorder   Severe tic disorder involving multiple sudden, involuntary motor movements and vocalizations.

transvestic behavior (transvestism)   Paraphilia in which a person is sexually aroused by dressing in clothing of the opposite sex.

Type A behavior   Pattern of behavior characterized by competitive, achievement-oriented behaviors; engaging in multiple tasks simultaneously; and a constant monitoring of the time. When this behavior pattern includes impatient and hostile behaviors, it is associated with high risk of cardiovascular disease.

well behaviors   Overt behaviors generally indicating that a person is not experiencing pain sensations; well behaviors are competing acceleration target behaviors for pain behaviors.

ABRAHMS, J. L. (1983). Cognitive-behavioral strategies to induce and enhance a collaborative set in distressed couples. In A. Freeman (Ed.), *Cognitive therapy with couples and groups* (pp. 125–155). New York: Plenum.

ABRAMOWITZ, J. S. (1996). Variants of exposure and response prevention in the treatment of obsessive-compulsive disorder: A meta-analysis. *Behavior Therapy, 27,* 583–600.

ABRAMOWITZ, J. S. (2001). Treatment of scrupulous obsessions and compulsions using exposure and response prevention: A case report. *Cognitive and Behavioral Practice, 8,* 79–85.

ABRAMS, M., & ELLIS, A. (1994). Rational emotive behaviour therapy in the treatment of stress. *British Journal of Guidance and Counselling, 22,* 39–50.

ACHENBACH, T. M. (1978). The Child Behavior Profile, I: Boys aged 6–11. *Journal of Consulting and Clinical Psychology, 46,* 478–488.

ACIERNO, R., HERSEN, M., VAN HASSELT, V. B., TREMONT, G., & MEUSER, K. T. (1994). Review of the validation and dissemination of eye-movement desensitization and reprocessing: A scientific and ethical dilemma. *Clinical Psychology Review, 14,* 287–299.

ACIERNO, R., TREMONT, G., LAST, C., & MONTGOMERY, D. (1994). Tripartite assessment of the efficacy of eye-movement desensitization in a multi-phobic patient. *Journal of Anxiety Disorders, 8,* 259–276.

ADAMS, C. D., & KELLEY, M. L. (1992). Managing sibling aggression: Overcorrection as an alternative to time-out. *Behavior Therapy, 23,* 707–717.

ADDIS, M. E., & CARPENTER, K. M. (1997). Treatment manuals and the future of behavior therapy. *the Behavior Therapist, 20,* 53–55.

ADDIS, M. E., & JACOBSON, N. S. (2000). A closer look at the treatment rationale and homework compliance in cognitive-behavioral therapy for depression. *Cognitive Therapy and Research, 24,* 313–326.

AESCHLEMAN, S. R., & IMES, C. (1999). Stress inoculation training for impulsive behaviors in adults with traumatic brain injury. *Journal of Rational-Emotive & Cognitive-Behavior Therapy, 17,* 51–65.

AGIGIAN, H. (1996, September 18). Personal communication.

AGRAS, W. S. (1976). Behavior modification in the general hospital psychiatric unit. In H. Leitenberg (Ed.), *Handbook of behavior modification and behavior therapy* (pp. 547–565). Englewood Cliffs, NJ: Prentice Hall.

AGRAS, W. S. (1981). Behavioral approaches to the treatment of essential hypertension. *International Journal of Obesity, 5* (Suppl. 1), 173–181.

AGRAS, W. S. (1993). Short-term psychological treatments for binge eating. In C. G. Fairburn & G. T. Wilson (Eds.), *Binge eating: Nature, assessment and treatment* (pp. 270–286). New York: Guilford.

AGRAS, W. S., & BERKOWITZ, R. I. (1994). Behavior therapy. In R. E. Hales, S. C. Yudofsky, & J. A. Talbott (Eds.), *The American Psychiatric Press textbook of psychiatry* (2nd ed., pp. 1061–1081). Washington, DC: American Psychiatric Press.

AGRAS, W. S., KAZDIN, A. E., & WILSON, G. T. (1979). *Behavior therapy: Toward an applied clinical science.* San Francisco: W. H. Freeman.

AGRAS, W. S., SCHNEIDER, J. A., ARNOW, B., RAEBURN, S. D., & TELCH, C. F. (1989). Cognitive-behavioral treatment with and without exposure plus response-prevention of bulimia nervosa: A reply to Leitenberg and Rosen. *Journal of Consulting and Clinical Psychology, 57,* 778–779.

AGRAS, W. S., SOUTHAM, M. A., & TAYLOR, C. B. (1983). Long-term persistence of relaxation-induced blood pressure lowering during the working day. *Journal of Consulting and Clinical Psychology, 51,* 792–794.

AGRAS, W. S., TAYLOR, C. B., KRAEMER, H. C., ALLEN, R. A., & SCHNEIDER, J. A. (1980). Relaxation training: Twenty-four-hour blood pressure reductions. *Archives of General Psychiatry, 37,* 859–863.

AGRAS, W. S., TAYLOR, C. B., KRAEMER, H. C., SOUTHAM, M. A., & SCHNEIDER, J. A. (1987). Relaxation treatment for essential hypertension at the worksite: II. The poorly controlled hypertensive. *Psychosomatic Medicine, 49,* 264–273.

AGRAS, W. S., TELCH, C. F., ARNOW, B., ELDREDGE, K., & MARNELL, M. (1997). One-year follow-up of cognitive-behavioral therapy for obese individuals with binge eating disorder. *Journal of Consulting and Clinical Psychology, 65,* 343–347.

AGRAS, W. S., WALSH, B. T., FAIRBURN, C. G., WILSON, G. T., & KRAEMER, H. C. (2000). A multicenter comparison of cognitive-behavioral therapy and interpersonal psychotherapy for bulimia nervosa. *Archives of General Psychiatry, 57,* 459–466.

AIKEN, L. R. (1996). *Personality assessment: Methods and practices* (2nd ed.). Seattle: Hogrefe & Huber.

AJIBOLA, O., & CLEMENT, P. W. (1995). Differential effects of methylphenidate and self-reinforcement on attention-deficit hyperactive disorder. *Behavior Modification, 19,* 211–233.

ALBERTI, R., & EMMONS, M. (2001). *Your perfect right: Assertiveness and equality in your life and relationships* (8th ed.). San Luis Obispo, CA: Impact Publishers.

ALFORD, B. A. (1986). Behavioral treatment of schizophrenic delusions: A single-case experimental analysis. *Behavior Therapy, 17,* 637–644.

ALFORD, B. A., & BECK, A. T. (1994). Cognitive therapy of delusional beliefs. *Behaviour Research and Therapy, 32,* 369–380.

ALFORD, B. A., & BECK, A. T. (1997). *The integrative power of cognitive therapy.* New York: Guilford.

ALFORD, B. A., & CORREIA, C. J. (1994). Cognitive therapy of schizophrenia: Theory and empirical status. *Behavior Therapy, 25,* 17–33.

ALFORD, B. A., FREEMAN, A., BECK, A. T., & WRIGHT, F. (1990). Brief focused cognitive therapy of panic disorder. *Psychotherapy, 27,* 230–234.

ALLEN, K. D. (1998). The use of an enhanced simplified habit-reversal procedure to reduce disruptive outbursts during athletic performance. *Journal of Applied Behavior Analysis, 31,* 489–492.

ALLEN, K. D., DANFORTH, J. S., & DRABMAN, R. S. (1989). Videotaped modeling and film distraction for fear reduction in adults undergoing hyperbaric oxygen therapy. *Journal of Consulting and Clinical Psychology, 57,* 554–558.

ALLEN, K. D., & SHRIVER, M. D. (1998). Role of parent-mediated pain behavior management strategies in biofeedback treatment of childhood migraines. *Behavior Therapy, 29,* 477–490.

ALLEN, K. D., & WARZAK, W. J. (2000). The problem of parental nonadherence in clinical behavior analysis: Effective treatment is not enough. *Journal of Applied Behavior Analysis, 33,* 373–391.

ALLEN, K. E., TURNER, K. K., & EVERETT, P. M. (1970). A behavior modification classroom for Head Start children with problem behaviors. *Exceptional Children, 37,* 119–127.

ALLEN, S. N., & BLOOM, S. L. (1994). Group and family treatment of post-traumatic stress disorder. *The Psychiatric Clinics of North America, 8,* 425–438.

ALTMAIER, E. M., & BERNSTEIN, D. N. (1981). Counselor trainees' problem-solving skills. *Counselor Education and Supervision, 20,* 285–291.

ALTMAIER, E. M., LEARY, M. R., HALPERN, S., & SELLERS, J. E. (1985). Effects of stress inoculation and participant modeling on confidence and anxiety: Testing predictions of self-efficacy theory. *Journal of Social and Clinical Psychology, 3,* 500–505.

ALVAREZ, M. F. (1997). Using REBT and supportive psychotherapy with post-stroke patients. *Journal of Rational-Emotive & Cognitive-Behavior Therapy, 15,* 231–245.

AMERICAN PSYCHIATRIC ASSOCIATION. (1987). *Diagnostic and statistical manual of mental disorders* (3rd ed., rev.). Washington, DC: Author.

AMERICAN PSYCHIATRIC ASSOCIATION. (1994). *Diagnostic and statistical manual of mental disorders* (4th ed.). Washington, DC: Author.

AMERICAN PSYCHIATRIC ASSOCIATION. (2000a). *Diagnostic and statistical manual of mental disorders* (4th ed., text rev.). Washington, DC: Author.

AMERICAN PSYCHIATRIC ASSOCIATION. (2000b). *Practice guidelines for the treatment of eating disorders.* Washington, DC: Author.

ANANT, S. S. (1968). The use of verbal aversion (negative conditioning) with an alcoholic: A case report. *Behaviour Research and Therapy, 6,* 695–696.

ANDERSON, C., & KATSIYANNIS, A. (1997). By what token economy? A classroom learning tool for inclusive settings. *Teaching Exceptional Children, 29,* 55–67.

ANDERSON, N. B., LAWRENCE, P. S., & OLSON, T. W. (1981). Within-subject analysis of autogenic training and cognitive coping training in the treatment of tension headache pain. *Journal of Behavior Therapy and Experimental Psychiatry, 12,* 219–223.

ANDERSON, T. P., COLE, T. M., GULLICKSON, G., HUDGENS, A., & ROBERTS, A. H. (1977). Behavior modification of chronic pain: A treatment program by a multidisciplinary team. *Clinical Orthopedics, 129,* 96–100.

ANDERSSON, G., MELIN, L., SCOTT, B., & LINDBERG, P. (1995). An evaluation of a behavioural treatment approach to hearing impairment. *Behaviour Research and Therapy, 33,* 283–292.

ANDRASIK, F., & BLANCHARD, E. B. (1987). Task force report on the biofeedback treatment of tension headache. In J. P. Hatch, J. D. Rugh, & J. G. Fisher (Eds.), *Biofeedback studies in clinical efficacy* (pp. 281–321). New York: Plenum.

ANDRASIK, F., LARSSON, B., & GRAZZI L. (2002). Biofeedback treatment of recurrent headaches in children and adolescents. In V. Guidetti, G. Russell, M. Sillanpaa, & P. Winner (Eds.), *Headache and migraine in childhood and adolescence* (pp. 317–332). London: Martin Dunitz.

ANESKO, K. M., & O'LEARY, S. G. (1982). The effectiveness of brief parent training for the management of children's homework problems. *Child & Family Behavior Therapy, 4,* 113–126.

ANTON, W. D. (1976). An evaluation of outcome variables in the systematic desensitization of test anxiety. *Behaviour Research and Therapy, 14,* 217–224.

ANTONI, M. H., KUMAR, M., IRONSON, G., CRUESS, D. G., LUTGENDORF, S., KLIMAS, N., FLETCHER, M., & SCHEIDERMAN, N. (2000). Cognitive-behavioral stress management intervention effects on anxiety, 24-hr urinary norepinephrine output, and T-cytotoxic/suppressor cells over time among symptomatic HIV-infected gay men. *Journal of Consulting and Clinical Psychology, 68,* 31–45.

ANTONI, M. H., LEHMAN, J. M., KILBOURN, K. M., BOYERS, A. E., CULVER, J. L., ALFERI, S. M., YOUNT, S. E., MCGREGOR, B. A., ARENA, P. L., HARRIS, S. D., PRICE, A. A., & CARVER, C. S. (2001). Cognitive-behavioral stress management intervention decreases the prevalence of depression and enhances benefit finding among woman under treatment for early-stage breast cancer. *Health Psychology, 20,* 20–32.

ANTONUCCIO, D. O., DANTON, W. G., & DENELSKY, G. Y. (1995). Psychotherapy versus medication for depression: Challenging the conventional wisdom with data. *Professional Psychology: Research and Practice, 26,* 574–585.

ANTONUCCIO, D. O., THOMAS, M., & DANTON, W. G. (1997). A cost-effectiveness analysis of cognitive behavior therapy and fluoxetine (Prozac) in the treatment of depressions. *Behavior Therapy, 28,* 187–210.

ANTONY, M. M., MCCABE, R. E., LEEUW, I., SANO, N., & SWINSON, R. P. (2001). Effect of distraction and coping styles on in vivo exposure for specific phobia of spiders. *Behaviour Research and Therapy, 39,* 1137–1150.

APPEL, M. A., SAAB, P. G., & HOLROYD, K. A. (1985). Cardiovascular disorders. In M. Hersen & A. S. Bellack (Eds.),

Handbook of clinical behavior therapy with adults (pp. 381–416). New York: Plenum.

AREAN, P. A., PERRI, M. G., NEZU, A. M., SCHEIN, R. L., CHRISTOPHER, F., & JOSEPH, T. X. (1993). Comparative effectiveness of social problem-solving therapy and reminiscence therapy as treatments for depression in older adults. *Journal of Consulting and Clinical Psychology, 61,* 1003–1010.

ARKOWITZ, H. (1992a). Integrative theories of therapy. In D. K. Freedheim (Ed.), *History of psychotherapy: A century of change* (pp. 261–303). Washington, DC: American Psychological Association.

ARKOWITZ, H. (1992b, Summer). Psychotherapy integration: Bringing psychotherapy back to psychology. *The General Psychologist, 20,* 11–20.

ARKOWITZ, H. (1995). Common factors or processes of change in psychotherapy? *Clinical Psychology: Science and Practice, 2,* 94–100.

ARMSTRONG, D., & RIMM, D. C. (1974). *Thought stopping-covert assertion vs. systematic desensitization in the treatment of snake phobias.* Unpublished master's thesis, Southern Illinois University, Carbondale.

ARMSTRONG, K. J., & DRABMAN, R. S. (1998). Treatment of a nine year old girl's masturbatory behavior. *Child & Family Behavior Therapy, 20,* 55–62.

ARNARSON, E. O. (1994). The saga of behavioural cognitive intervention. *Behavioural and Cognitive Psychotherapy, 22,* 105–109.

ARNKOFF, D. B., & GLASS, C. R. (1992). Cognitive therapy and psychotherapy: A century of change. In D. K. Freedheim (Ed.), *History of psychotherapy: A century of change* (pp. 657–694). Washington, DC: American Psychological Association.

ASARNOW, J. R., & CALLAN, J. W. (1985). Boys with peer adjustment problems: Social cognitive processes. *Journal of Consulting and Clinical Psychology, 53,* 80–87.

ASHBAUGH, R., & PECK, S. M. (1998). Treatment of sleep problems in a toddler: A replication of the faded bedtime with response cost protocol. *Journal of Applied Behavior Analysis, 31,* 127–129.

ASHEM, B., & DONNER, L. (1968). Covert sensitization with alcoholics: A controlled replication. *Behaviour Research and Therapy, 6,* 7–12.

Asylum on the front porch: Community life for the mentally retarded. (1974). *Innovations, 1,* 11–14.

ATTHOWE, J. M., JR., & KRASNER, L. (1968). Preliminary report on the application of contingent reinforcement procedures (token economy) on a "chronic" psychiatric ward. *Journal of Abnormal Psychology, 73,* 37–43.

AUSTIN, J., ALVERO, A. M., & OLSON, R. (1998). Prompting patron safety belt use at a restaurant. *Journal of Applied Behavior Analysis, 31,* 655–657.

AXELROD, S. (1998). *How to use group contingencies* (2nd ed.). Austin, TX: Pro-Ed.

AXELROD, S., BRANTNER, J. P., & MEDDOCK, T. D. (1978). Overcorrection: A review and critical analysis. *Journal of Special Education, 12,* 367–391.

AXELROD, S., & HALL, S. V. (1999). *Behavior modification: Basic principles* (2nd ed.). Austin, TX: Pro-Ed.

AYDIN, G., & YERIN, O. (1994). The effect of a story-based cognitive behavior modification procedure on reducing children's test anxiety before and after cancellation of an important examination. *International Journal for the Advancement of Counselling, 17,* 149–161.

AYLLON, T. (1963). Intensive treatment of psychotic behavior by stimulus satiation and food reinforcement. *Behaviour Research and Therapy, 1,* 53–61.

AYLLON, T. (1965). Some behavioral problems associated with eating in chronic schizophrenic patients. In L. P. Ullmann & L. Krasner (Eds.), *Case studies in behavior modification* (pp. 73–84). New York: Holt, Rinehart & Winston.

AYLLON, T., & AZRIN, N. H. (1965). The measurement and reinforcement of behavior of psychotics. *Journal of the Experimental Analysis of Behavior, 8,* 357–383.

AYLLON, T., & AZRIN, N. H. (1968). *The token economy: A motivational system for therapy and rehabilitation.* New York: Appleton-Century-Crofts.

AYLLON, T., LAYMAN, D., & KANDEL, H. J. (1975). A behavioral-educational alternative to drug control of hyperactive children. *Journal of Applied Behavior Analysis, 8,* 137–146.

AYLLON, T., & MICHAEL, J. (1959). The psychiatric nurse as a behavioral engineer. *Journal of the Experimental Analysis of Behavior, 2,* 323–334.

AYLLON, T., & ROBERTS, M. D. (1974). Eliminating discipline problems by strengthening academic performance. *Journal of Applied Behavior Analysis, 7,* 71–76.

AZAR, B. (2002, March). Helping older adults get on the technological bandwagon. *Monitor on Psychology, 33,* 28–29.

AZRIN, N. H., & BESALEL[-AZRIN], V. A. (1999). *How to use positive practice, self-correction, and overcorrection* (2nd ed.). Austin, TX: Pro-Ed.

AZRIN, N. H., GOTTLIEB, L., HUGHART, L., WESOLOWSKI, M. D., & RAHN, T. (1975). Eliminating self-injurious behavior by educative procedures. *Behaviour Research and Therapy, 13,* 101–111.

AZRIN, N. H., & HOLZ, W. C. (1966). Punishment. In W. K. Honig (Ed.), *Operant behavior: Areas of research and application* (pp. 380–447). New York: Appleton-Century-Crofts.

AZRIN, N. H., McMAHON, P. T., DONAHUE, B., BESALEL, V. A., LAPINSKI, K. J., KOGAN, E. S., ACIERNO, R. E., & GALLOWAY, E. (1994). Behavior therapy for drug abuse: A controlled treatment outcome study. *Behaviour Research and Therapy, 32,* 857–866.

AZRIN, N. H., & NUNN, R. G. (1973). Habit reversal: A method of eliminating nervous habits and tics. *Behaviour Research and Therapy, 11,* 619–628.

AZRIN, N. H., NUNN, R. G., & FRANTZ-RENSHAW, S. (1980). Habit reversal treatment of thumbsucking. *Behaviour Research and Therapy, 18,* 395–399.

AZRIN, N. H., & PETERSON, A. L. (1988a). Behavior therapy for Tourette's syndrome and tic disorders. In D. J. Cohen, R. D. Bruun, & J. F. Leckman (Eds.), *Tourette's syndrome and tic disorders: Clinical understanding and treatment* (pp. 238–255). New York: Wiley.

AZRIN, N. H., & PETERSON, A. L. (1988b). Habit reversal for the treatment of Tourette syndrome. *Behaviour Research and Therapy, 26,* 347–351.

AZRIN, N. H., & PETERSON, A. L. (1990). Treatment of Tourette syndrome by habit reversal: A waiting-list control group comparison. *Behavior Therapy, 21,* 305–318.

AZRIN, N. H., & POWELL, J. (1968). Behavioral engineering: The reduction of smoking behavior by a conditioning apparatus and procedure. *Journal of Applied Behavior Analysis, 1,* 193–200.

AZRIN, N. H., & POWELL, J. (1969). Behavioral engineering: The use of response priming to improve prescribed self-medication. *Journal of Applied Behavior Analysis, 2,* 39–42.

AZRIN, N. H., & POWERS, M. A. (1975). Eliminating classroom disturbances of emotionally disturbed children by positive practice procedures. *Behavior Therapy, 6,* 525–534.

AZRIN, N. H., SNEED, T. J., & FOXX, R. M. (1973). Dry bed: A rapid method of eliminating bedwetting (enuresis) of the retarded. *Behaviour Research and Therapy, 11,* 427–434.

AZRIN, N. H., SNEED, T. J., & FOXX, R. M. (1974). Dry-bed training: Rapid elimination of childhood enuresis. *Behaviour Research and Therapy, 12,* 147–156.

AZRIN, N., & TEICHNER, G. (1998). Evaluation of an instructional program for improving medication compliance for chronically mentally ill outpatients. *Behaviour Research and Therapy, 36,* 849–861.

AZRIN, N. H., & THIENES, P. (1978). Rapid elimination of enuresis by intensive learning without a conditioning apparatus. *Behavior Therapy, 9,* 342–354.

AZRIN, N. H., THIENES-HONTOS, P., & BESALEL-AZRIN, V. (1979). Elimination of enuresis without a conditioning apparatus: An extension by office instruction of the child and parents. *Behavior Therapy, 10,* 14–19.

AZRIN, N. H., & WESOLOWSKI, M. D. (1974). Theft reversal: An overcorrection procedure for eliminating stealing by retarded persons. *Journal of Applied Behavior Analysis, 7,* 577–581.

AZRIN, N. H., & WESOLOWSKI, M. D. (1975). Eliminating habitual vomiting in a retarded adult by positive practice and self-correction. *Journal of Behavior Therapy and Experimental Psychiatry, 6,* 145–148.

BABCOCK, R. A., SULZER-AZAROFF, B., SANDERSON, M., & SCIBAK, J. (1992). Increasing nurses' use of feedback to promote infection-control practices in a head-injury treatment center. *Journal of Applied Behavior Analysis, 25,* 621–627.

BACKHAUS, J., HOHAGEN, F., VODERHOLZER, U., & RIEMANN, D. (2001). Long-term effectiveness of a short-term cognitive-behavioral group treatment for primary insomnia. *European Archives of Psychiatry and Clinical Neuroscience, 25,* 35–41.

BAER, D. M. (1999). *How to plan for generalization* (2nd ed.). Austin, TX: Pro-Ed.

BAER, D. M., & GUESS, D. (1971). Receptive training of adjectival inflections in mental retardates. *Journal of Applied Behavior Analysis, 4,* 129–139.

BAER, D. M., & GUESS, D. (1973). Teaching productive noun suffixes to severely retarded children. *American Journal of Mental Deficiency, 77,* 498–505.

BAER, L., HURLEY, J. D., MINICHIELLO, W. E., OTT, B. D., PENZEL, F., & RICCIARDI, J. (1992). EMDR workshop: Disturbing issues? *the Behavior Therapist, 15,* 110–111.

BAER, R. A., OSNES, P. G., & STOKES, T. F. (1983). Training generalized correspondence between verbal behavior at school and nonverbal behavior at home. *Education and Treatment of Children, 6,* 379–388.

BAER, R. A., WILLIAMS, J. A., OSNES, P. G., & STOKES, T. F. (1983). Generalized verbal control and correspondence training. *Behavior Modification, 9,* 477–489.

BAGGS, K., & SPENCE, S. H. (1990). Effectiveness of booster sessions in the maintenance and enhancement of treatment gains following assertion training. *Journal of Consulting and Clinical Psychology, 58,* 845–854.

BAILEY, J. S., TIMBERS, G. D., PHILLIPS, E. L., & WOLF, M. M. (1971). Modification of articulation errors of pre-delinquents by their peers. *Journal of Applied Behavior Analysis, 4,* 265–281.

BAILEY, J. S., WOLF, M. M., & PHILLIPS, E. L. (1970). Home-based reinforcement and the modification of pre-delinquents' classroom behavior. *Journal of Applied Behavior Analysis, 3,* 223–233.

BAKKEN, J., MILTENBERGER, R. G., & SCHAUSS, S. (1993). Teaching parents with mental retardation: Knowledge versus skills. *American Journal of Mental Retardation, 97,* 405–417.

BALI, J., KEARNEY, B., WILHELM, K., DEWHURST-SAVELLIS, J., & BARTON, B. (2000). Cognitive behaviour therapy and assertion training groups for patients with depression and comorbid personality disorders. *Behavioural and Cognitive Psychotherapy, 28,* 71–85.

BALLARD, K. D., & CROOKS, T. J. (1984). Videotape modeling for preschool children with low levels of social interaction and low peer involvement in play. *Journal of Abnormal Child Psychology, 12,* 95–110.

BALTER, R., & UNGER, P. (1997). REBT stress management with patients with chronic fatigue syndrome. *Journal of Rational-Emotive & Cognitive-Behavior Therapy, 15,* 223–230.

BANARJEE, S. P. (1999). Behavioral psychotherapy in Singapore. *the Behavior Therapist, 22,* 80, 91.

BANDURA, A. (1969). *Principles of behavior modification.* New York: Holt, Rinehart & Winston.

BANDURA, A. (Ed.). (1971). *Psychological modeling: Conflicting theories.* Chicago: Aldine-Atherton.

BANDURA, A. (1976). Effecting change through participant modeling. In J. D. Krumboltz & C. E. Thoresen (Eds.), *Counseling methods* (pp. 248–265). New York: Holt, Rinehart & Winston.

BANDURA, A. (1977a). Self-efficacy: Toward a unifying theory of behavioral change. *Psychological Review, 84,* 191–215.

BANDURA, A. (1977b). *Social learning theory.* Englewood Cliffs, NJ: Prentice Hall.

BANDURA, A. (1978). Reflections on self-efficacy. In S. Rachman (Ed.), *Advances in behaviour research and therapy* (Vol. 1, pp. 237–269). Oxford, UK: Pergamon.

BANDURA, A. (1984). Recycling misconceptions of perceived self-efficacy. *Cognitive Therapy and Research, 8,* 231–255.

BANDURA, A. (1986a). From thought to action: Mechanisms of personal agency. *New Zealand Journal of Psychology, 15,* 1–17.

BANDURA, A. (1986b). *Social foundations of thought and action: A social cognitive theory.* Englewood Cliffs, NJ: Prentice Hall.

BANDURA, A. (1989). Human agency in social cognitive theory. *American Psychologist, 44,* 1175–1184.

BANDURA, A. (1997). *Self-efficacy: The exercise of control.* San Francisco: W. H. Freeman.

BANDURA, A. (2001, June). *On shaping one's future: The primacy of human agency.* Keynote address presented at the meeting of the American Psychological Society, Toronto.

BANDURA, A., JEFFERY, R. W., & GAJDOS, E. (1975). Generalizing change through participant modeling with self-directed mastery. *Behaviour Research and Therapy, 13,* 141–152.

BANDURA, A., JEFFERY, R. W., & WRIGHT, C. L. (1974). Efficacy of participant modeling as a function of response instruction aids. *Journal of Abnormal Psychology, 83,* 56–64.

BANDURA, A., & WALTERS, R. H. (1963). *Social learning and personality development.* New York: Holt, Rinehart & Winston.

BARCLAY, D. R., & HOUTS, A. C. (1995). Parenting skills: A review and developmental analysis of training content. In W. O'Donohue & L. Krasner (Eds.), *Handbook of psychological skills training: Clinical techniques and applications* (pp. 195–228). Boston: Allyn & Bacon.

BARKIN, R. M., & DUNCAN, R. (1975). Broken appointments: Questions, not answers. *Pediatrics, 55,* 747–748.

BARKLEY, R. A. (1987). *Defiant children: A clinician's manual for parent training.* New York: Guilford.

BARKLEY, R. A. (1989). *Defiant children.* New York: Guilford.

BARKLEY, R. A., GUEVREMONT, D. C., ANASTOPOULOS, A. D., & FLETCHER, K. (1992). A comparison of three family therapy programs for treating family conflicts in adolescents with attention deficit hyperactivity disorder. *Journal of Consulting and Clinical Psychology, 60,* 450–462.

BARLOW, D. H. (1988). *Anxiety and its disorders: The nature and treatment of anxiety and panic.* New York: Guilford.

BARLOW, D. H. (1993). Covert sensitization for paraphilia. In J. R. Cautela & A. J. Kearney (Eds.), *Covert conditioning casebook* (pp. 185–198). Pacific Grove, CA: Brooks/Cole.

BARLOW, D. H. (1994). Psychological interventions in the era of managed competition. *Clinical Psychology: Science and Practice, 1,* 109–122.

BARLOW, D. H., & CERNEY, J. A. (1988). *Psychological treatment of panic.* New York: Guilford.

BARLOW, D. H., CRASKE, M. G., CERNEY, J. A., & KLOSKO, J. S. (1989). Behavioral treatment of panic disorder. *Behavior Therapy, 20,* 261–282.

BARLOW, D. H., GORMAN, J. M., SHEAR, M. K., & WOODS, S. W. (2000). Cognitive-behavioral therapy, imipramine, or their combination for panic disorder. *Journal of the American Medical Association, 283,* 2529–2536.

BARLOW, D. H., & HERSEN, M. (1984). *Single case experimental designs: Strategies for studying behavior change* (2nd ed.). New York: Pergamon Press.

BARLOW, D. H., O'BRIEN, G. T., & LAST, C. A. (1984). Couples treatment of agoraphobia. *Behavior Therapy, 15,* 41–58.

BARNETT, J. E. (1996). Managed care: Time to fight or flee? *Psychotherapy Bulletin, 31,* 54–58.

BARR, R. F., LOVIBOND, S. H., & KATSAROS, E. (1972). Giles de la Tourette's syndrome in a brain-damaged child. *Medical Journal of Australia, 2,* 372–374.

BARRIOS, B. A. (1988). On the changing nature of behavioral assessment. In A. S. Bellack & M. Hersen (Eds.), *Behavioral assessment: A practical handbook* (3rd ed., pp. 3–41). Elmsford, NY: Pergamon.

BARRY, J. V. (1958). *Alexander Maconochie of Norfolk Island: A study of a pioneer in penal reform.* London: Oxford University Press.

BARRY, N. J., & OVERMANN, P. B. (1977). Comparison of the effectiveness of adult and peer models with EMR children. *American Journal of Mental Deficiency, 82,* 33–36.

BARTELS, S. J., MUESER, K. T., & MILES, K. M. (1997). Functional impairments in elderly patients with schizophrenia and major affective illness in the community: Social skills, living skills, and behavior problems. *Behavior Therapy, 28,* 43–63.

BARTON, E. J., & ASCIONE, F. R. (1984). Direct observation. In T. H. Ollendick & M. Hersen (Eds.), *Child behavioral assessment* (pp. 166–194). Elmsford, NY: Pergamon.

BARTON, E. S., GUESS, D., GARCIA, E., & BAER, D. M. (1970). Improvement of retardates' mealtime behaviors by time-out procedures using multiple base-line techniques. *Journal of Applied Behavior Analysis, 3,* 77–84.

BAUCOM, D. H., & EPSTEIN, N. (1990). *Cognitive-behavioral marital therapy.* New York: Brunner/Mazel.

BAUCOM, D. H., & HOFFMAN, J. A. (1986). The effectiveness of marital therapy: Current status and applications to the clinical setting. In N. S. Jacobson & A. S. Gurman (Eds.), *Clinical handbook of marital therapy* (pp. 597–620). New York: Guilford.

BAUCOM, D. H., SHOHAM, V., MUESER, K. T., DAIUTO, A. D., & STICKLE, T. R. (1998). Empirically supported couple and family interventions for marital distress and adult mental health problems. *Journal of Consulting and Clinical Psychology, 66,* 53–88.

BAUER, A. M., & SHEA, T. M. (1984). Tourette syndrome: A review and educational implications. *Journal of Autism and Developmental Disorders, 14,* 69–80.

BAUM, C. J., & FOREHAND, R. [L.] (1981). Long-term follow-up of parent training by use of multiple outcome measures. *Behavior Therapy, 12,* 643–652.

BAXTER, L. R., SCHWARTZ, J. M., BERGMAN, K. S., SZUBA, M. P., GUZE, B. H., MAZZIOTTA, J. C., AKAZRAJU, A., SELIN, C. E., FERNG, H. K., MUNFORD, P., & PHELPS, M. E. (1992). Caudate glucose metabolic rate changes with both drug and behavior therapy for obsessive-compulsive disorder. *Archives of General Psychiatry, 49,* 681–689.

BEACH, S. R. H., & O'LEARY, K. D. (1992). Treating depression in the context of marital discord: Outcome predictors of response of marital therapy versus cognitive therapy. *Behavior Therapy, 23,* 507–528.

BEACH, S. R. H., WHISMAN, M. A., & O'LEARY, K. D. (1994). Marital therapy for depression: Theoretical foundation, current status, and future directions. *Behavior Therapy, 25,* 345–371.

BEAUCHAMP, T. L., & WALTERS, L. (Eds.). (1978). *Contemporary issues in bioethics.* Encino, CA: Dickenson.

BEBKO, J. M., & LENNOX, C. (1988). Teaching the control of diurnal bruxism to two children with autism using a simple cueing procedure. *Behavior Therapy, 19,* 249–255.

BECK, A. T. (1963). Thinking and depression. *Archives of General Psychiatry, 9,* 324–333.

BECK, A. T. (1967). *Depression: Clinical, experimental, and theoretical aspects.* New York: Hoeber.

BECK, A. T. (1972). *Depression: Causes and treatment.* Philadelphia: University of Pennsylvania Press.

BECK, A. T. (1976). *Cognitive therapy and the emotional disorders.* New York: International Universities Press.

BECK, A. T. (1988). Cognitive approaches to panic disorder: Theory and therapy. In S. Rachman & J. D. Maser (Eds.), *Panic: Psychological perspectives* (pp. 91–109). Hillsdale, NJ: Erlbaum.

BECK, A. T. (1989). *Love is never enough.* New York: Harper & Row (Perennial Library).

BECK, A. T., & EMERY, G. (1985). *Anxiety disorders and phobias: A cognitive perspective.* New York: Basic Books.

BECK, A. T., & FREEMAN, A. (1989). *Cognitive therapy of personality disorders.* New York: Guilford.

BECK, A. T., RUSH, A. J., SHAW, B. F., & EMERY, G. (1979). *Cognitive therapy of depression*. New York: Guilford.

BECK, J. G., & STANLEY, M. A. (1997). Anxiety disorders in the elderly: The emerging role of behavior therapy. *Behavior Therapy, 28,* 83–100.

BECK, A. T., & STEER, R. A. (1993). *Beck Depression Inventory* (rev. ed.). San Antonio, TX: Psychological Corporation.

BECK, A. T., & WEISHAAR, M. [E.] (1989). Cognitive therapy. In A. Freeman, K. M. Simon, L. E. Beutler, & H. Arkowitz (Eds.), *Comprehensive handbook of cognitive therapy* (pp. 21–36). New York: Plenum.

BECK, A. T., WRIGHT, F. D., NEWMAN, C. F., & LIESE, B. S. (1993). *Cognitive therapy of substance abuse*. New York: Guilford.

BECK, J. G. (1997). Mental health in the elderly—Challenges for behavior therapy: Introduction to the special series. *Behavior Therapy, 28,* 1–2.

BECK, J. G., & STANLEY, M. A. (1997). Anxiety disorders in the elderly: The emerging role of behavior therapy. *Behavior Therapy, 28,* 83–100.

BECKER, R. E., & HEIMBERG, R. G. (1988). Assessment of social skills. In A. S. Bellack & M. Hersen (Eds.), *Behavioral assessment: A practical handbook* (3rd ed., pp. 365–395). Elmsford, NY: Pergamon.

BECKER, W. (1971). *Parents are teachers: A child management program*. Champaign, IL: Research Press.

BECKHAM, E. E., & WATKINS, J. T. (1989). Process and outcome in cognitive therapy. In A. Freeman, K. M. Simon, L. E. Beutler, & H. Arkowitz (Eds.), *Comprehensive handbook of cognitive therapy* (pp. 583–596). New York: Plenum.

BEIDEL, D. C., & TURNER, S. M. (1986). A critique of the theoretical bases of cognitive-behavioral theories and therapy. *Clinical Psychology Review, 6,* 177–197.

BEIDEL, D. C., & TURNER, S. M. (1998). *Shy children, phobic adults: The nature and treatment of social phobia*. Washington, DC: American Psychological Association.

BEIDEL, D. C., TURNER, S. M., & MORRIS, T. L. (1995). A new inventory to assess childhood social anxiety and phobia: The social phobia and anxiety inventory for children. *Psychological Assessment, 7,* 73–79.

BEIDEL, D. C., TURNER, S. M., & MORRIS, T. L. (2000). Behavioral treatment of childhood social phobia. *Journal of Consulting and Clinical Psychology, 68,* 1072–1080.

BEIMAN, I., ISRAEL, E., & JOHNSON, S. A. (1978). During training and posttraining effects of live and taped extended progressive relaxation, self-relaxation, and electromyogram biofeedback. *Journal of Consulting and Clinical Psychology, 46,* 314–321.

BELCHIC, J. K., & HARRIS, S. L. (1994). The use of multiple peer exemplars to enhance the generalization of play skills to the siblings of children with autism. *Child & Family Behavior Therapy, 16,* 1–24.

BELLACK, A. S., & HERSEN, M. (Eds.). (1988). *Behavioral assessment: A practical handbook* (3rd ed.). Elmsford, NY: Pergamon.

BELLACK, A. S., HERSEN, M., & TURNER, S. M. (1979). Relationship of role playing and knowledge of appropriate behavior to assertion in the natural environment. *Journal of Consulting and Clinical Psychology, 47,* 670–678.

BELLACK, A. S., MORRISON, R. L., WIXTED, J. T., & MUESER, K. T. (1990). An analysis of social competence in schizophrenia. *British Journal of Psychiatry, 156,* 809–818.

BELLACK, A. S., & MUESER, K. T. (1994). Schizophrenia. In L. W. Craighead, W. E. Craighead, A. E. Kazdin, & M. J. Mahoney (Eds.), *Cognitive and behavioral interventions: An empirical approach to mental health problems*. Needham Heights, MA: Allyn & Bacon.

BELL-DOLAN, D. J. (1995). Social cue interpretation of anxious children. *Journal of Clinical Child Psychology, 24,* 1–10.

BENNETT, W. (1987). Dietary treatments of obesity. In R. J. Wurtman & J. J. Wurtman (Eds.), *Human obesity* (pp. 250–263). New York: New York Academy of Sciences.

BENSON, H. (1975). *The relaxation response*. New York: Morrow.

BENTALL, R. P., HADDOCK, G., & SLADE, P. D. (1994). Cognitive behavior therapy for persistent auditory hallucinations: From theory to therapy. *Behavior Therapy, 25,* 51–66.

BENTALL, R. P., HIGSON, P., & LOWE, C. (1987). Teaching self-instructions to chronic schizophrenic patients: Efficacy and generalization. *Behavioural Psychotherapy, 15,* 58–76.

BENTON, M. K., & SCHROEDER, H. E. (1990). Social skills training with schizophrenics: A meta-analytic evaluation. *Journal of Consulting and Clinical Psychology, 58,* 741–747.

BERG, W. K., PECK, S. M., WACKER, D. P., HARDING, J., McCOMAS, J., RICHMAN, D. M., & BROWN, K. (2000). The effects of precession exposure to attention on the results of assessments of attention as a reinforcer. *Journal of Applied Behavior Analysis, 33,* 463–477.

BERGAN, J. (1995). Behavioral training and the new mental health: Are we learning what we need to know? *the Behavior Therapist, 18,* 161–164, 166.

BERGIN, A. E., & STRUPP, H. H. (Eds.). (1972). *Changing frontiers in the science of psychotherapy*. Chicago: Aldine-Atherton.

BERMAN, S. L., WEEMS, C. F., SILVERMAN, W. K., & KURTINES, W. M. (2000). Predictors of outcome of exposure-base cognitive and behavioral treatments for phobic and anxiety disorders in children. *Behavior Therapy, 31,* 713–731.

BERNARD, M. E. (1990). Rational-emotive therapy with children and adolescents: Treatment strategies. *School Psychology Review, 19,* 294–303.

BERNARD, M. E., & DiGIUSEPPE, R. [A.] (1989). Rational-emotive therapy today. In M. E. Bernard & R. [A.] DiGiuseppe (Eds.), *Inside rational-emotive therapy: A critical appraisal of the theory and therapy of Albert Ellis* (pp. 1–7). San Diego: Academic Press.

BERNARD, M. E., & JOYCE, M. R. (1984). *Rational-emotive therapy with children and adolescents: Theory, treatment strategies, preventative methods*. New York: Wiley.

BERNSTEIN, D. A., & BORKOVEC, T. D. (1973). *Progressive relaxation training: A manual for the helping professions*. Champaign, IL: Research Press.

BERNSTEIN, D. A., BORKOVEC, T. D., & HAZLETT-STEVENS, H. (2000). *New directions in progressive relaxation training: A guidebook for helping professionals*. Westport, CT: Praeger.

BERTAGNOLLI, A., & MORRIS, S. (1997). Cognitive-behavioral interventions with chronic fatigue syndrome: A single case study. *Journal of Cognitive Psychotherapy: An International Quarterly, 11,* 127–139.

BEUTLER, L. E., & GUEST, P. D. (1989). The role of cognitive change in psychotherapy. In A. Freeman, K. M.

Simon, L. E. Beutler, & H. Arkowitz (Eds.), *Comprehensive handbook of cognitive therapy* (pp. 123–142). New York: Plenum.

BIGELOW, G., LIEBSON, I., & GRIFFITHS, R. (1974). Alcoholic drinking: Suppression by a brief time-out procedure. *Behaviour Research and Therapy, 12,* 107–115.

BIGELOW, G., STRICKLER, D., LIEBSON, L., & GRIFFITHS, R. (1976). Maintaining disulfiram ingestion among outpatient alcoholics: A security-deposit contingency contracting procedure. *Behaviour Research and Therapy, 14,* 378–381.

BIGELOW, K. M., HUYNEN, K. B., & LUTZKER, J. R. (1993). Using a changing criterion design to teach fire escape to a child with developmental disabilities. *Journal of Developmental and Physical Disabilities, 5,* 121–128.

BIGELOW, K. M., & LUTZKER, J. R. (1998). Using video to teach planned activities to parents reported for child abuse. *Child & Family Behavior Therapy, 20,* 1–14.

BIGGAM, F. H., & POWER, K. G. (1999). Social problem-solving skills and psychological distress among incarcerated young offenders: The issue of bullying and victimization. *Cognitive Therapy and Research, 23,* 307–326.

BILLINGS, A. (1978). Self-monitoring in the treatment of tics: A single subject analysis. *Journal of Behavior Therapy and Experimental Psychiatry, 9,* 339–342.

BLACK, D. (1987). A minimal intervention program and a problem-solving program for weight control. *Cognitive Therapy and Research, 11,* 107–120.

BLACK, R. G. (1975). The chronic pain syndrome. *Surgical Clinics of North America, 55,* 4.

BLACKBURN, I. M. (1988). An appraisal of cognitive trials of cognitive therapy for depression. In C. Perris, I. M. Blackburn, & H. Perris (Eds.), *Cognitive psychotherapy* (pp. 329–364). Heidelberg, Germany: Springer.

BLAMPIED, N. M. (1999). Cognitive-behavior therapy in Aptearoa, New Zealand. *the Behavior Therapist, 22,* 173–178.

BLAMPIED, N. M., & FRANCE, K. G. (1993). A behavioral model of infant sleep disturbance. *Journal of Applied Behavior Analysis, 26,* 477–492.

BLAMPIED, N. M., & KAHAN, E. (1992). Acceptability of alternative punishments: A community survey. *Behavior Modification, 16,* 400–413.

BLANCHARD, E. B. (1970). The relative contributions of modeling, informational influences, and physical contact in the extinction of phobic behavior. *Journal of Abnormal Psychology, 76,* 55–61.

BLANCHARD, E. B. (1987). Long-term effects of behavioral treatment of chronic headache. *Behavior Therapy, 18,* 375–385.

BLANCHARD, E. B. (1992). Psychological treatment of benign headache disorders. *Journal of Consulting and Clinical Psychology, 60,* 537–551.

BLANCHARD, E. B., ANDRASIK, F., NEFF, D. F., ARENA, J. G., AHLES, T. A., JURISH, S. E., PALLMEYER, T. P., SAUNDERS, N. L., TEDERS, S. J., BARRON, K. D., & RODICHOK, L. D. (1982). Biofeedback and relaxation training with three kinds of headaches: Treatment effects and their prediction. *Journal of Consulting and Clinical Psychology, 50,* 562–575.

BLANCHARD, E. B., APPLEBAUM, K. A., RADNITZ, C. L., MORRILL, B., MICHULTKA, D., KIRSCH, C., GUARNIERI, P., HILLHOUSE, J., EVANS, D. D., JACCARD, J., & BARRON, K. D. (1990). A controlled evaluation of thermal biofeedback and thermal biofeedback combined with cognitive therapy in the treatment of vascular headache. *Journal of Consulting and Clinical Psychology, 58,* 216–224.

BLANCHARD, E. B., MCCOY, G. C., MUSSO, A., GERARDI, M. A., PALLMEYER, T. P., GERARDI, R. J., KOCH, P. A., SIRACUSA, K., & ANDRASIK, F. (1986). A controlled comparison of thermal biofeedback and relaxation training in the treatment of essential hypertension: I. Short-term and long-term outcome. *Behavior Therapy, 17,* 563–579.

BLANCHARD, E. B., THEOBALD, D. E., WILLIAMSON, D. A., SILVER, B. V., & BROWN, D. A. (1978). Temperature biofeedback in the treatment of migraine headaches. *Archives of General Psychiatry, 35,* 581–588.

BLANCHARD, E. B., YOUNG, L. D., & HAYNES, M. R. (1975). A simple feedback system for the treatment of elevated blood pressure. *Behavior Therapy, 6,* 241–245.

BLANKSTEIN, K. R., & SEGAL, Z. V. (2001). Cognitive assessment: Issues and methods. In K. S. Dobson (Ed.), *Handbook of cognitive-behavioral therapies* (2nd ed., pp. 40–85). New York: Guilford.

BLOCK, A. R., KREMER, E. F., & GAYLOR, M. (1980). Behavioral treatment of chronic pain: The spouse as a discriminative cue for pain behaviors. *Pain, 9,* 243–252.

BLOXHAM, G., LONG, C. G., ALDERMAN, N., & HOLLIN, C. R. (1993). The behavioral treatment of self-starvation and severe self-injury in a patient with borderline personality disorder. *Journal of Behavior Therapy and Experimental Psychiatry, 24,* 261–267.

BLUMBERG, E. J., HOVELL, M. F., WERNER, C. A., KELLEY, N. J., SIPAN, C. L., BURKHAM, S. M., & HOFFSTETTER, C. R. (1997). Evaluating AIDS-related social skills in Anglo and Latino adolescents. *Behavior Modification, 21,* 281–307.

BLY, R. (1990). *Iron John: A book about men.* Reading, MA: Addison-Wesley.

BONICA, J. J. (1986). Status of pain research and therapy. *Seminars in Anesthesia, 5,* 82–99.

BOOTZIN, R. R. (1972). Stimulus control treatment for insomnia. *Proceedings of the 80th annual convention of the American Psychological Association, 7,* 395–396.

BOOTZIN, R. R. (1975). *Behavior modification and therapy: An introduction.* Cambridge, MA: Winthrop.

BOOTZIN, R. R., & ENGLE-FRIEDMAN, M. (1987). Sleep disturbances. In B. Edelstein & L. Carstensen (Eds.), *Handbook of clinical gerontology* (pp. 238–251). Elmsford, NY: Pergamon.

BOOTZIN, R. R., & EPSTEIN, D. R. (2000). Stimulus control. In K. L. Lichstein & C. M. Morin (Eds.), *Treatment of late-life insomnia* (pp. 167–184). Thousand Oaks, CA: Sage.

BOOTZIN, R. R., EPSTEIN, D., & WOOD, J. M. (1991). Stimulus control instructions. In P. Hauri (Ed.), *Case studies in insomnia* (pp. 19–28). New York: Plenum.

BOOTZIN, R. R., & PERLIS, M. L. (1992). Nonpharmacologic treatments of insomnia. *Journal of Clinical Psychiatry, 53,* 37–41.

BORKOVEC, T. D. (1970). *The comparative effectiveness of systematic desensitization and implosive therapy and the effect of expectancy manipulation on the elimination of fear.* Unpublished doctoral dissertation, University of Illinois, Champaign.

BORKOVEC, T. D. (1972). Effects of expectancy on the outcome of systematic desensitization and implosive treatments for analogue anxiety. *Behavior Therapy, 3,* 29–40.

BORKOVEC, T. D., & COSTELLO, E. (1993). Efficacy of applied relaxation and cognitive-behavioral therapy in the treatment of generalized anxiety disorder. *Journal of Consulting and Clinical Psychology, 61,* 611–619.

BORKOVEC, T. D., GRAYSON, J. B., & O'BRIEN, G. T. (1979). Relaxation treatment of pseudoinsomnia and idiopathic insomnia: An electroencephalographic evaluation. *Journal of Applied Behavior Analysis, 12,* 37–54.

BORKOVEC, T. D., & MATHEWS, A. M. (1988). Treatment of nonphobic anxiety disorders: A comparison of nondirective, cognitive, and coping desensitization therapy. *Journal of Consulting and Clinical Psychology, 56,* 877–884.

BORKOVEC, T. D., & WHISMAN, M. A. (1996). Psychosocial treatment for generalized anxiety disorder. In M. R. Mavissakalian & R. F. Prien (Eds.), *Long term treatments of anxiety disorders* (pp. 171–199). Washington, DC: American Psychiatric Press.

BORNAS, X., FULLANA, M. A., TORTELLA-FELIU, M., LLABRÉS, J., & DE LA BANDA, G. G. (2001). Computer-assisted therapy in the treatment of flight phobia: A case report. *Cognitive and Behavioral Practice, 8,* 234–240.

BORNSTEIN, P. H., HAMILTON, S. B., & BORNSTEIN, M. T. (1986). Self-monitoring procedures. In A. Ciminero, K. Calhoun, & H. Adams (Eds.), *Handbook of behavioral assessment* (2nd ed., pp. 176–225). New York: Wiley.

BORREGO, J., & URQUIZA, A. J. (1998). Importance of therapist use of social reinforcement with parents as a model of parent-child relationships: An example with parent-child interaction therapy. *Child & Family Behavior Therapy, 20,* 27–54.

BOTELLA, C., BAÑOS, R. M., PERPIÑA, C., VILLA, H., ALCAÑIZ, M., & REY, A. (1998). Virtual reality treatment of claustrophobia: A case report. *Behaviour Research and Therapy, 36,* 239–246.

BOUDEWYNS, P. A., STWERTKA, S. A., HYER, L. A., ALBRECHT, J. W., & SPERR, E. V. (1993). Eye movement desensitization and reprocessing: A pilot study. *Behavior Therapy, 16,* 30–33.

BOUDIN, H. M. (1972). Contingency contracting as a therapeutic tool in deceleration of amphetamine use. *Behavior Therapy, 3,* 602–608.

BOUDJOUK, P. J., WOODS, D., MILTENBERGER, R. G., & LONG, E. S. (2000). Negative peer evaluation in adolescents: Effects of tic disorders and trichotillomania. *Child & Family Behavior Therapy, 22,* 17–28.

BOUHENIE, G., & MOORE, T. E. (2000). EMDR and the scientific perspective. *the Behavior Therapist, 23,* 154–158.

BOULOUGOURIS, J. C., MARKS, I. M., & MARSET, P. (1971). Superiority of flooding (implosion) to desensitization for reducing pathological fear. *Behaviour Research and Therapy, 9,* 7–16.

BOUTELLE, K. N. (1998). The use of exposure with response prevention in a male anorexic. *Journal of Behavior Therapy and Experimental Psychiatry, 29,* 79–84.

BOWERS, W. A. (1989). Cognitive therapy with inpatients. In A. Freeman, K. M. Simon, L. E. Beutler, & H. Arkowitz (Eds.), *Comprehensive handbook of cognitive therapy* (pp. 583–596). New York: Plenum.

BRACERO, W. (1996). The story hour: Narrative and multicultural perspectives on managed care and time-limited psychotherapy. *Psychotherapy Bulletin, 31,* 59–65.

BRADLEY, R. W., & HUGHES, H. (1979). *Blood pressure biofeedback and relaxation training: The effects of home practice on reduction of blood pressure in persons with essential hypertension.* Unpublished manuscript.

BRAET, C., & WINCKEL, M. V. (2000). Long-term follow-up of a cognitive behavioral treatment program for obese children. *Behavior Therapy, 31,* 55–74.

BRASWELL, L., & KENDALL, P. C. (2001). Cognitive-behavioral therapy with youth. In K. S. Dobson (Ed.), *Handbook of cognitive-behavioral therapies* (2nd ed., pp. 246–294). New York: Guilford.

BRAUER, A. P., NORLICK, L., NELSON, E., FARQUHAR, J. W., & AGRAS, W. S. (1979). Relaxation therapy for essential hypertension: A Veterans Administration outpatient study. *Journal of Behavioral Medicine, 2,* 21–29.

BRAUKMANN, C. J., & WOLF, M. M. (1987). Behaviorally based group homes for juvenile offenders. In E. K. Morris & C. J. Braukmann (Eds.), *Behavioral approaches to crime and delinquency: A handbook of applications, research, and concepts* (pp. 135–159). New York: Plenum.

BRAUKMANN, C. J., WOLF, M. M., & KIRIGIN RAMP, K. A. (1985). *Follow-up of group home youths into young adulthood* (Progress Report, Grant MH20030). Lawrence: Achievement Place Research Project, University of Kansas.

BRAY, M. A., & KEHLE, T. J. (1998). Self-modeling as an intervention for stuttering. *School Psychology Review, 27,* 587–598.

BRAY, M. A., & KEHLE, T. J. (2001). Long-term follow-up of self-modeling as an intervention for stuttering. *School Psychology Review, 30,* 135–141.

BRAZELTON, T. B. (1987, June). Are we frightening our children? *Family Circle,* pp. 98, 100, 124.

BREINER, J. L., & FOREHAND, R. [L.] (1981). An assessment of the effects of parent training on clinic-referred children's school behavior. *Behavioral Assessment, 3,* 31–42.

BRESTAN, E. V., EYBERG, S. M., BOGGS, S. R., & ALGINA, J. (1997). Parent-child interaction therapy: Parent's perceptions of untreated siblings. *Child & Family Behavior Therapy, 19,* 13–28.

BRICKES, W. A., & BRICKES, D. D. (1970). Development of receptive vocabulary in severely retarded children. *American Journal of Mental Deficiency, 74,* 599–607.

BRIGHAM, F. J., BAKKEN, J. P., SCRUGGS, T. E., & MASTROPIERE, M. A. (1992). Cooperative behavior management: Strategies for promoting a positive classroom environment. *Education and Training in Mental Retardation, 27,* 3–12.

BRISTOL, M. M., & SLOANE, H. N. (1974). Effects of contingency contracting on study rate and test performance. *Journal of Applied Behavior Analysis, 7,* 271–285.

BRODER, M. S. (2000). Making optimal use of homework to enhance your therapeutic effectiveness. *Journal of Rational-Emotive & Cognitive-Behavior Therapy, 18,* 3–18.

BROWN, D. K., KRATOCHWILL, T. R., & BERGAN, J. R. (1982). Teaching interviewing skills for problem identification: An analogue study. *Behavioral Assessment, 4,* 63–73.

BROWN, E. J., HEIMBERG, R. G., & JUSTER, H. R. (1995). Social phobia subtype and avoidant personality disorder: Effect on severity of social phobia, impairment, and outcome of cognitive-behavioral treatment. *Behavior Therapy, 26,* 467–486.

BROWN, K. A., WACKER, D. P., DERBY, K. M., PECK, S. M., RICHMAN, D. M., SASSO, G. M., KNUTSON, C. L., & HARDING, J. W. (2000). Evaluating the effects of functional communication training in the presence and absence of establishing operations. *Journal of Applied Behavior Analysis, 33,* 53–71.

BROWN, R. A., LICHTENSTEIN, E., MCINTYRE, K. O., & HARRINGTON-KOSTUR, J. (1984). Effects of nicotine fading and relapse prevention on smoking cessation. *Journal of Consulting and Clinical Psychology, 52,* 307–309.

BROWN, T. A., ANTONY, M. M., & BARLOW, D. H. (1995). Diagnostic comorbidity in panic disorder: Effect on treatment outcome and course of comorbid diagnoses following treatment. *Journal of Consulting and Clinical Psychology, 63,* 408–418.

BROWNELL, K. D., & COHEN, L. R. (1995). Adherence to dietary regimens 1: An overview of research. *Behavioral Medicine, 20,* 149–154.

BROWNING, R. M., & STOVER, D. O. (1971). *Behavior modification in child treatment: An experimental and clinical approach.* Chicago: Aldine-Atherton.

BRYANT, L. E., & BUDD, K. S. (1982). Self-instructional training to increase independent work performance in preschoolers. *Journal of Applied Behavior Analysis, 15,* 259–271.

BRYANT, M. J., SIMONS, A. D., & THASE, M. E. (1999). Therapist skill and patient variables in homework compliance: Controlled and uncontrolled variable in cognitive therapy outcome research. *Cognitive Therapy and Research, 23,* 381–399.

BUCELL, M. (1979). *An empirically derived self-report inventory for the assessment of assertive behavior.* Unpublished doctoral dissertation, Kent State University, Kent, OH.

BUCHER, B., & LOVAAS, O. I. (1968). Use of aversive stimulation in behavior modification. In M. R. Jones (Ed.), *Miami Symposium on the Prediction of Behavior 1967: Aversive stimulation* (pp. 77–145). Coral Gables, FL: University of Miami Press.

BUCKELEW, S. P., CONWAY, R., PARKER, J., DEUSER, W. E., READ, J., WITTY, T. E., HEWETT, J. E., MINOR, M., JOHNSON, J. C., VAN MALE, L., MCINTOSH, M. J., NIGH, M., & KAY, D. R. (1998). Biofeedback/relaxation training and exercise interventions for fibromyalgia: A prospective study. *Arthritis Care and Research, 11,* 169–209.

BUDD, K. S., WORKMAN, D. E., LEMSKY, C. M., & QUICK, D. M. (1994). The Children's Headache Assessment Scale (CHAS): Factor structure and psychometric properties. *Journal of Behavioral Medicine, 17,* 159–179.

BUDNEY, A. J., HIGGINS, S. T., RADONOVICH, K. J., & NOVY, P. L. (2000). Adding voucher-based incentives to coping skills and motivational enhancement improves outcomes during treatment for marijuana dependence. *Journal of Consulting and Clinical Psychology, 68,* 1051–1061.

BUGGEY, T., TOOMBS, K., GARDENER, P., & CERVETTI, M. (1999). Training responding behaviors in students with autism: Using videotaped self-modeling. *Journal of Positive Behavior Interventions, 1,* 205–214.

BUJOLD, A., LADOUCEUR, R., SYLVAIN, C., & BOISVERT, J. (1994). Treatment of pathological gamblers: An experimental study. *Journal of Behavior Therapy and Experimental Psychiatry, 25,* 275–282.

BURGESS, A. (1962). *A clockwork orange.* London: Heinemann.

BURGIO, L. D., WHITMAN, T. L., & JOHNSON, M. R. (1980). A self-instructional package for increasing attending behavior in educable mentally retarded children. *Journal of Applied Behavior Analysis, 13,* 443–459.

BURHAM, J. J., & GULLONE, E. (1997). The Fear Survey Schedule for Children-II: A psychometric investigation with American data. *Behaviour Research and Therapy, 35,* 165–173.

BURISH, T. G., & LYLES, J. N. (1979). Effectiveness of relaxation training in reducing the aversiveness of chemotherapy in the treatment of cancer. *Journal of Behavior Therapy and Experimental Psychiatry, 10,* 357–361.

BURISH, T. G., SHARTNER, C. D., & LYLES, J. N. (1981). Effectiveness of multiple-site EMG biofeedback and relaxation training in reducing the aversiveness of cancer chemotherapy. *Biofeedback and Self-Regulation, 6,* 523–535.

BURMAN, B., MARGOLIN, G., & JOHN, R. S. (1993). America's angriest home videos: Behavioral contingencies observed in home reenactments of marital conflict. *Journal of Consulting and Clinical Psychology, 61,* 28–39.

BURNS, D. [D.] (1980). *Feeling good.* New York: Morrow.

BURNS, D. D., & NOLEN-HOEKSEMA, S. (1992). Therapeutic empathy and recovery from depression in cognitive-behavioral therapy: A structural equation model. *Journal of Consulting and Clinical Psychology, 60,* 441–449.

BURNS, D. D., & SPRANGLER, D. L. (2000). Does psychotherapy homework lead to improvements in depression in cognitive-behavioral therapy or does improvement lead to increased homework compliance? *Journal of Consulting and Clinical Psychology, 69,* 46–56.

BUSHELL, D., JR. (1978). An engineering approach to the elementary classroom: The Behavior Analysis Follow Through Project. In C. A. Catania & T. A. Brigham (Eds.), *Handbook of applied behavior analysis: Social and instructional processes* (pp. 525–563). New York: Irvington.

BUSS, A. H., PLOMIN, R., & WILLERMAN, L. (1973). The inheritance of temperaments. *Journal of Personality, 41,* 513–524.

BUTLER, G. (1985). Exposure as a treatment for social phobia: Some instructive difficulties. *Behaviour Research and Therapy, 23,* 651–657.

CAHOON, D. D. (1968). Symptom substitution and the behavior therapies: A reappraisal. *Psychological Bulletin, 69,* 149–156.

CAIRNS, D., & PASINO, J. A. (1977). Comparison of verbal reinforcement and feedback in operant treatment of disability due to low back pain. *Behavior Therapy, 8,* 621–630.

CAIRNS, D., THOMAS, L., MOONEY, V., & PAU, J. B. (1976). A comprehensive treatment approach to chronic low back pain. *Pain, 2,* 301–308.

CALAMARI, J. E., FABER, S. D., HITSMAN, B. L., & POPPE, C. J. (1994). Treatment of obsessive compulsive disorder in the elderly: A review and case example. *Journal of Behavior Therapy and Experimental Psychiatry, 25,* 95–104.

CALLAHAN, E. J., & LEITENBERG, H. (1973). Aversion therapy for sexual deviation: Contingent electric shock and covert sensitization. *Journal of Abnormal Psychology, 81,* 60–73.

CAMP, B. W., & BASH, M. A. S. (1981). *Think aloud: Increasing social and cognitive skills—A problem-solving program for children (primary level)*. Champaign, IL: Research Press.

CAMP, B. W., BLOM, G. E., HERBERT, F., & VAN DOORWICK, W. J. (1977). "Think aloud": A program for developing self-control in young aggressive boys. *Journal of Abnormal Child Psychology, 5,* 157–169.

CAMPBELL, J. (1988). *The power of myth.* New York: Doubleday.

CAMPBELL, R. V., & LUTZKER, J. R. (1993). Using functional equivalence training to reduce severe challenging behavior: A case study. *Journal of Developmental and Physical Disabilities, 5,* 203–215.

CANAVAN, A. G. M., & POWELL, G. E. (1981). The efficacy of several treatments of Gilles de la Tourette's syndrome as assessed in a single case. *Behaviour Research and Therapy, 19,* 549–556.

CANTOR, D. W. (1995). Maintaining our professional integrity in the era of managed care. *Psychotherapy Bulletin, 30,* 27–28.

CAREY, M. P., BRAATEN, L. S., MAISTO, S. A., GLEASON, J. R., FORSYTH, A. D., DURANT, L. E., & JAWORSKI, B. C. (2000). Using information, motivation enhancement, and skills training to reduce the risk of HIV infection for low-income urban woman: A second randomized clinical trial. *Health Psychology, 19,* 3–11.

CAREY, R. G., & BUCHER, B. B. (1981). Identifying the educative and suppressive effects of positive practice and restitutional overcorrection. *Journal of Applied Behavior Analysis, 14,* 71–80.

CAREY, R. G., & BUCHER, B. B. (1986). Positive practice overcorrection: Effects of reinforcing correct performance. *Behavior Modification, 10,* 73–92.

CAREY, T. S. (1994). Chronic back pain: Behavioral interventions and outcomes in a changing healthcare environment. *Behavioral Medicine, 20,* 113–117.

CARLIN, A. S., HOFFMAN, H. G., & WEGHORST, S. (1997). Virtual reality and tactile augmentation in the treatment of spider phobia: A case report. *Behaviour Research and Therapy, 35,* 153–158.

CARLSON, C. L., MANN, M., & ALEXANDER, D. K. (2000). Effects of reward and response cost on the performance and motivation of children with ADHD. *Cognitive Therapy and Research, 24,* 87–98.

CARLSON, C. L., & TAMM, L. (2000). Responsiveness of children with attention deficit-hyperactivity disorder to reward and response cost: Differential impact on performance and motivation. *Journal of Consulting and Clinical Psychology, 68,* 73–83.

CARLSON, C. R., & BERNSTEIN, D. A. (1995). Relaxation skills training: Abbreviated progressive relaxation. In W. O'Donohue & L. Krasner (Eds.), *Handbook of psychological skills training: Clinical techniques and applications* (pp. 20–35). Boston: Allyn & Bacon.

CARLSON, C. R., & HOYLE, R. H. (1993). Efficacy of abbreviated progressive muscle relaxation training: A quantitative review of behavioral medicine research. *Journal of Consulting and Clinical Psychology, 61,* 1059–1067.

CARLSON, J. G., CHEMTOB, C. M., RUSNAK, K., HEDLUND, N. L., & MURAOKA, M. Y. (1998). Eye movement desensitization and reprocessing (EMDR) for combat-related posttraumatic stress disorder. *Journal of Traumatic Stress, 11,* 3–24.

CARMODY, T. P. (1978). Rational-emotive, self-instructional, and behavioral assertion training: Facilitating maintenance. *Cognitive Therapy and Research, 2,* 241–254.

CARMODY, T. P. (1992). Preventing relapse in the treatment of nicotine addiction: Current issues and future directions. *Journal of Psychoactive Drugs, 24,* 131–158.

CARR, E. G., & CARLSON, J. I. (1993). Reduction of severe behavior problems in the community using a multicomponent treatment approach. *Journal of Applied Behavior Analysis, 26,* 157–172.

CARR, E. G., & DURAND, V. M. (1985). Reducing behavior problems through functional communication training. *Journal of Applied Behavior Analysis, 18,* 111–126.

CARR, E. G., LEVIN, L., MCCONNACHIE, G., CARLSON, J. I., KEMP, D. C., & SMITH, C. E. (1994). *Communication-based intervention for problem behavior: A user's guide for producing positive change.* Baltimore: Brookes.

CARR, J. E. (1995). Competing responses for the treatment of Tourette syndrome and tic disorders. *Behaviour Research and Therapy, 33,* 455–456.

CARRINGTON, P. (1977). *Freedom in meditation.* New York: Anchor Press/Doubleday.

CARRINGTON, P., LEHRER, P. M., & WITTENSTROM, K. (1997). A children's self-management system for reducing homework-related problems: Parent efficacy ratings. *Child & Family Behavior Therapy, 19,* 1–22.

CARROLL, K. M. (1996). Relapse prevention as a psychosocial treatment: A review of controlled clinical trials. *Experimental and Clinical Psychopharmacology, 4,* 46–54.

CARROLL, K. M., ROUNSAVILLE, B. J., & GAWIN, F. H. (1991). A comparative trial of psychotherapies for ambulatory cocaine abusers: Relapse prevention and interpersonal psychotherapy. *American Journal of Drug and Alcohol Abuse, 17,* 229–247.

CARSTENSEN, L. L., & FISHER, J. E. (1991). Problems of the institutionalized elderly. In P. A. Wisocki (Ed.), *Handbook of clinical behavior therapy for the elderly client* (pp. 337–362). New York: Plenum.

CARTER, J. C., & FAIRBURN, C. G. (1998). Cognitive-behavioral self-help for binge eating disorder: A controlled effectiveness study. *Journal of Consulting and Clinical Psychology, 66,* 616–623.

CARTER, M. M., & BARLOW, D. H. (1993). Interoceptive exposure in the treatment of panic disorder. In L. VandeCreek, S. Knapp, & T. L. Jackson (Eds.), *Innovations in clinical practice: A source book* (Vol. 12, pp. 329–336). Sarasota, FL: Professional Resource Press/Professional Resource Exchange.

CARTER, M. M., & BARLOW, D. H. (1995). Learned alarms: The origins of panic. In W. O'Donohue & L. Krasner (Eds.), *Theories of behavior therapy: Exploring behavior change* (pp. 209–228). Washington, DC: American Psychological Association.

CARTWRIGHT, D. E. (1955). Effectiveness of psychotherapy: A critique of the spontaneous remission argument. *Journal of Counseling Psychology, 2,* 290–296.

CASH, T. F., & LAVALLEE, D. M. (1997). Cognitive-behavioral body-image therapy: Extended evidence of the efficacy of a self-directed program. *Journal of Rational-Emotive & Cognitive-Behavior Therapy, 15,* 281–294.

CASTANEDA, C. A. (1972). *A separate reality: Further conversations with Don Juan.* New York: Pocket Books.

CASTI, J. (1989). *Paradigms lost.* New York: Avon Books.

CAUCE, A. M. (1995, May). *Consequences of introducing culture/diversity into the research context.* Paper presented at the Conference on Marital and Family Therapy Outcome and Process Research: State of the Science, Philadelphia.

CAUTELA, J. R. (1966). Treatment of compulsive behavior by covert sensitization. *Psychological Record, 16,* 33–41.

CAUTELA, J. R. (1967). Covert sensitization. *Psychological Reports, 20,* 459–468.

CAUTELA, J. R. (1970). The use of covert sensitization in the treatment of alcoholism. *Psychotherapy: Theory, Research and Practice, 7,* 86–90.

CAUTELA, J. R. (1971). Covert sensitization for the treatment of sexual deviations. *Psychological Record, 21,* 37–48.

CAUTELA, J. R. (1972). Rationale and procedures for covert conditioning. In R. D. Rubin, H. Fensterheim, J. D. Henderson, & L. P. Ullmann (Eds.), *Advances in behavior therapy* (pp. 85–96). New York: Academic Press.

CAUTELA, J. R. (1982). Covert conditioning with children. *Journal of Behavior Therapy and Experimental Psychiatry, 13,* 209–214.

CAUTELA, J. R. (1993). Insight in behavior therapy. *Journal of Behavior Therapy and Experimental Psychiatry, 24,* 155–159.

CAUTELA, J. R., & KASTENBAUM, R. (1967). A reinforcement survey schedule for use in therapy, training, and research. *Psychological Reports, 20,* 1115–1130.

CAUTELA, J. R., & KEARNEY, A. J. (1993). *Covert conditioning casebook.* Pacific Grove, CA: Brooks/Cole.

CAUTELA, J. R., & WISOCKI, P. A. (1969). The use of male and female therapists in the treatment of homosexual behavior. In R. D. Rubin & C. M. Franks (Eds.), *Advances in behavior therapy* (pp. 165–174). New York: Academic Press.

CAVALIER, A. R., FERRETTI, R. P., & HODGES, A. E. (1997). Self-management within a classroom token economy with learning disabilities. *Research on Developmental Disabilities, 18,* 167–178.

CAVALIERE, F. (1995, October). Payers demand increased provider documentation. *APA Monitor, 26,* p. 41.

CAYNER, J. J., & KILAND, J. R. (1974). Use of brief time out with three schizophrenic patients. *Journal of Behavior Therapy and Experimental Psychiatry, 5,* 141–145.

CENTERS FOR DISEASE CONTROL AND PREVENTION. (1994). *HIV/AIDS surveillance report.* Atlanta: Author.

CERVONE, D., & PEAKE, P. K. (1986). Anchoring, efficacy, and action: The influence of judgmental heuristics on self-efficacy judgments and behavior. *Journal of Personality and Social Psychology, 50,* 492–501.

CERVONE, D., & SCOTT, W. D. (1995). Self-efficacy theory of behavioral change: Foundations, conceptual issues, and therapeutic implications. In W. O'Donohue & L. Krasner (Eds.), *Theories of behavior therapy* (pp. 349–383). Washington, DC: American Psychological Association.

CHADWICK, B. A., & DAY, R. C. (1971). Systematic reinforcement: Academic performance of underachieving students. *Journal of Applied Behavior Analysis, 4,* 311–319.

CHADWICK, P. D. J., & LOWE, C. F. (1990). Measurement and modification of delusional beliefs. *Journal of Consulting and Clinical Psychology, 58,* 225–232.

CHAMBLESS, D. L. (1985). Agoraphobia. In M. Hersen & A. S. Bellack (Eds.), *Handbook of clinical behavior therapy with adults* (pp. 49–87). New York: Plenum.

CHAMBLESS, D. L. (1996). In defense of dissemination of empirically supported psychological interventions. *Clinical Psychology: Science and Practice, 3,* 230–235.

CHAMBLESS, D. L., FOA, E. B., GROVES, G. A., & GOLDSTEIN, A. J. (1982). Exposure and communications training in the treatment of agoraphobia. *Behaviour Research and Therapy, 20,* 219–231.

CHAMBLESS, D. L., & HOLLON, S. D. (1998). Defining empirically supported therapies. *Journal of Consulting and Clinical Psychology, 66,* 7–18.

CHANDLER, G. M., BURCK, H. D., & SAMPSON, J. P. (1986). A generic computer program for systematic desensitization: Description, construction and case study. *Journal of Behavior Therapy and Experimental Psychiatry, 17,* 171–174.

CHANDLER, L. K., FOWLER, S. A., & LUBEK, R. C. (1992). An analysis of the effects of multiple setting events on the social behavior of preschool children with special needs. *Journal of Applied Behavior Analysis, 25,* 249–263.

CHANG, G., CARROLL, K. M., BEHR, H. M., & KOSTEN, T. R. (1992). Improving treatment outcome in pregnant opiate-dependent women. *Journal of Substance Abuse Treatment, 9,* 327–330.

CHAPMAN, S., FISHER, W., PIAZZA, C. C., & KURTZ, P. F. (1993). Functional assessment and treatment of life-threatening drug ingestion in a dually diagnosed youth. *Journal of Applied Behavior Analysis, 26,* 255–256.

CHARLOP, M. H., & MILSTEIN, J. P. (1989). Teaching autistic children conversational speech using video modeling. *Journal of Applied Behavior Analysis, 22,* 275–285.

CHARLOP, M. H., SCHREIBMAN, L., & TRYON, A. S. (1983). Learning through observation: The effects of peer modeling on acquisition and generalization in autistic children. *Journal of Abnormal Child Psychology, 11,* 355–366.

CHEMTOB, C. M., NOVACO, R. W., HAMADA, R. S., & GROSS, D. M. (1997). Cognitive-behavioral treatment for severe anger in posttraumatic stress disorder. *Journal of Consulting and Clinical Psychology, 65,* 184–189.

CHEN, C. P. (1995). Counseling applications of RET in a Chinese cultural context. *Journal of Rational-Emotive & Cognitive-Behavior Therapy, 13,* 117–129.

CHESNEY, M. A. (1994). Prevention of HIV and STD infections. *Preventive Medicine, 23,* 655–660.

CHESNEY, M. A., & FOLKMAN, S. (1994). Psychological impact of HIV disease and implications for intervention. *Psychiatric Clinics of North America, 17,* 163–182.

CHORPITA, B. F. (1995). Eventual responders: What do we do when treatments do not work? *the Behavior Therapist, 18,* 140–141.

CHORPITA, B. F., VITALI, A. E., & BARLOW, D. H. (1997). Behavioral treatment of choking phobia in an adolescent: An experimental analysis. *Journal of Behavior Therapy and Experimental Psychiatry, 28,* 307–315.

CHRISTENSEN, A., & DOBSON, K. (2001). Science and practice in clinical trials. *the Behavior Therapist, 24,* 141–143.

CHRISTENSEN, A., JACOBSON, N. S., & BABCOCK, J. C. (1995). Integrative behavioral couple therapy. In N. S. Jacobson & A. S. Gurman (Eds.), *Clinical handbook of marital therapy* (2nd ed., pp. 31–64). New York: Guilford.

CHRISTENSEN, A. P., & SANDERS, M. R. (1987). Habit reversal and differential reinforcement of other behaviour in the treatment of thumb-sucking: An analysis of generalization and side-effects. *Journal of Child Psychology and Psychiatry and Allied Disciplines, 28,* 281–295.

CHRISTIAN, L., & POLING, A. (1997). Using self-management procedures to improve the productivity of adults with developmental disabilities in a competitive employment setting. *Journal of Applied Behavior Analysis, 30,* 169–172.

CHRISTOPHERSEN, E. R. (1977). *Little people: Guidelines for common sense child rearing.* Lawrence, KS: H & H Enterprises.

CHURCH, P., FOREHAND, R. [L.], BROWN, C., & HOLMES, T. (1990). Prevention of drug abuse: Examination of the effectiveness of a program with elementary school children. *Behavior Therapy, 21,* 339–347.

CLARE, S. K., JENSON, W. R., KEHLE, T. J., & BRAY, M. A. (2000). Self-modeling as a treatment for increasing on-task behavior. *Psychology in the Schools, 37,* 517–522.

CLARK, D. F. (1966). Behaviour therapy of Gilles de la Tourette's syndrome. *British Journal of Psychiatry, 112,* 771–778.

CLARK, G. R., BUSSONE, A., & KIVITZ, M. S. (1974). Elwyn Institute's community living program. *The Challenge, 17,* 14–15.

CLARK, G. R., KIVITZ, M. S., & ROSEN, M. (1972). From research to community living. *Human Needs, 1,* 25–28.

CLARKE, G. N., HAWKINS, W., MURPHY, M., SHEEBER, L. B., LEWINSOHN, P. M., & SEELEY, J. R. (1995). Targeted prevention of unipolar depressive disorder in an at-risk sample of high school adolescents: A randomized trial of a group cognitive intervention. *Journal of the American Academy of Child and Adolescent Psychiatry, 34,* 312–321.

CLARKE, M. A., BRAY, M. A., KEHLE, T. J., & TRUSCOTT, S. D. (2001). A school-based intervention designed to reduce the frequency of tics in children with Tourette's syndrome. *School Psychology Review, 30,* 11–22.

CLAUDE, C. M., TOLIN, D., VAN DER KOLK, B. A., & PITMAN, R. K. (2000). Eye movement desensitization and reprocessing. In E. B. Foa, T. M. Keane, & M. J. Friedman (Eds.), *Effective treatments for PTSD* (pp. 139–154). New York: Guilford.

CLEES, T. J. (1994–95). Self-recording of students' daily schedules of teachers' expectancies: Perspectives on reactivity, stimulus control, and generalization. *Exceptionality, 5,* 113–129.

CLOITRE, M. (1995). An interview with Edna Foa. *the Behavior Therapist, 18,* 177–181.

CLOSE, J. M. (2000). Planned activities with and without a timeout component for families reported for child maltreatment. *Dissertation Abstracts International, 60,* 6350.

CLUM, G. A., CLUM, G. A., & SURLS, R. (1993). A meta-analysis of treatment for panic disorder. *Journal of Consulting and Clinical Psychology, 61,* 317–326.

COCCO, N., & SHARPE, L. (1993). An auditory variant of eye movement desensitization in a case of childhood post-traumatic stress disorder. *Journal of Behavior Therapy and Experimental Psychiatry, 24,* 373–377.

COE, D. A., BABBIT, R. L., WILLIAMS, K. E., HAJIMIHALIS, C., SNYDER, A. M., BALLARD, C., & EFRON, L. A. (1997). Use of extinction and reinforcement to increase food consumption and reduce expulsion. *Journal of Applied Behavior Analysis, 30,* 581–583.

COFER, C. N., & APPLEY, M. H. (1964). *Motivation: Theory and research.* New York: Wiley.

COHEN, D. J., LECKMAN, J. F., & SHAYWITZ, B. (1984). *A physician's guide to diagnosis and treatment of Tourette syndrome: A neurological multiple tic disorder.* New York: Tourette Syndrome Association.

COLDWELL, S. E., GETZ, T., MILGROM, P., PRALL, C. W., SPADAFORA, A., & RAMSAY, D. S. (1998). CARL: A LabVIEW 3 computer program for conducting exposure therapy for the treatment of dental injection fear. *Behaviour Research and Therapy, 36,* 429–441.

COLE, G. A., MONTGOMERY, R. W., WILSON, K. M., & MILAN, M. A. (2000). Parametric analysis of overcorrection duration effects: Is longer really better than shorter? *Behavior Modification, 24,* 359–377.

COLES, M. E., HART, T. A., & HEIMBERG, R. G. (2001). Cognitive-behavioral group treatment for social phobia. In R. Crozier & L. E. Alden (Eds.), *International handbook or social anxiety* (pp. 449–469). New York: Wiley.

COLLIER, W. C., & MARLATT, G. A. (1995). Relapse prevention. In A. J. Goreczny (Ed.), *Handbook of health and rehabilitation psychology* (pp. 307–321). New York: Plenum.

COMBS, M. L., & LAHEY, B. B. (1981). A cognitive social skills training program: Evaluation with young children. *Behavior Modification, 5,* 39–60.

COMPAS, B. E., HAAGA, D. A. [F.], KEEFE, F. J., LEITENBERG, H., & WILLIAMS, D. A. (1998). Sampling of empirically supported psychological treatments from health psychology: Smoking, chronic pain, cancer, and bulimia nervosa. *Journal of Consulting and Clinical Psychology, 66,* 89–112.

CONE, J. D. (1993). The current state of behavioral assessment. *European Journal of Psychological Assessment, 9,* 175–181.

CONE, J. D. (1998). Psychometric considerations: Concepts, contents, and methods. In M. Hersen & A. S. Bellack (Eds.), *Behavioral assessment: A practical handbook* (4th ed., pp. 22–46). Boston: Allyn & Bacon.

CONE, J. D., ALEXANDER, K., LICHTSZAJN, J. L., & MASON, R. L. (1996). Reengineering clinical training curricula to meet challenges beyond the year 2000. *the Behavior Therapist, 19,* 65–70.

CONNELL, M. C., CARTA, J. J., & BAER, D. M. (1993). Programming generalization of in-class transition skills: Teaching preschoolers with developmental delays to self-assess and recruit contingent teacher praise. *Journal of Applied Behavior Analysis, 26,* 345–352.

CONRIN, J., PENNYPACKER, H. S., JOHNSTON, J., & RAST, J. (1982). Differential reinforcement of other behavior to treat chronic rumination of mental retardates. *Journal of Behavior Therapy and Experimental Psychiatry, 13,* 325–329.

CONSTANTINO, G., MALGADY, R. G., & ROGLER, L. G. (1986). *Cuento* therapy: A culturally sensitive modality for Puerto Rican children. *Journal of Consulting and Clinical Psychology, 54,* 639–645.

COOK, D. (1999). Behavior bucks: A unique motivation program. *Intervention in School and Clinic, 34,* 307–308.

COOK, S., PETERSON, L., & DILILLO, D. (1999). Fear and exhilaration in response to risk: An extension of a model of injury risk in a real-world context. *Behavior Therapy, 30,* 5–15.

COON, D. W., & THOMPSON, L. W. (2002). Family caregivers for older adults: Ongoing and emergent themes for the behavior therapist. *the Behavior Therapist, 25,* 17–20.

COOPER, J. O., HERON, T. E., & HEWARD, W. L. (1987). *Applied behavior analysis.* Columbus, OH: Merrill.

COOPER, L. J., WACKER, D. P., BROWN, K., McCOMAS, J. J., PECK, S. M., DREW, J., ASMUS, J., & KAYSER, K. (1999). Use of a concurrent operants paradigm to evaluate positive reinforcers during treatment of food refusal. *Behavior Modification, 23,* 3–40.

CORRIGAN, P., SCHADE, M., & LIBERMAN, J. P. (1992). Social skills training. In R. P. Liberman (Ed.), *Handbook of psychiatric rehabilitation* (pp. 95–126). New York: Macmillan.

CORRIGAN, P. W. (2001). Getting ahead of the data: A threat to some behavior therapies. *the Behavior Therapist, 24,* 189–193.

CORRIGAN, S. A., THOMPSON, K. E., & MALOW, R. M. (1992). A psychoeducational approach to prevent HIV transmission among injection drug users. *Psychology of Addictive Behaviors, 6,* 114–119.

COSTENBADER, V., & READING-BROWN, M. (1995). Isolation timeout used with students with emotional disturbance. *Exceptional Children, 61,* 353–363.

COTHARIN, R. L., & MIKULAS, W. L. (1975). Systematic desensitization of racial emotional responses. *Journal of Behavior Therapy and Experimental Psychiatry, 6,* 347–348.

COTTER, L. H. (1967). Operant conditioning in a Vietnamese mental hospital. *American Journal of Psychiatry, 124,* 23–28.

COTTIER, C., SHAPIRO, K., & JULIUS, S. (1984). Treatment of mild hypertension with progressive muscle relaxation: Predictive value of indexes of sympathetic tone. *Archives of Internal Medicine, 144,* 1954–1958.

COTTRAUX, J. (1990). "*Cogito ergo sum*": Cognitive-behavior therapy in France. *the Behavior Therapist, 13,* 189–190.

COTTRAUX, J. (1993). Behavioral psychotherapy applications in the medically ill. *Psychotherapy and Psychosomatics, 60,* 116–128.

COTTRAUX, J., MOLLARD, E., BOUVARD, M., & MARKS, I. [M.] (1993). Exposure therapy, fluvoxamine, or combination treatment in obsessive-compulsive disorder: One-year follow up. *Psychiatry Research, 49,* 63–75.

COUSINS, N. (1979). *Anatomy of an illness.* New York: Norton.

COUSINS, N. (1989). *Head first: The biology of hope.* New York: Dutton.

COWLEY, G. (1994, June 20). Waving away the pain. *Newsweek, 123,* 70–71.

COX, B. J., FERGUS, K. D., & SWINSON, R. P. (1994). Patient satisfaction with behavioral treatments for panic disorder with agoraphobia. *Journal of Anxiety Disorders, 8,* 193–206.

COX, B. S., COX, A. B., & COX, D. J. (2000). Motivating signage prompts safety belt use among drivers exiting senior communities. *Journal of Applied Behavior Analysis, 33,* 635–638.

COYNE, L. W., FAUL, L. A., & GROSS, A. M. (2000). Harnessing environmental contingencies to enhance social skills: The case of Mike J. *Cognitive and Behavioral Practice, 7,* 231-235.

CRADOCK, C., COTLER, S., & JASON, L. A. (1978). Primary prevention: Immunization of children for speech anxiety. *Cognitive Therapy and Research, 2,* 389–396.

CRAIG, K. D. (1986). Social modeling influences: Pain in context. In R. A. Sternbach (Ed.), *The psychology of pain* (2nd ed., pp. 67–95). New York: Raven Press.

CRAIGHEAD, L. W. (1979). Self-instructional training for assertive-refusal behavior. *Behavior Therapy, 10,* 529–543.

CRAIGHEAD, W. E. (1990a). The changing nature of behavior therapy. *Behavior Therapy, 21,* 1–2.

CRAIGHEAD, W. E. (1990b). There's a place for us: All of us. *Behavior Therapy, 21,* 3–23.

CRAIGHEAD, W. E., KAZDIN, A. E., & MAHONEY, M. J. (1976). *Behavior modification: Principles, issues, and applications.* Boston: Houghton Mifflin.

CRAIGHEAD, W. E., KIMBALL, W. H., & REHAK, P. J. (1979). Mood changes, physiological responses, and self-statements during social rejection imagery. *Journal of Consulting and Clinical Psychology, 47,* 385–396.

CREER, T. L., & MIKLICH, D. R. (1970). The application of a self-modeling procedure to modify inappropriate behavior: A preliminary report. *Behaviour Research and Therapy, 8,* 91–92.

CRITCHFIELD, T. S., & VARGAS, E. A. (1991). Self-recording, instructions, and public self-graphing. *Behavior Modification, 15,* 95–112.

CSIKSZENTMIHALYI, M. (1990). *Flow: The psychology of optimal experience.* New York: Harper & Row.

CSIKSZENTMIHALYI, M., & CSIKSZENTMIHALYI, I. S. (Eds.). (1988). *Optimal experience: Psychological studies of flow in consciousness.* New York: Cambridge University Press.

CULLEN, J. W., FOX, B. H., & ISOM, R. N. (1976). *Cancer: The behavioral dimension.* New York: Raven Press.

CUNLIFFE, T. (1992). Arresting youth crime: A review of social skills training with young offenders. *Adolescence, 27,* 891–899.

CUNNINGHAM, C. E., & LINSCHEID, T. R. (1976). Elimination of chronic infant ruminating by electric shock. *Behavior Therapy, 7,* 231–234.

CURRIE, S. R., WILSON, K. G., PONTEFRACT, A. J., & deLAPLANTE, L. (2000). Cognitive-behavioral treatment of insomnia secondary to chronic pain. *Journal of Consulting and Clinical Psychology, 68,* 407–416.

DA COSTA, I. G., RAPOFF, M. A., & GOLDSTEIN, G. L. (1997). Improving adherence to medication regimens for children with asthma and its effect on clinical outcome. *Journal of Applied Behavior Analysis, 30,* 687–691.

DAHLQUIST, L. M., GIL, K. M., ARMSTRONG, F. D., GINSBERG, A., & JONES, B. (1985). Behavioral management of children's distress during chemotherapy. *Journal of Behavior Therapy and Experimental Psychiatry, 16,* 325–329.

DALEY, M. F. (1969). The "Reinforcement Menu": Finding effective reinforcers. In J. D. Krumboltz & C. E. Thoresen (Eds.), *Behavioral counseling: Cases and techniques* (pp. 42–45). New York: Holt, Rinehart & Winston.

DALTON, A. J., RUBINO, C. A., & HISLOP, M. W. (1973). Some effects of token rewards on school achievement of children with Down's syndrome. *Journal of Applied Behavior Analysis, 6,* 251–259.

DANAHER, B. G. (1974). Theoretical foundations and clinical applications of the Premack principle: Review and critique. *Behavior Therapy, 5,* 307–324.

DANFORTH, J. S. (1998). The outcome of parent training using the behavior management flow chart with mothers and their children with oppositional defiant disorder and attention-deficit hyperactivity disorder. *Behavior Modification, 22,* 443–473.

DAPCICH-MIURA, E., & HOVELL, M. F. (1979). Contingency management of adherence to a complex medical regimen in an elderly heart patient. *Behavior Therapy, 10,* 193–201.

DATE, A. (1996). On maintaining an empirical orientation in an "alternative ways of knowing" world. *the Behavior Therapist, 19,* 86.

DATTILIO, F. M. (1999). Cognitive behavior therapy in Cuba. *the Behavior Therapist, 22,* 78, 91.

DATTILIO, F. M., & PADESKY, C. A. (1990). *Cognitive therapy with couples.* Sarasota, FL: Professional Resource Exchange.

DAVIS, C. A., & FOX, J. (1999). Evaluating environmental arrangements as setting events: Review and implications of measurement. *Journal of Behavioral Education, 9,* 77–96.

DAVIS, P. K., & CHITTUM, R. (1994). A group-oriented contingency to increase leisure activities of adults with traumatic brain injury. *Journal of Applied Behavior Analysis, 27,* 553–554.

DAVIS, R. A. (1979). The impact of self-modeling on problem behaviors in school-age children. *School Psychology Digest, 8,* 128–132.

DAVISON, G. C. (1976). Homosexuality: The ethical challenge. *Journal of Consulting and Clinical Psychology, 44,* 157–162.

DAVISON, G. C. (1995). A failure of early behavior therapy (circa 1960): Or why I learned to stop worrying and to embrace psychotherapy integration. *Journal of Psychotherapy Integration, 5,* 107–112.

DAVISON, G. C., D'ZURILLA, T. J., GOLDFRIED, M. R., PAUL, G. L., & VALINS, S. (1968, August). In M. R. Goldfried (Chair), *Cognitive processes in behavior modification.* Symposium presented at the meeting of the American Psychological Association, San Francisco.

DAVISON, G. C., & LAZARUS, A. A. (1995). The dialectics of science and practice. In S. C. Hayes, V. M. Follette, R. M. Dawes, & K. E. Grady (Eds.), *Scientific standards of psychological practice: Issues and recommendations* (pp. 95–120). Reno, NV: Context Press.

DAVISON, G. C., NAVARRE, S. G., & VOGEL, R. S. (1995). The articulated thoughts in simulated situations paradigm: A think-aloud approach to cognitive assessment. *Current Directions in Psychological Science, 4,* 29–33.

DAVISON, G. C., & STUART, R. B. (1975). Behavior therapy and civil liberties. *American Psychologist, 30,* 755–763.

DAVISON, G. C., VOGEL, R. S., & COFFMAN, S. G. (1997). Think-aloud approaches to cognitive assessment and the Articulated Thoughts in Simulated Situations paradigm. *Journal of Consulting and Clinical Psychology, 65,* 950–958.

DAWE, G. F., & HART, D. S. (1986, June). *Covert modeling and rehearsal in the treatment of social anxiety.* Paper presented at the meeting of the Canadian Psychological Association, Toronto.

DAWLEY, H. H., & DILLENKOFFER, R. L. (1975). Minimizing the risks in rapid smoking treatment. *Journal of Behavior Therapy and Experimental Psychiatry, 6,* 174.

DAWSON, B., DE ARMAS, A., MCGRATH, M. L., & KELLY, J. A. (1986). Cognitive problem-solving training to improve child-care judgement of child neglectful parents. *Journal of Family Violence, 1,* 209–221.

DAY, L., & REZNIKOFF, M. (1980). Preparation of children and parents for treatment at a children's psychiatric clinic through videotaped modeling. *Journal of Consulting and Clinical Psychology, 48,* 303–304.

DE JONG, P. J., ANDREA, H., & MURIS, P. (1997). Spider phobia in children: Disgust and fear before and after treatment. *Behaviour Research and Therapy, 35,* 559–562.

DE JONG, P. J., VORAGE, I., & VAN DEN HOUT, M. A. (2000). Counterconditioning in the treatment of spider phobia: Effects on disgust, fear, and valence. *Behaviour Research and Therapy, 38,* 1055–1069.

DE KINKELDER, M., & BOELENS, H. (1998). Habit-reversal treatment for children's stuttering: Assessment in three settings. *Journal of Behavior Therapy and Experimental Psychiatry, 29,* 261–265.

DE L. HORNE, D. J., TAYLOR, M., & VARIGOS, G. (1999). The effects of relaxation with and without imagery in reducing anxiety and itchy skin in patients with eczema. *Behavioural and Cognitive Psychotherapy, 27,* 143–151.

DE L. HORNE, D. J., VATMANIDIS, P., & CARERI, A. (1994). Preparing patients for invasive medical and surgical procedures 1: Adding behavioral and cognitive interventions. *Behavioral Medicine, 20,* 5–13.

DE L. HORNE, D. J., WHITE, A. E., & VARIGOS, G. A. (1989). A preliminary study of psychological therapy in the management of atopic eczema. *British Journal of Medical Psychology, 62,* 241–248.

DE MOOR, W. (1970). Systematic desensitization versus prolonged high intensity stimulation (flooding). *Journal of Behavior Therapy and Experimental Psychiatry, 1,* 45–52.

DEALE, A., CHALDER, T., MARKS, I. [M.], & WESSELY, S. (1997). Cognitive behavior therapy for chronic fatigue syndrome: A randomized control trial. *American Journal of Psychiatry, 154,* 408–414.

DEANGELIS, T. (2002). Promising treatments for anorexia and bulimia. *Monitor on Psychology, 33,* 38–41.

DEFFENBACHER, J. L., DAHLEN, E. R., LYNCH, R. S., MORRIS, C. D., & GOWENSMITH, W. N. (2000). An application of Beck's cognitive therapy to general anger reduction. *Cognitive Therapy and Research, 24,* 689–697.

DEFFENBACHER, J. [L.], FILETTI, L., LYNCH, R., & DAHLEN, E. (2000, August). *Interventions for the reduction of driving anger.* Paper presented at the 108th Annual Convention of the American Psychological Association, Washington, DC.

DEFFENBACHER, J. [L.], HUFF, M., LYNCH, R., OETTING, E., & SALVATORE, N. (2000). Characteristics and treatment of high-anger drivers. *Journal of Counseling Psychology, 47,* 5–17.

DEITZ, S. M. (1977). An analysis of programming DRL schedules in educational settings. *Behaviour Research and Therapy, 15,* 103–111.

DEITZ, S. M., & REPP, A. C. (1973). Decreasing classroom misbehavior through the use of DRL schedules of reinforcement. *Journal of Applied Behavior Analysis, 6,* 457–463.

DEITZ, S. M., REPP, A. C., & DEITZ, D. E. D. (1976). Reducing inappropriate classroom behavior of retarded students through three procedures of differential reinforcement. *Journal of Mental Deficiency Research, 20,* 155–170.

DELEON, G., & MANDELL, W. (1966). A comparison of conditioning and psychotherapy in the treatment of functional enuresis. *Journal of Clinical Psychology, 22,* 326–330.

DELEON, G., & SACKS, S. (1972). Conditioning functional enuresis: A four-year follow-up. *Journal of Consulting and Clinical Psychology, 39,* 299–300.

DEMBER, W. N. (1974). Motivation and the cognitive revolution. *American Psychologist, 29,* 161–168.

DENNEY, D. R., SULLIVAN, B. J., & THIRY, M. R. (1977). Participant modeling and self-verbalization training in the reduction of spider fears. *Journal of Behavior Therapy and Experimental Psychiatry, 8,* 247–253.

DERBY, K. M., WACKER, D. P., BERG, W., DERAAD, A., ULRICH, S., ASMUS, J., HARDING, J., PROUTY, A., LAFFEY, P., & STONER, E. A. (1997). The long-term effects of functional communication training in home settings. *Journal of Applied Behavior Analysis, 30,* 587–531.

DERBY, K. M., WACKER, D. P., SASSO, G., STEEGE, M., NORTHUP, J., CIGLAND, K., & ASINUS, J. (1992). Brief functional assessment techniques to evaluate aberrant behavior in an outpatient setting: A summary of 79 cases. *Journal of Applied Behavior Analysis, 25,* 713–721.

DERISI, W. J., & BUTZ, G. (1975). *Writing behavioral contracts: A case simulation practice manual.* Champaign, IL: Research Press.

DERUBEIS, R. J., & CRITS-CHRISTOPH, P. (1998). Empirically supported individual and group psychological treatments for adult mental disorders. *Journal of Consulting and Clinical Psychology, 66,* 37–52.

DERUBEIS, R. J., TANG, T. Z., & BECK, A. T. (2001). Cognitive therapy. In K. S. Dobson (Ed.), *Handbook of cognitive-behavioral therapies* (2nd ed., pp. 349–392). New York: Guilford.

DEVILLY, G. J., SPENCE, S. H., & RAPEE, R. M. (1998). Statistical and reliable change with eye movement desensitization and reprocessing: Treating trauma within a veteran population. *Behavior Therapy, 29,* 435–455.

DEWHURST, D. T. (1993). Using the self-control triad to treat tension headache in a child. In J. R. Cautela & A. J. Kearney (Eds.), *Covert conditioning casebook* (pp. 75–81). Pacific Grove, CA: Brooks/Cole.

DICK-SISKIN, L. P. (2002). Cognitive-behavioral therapy with older adults. *the Behavior Therapist, 25,* 3–4, 6.

DIDDEN, R., CURFS, L. M. G., SIKKEMA, S. P. E., & DE MOOR, J. (1998). Functional assessment and treatment of sleeping problems with developmentally disabled children: Six case studies. *Journal of Behavior Therapy and Experimental Psychiatry, 29,* 85–97.

DIGIUSEPPE, R. A. (1981). Cognitive therapy with children. In G. Emery, S. D. Hollon, & R. C. Bedrosian (Eds.), *New directions in cognitive therapy: A casebook* (pp. 50–67). New York: Guilford.

DIGIUSEPPE, R. [A.] (1989). Cognitive therapy with children. In A. Freeman, K. M. Simon, L. E. Beutler, & H. Arkowitz (Eds.), *Comprehensive handbook of cognitive therapy* (pp. 515–533). New York: Plenum.

DITOMASSO, R. A., MARTIN, D. M., & KOVNAT, K. D. (2000). In F. M. Dattilio & A. Freeman (Eds.), *Cognitive-behavioral strategies for crisis intervention* (2nd ed., pp. 409–428). New York: Guilford.

DOBSON, K. S. (1989). A meta-analysis of the efficacy of cognitive therapy for depression. *Journal of Consulting and Clinical Psychology, 57,* 414–419.

DOBSON, K. S., & SHAW, B. F. (1989). The use of treatment manuals in cognitive therapy: Experiences and issues. *Journal of Consulting and Clinical Psychology, 56,* 673–681.

DOERFLER, L. A., MULLINS, L. L., GRIFFIN, N. J., SIEGEL, L. J., & RICHARDS, C. S. (1984). Problem-solving deficits in depressed children, adolescents, and adults. *Cognitive Therapy and Research, 8,* 489–500.

DOLCE, J. J., DOLEYS, D. M., RACZYNSKI, J. M., LOSSIE, J., POOLE, L., & SMITH, M. (1986). The role of self-efficacy expectancies in the prediction of pain tolerance. *Pain, 27,* 261–272.

DOLEYS, D. M. (1977). Behavioral treatment of nocturnal enuresis in children: A review of the recent literature. *Psychological Bulletin, 84,* 30–54.

DOLEYS, D. M., CROCKER, M., & PATTON, D. (1982). Response of patients with chronic pain to exercise quotas. *Physical Therapy, 62,* 1111–1114.

DOLEYS, D. M., & KURTZ, P. S. (1974). A behavioral treatment program for Gilles de la Tourette syndrome. *Psychological Reports, 35,* 43–48.

DONAHUE, B., THEVENIN, D. M., & RUNYON, M. K. (1997). Behavioral treatment of conversion disorder in adolescence: A case example of *Globus Hystericus. Behavior Modification, 21,* 231–251.

DONNER, L., & GUERNEY, B. G. (1969). Automated group desensitization for test anxiety. *Behaviour Research and Therapy, 7,* 1–13.

DONOHUE, B. C., VAN HASSELT, V. B., & HERSEN, M. (1994). Behavioral assessment and treatment of social phobia: An evaluative review. *Behavior Modification, 18,* 262–288.

DOOLEY, R. T., & HALFORD, W. K. (1992). A comparison of relapse prevention with nicotine gum or nicotine fading in modification of smoking. *Australian Psychologist, 27,* 186–191.

DOSTER, J. A. (1972). Effects of instructions, modeling, and role rehearsal on interview verbal behavior. *Journal of Consulting and Clinical Psychology, 39,* 202–209.

DOUGHER, M. J. (1993). Covert sensitization in the treatment of deviant sexual arousal. In J. R. Cautela & A. J. Kearney (Eds.), *Covert conditioning casebook* (pp. 199–207). Pacific Grove, CA: Brooks/Cole.

DOWNS, A. F. D., ROSENTHAL, T. L., & LICHSTEIN, K. L. (1988). Modeling therapies reduce avoidance of bath-time by the institutionalized elderly. *Behavior Therapy, 19,* 359–368.

DOWRICK, P. W. (1978). Suggestions for the use of edited video replay in training behavioral skills. *Journal of Practical Approaches to Developmental Handicap, 2,* 21–24.

DOWRICK, P. W. (1979). Single dose medication to create a self model film. *Child Behavior Therapy, 1,* 193–198.

DOWRICK, P. W. (1983). Video training of alternatives to cross-gender identity behaviors in a 4-year-old boy. *Child & Family Behavior Therapy, 5,* 59–65.

DOWRICK, P. W. (1986). *Social survival for children: A trainer's resource book.* New York: Brunner/Mazel.

DOWRICK, P. W. (1991). *Practical guide to using video in the behavioral sciences.* New York: Wiley.

DOWRICK, P. W. (1994). Video psychology. In R. J. Corsini (Ed.), *Encyclopedia of psychology* (2nd ed., pp. 566–567). New York: Wiley.

DOWRICK, P. W., & HOOD, M. (1978). Transfer of talking behaviours across settings using faked films. In T. Glynn

& S. McNaughton (Eds.), *Behaviour analysis in New Zealand* (pp. 78–87). Auckland, New Zealand: University of Auckland.

DOWRICK, P. W., & RAEBURN, J. M. (1977). Video editing and medication to produce a therapeutic self model. *Journal of Consulting and Clinical Psychology, 45,* 1156–1158.

DOWRICK, P. W., & RAEBURN, J. M. (1995). Self-modeling: Rapid skill training for children with physical disabilities. *Journal of Developmental and Physical Disabilities, 7,* 25–37.

DOWRICK, P. W., & WARD, K. M. (1997). Video feedforward in the support of a man with intellectual disability and inappropriate sexual behaviour. *Journal of Intellectual and Developmental Disability, 22,* 147–160.

DRYDEN, W., & ELLIS, A. (2001). Rational emotive behavior therapy. In K. S. Dobson (Ed.), *Handbook of cognitive-behavioral therapies* (2nd. ed., pp. 295–348). New York: Guilford.

DRYDEN, W., & HILL, L. K. (Eds.). (1993). *Innovations in rational-emotive therapy.* Newbury Park, CA: Sage.

DUBBERT, P. M. (1992). Exercise in behavioral medicine. *Journal of Consulting and Clinical Psychology, 60,* 613–618.

DUCHARME, D. E., & HOLBORN, S. W. (1997). Programming generalization of social skills in preschool children with hearing impairments. *Journal of Applied Behavior Analysis, 30,* 639–651.

DUCHARME, J. M., PONTES, E., GUGER, S., CROZIER, K., LUCAS, H., & POPYNICK, M. (1994). Errorless compliance to parental requests II: Increasing clinical practicality through abbreviation of treatment parameters. *Behavior Therapy, 25,* 469–487.

DUCHARME, J. M., & POPYNICK, M. (1993). Errorless compliance to parental requests: Treatment effects and generalization. *Behavior Therapy, 24,* 209–226.

DUCHARME, J. M., & VAN HOUTEN, R. (1994). Operant extinction in the treatment of severe maladaptive behavior: Adapting research to practice. *Behavior Modification, 18,* 139–170.

DULEY, S. M., CANCELLI, A. A., KRATOCHWILL, T. R., BERGAN, J. R., & MEREDITH, K. E. (1983). Training and generalization of motivational analysis interview assessment skills. *Behavioral Assessment, 5,* 281–293.

DUNKEL, L. D., & GLAROS, A. G. (1978). Comparison of self-instructional and stimulus control treatments for obesity. *Cognitive Therapy and Research, 2,* 75–78.

DUPAUL, G. J., GUEVREMONT, D. C., & BARKLEY, R. A. (1992). Behavioral treatment of attention-deficit hyperactivity disorder in the classroom: The use of the attention training system. *Behavior Modification, 16,* 204–225.

DURAN, V. M. (1999). Functional communication training using assistive devices: Recruiting natural communities of reinforcement. *Journal of Applied Behavior Analysis, 32,* 247–267.

DURAND, V. M., & MINDELL, J. A. (1990). Behavioral treatment of multiple childhood sleep disorders. *Behavior Modification, 14,* 37–49.

DURAND, V. M., & MINDELL, J. A. (1999). Behavioral interventions for childhood sleep terrors. *Behavior Therapy, 30,* 705–715.

DYCK, R. V., & SPINHOVEN, P. (1997). Does preference for type of treatment matter? A study of exposure in vivo with or without hypnosis in the treatment of panic disorder with agoraphobia. *Behavior Modification, 21,* 172–186.

DYER, W. (1977). *Your erroneous zones.* New York: Funk & Wagnalls.

D'ZURILLA, T. J. (1986). *Problem-solving therapy: A social competence approach to clinical intervention.* New York: Springer.

D'ZURILLA, T. J., & CHANG, E. C. (1995). The relations between social problem solving and coping. *Cognitive Therapy and Research 19,* 547–562.

D'ZURILLA, T. J., CHANG, E. C., NOTTINGHAM, E. J., & FACCINI, L. (1998). Social problem-solving deficits and hopelessness, depression, and suicide risk in college students and psychiatric inpatients. *Journal of Clinical Psychology, 54,* 1–17.

D'ZURILLA, T. J., & GOLDFRIED, M. R. (1971). Problem solving and behavior modification. *Journal of Abnormal Psychology, 78,* 107–126.

D'ZURILLA, T. J., & MASCHKA, G. (1988, November). *Outcome of a problem-solving approach to stress management: I. Comparison with social support.* Paper presented at the meeting of the Association for Advancement of Behavior Therapy, New York.

D'ZURILLA, T., & NEZU, A. (1982). Social problem solving in adults. In P. Kendall (Ed.), *Advances in cognitive-behavioral research and therapy* (Vol. 1, pp. 285–315). New York: Academic Press.

D'ZURILLA, T. J., & NEZU, A. M. (1999). *Problem-solving therapy: A social competence approach to clinical intervention* (2nd ed.). New York: Springer.

D'ZURILLA, T. J., & NEZU, A. M. (2001). Problem-solving therapies. In K. S. Dobson (Ed.), *Handbook of cognitive-behavioral therapies* (2nd ed., pp. 211–245). New York: Guilford.

D'ZURILLA, T. J., & SHEEDY, C. F. (1991). Relation between social problem-solving ability and subsequent level of psychological stress in college students. *Journal of Personality and Social Psychology, 61,* 841–846.

ECTON, R. B., & FEINDLER, E. L. (1990). Anger control training for temper control disorders. In E. L. Feindler & G. R. Kalfus (Eds.), *Adolescent behavior therapy handbook* (pp. 351–371). New York: Springer.

EDELMAN, R. E., & CHAMBLESS, D. L. (1993). Compliance during sessions and homework in exposure-based treatment of agoraphobia. *Behaviour Research and Therapy, 31,* 767–773.

EDELMAN, R. E., & CHAMBLESS, D. L. (1995). Adherence during sessions and homework in cognitive-behavioral group treatment of social phobia. *Behaviour Research and Therapy, 33,* 573–577.

EDGETTE, J. S., & PROUT, M. F. (1989). Cognitive and behavioral approaches to the treatment of anorexia nervosa. In A. Freeman, K. M. Simon, L. E. Beutler, & H. Arkowitz (Eds.), *Comprehensive handbook of cognitive therapy* (pp. 367–384). New York: Plenum.

EDINGER, J. D., & JACOBSEN, R. (1982). Incidence and significance of relaxation treatment side effects. *the Behavior Therapist, 5,* 137–138.

EGEL, A. L., RICHMAN, G. S., & KOEGEL, R. L., & ABRAHMS, J. L. (1983). Cognitive-behavioral strategies to induce and enhance a collaborative set in distressed couples. In A. Freeman (Ed.), *Cognitive therapy with couples and groups* (pp. 125–155). New York: Plenum.

EIFERT, G. H., SCHULTE, D., ZVOLENSKY, M. J., LEJUEZ, C. W., & LAU, A. (1997). Manualized behavior therapy: Merits and challenges. *Behavior Therapy, 28,* 499–509.

EIFERT, G. H., & WILSON, P. H. (1991). The triple response approach to assessment: A conceptual and methodological reappraisal. *Behaviour Research and Therapy, 29,* 283–292.

EISLER, R. M., HERSEN, M., & MILLER, P. M. (1973). Effects of modeling on components of assertive behavior. *Journal of Behavior Therapy and Experimental Psychiatry, 4,* 1–6.

EISLER, R. M., HERSEN, M., MILLER, P. M., & BLANCHARD, E. B. (1975). Situational determinants of assertive behaviors. *Journal of Consulting and Clinical Psychology, 43,* 330–340.

EITZEN, D. S. (1975). The effects of behavior modification on the attitudes of delinquents. *Behaviour Research and Therapy, 13,* 295–299.

ELDER, S. T., & EUSTIS, N. K. (1975). Instrumental blood pressure conditioning in outpatient hypertensives. *Behaviour Research and Therapy, 13,* 185–188.

ELDRIDGE, K. L., AGRAS, W. S., ARNOW, B., TELCH, C. F., BELL, S., CASTONGUAY, L., & MARNELL, M. (1997). The effects of extending cognitive-behavioral therapy for binge eating disorder among initial treatment nonresponders. *International Journal of Eating Disorders, 21,* 347–352.

ELKIN, I., SHEA, M. T., WATKINS, J. T., IMBER, S. D., SOTSKY, S. M., COLLINS, J. F., GLASS, D. R., PILKONIS, P. A., LEBER, W. R., DOCHERTY, J. P., FIESTER, S. J., & PARLOFF, M. B. (1989). National Institute of Mental Health Treatment of Depression Collaborative Research Program: General effectiveness of treatments. *Archives of General Psychiatry, 46,* 971–982.

ELLINGSON, S. A., MILTENBERGER, R. G., & LONG, E. S. (1999). A survey of the use of functional assessment procedures in agencies serving individuals with developmental disabilities. *Behavioral Interventions, 14,* 187–198.

ELLINGSON, S. A., MILTENBERGER, R. G., STRICKER, J., GALENSKY, T. L., & GARLINGHOUSE, M. (2000). Functional assessment and intervention for challenging behaviors in the classroom by general classroom teachers. *Journal of Positive Behavior Interventions, 2,* 85–97.

ELLINGSON, S. A., MILTENBERGER, R. G., STRICKER, J. M., GARLINGHOUSE, M. A., ROBERTS, J., & GALENSKY, T. L. (2000). Analysis and treatment of finger sucking. *Journal of Applied Behavior Analysis, 33,* 41–52.

ELLIOTT, A. J., MILTENBERGER, R. G., RAPP, J. T., LONG, E. S., & McDONALD, R. (1998). Brief application of simplified habit reversal to treat stuttering in children. *Journal of Behavior Therapy and Experimental Psychiatry, 29,* 289–302.

ELLIS, A. (1959). *Psychotherapy session with an eight year old female bedwetter.* Cassette recording. New York: Institute for Rational-Emotive Therapy.

ELLIS, A. (1962). *Reason and emotion in psychotherapy.* New York: Lyle Stuart.

ELLIS, A. (1970). *The essence of rational psychotherapy: A comprehensive approach in treatment.* New York: Institute for Rational Living.

ELLIS, A. (1989a). Comments on my critics. In M. E. Bernard & R. [A.] DiGiuseppe (Eds.), *Inside rational-emotive therapy: A critical appraisal of the theory and therapy of Albert Ellis* (pp. 199–233). San Diego: Academic Press.

ELLIS, A. (1989b). The history of cognition in psychotherapy. In A. Freeman, K. M. Simon, L. E. Beutler, & H. Arkowitz (Eds.), *Comprehensive handbook of cognitive therapy* (pp. 5–20). New York: Plenum.

ELLIS, A. (1993). Changing rational-emotive therapy (RET) to rational emotive behavior therapy (REBT). *the Behavior Therapist, 16,* 257–258.

ELLIS, A. (1994a). A corrective note on O'Donohue and Szymanski's study of logical analysis and REBT's use of empirical hypothesis testing as well as logical analysis. *Journal of Rational-Emotive & Cognitive-Behavior Therapy, 12,* 73–76.

ELLIS, A. (1994b). Ellis, Albert. *Current Biography, 65,* 6–10.

ELLIS, A. (1994c). General semantics and rational emotive behavior therapy. In P. D. Johnston, D. D. Bourland, & J. Klein (Eds.), *More E-prime: To be or not II* (pp. 213–240). Concord, CA: International Society for General Semantics.

ELLIS, A. (1994d). Post-traumatic stress disorder (PTSD): A rational emotive behavioral theory. *Journal of Rational-Emotive & Cognitive-Behavior Therapy, 12,* 3–25.

ELLIS, A. (1994e). Radical behavioral treatment of private events: A response to Michael Dougher. *the Behavior Therapist, 17,* 219–221.

ELLIS, A. (1995). Changing rational-emotive therapy (RET) to rational-emotive behavior therapy (REBT). *Journal of Rational-Emotive & Cognitive-Behavior Therapy, 13,* 85–89.

ELLIS, A. (1999). Rational emotive behavior therapy and cognitive behavior therapy for elderly people. *Journal of Rational-Emotive & Cognitive-Behavior Therapy, 17,* 5–18.

ELLIS, A., & BERNARD, M. E. (Eds.). (1983). *Rational-emotive approaches to the problems of childhood.* New York: Plenum.

ELLIS, A., & BERNARD, M. E. (1985). What is rational-emotive therapy (RET)? In A. Ellis & R. M. Grieger (Eds.), *Handbook of rational-emotive therapy* (pp. 1–30). New York: Springer.

ELLIS, A., & DRYDEN, W. (1987). *The practice of rational-emotive therapy.* New York: Springer.

ELLIS, A., & DRYDEN, W. (1993). A therapy by any other name? An interview. *The Rational Emotive Therapist, 1,* 34–37.

ELLIS, A., & HARPER, R. A. (1975). *A new guide to rational living.* North Hollywood, CA: Wilshire.

ELLIS, C. R., SINGH, N. N., CREWS, W. D., BONAVENTURA, S. H., GEHIN, J. M., & RICKETTS, R. W. (1997). Pica. In N. N. Singh (Ed.), *Prevention and treatment of severe behavior problems: Models and methods in developmental disabilities* (pp. 253–269). Pacific Grove, CA: Brooks/Cole.

ELSESSER, K., VAN BERKEL, M., SARTORY, G., BIERMANN-GÖCKE, W., & ÖHL, S. (1994). The effects of anxiety management training on psychological variables and immune parameters in cancer patients: A pilot study. *Behavioural and Cognitive Psychotherapy, 22,* 13–23.

EMERSON, E. (1993). Challenging behaviours and severe learning disabilities: Recent developments in behavioural analysis and intervention. *Behavioural and Cognitive Psychotherapy, 21,* 171–198.

EMMELKAMP, P. M. G. (1982). *Phobic and obsessive-compulsive disorders: Theory, research, and practice.* New York: Plenum.

EMMELKAMP, P. M. G. (1994). Behavior therapy with adults. In A. E. Bergin & S. L. Garfield (Eds.), *Handbook of psychotherapy and behavior change* (4th ed., pp. 379–427). New York: Wiley.

EMMELKAMP, P. M. G., DE HAAN, E., & HOOGDUIN, C. A. L. (1990). Marital adjustment and obsessive-compulsive disorder. *British Journal of Psychiatry, 156,* 55–60.

EMMELKAMP, P. M. G., & WESSELS, H. (1975). Flooding in imagination versus flooding *in vivo:* A comparison with agoraphobics. *Behaviour Research and Therapy, 13,* 7–15.

ENGERMAN, J. A., AUSTIN, J., & BAILEY, J. S. (1997). Prompting patron safety belt use at a supermarket. *Journal of Applied Behavior Analysis, 30,* 577–579.

ENGLE-FRIEDMAN, M., BOOTZIN, R. R., HAZLEWOOD, L., & TSAO, C. (1992). An evaluation of behavioral treatments for insomnia in the older adult. *Journal of Clinical Psychology, 48,* 77–90.

EPSTEIN, E. E., & MCCRADY, B. S. (1998). Behavioral couples treatment of alcohol and drug use disorders: Current status and innovations. *Clinical Psychology Review, 18,* 689–711.

EPSTEIN, L. H., BECK, S., FIGUEROA, J., FARKAS, G., KAZDIN, A. E., DANEMAN, D., & BECKER, D. (1981). The effects of targeting improvements in urine glucose on metabolic control in children with insulin dependent diabetes. *Journal of Applied Behavior Analysis, 14,* 365–375.

EPSTEIN, L. H., & MASEK, B. J. (1978). Behavioral control of medicine compliance. *Journal of Applied Behavior Analysis, 11,* 1–9.

EPSTEIN, N. (1983). Cognitive therapy with couples. In A. Freeman (Ed.), *Cognitive therapy with couples and groups* (pp. 107–123). New York: Plenum.

EPSTEIN, N., & BAUCOM, D. H. (1989). Cognitive-behavioral marital therapy. In A. Freeman, K. M. Simon, L. E. Beutler, & H. Arkowitz (Eds.), *Comprehensive handbook of cognitive therapy* (pp. 491–513). New York: Plenum.

ESPIE, C. A., LINDSAY, W. R., BROOKS, D. N., HOOD, E. H., & TURVEY, T. (1989). A controlled comparative investigation of psychological treatments for chronic sleep-onset insomnia. *Behaviour Research and Therapy, 27,* 79–88.

ESVELDT-DAWSON, K., & KAZDIN, A. E. (1998). *How to maintain behavior* (2nd ed.). Austin, TX: Pro-Ed.

Ethical issues for human services. (1977). *Behavior Therapy, 8,* v–vi.

EVANS, J. H., FERRE, L., FORD, L. A., & GREEN, J. L. (1995). Decreasing attention deficit hyperactivity disorder symptoms utilizing an automated classroom reinforcement device. *Psychology in the Schools, 32,* 210–219.

EVANS, P. D., & KELLAM, A. M. P. (1973). Semi-automated desensitization: A controlled clinical trial. *Behaviour Research and Therapy, 11,* 641–646.

EYSENCK, H. J. (1952). The effects of psychotherapy: An evaluation. *Journal of Consulting Psychology, 16,* 319–324.

FAIRBURN, C. G. (1995). *Overcoming binge eating.* New York: Guilford.

FAIRBURN, C. G., JONES, R., PEVELER, R. C., HOPE, R. A., & O'CONNOR, M. E. (1993). Psychotherapy and bulimia nervosa: The long-term effects of interpersonal psychotherapy, behavior therapy, and cognitive behavior therapy for bulimia nervosa. *Archives of General Psychiatry, 50,* 419–428.

FAIRBURN, C. G., MARCUS, M. D., & WILSON, G. T. (1993). Cognitive-behavioral therapy for binge eating and bulimia nervosa: A comprehensive treatment manual. In C. G. Fairburn & G. T. Wilson (Eds.), *Binge eating: Na-*

ture, assessment and treatment (pp. 361–404). New York: Guilford.

FAIRBURN, C. G., PEVELER, R. C., JONES, R., HOPE, R. A., & DOLL, H. (1993). Predictors of 12-month outcome in bulimia nervosa and the influence of attitudes to shape and weight. *Journal of Consulting and Clinical Psychology, 61,* 696–698.

FALLOON, I. R. H., & COVERDALE, J. H. (1994). Cognitive-behavioural family interventions for major mental disorders. Special issue: Behaviour therapy and schizophrenia: I. *Behaviour Change, 11,* 213–222.

FALS-STEWART, W., MARKS, A. P., & SCHAFER, J. (1993). A comparison of behavioral group therapy and individual behavior therapy in treating obsessive-compulsive disorder. *Journal of Mental and Nervous Disease, 181,* 189–193.

FANTUZZO, J. W., & THOMPSON, D. W. (1991). Behavioral community psychology: A timely and potent synergy. *the Behavior Therapist, 14,* 28.

FARQUHAR, J. W. (1978). The community-based model of lifestyle intervention trials. *American Journal of Epidemiology, 108,* 103–111.

FARQUHAR, J. W., MACCOBY, N., & SOLOMON, D. S. (1984). Community applications of behavioral medicine. In W. D. Gentry (Ed.), *Handbook of behavioral medicine* (pp. 437–478). New York: Guilford.

FARRELL, S. P., HAINS, A. A., & DAVIES, W. H. (1998). Cognitive behavioral interventions for sexually abused children exhibiting PTSD symptomology. *Behavior Therapy, 29,* 241–255.

FECTEAU, G., & NICKI, R. (1999). Cognitive behavioural treatment of post traumatic stress disorder after motor vehicle accident. *Behavioural and Cognitive Psychotherapy, 27,* 201–214.

FEINDLER, E. L., ECTON, R. B., KINGSLEY, D., & DUBEY, D. R. (1986). Group anger-control training for institutionalized psychiatric male adolescents. *Behavior Therapy, 17,* 109–123.

FEINDLER, E. L., MARRIOTT, S. A., & IWATA, M. (1984). Group anger-control training for junior high school delinquents. *Cognitive Therapy and Research, 8,* 299–311.

FELL, C. (Trans. and Ed.). (1975). *Egils saga.* London: Dent.

FERRITOR, D. E., BUCKHOLDT, D., HAMBLIN, R. L., & SMITH, L. (1972). The noneffects of contingent reinforcement for attending behavior on work accomplished. *Journal of Applied Behavior Analysis, 5,* 7–17.

FESKE, U., & GOLDSTEIN, A. J. (1997). Eye movement desensitization and reprocessing treatment for panic disorder: A controlled outcome and partial dismantling study. *Journal of Consulting and Clinical Psychology, 65,* 1026–1035.

FESTINGER, L. (1957). *A theory of cognitive dissonance.* Stanford, CA: Stanford University Press.

FEUERSTEIN, M., & GAINER, J. (1982). Chronic headache: Etiology and management. In D. M. Doleys, R. L. Meredith, & A. R. Ciminero (Eds.), *Behavioral medicine: Assessment and treatment strategies* (pp. 199–249). New York: Plenum.

FINNEY, J. W., MILLER, K. M., & ADLER, S. P. (1993). Changing protective and risky behaviors to prevent child-to-parent transmission of cytomegalovirus. *Journal of Applied Behavior Analysis, 26,* 471–472.

FINNEY, J. W., RAPOFF, M. A., HALL, C. L., & CHRISTOPHERSON, E. R. (1983). Replication and social validation of habit reversal treatment for tics. *Behavior Therapy, 14,* 116–126.

Fisher, E., & Thompson, J. K. (1994). A comparative evaluation of cognitive-behavioral therapy (CBT) versus exercise therapy (ET) for the treatment of body image disturbance: Preliminary findings. *Behavior Modification, 18,* 171–185.

Fisher, J. E., Swingen, D. N., & O'Donahue, W. (1997). Behavioral interventions for sexual dysfunction in the elderly. *Behavior Therapy, 28,* 65–82.

Fixsen, D. L., Phillips, E. L., Phillips, E. A., & Wolf, M. M. (1976). The teaching-family model of group home treatment. In W. E. Craighead, A. E. Kazdin, & M. J. Mahoney, *Behavior modification: Principles, issues, and applications* (pp. 310–320). Boston: Houghton Mifflin.

Flanagan, R., Povall, L., Dellino, M., & Byrne, L. (1998). A comparison of problem-solving with and without rational emotive behavior therapy to improve children's social skills. *Journal of Rational-Emotive & Cognitive-Behavior Therapy, 16,* 125–134.

Fleece, L. (1995). [Review of the book *The therapeutic relationship in behavioural psychotherapy*]. *the Behavior Therapist, 18,* 142.

Fleming, I. (1984). Habit reversal treatment for trichotillomania: A case study. *Behavioural Psychotherapy, 12,* 73–80.

Flor, H., Kerns, R. D., & Turk, D. C. (1987). The role of spouse reinforcement, perceived pain, and activity levels of chronic pain patients. *Journal of Psychosomatic Research, 31,* 251–259.

Foa, E. B., Dancu, C. V., Hembree, E. A., Jaycox, L. H., Meadows, E. A., & Street, G. P. (1999). A comparison of exposure therapy, stress inoculation training, and their combination for reducing posttraumatic stress disorder in female assault victims. *Journal of Consulting and Clinical Psychology, 67,* 194–200.

Foa, E. B., & Rothbaum, B. O. (1989). Behavioural psychotherapy for post-traumatic stress disorder. *International Review of Psychiatry, 1,* 219–226.

Foa, E. B., & Rothbaum, B. O. (1998). *Treating the trauma of rape: Cognitive-behavioral therapy for PTSD.* New York: Guilford.

Foa, E. B., Rothbaum, B. O., & Kozak, M. J. (1989). Behavioral treatments for anxiety and depression. In P. C. Kendall & D. Watson (Eds.), *Anxiety and depression: Distinctive and overlapping features* (pp. 413–454). New York: Academic Press.

Foa, E. B., Rothbaum, B. O., Riggs, D. S., & Murdock, T. B. (1991). Treatment of posttraumatic stress disorder in rape victims: A comparison between cognitive-behavioral procedures and counseling. *Journal of Consulting and Clinical Psychology, 59,* 715–723.

Foa, E. B., Steketee, G. S., Turner, R. M., & Fischer, S. C. (1980). Effectiveness of imaginal exposure to feared disasters in obsessive-compulsive checkers. *Behaviour Research and Therapy, 18,* 449–455.

Follansbee, D. J., LaGreca, A. M., & Citrin, W. S. (1983). Coping skills training for adolescents with diabetes. (Abstract) *Diabetes, 32*(Suppl. 1), 147.

Follick, M. J. (1979, September). *An outpatient based behaviorially oriented approach to the management of chronic pain.* Paper presented at the meeting of the American Psychological Association, New York.

Forbes, D., Creamer, M., & Rycroft, P. (1994). Eye movement desensitization and reprocessing in posttraumatic stress disorder: A pilot study using assessment measures. *Journal of Behavior Therapy and Experimental Psychiatry, 25,* 113–120.

Fordyce, W. [E.] (1976). *Behavioral methods for chronic pain and illness.* St. Louis: Mosby.

Fordyce, W. E. (1988). Pain and suffering: A reappraisal. *American Psychologist, 43,* 276–283.

Fordyce, W. E., Fowler, R. S., & deLateur, B. (1968). An application of behavior modification techniques to a problem of chronic pain. *Behaviour Research and Therapy, 6,* 105–107.

Fordyce, W. E., Fowler, R. S., Lehmann, J. F., deLateur, B. J., Sand, P. L., & Trieschmann, R. B. (1973). Operant conditioning in the treatment of chronic pain. *Archives of Physical Medicine and Rehabilitation, 54,* 399–408.

Fordyce, W. E., & Steger, J. C. (1979). Chronic pain. In O. F. Pomerleau & J. P. Brady (Eds.), *Behavioral medicine: Theory and practice* (pp. 125–153). Baltimore: Williams & Wilkins.

Forehand, R. [L.], & King, H. E. (1977). Noncompliant children: Effects of parent training on behavior and attitude. *Behavior Modification, 1,* 93–108.

Forehand, R. [L.], & Kotchik, B. A. (1996). Cultural diversity: A wake-up call for parent training. *Behavior Therapy, 27,* 187–206.

Forehand, R. [L.], & Long, N. (1988). Outpatient treatment of the acting-out child: Procedures, long-term follow-up data, and clinical problems. *Archives in Behaviour Research and Therapy, 10,* 129–177.

Forehand, R. L., & McMahon, R. J. (1981). *Helping the noncompliant child: A clinician's guide to parent training.* New York: Guilford.

Foreman, S. A. (1980). A comparison of cognitive training and response cost procedures in modifying aggressive behavior of elementary school children. *Behavior Therapy, 11,* 594–600.

Foreyt, J. P. (1987). The addictive disorders. In G. T. Wilson, C. M. Franks, P. C. Kendall, & J. P. Foreyt (Eds.), *Review of behavior therapy: Theory and practice* (Vol. 11, pp. 187–233). New York: Guilford.

Foreyt, J. P. (1990). The addictive disorders. In C. M. Franks, G. T. Wilson, P. C. Kendall, & J. P. Foreyt (Eds.), *Review of behavior therapy: Theory and practice* (Vol. 12, pp. 178–224). New York: Guilford.

Forsyth, J. P. (1997). It was the age of wisdom, it is the age of hope: Commentary on "It was the best of times, it was the worst of times." *Behavior Therapy, 28,* 397–401.

Foster, S. L., Bell-Dolan, D. J., & Burge, D. A. (1988). Behavioral observation. In A. S. Bellack & M. Hersen (Eds.), *Behavioral assessment: A practical handbook* (3rd ed., pp. 119–160). Elmsford, NY: Pergamon.

Foster, S. L., & Cone, J. D. (1980). Current issues in direct observation. *Behavioral Assessment, 2,* 313–338.

Foster, S. L., & Cone, J. D. (1986). Design and use of direct observation. In A. R. Ciminero, K. S. Calhoun, & H. A. Adams (Eds.), *Handbook of behavioral assessment* (2nd ed., pp. 253–324). New York: Wiley.

Foster, S. L., & Mash, E. J. (1999). Assessing social validity in clinical treatment research: Issues and procedures. *Journal of Consulting and Clinical Psychology, 67,* 308–319.

Fox, D. K., Hopkins, B. L., & Anger, W. K. (1987). The long-term effects of a token economy on safety performance in open-pit mining. *Journal of Applied Behavior Analysis, 20,* 215–224.

Fox, R. A., & deShaw, J. M. (1993a). Milestone reinforcer survey. *Education and Training in Mental Retardation, 28,* 257–261.

Fox, R. A., & deShaw, J. M. (1993b). *Milestone reinforcer survey manual.* Rockford, IL: Milestone Inc.

Foxx, R. M., & Azrin, N. H. (1972). Restitution: A method of eliminating aggressive-disruptive behavior of retarded and brain damaged patients. *Behaviour Research and Therapy, 10,* 15–27.

Foxx, R. M., & Azrin, N. H. (1973a). Dry pants: A rapid method of toilet training children. *Behaviour Research and Therapy, 11,* 435–442.

Foxx, R. M., & Azrin, N. H. (1973b). *Toilet training the retarded: A rapid program for day and night time independent toileting.* Champaign, IL: Research Press.

Foxx, R. M., & Faw, G. D. (1990). Long-term follow-up of echolalia and question answering. *Journal of Applied Behavior Analysis, 23,* 387–396.

Foxx, R. M., Faw, G. D., & Weber, G. (1991). Producing generalization of inpatient adolescents' social skills with significant adults in a natural environment. *Behavior Therapy, 22,* 85–99.

Foxx, R. M., & Hake, D. F. (1977). Gasoline conservation: A procedure for measuring and reducing the driving of college students. *Journal of Applied Behavior Analysis, 10,* 61–74.

Foxx, R. M., Martella, R. C., & Marchand-Martella, N. E. (1989). The acquisition, maintenance, and generalization of problem-solving skills by closed head-injured adults. *Behavior Therapy, 20,* 61–76.

Frame, C. L., & Matson, J. L. (1987). *Handbook of assessment in childhood psychopathology: Applied issues in differential diagnosis and treatment evaluation.* New York: Plenum.

France, K. G. (1992). Behavioral characteristics and security in sleep disturbed infants treated with extinction. *Journal of Pediatric Psychology, 17,* 467–475.

France, K. G., & Hudson, S. M. (1990). Behavior management of infant sleep disturbance. *Journal of Applied Behavior Analysis, 23,* 91–98.

France, K. G., & Hudson, S. M. (1993). Management of infant sleep disturbance: A review. *Clinical Psychology Review, 13,* 635–647.

Franco, D. D. (1981). Habit reversal and isometric tensing with motor tics. *Dissertation Abstracts International, 42,* 3418B.

Franco, D. P., Christoff, K. A., Crimmins, D. B., & Kelly, J. A. (1983). Social skills training for an extremely shy young adolescent: An empirical case study. *Behavior Therapy, 14,* 568–575.

Franco, H., Galanter, M., Casteeda, R., & Paterson, J. (1995). Combining behavioral and self-help approaches in the inpatient management of dually diagnosed patients. *Journal of Substance Abuse, 12,* 227–232.

Franklin, M. E., Abramowitz, J. S., Kozak, M. J., Levitt, J. T., & Foa, E. B. (2000). Effectiveness of exposure and ritual prevention for obsessive-compulsive disorder randomized compared with nonrandomized samples. *Journal of Consulting and Clinical Psychology, 68,* 594–602.

Franks, C. M. (1963). Behavior therapy, the principles of conditioning and the treatment of the alcoholic. *Quarterly Journal of Studies on Alcohol, 24,* 511–529.

Franks, C. M. (1969). Introduction: Behavior therapy and its Pavlovian origins: Review and perspectives. In C. M. Franks (Ed.), *Behavior therapy: Appraisal and status* (pp. 1–26). New York: McGraw-Hill.

Franks, C. M. (1995). RET, REBT and Albert Ellis. *Journal of Rational-Emotive & Cognitive-Behavior Therapy, 13,* 91–95.

Franks, C. M., & Wilson, G. T. (Eds.). (1973). *Annual review of behavior therapy: Theory and practice* (Vol. 1). New York: Brunner/Mazel.

Franks, C. M., & Wilson, G. T. (Eds.). (1975). *Annual review of behavior therapy: Theory and practice* (Vol. 3). New York: Brunner/Mazel.

Franks, C. M., & Wilson, G. T. (Eds.). (1976). *Annual review of behavior therapy: Theory and practice* (Vol. 4). New York: Brunner/Mazel.

Franks, C. M., & Wilson, G. T. (Eds.). (1978). *Annual review of behavior therapy: Theory and practice* (Vol. 6). New York: Brunner/Mazel.

Franks, C. M., Wilson, G. T., Kendall, P. C., & Foreyt, J. P. (1990). *Review of behavior therapy: Theory and practice* (Vol. 12). New York: Guilford.

Freeman, A., & Simon, K. M. (1989). Cognitive therapy of anxiety. In A. Freeman, K. M. Simon, L. E. Beutler, & H. Arkowitz (Eds.), *Comprehensive handbook of cognitive therapy* (pp. 347–365). New York: Plenum.

Freeman, A., & White, D. M. (1989). The treatment of suicidal behavior. In A. Freeman, K. M. Simon, L. E. Beutler, & H. Arkowitz (Eds.), *Comprehensive handbook of cognitive therapy* (pp. 321–346). New York: Plenum.

Freeston, M. H., Leger, E., & Ladouceur, R. (2001). Cognitive therapy for obsessive thoughts. *Cognitive and Behavioral Practice, 8,* 61–78.

Freud, S. (1955). Analysis of a phobia in a five-year-old boy. In J. Strachey (Ed. and Trans.), *The standard edition of the complete psychological works of Sigmund Freud* (Vol. 10). London: Hogarth. (Originally published 1909)

Friedberg, R. D., Crosby, L. E., Friedberg, B. A., Rutter, J. G., & Knight, K. R. (2000). Making cognitive behavioral therapy user-friendly to children. *Cognitive and Behavioral Practice, 6,* 189–200.

Friedberg, R. D., Viglione, D. J., Stinson, B. L., Beal, K. G., Fidaleo, R. A., & Celeste, B. (1999). Perceptions of treatment helpfulness and depressive symptamology in psychiatric inpatients on a cognitive therapy unit. *Journal of Rational-Emotive & Cognitive-Behavior Therapy, 17,* 33–50.

Friedman, R., Sobel, D., Myers, P., Caudill, M., & Benson, H. (1995). Behavioral medicine, clinical health psychology, and cost offset. *Health Psychology, 14,* 509–518.

Friedman, S. (1980). Self-control in the treatment of Gilles de la Tourette's syndrome: Case study with 18-month follow-up. *Journal of Consulting and Clinical Psychology, 48,* 400–402.

Friman, P. C. (2000). "Transitional objects" as establishing operations for thumb sucking: A case study. *Journal of Applied Behavior Analysis, 33,* 507–509.

Friman, P. C., Finney, J. W., & Christophersen, E. R. (1984). Behavioral treatment of trichotillomania: An evaluative review. *Behavior Therapy, 15,* 249–265.

FRIMAN, P. C., FINNEY, J. W., RAPOFF, M. A., & CHRISTOPHERSEN, E. R. (1985). Improving pediatric appointment keeping with reminders and reduced response requirements. *Journal of Applied Behavior Analysis, 18,* 315–321.

FRIMAN, P. C., & O'CONNOR, W. A. (1984). The integration of hypnotic and habit reversal techniques in the treatment of trichotillomania. *the Behavior Therapist, 7,* 166–167.

FRIMAN, P. C., & VOLLMER, D. (1995). The successful use of the nocturnal urine alarm for diurnal enuresis. *Journal of Applied Behavior Analysis, 28,* 89–90.

FRISBY, C. (1990). A teacher inservice model for problem solving in classroom discipline: Suggestions for the school psychologist. *School Psychology Quarterly, 5,* 211–232.

FRISCH, M. B., & FROBERG, W. (1987). Social validation of assertion strategies for handling aggressive criticism: Evidence for consistency across situations. *Behavior Therapy, 18,* 181–191.

FRUEH, B. C. (1995). Self-administered exposure therapy by a Vietnam veteran with PTSD. *American Journal of Psychiatry, 152,* 1831–1832.

FRUEH, B. C., TURNER, S. M., & BEIDEL, D. C. (1995). Exposure therapy for combat-related PTSD: A critical review. *Clinical Psychology Review, 15,* 799–817.

FRYE, A. A., & GOODMAN, S. H. (2000). Which social problem-solving components buffer depression in adolescent girls? *Cognitive Therapy and Research, 24,* 637–650.

FUDGE, R. C. (1996). The use of behavior therapy in the development of ethnic consciousness: A treatment model. *Cognitive and Behavioral Practice, 3,* 317–335.

GALE, B. M. (1996). Is this the year you become friends with technology? *the Behavior Therapist, 19,* 82–83.

GALLAGHER-THOMPSON, D., LOVETT, S., ROSE, J., MCKIBBIN, C., COON, D. W., FUTTERMAN, A., & THOMPSON, L. W. (2000). Impact of psychoeducational interventions on distressed family care-givers. *Journal of Clinical Geropsychology, 6,* 91–110.

GAMBRILL, E. [D.] (1985). Social skill training with the elderly. In L. L'Abate & M. A. Milan (Eds.), *Handbook of social skills training and research* (pp. 326–327). New York: Wiley.

GAMBRILL, E. [D.] (1995a). Assertion skills training. In W. O'Donohue & L. Krasner (Eds.), *Handbook of psychological skills training: Clinical techniques and applications* (pp. 81–118). Boston: Allyn & Bacon.

GAMBRILL, E. [D.] (1995b). Helping shy, socially anxious, and lonely adults: A skill-based contextual approach. In W. O'Donohue & L. Krasner (Eds.), *Handbook of psychological skills training: Clinical techniques and applications* (pp. 247–286). Boston: Allyn & Bacon.

GAMBRILL, E. D., & RICHEY, C. A. (1975). An assertion inventory for use in assessment and research. *Behavior Therapy, 6,* 550–561.

GANNON, P., HARMON, M., & WILLIAMS, B. F. (1997). An in-home token system for a student with attention deficit hyperactivity disorder. *Journal of Special Education, 21,* 33–40.

GARLAND, J. (1985). Adaptation skills in the elderly, their supporters and careers. Special issue: Sharing psychological skills: Training non-psychologists in the use of psychological techniques. *British Journal of Medical Psychology, 58,* 267–274.

GARNER, D. M., ROCKERT, W., DAVIS, R., GARNER, M. V., OLMSTEAD, M. P., & EAGLE, M. (1993). Comparison of cognitive-behavioral and supportive-expressive therapy for bulimia nervosa. *American Journal of Psychiatry, 150,* 37–46.

GASTON, L., GOLDFRIED, M. R., GREENBERG, L. S., HORVATH, A. O., RAUE, P. J., & WATSON, J. (1995). The therapeutic alliance in psychodynamic, cognitive-behavioral, and experimental therapies. *Journal of Psychotherapy Integration, 5,* 1–26.

GATCHEL, R. J. (1980). Effectiveness of two procedures for reducing dental fear: Group-administered desensitization and group education and discussion. *Journal of the American Dental Association, 101,* 634–637.

GEER, J. H. (1965). The development of a scale to measure fear. *Behaviour Research and Therapy, 3,* 45–53.

GEISS, S. K., & O'LEARY, K. D. (1981). Therapist ratings of frequency and severity of marital problems: Implications for research. *Journal of Marital and Family Therapy, 7,* 515–520.

GENEST, M., & TURK, D. C. (1981). Think-aloud approaches to cognitive assessment. In T. V. Merluzzi, C. R. Glass, & M. Genest (Eds.), *Cognitive assessment* (pp. 233–269). New York: Guilford.

GENTRY, W. D. (1971). Noncompliance to medical regimen. In R. B. Williams & W. D. Gentry (Eds.), *Behavioral approaches to medical treatment.* Cambridge, MA: Ballinger.

GETKA, E. J., & GLASS, C. R. (1992). Behavioral and cognitive-behavioral approaches to the reduction of dental anxiety. *Behavior Therapy, 23,* 433–448.

GIEBINK, J. W., STOVER, D., & FAHL, M. (1968). Teaching adaptive responses to frustration to emotionally disturbed boys. *Journal of Consulting and Clinical Psychology, 32,* 366–368.

GIL, K. M., CARSON, J. W., SEDWAY, J. A., PORTER, L. S., SCHAEFFER, J. J. W., & ORRINGER, E. (2000). Follow-up coping skills training in adults with sickle cell disease: Analysis of daily pain and coping practice diaries. *Journal of Consulting and Clinical Psychology, 68,* 85–90.

GIL, K. M., PORTER, L., READY, J., WORKMAN, E., SEDWAY, J., & ANTHONY, K. K. (2000). Pain in children and adolescents with sickle cell disease: An analysis of daily pain diaries. *Children's Health Care, 29,* 225–241.

GIL, K. M., WILSON, J. J., EDENS, J. L., WORKMAN, E., READY, J., SEDWAY, J., REDDING-LALLINGER, R., & DAESCHNER, C. W. (1997). Cognitive coping skills training with sickle cell disease pain. *International Journal of Behavioral Medicine, 4,* 364–377.

GILBERT, B. O., JOHNSON, S. B., SPILLAR, R., MCCALLUM, M., SILVERSTEIN, J. H., & ROSENBLOOM, A. (1982). The effects of a peer-modeling film on children learning to self-inject insulin. *Behavior Therapy, 13,* 186–193.

GILES, T. R. (1991). Managed mental health care and effective psychotherapy: A step in the right direction? *Journal of Behaviour Therapy and Experimental Psychiatry, 22,* 83–86.

GILES, T. R., PRIAL, E. M., & NEIMS, D. M. (1993). Evaluating psychotherapies: A comparison of effectiveness. *International Journal of Mental Health, 22,* 43–65.

GILLIES, L. A., HASHMALL, J. M., HILTON, N. Z., & WEBSTER, C. D. (1992). Relapse prevention in pedophiles: Clinical issues and program development. Special issue: Violence and its aftermath. *Canadian Psychology, 33,* 199–210.

GILLUM, R. F., & BARSKY, A. J. (1974). Diagnosis and management of patient noncompliance. *Journal of the American Medical Association, 228,* 1563–1567.

GIRARDEAU, F. L., & SPRADLIN, J. E. (1964). Token rewards in a cottage program. *Mental Retardation, 2,* 345–351.

GLANZ, M. D. (1989). Cognitive therapy with the elderly. In A. Freeman, K. M. Simon, L. E. Beutler, & H. Arkowitz (Eds.), *Comprehensive handbook of cognitive therapy* (pp. 467–489). New York: Plenum.

GLASER, B. A., KRONSNOBLE, K. M., & FORKNER, C. B. W. (1997). Parents and teachers as raters of children's problem behavior. *Child & Family Behavior Therapy, 19,* 1–13.

GLASGOW, R. E. (1975). *In vivo* prolonged exposure in treatment of urinary retention. *Behavior Therapy, 6,* 701–702.

GLASS, C. R., & ARNKOFF, D. B. (1989). Behavioral assessment of social anxiety and social phobia. *Clinical Psychology Review, 9,* 75–90.

GLASS, C. R., & ARNKOFF, D. B. (1992). Behavior therapy. In D. K. Freedheim (Ed.), *History of psychotherapy: A century of change* (pp. 587–628). Washington, DC: American Psychological Association.

GLASS, C. R., & ARNKOFF, D. B. (1994). Validity issues in self-statement measures of social phobia and social anxiety. *Behaviour Research and Therapy, 32,* 255–267.

GLASS, C. R., & ARNKOFF, D. B. (1997). Questionnaire methods of cognitive self-statement assessment. *Journal of Consulting and Clinical Psychology, 65,* 911–927.

GLASS, C. R., GOTTMAN, J. M., & SHMURAK, S. H. (1976). Response acquisition and cognitive self-statement modification approaches to dating skills training. *Journal of Counseling Psychology, 23,* 520–526.

GLASS, C. R., MERLUZZI, T. V., BIEVER, J. L., & LARSEN, K. H. (1982). Cognitive assessment of social anxiety: Development and validation of a self-statement questionnaire. *Cognitive Therapy and Research, 6,* 37–55.

GLENWICK, D., & JASON, L. [A.] (Eds.). (1980). *Behavioral community psychology: Progress and prospects.* New York: Praeger.

GLYNN, E. L. (1970). Classroom applications of self-determined reinforcement. *Journal of Applied Behavior Analysis, 3,* 123–132.

GLYNN, S. M. (1990). Token economy approaches for psychiatric patients. *Behavior Modification, 14,* 383–407.

GLYNN, S. M., ETH, S., RANDOLPH, E. T., FOY, D. W., URBAITIS, M., BOXER, L., PAZ, G. G., LEONG, G. B., FIRMAN, G., SALK, J. D., KATZMAN, J. W., & CROTHERS, J. (1999). A test of behavioral family therapy to augment exposure for combat-related posttraumatic stress disorder. *Journal of Consulting and Clinical Psychology, 67,* 243–251.

GOETZ, E. M., HOLMBERG, M. C., & LEBLANC, J. M. (1975). Differential reinforcement of other behavior and non-contingent reinforcement as control procedures during the modification of a preschooler's compliance. *Journal of Applied Behavior Analysis, 8,* 77–82.

GOLD, S. R., LETOURNEAU, E. J., & O'DONOHUE, W. (1995). Sexual interaction skills. In W. O'Donohue & L. Krasner (Eds.), *Handbook of psychological skills training: Clinical techniques and applications* (pp. 229–246). Boston: Allyn & Bacon.

GOLDFRIED, M. R. (1971). Systematic desensitization as training in self-control. *Journal of Consulting and Clinical Psychology, 37,* 228–234.

GOLDFRIED, M. R. (1988). Application of rational restructuring to anxiety disorders. *The Counseling Psychologist, 16,* 50–68.

GOLDFRIED, M. R. (1995). *From cognitive-behavior therapy to psychotherapy integration: An evolving view.* New York: Springer.

GOLDFRIED, M. R., & CASTONGUAY, L. G. (1993). Behavior therapy: Redefining strengths and limitations. *Behavior Therapy, 24,* 505–526.

GOLDFRIED, M. R., CASTONGUAY, L. G., & SAFRAN, J. D. (1992). Core issues and future directions in psychotherapy integration. In J. C. Norcross & M. R. Goldfried (Eds.), *Handbook of psychotherapy integration* (pp. 593–616). New York: Basic Books.

GOLDFRIED, M. R., & DAVISON, G. C. (1994). *Clinical behavior therapy* (expanded ed.). New York: Wiley.

GOLDFRIED, M. R., DECENTECEO, E. T., & WEINBERG, L. (1974). Systematic rational restructuring as a self-control technique. *Behavior Therapy, 5,* 247–254.

GOLDFRIED, M. R., GREENBERG, L. S., & MARMAR, C. (1990). Individual psychotherapy: Process and outcome. *Annual Review of Psychology, 41,* 659–688.

GOLDFRIED, M. R., & SPRAFKIN, J. N. (1974). *Behavioral personality assessment.* Morristown, NJ: General Learning Press.

GOLDFRIED, M. R., WISER, S. L., & RAUE, P. J. (1992). On the movement toward psychotherapy integration. *Journal of Psychotherapy Practice and Research, 1,* 213–224.

GOLDIAMOND, I. (1974). Toward a constitutional approach to social problems: Ethical and constitutional issues raised by applied behavior analysis. *Behaviorism, 2,* 1–79.

GOLDSTEIN, A. J., DE BEURS, E., CHAMBLESS, D. L., & WILSON, K. A. (2000). EMDR for panic disorder with agoraphobia: Comparison with waiting list and credible attention-placebo control conditions. *Journal of Consulting and Clinical Psychology, 68,* 947–956.

GOLDSTEIN, H., & MOUSETIS, L. (1989). Generalized language learning by children with severe mental retardation: Effects of peers' expressive modeling. *Journal of Applied Behavior Analysis, 22,* 245–259.

GOLDSTEIN, I. B., SHAPIRO, D., THANANOPAVARN, C., & SAMBHI, M. P. (1982). Comparison of drug and behavioral treatments of essential hypertension. *Health Psychology, 1,* 7–26.

GORDON, C. M., & CAREY, M. P. (1995). Penile tumescence monitoring during morning naps to assess male erectile functioning: An initial study of healthy men of varied ages. *Archives of Sexual Behavior, 24,* 291–307.

GORDON, P. K. (1983). Switching attention from obsessional thoughts: An illustrative case study. *Journal of Psychiatric Treatment and Evaluation, 5,* 171–174.

GOREN, E. (1975). *A comparison of systematic desensitization and self-instruction in the treatment of phobias.* Unpublished master's thesis, Rutgers University.

GOSSETTE, R. L., & O'BRIEN, R. M. (1993). Efficacy of rational emotive therapy (RET) with children: A critical reappraisal. *Journal of Behavior Therapy and Experimental Psychiatry, 24,* 15–25.

GOTTMAN, J. M., & MARKMAN, H. J. (1978). Experimental designs in psychotherapy research. In S. L. Garfield & A. E. Gergin (Eds.), *Handbook of psychotherapy and behavior change: An empirical analysis* (2nd ed., pp. 23–62). New York: Wiley.

GOTTMAN, J., [M.] & RUSHE, R. (1995). Communication skills and social skills approaches to treating ailing marriages: A recommendation for a new marital therapy called "Minimal Marital Therapy." In W. O'Donohue & L. Krasner (Eds.), *Handbook of psychological skills training: Clinical techniques and applications* (pp. 287–305). Boston: Allyn & Bacon.

GOULD, M. S., & SHAFFER, D. (1986). The impact of suicide in television movies: Evidence of imitation. *New UK Journal of Medicine, 31,* 690–694.

GOULD, R. A., & OTTO, M. W. (1995). Cognitive-behavioral treatment of social phobia and generalized anxiety disorder. In M. H. Pollack, M. W. Otto, & J. F. Rosenbaum (Eds.), *Challenges in psychiatric treatment: Pharmacological and psychosocial strategies* (pp. 171–200). New York: Guilford.

GOULD, R. A., OTTO, M. W., & POLLACK, M. H. (in press). A meta-analysis of treatment outcome for panic disorder. *Clinical Psychology Review.*

GRANDY, S. E., & PECK, S. M. (1997). The use of functional assessment and self-management with a first grader. *Child & Family Behavior Therapy, 19,* 29–43.

GRAUBARD, P. S., ROSENBERG, H., & MILLER, M. B. (1974). Student applications of behavior modification to teachers and environments or ecological approaches to social deviancy. In R. Ulrich, T. Stachnik, & J. Mabry (Eds.), *Control of human behavior* (Vol. 3, pp. 421–436). Glenview, IL: Scott Foresman.

GRAVE, D. G. (1999). Cognitive behavior therapy in obesity: Standard techniques and new trends. *Psicoterapia and Cognitiva e Comportamentale, 5,* 31–44.

GRAVES, R., OPENSHAW, D., & ADAMS, G. R. (1992). Adolescent sex offenders and social skills training. *International Journal of Offender Therapy and Comparative Criminology, 36,* 139–153.

GRAZIANO, A. M., deGIOVANNI, I. S., & GARCIA, K. A. (1979). Behavioral treatment of children's fears: A review. *Psychological Bulletin, 86,* 804–830.

GREAVES, D. (1997). The effects on rational-emotive parent education on the stress of mothers with young children with Down syndrome. *Journal of Rational-Emotive & Cognitive-Behavior Therapy, 15,* 249–267.

GREEN, L. (1978). Temporal and stimulus factors in self-monitoring of obese persons. *Behavior Therapy, 8,* 328–341.

GREENAN, E., POWELL, C., & VARNI, J. W. (1984). *Adherence to therapeutic exercise by children with hemophilia.* Unpublished manuscript. Cited in LaGreca, A. M. (1988). Adherence to prescribed medical regimens. In D. K. Routh (Ed.), *Handbook of pediatric psychology* (pp. 299–320). New York: Guilford.

GREENBERG, L. S. (1990, November). *The emotional bond: The therapeutic alliance in experiential therapy.* Paper presented at the meeting of the Association for Advancement of Behavior Therapy, San Francisco.

GREENE, L., KAMPS, D., WYBLE, J., & ELLIS, C. (1999). Home-based consultation for parents of young children with behavioral problems. *Child & Family Behavior Therapy, 21,* 19–45.

GREENE, R. W. (2001). *The explosive child* (2nd ed.). New York: HarperCollins.

GREYSON, J. B., FOA, E. A., & STEKETEE, G. (1985). Obsessive-compulsive disorder. In M. Hersen & A. S. Bellack (Eds.), *Handbook of clinical behavior therapy with adults* (pp. 133–165). New York: Plenum.

GRIFFITHS, D., FELDMAN, M. A., & TOUGH, S. (1997). Programming generalization of social skills in adults with developmental disabilities: Effects on generalization and social validity. *Journal of Applied Behavior Analysis, 28,* 253–269.

GRIFFITHS, R., BIGELOW, G., & LIEBSON, I. (1974). Suppression of ethanol self-administration in alcoholics by contingent time-out from social interactions. *Behaviour Research and Therapy, 12,* 327–334.

GRODEN, J. (1993). The use of covert procedures to reduce severe aggression in a person with retardation and behavioral disorders. In J. R. Cautela & A. J. Kearney (Eds.), *Covert conditioning casebook* (pp. 144–152). Pacific Grove, CA: Brooks/Cole.

GROSS, A. M., JOHNSON, W. G., WILDMAN, H. E., & MULLETT, M. (1981). Coping skills training with insulin dependent preadolescent diabetics. *Child Behavior Therapy, 3,* 141–153.

GROSS, A. M., & WIXTED, J. T. (1988). Assessment of child behavior problems. In A. S. Bellack & M. Hersen (Eds.), *Behavioral assessment: A practical handbook* (3rd ed., pp. 578–608). Elmsford, NY: Pergamon.

GROTH, A. N. (1980). *Men who rape: The psychology of the offender.* New York: Plenum.

GROTHBERG, E. H., FEINDLER, E. L., WHITE, C. B., & STUTMAN, S. S. (1991). Using anger management for prevention of child abuse. In P. Keller & S. Heyman (Eds.), *Innovations in clinical practice: A source book* (Vol. 10, pp. 5–21). Sarasota, FL: Professional Resource Press/Professional Resource Exchange.

GRUDER, C. L., MERMELSTEIN, R. J., KIRKENDOL, S., HEDEKER, D., WONG, S. C., SCHRECKENGOST, J., WARNECKE, R. B., BURZETTE, R., & MILLER, T. Q. (1993). Effects of social support and relapse prevention training as adjuncts to a televised smoking-cessation intervention. *Journal of Consulting and Clinical Psychology, 61,* 113–120.

GUESS, D. (1969). A functional analysis of receptive and productive speech: Acquisition of the plural morpheme. *Journal of Applied Behavior Analysis, 2,* 55–64.

GUESS, D., & BAER, D. M. (1973). An analysis of individual differences in generalization between receptive and productive language in retarded children. *Journal of Applied Behavior Analysis, 6,* 311–329.

GUEVREMONT, D. C. (1987). *A contingency contract to reduce fighting among siblings.* Unpublished manuscript, West Virginia University.

GUEVREMONT, D. C. (1990). Social skills and peer relationship training. In R. A. Barkley (Ed.), *Attention deficit hyperactivity disorder* (pp. 540–572). New York: Guilford.

GUEVREMONT, D. C., & DUMAS, M. C. (1996). *Impact of multiple setting events on social interactions of children with ADHD.* Unpublished manuscript, Blackstone Valley Psychological Institute, North Smithfield, RI.

GUEVREMONT, D. C., & DUMAS, M. C. (2002). *Impact of setting events on the social interactions of boys with attention deficit hyperactivity disorder.* Unpublished manuscript.

GUEVREMONT, D. C., DUPAUL, G. J., & BARKLEY, R. A. (1990). Diagnosis and assessment of attention deficit hyperactivity disorder in children. *Journal of School Psychology, 28,* 51–78.

GUEVREMONT, D. C., & FOSTER, S. L. (1992). Impact of social problem solving on the behavior of aggressive boys: Generalization, maintenance, and social validation. *Journal of Abnormal Child Psychology, 26,* 112–121.

GUEVREMONT, D. C., TISHELMAN, A. C., & HULL, D. B. (1985). Teaching generalized self-control to attention-deficit boys with mothers as adjunct therapists. *Child & Family Behavior Therapy, 7,* 23–36.

GUEVREMONT, D. C., OSNES, P. G., & STOKES, T. F. (1986a). Preparation for effective self-management: The development of generalized verbal control. *Journal of Applied Behavior Analysis, 19,* 99–104.

GUEVREMONT, D. C., OSNES, P. G., & STOKES, T. F. (1986b). Programming maintenance following correspondence training with children. *Journal of Applied Behavior Analysis, 19,* 215–219.

GUEVREMONT, D. C., OSNES, P. G., & STOKES, T. F. (1988). The functional role of verbalizations in the generalization of self-instructional training with children. *Journal of Applied Behavior Analysis, 21,* 45–55.

GUEVREMONT, D. C., & SPIEGLER, M. D. (1990, November). *What do behavior therapists really do? A survey of the clinical practice of AABT members.* Paper presented at the meeting of the Association for Advancement of Behavior Therapy, San Francisco.

GUMLEY, A. I., & POWER, K. G. (2000). Is targeting cognitive therapy during relapse in psychosis feasible? *Behavioural and Cognitive Psychotherapy, 28,* 161–174.

GUMPEL, T. P., & FRANK, R. (1999). An expansion of the peer-tutoring paradigm: Cross-age peer tutoring of social skills among social rejected boys. *Journal of Applied Behavior Analysis, 32,* 115–118.

GUTENTAG, S., & HAMMER, D. (2000). Shaping oral feeding in a gastronomy tube-dependent child in natural settings. *Behavior Modification, 24,* 395–410.

HAAGA, D. A. F. (1990). Issues in relating self-efficacy to smoking relapse: Importance of an "Achilles' heel" situation and of prior quitting experience. *Journal of Substance Abuse, 2,* 191–200.

HAAGA, D. A. F., & DAVISON, G. C. (1989a). Outcome studies of rational-emotive therapy. In M. E. Bernard & R. [A.] DiGiuseppe (Eds.), *Inside rational-emotive therapy: A critical appraisal of the theory and therapy of Albert Ellis* (pp. 155–197). San Diego: Academic Press.

HAAGA, D. A. F., & DAVISON, G. C. (1989b). Slow progress in rational-emotive therapy outcome research: Etiology and treatment. *Cognitive Therapy and Research, 13,* 493–508.

HAAGA, D. A. [F.], & DAVISON, G. C. (1993). An appraisal of rational-emotive therapy. *Journal of Consulting and Clinical Psychology, 61,* 215–220.

HAAGA, D. A. F., DAVISON, G. C., WILLIAMS, M. E., DOLEZAL, S. L., HALEBLIAN, J., ROSENBAUM, J., DWYER, J. H., BAKER, S., NEZAMI, E., & DEQUATTRO, V. (1994). Mode-specific impact of relaxation training for hypertensive men with Type A behavior pattern. *Behavior Therapy, 25,* 209–223.

HAAGA, D. A. [F.], DRYDEN, W., & DANCEY, C. P. (1991). Measurement of rational-emotive therapy in outcome studies. *Journal of Rational-Emotive & Cognitive-Behavior Therapy, 9,* 73–93.

HACKMANN, A., & McLEAN, C. (1975). A comparison of flooding and thought stopping in the treatment of obses-sional neurosis. *Behaviour Research and Therapy, 13,* 263–269.

HADDOCK, G., McCARRON, J., TARRIER, N., & FARAGHER, E. B. (1999). Scales to measure dimensions of hallucination and delusions: The Psychotic Symptom Rating Scale (PSYRATS). *Psychological Medicine, 29,* 879–889.

HAGOPIAN, L. P., CROCKETT, J. L., VAN STONE, M., DELEON, I. G., & BOWMAN, L. G. (2000). Effects of noncontingent reinforcement on problem behavior and stimulus engagement: The role of satiation, extinctions, and alternative reinforcement. *Journal of Applied Behavior Analysis, 33,* 433–449.

HAGOPIAN, L. P., & SLIFER, K. J. (1993). Treatment of separation anxiety disorder with graduated exposure and reinforcement targeting school attendance: A controlled case study. *Journal of Anxiety Disorders, 7,* 271–280.

HAHLWEG, K., & MARKMAN, H. J. (1988). Effectiveness of behavioral marital therapy: Empirical status of behavioral techniques in preventing and alleviating marital distress. *Journal of Consulting and Clinical Psychology, 56,* 440–447.

HALL, A. C., & NATHAN, P. R. (1992, July). *The management of night wakening and settling problems in young children: Efficacy of a behavioral group parent training programme.* Paper presented at the Fourth World Congress of Behavior Therapy, Queensland, Australia.

HALL, N. R. S. (1988). The virology of AIDS. *American Psychologist, 43,* 907–913.

HALL, R. V., & HALL, M. C. (1982). *How to negotiate a behavioral contract.* Austin, TX: Pro-Ed.

HALL, R. V., & HALL, M. L. (1998a). *How to select reinforcers* (2nd ed.). Austin, TX: Pro-Ed.

HALL, R. V., & HALL, M. L. (1998b). *How to use systematic attention and approval* (2nd ed.). Austin, TX: Pro-Ed.

HAMMOND, W. R., & PROTHOW-STITH, D. (1991, November). *Skills training for violence prevention with African American youth.* Clinical forum discussion presented at the meeting of the Association for Advancement of Behavior Therapy, New York.

HANNIE, T. J., JR., & ADAMS, H. E. (1974). Modification of agitated depression by flooding: A preliminary study. *Journal of Behavior Therapy and Experimental Psychiatry, 5,* 161–166.

HANSEN, D. J. (2001). Public education and media dissemination: An interview with Albert Ellis. *the Behavior Therapist, 24,* 117–121.

HANSEN, D. J., MACMILLAN, V. M., & SHAWCHUCK, C. R. (1990). Social isolation. In E. L. Feindler & G. R. Kalfus (Eds.), *Adolescent behavior therapy handbook* (pp. 165–190). New York: Springer.

HANSEN, D. J., ST. LAWRENCE, J. S., & CHRISTOFF, K. A. (1985). Effects of interpersonal problem-solving training with chronic aftercare patients on problem-solving component skills and effectiveness of solutions. *Journal of Consulting and Clinical Psychology, 53,* 167–174.

HANSEN, D. J., ZAMBOANGA, B. L., & SEDLAR, G. (2000). Cognitive-behavior therapy for ethnic minority adolescents: Broadening our perspectives. *Cognitive and Behavioral Practice, 7,* 54–60.

HARING, T. G., BREEN, C. G., WEINER, J., KENNEDY, C. H., & BEDNERAH, F. (1995). Using videotape modeling to facilitate generalized purchasing skills. *Journal of Behavioral Education, 5,* 29–53.

HARPER, G. W., & IWAMASA, G. Y. (2000). Cognitive-behavioral therapy with ethnic minority adolescents: Therapist perspectives. *Cognitive and Behavioral Practice, 7,* 37–53.

HARRIS, S. L., & ROMANCZYK, R. G. (1976). Treating self-injurious behavior of a retarded child by overcorrection. *Behavior Therapy, 7,* 235–239.

HARRIS, V. W., & SHERMAN, J. A. (1974). Homework assignments, consequences, and classroom performance in social studies and mathematics. *Journal of Applied Behavior Analysis, 7,* 505–519.

HARTL, T. L., & FROST, R. O. (1999). Cognitive-behavioral treatment of compulsive hoarding: A multiple baseline experimental case study. *Behaviour Research and Therapy, 37,* 451–461.

HARTMANN, D. P. (1982). Assessing the dependability of observational data. In D. P. Hartmann (Ed.), *New directions for methodology of social and behavioral science: Using observers to study behavior* (pp. 51–65). San Francisco: Jossey-Bass.

HARTMANN, D. P., & WOOD, D. D. (1982). Observational methods. In A. S. Bellack, M. Hersen, & A. E. Kazdin (Eds.), *International handbook of behavior modification and therapy* (pp. 109–138). New York: Plenum.

HATCH, M. L., FRIEDMAN, S., & PARADIS, C. M. (1996). Behavioral treatment of obsessive-compulsive disorder in African Americans. *Cognitive and Behavioral Practice, 3,* 303–315.

HAUGHTON, E., & AYLLON, T. (1965). Production and elimination of symptomatic behavior. In L. P. Ullmann & L. Krasner (Eds.), *Case studies in behavior modification* (pp. 94–98). New York: Holt, Rinehart & Winston.

HAURI, P. (1981). Treating psychophysiological insomnia with biofeedback: A replication study. *Biofeedback and Self-Regulation, 7,* 752–758.

HAUSER, R. (1974). Rapid smoking as a technique of behavior modification: Caution in selection of subjects. *Journal of Consulting and Clinical Psychology, 42,* 625.

HAWKINS, R. P. (1997). Can behavior therapy be saved from triviality? Commentary on "Thirty years of behavior therapy." *Behavior Therapy, 28,* 637–645.

HAWKINS, R. P., & FORSYTH, J. P. (1997). The behavior analytic perspective: Its nature, prospects, and limitations for behavior therapy. *Journal of Behavior Therapy and Experimental Psychiatry, 28,* 7–16.

HAY, W. M., HAY, L. R., & NELSON, R. O. (1977). The adaptation of covert modeling procedures in the treatment of chronic alcoholism and obsessive-compulsive behavior: Two case reports. *Behavior Therapy, 8,* 70–76.

HAYES, S. C. (1995). Working with managed care: Lessons from the acceptance and commitment therapy training project. *the Behavior Therapist, 18,* 184–186.

HAYES, S. C., STROSAHL, K. D., & WILSON, K. G. (1999). *Acceptance and commitment therapy: An experimental approach to behavior change.* New York: Guilford.

HAYNES, R. B., SACKETT, D. L., GIBSON, E. S., TAYLOR, D. W., HACKETT, B. C., ROBERTS, R. S., & JOHNSON, A. L. (1976). Improvement of medication compliance in uncontrolled hypertension. *Lancet, 1,* 1265–1268.

HAYNES, R. B., TAYLOR, D. W., & SACKETT, D. L. (Eds.). (1979). *Compliance with health care.* Baltimore: Johns Hopkins University Press.

HAYNES, S. N. (1978). *Principles of behavioral assessment.* New York: Gardner.

HAYNES, S. N., SPAIN, E. H., & OLIVEIRA, J. (1993). Identifying causal relationships in clinical assessment. *Psychological Assessment, 5,* 281–291.

HEARD, K., & WATSON, T. S. (1999). Reducing wandering by persons with dementia using differential reinforcement. *Journal of Applied Behavior Analysis, 32,* 381–384.

HEATHERTON, T. F., & BAUMEISTER, R. F. (1991). Binge eating as escape from self-awareness. *Psychological Bulletin, 110,* 86–108.

HEATON, R. C., & SAFER, D. J. (1982). Secondary school outcome following a junior high school behavioral program. *Behavior Therapy, 13,* 226–231.

HEDBERG, A. G., & CAMPBELL, L. (1974). A comparison of four behavioral treatments of alcoholism. *Journal of Behavior Therapy and Experimental Psychiatry, 5,* 251–256.

HEGEL, M. T., & FERGUSON, R. J. (2000). Differential reinforcement of other behavior (DRO) to reduce aggressive behavior following traumatic brain injury. *Behavior Modification, 24,* 94–101.

HEIMAN, G. A. (1995). *Research methods in psychology.* Boston: Houghton Mifflin.

HEIMBERG, R. G. (1998). Manual-based treatment: An essential ingredient of clinical practice in the 21st century. *Clinical Psychology: Science and Practice, 5,* 387–390.

HEIMBERG, R. G. (2001). Current status of psychotherapeutic interventions for social phobia. *Journal of Clinical Psychiatry, 62,* 36–42.

HEIMBERG, R. G., SALZMAN, D. G., HOLT, C. S., & BLENDELL, K. A. (1993). Cognitive-behavioral group treatment for social phobia: Effectiveness at five-year followup. *Cognitive Therapy and Research, 17,* 325–339.

HERBERT, J. D., & MUESER, K. T. (1992). Eye movement desensitization: A critique of the evidence. *Journal of Behavior Therapy and Experimental Psychiatry, 23,* 169–174.

HERMANN, C., BLANCHARD, E. B., & FLOR, H. (1997). Biofeedback treatment for pediatric migraine: Prediction of treatment outcome. *Journal of Consulting and Clinical Psychology, 65,* 611–616.

HERMANN, J. A., DE MONTES, A. I., DOMINGUEZ, B., MONTES, F., & HOPKINS, B. L. (1973). Effects of bonuses for punctuality on the tardiness of industrial workers. *Journal of Applied Behavior Analysis, 6,* 563–570.

HERRING, M., & NORTHUP, J. (1998). The generalization of social skills for a child with behavior disorders in the school setting. *Child & Family Behavior Therapy, 20,* 51–65.

HERSEN, M., EISLER, R. M., MILLER, P. M., JOHNSON, M. B., & PINKSTON, S. G. (1973). Effects of practice, instructions, and modeling on components of assertive behavior. *Behaviour Research and Therapy, 11,* 443–451.

HERSEN, M., KAZDIN, A. E., BELLACK, A. S., & TURNER, S. M. (1979). Effects of live modeling, covert modeling and rehearsal on assertiveness in psychiatric patients. *Behaviour Research and Therapy, 17,* 369–377.

HERSEN, M., & VAN HASSELT, V. (1992). Behavioral assessment and treatment of anxiety in the elderly. *Clinical Psychology Review, 12,* 619–640.

HESTER, R. K., & DELANEY, H. D. (1997). Behavioral self-control program for Windows: Results of a controlled clinical trial. *Journal of Consulting and Clinical Psychology, 65,* 686–693.

HEWARD, W. L., DARDIG, J. C., & ROSSETT, A. (1979). *Working with parents of handicapped children.* Columbus, OH: Merrill.

Hicks, D. J. (1965). Imitation and retention of film-mediated aggressive peer and adult models. *Journal of Personality and Social Psychology, 2,* 97–100.

Higgins, S. T., Budney, A. J., Bickel, W. K., Foerg, F. E., Donham, R., & Badger, G. J. (1994). Incentives improve outcome in outpatient behavioral treatment of cocaine dependence. *Archives of General Psychiatry, 51,* 568–576.

Higgins, S. T., Budney, A. J., Bickel, W. K., Hughes, J. R., Foerg, F., & Badger, G. (1993). Achieving cocaine abstinence with a behavioral approach. *American Journal of Psychiatry, 150,* 763–769.

Higgins, S. T., Wong, C. J., Badger, G. J., Ogden, D. H., & Dantona, R. (2000). Contingent reinforcement increases cocaine abstinence during outpatient treatment and 1 year of follow-up. *Journal of Consulting and Clinical Psychology, 68,* 64–72.

Hill, P. (1989). Behavioural psychotherapy with children. *International Review of Psychiatry, 1,* 257–266.

Hilliard, R. B. (1993). Single-case methodology in psychotherapy process and outcome research. *Journal of Consulting and Clinical Psychology, 61,* 373–380.

Himadi, B., Osteen, F., & Crawford, E. (1993). Delusional verbalizations and beliefs. *Behavioral Residential Treatment, 8,* 229–242.

Hobfoll, S. E., Jackson, A. P., Lavin, J., Britton, P. J., & Shepherd, J. B. (1994). Reducing inner-city women's AIDS risk activities: A study of single, pregnant women. *Health Psychology, 13,* 397–403.

Hodges, L. F., Rothbaum, B. O., Kooper, R., Opdyke, D., Meyer, T., de Graff, J. J., & Williford, J. S. (1994). *Presence as the defining factor in a VR application: Virtual reality graded exposure in the treatment of acrophobia.* (Tech. Rep. #GIT-GVU-94-6). Atlanta: Georgia Institute of Technology.

Hodgins, D. C., Wynne, H., & Makarchuck, K. (1999). Pathways to recovery from gambling problems: Follow-up from a general population survey. *Journal of Gambling Studies, 15,* 93–104.

Hodgson, R. J., & Rachman, S. (1970). An experimental investigation of the implosive technique. *Behaviour Research and Therapy, 8,* 21–27.

Hoelscher, T. J., Lichstein, K. L., Fischer, S., & Hegarty, T. B. (1987). Relaxation treatment of hypertension: Do home relaxation tapes enhance treatment outcome? *Behavior Therapy, 18,* 33–37.

Hoelscher, T. J., Lichstein, K. L., & Rosenthal, T. L. (1984). Objective vs. subjective assessment of relaxation compliance among anxious individuals. *Behaviour Research and Therapy, 22,* 187–193.

Hogan, R. A. (1968). The implosive technique. *Behaviour Research and Therapy, 6,* 423–432.

Hogan, R. A. (1969). Implosively oriented behavior modification: Therapy considerations. *Behaviour Research and Therapy, 7,* 177–184.

Hogan, R. A., & Kirchner, J. H. (1967). A preliminary report of the extinction of learned fears via a short term implosive therapy. *Journal of Abnormal Psychology, 72,* 106–111.

Holand, J., Plumb, M., Yates, J., Harris, S., Tuttolomondo, A., Holmes, J., & Holland, J. F. (1977). Psychological response of patients with acute leukemia to germ-free environments. *Cancer, 36,* 871–879.

Holden, A. E., & Barlow, D. H. (1986). Heart rate and heart rate variability recorded in vivo in agoraphobics and nonphobics. *Behavior Therapy, 17,* 26–42.

Hollon, S. D., & Beck, A. T. (1986). Research on cognitive therapies. In S. L. Garfield & A. E. Bergin (Eds.), *Handbook of psychotherapy and behavior change* (3rd ed., pp. 443–482). New York: Wiley.

Hollon, S. D., & Beck, A. T. (1994). Cognitive and cognitive behavioral therapies. In A. E. Bergin & S. L. Garfield (Eds.), *Handbook of psychotherapy and behavior change* (4th ed., pp. 428–466). New York: Wiley.

Hollon, S. D., Shelton, R. C., & Davis, D. D. (1993). Cognitive therapy for depression: Conceptual issues and clinical efficacy. *Journal of Consulting and Clinical Psychology, 61,* 270–275.

Hollon, S. D., Shelton, R. C., & Loosen, P. T. (1991). Cognitive therapy and pharmacotherapy for depression. *Journal of Consulting and Clinical Psychology, 59,* 88–99.

Holroyd, K. A. (1976). Cognition and desensitization in the group treatment of test anxiety. *Journal of Consulting and Clinical Psychology, 44,* 991–1001.

Holroyd, K. A., Andrasik, F., & Westbrook, T. (1977). Cognitive control of tension headache. *Cognitive Therapy and Research, 1,* 121–133.

Holroyd, K. A., & Penzien, D. B. (1994). Psychosocial interventions in the management of recurrent headache disorders 1: Overview and effectiveness. *Behavioral Medicine, 20,* 53–63.

Homme, L. E. (1971). *How to use contingency contracting in the classroom.* Champaign, IL: Research Press.

Homme, L. E., C'de Baca, P., Devine, J. V., Steinhorst, R., & Rickert, E. J. (1963). Use of the Premack principle in controlling the behavior of nursery school children. *Journal of the Experimental Analysis of Behavior, 6,* 544.

Honnen, T. J., & Kleinke, C. L. (1990). Prompting bar patrons with signs to take free condoms. *Journal of Applied Behavior Analysis, 23,* 215–217.

Horan, J. J., Hackett, G., Buchanan, J. D., Stone, C. I., & Stone, D. D. (1977). Coping with pain: A component analysis of stress inoculation. *Cognitive Therapy and Research, 1,* 211–221.

Horan, J. J., Hackett, G., Nicholas, W. C., Linberg, S. E., Stone, C. I., & Lukaski, H. C. (1977). Rapid smoking: A cautionary note. *Journal of Consulting and Clinical Psychology, 45,* 341–343.

Horan, J. J., & Johnson, R. G. (1971). Coverant conditioning through a self-management application of the Premack principle: Its effect on weight reduction. *Journal of Behavior Therapy and Experimental Psychiatry, 2,* 243–249.

Horne, A. M., & Matson, J. L. (1977). A comparison of modeling, desensitization, flooding, study skills, and control groups for reducing test anxiety. *Behavior Therapy, 8,* 1–8.

Horner, R. D., & Keilitz, I. (1975). Training mentally retarded adolescents to brush their teeth. *Journal of Applied Behavior Analysis, 8,* 301–309.

Hosford, R. (1974). *Using the self as a model to promote behavioral change.* Paper presented at the meeting of the University of Wisconsin Fourth Annual Symposium in Counseling, Madison.

Hosford, R., & Brown, S. (1975). Innovations in behavioral approaches to counseling. *Focus on Guidance, 8,* 1–11.

Houts, A. C., Berman, J. S., & Abramson, H. (1994). Effectiveness of psychological and pharmacological treatments for nocturnal enuresis. *Journal of Consulting and Clinical Psychology, 62,* 737–745.

Houts, A. C., Peterson, J. K., & Whelan, J. P. (1986). Prevention of relapse in Full-Spectrum Home Training for primary enuresis: A components analysis. *Behavior Therapy, 17,* 462–469.

Hrydowy, E. R., Stokes, T. F., & Martin, G. (1984). Training elementary students to prompt teacher praise. *Education and Treatment of Children, 7,* 99–108.

Huang, W., & Cuvo, A. J. (1997). Social skills training for adults with mental retardation in job-related settings. *Behavior Modification, 21,* 3–44.

Hughes, C., & Rusch, F. R. (1989). Teaching supported employees with severe mental retardation to solve problems. *Journal of Applied Behavior Analysis, 22,* 365–372.

Hummel, R. M., & Gross, A. M. (2001). Socially anxious children: An observational study of parent-child interaction. *Child & Family Behavior Therapy, 23,* 19–42.

Humphreys, L., Forehand, R. [L.], McMahon, R., & Roberts, M. (1978). Parent behavioral training to modify child noncompliance: Effects on untreated siblings. *Journal of Behavior Therapy and Experimental Psychiatry, 9,* 235–238.

Hunt, J. G., Fitzhugh, L. C., & Fitzhugh, K. B. (1968). Teaching "exit-ward" patients appropriate personal appearance by using reinforcement techniques. *American Journal of Mental Deficiency, 73,* 41–45.

Hunt, J. G., & Zimmerman, J. (1969). Stimulating productivity in a simulated sheltered workshop setting. *American Journal of Mental Deficiency, 74,* 43–49.

Hunter, J., & Schaecher, R. (1994). AIDS prevention for lesbian, gay, and bisexual adolescents. (Special Issue: HIV/AIDS). *Families in Society, 75,* 346–354.

Hunter, R. H. (1995). Benefits of competency-based treatment programs. *American Psychologist, 50,* 509–513.

Hutzell, R., Platzek, D., & Logue, P. (1974). Control of Gilles de la Tourette's syndrome by self-monitoring. *Journal of Behavior Therapy and Experimental Psychiatry, 5,* 71–76.

Iguchi, M. Y., Belding, M. A., Morral, A. R., Lamb, R. J., & Husband, S. D. (1997). Reinforcing operants other than abstinence in drug abuse treatment: An effective alternative for reducing drug use. *Journal of Consulting and Clinical Psychology, 65,* 421–428.

Information Please Almanac: Atlas and yearbook, 1990 (43rd ed.). (1989). Boston: Houghton Mifflin.

Ingham, R. J., & Andrews, G. (1973). An analysis of a token economy in stuttering therapy. *Journal of Applied Behavior Analysis, 6,* 219–229.

Irvin, J. E., Bowers, C. A., Dunn, M. E., & Wang, M. C. (1999). Efficacy of relapse prevention: A meta-analytic review. *Journal of Consulting and Clinical Psychology, 67,* 563–570.

Isaacs, W., Thomas, I., & Goldiamond, I. (1960). Application of operant conditioning to reinstate verbal behavior in psychotics. *Journal of Speech and Hearing Disorders, 25,* 8–12.

Israel, A. C., Guile, C. A., Baker, J. E., & Silverman, W. K. (1994). An evaluation of enhanced self-regulation training in the treatment of childhood obesity. *Journal of Pediatric Psychology, 19,* 737–749.

Itard, J. M. G. (1962). *The wild boy of Aveyron.* New York: Appleton-Century-Crofts.

Iwamasa, G. Y. (1996). Introduction to the special series: Ethnic and cultural diversity in cognitive and behavioral practice. *Cognitive and Behavioral Practice, 3,* 209–213.

Iwamasa, G. Y. (1997). Behavior therapy and a culturally diverse society: Forging an alliance. *Behavior Therapy, 28,* 347–358.

Iwamasa, G. Y. (1999). Behavior therapy and cultural diversity: Is there a commitment? *the Behavior Therapist, 22,* 193.

Iwamasa, G. Y., & Smith, S. K. (1996). Ethnic diversity in behavioral psychology. *Behavior Modification, 20,* 45–59.

Iwata, B. A. (1987). Negative reinforcement in applied behavior analysis: An emerging technology. *Journal of Applied Behavior Analysis, 20,* 361–378.

Iwata, B. A. (1994). Functional analysis methodology: Some closing comments. *Journal of Applied Behavior Analysis, 27,* 413–418.

Iwata, B. A., Vollmer, T. R., & Zarcone, J. R. (1990). The experimental (functional) analysis of behavior disorders: Methodology, applications, and limitations. In A. C. Repp & N. N. Singh (Eds.), *Perspectives on the use of nonaversive and aversive interventions for persons with developmental disabilities* (pp. 301–330). Sycamore, IL: Sycamore Publishing.

Iwata, B. A., Wallace, M. D., Kahng, S. W., Lindberg, J. S., Roscoe, E. M., Conners, J., Hanley, G. P., Thompson, R. H., & Worsdell, A. S. (2000). Skill acquisition in the implementation of functional analysis methodology. *Journal of Applied Behavior Analysis, 33,* 181–194.

Jackson, H. J., & Francey, S. M. (1985). The use of hypnotically induced covert modelling in the desensitization of an escalator phobia. *Australian Journal of Clinical and Experimental Hypnosis, 13,* 55–58.

Jacob, R. G., Shapiro, A. P., Reeves, R. A., Johnson, A. M., McDonald, R. H., & Coburn, C. (1986). Relaxation therapy for hypertension: Comparison of effects with concomitant placebo, diuretic and beta-blocker. *Archives of Internal Medicine, 146,* 2335–2340.

Jacob, R. G., Wing, R., & Shapiro, A. P. (1987). The behavioral treatment of hypertension: Long-term effects. *Behavior Therapy, 18,* 325–352.

Jacobs, G. D., Benson, H., & Friedman, R. (1993). Home-based central nervous system assessment of a multifactor behavioral intervention for chronic sleep-onset insomnia. *Behavior Therapy, 24,* 159–174.

Jacobs, G. D., Rosenberg, P. A., Friedman, R., Matheson, J., Peavy, G. M., Domar, A. D., & Benson, H. (1993). Multifactor behavioral treatment of chronic sleep-onset insomnia using stimulus control and the relaxation response: A preliminary study. *Behavior Modification, 17,* 498–509.

Jacobs, M. K., & Cochran, S. D. (1982). The effects of cognitive restructuring on assertive behavior. *Cognitive Therapy and Research, 6,* 63–76.

Jacobson, E. (1929). *Progressive relaxation.* Chicago: University of Chicago Press.

Jacobson, E. (1934). *You must relax.* Chicago: University of Chicago Press.

Jacobson, E. (1939). Variations of blood pressure with skeletal muscle tension and relaxation. *Annals of Internal Medicine, 12,* 1194–1212.

Jacobson, E. (1978). Relaxation technology applied to hypertensives. *Archives fur Arzneitherapie, 2,* 152. Cited in

J. Wolpe (1990), *The practice of behavior therapy* (4th ed.). Elmsford, NY: Pergamon.

JACOBSON, J. W., MULICK, J. A., & SCHWARTZ, A. A. (1995). A history of facilitated communication: Science, pseudoscience, and antiscience. *American Psychologist, 50,* 750–765.

JACOBSON, N. S. (1985). The role of observational measures in behavior therapy outcome research. *Behavioral Assessment, 7,* 297–308.

JACOBSON, N. S. (1988). Defining clinically significant change: An introduction. *Behavior Therapy, 10,* 131–132.

JACOBSON, N. S. (1989). The maintenance of treatment gains following social learning-based marital therapy. *Behavior Therapy, 20,* 325–336.

JACOBSON, N. S. (1991, September). *Marital therapy: Theory and treatment considerations.* Workshop sponsored by the Rhode Island Psychological Association, Warwick, RI.

JACOBSON, N. S. (1992). Behavioral couple therapy: A new beginning. *Behavior Therapy, 23,* 493–506.

JACOBSON, N. S. (1993). Introduction to special section on couples and couple therapy. *Journal of Consulting and Clinical Psychology, 61,* 5.

JACOBSON, N. S., & ADDIS, M. E. (1993). Research on couples and couple therapy: What do we know, where are we going? *Journal of Consulting and Clinical Psychology, 61,* 85–93.

JACOBSON, N. S., & CHRISTENSEN, A. (1996). *Acceptance and change in couple therapy: A therapist's guide to transforming relationships.* New York: Norton.

JACOBSON, N. S., CHRISTENSEN, A., PRINCE, S. E., CORDOVA, J., & ELDRIDGE, K. (2000). Integrative behavioral couple therapy: An acceptance-based, promising new treatment for couple discord. *Journal of Consulting and Clinical Psychology, 68,* 351–355.

JACOBSON, N. S., FOLLETTE, W. C., & REVENSTORF, D. (1984). Psychotherapy outcome research: Methods for reporting variability and evaluating clinical significance. *Behavior Therapy, 15,* 336–352.

JACOBSON, N. S., & MARGOLIN, G. (1979). *Marital therapy: Strategies based on social learning and behavior exchange principles.* New York: Brunner/Mazel.

JAMES, J. E. (1985). Desensitization treatment of agoraphobia. *British Journal of Clinical Psychology, 24,* 133–134.

JAMES, J. E. (1986). Review of the relative efficacy of imaginal and *in vivo* flooding in the treatment of clinical fear. *Behavioural Psychotherapy, 14,* 183–191.

JAMES, L. D., THORN, B. E., & WILLIAMS, D. A. (1993). Goal specification in cognitive-behavioral therapy for chronic headache pain. *Behavior Therapy, 24,* 305–320.

JAMES, S. D., & EGEL, A. L. (1986). A direct prompting strategy for increasing reciprocal interactions between handicapped and nonhandicapped siblings. *Journal of Applied Behavior Analysis, 19,* 173–186.

JANDA, L. H., & RIMM, D. C. (1972). Covert sensitization in the treatment of obesity. *Journal of Abnormal Psychology, 80,* 37–42.

JANNOUN, L., MUNBY, M., CATALAN, J., & GELDER, M. (1980). A home-based treatment program for agoraphobia: Replication and controlled evaluation. *Behavior Therapy, 11,* 294–305.

JANSEN, M. (1987). Women's health issues: An emerging priority for health psychology. In G. C. Stone, S. M. Weiss, J. D. Matarazzo, N. E. Miller, J. Rodin, C. D. Belar, M. J. Follick, & J. E. Singer (Eds.), *Health psychology: A discipline and a profession* (pp. 249–264). Chicago: University of Chicago Press.

JANSSON, L., & ÖST, L. G. (1982). Behavioral treatments for agoraphobia: An evaluation review. *Clinical Psychology Review, 2,* 42–58.

JASON, L. A. (1985). Using a token-actuated timer to reduce television viewing. *Journal of Applied Behavior Analysis, 18,* 269–272.

JASON, L. A., & GLENWICK, D. (1984). Behavioral community psychology: A review of recent research. In M. Hersen, R. M. Eisler, & P. M. Miller (Eds.), *Progress in behavior modification* (Vol. 18, pp. 85–121). New York: Academic Press.

JAY, S. M., & ELLIOTT, C. H. (1990). A stress inoculation program for parents whose children are undergoing painful medical procedures. *Journal of Consulting and Clinical Psychology, 58,* 799–804.

JAY, S. M., ELLIOTT, C. H., KATZ, E., & SIEGEL, E. (1987). Cognitive-behavioral and pharmacologic interventions for children's distress during painful medical procedures. *Journal of Consulting and Clinical Psychology, 55,* 860–865.

JAY, S. M., ELLIOTT, C. H., OZOLINS, M., OLSON, R. A., & PRUITT, S. D. (1985). Behavioral management of children's distress during painful medical procedures. *Behaviour Research and Therapy, 23,* 513–520.

JAYCOX, L. H., REIVICH, K. J., GILLHAM, J., & SELIGMAN, M. E. P. (1994). Prevention of depressive symptoms in school children. *Behaviour Research and Therapy, 32,* 801–816.

JENSEN, B. J., & HAYES, S. N. (1986). Self-report questionnaires and inventories. In A. R. Ciminero, K. S. Calhoun, & H. A. Adams (Eds.), *Handbook of behavioral assessment* (2nd ed., pp. 150–179). New York: Wiley.

JOHNSON, C. M., & LERNER, M. (1985). Amelioration of infant sleep disturbance: II. Effects of scheduled awakenings by compliant parents. *Infant Mental Health Journal, 6,* 21–30.

JOHNSON, S. M., & BOLSTAD, O. D. (1973). Methodological issues in naturalistic observation: Some problems and solutions for field research. In L. A. Hamerlynck, L. C. Handy, & E. J. Mash (Eds.), *Behavior change: Methodology, concepts, and practice.* Champaign, IL: Research Press.

JOHNSON, W. G., CORRIGAN, S. A., & MAYO, L. L. (1987). Innovative treatment approaches to bulimia nervosa. Special issue: Recent advances in behavioral medicine. *Behavior Modification, 11,* 373–388.

JONES, K. M., & FRIMAN, P. C. (1999). A case study of behavioral assessment and treatment of insect phobia. *Journal of Applied Behavior Analysis, 32,* 95–98.

JONES, M. C. (1924). A laboratory study of fear: The case of Peter. *Pedagogical Seminar, 31,* 308–315.

JONES, M. L., EYBERG, S. M., ADAMS, C. D., & BOGGS, S. R. (1998). Treatment acceptability of behavioral interventions for children: An assessment by mothers of children with disruptive behavior disorders. *Child & Family Behavior Therapy, 20,* 15–26.

JONES, R. J., & TIMBERS, G. D. (1983). *Professional parenting for juvenile offenders.* (Final Report, Grant MH15776). Morgantown, NC: BIABH Study Center.

JONES, R. T., KAZDIN, A. E., & HANEY, J. I. (1981). Social validation and training of emergency fire skills for potential injury prevention and life saving. *Journal of Applied Behavior Analysis, 14,* 249–260.

JORGENSEN, R. S., & CAREY, M. P. (1994). Supplementing relaxation training with "aromatherapy": An in-depth comparison of two clients. *Anxiety Disorders Practice Journal, 1,* 59–76.

JOYCE, M. R. (1995). Emotional relief for parents: Is rational-emotive parent education effective? *Journal of Rational-Emotive & Cognitive-Behavior Therapy, 13,* 55–75.

JURGELA, A. R. (1993). The use of covert conditioning to treat self-injurious behavior. In J. R. Cautela & A. J. Kearney (Eds.), *Covert conditioning casebook* (pp. 172–184). Pacific Grove, CA: Brooks/Cole.

KAESTLE, C. F. (Ed.). (1973). *Joseph Lancaster and the monitorial school movement: A documentary history.* New York: Teachers College Press.

KAHLE, A. L., & KELLEY, M. L. (1994). Children's homework problems: A comparison of goal setting and parent training. *Behavior Therapy, 25,* 275–290.

KAHN, J. S., KEHLE, T. J., JENSON, W. R., & CLARK, E. (1990). Comparison of cognitive-behavioral, relaxation, and self-modeling interventions for depression among middle-school students. *School Psychology Review, 19,* 196–211.

KAHNG, S. W., HENDRICKSON, D. J., & VU, C. P. (2000). Comparison of single and multiple functional communication training responses for the treatment of problem behavior. *Journal of Applied Behavior Analysis, 33,* 321–324.

KALAWSKY, R. S. (1993). *The science of virtual reality and virtual environments.* Reading, MA: Addison-Wesley.

KALICHMAN, S. C., CAREY, M. P., & JOHNSON, B. T. (1996). Prevention of sexually transmitted HIV infection: A meta-analytic review of the behavioral outcome literature. *Annals of Behavioral Medicine, 18,* 6–15.

KALICHMAN, S. C., CHERRY, C., & BROWNE-SPERLING, F. (1999). Effectiveness of a video-based motivational skills-building HIV-reduction intervention for inner-city African American men. *Journal of Consulting and Clinical Psychology, 67,* 959–966.

KALICHMAN, S. C., SIKKEMA, K., KELLY, J. A., & BULTO, M. (1995). Use of a brief behavioral skills intervention to prevent HIV infection among chronic mentally ill adults. *Psychiatric Services, 46,* 275–280.

KALLMAN, W. M., HERSEN, M., & O'TOOLE, D. H. (1975). The use of social reinforcement in a case of conversion reaction. *Behavior Therapy, 6,* 411–413.

KALMUSS, D. (1984). The intergenerational transmission of marital aggression. *Journal of Marriage and the Family, 46,* 11–19.

KAMINER, Y., & SHAHAR, A. (1987). The stress inoculation training management of self-mutilating behavior: A case study. *Journal of Behavior Therapy and Experimental Psychiatry, 18,* 289–292.

KANT, G. L., D'ZURILLA, T. J., & MAYDEU-OLIVARES, A. (1997). Social problem solving as a mediator of stress-related depression and anxiety in middle-aged and elderly community residents. *Cognitive Therapy and Research, 21,* 73–96.

KAPLAN, D. A. (1982). Behavioral, cognitive, and behavioral-cognitive approaches to group assertion training therapy. *Cognitive Therapy and Research, 6,* 301–314.

KAPLAN, H. S. (1974). *The new sex therapy: Active treatment of sexual dysfunctions.* New York: Brunner/Mazel.

KAPLAN, H. S. (1975). *The illustrated manual of sex therapy.* New York: Quadrangle.

KAPLAN, N. M. (1983). Mild hypertension: When and how to treat. *Archives of Internal Medicine, 143,* 255–259.

KAPLAN, R. M. (1990). Behavior as the central outcome in health care. *American Psychologist, 45,* 1211–1220.

KASL, S. V. (1975). Issues in patient adherence to health care regimens. *Journal of Human Stress, 1,* 5–17.

KASSIRER, L. B. (1974). Behavior modification for patients and prisoners: Constitutional ramifications of enforced therapy. *Journal of Psychiatry and Law, 2,* 245–302.

KATON, W. J., & WALKER, E. A. (1998). Medically unexplained symptoms in primary care. *Journal of Clinical Psychiatry, 59,* 15–21.

KATZ, E., KELLERMAN, J., & ELLENBERG, L. (1987). Hypnosis in the reduction of acute pain and distress in children with cancer. *Journal of Pediatric Psychology, 12,* 379–394.

KAZDIN, A. E. (1972). Response cost: The removal of conditioned reinforcers for therapeutic change. *Behavior Therapy, 3,* 533–546.

KAZDIN, A. E. (1973). Covert modeling and the reduction of avoidance behavior. *Journal of Abnormal Psychology, 81,* 87–95.

KAZDIN, A. E. (1974a). Comparative effects of some variations of covert modeling. *Journal of Behavior Therapy and Experimental Psychiatry, 5,* 225–231.

KAZDIN, A. E. (1974b). Covert modeling, model similarity, and reduction of avoidance behavior. *Behavior Therapy, 5,* 325–340.

KAZDIN, A. E. (1974c). The effect of model identity and fear-relevant similarity on covert modeling. *Behavior Therapy, 5,* 624–635.

KAZDIN, A. E. (1974d). Effects of covert modeling and model reinforcement on assertive behavior. *Journal of Abnormal Psychology, 83,* 240–252.

KAZDIN, A. E. (1974e). Reactive self-monitoring: The effects of response desirability, goal setting, and feedback. *Journal of Counsulting and Clinical Psychology, 5,* 704–716.

KAZDIN, A. E. (1976). Effects of covert modeling, multiple models, and model reinforcement on assertive behavior. *Behavior Therapy, 7,* 211–222.

KAZDIN, A. E. (1977a). Assessing the clinical or applied importance of behavior change through social validation. *Behavior Modification, 1,* 427–452.

KAZDIN, A. E. (1977b). Extensions of reinforcement techniques to socially and environmentally relevant behaviors. In M. Hersen, R. M. Eisler, & P. M. Miller (Eds.), *Progress in behavior modification* (Vol. 4, pp. 39–67). New York: Academic Press.

KAZDIN, A. E. (1977c). *The token economy: A review and evaluation.* New York: Plenum.

KAZDIN, A. E. (1978). *History of behavior modification: Experimental foundations of contemporary research.* Baltimore: University Park Press.

KAZDIN, A. E. (1979). Vicarious reinforcement and punishment in operant programs for children. *Child Behavior Therapy, 1,* 13–36.

KAZDIN, A. E. (1980). Acceptability of alternative treatments for deviant child behavior. *Journal of Applied Behavior Analysis, 13,* 259–273.

KAZDIN, A. E. (1987). *Conduct disorders in childhood and adolescence.* Newbury Park, CA: Sage.

KAZDIN, A. E. (1989). *Behavior modification in applied settings* (4th ed.). Pacific Grove, CA: Brooks/Cole.

KAZDIN, A. E. (1992). *Research design in clinical psychology* (2nd ed.). Boston: Allyn & Bacon.

KAZDIN, A. E. (1993). Evaluation in clinical practice: Clinically sensitive and systematic methods of treatment delivery. *Behavior Therapy, 24,* 11–45.

KAZDIN, A. E. (1994). *Behavior modification in applied settings* (5th ed.). Pacific Grove, CA: Brooks/Cole.

KAZDIN, A. E. (1999). The meanings and measurement of clinical significance. *Journal of Consulting and Clinical Psychology, 67,* 332–339.

KAZDIN, A. E., ESVELDT-DAWSON, K., FRENCH, N. H., & UNIS, A. S. (1987). Problem-solving skills training and relationship therapy in the treatment of antisocial child behavior. *Journal of Consulting and Clinical Psychology, 55,* 76–85.

KAZDIN, A. E., & GEESEY, S. (1977). Simultaneous-treatment design comparisons of the effects of reinforcers for one's peers versus for oneself. *Behavior Therapy, 8,* 682–693.

KAZDIN, A. E., & MASCITELLI, S. (1982). Behavioral rehearsal, self-instructions, and homework practice in developing assertiveness. *Behavior Therapy, 13,* 346–360.

KAZDIN, A. E., & WILCOXON, L. A. (1976). Systematic desensitization and nonspecific treatment effects: A methodological evaluation. *Psychological Bulletin, 83,* 729–758.

KAZDIN, A. E., & WILSON, G. T. (1978). *Evaluation of behavior therapy: Issues, evidence, and research strategies.* Cambridge, MA: Ballinger.

KEANE, T. M. (1998). Psychological and behavioral treatments of post traumatic stress disorder. In P. Nathan & J. Gorman (Eds.), *Guide to treatments that work* (pp. 398–407). Oxford, UK: Oxford University Press.

KEANE, T. M., FAIRBANK, J. A., CADDELL, J. M., & ZIMERING, R. T. (1989). Implosive (flooding) therapy reduces symptoms of PTSD in Vietnam combat veterans. *Behavior Therapy, 20,* 245–260.

KEANE, T. M., FAIRBANK, J. A., CADDELL, J. M., ZIMERING, R. T., & BENDER, M. E. (1985). A behavioral approach to assessing and treating post-traumatic stress disorder in Vietnam veterans. In C. R. Figley (Ed.), *Trauma and its wake* (pp. 257–294). New York: Brunner/Mazel.

KEARNEY, A. B. (1993). The use of covert conditioning in the treatment of obsessive compulsive disorder. In J. R. Cautela & A. J. Kearney (Eds.), *Covert conditioning casebook* (pp. 22–37). Pacific Grove, CA: Brooks/Cole.

KEARNEY, A. J. (1993). The use of covert conditioning in a hypnotic context to treat anticipatory anxiety and postoperative pain. In J. R. Cautela & A. J. Kearney (Eds.), *Covert conditioning casebook* (pp. 99–107). Pacific Grove, CA: Brooks/Cole.

KEARNEY, C. A., & SILVERMAN, W. K. (1999). Functionally based prescriptive and nonprescriptive treatment for children and adolescents with school refusal behavior. *Behavior Therapy, 30,* 673–695.

KEENEY, K. M., FISHER, W. W., ADELINIS, J. D., & WILDER, D. A. (2000). The effects of response cost in the treatment of aberrant behavior maintained by negative reinforcement. *Journal of Applied Behavior Analysis, 33,* 225–258.

KEHLE, T. J., CLARK, E., JENSON, W. R., & WAMPOLD, B. E. (1986). Effectiveness of self-observation with behavior disordered elementary school children. *School Psychology Review, 15,* 289–295.

KEHLE, T. J., MADAUS, R., BARATTA, V. S., & BRAY, M. A. (1998). Augmented self-modeling as a treatment for children with selective mutism. *Journal of School Psychology, 36,* 247–260.

KEHLE, T. J., OWEN, S. V., & CRESSY, E. T. (1990). The use of self-modeling as an intervention in school psychology: A case study of an elective mute. *School Psychology Review, 19,* 115–121.

KEIJSERS, G. P. J., SCHAAP, C. P. D. R., & HOOGDUIN, C. A. L. (2000). The impact of interpersonal patient and therapist behavior on outcome in cognitive-behavior therapy. *Behavior Modification, 24,* 264–297.

KELLAM, A. M. P. (1969). Shop lifting treated by aversion to a film. *Behaviour Research and Therapy, 7,* 125–127.

KELLER, F. S. (1968). "Good-bye, teacher . . . ." *Journal of Applied Behavior Analysis, 1,* 79–89.

KELLER, M. B., HERZOG, D. B., LAVORI, P. W., BRADBURN, I. S., & MAHONEY, E. M. (1992). The naturalistic history of bulimia nervosa: Extraordinary high rates of chronicity, relapse, recurrence, and psychosocial morbidity. *International Journal of Eating Disorders, 12,* 1–9.

KELLEY, M. L. (1990). *School-home notes: Promoting children's classroom success.* New York: Guilford.

KELLY, G. A. (1955). *The psychology of personal constructs.* New York: Norton.

KELLY, J. A., & MURPHY, D. A. (1992). Psychological interventions with AIDS and HIV: Prevention and treatment. *Journal of Consulting and Clinical Psychology, 60,* 576–585.

KELLY, J. A., MURPHY, D. [A.], WASHINGTON, C., WILSON, T., KOOB, J., DAVIS, D., LEPEZMA, G., & DAVANTES, B. (1994). Effects of HIV/AIDS prevention groups for high-risk women in urban primary health care clinics. *American Journal of Public Health, 84,* 1918–1922.

KELLY, J. A., & ST. LAWRENCE, J. [S.] (1987). The prevention of AIDS: Roles for behavioral intervention. *Scandinavian Journal of Behaviour Therapy, 16,* 5–19.

KELLY, J. A., & ST. LAWRENCE, J. S. (1988a). *The AIDS health crisis: Psychological and social intervention.* New York: Plenum.

KELLY, J. A., & ST. LAWRENCE, J. S. (1988b). AIDS prevention and treatment: Psychology's role in the health crisis. *Clinical Psychology Review, 8,* 255–284.

KELLY, J. A., & ST. LAWRENCE, J. S. (1990). The impact of community-based groups to help persons reduce HIV infection risk behaviours. *AIDS-Care, 2,* 25–36.

KELLY, J. A., ST. LAWRENCE, J. S., HOOD, H. V., & BRASFIELD, T. L. (1989). Behavioral intervention to reduce AIDS risk activities. *Journal of Consulting and Clinical Psychology, 57,* 60–67.

KENDALL, P. C. (1987a). Behavioral assessment and methodology. In G. T. Wilson, C. M. Franks, P. C. Kendall, & J. P. Foreyt (Eds.), *Review of behavior therapy: Theory and practice* (Vol. 11, pp. 40–83). New York: Guilford.

KENDALL, P. C. (1987b). Cognitive processes and procedures in behavior therapy. In G. T. Wilson, C. M. Franks, P. C. Kendall, & J. P. Foreyt (Eds.), *Review of behavior therapy: Theory and practice* (Vol. 11, pp. 114–153). New York: Guilford.

KENDALL, P. C. (1989). The generalization and maintenance of behavior change: Comments, considerations, and the "no-cure" criticism. *Behavior Therapy, 20,* 357–364.

KENDALL, P. C. (1993). Cognitive-behavioral therapies with youth: Guiding theory, current status, and emerging developments. *Journal of Consulting and Clinical Psychology, 61,* 235–247.

KENDALL, P. C. (1994). Treating anxiety disorders in children: Results of a randomized clinical trial. *Journal of Consulting and Clinical Psychology, 62,* 100–110.

KENDALL, P. C. (1998). Empirically supported psychological therapies. *Journal of Consulting and Clinical Psychology, 66,* 3–6.

KENDALL, P. C. (2000). *Child & adolescent therapy: Cognitive-behavioral procedures* (2nd ed.). New York: Guilford.

KENDALL, P. C., & BRASWELL, L. (1985). *Cognitive-behavioral therapy for impulsive children.* New York: Guilford.

KENDALL, P. C., & CHAMBLESS, D. L. (Eds.). (1998). Empirically supported psychological therapies. (Special Section). *Journal of Consulting and Clinical Psychology, 66*(1), 3–161.

KENDALL, P. C., CHU, B., PIMENTEL, S., & CHOUDHURY, M. (2000). Treating anxiety disorders in youth. In P. C. Kendall (Ed.), *Child and adolescent therapy: Cognitive-behavioral procedures* (2nd ed., pp. 235–287). New York: Guilford.

KENDALL, P. C., & FINCH, A. J. (1978). A cognitive-behavioral treatment for impulsivity: A group comparison study. *Journal of Consulting and Clinical Psychology, 46,* 110–118.

KENDALL, P. C., & GEROW, M. A. (1995). *Long-term follow-up of a cognitive-behavioral therapy for anxiety-disordered youth.* Unpublished manuscript.

KENDALL, P. C., HAAGA, D. A. F., ELLIS, A., BERNARD, M., DiGIUSEPPE, R. [A.], & KASSINOVE, H. (1995). Rational-emotive therapy in the 1990s and beyond: Current status, recent revisions, and research questions. *Clinical Psychology Review, 15,* 169–185.

KENDALL, P. C., NAY, W. R., & JEFFERS, J. (1975). Timeout duration and contrast effects: A systematic evaluation of a successive treatments design. *Behavior Therapy, 6,* 609–615.

KENDALL, P. C., & NORTON-FORD, J. D. (1982). Therapy outcome research methods. In P. C. Kendall & J. N. Butcher (Eds.), *Handbook of research methods in clinical psychology* (pp. 429–460). New York: Wiley.

KENDALL, P. C., & WILCOX, L. E. (1980). Cognitive-behavioral treatment for impulsivity: Concrete versus conceptual training in non-self-controlled problem children. *Journal of Consulting and Clinical Psychology, 48,* 80–91.

KENNEDY, C. H., & ITKONEN, T. (1993). Effects of setting events on the problem behavior of students with severe disabilities. *Journal of Applied Behavior Analysis, 26,* 321–327.

KENNEDY, C. H., & MEYER, K. A. (1998). Establishing operations and the motivation of challenging behavior. In J. K. Luiselli & M. J. Cameron (Eds.), *Antecedent control* (pp. 329–346). Baltimore: Brookes.

KENNEDY, S. H., KATZ, R., NEITZERT, C. S., RALEVSKI, E., & MENDLOWITZ, S. (1995). Exposure with response prevention treatment of anorexia nervosa-bulimic subtype and bulimia nervosa. *Behaviour Research and Therapy, 33,* 685–689.

KENNY, F. T., MOWBRAY, R. M., & LALANI, S. (1978). Faradic disruption of obsessive ideation in the treatment of obsessive neurosis. *Behavior Therapy, 9,* 209–221.

KENT, R. N., & FOSTER, S. (1977). Direct observational procedures: Methodological issues in naturalistic settings. In A. R. Ciminero, K. S. Calhoun, & H. E. Adams (Eds.), *Handbook of behavioral assessment* (pp. 279–328). New York: Wiley.

KEOGH, D. A., FAW, G. D., WHITMAN, T. L., & REID, D. H. (1984). Enhancing leisure skills in severely retarded adolescents through a self-instructional treatment package. *Analysis and Intervention in Developmental Disabilities, 4,* 333–351.

KERN, J. M. (1982). Predicting the impact of assertive, empathic-assertive, and nonassertive behavior: The assertiveness of the assertee. *Behavior Therapy, 13,* 486–498.

KERN, J. M., CAVELL, T. A., & BECK, B. (1985). Predicting differential reactions to males' versus females' assertions, empathic-assertions, and nonassertions. *Behavior Therapy, 16,* 63–75.

KERN, L., & DUNLAP, G. (1998). Curricular modifications to promote desirable classroom behavior. In J. K. Luiselli & M. J. Cameron (Eds.), *Antecedent control* (pp. 289–307). Baltimore: Brookes.

KERNS, R. D., TURK, D. C., HOLZMAN, A. D., & RUDY, T. E. (1986). Comparison of cognitive-behavioral and behavioral approaches to outpatient treatment of chronic pain. *Clinical Journal of Pain, 1,* 195–203.

KETTLEWELL, P. W., MIZES, J. S., & WASYLYSHYN, N. A. (1992). A cognitive-behavioral group treatment of bulimia. *Behavior Therapy, 23,* 657–670.

KIDD, A. H., & EUPHRAT, J. L. (1971). Why prospective outpatients fail to make or keep appointments. *Journal of Clinical Psychology, 27,* 94–95.

KILPATRICK, D. G., & BEST, C. L. (1984). Some cautionary remarks on treating sexual assault victims with implosion. *Behavior Therapy, 15,* 421–423.

KIMMEL, H. D., & KIMMEL, E. (1970). An instrumental conditioning method for treatment of enuresis. *Journal of Behavior Therapy and Experimental Psychiatry, 1,* 121–124.

KING, N. J., DUDLEY, A., MELVIN, G., PALLANT, J., & MORAWETZ, D. (2001). Empirically supported treatments for insomnia. (Special Issue). *Scandinavian Journal of Behaviour Therapy, 30,* 23–32.

KING, N. J., OLLENDICK, T. H., MURPHY, G. C., & TIBGE, B. (1997). Behavioural assessment of childhood phobias: A multi-method approach. *Scandinavian Journal of Behaviour Therapy, 26,* 3–10.

KING, N. J., TONGE, B. J., HEYNE, D., PRITCHARD, M., ROLLINGS, S., YOUNG, D., MYERSON, N., & OLLENDICK, T. H. (1998). Cognitive-behavioral treatment of school-refusing children: A controlled evaluation. *Journal of the Academy of Child and Adolescent Psychiatry, 37,* 395–403.

KIRBY, K. C., FOWLER, S. A., & BEAR, D. M. (1991). Reactivity in self-recording: Obtrusiveness of recording procedure and peer comments. *Journal of Applied Behavior Analysis, 24,* 487–498.

KIRBY, K. C., MARLOWE, D. B., CARRIGAN, D. R., & PLATT, J. J. (1998). Counselor prompts to increase condom taking during treatment for cocaine dependence. *Behavior Modification, 22,* 29–44.

KIRIGIN, K. A., BRAUKMANN, C. J., ATWATER, J., & WOLF, M. M. (1982). An evaluation of Achievement Place (Teaching-Family) group homes for juvenile offenders. *Journal of Applied Behavior Analysis, 15,* 1–16.

KIRKLAND, K., & HOLLANDSWORTH, J. G. (1980). Effective test taking: Skills-acquisition versus anxiety-reduction technique. *Journal of Consulting and Clinical Psychology, 48,* 431–439.

KIRKLEY, B. G., SCHNEIDER, J. A., AGRAS, W. S., & BACHMAN, J. A. (1985). Comparison of two group treatments for bulimia. *Journal of Consulting and Clinical Psychology, 53,* 43–48.

KITFIELD, E. B., & MASALSKY, C. J. (2000). Negative reinforcement-based treatment to increase food intake. *Behavior Modification, 24,* 600–608.

KLEINER, L., MARSHALL, W. L., & SPEVACK, M. (1987). Training in problem solving and exposure treatment for agoraphobic with panic attacks. *Journal of Anxiety Disorders, 1,* 219–238.

KLEINKNECHT, R. A. (1993). Rapid treatment of blood and injection phobias with eye movement desensitization. *Journal of Behavior Therapy and Experimental Psychiatry, 24,* 211–217.

KLEINKNECHT, R. A., & BERNSTEIN, D. A. (1979). Short term treatment of dental avoidance. *Journal of Behavior Therapy and Experimental Psychiatry, 10,* 311–315.

KLEINKNECHT, R. A., & MORGAN, M. P. (1992). Treatment of posttraumatic stress disorder with eye movement desensitization and reprocessing. *Journal of Behavior Therapy and Experimental Psychiatry, 23,* 43–49.

KLESGES, R. C., MALOTT, J. M., & UGLAND, M. (1984). The effects of graded exposure and parental modeling on the dental phobias of a four-year-old girl and her mother. *Journal of Behavior Therapy and Experimental Psychiatry, 15,* 161–164.

KLINGMAN, A., MELAMED, B. G., CUTHBERT, M. I., & HERMECZ, D. A. (1984). Effects of participant modeling on information acquisition and skill utilization. *Journal of Consulting and Clinical Psychology, 52,* 414–422.

KLORMAN, R., HILPERT, P. L., MICHAEL, R., LAGANA, C., & SVEEN, O. B. (1980). Effects of coping and mastery modeling on experienced and inexperienced pedodontic patients' disruptiveness. *Behavior Therapy, 11,* 156–168.

KNAPCZYK, D. R., & LIVINGSTON, G. (1973). Self-recording and student teacher supervision: Variables within a token economy structure. *Journal of Applied Behavior Analysis, 6,* 481–486.

KNAUS, W. [J.] (1974). *Rational-emotive education: A manual for elementary school teachers.* New York: Institute for Rational Living.

KNAUS, W. J. (1985). Student burnout: A rational-emotive education treatment approach. In A. Ellis & M. Bernard (Eds.), *Clinical applications of rational-emotive therapy* (pp. 257–276). New York: Plenum.

KNAUS, W. [J.], & EYMAN, W. (1974). Progress in rational-emotive education. *Rational Living, 9,* 27–29.

KNAUS, W. J., & HABERSTROH, N. (1993). A rational-emotive education program to help disruptive mentally retarded clients develop self-control. In W. Dryden & L. K. Hill (Eds.), *Innovations in rational-emotive therapy* (pp. 201–217). Newbury Park, CA: Sage.

KNAUS, W. [J.], & MCKEEVER, C. (1977). Rational-emotive education with learning disabled children. *Journal of Learning Disabilities, 10,* 10–14.

KNAUS, W. [J.], & WESSLER, R. (1976). Rational-emotive problem simulation. *Rational Living, 11,* 8–11.

KNIGHT, M. F., & MCKENZIE, H. S. (1974). Elimination of bedtime thumbsucking in home settings through contingent reading. *Journal of Applied Behavior Analysis, 7,* 33–38.

KOEGEL, L. K., STIEBEL, D., & KOEGEL, R. L. (1998). Reducing aggression in children with autism toward infant or toddler siblings. *Journal of the Association for Persons with Severe Handicaps, 23,* 111–118.

KOHLENBERG, R. J., & TSAI, M. (1991). *Functional analytic psychotherapy: Creating intense and curative therapeutic relationships.* New York: Plenum.

KOHLENBERG, R. J., & TSAI, M. (1994). Functional analytic psychotherapy: A radical behavioral approach to treatment and integration. *Journal of Psychotherapy Integration, 4,* 175–201.

KOHLENBERG, R. J., & TSAI, M. (1995). Functional analytic psychotherapy: A behavioral approach to intensive treatment. In W. T. O'Donohue & L. Krasner (Eds.), *Theories of behavior therapy: Exploring behavior change* (pp. 637–658). Washington, DC: American Psychological Association.

KOKOSZKA, A., POPIEL, A., & SITARZ, M. (2000). Cognitive-behavioral therapy in Poland. *the Behavior Therapist, 23,* 209–216.

KOLE-SNIJDERES, A. M. K., VLAEYEN, J. W. S., RUTTEN-VAN MOLKEN, M. P. M. H., HEUTS, P. H. T. G., VAN EEK, H., & VAN BREUKELEN, G. (1999). Chronic low-back pain: What does cognitive coping skills training add to operant behavioral treatment? Results of a randomized clinical trial. *Journal of Consulting and Clinical Psychology, 67,* 931–944.

KOPEC, A. M., BEAL, D., & DIGIUSEPPE, R. [A.] (1994). Training in RET: Disputational strategies. *Journal of Rational-Emotive & Cognitive-Behavior Therapy, 12,* 47–60.

KORNFELD, A. D. (1989). Mary Cover Jones and the Peter case: Social learning versus conditioning. *Journal of Anxiety Disorders, 3,* 187–195.

KORNHABER, R. C., & SCHROEDER, H. E. (1975). Importance of model similarity on extinction of avoidance behavior in children. *Journal of Consulting and Clinical Psychology, 43,* 601–607.

KOZAK, M. J., FOA, E. B., & STEKETEE, G. (1988). Process and outcome of exposure treatment with obsessive-compulsives: Psychophysiological indicators of emotional processing. *Behavior Therapy, 19,* 157–169.

KRAKAUER, J. (1995, October). Loving them to death. *Outside, 20,* pp. 72–80, 82, 142–143.

KRAMER, F. M., & STALKER, L. A. (1989). Treatment of obesity. In A. Freeman, K. M. Simon, L. E. Beutler, & H. Arkowitz (Eds.), *Comprehensive handbook of cognitive therapy* (pp. 385–401). New York: Plenum.

KRANTZ, P. J., & MCCLANNAHAN, L. E. (1998). Social interaction skills for children with autism: A script-fading procedure for beginning readers. *Journal of Applied Behavior Analysis, 31,* 191–202.

KRAPFL, J. E. (1967). *Differential ordering of stimulus presentation and semi-automated versus live treatment in the systematic desensitization of snake phobia.* Unpublished doctoral dissertation, University of Missouri.

KRASNER, L. (1976). Behavior modification: Ethical issues and future trends. In H. Leitenberg (Ed.), *Handbook of behavior modification and behavior therapy* (pp. 627–649). Englewood Cliffs, NJ: Prentice Hall.

KRISTT, D. A., & ENGEL, B. T. (1975). Learned control of blood pressure in patients with high blood pressure. *Circulation, 51,* 370–378.

KROENKE, K., & MANGELSDORF, A. D. (1989). Common symptoms in ambulatory care: Incidence, evaluation, therapy, and outcome. *American Journal of Medicine, 86,* 262–266.

KROP, H., & BURGESS, D. (1993a). Use of covert conditioning to treat excessive masturbation. In J. R. Cautela & A. J. Kearney (Eds.), *Covert conditioning casebook* (pp. 208–216). Pacific Grove, CA: Brooks/Cole.

KROP, H., & BURGESS, D. (1993b). The use of covert modeling in the treatment of a sexual abuse victim. In J. R. Cautela & A. J. Kearney (Eds.), *Covert conditioning casebook* (pp. 153–158). Pacific Grove, CA: Brooks/Cole.

KUTCHINS, H., & KIRK, S. A. (1995). Should DSM be the basis for teaching social work practice in mental health? No! *Journal of Social Work Education, 31,* 159–168.

LABERGE, B., GAUTHIER, J. G., COTE, G., PLAMONDON, J., & CORMIER, H. J. (1993). Cognitive-behavioral therapy of panic disorder with secondary major depression: A preliminary investigation. *Journal of Consulting and Clinical Psychology, 61,* 1028–1037.

LABOUVIE-VIEF, G., & GONDA, J. (1976). Cognitive strategy training and intellectual performance in the elderly. *Journal of Gerontology, 31,* 327–332.

LACKS, P., BERTELSON, A. D., GANS, L., & KUNKEL, J. (1983). The effectiveness of three behavioral treatments for different degrees of sleep-onset insomnia. *Behavior Therapy, 14,* 593–605.

LACKS, P., & MORIN, C. M. (1992). Recent advances in the assessment and treatment of insomnia. *Journal of Consulting and Clinical Psychology, 60,* 586–594.

LADOUCEUR, R. (1983). Participant modeling with or without cognitive treatment for phobias. *Journal of Consulting and Clinical Psychology, 51,* 942–944.

LAGGES, A. M., & GORDON, D. A. (1999). Use of an interactive laserdisc parent training program with teenage parents. *Child & Family Behavior Therapy, 21,* 19–35.

LAGRECA, A. M. (1988). Adherence to prescribed medical regimens. In D. K. Routh (Ed.), *Handbook of pediatric psychology* (pp. 299–320). New York: Guilford.

LAGRECA, A. M., & OTTINGER, D. R. (1979). Self-monitoring and relaxation training in the treatment of medically ordered exercise in a 12-year-old female. *Journal of Pediatric Psychology, 4,* 49–54.

LAHEY, B. B., & DRABMAN, R. S. (1974). Facilitation of the acquisition and retention of sight word vocabulary through token reinforcement. *Journal of Applied Behavior Analysis, 7,* 307–312.

LAHEY, B. B., MCNEES, M. P., & MCNEES, M. C. (1973). Control of an obscene "verbal tic" through time out in an elementary classroom. *Journal of Applied Behavior Analysis, 6,* 101–104.

LAKE, A. E., & PINGEL, J. D. (1988). Brief versus extended relaxation: Relationship to improvement at follow-up in mixed headache patients. *Medical Psychotherapy, 1,* 119–129.

LALLO, J. S., CASEY, S. D., & KATES, K. (1997). Noncontingent reinforcement as a treatment for severe problem behavior: Some procedural variations. *Journal of Applied Behavior Analysis, 30,* 127–137.

LAM, D. H., BRIGHT, J., JONES, S., HAYWARD, P., SCHUCK, N., CHISHOLM, D., & SHAM, P. (2000). Cognitive therapy for bipolar illness—A pilot study of relapse prevention. *Cognitive Therapy and Research, 24,* 503–520.

LAMAZE, F. (1970). *Painless childbirth.* Chicago: Henry Regery.

LAMONTAGNE, Y., & MARKS, I. M. (1973). Psychogenic urinary retention: Treatment of prolonged exposure. *Behavior Therapy, 4,* 581–585.

LANCASTER, J. (1805). *Improvements in education, as it respects the industrious classes of the community* (3rd ed.). London: Darton and Harvey.

LANDERS, S. (1990, March). Phobias: A stepchild garners new respect. *APA Monitor, 21,* 18.

LANDO, H. A. (1975). A comparison of excessive and rapid smoking in the modification of chronic smoking behavior. *Journal of Consulting and Clinical Psychology, 43,* 350–355.

LANDRINE, H., & KLONOFF, E. (1995). Cultural diversity and the silence of behavior therapy. *the Behavior Therapist, 18,* 187–189.

LANG, P. J. (1969). The mechanics of desensitization and the laboratory study of fear. In C. M. Franks (Ed.), *Behavior therapy: Appraisal and status* (pp. 160–191). New York: McGraw-Hill.

LANG, P. J., MELAMED, B. G., & HART, J. A. (1970). A psychophysiological analysis of fear modification using an automated desensitization procedure. *Journal of Abnormal Psychology, 76,* 220–234.

LARSON, K., & AYLLON, T. (1990). The effects of contingent music and differential reinforcement on infantile colic. *Behaviour Research and Therapy, 28,* 119–125.

LARSSON, B., & ANDRASIK, F. (2002). Relaxation treatment of recurrent headaches in children and adolescents. In V. Guidetti, G. Russell, M. Sillanpaa, & P. Winner (Eds.), *Headache and migraine in childhood and adolescence* (pp. 307–316). London: Martin Dunitz.

LASCELLES, M., CUNNINGHAM, S., MCGRATH, P., & SULLIVAN, M. (1989). Teaching coping skills to adolescents with migraine. *Journal of Pain and Symptom Management, 4,* 135–145.

LATNER, J. D., & WILSON, G. T. (2000). Cognitive-behavioral therapy and nutritional counseling in the treatment of bulimia nervosa and binge eating. *Eating Behaviors, 1,* 3–21.

LAUTERBACH, W. (1999). Cognitive behavior therapy in the Russian society. *the Behavior Therapist, 22,* 16.

LAVIGNA, G. W., & DONNELLAN, A. M. (1986). *Alternatives to punishment: Solving behavior problems with non-aversive strategies.* New York: Irvington.

LAVIN, N. I., THORPE, J. G., BARKER, J. C., BLAKEMORE, C. B., & CONWAY, C. G. (1961). Behaviour therapy in a case of transvestism. *Journal of Nervous and Mental Disease, 133,* 346–353.

LAWSON, D. M., & MAY, R. B. (1970). Three procedures for the extinction of smoking behavior. *Psychological Record, 20,* 151–157.

LAWTON, C., FRANCE, K. G., & BLAMPIED, N. M. (1991). Treatment of infant sleep disturbance by graduated extinction. *Child & Family Behavior Therapy, 13,* 39–56.

LAZARUS, A. A. (1959). The elimination of children's phobias by deconditioning. *Medical Proceedings, 5,* 261–265.

LAZARUS, A. A. (1961). Group therapy of phobic disorders by systematic desensitization. *Journal of Abnormal and Social Psychology, 63,* 505–510.

LAZARUS, A. A. (1966). Broad-spectrum behaviour therapy and the treatment of agoraphobia. *Behaviour Research and Therapy, 4,* 95–97.

LAZARUS, A. A. (1967). In support of technical eclecticism. *Psychological Reports, 21,* 415–416.

LAZARUS, A. A. (1971). *Behavior therapy and beyond.* New York: McGraw-Hill.

LAZARUS, A. A. (1973). On assertive behavior: A brief note. *Behavior Therapy, 4,* 697–699.

LAZARUS, A. A. (1976). *Multimodal behavior therapy.* New York: Springer.

LAZARUS, A. A. (Ed.). (1985). *Casebook of multimodal therapy.* New York: Guilford.

LAZARUS, A. A. (1989a). *The practice of multimodal therapy.* Baltimore: Johns Hopkins University Press.

LAZARUS, A. A. (1989b). The practice of rational-emotive therapy. In M. E. Bernard & R. [A.] DiGiuseppe (Eds.), *Inside rational-emotive therapy: A critical appraisal of the theory and therapy of Albert Ellis* (pp. 95–112). San Diego: Academic Press.

LAZARUS, A. A. (1989c). Why I am an eclectic (not an integrationist). *The British Journal of Guidance and Counselling, 17,* 248–258.

LAZARUS, A. A. (1995). Different types of eclecticism and integration: Let's be aware of the dangers. *Journal of Psychotherapy Integration, 5,* 27–39.

LAZARUS, A. A., & ABRAMOVITZ, A. (1962). The use of "emotive imagery" in the treatment of children's phobias. *Journal of Mental Science, 108,* 191–195.

LAZARUS, A. A., & BEUTLER, L. E. (1993). On technical eclecticism. *Journal of Counseling and Development, 71,* 381–385.

LAZARUS, A. A., DAVISON, G. C., & POLEFKA, D. A. (1965). Classical and operant factors in the treatment of a school phobia. *Journal of Abnormal Psychology, 70,* 225–229.

LAZARUS, R. S., & FOLKMAN, S. (1984). *Stress, appraisal, and coping.* New York: Springer.

LEDWIDGE, B. (1978). Cognitive behavior modification: A step in the wrong direction? *Psychological Bulletin, 85,* 353–375.

LEDWIDGE, B. (1979). Cognitive behavior modification: A rejoinder. *Cognitive Therapy and Research, 3,* 133–140.

LEE, E. S. (1951). Negro intelligence and selective migration: A Philadelphia test of the Klineberg hypothesis. *American Review, 16,* 227–232.

LEE, N. K., & OEI, T. P. S. (1993). Exposure and response prevention in anxiety disorders: Implications for treatment and relapse prevention in problem drinkers. *Clinical Psychology Review, 13,* 619–632.

LEHRER, P. M. (1982). How to relax and how not to relax: A reevaluation of the work of Edmund Jacobson—I. *Behaviour Research and Therapy, 20,* 417–428.

LEITENBERG, H. (1976). Behavioral approaches to treatment of neuroses. In H. Leitenberg (Ed.), *Handbook of behavior modification and behavior therapy* (pp. 124–167). Englewood Cliffs, NJ: Prentice Hall.

LEITENBERG, H. (1993). Treatment of bulimia nervosa. In T. R. Giles (Ed.), *Handbook of effective psychotherapy* (pp. 279–302). New York: Plenum.

LEITENBERG, H., BURCHARD, D., BURCHARD, N., FULLER, E. J., & LYSAGHT, T. V. (1977). Using positive reinforcement to suppress behavior: Some experimental comparisons with sibling conflict. *Behavior Therapy, 8,* 168–182.

LEITENBERG, H., GROSS, J., PETERSON, J., & ROSEN, J. C. (1984). Analysis of an anxiety model in the process of change during exposure plus response prevention treatment of bulimia nervosa. *Behavior Therapy, 15,* 3–20.

LEITENBERG, H., & ROSEN, J. C. (1988). Cognitive-behavioral treatment of bulimia nervosa. In M. Hersen, R. M. Eisler, & P. M. Miller (Eds.), *Progress in behavior modification* (Vol. 23, pp. 11–32). Newbury Park, CA: Sage.

LEITENBERG, H., ROSEN, J. C., WOLF, J., VARA, L. S., DETZER, M. J., & SREBNIK, D. (1994). Comparison of cognitive-behavior therapy and desipramine in the treatment of bulimia nervosa. *Behaviour Research and Therapy, 32,* 37–45.

LEMSKY, C. M. (1996). Adapting behavioral interventions for brain injured older adults. *the Behavior Therapist, 19,* 9–12.

LENNOX, D. B., MILTENBERGER, R. G., & DONNELLY, D. R. (1987). Response interruption and DRL for the reduction of rapid eating. *Journal of Applied Behavior Analysis, 20,* 279–284.

LERMAN, D. C., & IWATA, B. A. (1995). Prevalence of the extinction burst and its attenuation during treatment. *Journal of Applied Behavior Analysis, 28,* 93–94.

LERMAN, D. C., & IWATA, B. A. (1996). Developing a technology for the use of operant extinction in clinical settings: An examination of basic and applied research. *Journal of Applied Behavior Analysis, 29,* 345–382.

LERMAN, D. C., IWATA, B. A., & WALLACE, M. D. (1999). Side effects of extinction: Prevalence of bursting and aggression during the treatment of self-injurious behavior. *Journal of Applied Behavior Analysis, 32,* 1–8.

LERNER, J., FRANKLIN, M. E., MEADOWS, E. A., HEMBREE, E., & FOA, E. B. (1998). Effectiveness of a cognitive-behavioral treatment program for trichotillomania: An uncontrolled evaluation. *Behavior Therapy, 29,* 157–171.

LESTER, D. (1987). Indirect evidence for effects of suggestion in suicide: A critical mass hypothesis. *Psychological Reports, 61,* 576.

LEUNG, N., WALLER, G., & THOMAS, G. (2000). Outcome of group cognitive-behavioral therapy for bulimia nervosa: The role of core beliefs. *Behaviour Research and Therapy, 38,* 145–156.

LEVIN, R. B., & GROSS, A. M. (1984). Reactions to assertive versus nonassertive behavior. *Behavior Modification, 8,* 581–592.

LEVIS, D. J. (1980). Implementing the technique of implosive therapy. In A. Goldstein & E. B. Foa (Eds.), *Handbook of behavioral interventions: A clinical guide* (pp. 92–151). New York: Wiley.

LEVIS, D. J. (1988). Observations and experience from clinical practice: A critical ingredient for advancing behavioral theory and therapy. *the Behavior Therapist, 11,* 95–99.

LEVIS, D. J. (1993). The power of extrapolating basic laboratory principles: The behavioural-cognitive approach of implosive therapy. *Behaviour Change, 10,* 154–161.

LEVIS, D. J., & CARRERA, R. N. (1967). Effects of 10 hours of implosive therapy in the treatment of outpatients: A preliminary report. *Journal of Abnormal Psychology, 72,* 504–508.

LEVIS, D. J., & HARE, N. (1977). A review of the theoretical rationale and empirical support for the extinction approach of implosive (flooding) therapy. In M. Hersen, R. M. Eisler, & P. M. Miller (Eds.), *Progress in behavior modification* (Vol. 2, pp. 300–376). New York: Academic Press.

LEVIS, D. J., & MALLOY, P. F. (1982). Research in infrahuman and human conditioning. In G. T. Wilson & C. M. Franks (Eds.), *Contemporary behavior therapy: Conceptual and empirical foundations* (pp. 65–118). New York: Guilford.

LEVITT, E. E. (1957). The results of psychotherapy with children: An evaluation. *Journal of Consulting Psychology, 21,* 189–196.

LEVITT, E. E. (1963). Psychotherapy with children: A further evaluation. *Behaviour Research and Therapy, 1,* 45–51.

LEWINSOHN, P. M., CLARKE, G. N., & ROHDE, P. (1994). Psychological approaches to the treatment of depression in adolescents. In W. M. Reynolds & H. F. Johnston (Eds.), *Handbook of depression in children and adolescents* (pp. 309–344). New York: Plenum.

LEWINSOHN, P. M., & ROHDE, P. (1993). The cognitive-behavioral treatment of depression in adolescents: Research and suggestions. *The Clinical Psychologist, 46,* 177–183.

LIBB, J. W., & CLEMENTS, C. B. (1969). Token reinforcement in an exercise program for hospitalized geriatric patients. *Perceptual and Motor Skills, 28,* 957–958.

LIBERMAN, R. P., KOPELOWICZ, A., & YOUNG, A. S. (1994). Biobehavioral treatment and rehabilitation of schizophrenia. *Behavior Therapy, 25,* 89–107.

LIBERMAN, R. P., VACCARO, J. V., & CORRIGAN, P. W. (1995). Psychiatric rehabilitation. In H. I. Kaplan & B. J. Sadock (Eds.), *Comprehensive textbook of psychiatry* (6th ed., pp. 2696–2717). Baltimore: Williams & Wilkins.

LIBERMAN, R. P, WALLACE, C. J., BLACKWELL, G. [A.], ECKMAN, T. A., VACCARO, J. V., & KUEHNEL, T. G. (1993). Innovations in skills training for the seriously mentally ill: The UCLA social and independent living skills modules. *Innovations and Research, 2,* 43–60.

LIBERMAN, R. P., WALLACE, C. J., BLACKWELL, G. A., & VACCARO, J. V. (1993, November). *Integrating skills training with assertive case management in the rehabilitation of persons with schizophrenia.* Paper presented at a meeting of Psychiatric Research in the Department of Veterans Affairs, Washington, DC.

LICHSTEIN, K. L. (1988). *Clinical relaxation strategies.* New York: Wiley.

LICHSTEIN, K. L., PETERSON, B. A., RIEDEL, B. W., MEANS, M. K., EPPERSON, M. T., & AGUILLARD, R. N. (1999). Relaxation to assist sleep medication withdrawal. *Behavior Modification, 23,* 379–402.

LICHSTEIN, K. L., & RIEDEL, B. W. (1994). Behavioral assessment and treatment of insomnia: A review with an emphasis on clinical application. *Behavior Therapy, 25,* 659–688.

LICHSTEIN, K. L., WILSON, N. M., & JOHNSON, C. T. (2000). Psychological treatment of secondary insomnia. *Psychology and Aging, 15,* 232–240.

LICHTENSTEIN, E., & GLASGOW, R. E. (1977). Rapid smoking: Side effects and safeguards. *Journal of Consulting and Clinical Psychology, 45,* 815–821.

LICHTENSTEIN, E., HARRIS, D. E., BIRCHLER, G. R., WAHL, J. M., & SCHMAHL, D. P. (1973). Comparison of rapid smoking, warm, smoky air and attention-placebo in the modification of smoking behavior. *Journal of Consulting and Clinical Psychology, 40,* 92–98.

LICHTENSTEIN, E., & RODRIGUES, M. R. P. (1977). Long-term effects of rapid smoking treatment for dependent cigarette smokers. *Addictive Behaviors, 2,* 109–112.

LICK, J. R. (1975). Expectancy, false galvanic skin response feedback and systematic desensitization in the modification of a phobic behavior. *Journal of Consulting and Clinical Psychology, 43,* 557–567.

LIDDELL, A., DI FAZIO, L., BLACKWOOD, J., & ACKERMAN, C. (1994). Long-term follow-up of treated dental phobics. *Behaviour Research and Therapy, 32,* 605–610.

LIEBERT, R. M., & SPIEGLER, M. D. (1994). *Personality: Strategies and issues* (7th ed.). Pacific Grove, CA: Brooks/Cole.

LIESE, B. S. (1994). Brief therapy, crisis intervention and the cognitive therapy of substance abuse. *Crisis Intervention, 1,* 11–29.

LIMA, J., NAZARIAN, L., CHARNEY, E., & LAHTI, C. (1976). Compliance with short-term antimicrobial therapy: Some techniques that help. *Pediatrics, 57,* 383–386.

LINDBERG, J. S., IWATA, B. A., KAHNG, S. W., & DELEON, I. G. (1999). DRO contingencies: An analysis of variable-momentary schedules. *Journal of Applied Behavior Analysis, 32,* 123–136.

LINDSLEY, O. R. (1956). Operant conditioning methods applied to research in chronic schizophrenia. *Psychiatric Research Reports, 5,* 118–139.

LINDSLEY, O. R. (1960). Characteristics of the behavior of chronic psychotics as revealed by free-operant conditioning methods. *Diseases of the Nervous System (Monograph Supplement), 21,* 66–78.

LINDSLEY, O. R. (1963). Free-operant conditioning and psychotherapy. *Current Psychiatric Therapies, 3,* 47–56.

LINDSLEY, O. R. (1966). An experiment with parents handling behavior at home. *Johnstone Bulletin (Johnstone Training Center, Bordentown, NJ), 9,* 27–36.

LINDSLEY, O. R. (1968). A reliable wrist counter for recording behavior rates. *Journal of Applied Behavior Analysis, 1,* 77–78.

LINEHAN, M. M. (1993a). *Cognitive-behavioral treatment of borderline personality disorder.* New York: Guilford.

LINEHAN, M. M. (1993b). *Skill training manual for treating borderline personality disorder.* New York: Guilford.

LINEHAN, M. M., ARMSTRONG, H. E., SUAREZ, A., ALLMON, D., & HEARD, H. L. (1991). Cognitive-behavioral treatment of chronically parasuicidal borderline patients. *Archives of General Psychiatry, 48,* 1060–1064.

LINEHAN, M. M., HEARD, L., & ARMSTRONG, H. E. (1993). Naturalistic follow-up of a behavioral treatment for chronically parasuicidal borderline patients. *Archives of General Psychiatry, 50,* 971–974.

LINEHAN, M. M., & SCHMIDT, H., III. (1995). The dialectics of effective treatment of borderline personality disorders. In W. T. O'Donohue & L. Krasner (Eds.), *Theories of behavior therapy: Exploring behavior change* (pp. 553–584). Washington, DC: American Psychological Association.

LINSCHEID, T. R., HARTEL, F., & COOLEY, N. (1993). Are aversive procedures durable? A five year follow-up of three individuals treated with contingent electric shock. *Child and Adolescent Mental Health Care, 3,* 67–76.

LINSCHEID, T. R., IWATA, B. A., RICKETTS, R. W., WILLIAMS, D. E., & GRIFFIN, J. C. (1990). Clinical evaluation of the self-injurious behavior inhibiting system (SIBIS). *Journal of Applied Behavior Analysis, 23,* 53–78.

LINTON, S. J. (1982). Applied relaxation as a method of coping with chronic pain: A therapist's guide. *Scandinavian Journal of Behaviour Therapy, 11,* 161–174.

LINTON, S. J., & MELIN, L. (1983). Applied relaxation in the management of chronic pain. *Behavioural Psychotherapy, 11,* 337–350.

LIPKE, H., & BOTKIN, A. (1992). Brief case studies of eye movement desensitization and reprocessing with chronic post-traumatic stress disorder. *Psychotherapy, 29,* 591–595.

LITTLE, B. C., HAYWORTH, J., BENSON, P., HALL, F., BEARD, R. W., DEWHURST, V., & PRIEST, R. G. (1984). Treatment of hypertension in pregnancy by relaxation and biofeedback. *Lancet, 1,* 865–867.

LOCHMAN, J. E. (1985). Effects of different treatment lengths in cognitive behavioral interventions with aggressive boys. *Child Psychiatry and Human Development, 16,* 45–56.

LOCHMAN, J. E. (in press). Preventive intervention with precursors to substance abuse. In W. J. Bukowski & Z. Slabota (Eds.), *Handbook of drug abuse theory, science, and practice.* New York: Plenum.

LOCHMAN, J. E., & CURRY, J. F. (1986a). Effects of social problem-solving training and self-instruction training with aggressive boys. *Journal of Clinical Child Psychology, 15,* 159–164.

LOCHMAN, J. E., & CURRY, J. F. (1986b). Situational social problem-solving skills and self-esteem of aggressive and nonaggressive boys. *Journal of Abnormal Child Psychology, 14,* 605–617.

LOCHMAN, J. E., & LENHART, L. A. (1993). Anger coping intervention for aggressive children: Conceptual models and outcome effects. *Clinical Psychology Review, 13,* 785–805.

LOCHMAN, J. E., NELSON, W. M., III, & SIMS, J. P. (1981). A cognitive-behavioral program for use with aggressive children. *Journal of Clinical Child Psychology, 13,* 527–538.

LOCHMAN, J. E., WHIDBY, J. M., & FITZGERALD, D. P. (2000). Cognitive-behavioral assessment and treatment with aggressive children. In P. C. Kendall (Ed.), *Child and adolescent therapy: Cognitive-behavioral procedures* (2nd ed., pp. 31–87). New York: Guilford.

LOCKE, E. A. (1979). Behavior modification is not cognitive and other myths: A reply to Ledwidge. *Cognitive Therapy and Research, 3,* 119–126.

LODGE, J., TRIPP, G., & HARTE, D. K. (2000). Think-aloud, thought-listing, and video-mediated recall procedures in the assessment of children's self-talk. *Cognitive Therapy and Research, 24,* 399–418.

LOFTUS, E. (1979). *Eyewitness testimony.* Cambridge, MA: Harvard University Press.

LOHR, J. M., KLEINKNECHT, R. A., CONLEY, A. T., DAL CERRO, S., SCHMIDT, J., & SONNTAG, M. E. (1992). A methodological critique of the current status of eye movement desensitization (EMD). *Journal of Behavior Therapy and Experimental Psychiatry, 23,* 159–167.

LOHR, J., LILIENFELD, S. O., TOLIN, D. F., & HERBERT, J. D. (1999). Eye movement desensitization and reprocessing: An analysis of specific versus nonspecific treatment factors. *Journal of Anxiety Disorder, 13,* 185–207.

LOHR, J. M., TOLIN, D. F., & LILIENFELD, S. O. (1998). Efficacy of eye movement desensitization and reprocessing: Implications for behavior therapy. *Behavior Therapy, 29,* 123–156.

LOHR, J. M., TOLIN, D. F., & MONTGOMERY, R. W. (1996, January). Differing opinions on EMDR. [Letter to the editor]. *APA Monitor,* 3–4.

LONG, E. S., & MILTENBERGER, R. G. (1998). A review of behavioral and pharmacological treatments for habit disorders in individuals with mental retardation. *Journal of Behavior Therapy and Experimental Psychiatry, 29,* 143–156.

LONG, E. S., MILTENBERGER, R. G., ELLINGSON, S. A., & OTT, S. M. (1999). Augmenting simplified habit reversal in the treatment of oral-digital habits exhibited by individuals with mental retardation. *Journal of Applied Behavior Analysis, 32,* 353–365.

LONG, E. S., MILTENBERGER, R. G., & RAPP, J. T. (1998). A survey of habit behaviors exhibited by individuals with mental retardation. *Behavioral Interventions, 13,* 79–89.

LONG, E. S., MILTENBERGER, R. G., & RAPP, J. T. (1999). Simplified habit reversal plus adjunct contingencies in the treatment of thumb sucking and hair pulling in a young child. *Child & Family Behavior Therapy, 21,* 45–58.

LONG, E. S., WOODS, D. W., MILTENBERGER, R. [G.], FUQUA, R. W., & BOUDJOUK, P. J. (1999). Examining the social effects of habit behaviors exhibited by individuals with mental retardation. *Journal of Mental and Physical Disabilities, 11,* 295–312.

LONG, P., FOREHAND, R. [L.], WIERSON, M., & MORGAN, A. (1993). Does parent training with young noncompliant children have long-term effects? *Behaviour Research and Therapy, 32,* 101–107.

LOVAAS, O. I. (1977). *The autistic child: Language development through behavior modification.* New York: Irvington.

LOVAAS, O. I. (1987). Behavioral treatment and normal educational and intellectual functioning in young autistic children. *Journal of Consulting and Clinical Psychology, 55,* 3–9.

LOVAAS, O. I., & SIMMONS, J. Q. (1969). Manipulation of self-destruction in three retarded children. *Journal of Applied Behavior Analysis, 2,* 143–157.

LOVELL, K., FULLALOVE, L., GARVERY, R., & BROOKER, C. (2000). Telephone treatment of obsessive-compulsive disorder. *Behavioural and Cognitive Psychotherapy, 28,* 87–91.

LOVIBOND, S. H., & COOTE, M. A. (1970). Enuresis. In C. G. Costello (Ed.), *Symptoms of psychopathology: A handbook* (pp. 373–396). New York: Wiley.

LOWE, K., & LUTZKER, J. R. (1979). Increasing compliance to a medical regimen with a juvenile diabetic. *Behavior Therapy, 10,* 57–64.

LUBORSKY, L. (1954). A note on Eysenck's article "The effects of psychotherapy: An evaluation." *British Journal of Psychology, 45,* 129–131.

LUCIC, K. S., STEFFEN, J. J., HARRIGAN, J. A., & STUEBING, R. C. (1991). Progressive relaxation training: Muscle contraction before relaxation? *Behavior Therapy, 22,* 249–256.

LUISELLI, J. K. (1993). Training self-feeding skills in children who are deaf and blind. *Behavior Modification, 17,* 457–473.

LUISELLI, J. K. (1998). Intervention conceptualization and formulation. In J. K. Luiselli & M. J. Cameron (Eds.), *Antecedent control* (pp. 29–44). Baltimore: Brookes.

LUISELLI, J. K., & GREENRIDGE, A. (1982). Behavioral treatment of high-rate aggression in a rubella child. *Journal of Behavior Therapy and Experimental Psychiatry, 13,* 152–157.

LUKINS, R., DAVAN, I. G. P., & DRUMMOND, P. D. (1997). A cognitive behavioural approach to preventing anxiety during magnetic resonance imaging. *Journal of Behavior Therapy and Experimental Psychiatry, 28,* 97–104.

LUMLEY, V. A., MILTENBERGER, R. G., LONG, E. S., RAPP, J. T., & ROBERTS, J. A. (1998). Evaluation of a sexual abuse prevention program for adults with mental retardation. *Journal of Applied Behavior Analysis, 31,* 91–101.

LUNDQUIST, L. M., & HANSEN, D. J. (1998). Enhancing treatment adherence, social validity, and generalization of parent-training interventions with physically abusive and neglectful families. In J. Lutzker (Ed.), *Handbook of child abuse research and treatment* (pp. 449–471). New York: Plenum.

LUTGENDORF, S. K., STARR, K., MCCABE, P., ANTONI, M. H., IRONSON, G., KLIMAS, N., FLETCHER, M. A., KUMAR, M., SCHNEIDERMAN, N., & CLEVEN, K. (1997). Cognitive-behavioral stress management decreases dysphoric mood and herpes simplex virus-type 2 antibody titers in symptomatic HIV-seropositive gay men. *Journal of Consulting and Clinical Psychology, 65,* 31–43.

LUTZKER, J. R., HUYNEN, K. B., & BIGELOW, K. M. (1998). Parent training. In V. B. Van Hasselt & M. Michel (Eds.), *Handbook of psychological treatment protocols for children and adolescents* (pp. 467–500). Mahwah, NJ: Erlbaum.

LUTZKER, J. R., & STEED, S. E. (1998). Parent training for families of children with developmental disabilities. In J. M. Briesmeister & C. E Schaefer (Eds.), *Handbook of parent training: Parents as cotherapists for children's behavior problems* (2nd ed., pp. 281–307). New York: Wiley.

LYLES, J. M., BURISH, T. G., KROZELY, M. G., & OLDHAM, R. K. (1982). Efficacy of relaxation training and guided imagery in reducing the aversiveness of cancer chemotherapy. *Journal of Consulting and Clinical Psychology, 50,* 509–524.

LYNCH, D. J., BIRK, T. J., WEAVER, M. T., GOHARA, A. F., LEIGHTON, R. F., REPKA, F. J., & WALSH, M. E. (1992). Adherence to exercise interventions in the treatment of hypercholesterolemia. *Journal of Behavioral Medicine, 15,* 365–377.

LYONS, L. C., & WOODS, P. J. (1991). The efficacy of rational-emotive therapy: A quantitative view of the outcome research. *Clinical Psychology Review, 11,* 357–369.

MAAG, J. W., & KOTLASH, J. (1994). Review of stress inoculation training with children and adolescents: Issues and recommendations. *Behavior Modification, 18,* 443–469.

MACCOBY, N., FARQUHAR, J. W., WOOD, P. D., & ALEXANDER, J. (1977). Reducing the risk of cardiovascular disease: Effects of a community-based campaign on knowledge and behavior. *Journal of Community Health, 3,* 100–114.

MACCUBREY, J. (1971). Verbal operant conditioning with young institutionalized Down's syndrome children. *American Journal of Mental Deficiency, 75,* 676–701.

MACE, F. C. (1994). The significance and future of functional analysis methodologies. *Journal of Applied Behavior Analysis, 27,* 385–392.

MACKENZIE-KEATING, S. E., & MCDONALD, L. (1990). Overcorrection: Reviewed, revisited, and revised. *The Behavior Analyst, 13,* 39–48.

MACMILLAN, V., GUEVREMONT, D. C., & HANSEN, D. J. (1989). Problem-solving training with a multi-distressed abusive mother. *Journal of Family Violence, 3,* 69–81.

MACONOCHIE, A. (1848). *The mark system.* London: John Ollivier.

MACPHILLAMY, D., & LEWINSOHN, P. M. (1971). *The Pleasant Events Schedule.* (Mimeo). Eugene: University of Oregon.

MADSEN, C. H. (1965). Positive reinforcement in the toilet training of a normal child. In L. P. Ullmann & L. Krasner (Eds.), *Case studies in behavior modification* (pp. 305–307). New York: Holt, Rinehart & Winston.

MADSEN, C. H., HOFFMAN, M., THOMAS, D. R., KOROPSAK, E., & MADSEN, C. K. (1969). Comparison of toilet training techniques. In D. M. Gelfand (Ed.), *Social learning in childhood* (pp. 104–112). Pacific Grove, CA: Brooks/Cole.

MADSEN, C. K., GREER, R. D., & MADSEN, C. H. (1975). *Research in music behavior: Modifying music behavior in the classroom.* New York: Teachers College Press.

MAEDA, M. (1985). The effects of combinations of vicarious reinforcement on the formation of assertive behaviors in covert modeling. *Japanese Journal of Behavior Therapy, 10,* 34–44. (English abstract)

MAGEE, S. K., & ELLIS, J. (2000). Extinction effects during the assessment of multiple problem behaviors. *Journal of Applied Behavior Analysis, 33,* 313–316.

MAGRAB, P. R., & PAPADOPOULOU, Z. L. (1977). The effects of a token economy on dietary compliance for children on hemodialysis. *Journal of Applied Behavior Analysis, 10,* 573–578.

MAHONEY, K., VAN WAGENEN, R. K., & MEYERSON, L. (1971). Toilet training of normal and retarded children. *Journal of Applied Behavior Analysis, 4,* 173–181.

MAHONEY, M. J., & KAZDIN, A. E. (1979). Cognitive behavior modification: Misconceptions and premature evacuation. *Psychological Bulletin, 86,* 1044–1049.

MAHONEY, M. J., LYDDON, W. J., & ALFORD, D. J. (1989). An evaluation of the rational-emotive theory of psychotherapy. In M. E. Bernard & R. [A.] DiGiuseppe (Eds.), *Inside rational-emotive therapy: A critical appraisal of the theory and therapy of Albert Ellis* (pp. 69–94). San Diego: Academic Press.

MAHRER, A. R., NORDIN, S., & MILLER, L. S. (1995). If a client has this kind of problem, prescribe that kind of post-session behavior. *Psychotherapy, 32,* 194–203.

MALEC, J. F. (1995). Behavior therapy and cognitive decline in the elderly. *the Behavior Therapist, 18,* 161–169.

MALETZKY, B. M. (1974). "Assisted" covert sensitization in the treatment of exhibitionism. *Journal of Consulting and Clinical Psychology, 42,* 34–40.

MALETZKY, B. M. (1993). Assisted covert sensitization: Application to a bisexual pedophile. In J. R. Cautela & A. J. Kearney (Eds.), *Covert conditioning casebook* (pp. 217–234). Pacific Grove, CA: Brooks/Cole.

MALLESON, N. (1959). Panic and phobia. *Lancet, 1,* 225–227.

MALONEY, D. M., FIXSEN, D. L., & PHILLIPS, E. L. (1981). The Teaching-Family model: Research and dissemination in a service program. *Children and Youth Services Review, 3,* 343–355.

MALONEY, K. B., & HOPKINS, B. L. (1973). The modification of sentence structure and its relationship to subjective judgments of creativity in writing. *Journal of Applied Behavior Analysis, 6,* 425–433.

MANN, R. A. (1972). The behavior-therapeutic use of contingency contracting to control an adult behavior problem: Weight control. *Journal of Applied Behavior Analysis, 5,* 99–109.

MANN, R. A. (1976). The use of contingency contracting to facilitate durability of behavior change: Weight loss maintenance. *Addictive Behaviors, 1,* 245–249.

MANNE, S. L., BAKEMAN, R., JACOBSEN, P. B., GORFINKLE, K., & REDD, W. H. (1994). An analysis of a behavioral intervention for children undergoing venipuncture. *Health Psychology, 13,* 556–566.

MANNE, S. L., JACOBSEN, P. B., GORFINKLE, K., GERSTEIN, F., & REDD, W. H. (1993). Treatment adherence difficulties among children with cancer: The role of parenting style. *Journal of Pediatric Psychology, 18,* 47–62.

MANNE, S. L., REDD, W. H., JACOBSEN, P. B., GORFINKLE, K., SCHORR, O., & RABKIN, B. (1990). Behavioral interventions to reduce child and parent distress during venipuncture. *Journal of Consulting and Clinical Psychology, 58,* 565–572.

MANSDORF, I. J., CALAPAI, P., CASELLI, L., BURSTEIN, Y., & DIMANT, J. (1999). Reducing psychotropic medication usage in nursing home residents: The effects of behaviorally oriented psychotherapy. *the Behavior Therapist, 22,* 21–23, 29.

MARAFIOTE, R. A. (1993). On EMDR and controlled outcome studies. *the Behavior Therapist, 17,* 22–24.

MARCUS, B. A., & VOLLMER, T. R. (1995). Effects of differential negative reinforcement on disruption and compliance. *Journal of Applied Behavior Analysis, 28,* 229–230.

MARGOLIN, G., MICHELLI, J., & JACOBSON, N. (1988). Assessment of marital dysfunction. In A. S. Bellack & M. Hersen (Eds.), *Behavioral assessment: A practical handbook* (3rd ed., pp. 441–489). Elmsford, NY: Pergamon.

MARKMAN, H. J., FLOYD, F. J., STANLEY, S. M., & LEWIS, H. (1986). Prevention. In N. S. Jacobson & A. S. Gurman (Eds.), *Clinical handbook of marital therapy* (pp. 173–195). New York: Guilford.

MARKMAN, H. J., FLOYD, F. J., STANLEY, S. M., & STORAASLI, R. D. (1988). Prevention of marital distress: A longitudinal investigation. *Journal of Consulting and Clinical Psychology, 56,* 210–217.

MARKMAN, H. J., LEBER, B., CORDOVA, A. D., & ST. PETERS, M. (1995). Behavioral observation and family psychology: Strange bedfellows or happy marriage? *Journal of Family Psychology, 9,* 371–379.

MARKMAN, H. J., RENICK, M. J., FLOYD, F. J., STANLEY, S. M., & CLEMENTS, M. (1993). Preventing marital distress through communication and conflict management training: A 4-and 5-year follow-up. *Journal of Consulting and Clinical Psychology, 61,* 70–77.

MARKS, I. [M.] (1978). Behavioral psychotherapy of adult neurosis. In S. L. Garfield & A. E. Bergin (Eds.), *Handbook of psychotherapy and behavior change: An empirical analysis* (2nd ed., pp. 493–547). New York: Wiley.

MARKS, I. M. (1987). *Fears, phobias, and rituals: Panic, anxiety and their disorders.* New York: Oxford University Press.

MARLATT, G. A. (1982). Relapse prevention: A self-control program for the treatment of addictive behaviors. In R. B. Stuart (Ed.), *Adherence, compliance, and generalization in behavioral medicine* (pp. 329–378). New York: Brunner/Mazel.

MARLATT, G. A., & BARRETT, K. (1994). Relapse prevention. In M. Galanter & H. D. Kleber (Eds.), *The textbook of substance abuse treatment* (pp. 285–299). Washington, DC: American Psychiatric Press.

MARLATT, G. A., & GORDON, J. R. (Eds.). (1985). *Relapse prevention: Maintenance strategies in the treatment of addictive behaviors.* New York: Guilford.

MARLATT, G. A., & TAPERT, S. F. (1993). Harm reduction: Reducing the risks of addictive behaviors. In J. S. Baer, G. A. Marlatt, & R. J. McMahon (Eds.), *Addictive behaviors across the lifespan* (pp. 243–273). Newbury Park, CA: Sage.

MARLOW, A. G., TINGSTROM, D. H., OLMI, D. J., & EDWARDS, R. P. (1997). The effects of class-room based time-in/time-out on compliance rates in children with speech/language disabilities. *Child & Family Behavior Therapy, 19,* 1–14.

MARMAR, C. R. (1990, November). *Implications of empirical findings for the psychodynamic theory of the therapeutic alliance.* Paper presented at the meeting of the Association for Advancement of Behavior Therapy, San Francisco.

MARQUIS, J. N. (1972). An expedient model for behavior therapy. In A. A. Lazarus (Ed.), *Clinical behavior therapy* (pp. 41–72). New York: Brunner/Mazel.

MARQUIS, J. N. (1991). A report on seventy-eight cases treated by eye movement desensitization. *Journal of Behavior Therapy and Experimental Psychiatry, 22,* 187–192.

MARQUIS, J. N., MORGAN, W. G., & PIAGET, G. W. (1971). *A guidebook for systematic desensitization* (2nd ed.). Palo Alto, CA: Veterans' Workshop, Veterans Administration Hospital.

MARSHALL, W. L., GAUTHIER, J., CHRISTIE, M. M., CURRIE, D. W., & GORDON, A. (1977). Flooding therapy: Effectiveness, stimulus characteristics, and the value of brief *in vivo* exposure. *Behaviour Research and Therapy, 15,* 79–87.

MARSHALL, W. L., GAUTHIER, J., & GORDON, A. (1979). The current status of flooding therapy. In M. Hersen, R. M. Eisler, & P. M. Miller (Eds.), *Progress in behavior modification* (Vol. 7, pp. 205–275). New York: Academic Press.

MARSTON, M. V. (1970). Compliance with medical regimens: A review of the literature. *Nursing Research, 19,* 312–323.

MARTELL, C. R., & HOLLON, S. D. (2001). Working together on shifting ground: Researcher and clinician collaboration in clinical trials. *the Behavior Therapist, 24,* 144–146.

MARTIN, G., & PEAR, J. (1996). *Behavior modification: What it is and how to do it* (5th ed.). Upper Saddle River, NJ: Prentice Hall.

MARTIN, S. (1995, October). Ethnic issues deeply entwined in family therapy. *APA Monitor, 26,* p. 38.

MARTINEZ-TABOAS, A., & NAVAS-ROBLETO, J. J. (2000). Cognitive behavior therapy in Puerto Rico. *the Behavior Therapist, 23,* 184–187.

MASEK, B. J. (1982). Compliance and medicine. In D. M. Doleys, R. L. Meredith, & A. R. Ciminero (Eds.), *Behavioral medicine: Assessment and treatment strategies* (pp. 527–545). New York: Plenum.

MASON, L. W., GOOLKASIAN, P., & McCAIN, G. A. (1998). Evaluation of a multimodal treatment program for fibromyalgia. *Journal of Behavioral Medicine, 21,* 163–178.

MASTERS, J. C., BURISH, T. G., HOLLON, S. D., & RIMM, D. C. (1987). *Behavior therapy: Techniques and empirical findings* (3rd ed.). San Diego: Harcourt Brace Jovanovich.

MASTERS, W. H., & JOHNSON, V. E. (1970). *Human sexual inadequacy.* Boston: Little, Brown.

MATHEWS, A. M., GELDER, M. G., & JOHNSTON, D. W. (1981). *Agoraphobia: Nature and treatment.* New York: Guilford.

MATHEWS, A. M., JOHNSTON, D. W., LANCASHIRE, M., MUNBY, M., SHAW, P. M., & GELDER, M. G. (1976). Imaginal flooding and exposure to real phobic situations: Treatment outcome with agoraphobic patients. *British Journal of Psychology, 129,* 362–371.

MATHEWS, A. M., TEASDALE, J., MUNBY, M., JOHNSTON, D. W., & SHAW, P. A. (1977). A home-based treatment for agoraphobia. *Behavior Therapy, 8,* 915–924.

MATSON, J. L., BAMBURG, J., SMALLS, Y., & SMIROLDO, B. B. (1997). Evaluating behavioral techniques in training individuals with severe and profound mental retardation to use functional independent living skills. *Behavior Modification, 21,* 533–534.

MATSON, J. L., SEVIN, J. A., & BOX, M. L. (1995). Social skills in children. In W. O'Donohue & L. Krasner (Eds.). *Handbook of psychological skills training: Clinical techniques and applications* (pp. 36–53). Boston: Allyn & Bacon.

MATSON, J. L., SMALLS, Y., HAMPFF, A., SMIROLDO, B. B., & ANDERSON, S. J. (1998). A comparison of behavioral techniques to teach functional independent-living skills to individuals with severe and profound mental retardation. *Behavior Modification, 22,* 298–306.

MATTICK, R. P., & PETERS, L. (1988). Treatment of severe social phobia: Effects of guided exposure with and without cognitive restructuring. *Journal of Consulting and Clinical Psychology, 56,* 251–260.

MAUDE-GRIFFEN, P. M., HOHENSTEIN, J. M., HUMFLEET, G. L., REILLY, P. M., TUSEL, D. J., & HALL, S. M. (1998). Superior efficacy of cognitive-behavioral therapy for urban crack cocaine abusers: Main and matching effects. *Journal of Consulting and Clinical Psychology, 66,* 832–837.

MAVISSAKALIAN, M., & BARLOW, D. H. (Eds.). (1981). *Phobia: Psychological and pharmacological treatment.* New York: Guilford.

MAYDEU-OLIVARES, A., & D'ZURILLA, T. J. (1997). The factor structure of the Problem Solving Inventory. *European Journal of Psychological Assessment, 13,* 206–215.

MAYDEU-OLIVARES, A., RODRIGUEZ-FORNELLS, A., GOMEZ-BENITO, J., & D'ZURILLA, T. J. (2000). Psychometric properties of the Spanish adaptation of the Social Problem-Solving Inventory-Revised (SPSI-R). *Personality and Individual Differences, 29,* 699–708.

MAYER, J. A., & FREDERIKSEN, L. W. (1986). Encouraging long-term compliance with breast self-examination: The evaluation of prompting strategies. *Journal of Behavioral Medicine, 9,* 179–189.

MAYHEW, G. L., & HARRIS, F. C. (1978). Some negative side effects of a punishment procedure for stereotyped behavior. *Journal of Behavior Therapy and Experimental Psychiatry, 9,* 245–251.

MAZALESKI, J. L., IWATA, B. A., VOLLMER, T. R., ZARCONE, J. R., & SMITH, R. G. (1993). Analysis of the reinforcement and extinction components in contingencies with self-injury. *Journal of Applied Behavior Analysis, 26,* 143–156.

MAZUR, T., & MICHAEL, P. M. (1992). Outpatient treatment for adolescents with sexually inappropriate behavior. *Journal of Offender Rehabilitation, 18,* 191–203.

MCADAM, D. B., & CUVO, A. J. (1994). Textual prompts as an antecedent cue self-management strategy for persons with mild disabilities. *Behavior Modification, 18,* 47–65.

MCCABE, R. E., BLANKSTEIN, K. R., & MILLS, J. S. (1999). Interpersonal sensitivity and social problem-solving: Relation with academic and social self-esteem, depressive symptoms, and academic performance. *Cognitive Therapy and Research, 23,* 587–604.

MCCAIN, A. P., & KELLEY, M. L. (1993). Managing the classroom behavior of an ADHD preschooler: The efficacy of a school-home note intervention. *Child & Family Behavior Therapy, 15,* 33–44.

MCCAIN, A. P., & KELLEY, M. L. (1994). Improving classroom performance in underachieving adolescents: The additive effects of response cost to a school-home note system. *Child & Family Behavior Therapy, 16,* 27–41.

MCCANN, D. L. (1992). Post-traumatic stress disorder due to devastating burns overcome by a single session of eye movement desensitization. *Journal of Behavior Therapy and Experimental Psychiatry, 23,* 319–323.

MCCARTHY, B. [W.] (1989). A cognitive-behavioral approach to sex therapy. In A. Freeman, K. M. Simon, L. E. Beutler, & H. Arkowitz (Eds.), *Comprehensive handbook of cognitive therapy* (pp. 435–447). New York: Plenum.

MCCARTHY, B. W. (2001). Relapse prevention strategies and techniques with erectile dysfunction. *Journal of Sex & Marital Therapy, 27,* 1–8.

MCCARTHY, G. W., & CRAIG, K. D. (1995). Flying therapy for flying phobia. *Aviation, Space, and Environmental Medicine, 66,* 1179–1184.

MCCATHIE, H., & SPENCE, S. H. (1991). What is the Revised Fear Survey Schedule for Children measuring? *Behaviour Research and Therapy, 29,* 495–502.

MCCOMAS, J. J., WACKER, D. P., & COOPER, L. J. (1998). Increasing compliance with medical procedures: Application of the high-probability request procedure for a toddler. *Journal of Applied Behavior Analysis, 31,* 287–290.

MCCONAGHY, N. (1988). Assessment of sexual dysfunction and deviation. In A. S. Bellack & M. Hersen (Eds.), *Behavioral assessment: A practical handbook* (3rd ed., pp. 490–541). Elmsford, NY: Pergamon.

MCCONNACHIE, G., & CARR, E. G. (1997). The effects of child behavior problems on the maintenance of intervention fidelity. *Behavior Modification, 21,* 123–158.

MCCONNELL, J. V. (1990). Negative reinforcement and positive punishment. *Teaching of Psychology, 17,* 247–249.

MCCORDICK, S. M., KAPLAN, R. M., FINN, M. E., & SMITH, S. H. (1979). Cognitive behavior modification and modeling for test anxiety. *Journal of Consulting and Clinical Psychology, 47,* 419–420

MCFALL, R. M., & LILLESAND, D. B. (1971). Behavior rehearsal with modeling and coaching in assertion training. *Journal of Abnormal Psychology, 77,* 313–323.

MCFALL, R. M., & MARSTON, A. R. (1970). An experimental investigation of behavior rehearsal in assertive training. *Journal of Abnormal Behavior, 76,* 295–303.

MCGINN, L. K., & YOUNG, J. E. (1996). Schema-focused therapy. In P. M. Salkovskis (Ed.), *Frontiers of cognitive therapy* (pp. 182–207). New York: Guilford.

MCGINN, L. K., YOUNG, J. E., & SANDERSON, W. C. (1995). When and how to do longer term therapy without feeling guilty. *Cognitive and Behavioral Practice, 2,* 187–212.

McGinnis, J. C., Friman, P. C., & Carlyon, W. D. (1999). The effect of token awards on "intrinsic" motivation for doing math. *Journal of Applied Behavior Analysis, 32,* 375–379.

McGlynn, F. D., & Cornell, C. E. (1985). Simple phobia. In M. Hersen & A. S. Bellack (Eds.), *Handbook of clinical behavior therapy with adults* (pp. 23–48). New York: Plenum.

McGlynn, F. D., Moore, P. M., Rose, M. P., & Lazarte, A. (1995). Effects of relaxation training on fear and arousal during in vivo exposure to a caged snake among DSM-III-R simple (snake) phobics. *Journal of Behavior Therapy and Experimental Psychiatry, 26,* 1–8.

McGoey, K. E., & DuPaul, G. J. (2000). Token reinforcement and response cost procedures: Reducing the disruptive behavior of preschool children with attention-deficit/hyperactivity disorder. *School Psychology Quarterly, 15,* 330–343.

McGrady, A. (1994). Effects of group relaxation training and thermal biofeedback on blood pressure and related physiological and psychological variables in essential hypertension. *Biofeedback and Self-Regulation, 19,* 51–66.

McGrady, A., Olson, R. P., & Kroon, J. S. (1995). Biobehavioral treatment of essential hypertension. In M. S. Schwartz (Ed.), *Biofeedback: A practitioner's guide* (pp. 445–467). New York: Guilford.

McGrady, A., Wauquier, A., McNeil, A., & Gerard, G. (1994). Effects of biofeedback-assisted relaxation on migraine headache and changes in cerebral blood flow velocity in the middle cerebral artery. *Headache, 34,* 424–428.

McGrady, A. V., Andrasik, F., Davies, T., Striefel, S., Wickramasekera, I., Baskin, S. M., Penzien, D. B., & Tietjen, G. (1999). Psychophysiologic therapy for chronic headache in primary care. *Primary Care Companion Journal of Clinical Psychiatry, 1,* 96–102.

McKay, D. (1997). A maintenance program for obsessive-compulsive disorder using exposure with response prevention: 2 year follow-up. *Behaviour Research and Therapy, 35,* 367–369.

McKay, D. (1999). Two-year follow-up of behavioral treatment and maintenance for body dysmorphic disorder. *Behavior Modification, 23,* 620–629.

McKay, D., Todaro, J., Neziroglu, F., Campisi, T., Moritz, E. K., & Yaryura-Tobias, J. A. (1997). Body dysmorphic disorder: A preliminary evaluation of treatment and maintenance using exposure with response prevention. *Behaviour Research and Therapy, 35,* 67–70.

McKusick, L., Wiley, J., Coates, T. J., & Morin, S. F. (1986, November). *Predictors of AIDS behavioral risk reduction: The AIDS behavioral research project.* Paper presented at the New Zealand AIDS Foundation Prevention Education Planning Workshop, Auckland.

McLaughlin, T. F. (1982). An analysis of token reinforcement: A control group comparison with special education youth employing measures of clinical significance. *Child & Family Behavior Therapy, 3,* 43–50.

McNair, L. D. (1996). African American women and behavior therapy: Integrating theory, culture, and clinical practice. *Cognitive and Behavioral Practice, 3,* 337–349.

McNally, R. J. (1994). Introduction to the special series: Innovations in cognitive-behavioral approaches to schizophrenia. *Behavior Therapy, 25,* 1–4.

McNamee, G., O'Sullivan, G., Lelliott, P., & Marks, I. M. (1989). Telephone-guided treatment for housebound agoraphobics with panic disorder: Exposure vs. relaxation. *Behavior Therapy, 20,* 491–497.

McNees, M. P., Egli, D. S., Marshall, D. S., Schnelle, R. S., Schnelle, J. F., & Risley, T. R. (1976). Shoplifting prevention: Providing information through signs. *Journal of Applied Behavior Analysis, 9,* 399–405.

McNeil, C. B., Clemens-Mowrer, L., Gurwitch, R. H., & Funderburk, B. W. (1994). Assessment of a new procedure to prevent timeout escape in preschoolers. *Child & Family Behavior Therapy, 16,* 27–35.

Meadowcroft, P., Hawkins, R. P., Trout, B. A., Grealish, E. M., & Stark, L. J. (1982, September). *Making foster-family-based treatment accountable: The issue of quality control.* Paper presented at the meeting of the American Psychological Association, Washington, DC.

Meadows, E. A., & Foa, E. B. (1998). Intrusion, arousal, and avoidance. In V. M. Follette, J. I. Ruzek, & F. R. Abueg (Eds.), *Cognitive-behavioral therapies for trauma* (pp. 100–123). New York: Guilford.

Mealiea, W. L., & Nawas, M. M. (1971). The comparative effectiveness of systematic desensitization and implosive therapy in the treatment of snake phobia. *Journal of Behavior Therapy and Experimental Psychiatry, 2,* 85–94.

Means, M. K., Lichstein, K. L., Epperson, M. T., & Johnson, C. T. (2000). Relaxation therapy for insomnia: Nighttime and day time effects. *Behaviour Research and Therapy, 38,* 665–678.

Meharg, S. S., & Woltersdorf, M. A. (1990). Therapeutic uses of videotape self-modeling: A review. *Advances in Behaviour Research and Therapy, 12,* 85–99.

Mehta, M. (1990). A comparative study of family-based and patient-based behavioral management in obsessive-compulsive disorder. *British Journal of Psychiatry, 157,* 133–135.

Meichenbaum, D. [H.] (1971). Examination of model characteristics in reducing avoidance behavior. *Journal of Personality and Social Psychology, 17,* 298–307.

Meichenbaum, D. [H.] (1974). Self-instructional training: A cognitive prosthesis for the aged. *Human Development, 17,* 273–280.

Meichenbaum, D. [H.] (1975). Enhancing creativity by modifying what subjects say to themselves. *American Educational Research Journal, 12,* 129–145.

Meichenbaum, D. [H.] (1977). *Cognitive-behavior modification: An integrative approach.* New York: Plenum.

Meichenbaum, D. [H.] (1979). Cognitive behavior modification: The need for a fairer assessment. *Cognitive Therapy and Research, 3,* 127–132.

Meichenbaum, D. H. (1985). *Stress inoculation training.* Elmsford, NY: Pergamon.

Meichenbaum, D. [H.] (1991, February–March). *Cognitive behavioral therapy.* Workshop sponsored by the Institute for the Advancement of Human Behavior (Portola Valley, CA), Chicago.

Meichenbaum, D. [H.] (1994). *A clinical handbook/practical therapist manual for assessing and treating adults with post-traumatic stress disorder (PTSD).* Waterloo, Ontario: Institute Press.

Meichenbaum, D. [H.], & Cameron, R. (1972). *Stress inoculation: A skills training approach to anxiety management.* Unpublished manuscript, University of Waterloo, Ontario.

MEICHENBAUM, D. [H.], & CAMERON, R. (1973). Training schizophrenics to talk to themselves: A means of developing attentional controls. *Behavior Therapy, 4,* 515–534.

MEICHENBAUM, D. H., & DEFFENBACHER, J. L. (1988). Stress inoculation training. *The Counseling Psychologist, 16,* 69–90.

MEICHENBAUM, D. [H.], GILMORE, B., & FEDORAVICIUS, A. (1971). Group insight vs. group desensitization in treating speech anxiety. *Journal of Consulting and Clinical Psychology, 36,* 410–421.

MEICHENBAUM, D. [H.], & GOODMAN, J. (1971). Training impulsive children to talk to themselves: A means of developing self-control. *Journal of Abnormal Psychology, 77,* 115–126.

MEICHENBAUM, D. [H.], & JAREMKO, M. E. (Eds.). (1982). *Stress prevention and management: A cognitive-behavioral approach.* New York: Plenum.

MEICHENBAUM, D. [H.], & TURK, D. [C.] (1976). The cognitive-behavioral management of anxiety, anger and pain. In J. Davison (Ed.), *The behavioral management of anxiety, depression and pain* (pp. 1–34). New York: Brunner/Mazel.

MEICHENBAUM, D. [H.], & TURK, D. [C.] (1987). *Facilitating treatment adherence: A practitioner's guidebook.* New York: Plenum.

MELAMED, B. G. (1979). Behavioral approaches to fear in dental settings. In M. Hersen, R. M. Eisler, & P. M. Miller (Eds.), *Progress in behavior modification* (Vol. 7, pp. 172–205). New York: Academic Press.

MELAMED, B. G., HAWES, R. R., HELBY, E., & GLICK, J. (1975). Use of filmed modeling to reduce uncooperative behavior of children during dental treatment. *Journal of Dental Research, 54,* 797–801.

MELAMED, B. G., & SIEGEL, L. J. (1975). Reduction of anxiety in children facing hospitalization and surgery by use of filmed modeling. *Journal of Consulting and Clinical Psychology, 43,* 511–521.

MELAMED, B. G., WEINSTEIN, D., HAWES, R., & KATKIN-BORLAND, M. (1975). Reduction of fear-related dental management problems with use of filmed modeling. *Journal of the American Dental Association, 90,* 822–826.

MENZIES, R. G., & CLARKE, J. C. (1993). A comparison of in vivo and vicarious exposure in the treatment of childhood water phobia. *Behaviour Research and Therapy, 31,* 9–15.

MESSER, S. C., & GROSS, A. M. (1995). Childhood depression and family interaction: A naturalistic observation study. *Journal of Clinical Child Psychology, 24,* 77–88.

METZ, J. R. (1965). Conditioning generalized imitation in autistic children. *Journal of Experimental Child Psychology, 2,* 389–399.

METZLER, C. W., BIGLAN, A., NOELL, J., ARY, D. V., & OCHS, L. (2000). A randomized controlled trial of a behavioral intervention to reduce high-risk sexual behavior among adolescents in STD clinics. *Behavior Therapy, 31,* 27–54.

MEYER, A. J., NASH, J. D., McALISTER, A. L., MACCOBY, N., & FARQUHAR, J. W. (1980). Skills training in a cardiovascular health education campaign. *Journal of Consulting and Clinical Psychology, 48,* 129–142.

MEYER, R. G. (1975). A behavioral treatment of sleepwalking associated with test anxiety. *Journal of Behavior Therapy and Experimental Psychiatry, 6,* 167–168.

MEYER, V., ROBERTSON, J., & TATLOW, A. (1975). Home treatment of an obsessive-compulsive disorder by response prevention. *Journal of Behavior Therapy and Experimental Psychiatry, 6,* 37–38.

MEYERS, A., MERCATORIS, M., & SIROTA, A. (1976). Use of covert self-instruction for the elimination of psychotic speech. *Journal of Consulting and Clinical Psychology, 44,* 480–483.

MICHAEL, J. (1975). Positive and negative reinforcement, a distinction that is no longer necessary; or, a better way to talk about bad things. *Behaviorism, 3,* 33–44.

MICHAEL, J. (2000). Implications and refinements of the establishing operations concept. *Journal of Applied Behavior Analysis, 33,* 401–410.

MIDDLETON, M. B., & CARTLEDGE, G. (1995). The effects of social skills instruction and parental involvement on the aggressive behaviors of African American males. *Behavioral Medicine, 19,* 192–210.

MIKULAS, W. L., & COFFMAN, M. F. (1989). Home-based treatment of children's fear of the dark. In C. E. Schaefer & J. M. Briesmeister (Eds.), *Handbook of parent training: Parents as co-therapists for children's behavior problems* (pp. 179–202). New York: Wiley.

MIKULAS, W. L., COFFMAN, M. F., DAYTON, D., FRAYNE, C., & MAIER, P. L. (1985). Behavioral bibliotherapy and games for treating fear of the dark. *Child & Family Behavior Therapy, 7,* 1–7.

MILAN, M. A. (1987). Token economy programs in closed institutions. In E. K. Morris & C. J. Braukmann (Eds.), *Behavioral approaches to crime and delinquency: A handbook of applications, research, and concepts* (pp. 195–222). New York: Plenum.

MILGROM, P., MANCL, L., KING, B., & WEINSTEIN, P. (1995). Origins of childhood dental fear. *Behaviour Research and Therapy, 33,* 313–319.

MILLER, A. L. (1970). Treatment of a child with Gilles de la Tourette's syndrome using behavior modification techniques. *Journal of Behavior Therapy and Experimental Psychiatry, 1,* 319–321.

MILLER, D. L., & KELLEY, M. L. (1992). Treatment acceptability: The effects, marital adjustment, and child behavior. *Child & Family Behavior Therapy, 14,* 11–23.

MILLER, D. L., MANNE, S., & PALEVSKY, W. (1998). Acceptance of behavioral interventions for children with cancer: Perceptions of parents, nurses, and community controls. *Journal of Pediatric Psychology, 23,* 267–271.

MILLER, D. N., & COLE, C. L. (1998). Effects of social skills training on an adolescent with comorbid conduct disorder and depression. *Child & Family Behavior Therapy, 20,* 35–53.

MILLER, H. R., & NAWAS, M. M. (1970). Control of aversive stimulus termination in systematic desensitization. *Behaviour Research and Therapy, 8,* 57–61.

MILLER, N. E. (1978). Biofeedback and visceral learning. *Annual Review of Psychology, 29,* 373–404.

MILLER, P. M. (1972). The use of behavioral contracting in the treatment of alcoholism: A case report. *Behavior Therapy, 3,* 593–596.

MILNE, D., & KENNEDY, S. (1993). The utility of consumer satisfaction data: A case study in organizational behaviour management. *Behavioural and Cognitive Psychotherapy, 21,* 281–291.

Miltenberger, R. G. (2000). Behavioral skills training to remediate deviant social behavior of an adolescent in residential treatment. *Cognitive and Behavioral Practice, 7,* 236–238.

Miltenberger, R. G., & Fuqua, R. W. (1985). A comparison of contingent vs. non-contingent competing response practice in the treatment of nervous habits. *Journal of Behavior Therapy and Experimental Psychiatry, 16,* 195–200.

Miltenberger, R. G., Fuqua, R. W., & McKinley, T. (1985). Habit reversal with muscle tics: Replication and component analysis. *Behavior Therapy, 16,* 39–50.

Miltenberger, R. G., Fuqua, R. W., & Woods, D. W. (1998). Applying behavior analysis to clinical problems: Review and analysis of habit reversal. *Journal of Applied Behavior Analysis, 31,* 447–469.

Miltenberger, R. G., Roberts, J. A., Ellingson, S., Galensky, T., Rapp, J. T., Long, E. S., & Lumley, V. A. (1999). Training and generalization of sexual abuse prevention skills for woman with mental retardation. *Journal of Applied Behavior Analysis, 32,* 385–388.

Miltenberger, R. G., & Thiesse-Duffy, E. (1988). Evaluation of home-based programs for teaching personal safety skills to children. *Journal of Applied Behavior Analysis, 21,* 81–87.

Minkin, N., Braukmann, C. J., Minkin, B. L., Timbers, G. D., Timbers, B. J., Fixsen, D. L., Phillips, E. L., & Wolf, M. M. (1976). The social validation and training of conversational skills. *Journal of Applied Behavior Analysis, 9,* 127–139.

Minneker-Hugel, E., Unland, H., & Buchkremer, G. (1992). Behavioral relapse prevention strategies in smoking cessation. *The International Journal of the Addictions, 27,* 627–634.

Minor, S. W., Leone, C., & Baldwin, R. T. (1984). A comparison of in vivo and imaginal participant modeling. *Journal of Clinical Psychology, 40,* 717–720.

Minor, S. W., Minor, J. W., & Williams, P. P. (1983). A participant modeling procedure to train parents of developmentally disabled infants. *Journal of Psychology, 115,* 107–111.

Mischel, W. (1968). *Personality and assessment.* New York: Wiley.

Mischel, W. (1973). On the empirical dilemmas of psychodynamic approaches: Issues and alternatives. *Journal of Abnormal Psychology, 82,* 335–344.

Mitchell, J. E., Pyle, R. L., Hatsukami, D., Goff, G., Glotter, D., & Harper, J. (1989). A 2–5 year follow-up study of patients treated for bulimia nervosa. *International Journal of Eating Disorders, 8,* 157–165.

Mitchell, J. E., Raymond, N., & Specker, S. (1993). A review of the controlled trials of pharmacotherapy and psychotherapy in the treatment of bulimia nervosa. *International Journal of Eating Disorders, 14,* 229–247.

Mohr, D. C., Likosky, W., Bertagnolli, A., Goodkin, D. E., Van Der Wende, J., Dwyer, P., & Dick, L. P. (2000). Telephone-administered cognitive-behavioral therapy for the treatment of depressive symptomology in multiple sclerosis. *Journal of Consulting and Clinical Psychology, 68,* 356–361.

Montgomery, R. W. (1993). *An empirical investigation of eye movement desensitization.* Unpublished dissertation, Georgia State University.

Monti, P. M., Abrams, D. B., Kadden, R. M., & Cooney, N. L. (1989). *Treating alcohol dependence.* New York: Guilford.

Monti, P. M., Rohsenow, D. J., Rubonis, A. V., Niaura, R. S., Sirota, A. D., Colby, S. M., Goddard, P., & Abrams, D. B. (1993). Cue exposure with coping skills treatment for male alcoholics: A preliminary investigation. *Journal of Consulting and Clinical Psychology, 61,* 1011–1019.

Moore, N. (1965). Behavior therapy in bronchial asthma: A controlled study. *Journal of Psychosomatic Research, 9,* 257–276.

Moore, V., & Callias, M. (1987). A systematic approach to teaching reading and spelling to a nine-year-old boy with severely impaired literacy skills. *Educational Psychology, 7,* 103–115.

Morgan, D. L., & Morgan, R. K. (2001). Single-subject research design: Bringing science to managed care. *American Psychologist, 56,* 119–127.

Morgan, W. G. (1974). The shaping game: A teaching technique. *Behavior Therapy, 5,* 271–272.

Morganstern, K. P. (1973). Implosive therapy and flooding procedures: A critical review. *Psychological Bulletin, 79,* 318–334.

Morganstern, K. P. (1976). Behavioral interviewing: The initial stages of assessment. In M. Hersen & A. S. Bellack (Eds.), *Behavioral assessment: A practical approach* (pp. 51–76). Oxford, UK: Pergamon.

Morin, C. D., Culvert, J. P., & Schwartz, S. M. (1994). Nonpharmacological interventions for insomnia: A meta-analysis of treatment efficacy. *American Journal of Psychiatry, 151,* 1172–1180.

Morin, C. M. (1993). *Insomnia: Psychological assessment and management.* New York: Guilford.

Morin, C. M., & Azrin, N. H. (1987). Stimulus control and imagery training in treating sleep-maintenance insomnia. *Journal of Consulting and Clinical Psychology, 55,* 260–262.

Morin, C. M., & Azrin, N. H. (1988). Behavioral and cognitive treatments of geriatric insomnia. *Journal of Consulting and Clinical Psychology, 56,* 748–753.

Morin, C. M., Kowatch, R. A., Barry, T., & Walton, E. (1993). Cognitive-behavior therapy for late-life insomnia. *Journal of Consulting and Clinical Psychology, 61,* 137–146.

Morin, C. M., Stone, J., McDonald, K., & Jones, S. (1994). Psychological management of insomnia: A clinical replication series with 100 patients. *Behavior Therapy, 25,* 291–309.

Morris, C. W., & Cohen, R. (1982). Cognitive considerations in cognitive behavior modification. *School Psychological Review, 11,* 14–20.

Morris, R. J., & Kratochwill, T. R. (1983). *Treating children's fears and phobias.* Elmsford, NY: Pergamon.

Morrison, A. P. (1998). A cognitive analysis of auditory hallucinations: Are voices to schizophrenia what bodily sensations are to panic? *Behavioural and Cognitive Psychotherapy, 26,* 289–302.

Morrison, A. P., & Renton, J. C. (2001). Cognitive therapy for auditory hallucinations: A theory-based approach. *Cognitive and Behavioral Practice, 8,* 147–160.

Morrison, A. P., Renton, J., Williams, S., & Dunn, H. (1999). *An effectiveness study of cognitive therapy for psychosis: Preliminary findings.* Paper presented at the 3rd International Conference on Psychological Treatment of Schizophrenia, Oxford, UK.

Morrison, R. L. (1988). Structured interviews and rating scales. In A. S. Bellack & M. Hersen (Eds.), *Behavioral assessment: A practical handbook* (3rd ed., pp. 252–277). Elmsford, NY: Pergamon.

Morrow, G. R. (1986). Effect of the cognitive hierarchy in the systematic desensitization treatment of anticipatory nausea in cancer patients: A component comparison with relaxation only, counseling, and no treatment. *Cognitive Therapy and Research, 10,* 421–446.

Morrow, G. R., Asbury, R., Hammon, S., Dobkin, P., Caruso, L., Pandya, K., & Rosenthal, S. (1992). Comparing the effectiveness of behavioral treatment for chemotherapy-induced nausea and vomiting when administered by oncologists, oncology nurses, and clinical psychologists. *Health Psychology, 11,* 250–256.

Morrow, G. R., & Morrell, C. (1982). Behavioral treatment for the anticipatory nausea and vomiting induced by cancer chemotherapy. *New UK Journal of Medicine, 307,* 1476–1480.

Moses, A. N., & Hollandsworth, J. G. (1985). Relative effectiveness of education alone versus stress inoculation training in treatment of dental phobia. *Behavior Therapy, 16,* 531–537.

Mowrer, O. H. (1960). *Learning theory and the symbolic processes.* New York: Wiley.

Mowrer, O. H., & Mowrer, W. M. (1938). Enuresis: A method for its study and treatment. *American Journal of Orthopsychiatry, 8,* 436–447.

Mudford, O. C. (1995). An intrusive and restrictive alternative to contingent shock. *Behavioral Interventions, 10,* 87–99.

Munby, M., & Johnston, D. W. (1980). Agoraphobia: The long-term follow-up of behavioural treatment. *British Journal of Psychiatry, 137,* 418–427.

Muran, E., & DiGiuseppe, R. [A.] (2000). Rape trauma. In F. M. Dattilio & A. Freeman (Eds.), *Cognitive-behavioral strategies for crisis intervention* (2nd ed., pp. 84–125). New York: Guilford.

Muris, P., Merckelbach, H., Holdrinet, I., & Sijsenaar, M. (1998). Treating phobic children: Effects of EMDR versus exposure. *Journal of Consulting and Clinical Psychology, 66,* 193–198.

Murtagh, D. R. R., & Greenwood, K. M. (1995). Identifying effective psychological treatments for insomnia: A meta-analysis. *Journal of Consulting and Clinical Psychology, 63,* 79–89.

Mylott, K. (1994). Twelve irrational ideas that drive gay men and women crazy. *Journal of Rational-Emotive & Cognitive-Behavior Therapy, 12,* 61–71.

Nangle, D. W., Carr-Nangle, R. E., & Hansen, D. J. (1994). Enhancing generalization of a contingency-management intervention through the use of family problem-solving training: Evaluation with a severely conduct-disordered adolescent. *Child & Family Behavior Therapy, 15,* 65–76.

Nangle, D. W., & Hansen, D. J. (1998). Adolescent heterosocial competence revisited: Implications for an expanded conceptualization for the prevention of high-risk sexual interactions. *Education and Treatment of Children, 21,* 431–446.

Nathan, P. E. (1976). Alcoholism. In H. Leitenberg (Ed.), *Handbook of behavior modification and behavior therapy* (pp. 3–44). Englewood Cliffs, NJ: Prentice Hall.

National Center for HIV, STD and TB Prevention. (2001). *HIV/AIDS Surveillance Report.* Retrieved February 17, 2002, from http://www.cdc.gov/hiv stats/hasr1202.htm

Nawas, M. M., Welsch, W. V., & Fishman, S. T. (1970). The comparative effectiveness of pairing aversive imagery with relaxation, neutral tasks and muscular tension in reducing snake phobia. *Behaviour Research and Therapy, 6,* 63–68.

Nazarian, L. F., Mechaber, J., Charney, E., & Coulter, M. P. (1974). Effects of a mailed appointment reminder on appointment keeping. *Pediatrics, 5,* 49–52.

Neal-Barnett, A. M., & Smith, J. M., Sr. (1996). African American children and behavior therapy: Considering the Afrocentric approach. *Cognitive and Behavioral Practice, 3,* 351–369.

Neef, N. A., Bill-Harvey, D., Shade, D., Iezzi, M., & deLorenzo, T. (1995). Exercise participation with videotaped modeling: Effects on balance and gait in elderly residents of care facilities. *Behavior Therapy, 26,* 135–151.

Neimeyer, R. A. (2000). Constructivist psychotherapies. In *Encyclopedia of psychology.* Washington, DC: American Psychological Association.

Neimeyer, R. A., & Raskin, J. D. (Eds.). (2000). *Constructions of disorder: Meaning-making frameworks for psychotherapy.* Washington, DC: American Psychological Association.

Neimeyer, R. A., & Raskin, J. D. (2001). Varieties of constructivism in psychotherapy. In K. S. Dobson (Ed.), *Handbook of cognitive-behavioral therapies* (2nd ed., pp. 393–430). New York: Guilford.

Neisworth, J. T., & Moore, F. (1972). Operant treatment of asthmatic responding with the parent as therapist. *Behavior Therapy, 3,* 95–99.

Nelson, W. M., III, & Finch, A. J., Jr. (2000). Managing anger in youth. In P. C. Kendall (Ed.), *Child and adolescent therapy: Cognitive-behavioral procedures* (2nd ed., pp. 129–170). New York: Guilford.

Nelson, W. M., III, & Politano, P. M. (1993). The goal is to say "goodbye" and have the treatment effects generalize and maintain: A cognitive-behavioral view of termination. *Journal of Cognitive Psychotherapy, 7,* 251–263.

Nemetz, G. H., Craig, K. D., & Reith, G. (1978). Treatment of female sexual dysfunction through symbolic modeling. *Journal of Consulting and Clinical Psychology, 46,* 62–73.

Nesbitt, E. B. (1973). An escalator phobia overcome in one session of flooding *in vivo. Journal of Behavior Therapy and Experimental Psychiatry, 4,* 405–406.

Nevo, O., & Shapira, J. (1988). The use of humor by pediatric dentists. *Journal of Children in Contemporary Society, 20,* 171–178.

New tool: "Reinforcement" for good work. (1971, December 18). *Business Week,* 76–77.

Newman, C. F., & Haaga, D. A. F. (1995). Cognitive skills training. In W. O'Donohue & L. Krasner (Eds.), *Handbook of psychological skills training: Clinical techniques and applications* (pp. 119–143). Boston: Allyn & Bacon.

Newman, M. G., Consoli, A., & Taylor, C. B. (1997). Computers in assessment and cognitive behavior treatment of clinical disorders: Anxiety as a case in point. *Behavior Therapy, 28,* 211–235.

NEWMAN, M. G., CONSOLI, A., & TAYLOR, C. (1999). A palmtop computer program for the treatment of generalized anxiety disorder. *Behavior Modification, 23,* 597–619.

NEWMAN, M. G., HOFMANN, S. G., TRABERT, W., ROTH, W. T., & TAYLOR, C. B. (1994). Does behavioral treatment of social phobia lead to cognitive changes? *Behavior Therapy, 25,* 503–517.

NEWMAN, M. G., KENARDY, J., HERMAN, S., & TAYLOR, C. B. (1996). The use of hand-held computers as an adjunct to cognitive-behavior therapy. *Computers in Human Behavior, 12,* 135–143.

NEWMAN, M. G., KENARDY, J., HERMAN, S., & TAYLOR, C. B. (1997a). Comparison of palmtop computer assisted brief cognitive behavioral treatment to cognitive behavioral treatment for panic disorder. *Journal of Consulting and Clinical Psychology, 65,* 178–183.

NEWMAN, M. G., KENARDY, J., HERMAN, S., & TAYLOR, C. B. (1997b). Comparison of palmtop-computer-assisted brief cognitive-behavioral treatments to cognitive-behavioral treatment of panic disorder. *Journal of Applied Behavior Analysis, 65,* 178–183.

NEWSTROM, J., MCLAUGHLIN, T. F., & SWEENEY, W. J. (1999). The effects of contingency contracting to improve the mechanics of written language with a middle school student with behavior disorders. *Child & Family Behavior Therapy, 21,* 39–48.

NEWTON, T., HARTLEY, P., & STURMEY, P. (1993). Treatment evaluation for eating disorders by clients with eating disorders. *Behavioural and Cognitive Psychotherapy, 21,* 371–374.

NEZIROGLU, F. A., & YARYURA-TOBIAS, J. A. (1993). Exposure, response prevention, and cognitive therapy in the treatment of body dysmorphic disorder. *Behavior Therapy, 24,* 431–438.

NEZU, A. (1996). The main thing. *the Behavior Therapist, 19,* 36–39.

NEZU, A. M., & D'ZURILLA, T. J. (1989). Social problem solving and negative affective conditions. In P. C. Kendall & D. Watson (Eds.), *Anxiety and depression: Distinctive and overlapping features* (pp. 285–315). San Diego: Academic Press.

NEZU, A. M., NEZU, C. M., D'ZURILLA, T. J., & ROTHENBERG, J. L. (1996). Problem-solving therapy. In J. S. Kantor (Ed.), *Clinical depression during addiction recovery: Processes, diagnosis, and treatment* (pp. 187–219). New York: Marcel Dekker.

NEZU, A. M., NEZU, C. M., & LOMBARDO, E. R. (2001). Cognitive-behavioral therapy for medically unexplained symptoms: A critical review of the treatment literature. *Behavior Therapy, 32,* 537–583.

NEZU, A. M., NEZU, C. M., & PERRI, M. G. (1989). *Problem-solving therapy for depression: Theory, research, and clinical guidelines.* New York: Wiley.

NEZU, C. M., NEZU, A. M., & HOUTS, P. S. (1993). Multiple applications of problem-solving principles in clinical practice. In K. T. Kuehlwein & H. Rosen (Eds.), *Cognitive therapies in action: Evolving innovative practice* (pp. 353–378). San Francisco: Jossey-Bass.

NICASSIO, P. M., BOYLAN, M. B., & MCCABE, T. G. (1982). Progressive relaxation, EMG biofeedback and biofeedback placebo in the treatment of sleep-onset insomnia. *British Journal of Medical Psychology, 55,* 159–166.

NICASSIO, P. M., RADOJEVIC, V., WEISMAN, M. H., SHUMAN, C., KIM, J., SCHOENFELD-SMITH, K., & KRALL, T. (1997). A comparison of behavioral and educational interventions for fibromyalgia. *The Journal of Rheumatology, 24,* 2000–2007.

NICHOLSON, N. L., & BLANCHARD, E. B. (1993). A controlled evaluation of behavioral treatment of chronic headache in the elderly. *Behavior Therapy, 24,* 395–408.

NIELSEN, S. L. (2001). Accommodating religion and integrating religious material during rational emotive behavior therapy. *Cognitive and Behavior Practice, 8,* 34–39.

NIETZEL, M. T., BERNSTEIN, D. A., & RUSSELL, R. L. (1988). Assessment of anxiety and fear. In A. S. Bellack & M. Hersen (Eds.), *Behavioral assessment: A practical handbook* (3rd ed., pp. 280–312). Elmsford, NY: Pergamon.

NINNESS, H. A. C., ELLIS, J., & NINNESS, S. K. (1999). Self-assessment as a learned reinforcer during computer interactive math performance: An experimental analysis. *Behavior Modification, 23,* 403–418.

NOCELLA, J., & KAPLAN, R. (1982). Training children to cope with dental treatment. *Journal of Pediatric Psychology, 7,* 175–178

NOMELLINI, S., & KATZ, R. C. (1983). Effects of anger control training on abusive parents. *Cognitive Therapy and Research, 7,* 57–68.

NORCROSS, J. C., & GOLDFRIED, M. R. (Eds.). (1992). *Handbook of psychotherapy integration.* New York: Basic Books.

NORTH, M. M., NORTH, S. M., & COBLE, J. R. (1998). Virtual reality therapy: An effective treatment for phobias. In G. Riva & B. K. Wiederhold (Eds.), *Virtual environments in clinical psychology and neuroscience: Methods and techniques in advanced patient-therapist interaction.* Amsterdam: IOS Press.

NOVACO, R. W. (1975). *Anger control: The development and evaluation of an experimental treatment.* Lexington, MA: Lexington Books.

NOVACO, R. [W.] (1977a). A stress-inoculation approach to anger management in the training of law enforcement officers. *American Journal of Community Psychology, 5,* 327–346.

NOVACO, R. [W.] (1977b). Stress inoculation: A cognitive therapy for anger and its application to a case of depression. *Journal of Consulting and Clinical Psychology, 45,* 600–608.

NOVICK, J. (1966). Symptomatic treatment of acquired and persistent enuresis. *Journal of Abnormal Psychology, 71,* 363–368.

NUNES, D. L., MURPHY, R. J., & RUPRECHT, M. L. (1977). Reducing self-injurious behavior of severely retarded individuals through withdrawal-of-reinforcement procedures. *Behavior Modification, 1,* 499–516.

NUNN, R. G., NEWTON, K. S., & FAUCHER, P. (1992). 2.5 year follow-up of weight and body mass index values in the Weight Control for Life Program: A descriptive analysis. *Addictive Behaviors, 17,* 579–585.

O'BANION, D. R., & WHALEY, D. L. (1981). *Behavior contracting: Arranging contingencies of reinforcement.* New York: Springer.

O'CALLAGHAN, M. E., & COUVADELLI, B. (1998). Use of self-instructional strategies with three neurologically impaired adults. *Cognitive Therapy and Research, 22,* 91–107.

OCKENE, J. K., EMMONS, K. M., MERMELSTEIN, R. J., PERKINS, K. A., BONOLLO, D. S., VOORHEES, C. C., & HOLLIS, J. F. (2000). Relapse and maintenance issues for smoking cessation. *Health Psychology, 19,* 17–31.

O'CONNOR, R. D. (1969). Modification of social withdrawal through symbolic modeling. *Journal of Applied Behavior Analysis, 2,* 15–22.

O'DONOHUE, W., & KRASNER, L. (Eds.). (1995a). *Handbook of psychological skills training: Clinical techniques and applications.* Boston: Allyn & Bacon.

O'DONOHUE, W., & KRASNER, L. (1995b). Psychological skills training. In W. O'Donohue & L. Krasner (Eds.), *Handbook of psychological skills training: Clinical techniques and applications* (pp. 1–19). Boston: Allyn & Bacon.

O'DONOHUE, W., & NOLL, J. (1995). Problem-solving skills. In W. O'Donohue & L. Krasner (Eds.), *Handbook of psychological skills training: Clinical techniques and applications* (pp. 144–160). Boston: Allyn & Bacon.

OEI, T. P. S., & SHUTTLEWOOD, G. J. (1997). Comparison of specific and nonspecific factors in group cognitive therapy for depression. *Journal of Behavior Therapy and Experimental Psychiatry, 28,* 221–231.

O'FARRELL, T. J. (1994). Marital therapy and spouse-involved treatment with alcoholic patients. *Behavior Therapy, 25,* 391–406.

O'FARRELL, T. J., CUTTER, H. S. G., CHOQUETTE, K. A., FLOYD, F. J., & BAYOG, R. D. (1992). Behavioral marital therapy for male alcoholics: Marital and drinking adjustment during the two years after treatment. *Behavior Therapy, 23,* 529–549.

O'FARRELL, T. J., & FALS-STEWART, W. (2000). Behavioral couples therapy for alcoholism and drug abuse. *the Behavior Therapist, 23,* 49–54, 70.

OFFICE OF INSPECTOR GENERAL. (1996, May). *Mental health services in nursing facilities.* (Publication OEI-02-91-00860). Washington, DC: U.S. Department of Health and Human Services.

OLDENBURG, D. (1994, April 12). In the eye of the beholder. *The Washington Post,* p. E5.

O'LEARY, K. D. (1972). The assessment of psychopathology in children. In H. C. Quay & J. S. Werry (Eds.), *Psychopathological disorders of childhood* (pp. 234–272). New York: Wiley.

O'LEARY, K. D., & RATHUS, J. H. (1993). Clients' perceptions of therapeutic helpfulness in cognitive and marital therapy for depression. *Cognitive Therapy and Research, 17,* 225–233.

O'LEARY, K. D., & TURKEWITZ, H. (1978). Marital therapy from a behavioral perspective. In T. J. Paolino & B. S. McCrady (Eds.), *Marriage and marital therapy: Psychoanalytic, behavioral and systems theory perspectives* (pp. 240–297). New York: Brunner/Mazel.

O'LEARY, K. D., & WILSON, G. T. (1975). *Behavior therapy: Application and outcome.* Englewood Cliffs, NJ: Prentice Hall.

OLLENDICK, T. H. (1979). Fear reduction techniques with children. In M. Hersen, R. M. Eisler, & P. M. Miller (Eds.), *Progress in behavior modification* (Vol. 8, pp. 127–168). New York: Academic Press.

OLLENDICK, T. H. (1983). Reliability and validity of the Revised Fear Survey Schedule for Children (FSSC-R). *Behaviour Research and Therapy, 21,* 685–692.

OLLENDICK, T. H., & CERNY, J. A. (1981). *Clinical behavior therapy with children.* New York: Plenum.

OLLENDICK, T. H., & GREENE, R. W. (1998). Principles and practices of behavioral assessment with children. In C. R. Reynolds (Ed.), *Comprehensive clinical psychology: Assessment* (Vol. 4, pp. 131–155). Oxford: Elsevier Science.

OLLENDICK, T. H., HAGOPIAN, L. P., & KING, N. J. (1997). Specific phobias in children. In G. C. L. Davey (Ed.), *Phobia: A handbook of theory, research, and treatment* (pp. 201–224). New York: Wiley.

OLLENDICK, T. H., & MATSON, J. L. (1978). Overcorrection: An overview. *Behavior Therapy, 9,* 830–842.

OLMSTED, M. P., DAVIS, R., ROCKERT, W., IRVINE, M. J., EAGLE, M., & GARNER, D. M. (1991). Efficacy of a brief group psychoeducational intervention for bulimia nervosa. *Behaviour Research and Therapy, 29,* 71–83.

OLSON, R. L., & ROBERTS, M. W. (1987). Alternative treatments for sibling aggression. *Behavior Therapy, 18,* 243–250.

OMIZO, M. M., CUBBERLY, W. E., & OMIZO, S. A. (1985). The effects of rational-emotive education groups on self-concept and locus of control among learning disabled children. *Exceptional Child, 32,* 13–19.

OMIZO, M. M., LO, F. G., & WILLIAMS, E. (1986). Rational-emotive education, self-concept, and locus of control among learning disabled students. *Journal of Humanistic Education and Development, 25,* 58–69.

O'NEILL, R. E., HORNER, R. H., ALBIN, R. W., STOREY, K., & SPRAGUE, J. R. (1990). *Functional analysis of problem behavior: A practical assessment guide.* Pacific Grove, CA: Brooks/Cole.

OPPEL, W. C., HARPER, P. A., & RIDER, R. V. (1968). Social, psychological and neurological factors associated with nocturnal enuresis. *Pediatrics, 42,* 627–641.

O'REILLY, D., & DILLENBURGER, K. (1997). Compliance training as an intervention for antisocial behaviour: A pilot study. In K. Dillenburger, M. F. O'Reilly, & M. Keenan (Eds.), *Advances in behaviour analysis* (pp. 134–156). Dublin, Ireland: University College Dublin Press.

ORGANISTA, K. C., & MUÑOZ, R. F. (1996). Cognitive behavioral therapy with Latinos. *Cognitive and Behavioral Practice, 3,* 255–270.

ORLEANS, C. T. (2000). Promoting the maintenance of health behavior change: Recommendations for the next generation of research and practice. *Health Psychology, 19,* 76–83.

OSBORN, E. L. (1986). Effects of participant modeling and desensitization on childhood warm water phobia. *Journal of Behavior Therapy and Experimental Psychiatry, 17,* 117–119.

OSMAN, A., BARRIOS, F. X., OSMAN, J. R., SCHNEKLOTH, R., & TROUTMAN, J. A. (1994). The pain anxiety symptoms scale: Psychometric properties in a community sample. *Journal of Behavioral Medicine, 17,* 511–522.

ÖST, L. G. (1989). One-session treatment for specific phobias. *Behaviour Research and Therapy, 27,* 1–7.

ÖST, L., BRANDENBERG, M., & ALM, T. (1997). One versus five sessions of exposure in the treatment of flying phobia. *Behaviour Research and Therapy, 35,* 987–996.

ÖST, L., & BREITHOLZ, E. (2000). Applied relaxation vs. cognitive therapy in the treatment of generalized anxiety disorder. *Behaviour Research and Therapy, 38,* 777–790.

ÖST, L., FEREBEE, I., & FURMARK, T. (1997). One-session group therapy of spider phobia: Direct versus indirect treatments. *Behaviour Research and Therapy, 35,* 721–732.

Öst, L., Westling, B. E., & Hellstrom, K. (1993). Applied relaxation, exposure in vivo and cognitive methods in the treatment of panic disorder with agoraphobia. *Behaviour Research and Therapy, 31,* 383–394.

Osterweis, M., Mechanic, D., & Kleinman, A. (1987). *Pain and disability: Clinical, behavioral, and public policy perspectives.* New York: National Academy Press.

Ostroff, R. B., & Boyd, J. H. (1987). Television and suicide: Comment. *New UK Journal of Medicine, 316,* 876–877.

Otto, M. W., & Gould, R. A. (1995). Maximizing treatment-outcome for panic disorder: Cognitive-behavioral strategies. In M. H. Pollack, M. W. Otto, & J. F. Rosenbaum (Eds.), *Challenges in psychiatric treatment: Pharmacological and psychosocial strategies* (pp. 113–140). New York: Guilford.

Otto, M. W., Gould, R. A., & Pollack, M. H. (1994). Cognitive-behavioral treatment of panic disorder: Considerations for the treatment of patients over the long term. *Psychiatric Annals, 24,* 307–315.

Otto, M. W., Pava, J. A., & Sprich-Buckminster, S. (1995). Treatment of major depression: Applications and efficacy of cognitive-behavior therapy. In M. H. Pollack, M. W. Otto, & J. F. Rosenbaum (Eds.), *Challenges in psychiatric treatment: Pharmacological and psychosocial strategies* (pp. 31–52). New York: Guilford.

Otto, M. W., Penava, S. J., Pollack, R. A., & Smoller, J. W. (1995). Cognitive-behavioral and pharmacologic perspectives on the treatment of post-traumatic stress disorder. In M. H. Pollack, M. W. Otto, & J. F. Rosenbaum (Eds.), *Challenges in psychiatric treatment: Pharmacological and psychosocial strategies* (pp. 219–260). New York: Guilford.

Otto, M. W., & Pollack, M. H. (1994). Treatment strategies for panic disorder: A debate. *Harvard Review of Psychiatry, 2,* 166–170.

Otto, M. W., Pollack, M. H., Gould, R. A., Worthington, J. J., McArdle, E. T., & Rosenbaum, J. F. (2000). A comparison of the efficacy of clonazepam and cognitive-behavioral group therapy for the treatment of social phobia. *Journal of Anxiety Disorders, 14,* 345–358.

Otto, M. W., Pollack, M. H., Meltzer-Brody, S., & Rosenbaum, J. F. (1992). Cognitive-behavioral therapy for benzodiazepine discontinuation in panic disorder patients. *Psychopharmacology Bulletin, 28,* 123–130.

Otto, M. W., Pollack, M. H., Sachs, G. S., Reiter, S. R., Meltzer-Brody, S., & Rosenbaum, J. F. (1993). Discontinuation of benzodiazepine treatment: Efficacy of cognitive-behavioral therapy for patients with panic disorder. *American Journal of Psychiatry, 150,* 1485–1490.

Ouimette, P. C., Finney, J. W., & Moos, R. H. (1997). Twelve-step and cognitive-behavioral treatment for substance abuse: A comparison of treatment effectiveness. *Journal of Consulting and Clinical Psychology, 65,* 230–240.

Overhoser, J. C., & Fine, M. A. (1994). Cognitive-behavioral treatment of excessive interpersonal dependency: A four-stage psychotherapy model. *Journal of Cognitive Psychotherapy: An International Quarterly, 8,* 55–70.

Owusu-Bempah, J. P., & Howitt, D. (1985). The effects of self-modeling on cigarette smoking behavior. *Current Psychological Research and Reviews, 4,* 133–142.

Ozer, E. M., & Bandura, A. (1990). Mechanisms governing empowerment effects: A self-efficacy analysis. *Journal of Personality and Social Psychology, 58,* 472–486.

Pace, G. M., Ivancic, M. T., Edwards, J. L., Iwata, B. A., & Page, T. J. (1985). Assessment of stimulus preference and reinforcer value with profoundly retarded individuals. *Journal of Applied Behavior Analysis, 18,* 249–255.

Pace, T. M., & Dixon, D. N. (1993). Changes in depressive self-schemata and depressive symptoms following cognitive therapy. *Journal of Counseling Psychology, 40,* 288–294.

Page, A. C., & Crino, R. D. (1993). Eye-movement desensitisation: A simple treatment for post-traumatic stress disorder? *Australian and New Zealand Journal of Psychiatry, 27,* 288–293.

Paniagua, F. A. (1998). *Assessing and treating culturally diverse clients: A practical guide* (2nd ed.). Thousand Oaks, CA: Sage.

Paradis, C. M., Friedman, S., Hatch, M. L., & Ackerman, R. (1996). Cognitive behavioral treatment of anxiety disorders in Orthodox Jews. *Cognitive and Behavioral Practice, 3,* 271–288.

Park, W. D., & Williams, G. T. (1986). Encouraging elementary school children to refer themselves for counseling. *Elementary School Guidance and Counseling, 21,* 8–14.

Paschalis, A. P., Kimmel, H. D., & Kimmel, E. (1972). Further study of diurnal instrumental conditioning in the treatment of enuresis nocturna. *Journal of Behavior Therapy and Experimental Psychiatry, 3,* 253–256.

Patel, C. (1977). Biofeedback-aided relaxation and meditation in the management of hypertension. *Biofeedback and Self-Regulation, 2,* 1–41.

Patterson, G. R. (1974). Interventions for boys with conduct problems: Multiple settings, treatments, and criteria. *Journal of Consulting and Clinical Psychology, 42,* 471–481.

Patterson, G. R. (1975). *Families: Applications of social learning to family life.* Champaign, IL: Research Press.

Patterson, G. R. (1982). *Coercive family processes.* Eugene, OR: Castalia Press.

Patterson, G. R., Chamberlain, P., & Reid, J. B. (1982). A comparative evaluation of a parent-training program. *Behavior Therapy, 13,* 638–650.

Patterson, G. R., & Forgatch, M. S. (1985). Therapist behavior as a determinant for client noncompliance: A paradox for the behavior modifier. *Journal of Consulting and Clinical Psychology, 53,* 846–851.

Patterson, G. R., & Gullion, M. E. (1976). *Living with children: New methods for parents and teachers.* Champaign, IL: Research Press.

Patterson, G. R., Ray, R. S., Shaw, D. A., & Cobb, T. A. (1969). *A manual for coding of family interactions.* New York: Microfiche Publications.

Patterson, G. R., & Reid, J. B. (1970). Reciprocity and coercion: Two facets of social systems. In C. Neuringer & J. L. Michael (Eds.), *Behavior modification in clinical psychology* (pp. 133–177). New York: Appleton-Century-Crofts.

Patterson, G. R., & Reid, J. B. (1973). Interventions for families of aggressive boys: A replication study. *Behaviour Research and Therapy, 11,* 383–394.

Patterson, G. R., Reid, J. B., & Dishion, T. J. (1992). *Antisocial boys.* Eugene, OR: Castalia Press.

Paul, G. L. (1966). *Insight vs. desensitization in psychotherapy.* Stanford, CA: Stanford University Press.

PAUL, G. L. (1967). Insight vs. desensitization in psychotherapy two years after termination. *Journal of Consulting Psychology, 31,* 333–348.

PAUL, G. L. (1969a). Behavior modification research: Design and tactics. In C. M. Franks (Ed.), *Behavior therapy: Appraisal and status* (pp. 29–62). New York: McGraw-Hill.

PAUL, G. L. (1969b). Outcome of systematic desensitization: II. Controlled investigations of individual treatment, technique variations, and current status. In C. M. Franks (Ed.), *Behavior therapy: Appraisal and status* (pp. 105–159). New York: McGraw-Hill.

PAUL, G. L., & LENTZ, R. J. (1977). *Psychosocial treatment of chronic mental patients: Milieu vs. social learning programs.* Cambridge, MA: Harvard University Press.

PAUL, G. L., & SHANNON, D. T. (1966). Treatment of anxiety through systematic desensitization in therapy groups. *Journal of Abnormal Psychology, 71,* 124–135.

PAVLOV, I. P. (1927). *Conditioned reflexes.* New York: Liveright.

PEDALINO, E., & GAMBOA, V. U. (1974). Behavior modification and absenteeism: Intervention in one industrial setting. *Journal of Applied Psychology, 59,* 694–698.

PEED, S., ROBERTS, M., & FOREHAND, R. [L.] (1977). Evaluation of the effectiveness of a standardized parent training program in altering the interaction of mothers and their noncompliant children. *Behavior Modification, 1,* 323–350.

PENAVA, S. J., OTTO, M. W., MAKI, K. M., & POLLACK, M. H. (1998). Rate of improvement during cognitive-behavioral group treatment for panic disorder. *Behaviour Research and Therapy, 36,* 665–673.

PENISTON, E. (1975). Reducing problem behaviors in the severely and profoundly retarded. *Journal of Behavior Therapy and Experimental Psychiatry, 6,* 295–299.

PENZIEN, D. B., & HOLROYD, K. A. (1994). Psychosocial interventions in the management of recurrent headache disorders 2: Description of treatment techniques. *Behavioral Medicine, 20,* 64–73.

PERLIS, M., ALOIA, M., MILLIKAN, A., BOEHMLER, J., SMITH, M., GREENBLATT, D., & GILES, D. (2000). Behavioral treatment of insomnia: A clinical case series study. *Journal of Behavioral Medicine, 23,* 149–161.

PERRIS, C. (1989). *Cognitive therapy with schizophrenic patients.* New York: Guilford.

PERSONS, J. B. (1989). *Cognitive therapy in practice: A case formulation approach.* New York: Norton.

PERSONS, J. [B.] (1994). Is behavior therapy boring? *the Behavior Therapist, 17,* 190.

PERSONS, J. B. (1995). Why practicing psychologists are slow to adopt empirically-validated treatments. In S. C. Hayes, V. M. Follette. R. M. Dawes, & K. E. Grady (Eds.), *Scientific standards of psychological practice: Issues and recommendations* (pp. 141–157). Reno, NV: Context Press.

PERSONS, J. B. (1997). Dissemination of effective methods: Behavior therapy's next challenge. *Behavior Therapy, 28,* 465–471.

PERSONS, J. B., BOSTROM, A., & BERTAGNOLLI, A. (1999). Results of randomized controlled trials of cognitive therapy for depression generalize to private practice. *Cognitive Therapy and Research, 23,* 535–548.

PETERS, L. (2000). Discriminant validity of the Social Phobia and Anxiety Inventory (SPAI), the Social Phobias Scale (SPS) and the Social Interaction Anxiety Scale (SIAS). *Behaviour Research and Therapy, 38,* 943–950.

PETERSON, A. L., & AZRIN, N. H. (1990, November). *A comparison of behavioral procedures for the treatment of Tourette syndrome.* Paper presented at the meeting of the Association for Advancement of Behavior Therapy, San Francisco.

PETERSON, A. L., & AZRIN, N. H. (1993). Behavioral and pharmacological treatments for Tourette syndrome: A review. *Applied and Preventive Psychology, 2,* 231–242.

PETERSON, A. L., CAMPISE, R. L., & AZRIN, N. H. (1994). Behavioral and pharmacological treatments for tic and habit disorders: A review. *Developmental and Behavioral Pediatrics, 15,* 430–441.

PETERSON, A. L., DIXON, D. C., TALCOTT, W., & KELLEHER, W. J. (1993). Habit reversal treatment of temporomandibular disorders: A pilot investigation. *Journal of Behavior Therapy and Experimental Psychiatry, 24,* 49–55.

PETERSON, D. R. (1968). *The clinical study of social behavior.* New York: Appleton-Century-Crofts.

PETERSON, L. (1992). Behavior therapy—Not just "behavior therapy." *the Behavior Therapist, 15,* 87.

PETERSON, L., & BELL-DOLAN, D. (1995). Treatment outcome research in child psychology: Realistic coping with the "Ten Commandments of Methodology." *Journal of Clinical Child Psychology, 24,* 149–162.

PETERSON, L., CROWSON, J., SALDANA, L., & HOLDRIDGE, S. (1999). Of needles and skinned knees: Children's coping with medical procedures and minor injuries for self and others. *Health Psychology, 18,* 197–200.

PETERSON, L., & RIDLEY-JOHNSON, R. (1980). Pediatric hospital response to survey on prehospital preparation for children. *Journal of Pediatric Psychology, 5,* 1–7.

PETERSON, L., SCHULTHEIS, K., RIDLEY-JOHNSON, R., MILLER, D. J., & TRACY, K. (1984). Comparison of three modeling procedures on the presurgical and postsurgical reactions of children. *Behavior Therapy, 15,* 197–203.

PETERSON, L., & SHIGETOMI, C. (1981). The use of coping techniques to minimize anxiety in hospitalized children. *Behavior Therapy, 12,* 1–14.

PETERSON, L., & TREMBALY, G. (1999). Self-monitoring in behavioral medicine: Children. *Psychological Assessment, 11,* 458–465.

PETERSON, P. L., & LOWE, J. B. (1992). Preventing fetal alcohol exposure: A cognitive behavioral approach. *The International Journal of the Addictions, 27,* 613–626.

PETRONKO, M. R., HARRIS, S. L., & KORMANN, R. J. (1994). Community-based behavioral training approaches for people with mental retardation and mental illness. *Journal of Consulting and Clinical Psychology, 62,* 49–54.

PETRY, N. M., MARTIN, B., COONEY, J. L., & KRANZIER, H. R. (2000). Give them prizes, and they will come: Contingency management for treatment of alcohol dependence. *Journal of Consulting and Clinical Psychology, 68,* 250–257.

PHILLIPS, D., FISCHER, S. C., & SINGH, R. (1977). A children's reinforcement survey schedule. *Journal of Behavior Therapy and Experimental Psychiatry, 8,* 131–134.

PHILLIPS, E. L. (1968). Achievement Place: Token reinforcement procedures in a home-style rehabilitation setting for "pre-delinquent" boys. *Journal of Applied Behavior Analysis, 1,* 213–223.

PHILLIPS, E. L., PHILLIPS, E. A., FIXSEN, D. L., & WOLF, M. M. (1971). Achievement Place: Modification of the behaviors of pre-delinquent boys within a token economy. *Journal of Applied Behavior Analysis, 4,* 45–59.

PHILLIPS, E. L., PHILLIPS, E. A., WOLF, M. M., & FIXSEN, D. L. (1973). Achievement Place: Development of the elected manager system. *Journal of Applied Behavior Analysis, 6,* 541–561.

PICKERING, T. G. (1982). Nonpharmacologic methods of treatment of hypertension: Promising but unproved. *Cardiovascular Reviews and Reports, 3,* 82–88.

PIERCE, K. L., & SCHREIBMAN, L. (1994). Teaching daily living skills to children with autism in unsupervised settings through pictorial self-management. *Journal of Applied Behavior Analysis, 27,* 471–481.

PIERCE, T. W. (1995). Skills training in stress management. In W. O'Donohue & L. Krasner (Eds.), *Handbook of psychological skills training: Clinical techniques and applications* (pp. 306–319). Boston: Allyn & Bacon.

PIGOTT, H. E., & GONZALES, F. P. (1987). The efficacy of videotape self-modeling to treat an electively mute child. *Journal of Clinical Child Psychology, 16,* 106–110.

PIGOTT, H. E., & HEGGIE, D. L. (1986). Interpreting the conflicting results of individual versus group contingencies on classrooms: The targeted behavior as a mediating variable. *Child & Family Behavior Therapy, 7,* 1–15.

PINKERTON, S. S., HUGHES, H., & WENRICH, W. W. (1982). *Behavioral medicine: Clinical applications.* New York: Wiley.

PINKSTON, E. M., LINSK, N. L., & YOUNG, R. N. (1988). Home-based behavioral family therapy of the impaired elderly. *Behavior Therapy, 19,* 331–344.

PITMAN, R. K., ALTMAN, B., GREENWALD, E., LONGPRE, R. E., MACKLIN, M. L., POIRE, R. E., & STEKETEE, G. S. (1991). Psychiatric complications during flooding therapy for post-traumatic stress disorder. *Journal of Clinical Psychiatry, 52,* 17–20.

PITMAN, R. K., ORR, S. P., ALTMAN, B., LONGPRE, R. E., POIRE, R. E., & LASKO, N. B. (1993, May). *A controlled study of EMDR treatment for post-traumatic stress disorder.* Paper presented at the 146th annual meeting of the American Psychiatric Association, Washington, DC.

PITTS, C. E. (1976). Behavior modification—1787. *Journal of Applied Behavior Analysis, 9,* 146.

POCHE, C., BROUWER, R., & SWEARINGEN, M. (1981). Teaching self-protection to young children. *Journal of Applied Behavior Analysis, 14,* 169–176.

POCHE, C., YODER, P., & MILTENBERGER, R. [G.] (1988). Teaching self-protection to children using television techniques. *Journal of Applied Behavior Analysis, 21,* 253–261.

POLAHA, J. A., & ALLEN, K. D. (2000). Using technology to automate off-task behavior: Classroom management made simple. *Proven Practice, 2,* 52–56.

POLING, A., & RYAN, C. (1982). Differential-reinforcement-of-other-behavior schedules. *Behavior Modification, 6,* 3–21.

POLLACK, M. H., OTTO, M. W., KASPI, S. P., HAMMERNESS, P. G., & ROSENBAUM, J. F. (1994). Cognitive behavior therapy for treatment-refractory panic disorder. *Journal of Clinical Psychiatry, 55,* 200–205.

POLLACK, M. J., FLEMING, R. K., & SULZER-AZAROFF, B. (1994). Enhancing professional performance through organizational change. *Behavioral Interventions, 9,* 27–42.

POLLARD, N. L. (1998). Development of social interaction skills in preschool children with autism: A review of the literature. *Child & Family Behavior Therapy, 20,* 1–16.

POOLE, A. D., SANSON-FISHER, R. W., GERMAN, G. A., & HARKER, J. (1980). The rapid-smoking technique: Some physiological effects. *Behaviour Research and Therapy, 18,* 581–586.

POSAVAC, H. D., SHERIDAN, S. M., & POSAVAC, S. S. (1999). A cueing procedure to control impulsivity in children with attention deficit hyperactivity disorder. *Behavior Modification, 23,* 234–253.

POSER, E. G. (1970). Toward a theory of behavioral prophylaxis. *Journal of Behavior Therapy and Experimental Psychiatry, 1,* 39–43.

POSER, E. [G.], & KING, M. (1975). Strategies for the prevention of maladaptive fear responses. *Canadian Journal of Behavioural Science, 7,* 279–294.

POSSELL, L. E., KEHLE, T., MCLOUGHLIN, C. S., & BRAY, M. A. (1999). Self-modeling as an intervention to reduce disruptive classroom behavior. *Cognitive and Behavioral Practice, 6,* 99–105.

POTTS, S. G., & BASS, C. M. (1995). Psychological morbidity in patients with chest pain and normal or near-normal coronary arteries: A long-term follow-up study. *Psychological Medicine, 25,* 339–347.

POWELL, E. (1996). *Sex on your terms.* Boston: Allyn & Bacon.

POWERS, L. E., SINGER, G. H. S., STEVENS, T., & SOWERS, J. (1992). Behavioral parent training in home and community generalization settings. *Education and Training in Mental Retardation, 27,* 13–27.

POWERS, S. W., & ROBERTS, M. W. (1995). Simulation training with parents of oppositional children: Preliminary findings. *Journal of Clinical Child Psychology, 24,* 89–97.

PRATT, J., & JONES, T. (1995). Noncompliance with therapy: An ongoing problem in treating hypertension. *Primary Cardiology, 21,* 34–38.

PRECIADO, J. (1999). Behavior therapy's commitment to cultural diversity: The case of Hispanics. *the Behavior Therapist, 22,* 199–200, 207.

PREMACK, D. (1965). Reinforcement theory. In D. Levine (Ed.), *Nebraska symposium on motivation* (pp. 123–180). Lincoln: University of Nebraska Press.

PRINCE, D., & DOWRICK, P. W. (1984, November). *Self-modeling in the treatment of depression: Implications for video in behavior therapy.* Paper presented at the meeting of the Association for Advancement of Behavior Therapy, Philadelphia.

PRINCE, H. T., II. (1975). *The effects of covert behavioral rehearsal, modeling, and vicarious consequences in assertive training.* Unpublished doctoral dissertation, University of Texas at Austin.

PRITCHARD, A., & APPLETON, P. (1988). Management of sleep problems in preschool children. *Early Child Development and Care, 34,* 227–240.

PROCHASKA, J., SMITH, N., MARZILLI, R., COLBY, J., & DONOVAN, W. (1974). Remote-control aversive stimulation in the treatment of head-banging in a retarded child. *Journal of Behavior Therapy and Experimental Psychiatry, 5,* 285–289.

PROPST, L. R., OSTROM, R., WATKINS, P., DEAN, T., & MASHBURN, D. (1992). Comparative efficacy of religious and nonreligious cognitive-behavioral therapy for the treatment of clinical depression in religious individuals. *Journal of Consulting and Clinical Psychology, 60,* 94–103.

Puder, R., Lacks, P., Bertelson, A. D., & Storandt, M. (1983). Short-term stimulus control treatment of insomnia in older adults. *Behavior Therapy, 14,* 424–429.

Puk, G. (1991). Treating traumatic memories: A case report on the eye movement desensitization procedure. *Journal of Behavior Therapy and Experimental Psychiatry, 22,* 149–151.

Pumroy, D. K., & Pumroy, S. S. (1965). Systematic observation and reinforcement technique in toilet training. *Psychological Reports, 16,* 467–471.

Purcell, D. W., Campos, P. E., & Perilla, J. L. (1996). Therapy with lesbians and gay men: A cognitive behavioral perspective. *Cognitive and Behavioral Practice, 3,* 391–415.

Rabavilas, A. D., Boulougouris, J. C., & Stefanis, C. (1976). Duration of flooding sessions in the treatment of obsessive-compulsive patients. *Behaviour Research and Therapy, 14,* 349–355.

Rachman, S. (1959). The treatment of anxiety and phobic reactions by systematic desensitization psychotherapy. *Journal of Abnormal and Social Psychology, 58,* 259–263.

Rachman, S. (1967). Systematic desensitization. *Psychological Bulletin, 67,* 93–103.

Rachman, S. (1972). Clinical application of observational learning, imitation and modeling. *Behavior Therapy, 3,* 379–397.

Rachman, S. (1990). *Fear and courage* (2nd ed.). New York: W. H. Freeman.

Rachman, S., & Eysenck, H. J. (1966). Reply to a "critique and reformulation" of behavior therapy. *Psychological Bulletin, 65,* 165–169.

Rachman, S., & Hodgson, R. (1980). *Obsessions and compulsions.* Englewood Cliffs, NJ: Prentice Hall.

Rachman, S., & Teasdale, J. (1969). *Aversion therapy and behaviour disorders: An analysis.* Coral Gables, FL: University of Miami Press.

Rachman, S. J., & Wilson, G. T. (1980). *The effects of psychological therapy* (2nd, enlarged ed.). Oxford: Pergamon.

Rains, J. C. (1995). Treatment of obstructive sleep apnea in pediatric patients: Behavioral intervention for compliance with nasal continuous positive airway pressure. *Clinical Pediatrics, 34,* 535–541.

Ramirez, S. Z., & Kratochwill, T. R. (1990). Development of the Fear Survey Schedule for Children With and Without Mental Retardation. *Behavioral Assessment, 12,* 457–470.

Rankin, W. H. (1960). *The man who rode the thunder.* Englewood Cliffs, NJ: Prentice Hall.

Rao, N., Moely, B. E., & Lockman, J. J. (1987). Increasing social participation in preschool social isolates. *Journal of Clinical Child Psychology, 16,* 178–183.

Rapp, J. T., Miltenberger, R. G., Galensky, T. L., Ellingson, S. A., & Long, E. S. (1999). A functional analysis of hair pulling. *Journal of Applied Behavior Analysis, 32,* 329–337.

Rapp, J. T., Miltenberger, R. G., Galensky, T. L., Roberts, J., & Ellingson, S. A. (1999). Brief functional analysis and simplified habit reversal treatment of thumb sucking in fraternal twin brothers. *Child & Family Behavior Therapy, 21,* 1–17.

Rapp, J. T., Miltenberger, R. G., Long, E. S., Elliott, A. J., & Lumley, V. A. (1998). Simplified habit reversal treatment for chronic hair pulling in three adolescents: A clinical replication with direct observation. *Journal of Applied Behavior Analysis, 31,* 299–302.

Rasing, E. J., Coninx, F., Duker, P. C., & van Den Hurk, A. J. (1994). Acquisition and generalization of social behavior in language-disabled deaf adolescents. *Behavior Modification, 18,* 411–442.

Rathus, S. A. (1973). A 30-item schedule for assessing assertive behavior. *Behavior Therapy, 4,* 398–406.

Raue, P. J., Castonguay, L. G., & Goldfried, M. R. (1993). The working alliance: A comparison of two therapies. *Psychotherapy Research, 3,* 197–207.

Raue, P. J., & Goldfried, M. R. (1994). The therapeutic alliance in cognitive-behavior therapy. In A. O. Horvath & L. S. Greenberg (Eds.), *The working alliance: Theory, research, and practice* (pp. 131–152). New York: Wiley.

Raw, M., & Russell, M. A. H. (1980). Rapid smoking, cue exposure and support in the modification of smoking. *Behaviour Research and Therapy, 18,* 363–372.

Raw, S. D. (1993). Does psychotherapy research teach us anything about psychotherapy? *the Behavior Therapist, 16,* 75–76.

Redd, W. [H.] (1980). Stimulus control and extinction of psychosomatic symptoms in cancer patients in protective isolation. *Journal of Consulting and Clinical Psychology, 48,* 448–455.

Redd, W. H., & Andrykowski, M. A. (1982). Behavioral intervention in cancer treatment: Controlling aversion reactions to chemotherapy. *Journal of Consulting and Clinical Psychology, 50,* 1018–1029.

Redd, W. H., Manne, S. L., Peters, B., Jacobsen, P. B., & Schmidt, H. (1994). Fragrance administration to reduce anxiety during MR imaging. *Journal of Magnetic Resonance, 4,* 623–626.

Reeves, J. L. (1976). EMG-biofeedback reduction of tension headache: A cognitive skills-training approach. *Biofeedback and Self-Regulation, 1,* 217–225.

Rehm, L. P. (1988). Assessment of depression. In A. S. Bellack & M. Hersen (Eds.), *Behavioral assessment: A practical handbook* (3rd ed., pp. 313–364). Elmsford, NY: Pergamon.

Rehm, L. P., & Rokke, P. D. (1988). Self-management therapies. In K. S. Dobson (Ed.), *Handbook of cognitive-behavioral therapies* (pp. 136–166). New York: Guilford.

Reid, J. B., Eddy, M., Bank, L., & Fetrow, R. (1994, November). *Some preliminary findings from a universal prevention program for conduct disorder.* Paper presented at the Fourth Annual National Prevention Conference, Washington, DC.

Reid, J. B., Hinjosa-Rivera, G., & Loeber, R. A. (1980). *A social learning approach to the outpatient treatment of children who steal.* Unpublished manuscript, Oregon Social Learning Center, Eugene.

Reid, R. (1996). Research in self-monitoring with students with learning disabilities: The present, the prospects, the pitfalls. *Journal of Learning Disabilities, 29,* 317–331.

Reid, R. (1999). Attention deficit hyperactivity disorder: Effective methods for the classroom. *Focus on Exceptional Children, 32,* 1–20.

Reidel, B. W., & Lichstein, K. L. (2000). Insomnia in older adults. In W. K. Whitbourne (Ed.), *Psychopathology in later adulthood* (pp. 299–322). New York: Wiley.

REIMRINGER, M. J., MORGAN, S. W., & BRAMWELL, P. F. (1970). Succinylcholine as a modifier of acting-out behavior. *Clinical Medicine, 77,* 28–29.

REINCKE, M. A. (2000). Suicide and depression. In F. M. Dattilio & A. Freeman (Eds.), *Cognitive-behavioral strategies for crisis intervention* (2nd ed., pp. 84–125). New York: Guilford.

REISINGER, J. J., & ORA, J. P. (1977). Parent-child and home interaction during toddler management training. *Behavior Therapy, 8,* 771–786.

REITMAN, D., HUMMEL, R., FRANZ, D. Z., & GROSS, A. M. (1998). A review of methods and instruments for assessing externalizing disorders: Theoretical and practical considerations in rendering a diagnosis. *Clinical Psychology Review, 18,* 555–584.

RENFREY, G., & SPATES, C. R. (1994). Eye movement desensitization: A partial dismantling study. *Journal of Behavior Therapy and Experimental Psychiatry, 23,* 231–239.

RENFREY, G. S. (1992). Cognitive-behavior therapy and the Native American client. *Behavior Therapy, 23,* 321–340.

REYNA, T. (1996). Personal communication.

REYNOLDS, L. K., & KELLEY, M. L. (1997). The efficacy of a response cost-based treatment package for managing aggressive behavior in preschoolers. *Behavior Modification, 21,* 216–230.

RICE, J. M., & LUTZKER, J. R. (1984). Reducing noncompliance to follow-up appointment keeping at a family practice center. *Journal of Applied Behavior Analysis, 17,* 303–311.

RICHARD, J. (1995). Behavioral treatment of an atypical case of obsessive compulsive disorder. *the Behavior Therapist, 18,* 134–135.

RICHARDS, D. A., LOVELL, K., & MARKS, I. M. (1994). Posttraumatic stress disorder: Evaluation of a behavioral treatment program. *Journal of Traumatic Stress, 7,* 669–680.

RIECKERT. J., & MOLLER, A. T. (2000). Rational-emotive behavior therapy in the treatment of adult victims of childhood sexual abuse. *Journal of Rational-Emotive & Cognitive-Behavior Therapy, 18,* 87–101.

RIETVELD, C. M. (1983). The training of choice behaviours in Down's syndrome and nonretarded preschool children. *Australia and New Zealand Journal of Developmental Disabilities, 9,* 75–83.

RIMM, D. C., DEGROOT, J. C., BOORD, P., HEIMAN, J., & DILLOW, P. V. (1971). Systematic desensitization of an anger response. *Behaviour Research and Therapy, 9,* 273–280.

RIMM, D. C., & MASTERS, J. C. (1979). *Behavior therapy: Techniques and empirical findings* (2nd ed.). New York: Academic Press.

RIMM, D. C., SAUNDERS, W. D., & WESTEL, W. (1975). Thought stopping and covert assertion in the treatment of snake phobias. *Journal of Consulting and Clinical Psychology, 43,* 92–93.

RISLEY, T. R. (1968). The effects and side effects of punishing the autistic behaviors of a deviant child. *Journal of Applied Behavior Analysis, 1,* 21–34.

RISLEY, T. R. (1995). Get a life! Positive behavioral intervention for challenging behavior through Life Arrangement and Life Coaching. In L. K. Koegel, R. L. Koegel, & G. Dunlap (Eds.), *Community, school, family, and social inclusion through positive behavioral support.* Baltimore: Brookes.

RISLEY, T. R., & TWARDOSZ, S. (1974, January). *Suggesting guidelines for the humane management of the behavior problems of the retarded.* Unpublished manuscript, Johnny Cake Child Study Center, Mansfield, AR.

RITTER, B. (1968a). Effect of contact desensitization on avoidance behavior, fear ratings, and self-evaluative statements. *Proceedings of the American Psychological Association* (pp. 527–528). Washington, DC: American Psychological Association.

RITTER, B. (1968b). The group desensitization of children's snake phobias using vicarious and contact desensitization procedures. *Behaviour Research and Therapy, 6,* 1–6.

RITTER, B. (1969a). Eliminating excessive fears of the environment through contact desensitization. In J. D. Krumboltz & C. E. Thoresen (Eds.), *Behavioral counseling: Cases and techniques* (pp. 168–178). New York: Holt, Rinehart & Winston.

RITTER, B. (1969b). Treatment of acrophobia with contact desensitization. *Behaviour Research and Therapy, 7,* 41–45.

RITTER, B. (1969c). The use of contact desensitization, demonstration-plus-relaxation and demonstration alone in the treatment of acrophobia. *Behaviour Research and Therapy, 7,* 157–164.

RIVERA, D., & SMITH, D. D. (1988). Using a demonstration strategy to teach midschool students with learning disabilities how to compute long division. *Journal of Learning Disabilities, 21,* 77–81.

ROBB, H. B. (2001). Facilitating rational emotive behavior therapy by including religious beliefs. *Cognitive and Behavioral Practice, 8,* 29–34.

ROBERTS, A. (1979). The behavioral treatment of pain. In M. Ferguson & C. B. Taylor (Eds.), *A comprehensive handbook of behavioral medicine* (pp. 171–189). New York: Spectrum.

ROBERTS, A. E. (1969). Development of self-control using Premack's differential rate hypothesis: A case study. *Behaviour Research and Therapy, 7,* 341–344.

ROBERTS, M., WHITE, R., & McLAUGHLIN, T. F. (1997). Useful classroom accommodations for teaching children with ADD and ADHD. *Journal of Special Education, 21,* 71–84.

ROBIN, A. L., & FOSTER, S. L. (1989). *Negotiating parent adolescent conflict: A behavioral-family-systems approach.* New York: Guilford.

ROBINS, C. J., & HAYES, A. M. (1993). An appraisal of cognitive therapy. *Journal of Consulting and Clinical Psychology, 61,* 205–214.

ROFFMAN, R. A., GILCHRIST, L. D., STEPHENS, R. S., & KIRKHAM, M. A. (1988, November). Relapse prevention with gay or bisexual males at risk for AIDS due to ongoing unsafe sexual behavior. In J. A. Kelly (Chair), *Behavioral intervention to prevent AIDS: Current status and future directions.* Symposium presented at the meeting of the Association for Advancement of Behavior Therapy, New York.

ROHSENOW, D. J., MONTI, P. M., MARTIN, R. A., MICHALEC, E., & ABRAMS, D. B. (2000). Brief coping skills treatment for cocaine abuse: 12-month substance use outcomes. *Journal of Consulting and Clinical Psychology, 68,* 515–520.

ROJAHN, J., HAMMER, D., & KROEGER, T. L. (1997). Stereotypy. In N. N. Singh (Ed.), *Prevention and treatment of severe behavior problems: Models and methods in developmental disabilities* (pp. 199–216). Pacific Grove, CA: Brooks/Cole.

ROKKE, P. D., & AL'ABSI, M. (1992). Matching pain coping strategies to the individual: A prospective validation of the cognitive coping strategy inventory. *Journal of Behavioral Medicine, 15,* 611–625.

ROKKE, P. D., TOMHAVE, J. A., & JOCIC, Z. (1999). The role of client choice and target selection in self-management therapy for depression in older adults. *Psychology and Aging, 14,* 155–169.

ROKKE, P. D., TOMHAVE, J. A., & JOCIC, Z. (2000). Self-management therapy and educational group therapy for depressed elders. *Cognitive Therapy and Research, 24,* 99–119.

ROLIDER, A., & VAN HOUTEN, R. (1984). Training parents to use extinction to eliminate nighttime crying by gradually increasing the criteria for ignoring crying. *Education and Treatment of Children, 7,* 119–124.

ROLLINGS, J. P., BAUMEISTER, A. A., & BAUMEISTER, A. A. (1977). The use of overcorrection procedures to eliminate the stereotyped behaviors of retarded individuals: An analysis of collateral behaviors and generalization of suppressive effects. *Behavior Modification, 1,* 29–46.

ROMANO, J. M., & BELLACK, A. S. (1980). Social validation of a component model of assertive behavior. *Journal of Consulting and Clinical Psychology, 48,* 478–490.

RONAN, K., KENDALL, P. C., & ROWE, M. (1994). Negative affectivity in children: Development and validation of a self-statement questionnaire. *Cognitive Therapy and Research 18,* 509–528.

RORTVEDT, A. K., & MILTENBERGER, R. G. (1994). Analysis of a high-probability instructional sequence and time-out in the treatment of child noncompliance. *Journal of Applied Behavior Analysis, 27,* 327–330.

ROSALES-RUIZ, J., & BAER, D. M. (1997). Behavioral cusps: A developmental and pragmatic concept for behavior analysis. *Journal of Applied Behavior Analysis, 30,* 533–544.

ROSEKRANS, M. A. (1967). Imitation of children as a function of perceived similarity to a social model and vicarious reinforcement. *Journal of Personality and Social Psychology, 7,* 307–315.

ROSEN, G. M. (1995). On the origin of eye movement desensitization. *Journal of Behavior Therapy and Experimental Psychiatry, 26,* 121–122.

ROSEN, G. M. (1996). Level II training for EMDR: One commentator's view. *the Behavior Therapist, 19,* 76–77.

ROSEN, G. M., GLASGOW, R. E., & BARRERA, M. (1976). A controlled study to assess the clinical efficacy of totally self-administered systematic desensitization. *Journal of Consulting and Clinical Psychology, 44,* 208–217.

ROSEN, H. S., & ROSEN, L. A. (1983). Eliminating stealing: Use of stimulus control with an elementary student. *Behavior Modification, 7,* 56–63.

ROSENHAN, D. L. (1973). On being sane in insane places. *Science, 179,* 250–258.

ROSENTHAL, R. (1969). Interpersonal expectations: Effects of the experimenter's hypothesis. In R. Rosenthal & R. L. Rosnow (Eds.), *Artifact in behavioral research* (pp. 181–277). New York: Academic Press.

ROSENTHAL, T. L., LINEHAN, K. S., KELLEY, J. E., ROSENTHAL, R. H., THEOBALD, D. E., & DAVIS, A. F. (1978). Group aversion by imaginal, vicarious and shared recipient-observer shocks. *Behaviour Research and Therapy, 16,* 421–427.

ROSENTHAL, T. L., & REESE, S. L. (1976). The effects of covert and overt modeling on assertive behavior. *Behaviour Research and Therapy, 14,* 463–470.

ROSENTHAL, T. L., ROSENTHAL, R. H., & CHANG, A. F. (1977). Vicarious, direct and imaginal aversion in habit control: Outcomes, heart rates, and subjective perceptions. *Cognitive Therapy and Research, 1,* 143–159.

ROSENTHAL, T. L., & STEFFEK, B. D. (1991). Modeling applications. In F. H. Kanfer & A. P. Goldstein (Eds.), *Helping people change* (4th ed., pp. 70–122). New York: Pergamon.

ROSS, L. (1977). The intuitive psychologist and his shortcomings. In L. Berkowitz (Ed.), *Advances in experimental social psychology* (Vol. 10, pp. 173–220). New York: Academic Press.

ROSS, M. S., & MOLDOFSKY, H. (1978). A comparison of pimozide and haloperidol in the treatment of Gilles de la Tourette's Syndrome. *American Journal of Psychiatry, 135,* 585–587.

ROSSELLO, J., & BERNAL, G. (1999). The efficacy of cognitive-behavioral and interpersonal treatments for depression in Puerto Rican adolescents. *Journal of Consulting and Clinical Psychology, 67,* 734–745.

ROTH, A., & FONAGY, P. (1997). *What works for whom? A critical review of psychotherapy research.* London: Guilford.

ROTHBAUM, B. O. (1992). The behavioral treatment of trichotillomania. *Behavioural Psychotherapy, 20,* 85–90.

ROTHBAUM, B. O. (1997). A controlled study of eye movement desensitization and reprocessing in the treatment of posttraumatic stress disordered sexual assault victims. *Bulletin of the Menninger Clinic, 61,* 1–18.

ROTHBAUM, B. O., & HODGES, L. F. (1999). The use of virtual reality exposure in the treatment of anxiety disorders. *Behavior Modification, 23,* 507–525.

ROTHBAUM, B. O., HODGES, L. F., KOOPER, R., OPDYKE, D., WILLIFORD, J. S., & NORTH, M. (1995a). Effectiveness of computer-generated (virtual reality) graded exposure in the treatment of acrophobia. *The American Journal of Psychiatry, 152,* 626–628.

ROTHBAUM, B. O., HODGES, L. F., KOOPER, R., OPDYKE, D., WILLIFORD, J. S., & NORTH, M. (1995b). Virtual reality graded exposure in the treatment of acrophobia: A case report. *Behavior Therapy, 26,* 547–554.

ROTHBAUM, B. O., HODGES, L. [F.], SMITH, S., LEE, J. H., & PRICE, L. (2000). A controlled study of virtual reality exposure therapy for the fear of flying. *Journal of Consulting and Clinical Psychology, 68,* 1020–1026.

ROTHBAUM, B. O., MEADOWS, E. A., RESICK, P., & FOY, D. W. (2000). Cognitive-behavioral therapy. In E. B. Foa, T. M. Keane, & M. J. Friedman (Eds.), *Effective treatments for PTSD* (pp. 60–83). New York: Guilford.

ROTHBAUM, B. O., & NINAN, P. T. (1999). Manual for the cognitive-behavioral treatment of trichotillomania. In D. J. Stein & G. A. Christenson (Eds.), *Trichotillomania* (pp. 263–284). Washington, DC: American Psychiatric Press.

ROTHERAM-BORUS, M. J., KOOPMAN, C., HAIGNERE, C., & DAVIES, M. (1991). Reducing HIV sexual risk behaviors among runaway adolescents. *Journal of the American Medical Association, 266,* 1237–1241.

ROWA, K., ANTONY, M. M., & SWINSON, R. P. (2000). Behavioural treatment of obsessive compulsive disorder. *Behavioural and Cognitive Psychotherapy, 28,* 353–360.

ROWAN-SZAL, G. A., JOE, G. W., CHATHAM, L. R., & SIMPSON, D. D. (1994). A simple reinforcement system for methadone clients in a community-based treatment program. *Journal of Substance Abuse Treatment, 11,* 217–223.

RUDD, M. D., JOINER, T., & RAJAB, M. H. (2001). *Treating suicidal behavior: An effective, time-limited approach.* New York: Guilford.

RUSCH, F. R., HUGHES, C., & WILSON, P. G. (1995). Utilizing cognitive strategies in the acquisition of employment skills. In W. O'Donohue & L. Krasner (Eds.), *Handbook of psychological skills training: Clinical techniques and applications* (pp. 363–382). Boston: Allyn & Bacon.

RUSCH, F. R., MARTIN, J. E., LAGOMARCINO, T. R., & WHITE, D. M. (1987). Teaching task sequencing via verbal mediation. *Education and Training in Mental Retardation, 22,* 229–235.

RUSCH, F. R., MORGAN, T. K., MARTIN, J. E., RIVA, M., & AGRAN, M. (1985). Competitive employment: Teaching mentally retarded employees self-instructional strategies. *Applied Research in Mental Retardation, 6,* 389–407.

RUSCH, M. D., GRUNERT, B. K., MENDELSOHN, R. A., & SMUCKER, M. R. (2000). Imagery rescripting for recurrent, distressing images. *Cognitive and Behavioral Practice, 7,* 173–182.

RUSHALL, B. S., & SIEDENTOP, D. (1972). *The development and control of behavior in sport and physical education.* Philadelphia: Lea & Febiger.

RUSHTON, H. G. (1989). Nocturnal enuresis: Epidemiology, evaluation, and currently available treatment options. *The Journal of Pediatrics, 114,* 691–696.

RYCHTARIK, R. G., SILVERMAN, W. K., LANDINGHAM, W. P. V., & PRUE, D. M. (1984). Treatment of an incest victim with implosive therapy: A case study. *Behavior Therapy, 15,* 410–420.

SACHS, D. A. (1975). Behavioral techniques in a residential nursing home facility. *Journal of Behavior Therapy and Experimental Psychiatry, 26,* 123–127.

SACKETT, D. L., & HAYNES, R. B. (Eds.). (1976). *Compliance with therapeutic regimens.* Baltimore: Johns Hopkins University Press.

SACKETT, D. L., & SNOW, J. C. (1979). The magnitude of compliance and noncompliance. In R. B. Haynes, D. W. Taylor, & D. L. Sackett (Eds.), *Compliance with health care* (pp. 11–22). Baltimore: Johns Hopkins University Press.

SAFREN, S. A. (2001). The continuing need for diversity in cognitive-behavioral therapy training and research. *the Behavior Therapist, 24,* 209.

SAFREN, S. A., HOLLANDER, G., HART, T. A., & HEIMBERG, R. G. (2001). Cognitive-behavioral therapy with lesbian, gay, and bisexual youth. *Cognitive and Behavioral Practice, 8,* 215–223.

SAHAKIAN, B., & CHARLESWORTH, G. (1994). Masked bereavement presenting as agoraphobia. *Behavioural and Cognitive Psychotherapy, 22,* 177–180.

SAIGH, P. A. (1986). *In vitro* flooding in the treatment of a 6-yr-old boy's posttraumatic stress disorder. *Behaviour Research and Therapy, 24,* 685–688.

SAIGH, P. A. (1987). *In vitro* flooding of an adolescent's posttraumatic stress disorder. *Journal of Clinical Child Psychology, 16,* 147–150.

SAKUTA, T. (1999). Recent progress in behavioral psychotherapy in Japan. *the Behavior Therapist, 22,* 76–77, 91

SANAVIO, E. (1999). Behavioral and cognitive therapy in Italy. *the Behavior Therapist, 22,* 69–75.

SANDERS, M. R., MARKIE-DADDS, C., TULLY, L. A., & BOR, W. (2000). The Triple P-Positive Parenting Program: A comparison of enhanced, standard, and self-directed behavioral family intervention for parents and children with early onset conduct problems. *Journal of Consulting and Clinical Psychology, 68,* 624–640.

SANDERSON, A., & CARPENTER, R. (1992). Eye movement desensitization versus image confrontation: A single-session crossover study of 58 phobic subjects. *Journal of Behavior Therapy and Experimental Psychiatry, 23,* 269–275.

SANDERSON, W. C., BECK, A. T., & MCGINN, L. K. (1994). Cognitive therapy for generalized anxiety disorder: Significance of comorbid personality disorders. *Journal of Cognitive Psychotherapy, 8,* 13–18.

SAPER, Z., BLANK, M. K., & CHAPMAN, L. (1995). Implosive therapy as an adjunct treatment in a psychotic disorder: A case report. *Journal of Behavior Therapy and Experimental Psychiatry, 26,* 157–160.

SARASON, I. G. (1975). Test anxiety and the self-disclosing coping model. *Journal of Consulting and Clinical Psychology, 43,* 148–153.

SASSO, G. M., MUNDSCHENK, N. A., MELLOY, K. J., & CASEY, S. D. (1998). A comparison of the effects of organismic and setting variables on the social interaction behavior of children with developmental disabilities and autism. *Focus on Autism and Other Developmental Disabilities, 13,* 2–16.

SATTERFIELD, J. H., SATTERFIELD, B. T., & CANTWELL, D. P. (1981). Three-year multi-modality treatment of 100 hyperactive boys. *Journal of Pediatrics, 98,* 650–655.

SAUNDERS, D. G. (1976). A case of motion sickness treated by systematic desensitization and *in vivo* relaxation. *Journal of Behavior Therapy and Experimental Psychiatry, 7,* 381–382.

SAYERS, M. D., BELLACK, A. S., WADE, J. H., BENNETT, M. E., & FONG, P. (1995). An empirical method for assessing social problem solving in schizophrenia. *Behavior Modification, 19,* 267–289.

SCHAPP, C., BENNUN, I., SCHINDLER, L., & HOOGDUIN, K. (1993). *The therapeutic relationship in behavioural psychotherapy.* New York: Wiley.

SCHELL, B. J. (1996). Chronic disease and psychotherapy: Part I. *Psychotherapy Bulletin, 31,* 21–25.

SCHERER, M. W., & NAKAMURA, C. Y. (1968). A fear survey schedule for children (FSS-C): A factor analytic comparison with manifest anxiety. *Behaviour Research and Therapy, 6,* 173–182.

SCHLESER, R., MEYERS, A., & COHEN, R. (1981). Generalization of self-instructions: Effects of general versus specific content, active rehearsal, and cognitive level. *Child Development, 52,* 335–340.

SCHMIDT, A. J. M., GIERLINGS, R. E. H., & PETERS, M. L. (1989). Environment and interoceptive influences on chronic low back pain behavior. *Pain, 38,* 137–143.

SCHMIDT, N. B., JOINER, T. E., YOUNG, J. E., & TELCH, M. J. (1995). The Schema Questionnaire: Investigation of psychometric properties and the hierarchical structure of a measure of maladaptive schemas. *Cognitive Therapy and Research, 19,* 295–321.

SCHMIDT, N. B., & WOOLAWAY-BICKEL, K. (2000). The effects of treatment compliance on outcome in cognitive-behavioral therapy for panic disorder: Quality versus quantity. *Journal of Consulting and Clinical Psychology, 68,* 13–18.

SCHMIDT, U. (1989). Behavioural psychotherapy for eating disorders. *International Review of Psychiatry, 1,* 245–256.

SCHMITZ, J. M., RHOADES, H., & GRABOWSKI, J. (1994). A menu of potential reinforcers in a methadone maintenance program. *Journal of Substance Abuse Treatment, 11,* 425–431.

SCHNEIDERMAN, N., ANTONI, M. H., IRONSON, G., LAPERRIERE, A., & FLETCHER, M. A. (1992). Applied psychological science and HIV-1 spectrum disease. *Applied and Preventive Psychology, 1,* 67–82.

SCHNELLE, J. F., KIRCHNER, R. E., MACRAE, J. W., MCNEES, M. P., ECK, R. H., SNODGRASS, S., CASEY, J. D., & USELTON, P. H. (1978). Police evaluation research: An experimental and cost-benefit analysis of a helicopter patrol in a high crime area. *Journal of Applied Behavior Analysis, 11,* 11–21.

SCHNELLE, J. F., KIRCHNER, R. E., MCNEES, M., & LAWLER, J. M. (1975). Social evaluation research: The evaluation of two police patrolling strategies. *Journal of Applied Behavior Analysis, 8,* 353–365.

SCHOLING, A., & EMMELKAMP, P. M. G. (1993a). Cognitive and behavioural treatments of fear of blushing, sweating or trembling. *Behaviour Research and Therapy, 31,* 155–170.

SCHOLING, A., & EMMELKAMP, P. M. G. (1993b). Exposure with and without cognitive therapy for generalized social phobia: Effects of individual and group treatment. *Behaviour Research and Therapy, 31,* 667–681.

SCHROEDER, H. E., & BLACK, M. J. (1985). Unassertiveness. In M. Hersen & A. S. Bellack (Eds.), *Handbook of clinical behavior therapy with adults* (pp. 509–530). New York: Plenum.

SCHULMAN, M. (1974). Control of tics by maternal reinforcement. *Journal of Behavior Therapy and Experimental Psychiatry, 5,* 95–96.

SCHUMAKER, J., & SHERMAN, J. A. (1970). Training generative verb usage by imitation and reinforcement procedures. *Journal of Applied Behavior Analysis, 3,* 273–287.

SCHWARTZ, C., HOULIHAN, D., KRUEGER, K. F., & SIMON, D. A. (1997). The behavioral treatment of a young adult with post traumatic stress disorder for fear of children. *Child & Family Behavior Therapy, 19,* 37–49.

SCHWARTZ, J. M., STOESSEL, P. W., BAXTER, L. R., MARTIN, K. M., & PHELPS, M. E. (1996). Systematic changes in cerebral glucose metabolic rate after successful behavior modification treatment of obsessive-compulsive disorder. *Archives of General Psychiatry, 53,* 109–113.

SCHWARZER, R. (Ed.). (1992). *Self-efficacy: Thought control of action.* New York: Hemisphere.

SCHWITZGEBEL, L., & SCHWITZGEBEL, K. (1973). *Psychotechnology: Electronic control of mind and behavior.* New York: Holt, Rinehart & Winston.

SCOGIN, F., & MCELREATH, L. (1994). Efficacy of psychosocial treatments for geriatric depression: A quantitative review. *Journal of Consulting and Clinical Psychology, 62,* 69–74.

SCOTT, C. S., SCOTT, J. L., TACCHI, M. J., & JONES, R. H. (1994). Abbreviated cognitive therapy for depression: A pilot study in primary care. *Behavioural and Cognitive Psychotherapy, 22,* 57–64.

SEDLAR, G., & HANSEN, D. J. (2001). Anger, child behavior, and family distress: Further evaluation of the Parental Anger Inventory. *Journal of Family Violence, 16,* 361–373.

SELIGMAN, M. E. P. (1995). The effectiveness of psychotherapy: The Consumer Reports *study. American Psychologist, 50,* 965–974.

SELIGSON, M. R., & PETERSON, K. E. (Eds.). (1992). *AIDS prevention and treatment: Hope, humor, & healing.* New York: Hemisphere.

SERGIS-DEAVENPORT, E., & VARNI, J. W. (1982). Behavioral techniques in teaching hemophilia factor replacement procedures to families. *Pediatric Nursing, 8,* 416–419.

SERGIS-DEAVENPORT, E., & VARNI, J. W. (1983). Behavioral assessment and management of adherence to factor replacement therapy in hemophilia. *Journal of Pediatric Psychology, 8,* 367–377.

SHAFFER, H., BECK, J., & BOOTHROYD, P. (1983). The primary prevention of smoking onset: An inoculation approach. *Journal of Psychoactive Drugs, 15,* 177–184.

SHAFTO, F., & SULZBACHER, S. (1977). Comparing treatment tactics with a hyperactive preschool child: Stimulant medication and programmed teacher intervention. *Journal of Applied Behavior Analysis, 10,* 13–20.

SHAH, M., COYLE, Y., KAVANAUGH, A., ADAMS-HUET, B., & LIPSKEY, P. E. (2000). Development and initial evaluation of a culturally sensitive cholesterol-lowering diet program for Mexican and African American patients with systemic lupus erythematosus. *Arthritis Care and Research: Special Issue, 13,* 205–212.

SHANER, A., ECKMAN, T. A., & ROBERTS, L. (1994, November). *Monetary reinforcement for cocaine abstinence in cocaine dependent schizophrenia.* Poster presented at the meeting of the Association for Advancement of Behavior Therapy, San Diego.

SHANNON, H. D., & ALLEN, T. W. (1998). The effectiveness of a REBT training program in increasing the performance of high school students mathematics. *Journal of Rational-Emotive & Cognitive-Behavior Therapy, 16,* 197–209.

SHAPIRO, A. K., & SHAPIRO, E. (1984). Controlled study of pimozide vs. placebo in Tourette's syndrome. *Journal of the American Academy of Child Psychiatry, 23,* 161–173.

SHAPIRO, D. A., REES, A., BARKHAM, M., HARDY, G., REYNOLDS, S., & STARTUP, M. (1995). Effects of treatment duration and severity of depression on the maintenance of gains after cognitive-behavioral and psychodynamic-interpersonal psychotherapy. *Journal of Consulting and Clinical Psychology, 63,* 378–387.

SHAPIRO, E., SHAPIRO, A. K., FULOP, G., HUBBARD, M., MANDELI, J., NORDLIE, J., & PHILLIPS, R. A. (1989). Controlled study of haloperidol, pimozide, and placebo for the treatment of Gilles de la Tourette's syndrome. *Archives of General Psychiatry, 46,* 722–730.

SHAPIRO, E. S., ALBRIGHT, T. S., & AGER, C. L. (1986). Group versus individual contingencies in modifying two disruptive adolescents' behavior. *Professional School Psychology, 1,* 105–116.

SHAPIRO, F. (1989a). Efficacy of the eye movement desensitization procedure in the treatment of traumatic memories. *Journal of Traumatic Stress Studies, 2,* 199–223.

SHAPIRO, F. (1989b). Eye movement desensitization: A new treatment for post-traumatic stress disorder. *Journal of Behavior Therapy and Experimental Psychiatry, 20,* 211–217.

SHAPIRO, F. (1995). *Eye movement desensitization and reprocessing: Basic principles, protocols, and procedures.* New York: Guilford.

SHAPIRO, M. B. (1951). An experimental approach to diagnostic psychological testing. *Journal of Mental Science, 98,* 748–764.

SHAPIRO, M. B. (1952). Experimental studies of a perceptual anomaly. II. Confirmatory and explanatory experiments. *Journal of Mental Science, 98,* 605–617.

SHAPIRO, M. B. (1957). Experimental method in the psychological description of the individual psychiatric patient. *International Journal of Social Psychiatry, 3,* 89–102.

SHAPIRO, M. B. (1961a). A method of measuring psychological changes specific to the individual psychiatric patient. *British Journal of Medical Psychology, 34,* 151–155.

SHAPIRO, M. B. (1961b). The single case in fundamental clinical research. *British Journal of Medical Psychology, 34,* 255–262.

SHAPIRO, M. B. (1966). The single case of clinical-psychological research. *Journal of General Psychology, 74,* 3–23.

SHARP, K. (1981). Impact of interpersonal problem-solving training on preschoolers' social competency. *Journal of Applied Developmental Psychology, 2,* 129–143.

SHEA, M. T. (Panelist). (1990, November). In K. S. Dobson (Moderator), *Cognitive therapy and interpersonal therapy: What do the collaborative study results tell us and where do we go from here?* Panel discussion presented at the meeting of the Association for Advancement of Behavior Therapy, San Francisco.

SHEA, M. T., ELKIN, I., IMBER, S. D., SOTSKY, S. M., WATKINS, J. T., COLLINS, J. F., PILKONIS, P. A., BECKHAM, E., GLASS, D. R., DOLAN, R. T., & PARLOFF, M. B. (1992). Course of depressive symptoms over follow-up: Findings from the National Institute of Mental Health Treatment of Depression Collaborative Research Program. *Archives of General Psychiatry, 49,* 782–787.

SHIPLEY, R. H., & BOUDEWYNS, P. A. (1980). Flooding and implosive therapy: Are they harmful? *Behavior Therapy, 11,* 503–508.

SHIPLEY, R. H., BUTT, J. H., & HORWITZ, E. A. (1979). Preparation to re-experience a stressful medical examination: Effect of repetitious videotape exposure and coping style. *Journal of Consulting and Clinical Psychology, 47,* 485–492.

SHIPLEY, R. H., BUTT, J. H., HORWITZ, B., & FARBRY, J. E. (1978). Preparation for a stressful medical procedure: Effect of stimulus pre-exposure and coping style. *Journal of Consulting and Clinical Psychology, 46,* 499–507.

SHIRLEY, M. J., IWATA, B. A., KAHNG, S. W., MAZALESKI, J. L., & LERMAN, D. C. (1997). Does functional communication training compete with ongoing contingencies of reinforcement? An analysis during response acquisition and maintenance. *Journal of Applied Behavior Analysis, 30,* 93–104.

SHORKEY, C., & HIMLE, D. P. (1974). Systematic desensitization treatment of a recurring nightmare and related insomnia. *Journal of Behavior Therapy and Experimental Psychiatry, 5,* 97–98.

SHURE, M. B., & SPIVACK, G. (1980). Interpersonal problem-solving as a mediator of behavioral adjustment in preschool and kindergarten children. *Journal of Applied Developmental Psychology, 1,* 29–44.

SIEGEL, L. J., & PETERSON, L. (1980). Stress reduction in young dental patients through coping skills and sensory information. *Journal of Consulting and Clinical Psychology, 48,* 785–787.

SIKKEMA, K., WINETT, R. A., & LOMBARD, D. N. (1995). Development and evaluation of an HIV risk reduction program for female college students. *AIDS Education and Prevention, 7,* 145–159.

SILVER, B. V., BLANCHARD, E. B., WILLIAMSON, D. A., THEOBALD, D. E., & BROWN, D. A. (1979). Temperature biofeedback and relaxation training in the treatment of migraine headache: One year follow-up. *Biofeedback and Self-Regulation, 4,* 359–366.

SILVERMAN, W. H. (1986). Client-therapist cooperation in the treatment of compulsive hand washing. *Journal of Behavior Therapy and Experimental Psychiatry, 17,* 39–42.

SILVERMAN, W. K., GINSBURG, G. S., & KURTINES, W. M. (1995). Clinical issues in treating children with anxiety and phobic disorders. *Cognitive and Behavioral Practice, 2,* 93–117.

SILVERMAN, W. K., KURTINES, W. M., GINSBURG, G. S., WEEMS, C. F., LUMPKIN, P. W., & CARMICHAEL, D. H. (1999). Treating anxiety disorders in children with group cognitive-behavioral therapy: A randomized clinical trial. *Journal of Consulting and Clinical Psychology, 67,* 995–1003.

SILVERMAN, W. K., KURTINES, W. M., GINSBURG, G. S., WEEMS, C. F., RABIAN, B., & SERAFINI, L. T. (1999). Contingency management, self-control, and education support in the treatment of childhood phobic disorders: A randomized clinical trial. *Journal of Consulting and Clinical Psychology, 67,* 675–687.

SILVERMAN, W. K., & RABIAN, B. (1994). Specific phobias. In T. H. Ollendick, N. J. King, & W. Yule (Eds.), *International handbook of phobic and anxiety disorders in children and adolescents* (pp. 87–109). New York: Plenum.

SIMMONS, T. (1993). *A season in the air.* New York: Fawcett Columbine.

SIMON, K. M. (1994). A rapid stabilization cognitive group therapy program for psychiatric inpatients. *Clinical Psychology and Psychotherapy, 1,* 286–297.

SIMOS, G., & DIMITRIOU, E. (1994). Cognitive-behavioural treatment of culturally bound obsessional ruminations: A case report. *Behavioural and Cognitive Psychotherapy, 2,* 325–330.

SINGH, N. N., DAWSON, M. J., & MANNING, P. (1981). Effects of spaced responding DRL on the stereotyped behavior of profoundly retarded persons. *Journal of Applied Behavior Analysis, 14,* 521–526.

SIPICH, J. F., RUSSELL, R. K., & TOBIAS, L. L. (1974). A comparison of covert sensitization and "non-specific" treatment in the modification of smoking behavior. *Journal of Behavior Therapy and Experimental Psychiatry, 5,* 201–203.

SISSON, L. A., VAN HASSELT, V. B., & HERSEN, M. (1993). Behavioral interventions to reduce maladaptive responding in youth with dual sensory impairment: An analysis of direct and concurrent effects. *Behavior Modification, 17,* 164–188.

SKEELS, H. M. (1966). Adult status of children with contrasting early life experiences. *Monographs of the Society for Research in Child Development, 31*(Whole No. 3).

SKINNER, B. F. (1953). *Science and human behavior.* New York: Macmillan.

SKINNER, B. F. (1954). A new method for the experimental analysis of the behavior of psychotic patients. *Journal of Nervous and Mental Disease, 120,* 403–406.

SKINNER, B. F., SOLOMON, H. C., & LINDSLEY, O. R. (1953, November 30). *Studies in behavior therapy: Status Report I.* Waltham, MA: Metropolitan State Hospital.

SKINNER, B. F., SOLOMON, H. C., LINDSLEY, O. R., & RICHARDS, M. E. (1954, May 31). *Studies in behavior therapy: Status Report II.* Waltham, MA: Metropolitan State Hospital.

SKINNER, B. F., & VAUGHAN, M. E. (1983). *Enjoy old age.* New York: Norton.

SLIFER, K. J., BABBITT, R. L., & CATALDO, M. D. (1995). Simulation and counterconditioning as adjuncts to pharmacotherapy for invasive pediatric procedures. *Journal of Developmental and Behavioral Pediatrics, 16,* 133–141.

SLIFER, K. J., CATALDO, M. F., CATALDO, M. D., LLORENTE, A. M., & GERSON, A. C. (1993). Behavior analysis of motion control for pediatric neuroimaging. *Journal of Applied Behavior Analysis, 26,* 469–470.

SLOAN, E. P., HAURIS, P., BOOTZIN, R., MORIN, C., STEVENSON, M., & SHAPIRO, C. M. (1993). The nuts and bolts of behavioral therapy for insomnia. *Journal of Psychosomatic Research, 37* (Suppl. 1), 19–37.

SLOAN, E. P., & SHAPIRO, C. M. (1993). [Editorial] *Journal of Psychosomatic Research, 37,* 1–2.

SLOANE, R. B., STAPLES, F. R., CRISTOL, A. H., YORKSTON, N. H., & WHIPPLE, K. (1975). *Psychotherapy versus behavior therapy.* Cambridge, MA: Harvard University Press.

SMITH, B. H., PELHAM, W. E., GNAGY, E., MOLINA, B., & EVANS, S. (2000). The reliability, validity, and unique contribution of self report by adolescents receiving treatment for attention-deficit/hyperactivity disorder. *Journal of Consulting and Clinical Psychology, 68,* 489–499.

SMITH, D. D., & LOVITT, T. C. (1975). The use of modeling techniques to influence acquisition of computational arithmetic skills in learning disabled children. In E. Ramp & G. Semb (Eds.), *Behavior analysis: Areas of research and application* (pp. 283–308). Englewood Cliffs, NJ: Prentice Hall.

SMITH, D. E., MARCUS, M. D., & ELDREDGE, K. L. (1994). Binge eating syndromes: A review of assessment and treatment with an emphasis on clinical application. *Behavior Therapy, 25,* 635–658.

SMITH, F. A., & LINSCHEID, T. R. (1994). Effect of parental acceptance or rejection of a proposed aversive intervention on treatment acceptability. *American Journal on Mental Retardation, 99,* 262–269.

SMITH, M. L., & GLASS, G. V. (1977). Meta-analysis of psychotherapy outcome studies. *American Psychologist, 32,* 752–760.

SMITH, R. E. (1973). The use of humor in the counterconditioning of anger responses: A case study. *Behavior Therapy, 4,* 576–580.

SMITH, R. E., & GREGORY, P. B. (1976). Covert sensitization by induced anxiety in the treatment of an alcoholic. *Journal of Behavior Therapy and Experimental Psychiatry, 7,* 31–33.

SMITH, R. G., & IWATA, B. A. (1997). Antecedent influences on behavior disorders. *Journal of Applied Behavior Analysis, 30,* 343–375.

SMITH, R. G., IWATA, B. A., VOLLMER, T. R., & ZARCONE, J. R. (1993). Experimental analysis and treatment of multiply controlled self-injury. *Journal of Applied Behavior Analysis, 26,* 183–196.

SMITH, S. G., ROTHBAUM, B. O., & HODGES, L. [F.] (1999). Treatment of fear of flying using virtual reality exposure therapy: A single case study. *the Behavior Therapist, 22,* 154–160.

SMITH, T., KLEVSTRAND, M., & LOVAAS, O. I. (1995). Behavioral treatment of Rett's disorder: Ineffectiveness in three cases. *American Journal of Mental Retardation, 100,* 317–322.

SMUCKER, M. R., DANCU, C., FOA, E. B., & NIEDEREE, J. L. (1995). Imagery rescripting: A new treatment for survivors of childhood sexual abuse suffering from posttraumatic stress. *Journal of Cognitive Psychotherapy: An International Quarterly, 9,* 3–17.

SOBELL, L. C. (1994). AABT coming of middle age. *the Behavior Therapist, 17,* 179–180.

SOBELL, M. B., & SOBELL, L. C. (2000). Stepped care as a heuristic approach to the treatment of alcohol problems. *Journal of Consulting and Clinical Psychology, 68,* 573–579.

SOBELL, M. B., SOBELL, L. C., & LEO, G. I. (2000). Does enhanced social support improve outcomes for problem drinkers in guided self-change treatment? *Journal of Behavior Therapy and Experimental Psychiatry, 31,* 41–54.

SOKOLOV, A. N. (1972). *Inner speech and thought.* New York: Plenum.

SOLOMON, A., & HAAGA, D. A. F. (1995). Rational-emotive behavior therapy research: What we know and what we need to know. *Journal of Rational-Emotive & Cognitive-Behavior Therapy, 13,* 179–191.

SOLOMON, L. J., FLYNN, B. S., WORDEN, J. K., MICKEY, R. M., SKELLY, J. M., GELLER, B. M., PELUSO, N. W., & WEBSTER, J. A. (1998). Assessment of self-reward strategies for maintenance of breast self-examinations. *Journal of Behavioral Medicine, 21,* 83–102.

SOLOMON, R. L. (1964). Punishment. *American Psychologist, 19,* 239–253.

SOLOMON, R. W., & WAHLER, R. G. (1973). Peer reinforcement control of classroom problem behavior. *Journal of Applied Behavior Analysis, 6,* 49–56.

SOMERS, J. M., & MARLATT, G. A. (1992). Alcohol problems. In P. H. Wilson (Ed.), *Principles and practice of relapse prevention* (pp. 23–42). New York: Guilford.

SOROCCO, K. H., KASL-GODLEY, J., & ZEISS, A. M. (2002). Fostering sexual intimacy in older adults: The role of the behavior therapist. *the Behavior Therapist, 25,* 21–22.

SOUTHAM, M. A., AGRAS, W. S., TAYLOR, C. B., & KRAEMER, H. C. (1982). Relaxation training: Blood pressure lowering during the working day. *Archives of General Psychiatry, 39,* 715–717.

SOWERS, J., RUSCH, F. R., CONNIS, R. T., & CUMMINGS, L. E. (1980). Teaching mentally retarded adults to time manage in a vocational setting. *Journal of Applied Behavior Analysis, 13,* 119–128.

SPECTOR, I. P., CAREY, M. P., JORGENSEN, R. S., MEISLER, A. W., & CARNRIKE, C. L. M., II. (1993). Cue-controlled relaxation and "Aromatherapy" in the treatment of speech anxiety. *Behavioural and Cognitive Psychotherapy, 21,* 239–253.

Spiegler, M. D. (1970, January). A modeling approach. In J. Schwartz (Chair), *Alternatives within behavior modification.* Symposium presented at the meeting of the California State Psychological Association, Monterey.

Spiegler, M. D. (1980, November). Behavioral primary prevention: Introduction and overview. In M. D. Spiegler (Chair), *Behavioral primary prevention: A challenge for the 1980s.* Symposium presented at the meeting of the Association for Advancement of Behavior Therapy, New York.

Spiegler, M. D. (1983). *Contemporary behavioral therapy.* Palo Alto, CA: Mayfield.

Spiegler, M. D. (1989, March). *Teaching behavior modification experientially through individual behavior change projects: A five-year study.* Paper presented at Teaching of Psychology: Ideas and Innovations, Philadelphia.

Spiegler, M. D. (2000, November). *An analogue model to teach behavior therapy experientially.* Paper to be presented at the meeting of the Association for Advancement of Behavior Therapy, New Orleans.

Spiegler, M. D., & Agigian, H. (1977). *The Community Training Center: An educational-behavioral-social systems model for rehabilitating psychiatric patients.* New York: Brunner/Mazel.

Spiegler, M. D., Cooley, E. J., Marshall, G. J., Prince, H. T., II, Puckett, S. P., & Skenazy, J. A. (1976). A self-control versus a counterconditioning paradigm for systematic desensitization: An experimental comparison. *Journal of Counseling Psychology, 23,* 83–86.

Spiegler, M. D., & Guevremont, D. C. (1994, November). *The relationship between behavior therapy practice and research.* Paper to be presented at the meeting of the Association for Advancement of Behavior Therapy, San Diego.

Spiegler, M. D., & Guevremont, D. C. (1998). *Contemporary behavior therapy* (3rd ed.). Pacific Grove, CA: Brooks/Cole.

Spiegler, M. D., & Guevremont, D. C. (2002). *Current use of behavior therapies in clinical practice.* Unpublished manuscript.

Spiegler, M. D., & Liebert, R. M. (1970). Some correlates of self-reported fear. *Psychological Reports, 26,* 691–695.

Spiegler, M. D., Liebert, R. M., McMains, M. J., & Fernandez, L. E. (1969). Experimental development of a modeling treatment to extinguish persistent avoidance behavior (pp. 45–51). In R. D. Rubin & C. M. Franks (Eds.), *Advances in behavior therapy, 1968.* New York: Academic Press.

Spivack, G., & Shure, M. B. (1974). *Social adjustment of young children.* San Francisco: Jossey-Bass.

Spradlin, J. E., & Girardeau, F. L. (1966). The behavior of moderately and severely retarded persons. In N. R. Ellis (Ed.), *International review of research in mental retardation* (Vol. 1, pp. 257–298). New York: Academic Press.

Spring, F. L., Sipich, J. F., Trimble, R. W., & Goeckner, D. J. (1978). Effects of contingency and noncontingency contracts in the context of a self-control-oriented smoking modification program. *Behavior Therapy, 9,* 967–968.

St. Lawrence, J. S. (1987). Assessment of assertion. In M. Hersen, R. M. Eisler, & P. M. Miller (Eds.). *Progress in behavior modification* (Vol. 12, pp. 152–190). Newbury Park, CA: Sage.

St. Lawrence, J. S., Brasfield, T. L., Jefferson, K. W., Alleyne, E., O'Bannon, R. E., & Shirley, A. (1995). Cognitive behavioral intervention to reduce African American adolescents' risk for HIV infection. *Journal of Consulting and Clinical Psychology, 58,* 432–436.

St. Lawrence, J. S., Hansen, D. J., Cutts, T. F., Tisdelle, D. A., & Irish, J. D. (1985). Situational context: Effects on perceptions of assertive and unassertive behavior. *Behavior Therapy, 16,* 51–62.

St. Lawrence, J. S., Jefferson, K. W., Alleyne, E., & Brasfield, T. L. (1995). Comparison of education versus behavioral skills training interventions in lowering sexual HIV-risk behavior of substance-dependent adolescents. *Journal of Consulting and Clinical Psychology, 63,* 154–157.

Stambaugh, E. E., II. (1977). Audio-taped flooding in outpatient treatment of somatic complaints. *Journal of Behavior Therapy and Experimental Psychiatry, 8,* 173–176.

Stampfl, T. G. (1961, May). *Implosive therapy: A learning theory derived psychodynamic therapeutic technique.* Colloquium presented at the University of Illinois, Champaign.

Stampfl, T. G. (1966). Implosive therapy, Part I: The theory. In S. G. Armitage (Ed.), *Behavioral modification techniques in the treatment of emotional disorder* (pp. 12–21). Battle Creek, MI: V. A. Hospital Publications.

Stampfl, T. G. (1970). Implosive therapy: An emphasis on covert stimulation. In D. J. Levis (Ed.), *Learning approaches to therapeutic behavior change.* Chicago: Aldine.

Stampfl, T. G., & Levis, D. J. (1967). Essentials of implosive therapy: A learning-theory-based psychodynamic behavioral therapy. *Journal of Abnormal Psychology, 72,* 496–503.

Stampfl, T. G., & Levis, D. J. (1973). *Implosive therapy: Theory and technique.* Morristown, NJ: General Learning Press.

Stanley, M. A., & Turner, S. M. (1995). Current status of pharmacological and behavioral treatment of obsessive-compulsive disorder. *Behavior Therapy, 26,* 163–186.

Stanley, S. M., Markman, H. J., St. Peters, M., & Leber, D. (1995). Strengthening marriages and preventing divorce: New directions in prevention research. *Family Relations, 44,* 392–401.

Star, T. Z. (1986). Group social skills training: A comparison of two coaching programs. *Techniques, 2,* 24–38.

Stark, L. J., Collins, F. L., Osnes, P. G., & Stokes, T. F. (1986). Using reinforcement and cueing to increase healthy snack food choices in preschoolers. *Journal of Applied Behavior Analysis, 19,* 367–379.

Stark, L. J., Knapp, L. G., Bowen, A. M., Powers, S. W., Jelalian, E., Evans, S., Passero, M. A., Mulvihill, M. M., & Hovell, M. (1993). Increasing calorie consumption in children with cystic fibrosis: Replication with 2-year follow-up. *Journal of Applied Behavior Analysis, 26,* 435–450.

Stark, L. J., Powers, S. W., Jelalian, E., Rape, R. N., & Miller, D. L. (1994). Modifying problematic mealtime interactions of children with cystric fibrosis and their parents via behavioral parent training. *Journal of Pediatric Psychology, 19,* 751–768.

Startup, M., & Edmonds, J. (1994). Compliance with homework assignments in cognitive-behavioral psychotherapy for depression: Relation to outcome and methods of enhancement. *Cognitive Therapy and Research, 18,* 567–579.

STEED, S. E., BIGELOW, K. M., HUYNEN, K. B., & LUTZKER, J. R. (1995). The effects of planned activities training, low-demand schedule, and reinforcement sampling on adults with developmental disabilities who exhibit challenging behaviors. *Journal of Developmental and Physical Disabilities, 7,* 303–316.

STEGER, J., & HARPER, R. (1977, April). *EMG biofeedback versus* in vivo *self-monitored relaxation training in the treatment of tension headaches.* Paper presented at the meeting of the Western Psychological Association, Seattle.

STEINMARK, S. W., & BORKOVEC, T. D. (1974). Active and placebo treatment effects on moderate insomnia under counterdemand and positive demand instructions. *Journal of Abnormal Psychology, 83,* 157–163.

STEKETEE, G. (1994). Behavioral assessment and treatment planning with obsessive compulsive disorder: A review emphasizing clinical application. *Behavior Therapy, 25,* 613–633.

STEKETEE, G., & LAM, J. (1993). Obsessive-compulsive disorder. In T. R. Giles (Ed.), *Handbook of effective psychotherapy* (pp. 253–278). New York: Plenum.

STEPHENS, R. S., ROFFMAN, R. A., & SIMPSON, E. E. (1994). Treating adult marijuana dependence: A test of the relapse prevention model. *Journal of Consulting and Clinical Psychology, 62,* 92–99.

STERN, R. S., LIPSEDGE, M. S., & MARKS, I. M. (1973). Obsessive ruminations: A controlled trial of thought-stopping technique. *Behaviour Research and Therapy, 11,* 659–662.

STEWART, M. A. (1961). Psychotherapy by reciprocal inhibition. *American Journal of Psychiatry, 118,* 175–177.

STITZER, M., BIGELOW, G., LAWRENCE, C., COHEN, J., D'LUGOFF, B., & HAWTHORNE, J. (1977). Medication take-home as a reinforcer in a methadone maintenance program. *Addictive Behaviors, 2,* 9–14.

STOLZ, S. B. (1977). Why no guidelines for behavior modification? *Journal of Applied Behavior Analysis, 10,* 349–367.

STOLZ, S. B., & ASSOCIATES. (1978). *Ethical issues in behavior modification: Report of the American Psychological Association Commission.* San Francisco: Jossey-Bass.

STONE, G. W. (1994, May 9). Magic fingers. *New York, 27,* pp. 32–37.

STOREY, K., DANKO, C. D., ASHWORTH, R., & STRAIN, P. S. (1994). Generalization of social skills intervention for preschoolers with social delays. *Education and Treatment of Children, 17,* 29–51.

STOREY, K., LAWRY, J. R., ASHWORTH, R., DANKO, C. D., & STRAIN, P. S. (1994). Functional analysis and intervention for disruptive behaviors of a kindergarten student. *Journal of Educational Research, 87,* 361–370.

STORMS, L. (1985). Massed negative practice as a behavioral treatment of Gilles de la Tourette's syndrome. *American Journal of Psychotherapy, 39,* 277–281.

STRAHLEY, R. F. (1965). *Systematic desensitization and counterphobic treatment of an irrational fear of snakes.* Unpublished doctoral dissertation, University of Tennessee, Knoxville.

STRAIN, P. S. (Ed.). (1981). *The utilization of classroom peers as behavior change agents.* New York: Plenum.

STRAIN, P. S., SHORES, R. E., & KERR, M. M. (1976). An experimental analysis of "spillover" effects on the social interaction of behaviorally handicapped preschool children. *Journal of Applied Behavior Analysis, 9,* 31–40.

STRAUSS, C. A. (1986). An operant approach to increasing performance of household chores: A case study using behavioral consultation. *Psychological Reports, 58,* 738.

STRAVYNSKI, A., & GREENBERG, D. (1989). Behavioural psychotherapy for social phobia and dysfunction. *International Review of Psychiatry, 1,* 207–217.

STROSAHL, K. (1995). Behavior therapy 2000: A perilous journey. *the Behavior Therapist, 18,* 130–133.

STROSAHL, K. (1996). Behavior therapy 2000: Three "gold mine-land mine" themes in Generation 2 of health care reform. *the Behavior Therapist, 19,* 52–54.

STRUPP, H. H. (1966). *Who needs intrapsychic factors in clinical psychology?* Paper presented at the Albert Einstein College of Medicine, New York.

STRUPP, H. H. (1978). Psychotherapy research and practice: An overview. In S. L. Garfield & A. E. Gergin (Eds.), *Handbook of psychotherapy and behavior change: An empirical analysis* (2nd ed., pp. 3–22). New York: Wiley.

STRUPP, H. H. (1995). The psychotherapist's skills revisited. *Clinical Psychology: Science and Practice, 2,* 70–74.

STUART, G. L., TREAT, T. A., & WADE, W. A. (2000). Effectiveness of an empirically based treatment for panic disorder delivered in a service clinic setting: One year follow-up. *Journal of Consulting and Clinical Psychology, 68,* 506–512.

STUART, R. B. (1967). Behavioral control of overeating. *Behaviour Research and Therapy, 5,* 357–365.

STUART, R. B. (1969). Operant-interpersonal treatment for marital discord. *Journal of Consulting and Clinical Psychology, 33,* 675–682.

STUART, R. B. (1971). Behavioral contracting with the families of delinquents. *Journal of Behavior Therapy and Experimental Psychiatry, 2,* 1–11.

STUART, R. B. (1980). *Helping couples change: A social learning approach to marital therapy.* New York: Guilford.

STUART, R. B., & LOTT, L. A., JR. (1972). Behavioral contracting with delinquents: A cautionary note. *Journal of Behavior Therapy and Experimental Psychiatry, 3,* 161–169.

STURGES, J. W., & STURGES, L. V. (1998). In vivo systematic desensitization in a single-session treatment of an 11-year old girl's elevator phobia. *Child & Family Behavior Therapy, 20,* 55–62.

STURGIS, E. T., & GRAMLING, S. (1988). Psychophysiological assessment. In A. S. Bellack & M. Hersen (Eds.), *Behavioral assessment: A practical handbook* (3rd ed., pp. 213–251). Elmsford, NY: Pergamon.

STURMEY, P. (1992). Treatment acceptability for anorexia nervosa: Effect of treatment type, problem severity, and treatment outcome. *Behavioural Psychotherapy, 20,* 91–93.

SUAREZ, Y., MCCUTCHEON, B. A., & ADAMS, H. E. (1976). Flooding and systematic desensitization: Efficacy in subclinical phobias as a function of arousal. *Journal of Consulting and Clinical Psychology, 44,* 872.

SUAREZ, Y., PETERS, R. D., CROWE, M. J., EASTERLING, K., & ADAMS, C. (1988, August). *Self vs. therapist control of escape for treatment of phobias.* Paper presented at the meeting of the American Psychological Association, Atlanta.

SUINN, R. M. (2001). The terrible twos—Anger and anxiety: Hazardous to your health. *American Psychologist, 56,* 27–36.

SUINN, R. [M.], & DEFFENBACHER, J. L. (in press). Anxiety management training. In M. Hersen & W. Sledge (Eds.), *Encyclopedia of psychotherapy.* New York: Academic Press.

SUINN, R. M., & RICHARDSON, F. (1971). Anxiety Management Training: A nonspecific behavior therapy program for anxiety control. *Behavior Therapy, 2,* 498–510.

SULLAWAY, M., & HENRY, C. J. (2001). The impact on a private practitioner of being in a clinical trial. *the Behavior Therapist, 24,* 149–150.

SULLIVAN, K. T., & BRADBURY, T. N. (1996). Preventing marital dysfunction: The primacy of secondary strategies. *the Behavior Therapist, 19,* 33–36.

SULLIVAN, M. A., & O'LEARY, S. G. (1990). Maintenance following reward and cost token programs. *Behavior Therapy, 21,* 139–149.

SUTHERLAND, A., AMIT, Z., GOLDEN, N., & ROSENBERGER, Z. (1975). Comparison of three behavioral techniques in the modification of smoking behavior. *Journal of Consulting and Clinical Psychology, 43,* 443–447.

SUZMAN, K. B., MORRIS, R. D., MORRIS, M. K., & MILAN, M. A. (1997). Cognitive-behavioral remediation of problem solving deficits in children with acquired brain injury. *Journal of Behavior Therapy and Experimental Psychiatry, 28,* 202–212.

SWAGGART, B., GAGNON, E., BOCK, S. J., EARLES, T. L., QUINN, C. P., MYLES, B. S., & SIMPSON, R. L. (1995). Using social stories to teach social and behavioral skills to children with autism. *Focus on Autistic Behavior, 10,* 1–16.

SWAN, G. E., & MACDONALD, M. L. (1978). Behavior therapy in practice: A national survey of behavior therapists. *Behavior Therapy, 9,* 799–807.

SWINSON, R. P., FERGUS, K. D., COX, B. J., & WICKWIRE, K. (1995). Efficacy of telephone-administered behavioral therapy for panic disorder with agoraphobia. *Behaviour Research and Therapy, 33,* 465–469.

SWINSON, R. P., & KUCH, K. (1989). Behavioural psychotherapy for agoraphobia. *International Review of Psychiatry, 1,* 195–205.

SZYMANSKI, J., & O'DONOHUE, W. (1995). Self-appraisal skills. In W. O'Donohue & L. Krasner (Eds.). *Handbook of psychological skills training: Clinical techniques and applications* (pp. 161–179). Boston: Allyn & Bacon.

TANAKA-MATSUMI, J., & HIGGINBOTHAM, H. N. (1994). Clinical application of behavior therapy across ethnic and cultural boundaries. *the Behavior Therapist, 17,* 123–126.

TANAKA-MATSUMI, J., HIGGINBOTHAM, H. N., & CHANG, R. (2002). Cognitive-behavioral approaches to counseling across cultures: A functional analytic approach for clinical applications. In P. B. Pedersen, J. G. Draguns, W. J. Lonner, & J. E. Trimble (Eds.), *Counseling across cultures* (5th ed., pp. 337–354). Thousand Oaks, CA: Sage.

TANAKA-MATSUMI, J., & SEIDEN, D. Y. (1994, November). *Functional analytic approaches to cross-cultural therapy.* Paper presented at the meeting of the Association for Advancement of Behavior Therapy, San Diego.

TANAKA-MATSUMI, J., SEIDEN, D., & LAM, K. N. (1996). The Culturally Informed Functional Assessment (CIFA) Interview: A strategy for cross-cultural behavioral practice. *Cognitive and Behavioral Practice, 3,* 215–233.

TARAS, M. E., MATSON, J. L., & LEARY, C. (1988). Training social interpersonal skills in two autistic children. *Journal of Behavior Therapy and Experimental Psychiatry, 19,* 275–280.

TARNOWSKI, K. J., ROSEN, L. A., McGRATH, M. L., & DRABMAN, R. S. (1987). A modified habit reversal procedure in a recalcitrant case of trichotillomania. *Journal of Behavior Therapy and Experimental Psychiatry, 18,* 157–163.

TARNOWSKI, K. J., SIMONIAN, S. J., BEKENY, P., & PARK, A. (1992). Acceptability of interventions for childhood depression. *Behavior Modification, 16,* 103–117.

TARRIER, N. (1992). Management and modification of residual positive psychotic symptoms. In M. Birchwood & N. Tarrier (Eds.), *Innovations in the psychological management of schizophrenia* (pp. 147–169). Chichester, UK: Wiley.

TARRIER, N., KINNEY, C., McCARTHY, E., HUMPHREYS, L., WITTKOWSKI, A., & MORRIS, J. (2000). Two-year follow-up on cognitive-behavioral therapy and supportive counseling in the treatment of persistent symptoms in chronic schizophrenia. *Journal of Consulting and Clinical Psychology, 68,* 917–922.

TARRIER, N., PILGRIM, H., SOMMERFIELD, C., FARAGHER, B., REYNOLDS, M., GRAHAM, E., & BARROWCLOUGH, C. (1999). A randomized trial of cognitive therapy and imaginal exposure in the treatment of chronic posttraumatic stress disorder. *Journal of Consulting and Clinical Psychology, 67,* 13–18.

TARRIER, N., SOMMERFIELD, C., PILGRIM, H., & FARAGHER, B. (2000). Factors associated with outcome of cognitive-behavioural treatment of chronic post-traumatic stress disorder. *Behaviour Research and Therapy, 38,* 191–202.

TARRIER, N., SOMMERFIELD, C., REYNOLDS, M., & PILGRIM, H. (1999). Symptom self-monitoring in the treatment of posttraumatic stress disorder. *Behavior Therapy, 30,* 597–605.

TASK FORCE ON PROMOTION AND DISSEMINATION OF PSYCHOLOGICAL PROCEDURES. (1995). Training in and dissemination of empirically-validated psychological treatments: Report and recommendations. *The Clinical Psychologist, 48,* 3–23.

TATE, B. G., & BAROFF, G. S. (1966). Aversive control of self-injurious behavior in a psychotic boy. *Behaviour Research and Therapy, 4,* 281–287.

TAYLOR, C. B., AGRAS, W. S., SCHNEIDNER, J. A., & ALLEN, R. A. (1983). Adherence to instructions to practice relaxation exercises. *Journal of Consulting and Clinical Psychology, 51,* 952–953.

TAYLOR, C. B., FARQUHAR, J. W., NELSON, E., & AGRAS, W. S. (1977). Relaxation therapy and high blood pressure. *Archives of General Psychiatry, 34,* 339–342.

TAYLOR, D. W. A. (1971). A comparison of group desensitization with two control procedures in the treatment of test anxiety. *Behaviour Research and Therapy, 9,* 281–284.

TAYLOR, T. K., SCHMIDT, F., PEPLER, D., & HODGINS, C. (1998). A comparison of eclectic treatment with Webster-Stratton's parents and children series in a children's mental health center: A randomized controlled trial. *Behavior Therapy, 29,* 221–240.

TEASDALE, J. D., SEGAL, Z., & WILLIAMS, J. M. G. (1995). How does cognitive therapy prevent depressive relapse and why should attention control (mindfulness) training help? *Behaviour Research and Therapy, 33,* 25–39.

TERI, L., CURTIS, J., GALLAGHER-THOMPSON, D., & THOMPSON, L. (1994). Cognitive-behavioral therapy with depressed older adults. In L. S. Schneider, C. F. Reynolds, D. B. Lebowitz, & A. J. Friedhoff (Eds.), *Diagnosis and treatment of depression in late life: Results of the NIH consensus development conference* (pp. 279–291). Washington, DC: American Psychiatric Press.

TESTAL, R., FRANCISCO, J., ORTIZ, C., ANGEL, M., SANTOS, R., & DOLORES, M. (1998). Application of a multimodal programme on a set of disruptive behaviours in a case of mental retardation. *Apuntes de Psicologia, 16,* 5–19.

THACKWRAY, D. E., SMITH, M. C., BODFISH, J. W., & MEYERS, A. W. (1993). A comparison of behavioral and cognitive-behavioral interventions for bulimia nervosa. *Journal of Consulting and Clinical Psychology, 61,* 639–645.

THASE, M. E. (1994). After the fall: Perspectives on cognitive behavioral treatment of depression in the "post-collaborative" era. *the Behavior Therapist, 17,* 48–52.

THASE, M. E., BOWLER, K., & HARDEN, T. (1991). Cognitive behavior therapy of endogenous depression: Part 2: Preliminary findings in 16 unmedicated inpatients. *Behavior Therapy, 22,* 469–477.

THASE, M. E., REYNOLDS, C. F., FRANK, E., SIMONS, A. D., GARAMONI, G. D., MCGEARY, J., HARDEN, T., FASICZKA, A. L., & CAHALANE, J. F. (1994). Response to cognitive-behavioral therapy in chronic depression. *The Journal of Psychotherapy Practice and Research, 3,* 204–214.

THASE, M. E., REYNOLDS, C. F., FRANK, E., SIMONS, A. D., MCGEARY, J., FASICZKA, A. L., GARAMONI, G. G., JENNINGS, J. R., & KUPFER, D. J. (1994). Do depressed men and women respond similarly to cognitive behavior therapy? *The American Journal of Psychiatry, 151,* 500–505.

THASE, M. E., SIMONS, A. D., CAHALANE, J. F., & MCGEARY, J. (1991). Cognitive behavior therapy of endogenous depression: Part 1: An outpatient clinical replication series. *Behavior Therapy, 22,* 457–467.

THASE, M. E., & WRIGHT, J. H. (1991). Cognitive behavior therapy manual for depressed inpatients: A treatment protocol outline. *Behavior Therapy, 22,* 579–595.

THELEN, M. H., FRY, R. A., FEHRENBACH, P. A., & FRAUTSCHI, N. M. (1979). Therapeutic videotape and film modeling: A review. *Psychological Bulletin, 86,* 701–720.

THOM, A., SARTORY, G., & JOHREN, P. (2000). Comparison between one-session psychological treatment and benzodiazepine in dental phobia. *Journal of Consulting and Clinical Psychology, 68,* 378–387.

THOMAS, D. R., BECKER, W. C., & ARMSTRONG, M. (1968). Production and elimination of disruptive classroom behavior by systematically varying teacher's behavior. *Journal of Applied Behavior Analysis, 1,* 35–45.

THOMAS, E. J., ABRAMS, K. S., & JOHNSON, J. (1971). Self-monitoring and reciprocal inhibition in the modification of multiple tics of Gilles de la Tourette's syndrome. *Journal of Behavior Therapy and Experimental Psychiatry, 2,* 159–171.

THOMPSON, J. K. (1992). Body image: Extent of disturbance, associated features, theoretical models, assessment methodologies, intervention strategies, and a proposal for a new DSM-IV diagnostic category—Body image disorder. In M. Hersen, R. M. Eisler, & P. M. Miller (Eds.), *Progress in behavior modification* (Vol. 28, pp. 3–54). Sycamore, IL: Sycamore Publishing.

THOMPSON, L., W., GALLAGHER-THOMPSON, D., & BRECKENRIDGE, J. (1987). Comparative effectiveness of psychotherapies for depressed elders. *Journal of Consulting and Clinical Psychology, 55,* 385–390.

THOMPSON, R. H., IWATA, B. A., CONNERS, J., & ROSCOE, E. M. (1999). Effects of reinforcement for alternative behavior during punishment of self-injury. *Journal of Applied Behavior Analysis, 32,* 317–328.

THORESEN, C. E., & MAHONEY, M. J. (1974). *Behavioral self-control.* New York: Holt, Rinehart & Winston.

THORNDIKE, E. L. (1911). *Animal intelligence: Experimental studies.* New York: Macmillan.

THORNDIKE, E. L. (1931). *Human learning.* New York: Century.

THORNDIKE, E. L. (1933). *An experimental study of rewards.* New York: Teachers College Press.

THYER, B. A. (1985). Audio-taped exposure therapy in a case of obsessional neurosis. *Journal of Behavior Therapy and Experimental Psychiatry, 16,* 271–273.

TIMBERLAKE, E. M. (1981). Child abuse and externalized aggression: Preventing a delinquent lifestyle. In R. J. Hunner & Y. E. Walker (Eds.), *Exploring the relationship between child abuse and delinquency* (pp. 43–51). Montclair, NJ: Allanheld, Osmun.

TIMBERLAKE, W., & FARMER-DOUGAN, V. A. (1991). Reinforcement in applied settings: Figuring out ahead of time what will work. *Psychological Bulletin, 110,* 379–391.

TIMBERS, G. D., TIMBERS, B. J., FIXSEN, D. L., PHILLIPS, E. L., & WOLF, M. M. (1973, August). *Achievement Place for predelinquent girls: Modification of inappropriate emotional behaviors with token reinforcement and instructional procedures.* Paper presented at the meeting of the American Psychological Association, Montreal.

TINCH, C. S., & FRIEBERG, R. D. (1998). The Schema Identification Worksheet. In L. Vanderreek & T. J. Jackson (Eds.), *Innovations in clinical practice* (pp. 247–258). Sarasota, FL: Professional Resource Press.

TOLIN, D. F., & FOA, E. B. (1999). Treatment of a police officer with PTSD using prolonged exposure. *Behavior Therapy, 30,* 527–538.

TONER, B. B., SEGAL, Z. V., EMMOTT, S. D., & MYRAN, D. (2000). *Cognitive-behavioral treatment of irritable bowel syndrome: The brain-gut connection.* New York: Guilford.

TOOLEY, J. T., & PRATT, S. (1967). An experimental procedure for the extinction of smoking behavior. *Psychological Record, 17,* 209–218.

TOPHOFF, M. (1973). Massed practice, relaxation, and assertion training in the treatment of Gilles de la Tourette's syndrome. *Journal of Behavior Therapy and Experimental Psychiatry, 4,* 71–73.

TORGERSEN, A. M. (1985). Temperamental differences in infants and 6-year-old children: A follow-up study of twins. In J. Strelau, F. Farley, & A. Gale (Eds.), *The biological bases of personality and behavior* (Vol. 1, pp. 227–239). New York: Hemisphere.

TORRES-MARTINEZ, E., & SPINETTA, M. (1997). Behavior therapy in Argentina. *the Behavior Therapist, 20,* 171–174.

TOYOKAWA, T., & NEDATE, K. (1996). Application of cognitive behavior therapy to interpersonal problems: A case study of a Japanese female client. *Cognitive and Behavioral Practice, 3,* 289–302.

TREMBLAY, G. C., & DRABMAN, R. S. (1997). An intervention for childhood stealing. *Child & Family Behavior Therapy, 19,* 33–40.

TROWER, P. (1995). Adult social skills: State of the art and future directions. In W. O'Donohue & L. Krasner (Eds.), *Handbook of psychological skills training: Clinical techniques and applications* (pp. 54–80). Boston: Allyn & Bacon.

TRUAX, C. B., SHAPIRO, J. G., & WARGO, D. G. (1968). The effects of alternate sessions and vicarious therapy pretraining on group psychotherapy. *International Journal of Group Psychotherapy, 18,* 186–198.

TRULL, T. J., NIETZEL, M. T., & MAIN, A. (1988). The use of meta-analysis to assess the clinical significance of behavior therapy for agoraphobia. *Behavior Therapy, 19,* 527–538.

TRYON, G. S. (1979). A review and critique of thought stopping research. *Journal of Behavior Therapy and Experimental Psychiatry, 10,* 189–192.

TRYON, W. W. (1999). Behavioral diagnosis versus the *Diagnostic and Statistical Manual. the Behavior Therapist, 22,* 3–4, 19.

TRYON, W. W., & PINTO, L. P. (1994). Comparing activity measurements and ratings. *Behavior Modification, 18,* 251–261.

TUCKER, M., SIGAFOOS, J., & BUSHELL, H. (1998). Use of noncontingent reinforcement in the treatment of challenging behavior. *Behavior Modification, 22,* 529–547.

TURK, C. L., COLES, M. E., & HEIMBERG, R. G. (2002). Psychotherapy for social phobia. In D. J. Stein & E. Hollander (Eds.), *Anxiety disorders* (pp. 323–339). Washington, DC: American Psychiatric Press.

TURK, D. [C.] (1975). *Cognitive control of pain: A skill training approach.* Unpublished manuscript, University of Waterloo, Ontario.

TURK, D. [C.] (1976). *An expanded skills training approach for the treatment of experimentally induced pain.* Unpublished doctoral dissertation, University of Waterloo, Ontario.

TURK, D. C., & GENEST, M. (1979). Regulation of pain: The application of cognitive and behavioral techniques for prevention and remediation. In P. Kendall & S. Hollon (Eds.), *Cognitive behavioral interventions: Theory, research, and prevention* (pp. 287–319). New York: Academic Press.

TURK, D. C., & MEICHENBAUM, D. [H.] (1989). A cognitive-behavioural approach to pain management. In P. D. Wall & R. Melzack (Eds.), *Textbook of pain* (2nd ed.). London: Churchill Livingstone.

TURK, D. C., MEICHENBAUM, D. [H.], & GENEST, M. (1983). *Pain and behavioral medicine.* New York: Guilford.

TURK, D. C., & RUDY, T. E. (1995). Strategies and tactics in the treatment of persistent pain patients. In W. O'Donohue & L. Krasner (Eds.), *Handbook of psychological skills training: Clinical techniques and applications* (pp. 339–362). Boston: Allyn & Bacon.

TURKAT, I. D., & FEUERSTEIN, M. (1978). Behavior modification and the public misconception. *American Psychologist, 33,* 194.

TURNER, A. J., & VERNON, J. C. (1976). Prompts to increase attendance in a community mental health center. *Journal of Applied Behavior Analysis, 9,* 141–145.

TURNER, J. A. (1982). Comparison of group progressive-relaxation training and cognitive-behavioral group therapy. *Journal of Consulting and Clinical Psychology, 50,* 757–765.

TURNER, J. A., & CLANCY, S. (1988). Comparison of operant behavioral and cognitive-behavioral group treatment for chronic low back pain. *Journal of Consulting and Clinical Psychology, 56,* 261–266.

TURNER, J. [A.], HEINRICH, R., MCCREARY, C., & DAWSON, E. (1979, April). *Evaluation of two behavioral interventions for chronic low back pain.* Paper presented at the meeting of the Society of Behavioral Medicine, San Francisco.

TURNER, S. M., BEIDEL, D. C., & COOLEY-QUILLE, M. R. (1997). *Social effectiveness therapy: A program for overcoming social anxiety and social phobia.* Toronto, Ontario: Multi-Health Systems.

TURNER, S. M., BEIDEL, D. C., & JACOB, R. G. (1994). Social phobia: A comparison of behavior therapy and atenolol. *Journal of Consulting and Clinical Psychology, 62,* 350–358.

TURNER, S. M., BEIDEL, D. C., SPAULDING, S. A., & BROWN, J. M. (1995). The practice of behavior therapy: A national survey of cost and methods. *the Behavior Therapist, 18,* 1–4.

TURPIN, G. (1983). The behavioral management of tic disorders: A critical review. *Advances in Behaviour Research and Therapy, 5,* 203–245.

TURSKY, B., SHAPIRO, D., & SCHWARTZ, G. E. (1972). Automated constant cuff pressure system to measure average systolic blood pressure in men. *IEEE Transactions on Biomedical Engineering, 19,* 271–276.

TUSTIN, R. D., PENNINGTON, B., & BYRNE, M. (1994). Intrusiveness of interventions: Ratings by psychologists. *Behaviour Change, 11,* 68–100.

TWYMAN, J. S., JOHNSON, H., BUIE, J. D., & NELSON, C. M. (1994). The use of a warning procedure to signal a more intrusive timeout contingency. *Behavioral Disorders, 19,* 243–253.

ULLMANN, L. P., & KRASNER, L. (Eds.). (1965). *Case studies in behavior modification.* New York: Holt, Rinehart & Winston.

ULMAN, J. D., & KLEM, J. L. (1975). (Communication). *Journal of Applied Behavior Analysis, 8,* 210.

UPPER, D. (1993). The use of covert reinforcement and thought stopping in treating a young woman's sexual anxiety. In J. R. Cautela & A. J. Kearney (Eds.), *Covert conditioning casebook* (pp. 235–244). Pacific Grove, CA: Brooks/Cole.

USSHER, J. M. (1990). Cognitive behavioural couples therapy with gay men referred for counselling in an AIDS setting: A pilot study. *AIDS-Care, 2,* 43–51.

VAAL, J. J. (1973). Applying contingency contracting to a school phobic: A case study. *Journal of Behavior Therapy and Experimental Psychiatry, 4,* 371–373.

VALINS, S., & RAY, A. (1967). Effects of cognitive desensitization on avoidance behavior. *Journal of Personality and Social Psychology, 7,* 345–350.

VALLIS, T. M. (1984). A complete component analysis of stress inoculation for pain tolerance. *Cognitive Therapy and Research, 8,* 313–329.

VALLIS, T. M., HOWES, J. L., & STANDAGE, K. (2000). Is cognitive therapy suitable for treating individuals with personality dysfunction? *Cognitive Therapy and Research, 24,* 595–606.

VAN BALKOM, A. J. L. M., VAN OPPEN, P., VERMEULEN, A. W. A., VAN DYCK, R., NAUTA, M. C. E., & VORST, H. C. M. (1994). A meta-analysis on the treatment of obsessive compulsive disorder: A comparison of antidepressants, behavior, and cognitive therapy. *Clinical Psychology Review, 14,* 359–381.

VAN HOUTEN, R. (1998). *How to use prompts to initiate behavior* (2nd ed.). Austin, TX: Pro-Ed.

VAN OPPEN, P., & ARNTZ, A. (1994). Cognitive therapy for obsessive-compulsive disorder. *Behaviour Research and Therapy, 32,* 79–87.

VAN OPPEN, P., DE HANN, E., VAN BALKOM, A. J. L. M., SPINHOVEN, P., HOOGDUIN, K., & VAN DYCK, R. (1995). Cognitive therapy and exposure *in vivo* in the treatment of obsessive-compulsive disorder. *Behaviour Research and Therapy, 33,* 379–390.

VAN PESKI-OOSTERBAAN, A. S., SPINHOVEN, P., VAN DER DOES, A. J., BRUSHKE, A. V. G., & ROOIJMANS, H. G. M. (1999). Cognitive change following cognitive behavioural therapy for non-cardiac chest pain. *Psychotherapy and Psychosomatics, 68,* 214–220.

VAN SON, M., VAN HEESCH, N., MULDER, G., & VAN LONDEN, A. (1995). The effectiveness of dry bed training for nocturnal enuresis in adults: A 3, 5, and 6 years follow-up. *Behaviour Research and Therapy, 33,* 557–559.

VARGAS, J. S., & SHANLEY, D. (1995). Academic skills. In W. O'Donohue & L. Krasner (Eds.), *Handbook of psychological skills training: Clinical techniques and applications* (pp. 180–194). Boston: Allyn & Bacon.

VARNI, J. W., BOYD, E. F., & CATALDO, M. F. (1978). Self-monitoring, external reinforcement, and timeout procedures in the control of high rate tic behaviors in a hyperactive child. *Journal of Behavior Therapy and Experimental Psychiatry, 9,* 353–358.

VARNI, J. W., KATZ, E. R., COLEGROVE, R., JR., & DOLGIN, M. (1993). The impact of social skills training on the adjustment of children with newly diagnosed cancer. *Journal of Pediatric Psychology, 18,* 751–767.

VARNI, J. W., LA GRECA, A. M., & SPIRITO, A. (2000). Cognitive-behavioral interventions for children with chronic health conditions. In K. S. Dobson (Ed.), *Handbook of cognitive-behavioral therapies* (2nd ed., pp. 291–333). New York: Guilford.

VAUGHAN, K., ARMSTRONG, M. F., GOLD, R., O'CONNOR, N., JENNEKE, W., & TARRIER, N. (1994). A trial of eye movement desensitization compared to image habituation training and applied muscle relaxation in post-traumatic stress disorder. *Journal of Behavior Therapy and Experimental Psychiatry, 25,* 283–291.

VENTIS, W. L. (1973). Case history: The use of laughter as an alternative response in systematic desensitization. *Behavior Therapy, 4,* 120–122.

VERNON, A. (1983). Rational-emotive education. In A. Ellis & M. Bernard (Eds.), *Rational-emotive approaches to the problems of childhood* (pp. 467–484). New York: Plenum.

VERNON, D. T. A. (1974). Modeling and birth order in responses to painful stimuli. *Journal of Personality and Social Psychology, 29,* 794–799.

VINCELLI, F., & MOLINARI, E. (1998). Virtual reality and imaginative techniques in clinical psychology. In G. Riva & B. K. Wiederhold (Eds.), *Virtual environments in clinical psychology and neuroscience: Methods and techniques in advanced patient-therapist interaction.* Amsterdam: IOS Press.

VOEGTLIN, W. L., LEMERE, F., BROZ, W. R., & O'HOLLAREN, P. (1941). Conditioned reflex therapy of chronic alcoholism. *Quarterly Journal of Studies on Alcohol, 2,* 505–511.

VOELTZ, L. M., & EVANS, I. M. (1982). The assessment of behavioral interrelationships in child behavior therapy. *Behavioral Assessment, 4,* 131–165.

VOLLMER, A., & BLANCHARD, E. B. (1998). Controlled comparison of individual versus group cognitive therapy for irritable bowel syndrome. *Behavior Therapy, 29,* 19–33.

VOLLMER, T. R., IWATA, B. A., ZARCONE, J. R., SMITH, R. G., & MAZALESKI, J. L. (1993). The role of attention in the treatment of attention-maintained self-injurious behavior: Noncontingent reinforcement and differential reinforcement of other behavior. *Journal of Applied Behavior Analysis, 26,* 9–21.

VOLMER, T. R., ROANE, H. S., RINGDAHL, J. E., & MARCUS, B. A. (1999). Evaluating treatment challenges with differential reinforcement of alternative behavior. *Journal of Applied Behavior Analysis, 32,* 9–23.

WADE, T. C., BAKER, T. B., & HARTMANN, D. P. (1979). Behavior therapists' self-reported views and practices. *the Behavior Therapist, 2,* 3–6.

WAGAMAN, J. R., MILTENBERGER, R. G., & ARNDORFER, R. E. (1993). Analysis of a simplified treatment for stuttering in children. *Journal of Applied Behavior Analysis, 26,* 53–61.

WAGAMAN, J. R., MILTENBERGER, R. G., & WILLIAMS, D. E. (1995). Treatment of a vocal tic by differential reinforcement. *Journal of Behavior Therapy and Experimental Psychiatry, 26,* 35–39.

WAGAMAN, J. R., MILTENBERGER, R. G., & WOODS, D. (1995). Long-term follow-up of a behavioral treatment for stuttering in children. *Journal of Applied Behavior Analysis, 28,* 233–234.

WAGGONER, C. D., & LELIEUVRE, R. B. (1981). A method to increase compliance to exercise regimens in rheumatoid arthritis patients. *Journal of Behavioral Medicine, 4,* 191–201.

WAGNER, J. (1998). Improving adherence to diabetes blood glucose monitoring regimens with prompts and unit dose packaging. *the Behavior Therapist, 21,* 157–159.

WAGNER, M. K., & BRAGG, R. A. (1970). Comparing behavior modification approaches to habit decrement—Smoking. *Journal of Consulting and Clinical Psychology, 34,* 258–263.

WAGNER, W., JOHNSON, S. B., WALKER, D., CARTER, R., & WITNER, J. (1982). A controlled comparison of two treatments of nocturnal enuresis. *Journal of Pediatrics, 101,* 302–307.

WAHLER, R. G. (1969). Oppositional children: A quest for parental reinforcement control. *Journal of Applied Behavior Analysis, 2,* 159–170.

WAHLER, R. G., & GRAVES, M. G. (1983). Setting events in social networks: Ally or enemy in child behavior therapy? *Behavior Therapy, 14,* 19–36.

WALKER, C. E., HEDBERG, A., CLEMENT, P. W., & WRIGHT, L. (1981). *Clinical procedures for behavior therapy.* Englewood Cliffs, NJ: Prentice Hall.

WALKER, C. E., MILLING, L. S., & BONNER, B. L. (1988). Incontinence disorders: Enuresis and encopresis. In D. K. Routh (Ed.), *Handbook of pediatric psychology* (pp. 363–397). New York: Guilford.

WALKER, W. R., FREEMAN, R. F., & CHRISTENSEN, D. K. (1994). Restricting environmental stimulation (REST) to enhance cognitive behavioral treatment for obsessive compulsive disorder with schizotypal personality disorder. *Behavior Therapy, 25,* 709–719.

WALLACE, B. C. (1992). Treating crack cocaine dependence: The critical role of relapse prevention. *Journal of Psychoactive Drugs, 24,* 131–158.

WALLER, M. A., & SPIEGLER, M. D. (1997). A cross-cultural perspective on couple differences. *Journal of Couples Therapy, 7,* 83–98.

WALSH, P., DALE, A., & ANDERSON, D. E. (1977). Comparison of biofeedback pulse wave velocity and progressive relaxation in essential hypertensives. *Perceptual and Motor Skills, 44,* 839–843.

WALTER, H., & VAUGHAN, R. (1993). AIDS risk reduction among a multiethnic sample of urban high school students. *Journal of the American Medical Association, 270,* 725–730.

WALTON, D., & MATHER, M. D. (1963). The relevance of generalization techniques to the treatment of stammering and phobic symptoms. *Behaviour Research and Therapy, 1,* 121–125.

WASIK, B. H. (1970). The application of Premack's generalization on reinforcement to the management of classroom behavior. *Journal of Experimental Child Psychology, 10,* 33–43.

WASSERMAN, I. M. (1984). Imitation and suicide: A reexamination of the Werther effect. *American Sociological Review, 49,* 427–436.

WATSON, D. L., & THARP, R. G. (1972). *Self-directed behavior: Self-modification for personal adjustment.* Pacific Grove, CA: Brooks/Cole.

WATSON, D. L., & THARP, R. G. (1989). *Self-directed behavior: Self-modification for personal adjustment* (5th ed.). Pacific Grove, CA: Brooks/Cole.

WATSON, J. B. (1914). *Behavior: An introduction to comparative psychology.* New York: Holt.

WATSON, J. P., MULLETT, G. E., & PILLAY, H. (1973). The effects of prolonged exposure to phobic situations upon agoraphobic patients treated in groups. *Behaviour Research and Therapy, 11,* 531–545.

WATSON, T. S., & KRAMER, J. J. (1995). Teaching problem solving skills to teachers-in-training: An analogue experimental analysis of three methods. *Journal of Behavioral Education, 5,* 295–317.

WAUQUIER, A., MCGRADY, A., ALOE, L., KLAUSNER, T., & COLLINS, B. (1995). Changes in cerebral blood flow velocity, associated with biofeedback-assisted relaxation treatment of migraine headaches, are specific for the middle cerebral artery. *Headache, 35,* 358–362.

WEBSTER-STRATTON, C. (1981a). Modification of mothers' behaviors and attitudes through videotape modeling group discussion. *Behavior Therapy, 12,* 634–642.

WEBSTER-STRATTON, C. (1981b). Videotape modeling: A method of parent education. *Journal of Clinical Child Psychology, 10,* 93–97.

WEBSTER-STRATTON, C. (1982a). Long-term effects of a videotape modeling parent education program: Comparison of immediate and 1-year follow-up results. *Behavior Therapy, 13,* 702–714.

WEBSTER-STRATTON, C. (1982b). Teaching mothers through videotape modeling to change their children's behaviors. *Journal of Pediatric Psychology, 7,* 279–294.

WEBSTER-STRATTON, C. (1984). Randomized trial of two parent-training programs for families with conduct disordered children. *Journal of Consulting and Clinical Psychology, 52,* 666–678.

WEBSTER-STRATTON, C., KOLPACOFF, M., & HOLLINGSWORTH, T. (1988). Self-administered videotape therapy for families with conduct problem children: Comparison with two cost-effective treatments and a control group. *Journal of Consulting and Clinical Psychology, 57,* 558–566.

WEIDNER, F. (1970). *In vivo* desensitization of a paranoid schizophrenic. *Journal of Behavior Therapy and Experimental Psychiatry, 1,* 79–81.

WEINHARDT, L. S., CAREY, M. P., CAREY, K. B., & VERDECIAS, R. N. (1998). Increasing assertiveness skills to reduce HIV risk among woman living with a severe and persistent mental illness. *Journal of Consulting and Clinical Psychology, 66,* 680–684.

WEINRACH, S. G. (1995). Rational emotive behavior therapy: A tough-minded therapy for a tender-minded profession. *Journal of Counseling and Development, 73,* 296–300.

WEINSTEIN, M. (1988). Preparation of children for psychotherapy through videotaped modeling. *Journal of Clinical Child Psychology, 17,* 131–136.

WEISENBERG, R. P., GESTEN, E. L., CARNIKE, C. L., TORO, P. A., RAPKIN, B. D., DAVIDSON, E., & COWEN, E. L. (1981). Social problem-solving skills training: A competence-building intervention with second-to-fourth-grade children. *American Journal of Community Psychology, 9,* 411–423.

WEISHAAR, M. E. (1996). Developments in cognitive therapy: 1960–1996. In W. Dryden (Ed.), *Developments in psychotherapy: Historical perspectives* (pp. 188–212). London: Sage.

WEISSBERG, N. C., & OWEN, D. R. (1999). Behavior therapy and behavioral genetics are not enemies: A reply to Hayes. *the Behavior Therapist, 22,*

WELCH, M. W., & GIST, J. W. (1974). *The open token economy system: A handbook for a behavioral approach to rehabilitation.* Springfield, IL: Charles C Thomas.

WELLS, E. A., PETERSON, P. L., GAINEY, R. R., HAWKINS, J. D., & CATALANO, R. F. (1994). Outpatient treatment for cocaine abuse: A controlled comparison of relapse prevention and twelve-step approaches. *American Journal of Drug and Alcohol Abuse, 20,* 1–17.

WELLS, J. K., HOWARD, G. S., NOWLIN, W. F., & VARGAS, M. J. (1986). Presurgical anxiety and postsurgical pain and adjustment: Effects of a stress inoculation procedure. *Journal of Consulting and Clinical Psychology, 54,* 831–835.

WELLS, K. C. (1994). Parent and family management training. In L. W. Craighead, W. E. Craighead, A. E. Kazdin, & M. J. Mahoney (Eds.), *Cognitive and behavioral interventions: An empirical approach to mental health problems* (pp. 251–266). Boston: Allyn & Bacon.

WELLS, K. C., & EGAN, J. (1988). Social learning and systems family therapy for childhood oppositional disorder: Comparative treatment outcome. *Comprehensive Psychiatry, 29,* 138–146.

WELLS, K. C., GRIEST, D. C., & FOREHAND, R. [L.] (1980). The use of a self-control package to enhance temporal generality of a parent training program. *Behaviour Research and Therapy, 18,* 347–353.

WERRY, J. S., & COHRSSEN, J. (1965). Enuresis: An etiologic and therapeutic study. *Journal of Pediatrics, 67,* 423–431.

WETHERELL, J. L. (2002). Behavior therapy for anxious older adults. *the Behavior Therapist, 25,* 16–17.

WHISMAN, M. A. (1993). Mediators and moderators of change in cognitive therapy of depression. *Psychological Bulletin, 114,* 248–265.

WHITAL, M. L., AGRAS, W. S., & GOULD, R. A. (1999). Bulimia nervosa: A meta-analysis of psychosocial and pharmacological treatments. *Behavior Therapy, 30,* 117–135.

WHITE, G. D., NIELSON, G., & JOHNSON, S. M. (1972). Timeout duration and the suppression of deviant behavior in children. *Journal of Applied Behavior Analysis, 5,* 111–120.

WHITE, J. A., DAVISON, G. C., HAAGA, D. A. F., & WHITE, K. L. (1992). Cognitive bias in the articulated thoughts of depressed and nondepressed psychiatric patients. *Journal of Nervous and Mental Disease, 180,* 77–81.

WHITE, M. (1989). *Selected papers.* Adelaide, South Australia: Dulwich Centre Publications.

WHITE, M. (1995, March). *Re-authoring lives.* Workshop presented in Mansfield, MA.

WHITE-BLACKBURN, G., SEMB, S., & SEMB, G. (1977). The effects of a good-behavior contract on the classroom behaviors of sixth-grade students. *Journal of Applied Behavior Analysis, 10,* 312.

WICKRAMASEKERA, I. (1976). Aversive behavior rehearsal for sexual exhibitionism. *Behavior Therapy, 7,* 167–176.

WIJMA, K., MELIN, A., NEDSTRAND, E., & HAMMAR, M. (1997). Treatment of menopausal symptoms with applied relaxation: A pilot study. *Journal of Behavior Therapy and Experimental Psychiatry, 28,* 251–261.

WILDER, D. A., HIGBEEN, T. S., WILLIAMS, W. L., & NACHTWEY, A. (1997). A simplified method of toilet training adults in residential settings. *Journal of Behavior Therapy and Experimental Psychiatry, 28,* 241–246.

WILFLEY, D. E., SCHWARTZ, M. B., SPURRELL, E. B., & FAIRBURN, C. G. (1997). Assessing the specific psychopathology of binge eating disorder patients: Interview or self-report? *Behaviour Research and Therapy, 35,* 1151–1159.

WILKIE, E. A., KIVITZ, M. S., CLARK, G. R., BYER, M. J., & COHEN, J. S. (1968). Developing a comprehensive rehabilitation program within an institutional setting. *Mental Retardation, 6,* 35–38.

WILLERMAN, L. (1979). *The psychology of individual and group differences.* San Francisco: W. H. Freeman.

WILLIAMS, C. D. (1959). The elimination of tantrum behavior by extinction procedures: Case report. *Journal of Abnormal and Social Psychology, 59,* 269.

WILLIAMS, D. E., KIRKPATRICK-SANCHEZ, S., & CROCKER, W. T. (1994). A long-term follow-up of treatment for severe self-injury. *Research in Developmental Disabilities, 15,* 487–501.

WILLIAMS, D. E., & WILLIAMS, J. W. (1995). Contingencies for dangerous behavior. *American Journal of Psychiatry, 152,* 1696.

WILLIAMS, K. E., CHAMBLESS, D. L., & STEKETEE, G. (1998). Behavioral treatment of obsessive compulsive disorder in African Americans: Clinical issues. *Journal of Behavior Therapy and Experimental Psychiatry, 29,* 163–170.

WILLIAMS, S. L., DOOSEMAN, G., & KLEIFIELD, E. (1984). Comparative effectiveness of guided mastery and exposure treatments for intractable phobias. *Journal of Consulting and Clinical Psychology, 52,* 505–518.

WILLIAMS, S. L., TURNER, S. M., & PEER, D. F. (1985). Guided mastery and performance desensitization treatments for severe acrophobia. *Journal of Consulting and Clinical Psychology, 53,* 237–247.

WILLIAMS, S. L., & ZANE, G. (1989). Guided mastery and stimulus exposure treatments for severe performance anxiety in agoraphobics. *Behaviour Research and Therapy, 27,* 237–245.

WILLIAMSON, D. A., DAVIS, C. J., & PRATHER, R. C. (1988). Assessment of health-related disorders. In A. S. Bellack & M. Hersen (Eds.), *Behavioral assessment: A practical handbook* (3rd ed., pp. 396–440). Elmsford, NY: Pergamon.

WILLIAMSON, D. A., WILLIAMSON, S. H., WATKINS, P. C., & HUGHES, H. H. (1992). Increasing cooperation among children using dependent group-oriented reinforcement contingencies. *Behavior Modification, 16,* 414–425.

WILLIS, R. W., & EDWARDS, J. A. (1969). A study of the comparative effectiveness of systematic desensitization and implosive therapy. *Behaviour Research and Therapy, 7,* 387–395.

WILSON, D. D., ROBERTSON, S. J., HERLONG, L. H., & HAYNES, S. N. (1979). Vicarious effects of time out in the modification of aggression in the classroom. *Behavior Modification, 3,* 97–111.

WILSON, G. T. (1978). On the much discussed nature of the term "behavior therapy." *Behavior Therapy, 9,* 89–98.

WILSON, G. T. (1982). Adult disorders. In G. T. Wilson & C. M. Franks (Eds.), *Contemporary behavior therapy: Conceptual and empirical foundations* (pp. 505–562). New York: Guilford.

WILSON, G. T. (1984). Fear reduction methods and the treatment of anxiety disorders. In C. M. Franks, G. T. Wilson, P. C. Kendall, & K. D. Brownell (Eds.), *Review of behavior therapy: Theory and practice* (Vol. 10, pp. 87–122). New York: Guilford.

WILSON, G. T. (1997a). Behavior therapy at century close. *Behavior Therapy, 28,* 18–23.

WILSON, G. T. (1997b). Treatment manuals in clinical practice. *Behaviour Research and Therapy, 35,* 305–310.

WILSON, G. T., ELDREDGE, K. L., SMITH, D. E., & NILES, B. (1991). Cognitive-behavioral treatment with and without response prevention for bulimia. *Behaviour Research and Therapy, 29,* 575–583.

WILSON, G. T., & FAIRBURN, C. G. (1993). Cognitive treatment for eating disorders. *Journal of Consulting and Clinical Psychology, 61,* 261–269.

WILSON, G. T., & FAIRBURN, C. G. (1998). Treatments for eating disorders. In P. E. Nathan & J. M. Gorman (Eds.), *A guide to treatments that work* (pp. 501–530). New York: Oxford University Press.

WILSON, G. T., LOEB, K. L., WALSH, B. T., LABOUVIE, E., PETKOVA, E., LIU, X., & WATERNAUX, C. (1999). Psychological versus pharmacological treatments of bulimia nervosa: Predictors and processes of change. *Journal of Consulting and Clinical Psychology, 67,* 451–459.

WILSON, G. T., O'LEARY, K. D., & NATHAN, P. E. (1992). *Abnormal psychology.* Englewood Cliffs, NJ: Prentice Hall.

WILSON, G. T., ROSSITER, E., KLEIFIELD, E. I., & LINDHOLM, L. (1986). Cognitive-behavioral treatment of bulimia nervosa: A controlled evaluation. *Behaviour Research and Therapy, 24,* 277–288.

WILSON, G. T., & TRACEY, D. A. (1976). An experimental analysis of aversive imagery versus electrical aversive conditioning in the treatment of chronic alcoholics. *Behaviour Research and Therapy, 14,* 41–51.

WILSON, G. T., VITOUSEK, K. M., & LOEB, K. L. (2000). Stepped care treatment for eating disorders. *Journal of Consulting and Clinical Psychology, 68,* 564–572.

WILSON, J. Q., & HERRNSTEIN, R. J. (1985). *Crime and human nature*. New York: Simon & Schuster.

WILSON, K., & GALLOIS, C. (1993). *Assertion and its social context*. New York: Pergamon.

WILSON, M. D., & MCREYNOLDS, L. V. (1973). A procedure for increasing oral reading rate in hard of hearing children. *Journal of Applied Behavior Analysis, 6*, 231–239.

WILSON, S. A., BECKER, L. A., & TINKER, R. (1997). Fifteen-month follow-up of eye movement desensitization and reprocessing (EMDR) treatment for posttraumatic stress disorder and psychological trauma. *Journal of Consulting and Clinical Psychology, 65*, 1047–1056.

WINCZE, J. P., & CAIRD, W. K. (1976). The effects of systematic desensitization and video desensitization in the treatment of sexual dysfunction in women. *Behavior Therapy, 7*, 335–342.

WINETT, R. A., & WINKLER, R. C. (1972). Current behavior modification in the classroom: Be still, be quiet, be docile. *Journal of Applied Behavior Analysis, 5*, 499–504.

WISOCKI, P. A. (1994). The experience of worry among the elderly. In G. C. L. Davey & F. Tallis (Eds.), *Worrying: Perspectives on theory, assessment and treatment* (pp. 247–261). Chichester, UK: Wiley.

WITTROCK, D. A., & BLANCHARD, E. B. (1992). Thermal biofeedback treatment of mild hypertension: A comparison of effects on conventional and ambulatory blood pressure measures. *Behavior Modification, 16*, 283–304.

WITTROCK, D. A., BLANCHARD, E. B., & MCCOY, G. C. (1988). Three studies on the relation of process to outcome in the treatment of essential hypertension with relaxation and thermal biofeedback. *Behaviour Research and Therapy, 26*, 53–66.

WOLF, E. M., & CROWTHER, J. H. (1992). An evaluation of behavior and cognitive-behavioral group interventions for the treatment of bulimia nervosa in women. *International Journal of Eating Disorder, 22*, 503–517.

WOLF, M. M. (1978). Social validity: The case for subjective measurement or how applied behavior analysis is finding its heart. *Journal of Applied Behavior Analysis, 11*, 203–214.

WOLF, M. M., BRAUKMANN, C. J., & RAMP, K. A. (1987). Serious delinquent behavior as part of a significantly handicapping condition: Cures and supportive environments. *Journal of Applied Behavior Analysis, 20*, 347–359.

WOLFE, D. A., & SANDLER, J. (1981). Training abusive parents in effective child management. *Behavior Modification, 5*, 320–335.

WOLFE, D. A., & WEKERLE, C. (1993). Treatment strategies for child physical abuse and neglect: A critical progress report. *Clinical Psychology Review, 13*, 473–500.

WOLFSON, A., LACKS, P., & FUTTERMAN, A. (1992). Effects of parent training on infant sleeping patterns, parents' stress, and perceived parental competence. *Journal of Consulting and Clinical Psychology, 60*, 41–48.

WOLPE, J. (1958). *Psychotherapy by reciprocal inhibition*. Stanford, CA: Stanford University Press.

WOLPE, J. (1976). Behavior therapy and its malcontents: II. Multimodal eclecticism, cognitive exclusivism and "exposure" empiricism. *Journal of Behavior Therapy and Experimental Psychiatry, 7*, 109–116.

WOLPE, J. (1990). *The practice of behavior therapy* (4th ed.). Elmsford, NY: Pergamon.

WOLPE, J., & ABRAMS, J. (1991). Post-traumatic stress disorder overcome by eye movement desensitization: A case report. *Journal of Behavior Therapy and Experimental Psychiatry, 22*, 39–43.

WOLPE, J., & LANG, P. J. (1964). A fear survey schedule for use in behavior therapy. *Behaviour Research and Therapy, 2*, 27–30.

WOLPE, J., & LAZARUS, A. A. (1966). *Behavior therapy techniques: A guide to the treatment of neurosis*. New York: Pergamon.

WONG, S. E., MARTINEZ-DIAZ, J. A., MASSEL, H. K., EDELSTEIN, B. A., WIEGAND, W., BOWEN, L., & LIBERMAN, R. P. (1993). Conversation skills training with schizophrenic inpatients: A study of generalization across settings and conversants. *Behavior Therapy, 24*, 285–304.

WONG, S. E., SEROKA, P. L., & OGISI, J. (2000). Effects of a checklist on self-assessment of blood glucose level by a memory-impaired woman with diabetes mellitus. *Journal of Applied Behavior Analysis, 33*, 251–254.

WOODS, D. W., & MILTENBERGER, R. G. (1995). Habit reversal: A review of applications and variations. *Journal of Behavior Therapy and Experimental Psychiatry, 26*, 123–131.

WOODS, D. W., MURRAY, L. K., FUQUA, W., SEIF, T. A., BOYER, L. J., & SIAH, A. (1999). Comparing the effectiveness of similar and dissimilar competing responses in evaluating the habit reversal treatment of oral-digital habits in children. *Journal of Behavior Therapy and Experimental Psychiatry, 30*, 289–300.

WOODWARD, R., & JONES, R. B. (1980). Cognitive restructuring treatment: A controlled trial with anxious patients. *Behaviour Research and Therapy, 18*, 401–407.

WOOLFOLK, A. E., WOOLFOLK, R. L., & WILSON, G. T. (1977). A rose by another name . . . : Labeling bias and attitudes toward behavior modification. *Journal of Consulting and Clinical Psychology, 45*, 184–191.

WOOLFOLK, R. L., & DEVER, S. (1979). Perceptions of assertion: An empirical analysis. *Behavior Therapy, 10*, 404–411.

WORLD HEALTH ORGANIZATION. (1992). *International classification of diseases and related health problems* (10th rev.). Geneva: Author.

WORSDELL, A. S., IWATA, B. A., CONNERS, J., KAHNG, S. W., & THOMPSON, R. H. (2000). Relative influences of establishing operations and reinforcement contingencies on self-injurious behavior during functional analyses. *Journal of Applied Behavior Analysis, 33*, 451–461.

WORSDELL, A. S., IWATA, B. A., HANLEY, G. P., THOMPSON, R. H., & KAHNG, S. W. (2000). Effects of continuous and intermittent reinforcement for problem behavior during functional communication training. *Journal of Applied Behavior Analysis, 33*, 167–179.

WURTELE, S. K. (1990). Teaching personal safety skills to four-year-old children: A behavioral approach. *Behavior Therapy, 21*, 25–32.

WURTELE, S. K., CURRIER, L. L., GILLISPIE, E. I., & FRANKLIN, C. F. (1991). The efficacy of a parent-implemented program for teaching preschoolers personal safety skills. *Behavior Therapy, 22*, 69–83.

WURTELE, S. K., MARRS, S. R., & MILLER-PERRIN, C. J. (1987). Practice makes perfect? The role of participant modeling in sexual abuse prevention programs. *Journal of Consulting and Clinical Psychology, 55,* 599–602.

Wysocki, T., Hall, G., Iwata, B., & Riordan, M. (1979). Behavioral management of exercise: Contracting for aerobic points. *Journal of Applied Behavior Analysis, 12,* 55–64.

Yates, A. J. (1958). The application of learning theory to the treatment of tics. *Journal of Abnormal and Social Psychology, 56,* 175–182.

Yates, A. J. (1970). *Behavior therapy.* New York: Wiley.

Young, J. E. (1990). *Cognitive therapy for personality disorders: A schema-focused approach* (rev. ed.). Sarasota, FL: Professional Resource Exchange.

Young, J. E. (1994). *Cognitive therapy for personality disorders: A schema-focused approach* (rev. ed.). Sarasota, FL: Professional Resource Press.

Young, J. E., Beck, A. T., & Weinberger, A. (1993). Depression. In D. H. Barlow (Ed.), *Clinical handbook of psychological disorders* (2nd ed., pp. 240–277). New York: Guilford.

Yu, P., Harris, G. E., Solovitz, B. L., & Franklin, L. (1986). A social problem-solving intervention for children at high risk for later psychopathology. *Journal of Clinical Child Psychology, 13,* 30–40.

Yule, W., Sacks, B., & Hersov, L. (1974). Successful flooding treatment of a noise phobia in an eleven-year-old. *Journal of Behavior Therapy and Experimental Psychiatry, 5,* 209–211.

Zanolli, K., & Daggett, J. (1998). The effects of reinforcement rate on the spontaneous social initiations of socially withdrawn preschoolers. *Journal of Applied Behavior Analysis, 31,* 117–125.

Zeiss, A. M., & Steffen, A. (1996). Treatment issues with elderly clients. *Cognitive and Behavioral Practice, 3,* 371–389.

Zeitlin, S. B., Netten, K. A., & Hodder, S. L. (1995). Thought suppression: An experimental investigation of spider phobics. *Behaviour Research and Therapy, 33,* 407–413.

Zettle, R. D., & Hayes, S. C. (1982). Rule-governed behavior: A potential theoretical framework for cognitive-behavioral therapy. In P. C. Kendall (Ed.), *Advances in cognitive-behavioral research and therapy* (Vol. 1, pp. 73–118). New York: Academic Press.

Zifferblatt, S. M. (1975). Increasing patient compliance through the applied analysis of behavior. *Preventive Medicine, 4,* 173–182.

Zimmerman, J., Stuckey, T. E., Garlick, B. J., & Miller, M. (1969). Effects of token reinforcement on productivity in multiple handicapped clients in a sheltered workshop. *Rehabilitation Literature, 30,* 34–41.

Zionts, P. (1983). A strategy for understanding and correcting irrational beliefs in pupils: The rational-emotive approach. *Pointer, 27,* 13–17.

Name Index

Subject Index

Credits

This page constitutes an extension of the copyright page. We have made every effort to trace the ownership of all copyrighted material and to secure permission from copyright holders. In the event of any question arising as to the use of any material, we will be pleased to make the necessary corrections in future printings. Thanks are due to the following authors, publishers, and agents for permission to use the material indicated.

Text Credits
Chapter 2. 21: Adapted from Haughton, E., & Ayllon, T. (1965). Production and elimination of symptomatic behavior. In L. P. Ullmann & L. Krasner (Eds.), *Case studies in behavior modification* (pp. 94–98). New York: Holt, Rinehart & Winston.
Chapter 3. 37: CALVIN & HOBBES copyright 1990 Watterson. Dist. by UNIVERSAL PRESS SYNDICATE. Reprinted with permission. All rights reserved. **41:** PEANUTS Reprinted by permission of UFS, Inc.
Chapter 4. 46: From Lazarus, A. A., Davison, G. C., & Polefka, D. A. (1965). Classical and operant factors in the treatment in a school phobia. *Journal of Abnormal Psychology, 70,* 225–229. © 1965 by the American Psychological Association. Reprinted with permission. **50:** © Michael Spiegler and David C. Guevremont. **52:** © Michael Spiegler and David C. Guevremont.
Chapter 5. 76: Most frequently used methods of behavioral assessment. From Guevremont, D. C., & Spiegler, M. D. (1990, November). *What do behavior therapists really do? A survey of the clinical practice of AABT members.* Paper presented at the meeting of the Association for Advancement of Behavior Therapy, San Francisco. Reprinted by permission. **90:** From Liebert, R. M., & Spiegler, M. D. (1994). *Personality: Strategies and issues* (7th ed.). Pacific Grove, CA: Brooks/Cole. Reprinted with permission. **92:** Dr. Craig Edelbrock. **96:** THE FAR SIDE copyright 1984 UNIVERSAL PRESS SYNDICATE. Reprinted with permission of Creators Syndicate. All rights reserved.
Chapter 6. 114: HAGAR reprinted with special permission of King Features Syndicate, Inc. **122:** From Kallman, W. M., Hersen, M., & O'Toole, D. H. (1975). The use of social reinforcement in a case of conversation reaction. *Behavioral Therapy, 6,* 411–413, Fig. 1, p. 412. Reprinted with permission from the Association for Advancement of Behavior Therapy. **127:** From Behavioral Counseling: Cases and Techniques by Krumboltz © 1969. Reprinted with permission of Wadsworth. **133:** Reprinted with permission of Mal Hancock. **134:** © Michael D. Spiegler and David C. Guevremont.
Chapter 7. 147: From Williams, C. D. (1959). The elimination of tantrum behavior by extinction procedures: Case report. *Journal of Abnormal and Social Psychology, 59,* 269. **153:** CALVIN & HOBBES copyright 1986 Watterson. Dist. by UNIVERSAL PRESS SYNDICATE. Reprinted with permission. All rights reserved. **155:** From Azrin, N. H., & Wesolowski, M. D. (1974). Theft reversal: An overcorrection procedure for eliminating stealing by retarded persons. *Journal of Applied Behavior Analysis, 7,* 577–581. Copyright © 1974 Society for the Experimental Analysis of Behavior, Inc. Reprinted by Permission. **158:** From Risley, T. R. (1968). The effects and side effects of punishing the autistic behaviors of a deviant child. *Journal of Applied Behavior Analysis, 1,* 21–34. Copyright © 1968 by the Society for the Experimental Analysis of Behavior, Inc. Reprinted by Permission. **159:** From Risley, T. R. (1968). The effects and side effects of punishing the autistic behaviors of a deviant child. *Journal of Applied Behavior Analysis, 1,* 21–34. Copyright © 1968 by the Society for the Experimental Analysis of Behavior, Inc. Reprinted by Permission. **164:** From Cunningham, C. E., & Linscheid, T. R. (1976). Elimination of chronic infant ruminating by electric shock. *Behavior Therapy, 7,* 231–234. Reprinted by permission of the Association for Advancement of Behavior Therapy.
Chapter 8. 179: From "Example of a credit card used by trainees in the Community Training Center credit system (token community)." In Spiegler, M. D., & Agigian, H. (1977). *The Community Training Center: An educational-behavioral-social systems model for rehabilitating psychiatric patients.* New York: Brunner/Mazel. Used by permission of the author. **180:** From "Example of reinforcing activities and their credit costs at the Community Training Center." In Spiegler, M. D., & Agigian, H. (1977). *The Community Training Center: An educational-behavioral-social systems model for rehabilitating psychiatric patients.* New York: Brunner/Mazel. Used by permission of the author. **181:** From " Example of undesirable behaviors and the average number of credits trainees at the Community Training Center paid to engage in them." In Spiegler, M. D., & Agigian, H. (1977). *The Community Training Center: An educational-behavioral-social systems model for rehabilitating psychiatric patients.* New York: Brunner/Mazel. Used by permission of the author. **182:** From "Comparison of personal adjustment between Community Training Center graduates and a comparable sample of outpatients." In Spiegler, M. D., & Agigian, H. (1977). *The Community Training Center: An educational-behavioral-social systems model for rehabilitating psychiatric patients.* New York: Brunner/Mazel. Used by permission of the author. **183:** From Phillips, E. L.

(1968). Achievement Place: Token reinforcement procedures in a home-style rehabilitation setting for "pre-delinquent" boys. *Journal of Applied Behavior Analysis, 1,* 215. Copyright © 1968 by the Society for the Experimental Analysis of Behavior, Inc. **184:** From Phillips, E. L., Phillips, E. A., Fixsen, D. L., & Wolf, M. M. (1971). Achievement Place: Modification of the behaviors of pre-delinquent boys within a token economy. *Journal of Applied Behavior Analysis, 4,* 46. Copyright © 1971 by the Society for the Experimental Analysis of Behavior, Inc. **187:** From Maloney, K. B., & Hopkins, B. L. (1973). The modification of sentence structure and its relationship to subjective judgments of creativity in writing. *Journal of Applied Behavior Analysis, 6,* 429. Copyright © 1973 by the Society for the Experimental Analysis of Behavior, Inc. **189:** From Dapcich-Miura, E., & Hovell, M. F. (1979). Contingency management of adherence to a complex medical regimen in an elderly heart patient. *Behavior Therapy, 10,* 193–201. Copyright © 1979 by Association for Advancement of Behavior Therapy. Reprinted by Permission of the Publisher and author. **193:** CALVIN & HOBBES copyright 1986 Watterson. Dist. by UNIVERSAL PRESS SYNDICATE. Reprinted with permission. All rights reserved. **194:** © 2002 Michael Spiegler and David Guevremont
Chapter 9. 207: From Spiegler, M. D., & Liebert, R. M. (1970). Some correlates of self-reported fear. *Psychological Reports, 26,* 691–695. Used with permission from the author. **211:** THE FAR SIDE copyright 1987 UNIVERSAL PRESS SYNDICATE. Reprinted with permission of Creators Syndicate. All rights reserved. **212:** Excerpted from Wolpe, J., & Lazarus, A. A. (1996). Behavior therapy techniques: A guide to treatment to neurosis (p. 81). New York: Pergamon. Copyright © 1973 by Pergamon Press. Reprinted by permission of J. Wolpe. **220:** From Paul, G. L. (1966). *Insight vs. desensitization in psychotherapy* (p. 109). Stanford, CA: Stanford University Press. Copyright © 1966 by Stanford University Press. Reprinted by permission. **220:** Data from Paul, G. L. (1966). *Insight vs. desensitization in psychotherapy* (p. 109). Stanford, CA: Stanford University Press. © 1966 Stanford University Press. Used with permission.
Chapter 10. 238: Reprinted with permission from Nesbitt, E. B. (1973). An escalator phobia overcome in one session of flooding *in vivo. Journal of Behavior Therapy and Experimental Psychiatry, 4,* 405–406. Copyright © 1973, Elsevier Science. **243:** From Saigh, P. A. (1987). *In vitro* flooding of an adolescent's posttraumatic stress disorder. *Journal of Clinical Child Psychology, 16,* 148. Copyright by Lawrence Erlbaum, Inc. Reprinted by permission. **244:** From Saigh, P. A. (1987). *In vitro* flooding of an adolescent's posttraumatic stress disorder. *Journal of Clinical Child Psychology, 16,* 148. Copyright by Lawrence Erlbaum, Inc. Reprinted by permission. **246:** From Levis, D. J. (1980). Implementing the technique of implosive therapy. In A. Goldstein & E. B. Foa (Eds.), *Handbook of behavioral interventions: A clinical guide* (pp. 125–126). New York: Wiley. Copyright © 1980 by John Wiley and Sons. Reprinted with permission.
Chapter 11. 269: © Michael D. Spiegler and David C. Guevremont. **280:** From McFall, R. M., & Lillesand, D. B. (1971). Behavior rehearsal with modeling and coaching in assertion training. *Journal of Abnormal Psychology, 77,* 313–323. © 1971 by the American Psychological Association. Reprinted with permission. **293:** Bob Knight and Associates, 1969. **294:** Used with permission from Mary F. Coffman; drawn by Dianne Dusevitch.
Chapter 12. 320: From Beck, A. T., & Weishaar M. (1989). *Comprehensive handbook of cognitive therapy* (pp. 21–36). New York: Plenum. © 1989 by Kluwer Academic. Used by permission. **325:** From Beck, A. T. (1976). *Cognitive therapy and the emotional disorders* (pp. 284–286). New York: International Universities Press. Reprinted with permission from International Universities Press, Inc. **336:** CALVIN & HOBBES copyright 1986 Watterson. Dist. by UNIVERSAL PRESS SYNDICATE. Reprinted with permission. All rights reserved.
Chapter 13. 345: From Camp, B. W., & Bash, M. A. S. (1981). *Think aloud: Increasing social and cognitive skills—A problem-solving program for children (primary level).* Champaign, IL: Research Press. Reprinted by permission. **346:** From Guevremont, D. C., Osnes, P. G., & Stokes, T. F. (1988). The functional role of verbalizations in the generalization of self-instructional training with children. *Journal of Applied Behavior Analysis, 21,* 45–55. **356:** Abbreviated guidelines for rating children's problem-solving skills. From Impact of social problem solving on the behavior of aggressive boys: Generalization, maintenance, and social validation. *Journal of Abnormal Child Psychology, 26,* 112–121. Reprinted by permission of the author. **362:** THE FAR SIDE copyright 1988 UNIVERSAL PRESS SYNDICATE. Reprinted with permission of Creators Syndicate. All rights reserved.
Chapter 14. 391: CALVIN & HOBBES copyright 1988 Watterson. Dist. by UNIVERSAL PRESS SYNDICATE. Reprinted with permission. All rights reserved. **391:** From Fordyce, W. E. (1975). *Behavioral methods for chronic pain and illness* (p. 89). St. Louis: Mosby. Copyright © 1975 by Wlibert E. Fordyce. Reprinted by permission.
Chapter 15. 420: From Azrin, N. H., Thienes-Hontos, P., & Besalel-Azrin, V. (1979). Eliminating of enuresis without a conditioning apparatus: An extension by office instruction of the child and parents. *Behavior Therapy, 10,* 18. Copyright ©1979 by the Association for the Advancement of Behavior Therapy. Reprinted by permission of the publisher and author.

Photo Credits
Chapter 2. 17: Bettmann Archive/Corbis. **18:** Archives of the History of American Psychology, University of Akron. **18:** Archives of the History of American Psychology, University of Akron. **18:** Courtesy of the University of Illinois Archives, record series 15/19/25, Box 1. **19:** Archives of the History of American Psychology, University of Akron. **19:** Courtesy of the University of London British Postgraduate Medical Federation. **20:** Courtesy of Harvard University Archives. **20:** Courtesy of University of Kansas, University Archives. **22:** Courtesy of Arnold Lazarus. **22:** Courtesy of Stanley Rachman. **24:** Chuck Painter, Stanford University News Service. **24:** Courtesy of Cyril Franks.
Chapter 4. 54: Elizabeth Crews/Stock, Boston. **54:** Barbara Alper/Stock, Boston.
Chapter 5. 87: © 1997 Michael D. Spiegler and David C. Guevremont. **97:** © 1997 Michael D. Spiegler and David C. Guevremont. **98:** Cary Wolinsky/Stock, Boston. **101:** © 1997 Michael D. Spiegler and David C. Guevremont. **101:** © 1997 Michael D. Spiegler and David C. Guevremont.

Chapter 6. 115: © 1997 Michael D. Spiegler and David C. Guevremont.

Chapter 7. 149: © 1997 Michael D. Spiegler and David C. Guevremont. **152:** © 1997 Michael D. Spiegler and David C. Guevremont. **159:** The John Hopkins University Applied Physics Laboratory.

Chapter 8. 177: Courtesy of Teodoro Ayllon. **177:** Courtesy of Nathan Azrin. **188:** © 1997 Michael D. Spiegler and David C. Guevremont. **196:** Courtesy of Gerald Patterson. **196:** Courtesy of Rex Forehand.

Chapter 9. 204: Courtesy of Joseph Wolpe. **205:** © 1997 Michael D. Spiegler and David C. Guevremont. **216:** Courtesy of Marvin R. Goldfried. **227:** Courtesy of Georgia Tech Telephoto.

Chapter 10. 245: Courtesy of the University of Wisconsin, Milwaukee. **245:** Courtesy of Donald Levis.

Chapter 11. 270: Courtesy of the Eden Institute. **271:** © 1997 Michael D. Spiegler and David C. Guevremont. **290:** Courtesy of Barbara Melamed.

Chapter 12. 308: Courtesy of Albert Ellis, Institute for Rational-Emotive Therapy. **318:** Courtesy of the University of Pennsylvania Medical Center.

Chapter 13. 344: Courtesy of the University of Waterloo, Ontario, Canada. **350:** Courtesy of Thomas D'Zurilla. **368:** Courtesy of Virginia Rutter. **368:** Courtesy of Andrew Christensen, UCLA.

Chapter 14. 381: Visual Image Presentations. **387:** © 1997 Michael D. Spiegler and David C. Guevremont. **398:** © 1997 Michael D. Spiegler and David C. Guevremont.

Chapter 15. 419: © 1997 Michael D. Spiegler and David C. Guevremont. **435:** © 1997 Michael D. Spiegler and David C. Guevremont.